FRIENDS
WITH
BOOKS

2015 · Studio Claus Due (DK) · Logo · Art Book
Fair Berlin

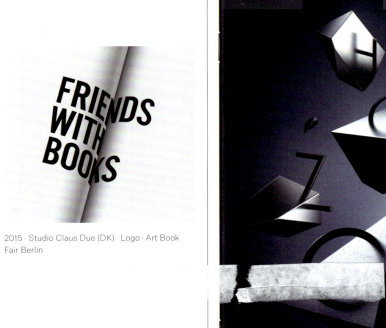

2016 · Sawdust · UK · Magazine cover

ZENEX

1981 · Tony Forster · UK · Logo · Zenex

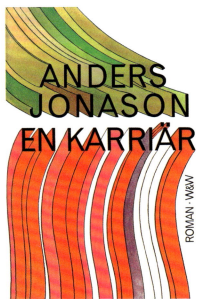
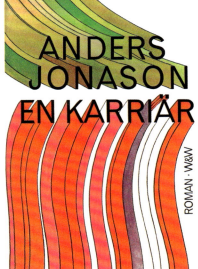

ANDERS
JONASON
EN KARRIÄR

1969 · Per Åhlin · SE · Book cover

2014 · Frost* Design · AU · Poster

MIT
MEDIA
LAB

1990 · Muriel Cooper · US · Logo · MIT Media Lab

2003 · Uwe Loesch · DE · Poster

Getting Around

2016 · Karlssonwilker · US · Brochure

1975 · Anonymous · DE · Record cover

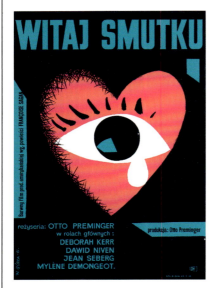

1961 · Wiktor Górka · PL · Poster

1970 · Georges Beaupré · CA · Logo · National Film Board of Canada

Newsweek

SPECIAL EDITION

ISSUES 2013

2013 · Edel Rodriguez · CU/US · Magazine cover

1968 · Tadahito Nadamoto · JP · Poster

1990 · Steff Geissbuhler · US · Logo · Time Warner Cable

1960 · Anonymous · US · Record cover

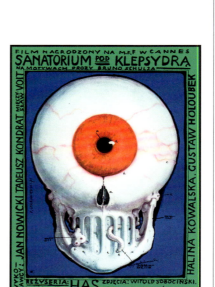

1973 · Franciszek Starowieyski · PL · Poster

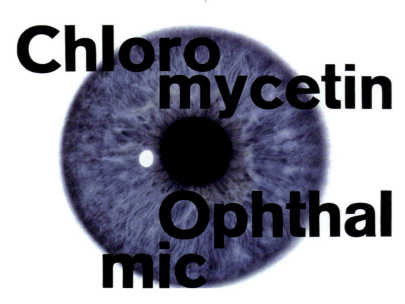

Chloro mycetin Ophthal mic

1960 · Michael Engelmann · DE/CH · Leaflet

KAIBOSH EYEWEAR STORE

2016 · Snask · SE · Poster/Identity

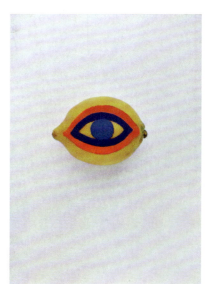

1966 · Hans Hillmann · DE · New year's card

𝑛VIDIA®

1993 · Anonymous · US · Logo · Nvidia

1968 · Václav Ševčík · CZ · Poster

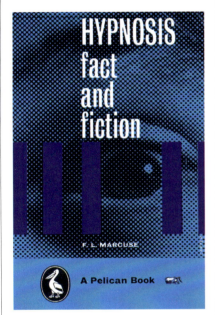

1961 · Larry Carter · UK · Book cover

1987 · Ott+Stein · DE · Poster

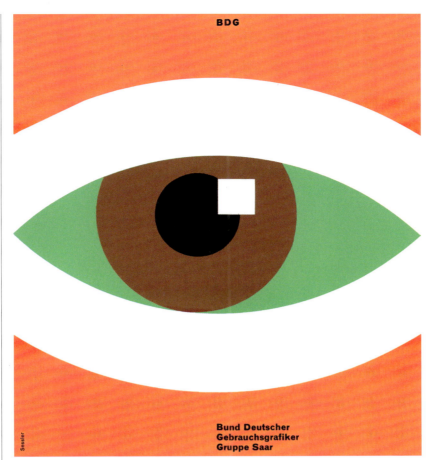

1961 · Robert Sessler · DE · Brochure cover

1983 · Vladislav Rostoka · SK · Book cover

2003 · Alireza Mostafazadeh Ebrahimi · IR · Poster

2008 · Jorge Silva, Silvadesigners · PT · Book cover

1987 · Malcolm Swatridge, Stephen Gibbons, The Partners · UK · Logo · Cambridge Contact Lenses

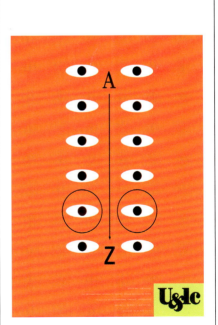

1992 · Gunter Rambow · DE/BR · Poster

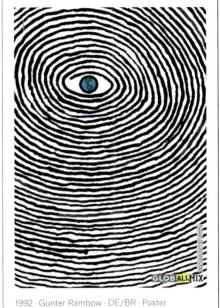

1996 · Carin Goldberg · US · Magazine cover

THE HISTORY OF

1983 · Jörg Hamburger · CH · Poster

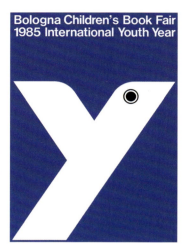

1985 · Gianni Bortolotti · IT · Poster

1969 · Anonymous · BR · Poster

1978 · Gerhard Preiß · DE · Poster

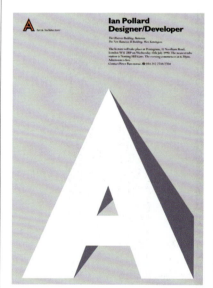

1988 · John Powner · UK · Poster

Jens Müller
Julius Wiedemann (Ed.)

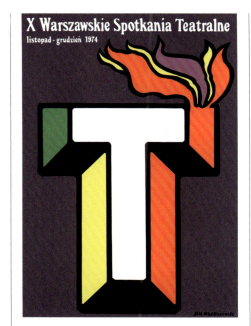

1974 · Jan Młodozeniec · PL · Poster

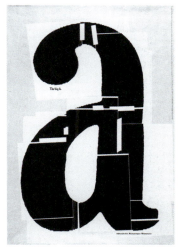

1992 · Paula Scher, Pentagram · US · Poster

GRAPHIC DESIGN

Vol. 2
1960–TODAY

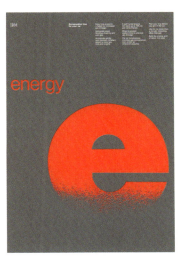

1980 · Kurt W. Gibson · US · Poster

TASCHEN

CONTENTS

1982 · Rostislav Vaněk · CZ · Poster

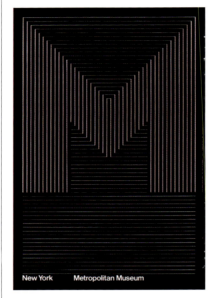

New York   Metropolitan Museum

1970 · Peter Teubner · US · Poster

8.—15. September 1963

Wiener
Internationale
Messe

1963 · Anonymous · AT · Poster

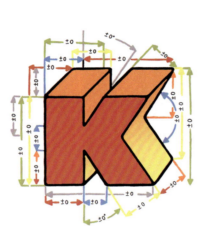

КАЧЕСТВО ВЪВ ВСИЧКИ ИЗМЕРЕНИЯ

1984 · Dimiter Tassew · BG · Poster

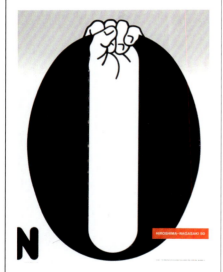

1995 · Shigeo Fukuda · JP · Poster

c channel   the promise of performance

1984 · Jennifer Gyles · CA · Poster

GRAPHIC DESIGN AND BEYOND

7

GRAFIKDESIGN UND SO WEITER

11

LE GRAPHISME ET PLUS ENCORE

15

1964 · Walter Breker · DE · Poster

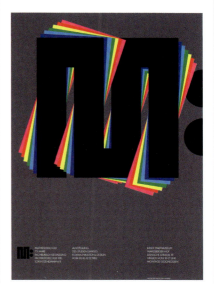

1982 · Ulrike Tetzlaff Werner · DE · Poster

1988 · Erkki Ruuhinen · FI · Poster

1986 · Jaroslav Chadima · CZ · Poster

The Brazilian graphic designer
Aloísio Magalhães working on
brand identities in his studio
in the mid-1960s.

As early as 1991, Berlin-based
MetaDesign was installing
computers for all its workers.

The design and coding
studio Lundgren+Lindqvist
in Gothenburg.

Der brasilianische Grafikdesigner Aloisio Magalhães bei
der Arbeit an Erscheinungs-
bildern in seinem Studio Mitte
der 1960er-Jahre.

Das Berliner Designbüro
MetaDesign setzte bereits 1991
an fast jedem Arbeitsplatz
Computer ein.

Blick in das Studio Lundgren
+Lindqvist in Göteborg, das
sich auf Design und Coding
spezialisiert hat.

Le graphiste brésilien Aloísio
Magalhães travaillant sur des
images de marque dans son studio, au milieu des années 1960.

Dès 1991, l'agence de graphisme
berlinoise MetaDesign instal-
lait des ordinateurs à chaque
poste de travail.

Vue de l'agence Lundgren+
Lindqvist à Göteborg spécialisée en graphisme et codage.

Introduction

GRAPHIC DESIGN AND BEYOND

Introduction by Jens Müller

Anyone who walked into a design studio in the 1980s, and then did not return for another 10 years would, on that second visit, think they had walked in on a totally different profession. Drafting tables, adhesives, and pencil holders would have made way for screens, keyboards, and other gray pieces of equipment. In the field of graphic design, the much-talked-about digitalization of the economy was already under way some three decades ago. Within a very short time, software and hardware solutions became available, making it possible to create complete, and perfect artworks onscreen. The analog tools once essential to the production process became superfluous, as did the many outside contractors who had contributed to the job at every stage, from design to printing. At the same time, in the 1990s the internet arrived as the new mass medium, thus paving the way for the next stage of the digital revolution. The fact that most designers were obviously ready to sign up for this existential transformation is best explained by the constant eagerness for change which is to some extent embedded in the DNA of their profession.

As they interacted over the course of the 20th century with continuing technological advances and changing economic conditions, designers consistently found new fields of activity in which to engage—from entire corporate identities, through signage for buildings, to website design. Cross-over artists also emerged, who embarked on product and communication design or whose work combined, for example, architecture and graphic design. With the passage of time, this diversity of interests guaranteed that the profession itself was seen to have an increasingly broad range. Today, clients regard designers as service providers, creative partners, strategic advisers, and, every now and then, as artists.

Even well-established and internationally sought-after professionals have to live with the situation that for some commissions they can work with full artistic freedom while, on the other hand, many of their other projects require them to deliver a very specifically defined job.

The opportunity to create digital designs much faster by using technically simpler methods has made it easier for clients to intervene in the design process compared with the same situation in the analog era. In times when it is becoming increasingly difficult in many areas to maintain the status of being an "expert", it seems logical to conclude that this profession too is changing. The search for a new role for the designer is well under way. For more than a decade now, attention has been focused on the question of authorship. A designer with only the basic skills—such as knowing how to conceive content and how to put it all together in a way that will appeal to the public—was now able to accomplish the whole task. Thanks to digitization, it has not only become much easier for all of us to design our own books and magazines, but also to produce and sell them. Both non-commercial side projects and business-oriented start-ups have led to the development of many exciting publications, such as the London-based movie magazine *Little White Lies*, to name but one example, and even to the setting-up of independent publishers, such as Spector Books.

Despite these substantial developments, designers succeeded in taking on new roles in quite different fields. For example, Stefan Sagmeister achieved international success with his traveling exhibition *The Happy Show*, which set out to explore several aspects of society's and the designer's own happiness. He followed it up with the movie documentary *The Happy Film*, which was shown in cinemas in several countries. In 2008, Tina Roth-Eisenberg devised *Creative-Mornings*, a monthly talk over breakfast for people from all walks of the design community that has spread to some 180 towns and cities across the world. A few years later, she also launched Tattly, a business selling temporary tattoos created by designers and illustrators. In a project for the Japanese manufacturer Honda, Kashiwa Sato was made Total Creative Director and given the responsibility of developing a new model of space-saving micro car. For this "N" series small car he oversaw the general vehicle design as well as producing the graphic design for it and leading the product launch campaign in 2011. After graduating from the Rhode Island School of Design in 2005, Joe Gebbia got together with friends to develop a website where people could advertise temporary accommodation to let. Today their platform, Airbnb, is available in 190 different countries and is used by more than 150 million people.

With a certain degree of hesitation, it should be said, companies operating in the mainstream economy are now coming to realize that designers can do much more for them than the traditional range of tasks they have come to expect. In recent years, the not uncontroversial term "design thinking" has appeared, although sadly this does not always mean that the designer is perceived as an integral part of new project developments, or as someone who can influence things in a different way from management and specialist staff. All too often the term indicates nothing more than a new management style which functions by using creative technologies and processes borrowed from the design industry. By contrast, successful start-ups, in which designers have been allowed to apply their knowledge from the outset, amply demonstrate the potential inherent in this kind of working environment.

Let us take another look at classic graphic design, which, amid all the new developments, naturally continues to offer the same services it has always done—albeit perhaps in increased abundance and in ways that are more powerful than ever before. On first consideration, it is apparent that it is not that simple to present an overview of current trends and developments. Countless websites, blogs, social media streams, and printed publications provide a massive amount of information about the most recent work of creatives from all over the world. The need to classify what is relevant, and what may have lasting significance, makes the task even more problematic. However, despite constant changes in typography, imagery, and designers' personal style, it is still possible to spot trends that will likely define the future. Even traditional media such as posters are progressively shifting towards moving images and, alongside standard wall posters, more and more animated versions are appearing on display stands or on the web. The term "art direction", which took hold in the 1940s in the field of magazine design, has come to stand for a new way of working in graphic design, which includes the use of photography and illustration in brand presentations. The infographic, which already flourished in medieval books, is living through a new golden age and, under the label of "visual journalism", is deployed in many printed and online magazines as a new narrative form which helps with the interpretation of editorial content. Similarly, the field of corporate design has undergone visible and lasting changes. Rules laid down in the 1960s, which demanded uniformity and rigor, seem to have fallen out of fashion, gradually making way for a flexible and playful approach to branding.

The much-vaunted transition from the industrial age—which created the need in the first place amongst key industries for visual communication—to the digital age has shaped the history of graphic design in the 20th century. Consequently, most recent developments can only be understood in the context of a tradition dating back more than a century. They can be seen as an alternative strategy but also as a step forward. Without the culture of the poster that flourished in the 1890s, today's fashion campaigns would be unthinkable, as would the user interface on a smartphone were it not for the modernizations of the 1920s. However, we can only hazard a guess as to how future developments will look. And we can scarcely begin to predict what a visitor to a design studio will observe 10 years from now.

Continuing technological change, in conjunction with the still not finally determined definition of the designer's job, are together creating a very special framework which, in the future, will make it possible to explore endless new avenues. Whether virtual reality, 3D printing, artificial intelligence, or still undreamt-of innovations—designers will be there, ready to turn their hands to all kinds of challenges and to use their talents and skills to find fascinating solutions.

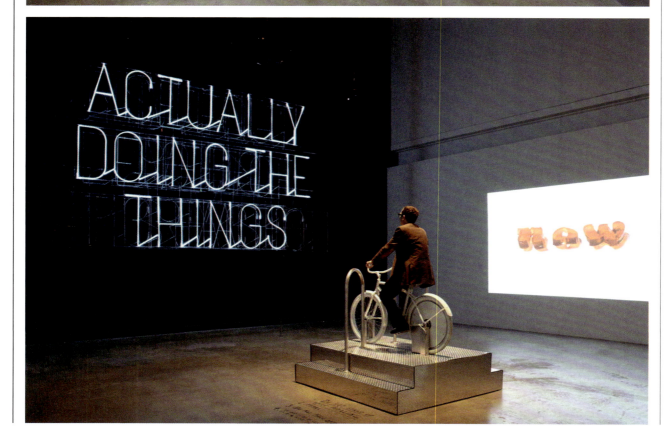

Graphic designer Stefan Sagmeister first set up his traveling exhibition *The Happy Show* in 2012, which was followed four years later by *The Happy Film*, his documentary on the same subject, the things that make people happy.

Der Grafikdesigner Stefan Sagmeister realisierte 2012 zunächst die Wanderausstellung *The Happy Show*. Vier Jahre später stellte er unter dem Titel *The Happy Film* einen Dokumentarfilm fertig, der sich ebenfalls damit beschäftigt, was Menschen glücklich macht.

En 2012, le graphiste Stefan Sagmeister présentait l'exposition itinérante *The Happy Show*. Quatre ans plus tard, il a réalisé un documentaire intitulé *The Happy Film*, qui aborde à son tour ce qui rend les gens heureux.

GRAFIKDESIGN UND SO WEITER

Einleitung von Jens Müller

Betrat man Mitte der 1980er-Jahre ein Designstudio und dann erst wieder zehn Jahre später, erhielt man beim zweiten Besuch den Eindruck eines völlig neuen Berufs. Zeichentische, Klebeutensilien und Behälter voller Stifte waren Bildschirmen, Tastaturen und anderen grauen Gerätschaften gewichen. Der heute viel beschworene digitale Wandel der Wirtschaft – er fand im Grafikdesign bereits vor rund drei Jahrzehnten statt. Innerhalb kürzester Zeit standen Soft- und Hardwarelösungen zur Verfügung, die es erlaubten, perfekte Druckvorlagen komplett am Bildschirm zu erstellen. Die zuvor im Produktionsprozess benötigten analogen Hilfsmittel wurden genauso überflüssig wie zahlreiche externe Dienstleister, die bis dahin ganz selbstverständlich die Arbeit vom Entwurf bis zur Drucklegung begleitet hatten. Parallel setzte sich in den 1990er-Jahren das Internet als neues Massenmedium durch und bildete die Basis für die nächste Stufe der digitalen Revolution. Dass die meisten Gestalterinnen und Gestalter diesen existenziellen Umbruch ganz selbstverständlich mitmachten, ist durch eine konstante Bereitschaft zur Transformation, die gewissermaßen in der DNA des Berufs verankert ist, am besten zu erklären.

In Wechselwirkung mit technischen Weiterentwicklungen und veränderten wirtschaftlichen Bedingungen entdeckte und erschloss die Designszene im Laufe des 20. Jahrhunderts immer wieder neue Aufgabenfelder für sich – von einheitlichen Firmenidentitäten über Leitsysteme für Gebäude bis hin zur Gestaltung von Websites. Dazu kamen individuelle Grenzgänger, die an der Schwelle von Produkt- und Kommunikationsdesign arbeiteten oder in ihrer Arbeit beispielsweise Architektur und Grafikdesign verbanden. Diese Vielfalt sorgte im Laufe der Zeit für eine zunehmend heterogene Wahrnehmung der Profession. Heute werden Designer mal als rein ausführende Dienstleister, kreative Partner, strategische Berater oder visuelle Ideengeber, zuweilen auch als Künstler von ihren Auftraggebern wahrgenommen. Selbst etablierte und international gefragte Kolleginnen und Kollegen leben mit der Situation, dass sie bei manchen Aufträgen mit absoluter gestalterischer Freiheit arbeiten können und bei anderen Projekten wiederum eine sehr spezifisch definierte Leistung abzuliefern haben.

Die Möglichkeit, digitale Entwürfe viel schneller und technisch einfacher umzusetzen, hat dafür gesorgt, dass Auftraggeber stärker in den Designprozess eingreifen als im analogen Zeitalter. Zu Zeiten, in denen es also zunehmend schwer wird, den Expertenstatus aufrechtzuerhalten, scheint es eine logische Schlussfolgerung, dass sich der Beruf verändert. Die Suche nach einer neuen Rolle des Designers läuft auf vollen Touren. Bereits vor mehr als einem Jahrzehnt rückte das Thema Autorenschaft in den Fokus. Grundlegende Fähigkeiten wie das Wissen um die publikumswirksame Aufbereitung und Zusammenstellung von Inhalten wurden nun auch in eigener Sache eingesetzt. Dank der Digitalisierung war es auf einmal nicht nur viel einfacher, eigene Bücher und Zeitschriften zu gestalten, sondern diese auch selbst herzustellen und zu vertreiben. Sowohl aus nicht kommerziellen Side Projects als auch aus businessorientierten Start-ups entwickelten sich zahlreiche spannende Publikationen – darunter Magazine wie die britische Filmzeitschrift *Little White Lies* oder sogar eigenständige Verlage wie Spector Books.

Aber auch in ganz anderen Bereichen wurden Gestalterinnen und Gestalter in neuer Rolle tätig: Stefan Sagmeister erzielte beispielsweise mit der Wanderausstellung *The Happy Show*, in der er sich mit der großen Frage nach dem Glück befasst, einen internationalen Publikumserfolg – und ließ auch noch den Dokumentarfilm *The Happy Film* folgen, der in vielen Ländern in den Kinos lief. Tina Roth-Eisenberg entwickelte 2008 die Vortragsreihe *Creative-Mornings*, die inzwischen in rund 180 Städten auf der ganzen Welt veranstaltet wird. Einige Jahre später gründete sie zudem das Start-up Tattly, das temporäre Tattoos mit Entwürfen von Designern und Illustratoren vertreibt. Kashiwa Sato entwickelte für den japanischen Automobilhersteller Honda ein neues Segment platzsparender Microcars, für die er mit seinem Studio die „Total Creative Direction" übertragen bekam. Unter dem Namen „N" verantwortete er das Fahrzeugdesign, das Grafikdesign sowie die Kampagne zur Einführung im Jahr 2011. Joe Gebbia, der 2005 sein Studium an der Rhode Island School of Design abgeschlossen hatte, entwickelte im Anschluss mit Freunden eine Website, auf der man Wohnungen zur Zwischenmiete anbieten konnte. Heute wird seine Plattform Airbnb in über 190 Ländern und von über 150 Millionen Menschen genutzt.

Zögerlich setzt sich auch in der etablierten Wirtschaft die Erkenntnis durch, dass Designerinnen und Designer viel mehr für Unternehmen tun können, als es das traditionelle Aufgabenspektrum mit sich bringt. In den letzten Jahren ist der nicht unumstrittene Begriff „Design Thinking" aufgetaucht. Leider ist damit nicht immer gemeint, den Designer als integralen Bestandteil neuer Projektentwicklungen zu begreifen, der diese durch eine andere Sichtweise als das Fach- und Wirtschaftspersonal mitprägt. Allzu oft bezeichnet der Begriff nur eine neue Managementmethode, die mit kreativen Techniken und Abläufen aus der Designbranche arbeitet. Erfolgreiche Start-ups, in denen Gestalter von Anfang an und gleichberechtigt ihr Wissen einbringen, beweisen hingegen, welches Potenzial dieser Arbeitskonstellation innewohnt.

Wenden wir uns noch einmal dem klassischen Grafikdesign zu, das es bei allen Neuentwicklungen natürlich nach wie vor gibt und vielleicht sogar in größerer Fülle und mit stärkeren Ausprägungen als je zuvor. Zunächst ist es gar nicht so einfach, sich einen Überblick über aktuelle Tendenzen und Entwicklungen zu verschaffen. Zahllose Websites, Blogs, Social Media Streams und gedruckte Publikationen bilden zwar in hoher Dichte die neuesten Arbeiten von Kreativen aus aller Welt ab, die Einordnung, was relevant ist und nachhaltige Bedeutung haben könnte, fällt aber umso schwerer. Unabhängig von sich ständig wandelnder Typografie oder Bildsprache sowie von individuellen Handschriften lassen sich aktuell dennoch einige prägende Trends für die Zukunft erkennen: Auch traditionelle Medien wie Plakate orientieren sich verstärkt in Richtung Bewegtbild und werden zusätzlich zum klassischen Aushang immer häufiger auch in animierter Form auf Displays oder im Web verwendet. Der Begriff „Artdirection", der sich in den 1940er-Jahren im Bereich der Magazingestaltung etabliert hat, steht immer häufiger für eine neue Arbeitsweise im Grafikdesign, unter der die Inszenierung von Marken mit den Mitteln der Fotografie und der Illustration verstanden wird. Die Informationsgrafik, die bereits in mittelalterlichen Büchern Anwendung fand, erlebt eine neue Blütezeit und wird unter dem Stichwort „Visual Journalism" von zahlreichen Print- und Onlinemagazinen als moderne Erzählform redaktioneller Inhalte eingesetzt. Wirklich nachhaltige Veränderungen sind dagegen im Bereich Corporate Design festzustellen. In den 1960er-Jahren definierte Regeln zu Vereinheitlichung und Strenge scheinen überholt und weichen zunehmend einem flexiblen und spielerischen Umgang mit Branding.

Der viel beschworene Übergang vom Industriezeitalter, das wesentliche Bereiche der visuellen Kommunikation überhaupt erst notwendig gemacht hat, hin zum Informationszeitalter prägt die Geschichte des Grafikdesigns im 20. Jahrhundert. Ganz aktuelle Entwicklungen sind daher nur im Kontext der inzwischen mehr als hundertjährigen Tradition zu verstehen. Ob als Gegenentwurf oder als Evolution: Aktuelle Modekampagnen wären ohne die Plakatkultur der 1890er-Jahre genauso wenig denkbar wie die grafische Benutzeroberfläche eines Smartphones ohne die visuellen Modernisierungen der 1920er-Jahre. Wie zukünftige Entwicklungen im Detail aussehen werden, können wir dennoch nur sehr bedingt erahnen. Was ein Besucher in zehn Jahren in einem Designstudio erblicken wird, lässt sich also kaum prognostizieren.

Der fortschreitende technische Wandel und die nicht abschließend festgelegte Definition des Designerberufes bilden jedoch eine besondere Konstellation, die es auch in der Zukunft immer wieder ermöglichen wird, ganz neue Wege zu beschreiten. Ob Virtual Reality, 3-D-Druck, künstliche Intelligenz oder heute noch gar nicht vorstellbare Neuerungen – Designerinnen und Designer werden dabei sein, sich veränderten Herausforderungen zuwenden und mit ihren Talenten und Kenntnissen faszinierende Lösungen finden.

In the past the term "art direction" had come to describe a new way of working in the world of graphic design. Creative agencies such as Snask of Stockholm nowadays develop lavish imagery in the photographic studio, paying close attention to every detail of the production, as in this one for the fashion label Monki.

In den vergangenen Jahren wurde unter dem Begriff „Art-direction" eine neue Arbeits-weise im Grafikdesign populär. Designbüros wie Snask aus Stockholm konzipieren aufwen-dige Bildmotive im Fotostudio und kontrollieren jedes Detail der Inszenierung, wie hier für das Modelabel Monki.

Le terme «direction artistique» a pendant un temps désigné un nouveau mode de travail dans le monde du graphisme. Dans des studios photo, des agences de création comme Snask, à Stockholm, conçoivent de splen-dides images et contrôlent chaque détail de la production, comme ici pour le label de mode Monki.

LE GRAPHISME ET PLUS ENCORE

Introduction de Jens Müller

Une personne qui, après avoir visité un studio de graphisme au milieu des années 1980, n'y serait retournée que dix ans plus tard, aurait eu le sentiment d'avoir affaire à un tout autre métier. Les tables à dessin, adhésifs et gobelets remplis de crayons et de stylos en tous genres ont cédé la place à des moniteurs, des claviers et autres appareils. Dans le monde du graphisme, le passage à l'économie numérique si rebattu s'est produit voici une trentaine d'années. Du jour au lendemain sont apparues des solutions logicielles et matérielles permettant de réaliser entièrement à l'écran des matrices d'impression parfaites. Les outils de travail analogiques autrefois nécessaires à la production sont soudain devenus aussi superflus que la foule de prestataires externes qui intervenaient autrefois tout naturellement – de la conception à la mise sous presse. Parallèlement, dans les années 1990, Internet s'est imposé comme un nouveau média de masse et a posé les bases de l'étape suivante de la révolution numérique. Le fait que la plupart des graphistes ont tout naturellement entériné ces changements s'explique le mieux par la constante disposition aux innovations qui est en quelque sorte ancrée dans l'ADN de la profession.

Tout au long du XXe siècle, la scène du graphisme n'a cessé d'adopter de nouveaux champs d'application en synergie avec les évolutions technologiques et économiques – des images de marque globales aux signalétiques de bâtiments et à la conception de sites web. Elle s'est enrichie d'électrons libres qui travaillaient à la croisée entre design de produit et communication ou qui conjuguaient par exemple dans leurs projets architecture et design graphique. Au fil du temps, cette diversité a entraîné une perception de plus en plus hétérogène de la profession. Aujourd'hui, leurs commanditaires perçoivent les graphistes comme de simples prestataires, des partenaires créatifs, des conseillers stratégiques ou parfois des artistes. Les confrères bien établis et internationalement sollicités doivent eux-mêmes s'accommoder d'une situation dans laquelle certaines commandes leur permettent de travailler en toute liberté créative, alors que de nombreux projets leur imposent des prestations encadrées par des contraintes spécifiques.

En pouvant réaliser des projets numériques de manière beaucoup plus rapide et techniquement plus simple, les commanditaires interviennent aujourd'hui plus fortement dans le processus graphique qu'à l'ère analogique. À une époque où il devient chaque fois plus difficile de préserver un statut d'expert, ce métier se retrouve logiquement aussi en pleine évolution. La recherche d'un nouveau rôle du graphiste tourne à plein régime, et voici déjà plus de dix ans que la notion d'autorat est d'actualité. Des compétences de base, à savoir l'élaboration des contenus et une présentation attirante au public, suffisent au graphiste pour livrer un projet. Grâce à la numérisation, il est devenu beaucoup plus facile non seulement de concevoir ses propres livres et magazines, mais aussi de les produire et de les diffuser sans intervenants externes. En parallèle, des projets non commerciaux et des startups ont motivé l'apparition de nombreuses publications passionnantes (comme la revue de cinéma *Little White Lies* d'une agence londonienne, pour ne citer qu'un exemple) et de maisons d'édition indépendantes (comme Spector Books).

Mais dans bien d'autres domaines encore les graphistes sont devenus actifs en endossant des rôles inédits: avec son exposition itinérante *The Happy Show,* dans laquelle il abordait la grande question du bonheur, Stefan Sagmeister a connu un succès public international et l'a même fait suivre du documentaire *The Happy Film,* projeté dans les salles de nombreux pays. En 2008, Tina Roth-Eisenberg lançait la série de conférences *CreativeMornings,* organisée aujourd'hui dans quelque 180 villes du monde entier. Quelques années plus tard, elle fondait en outre la startup Tattly, qui distribue des tatouages éphémères dessinés par des graphistes et des illustrateurs. Kashiwa Sato a développé pour le compte du constructeur automobile japonais Honda un nouveau modèle de voiture compacte dont il a reçu la direction créative absolue avec son studio. Sous l'appellation «N», il a signé le design de la voiture, le graphisme et la campagne de lancement en 2011. En 2005, au sortir de ses études de graphisme à la Rhode Island School of Design, Joe Gebbia développait avec quelques amis un site web sur lequel proposer des appartements à la location temporaire. Sa plate-forme Airbnb est aujourd'hui utilisée par plus de 150 millions d'utilisateurs dans plus de 190 pays.

Dans l'économie courante s'impose peu à peu, et non sans réticences, l'acceptation que les graphistes peuvent faire beaucoup plus pour les entreprises que le traditionnel éventail de missions de la profession. Ces dernières années est apparu le concept controversé de «design thinking», qui ne veut pas toujours dire hélas que le designer est compris comme un acteur intégré à part entière dans le lancement de projets ou comme capable d'imprimer sa marque avec une vision différente de celle de la direction et des spécialistes. Le concept ne désigne bien trop souvent qu'une nouvelle méthode de management qui applique des techniques et des processus créatifs propres aux métiers graphiques. Inversement, des startups couronnées de succès, dans lesquelles les créatifs apportent d'emblée leur expertise, démontrent le potentiel inhérent à ce genre d'environnement de travail.

Mais revenons au graphisme classique, qui continue bien sûr d'exister au milieu de toutes ces nouvelles évolutions, peut-être encore davantage et sous des formes plus affirmées que jamais. La première chose à dire, c'est qu'il n'est pas si facile de se faire une idée globale des tendances et développements actuels. Si d'innombrables sites web, blogs, flux de médias sociaux et publications imprimées relaient en masse les travaux les plus récents des créatifs du monde entier, le tri de ce qui est pertinent et pourrait avoir une valeur durable n'est pas une tâche aisée. Mais en dépit des changements constants en matière de typographies, d'images et de styles individuels, on n'en discerne pas moins quelques tendances déterminantes pour l'avenir: les supports traditionnels comme l'affiche s'orientent eux aussi de plus en plus fortement vers l'image animée et à côté de l'affichage classique, les versions animées sont chaque fois plus fréquentes sur les écrans d'affichage ou sur le web. La notion de direction artistique, qui s'était établie dans les années 1940 dans le domaine de la création de magazines, s'affirme comme une nouvelle méthode de travail graphique assurant les présentations de marques par le truchement de la photographie et de l'illustration. Le graphisme d'information, déjà présent dans les ouvrages médiévaux, connaît une nouvelle floraison sous l'appellation de journalisme visuel dans de nombreux magazines imprimés ou en ligne comme forme narrative moderne de contenus rédactionnels. Cela dit, des changements vraiment durables sont aussi clairement perceptibles dans le domaine du design corporatif. Les règles établies dans les années 1960 sous le signe de la rigueur et de l'homogénéisation semblent aujourd'hui dépassées et cèdent souvent la place à un traitement souple et ludique de l'image de marque.

Le passage si souvent invoqué de l'ère industrielle – à l'origine du besoin pour les principaux secteurs d'une communication visuelle – à l'ère numérique marque l'histoire du graphisme au XXᵉ siècle. Les évolutions les plus récentes doivent donc être comprises dans le contexte d'une tradition plus que séculaire. Que ce soit comme contre-projet ou comme évolution, les campagnes de mode actuelles seraient tout aussi peu concevables sans la culture de l'affiche des années 1890 que l'interface graphique d'un smartphone sans les modernisations des années 1920. À quoi ressembleront les évolutions futures? Nous ne pouvons l'imaginer qu'avec toutes les réserves d'usage: ce que découvrira le visiteur d'un studio de design dans dix ans ne peut guère être prédit.

Le changement technologique imparable et la définition encore en suspens du métier de graphiste forment néanmoins une configuration particulière qui permettra d'ouvrir des voies entièrement nouvelles. Qu'il s'agisse de la réalité virtuelle, de l'impression 3D, de l'intelligence artificielle ou d'innovations encore inimaginables aujourd'hui, les graphistes seront présents, relèveront les nouveaux défis et élaboreront des solutions fascinantes grâce à leur talent et leur savoir.

1967 · M. Katzourakis · GR · Poster

1960s · Anonymous · DE · Poster

1960 ————

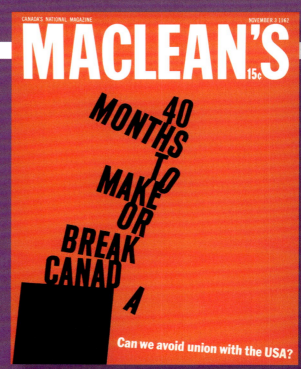

1962 · Allan Robb Fleming · CA · Magazine cover

1962 · Paul Rand · US · Logo · ABC Television

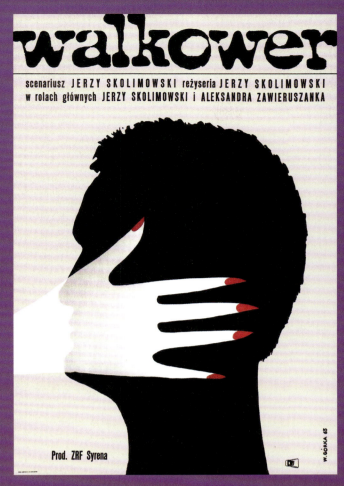

1965 · Wiktor Górka · PL · Poster

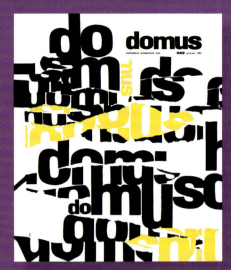

1960 · William Klein · IT · Magazine cover

1969

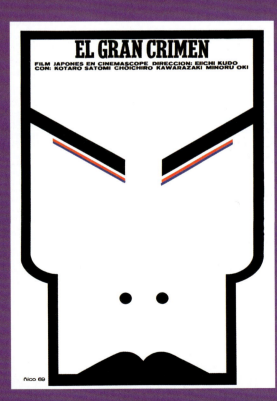

1969 · "Nico" (Antonio Perez Gonzalez) · CU · Poster

1963 · Benno Wissing · NL · Poster

The 1960s saw the heyday of modernist-minimalist graphic design, and at first, Switzerland was in the vanguard. The wide-ranging new style was used in a whole series of different ways—from food packaging and magazine design to signage systems for airports—and was soon picked up right across the world, earning itself the name of International Style. At about the same time the merits of powerful imagery were at last becoming widely accepted, leading to a new standard in brand communication. An international group of designers, including Paul Rand, Otl Aicher, F.H.K. Henrion, and Yusaku Kamekura, made a defining impression on all aspects of graphics, and alongside the austerity of the International Style, the second half of the decade also produced an innovative, emotionally charged visual vocabulary that defied all previous convention. Set against a musical backdrop of jazz, pop, and rock, a new kind of imagery was created which began in western subculture but quickly found its way into the mainstream.

Die 1960er-Jahre waren die Blütezeit der modernistisch-reduzierten Grafik. Tonangebend war hier zunächst vor allem die Schweiz. Der neue Stil fand sich in einem breiten Spektrum unterschiedlichster Anwendungsformen – von Lebensmittelverpackungen und Magazinen bis zu Leitsystemen auf Flughäfen, verbreitete sich aber auch in rasanter Geschwindigkeit überall in der Welt, was ihm den Namen „International Style" einbrachte. Gleichzeitig setzten sich die Vorzüge eines konsequenten Erscheinungsbildes endgültig durch und führten zu einer neuen Qualität in der Markenkommunikation. Eine Riege internationaler Gestalter wie Paul Rand, Otl Aicher, F.H.K. Henrion oder Yusaku Kamekura prägten dieses neue Arbeitsfeld nachhaltig. Neben aller Strenge stand besonders die zweite Hälfte des Jahrzehnts gleichermaßen auch für ein neuartiges konventionsfreies und emotionsgeladenes Design. Besonders im Umfeld von Jazz-, Pop- und Rockmusik entwickelten sich neue Bildsprachen, die, ausgehend von der westlichen Subkultur, schnell ihren Weg in den Mainstream fanden.

Les années 1960 marquent l'apogée d'un graphisme à la fois minimaliste et moderniste, et le ton est d'abord donné par la Suisse. Le nouveau style trouve alors son application dans les domaines les plus divers, des emballages alimentaires et du graphisme éditorial à la signalétique dans les aéroports, et il se répand à une vitesse effrénée dans le monde entier, ce qui lui vaut le nom de «style international». En même temps, les avantages d'une image plus cohérente s'imposent enfin et conduisent à une nouvelle norme dans la communication de marque. Une série de créateurs internationaux comme Paul Rand, Otl Aicher, F.H.K. Henrion ou Yusaku Kamekura marquent durablement de leur empreinte ce nouveau champ d'activité. À côté de toute cette rigueur, la seconde moitié de la décennie voit aussi émerger un graphisme inédit, libéré des conventions et véhiculé par un vocabulaire visuel plein d'émotions. Dans le contexte du jazz, de la pop et du rock se développe une nouvelle imagerie qui, partant de la sous-culture, entre rapidement dans le *mainstream*.

1960

The United States successfully sends the first weather and navigation satellites into space

The first episode of *The Flintstones* is aired on TV

OPEC (Organization of the Petroleum Exporting Countries) is founded in Baghdad

John F. Kennedy is elected U.S. president

The first birth control pills go on sale under the name Enovid

Alfred Hitchcock's *Psycho* goes on general release

The Summer Olympic Games are held in Rome

American engineer Theodore Maiman demonstrates the first working laser

Filming of Federico Fellini's *La Dolce Vita* takes place in Rome

The European Free Trade Association (EFTA) is formed in reaction to the European Union

1961

Audrey Hepburn stars in *Breakfast at Tiffany's*

At the Vienna Summit between Kennedy and Soviet Premier Nikita Khrushchev the Berlin question is discussed

In New York, the name Fluxus is given to a new art movement

Soviet Yuri Gagarin becomes the first person to travel into space

The World Wildlife Fund (WWF) is established

Construction of the Berlin Wall begins

The film musical *West Side Story* premieres

American Melvin Calvin receives the Nobel Prize in Chemistry

Amnesty International is formed in London

1962

Andy Warhol opens his New York studio, the Factory

The first live transatlantic TV program is broadcast from the United States to Britain via Telstar

Marilyn Monroe is found dead in her apartment in Los Angeles

The Cuban Missile Crisis has the world on edge for 13 days in October

The first Wal-Mart store opens

The U.S. Supreme Court rules that photographs of naked men are not obscene, decriminalizing male pornographic magazines

Sean Connery stars as 007 in *Dr. No*, the first film in the James Bond series

The Space Needle in Seattle is completed in time for the 1962 World's Fair

1963

American Edward Lorenz publishes his study on the "butterfly effect" which has great significance in the development of chaos theory

The Beach Boys song "Surfin' USA" is released

Martin Luther King, Jr. delivers his "I Have a Dream" speech in Washington, DC

Maurice Sendak's *Where the Wild Things Are* is first published

CLEOPATRA

Cleopatra with Elizabeth Taylor and Richard Burton becomes the most expensive film ever made (until 1999)

English accountant Edward Craven Walker invents the lava lamp

Kennedy is assassinated in Dallas on November 22

American Harvey Ball designs the smiley face for the State Mutual Life Assurance Company

1964

Ranger 7 sends back the first close-up photographs of the Moon

Petula Clark's song "Downtown" becomes an international hit

Nelson Mandela is sentenced to life in prison

The original BASIC language is designed by John G. Kemeny, Thomas E. Kurtz, and Mary Kenneth Keller

U.S. Congress signs in the Civil Rights Act of 1964

The TV quiz show *Jeopardy!* airs for the first time on NBC

A military coup takes place in Brazil

Chairman Mao's *Little Red Book* is first published

Inspired by the Free Speech Movement, students in California stage various protests

The first Ford Mustang goes into production

1965

Robert Indiana's *LOVE* is commissioned as a Christmas card by MoMA

Malcolm X is assassinated

The Beatles release the film and album versions of *Help!*

Operation Rolling Thunder increases U.S. aerial bombardment of Vietnam

The Russian Alexey Leonov becomes the first person to walk in space

The first commercially successful minicomputer, the 12-bit PDP-8, is launched by the Digital Equipment Corporation

London-based fashion designer Mary Quant introduces the miniskirt

David Lean's film *Doctor Zhivago* is released

The Selma to Montgomery marches are organized to demonstrate in support of the right to vote for African-Americans

1966

Mao Zedong launches the Cultural Revolution

American sexologists William Masters and Virginia Johnson publish the first findings of their research in *Human Sexual Response*

The first episode of *Star Trek* is aired on NBC

Simon & Garfunkel's album *Sounds of Silence* is released

The unmanned Soviet *Luna 9* spacecraft makes the first controlled, rocket-assisted landing on the Moon

Franco Nero stars in the original *Django* movie, directed by Sergio Corbucci

England wins the soccer World Cup

Dutch crown princess Beatrix marries Claus von Amsberg

The Salazar Bridge is opened in Lisbon

1967

Disney's version of *The Jungle Book* is released in cinemas

Christiaan Barnard performs the first successful heart transplant operation in a hospital in Cape Town

The Boeing 737 airliner makes its first flight

Che Guevara is shot dead in Bolivia

The first issue of *Rolling Stone* magazine is published

Washoe the chimpanzee begins to learn American Sign Language

In the Six-Day War, Israel captures the Gaza Strip and the Sinai Peninsula from Egypt, the West Bank from Jordan, and the Golan Heights from Syria

The Doors release their self-titled debut studio album

1968

McDonald's introduces the Big Mac across the United States

Intel, the semiconductor chip manufacturer, is founded

Widespread civil unrest occurs in France, later known as the events of May 68

The U.S. edition of Andrew Garve's thriller *The Long Short Cut* is the first book to be printed completely using automated typesetting

Stanley Kubrick's *2001: A Space Odyssey* is released

Martin Luther King, Jr. is assassinated in Memphis, Tennessee

Richard Nixon is elected the 37th President of the United States after the first campaign that relied on TV

The Winter Olympics is held in Grenoble, France

Jane Fonda stars in the kitsch classic *Barbarella*

1969

The Woodstock Music & Art Fair is held in White Lake, NY

On July 20, Neil Armstrong becomes the first person to walk on the surface of the Moon

John Lennon and Yoko Ono hold two week-long Bed-Ins for Peace to protest against the Vietnam War

The first episode of *Sesame Street* appears on TV

The Stonewall riots in Christopher Street, New York, become the most important event leading to the gay liberation movement

Yasser Arafat becomes leader of the Palestine Liberation Organization

Dennis Hopper and Peter Fonda star in *Easy Rider*

Muammar Gaddafi leads a military coup in Libya which overthrows the monarchy and replaces it with the Libyan Arab Republic

The supersonic airliner Concorde makes its first flight

1960

A **World Design Conference** (Sekai Dezain Kaigi) is held in Tokyo, featuring speakers from all over the world

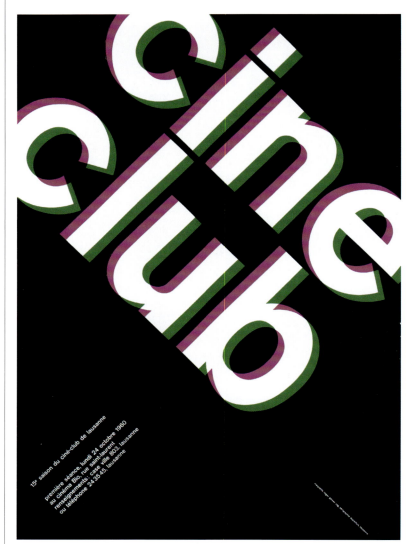

1960 · Roger-Virgil Geiser · CH · Poster

1960 · Kazumasa Nagai · JP · Logo · Nippon Design Center

1960 · Anton Stankowski · DE · Logo · Viessmann

1960 · Yusaku Kamekura · JP · Logo · Japan Architects Association

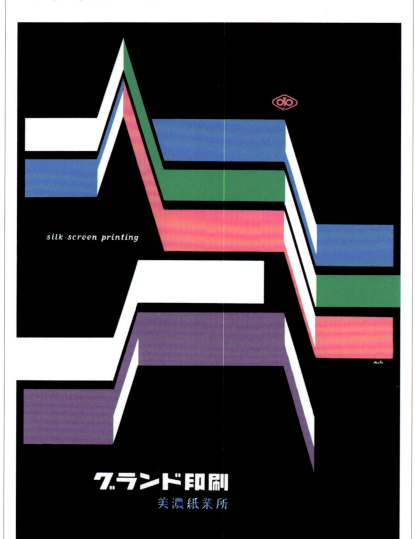

1960 · Mitsutomo Ishikawa · JP · Poster

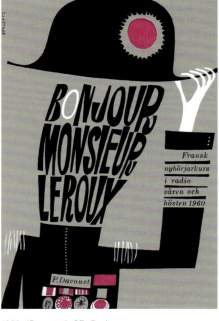

1960 · "Bergentz" · SE · Book cover

1960 · Erik Bruun · FI · Poster

1960 · "KTG" · CZ · Poster

1960 · Victor Palla · PT · Book cover

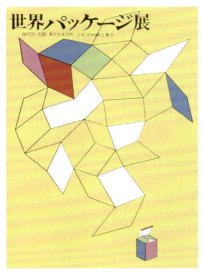

1960 · Isao Arimoto · JP · Poster

1960 · Ryuichi Yamashiro · JP · Poster

1960 · Franz Fässler · CH · Poster

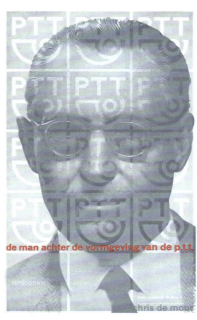

1960 · Pieter Brattinga · NL · Poster

1960 · Karl Gerstner · CH · Poster

1960 · Maurice Binder · US · Poster

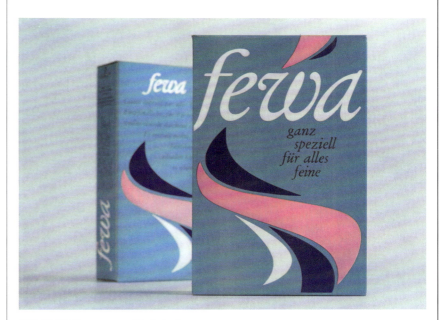

1960 · Wolf D. Zimmermann · DE · Packaging

1960 · Wojciech Zamecznik · PL · Poster

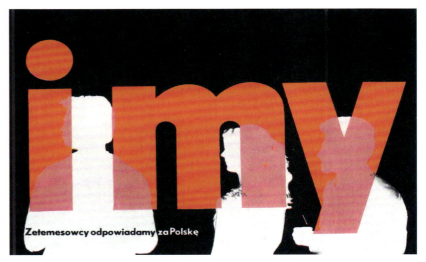

1960 · Wojciech Zamecznik · PL · Poster

Gewerbemuseum Basel
Ausstellung «die Zeitung»
9. April bis 18. Mai 1958
Geöffnet
werktags 10-12 und 14-18
sonntags 10-12 und 14-17
Eintritt frei

die
Zeitung

Entwurf Ruder · Druck Gewerbeschule Basel

1958 · Emil Ruder · CH · Poster

Emil Ruder (1914, Zurich – 1970, Basel) was a Swiss typographer and designer, and one of the major contributors to what is referred to as the Swiss Style. After an apprenticeship as a compositor, Ruder attended the Zurich School of Arts and Crafts, later becoming a teacher at the Basel School of Design alongside Armin Hofmann. He became well known for his individual and holistic approach to design and teaching, regularly applying a systematic combination of practice, theory, and philosophy. After WWII, Ruder was one of the first to introduce new laws of composition in place of traditional typography, in order to focus on usability and legibility.

Emil Ruder (1914, Zürich – 1970, Basel) war ein Schweizer Typograf und Grafikdesigner, der zu den bedeutendsten Vertretern des sogenannten Swiss Style gehörte. Nach seiner Ausbildung zum Schriftsetzer besuchte Ruder die Kunstgewerbeschule in Zürich und lehrte später, wie auch Armin Hofmann, an der Allgemeinen Gewerbeschule Basel. Bekannt wurde Ruder für seinen individuellen, ganzheitlichen Ansatz bei Design und Unterricht, der stets bestimmt war von einer systematischen Kombination aus Praxis, Theorie und Philosophie. Nach dem Zweiten Weltkrieg führte Ruder als einer der Ersten zum Zweck besserer Verwendbarkeit und Lesbarkeit neue Gesetze der Komposition anstelle traditioneller Typografie ein.

Emil Ruder (1914, Zurich – 1970, Bâle) fut un typographe et graphiste suisse et un protagoniste majeur du style suisse. Après une formation d'apprenti compositeur et des études à l'École des arts et métiers de Zurich, Ruder devint plus tard professeur à l'École de design de Bâle avec Armin Hofmann. Il se fit connaître par son approche personnelle et holistique du design et de l'enseignement, appliquant régulièrement une combinaison systématique de pratique, de théorie et de philosophie. Après la Seconde Guerre mondiale, Ruder fut un des premiers à introduire de nouvelles règles de composition pour remplacer la typographie traditionnelle et concentrer l'attention sur l'utilité et la lisibilité.

1961 · Emil Ruder · CH · Magazine covers

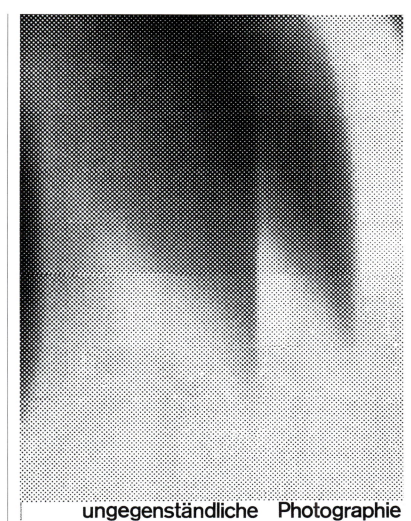

ungegenständliche Photographie

Gewerbemuseum Basel 27. Februar bis 10. April 1960   Täglich 10-12 und 14-17 Uhr Eintritt frei

1960 · Emil Ruder · CH · Poster

sammlung
richard doetsch-
benziger
bücher
ostasiatische
kleinkunst
gewerbemuseum
basel
26.januar bis
3.märz 1957

täglich 10-12 14-18
eintritt fr.1.-
studierende und
schüler 50 rp.
schüler mit lehrer
eintritt frei

1957 · Emil Ruder · CH · Poster

Swiss graphic design is a particularly telling example of how, in the age of analog technology, developments in visual imagery could catch on internationally and rapidly spread from one country to another. Only a few years after it was first conceived in its native Switzerland in the mid-1950s, similar, or in some cases identical forms of visual expression emerged worldwide. In the course of the 1960s, in Poland, as in Greece, Argentina, or Japan, the functional style first coined in Basel and Zurich became globally accepted as one that could be applied without restriction in any number of contexts. Consequently, the name "Swiss Style" was quickly replaced by the term "International Style."

Wie schnell und über nationale Grenzen hinweg sich bereits im analogen Zeitalter visuelle Entwicklungen verbreiteten, zeigt die Internationalisierung der Schweizer Grafik besonders eindrucksvoll. Nur wenige Jahre nach ihrer nationalen Etablierung Mitte der 1950er-Jahre tauchten weltweit vergleichbare Arbeiten auf, die ähnliche oder sogar identische Gestaltungsmaximen zeigten. Ob in Polen, Griechenland, Argentinien oder Japan: Die in Basel und Zürich geprägte funktionale Stilistik fand im Laufe der 1960er-Jahre globale und vor allem thematisch uneingeschränkte Anwendung. Der Name „Swiss Style" wurde folgerichtig bald durch den Begriff „International Style" vielfach abgelöst.

La vitesse à laquelle les évolutions visuelles ont pu se diffuser au-delà des frontières nationales dès l'ère analogique est illustrée de manière saisissante par le cas du graphisme suisse. Quelques années après l'avènement du style suisse dans son pays d'origine au milieu des années 1950, des travaux similaires, voire identiques, apparaissent déjà un peu partout dans le monde. Que ce soit en Pologne, en Grèce, en Argentine ou au Japon, le style fonctionnel d'empreinte bâloise ou zurichoise connaît dans les années 1960 une application globale et surtout thématiquement illimitée. Très logiquement, l'appellation «style suisse» devient alors «style international».

1960s · Waldemar Świerzy · PL · Poster

1963 · Iannis Svoronos · GR · Poster

1964 · Leif Frimann Anisdahl · NO · Book cover

1968 · Heinz Lippert, Winfried Holtz, Hans Buschfeld, Siegfried Himmer, Coordt von Mannstein, Graphicteam · DE · Packaging

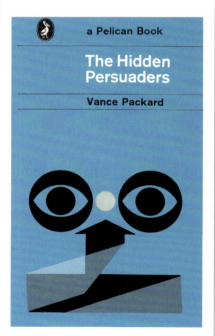

1962 · Larry Carter · UK · Book cover

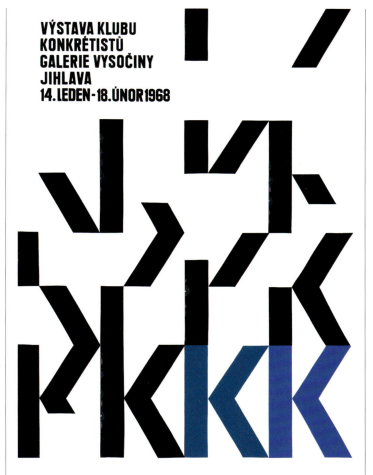

VÝSTAVA KLUBU KONKRÉTISTŮ GALERIE VYSOČINY JIHLAVA 14. LEDEN - 18. ÚNOR 1968

1968 · Jiří Hilmar · CZ · Poster

8 BIENNALE MIDDELHEIM ANTWERPEN

1965 · Paul Ibou · BE · Brochure cover

El hombre crece a través de las empresas del hombre; ellas son la ciencia y el esfuerzo acumulados por la tarea en común. La empresa es ... el hombre. Vive y avanza. Crece para servir.

SIAM

1962 · Juan Carlos Distéfano · AR · Ad

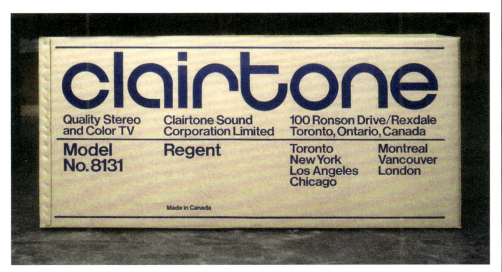

clairtone

Quality Stereo and Color TV

Clairtone Sound Corporation Limited

100 Ronson Drive/Rexdale Toronto, Ontario, Canada

Model No. 8131

Regent

Toronto New York Los Angeles Chicago

Montreal Vancouver London

Made in Canada

1966 · Burton Kramer · CA · Packaging

In 1959, Adolf Theobald and Stephan Wolf came up with the idea of a new magazine designed for young adults. Without the backing of a publisher, the two of them put together a batch of advertising orders and printed and distributed issue one of *twen* without knowing whether a second would be forthcoming. In the years that followed, the magazine became the mouthpiece for an entire generation, dealing with a range of social and cultural issues. Willy Fleckhaus's design played a major role in this success story. From the very first issue, the young art director defined the look of the magazine with its striking black covers and pioneering layouts. *twen*'s uncompromising creativity gave it international resonance and made it a trailblazer for modern magazine design.

Adolf Theobald und Stephan Wolf hatten 1959 die Idee zu einem neuartigen Magazin für junge Erwachsene. Ohne den Rückhalt eines Verlages sammelten die beiden Anzeigenaufträge und realisierten in Eigenregie den Druck einer Nullnummer. In den folgenden Jahren wurde *twen* zum Sprachrohr einer ganzen Generation, behandelt wurden gesellschaftliche wie kulturelle Themen. Eine wesentliche Rolle in dieser Erfolgsgeschichte spielte die Gestaltung von Willy Fleckhaus. Von der ersten Ausgabe an definierte der junge Artdirector das Aussehen des Hefts mit seinen markanten schwarzen Covern und radikal modernen Layouts. Die kompromisslose Gestaltung machte *twen* zum Vorreiter moderner Magazingestaltung und erfuhr internationale Resonanz.

En 1959, Adolf Theobald et Stephan Wolf eurent l'idée de créer un magazine d'un genre inédit destiné à de jeunes adultes. Sans le soutien d'aucun éditeur, il recueillirent des commandes publicitaires et réalisèrent l'impression d'un numéro un sans savoir si un deuxième suivrait. Au cours des années suivantes, *twen* devint le porte-parole de toute une génération grâce à ses sujets de société et culturels. Le graphisme de Willy Fleckhaus a joué un rôle essentiel dans cette éclatante réussite: dès le premier numéro, le jeune directeur artistique définit l'aspect visuel de la revue, avec ses couvertures noires marquantes et ses mises en pages inédites. Son graphisme sans concession fit de *twen* un précurseur du design éditorial de magazines et connut un impact international.

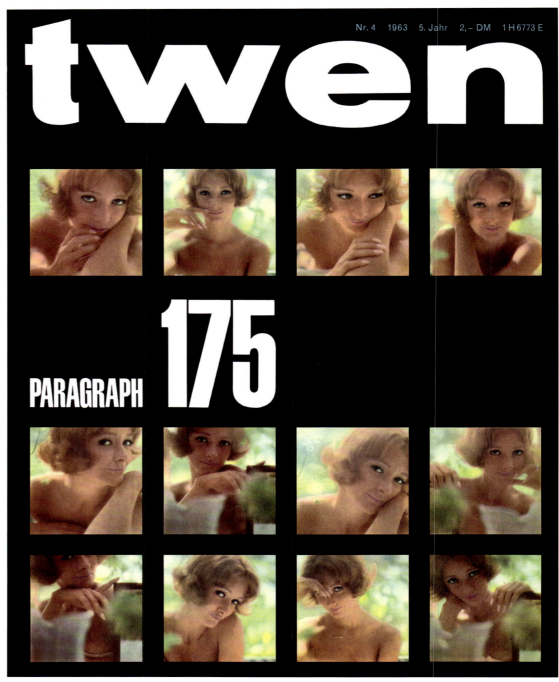

1963 · Willy Fleckhaus · DE · Magazine cover

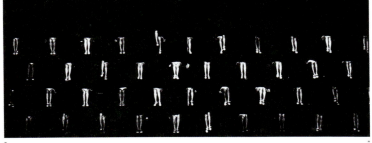

1963 · Willy Fleckhaus · DE · Magazine spreads

Willy Fleckhaus (1925, Velbert, Germany – 1983, Castelfranco di Sopra, Italy) was one of the most influential German designers from the 1950s to the 1980s. Also a journalist, Fleckhaus was a prominent book and newspaper designer, and professor of visual communications in the universities of Essen and Wuppertal. After serving in the military in WWII, he worked in various editorial positions before taking over the design direction for *Aufwärts* magazine in 1953. Fleckhaus worked closely with the Photokina photography fair for over two decades, co-founded *twen* magazine, and served as president of the German Art Directors Club from 1972–73.

Willy Fleckhaus (1925, Velbert, Deutschland – 1983, Castelfranco di Sopra, Italien) war ab den 1950er-Jahren bis zu seinem Tod einer der einflussreichsten deutschen Grafikdesigner. Zudem war er Journalist, Buch- und Zeitungsgestalter und Professor für Kommunikationsdesign an den Universitäten Essen und Wuppertal. Nach dem Militärdienst im Zweiten Weltkrieg arbeitete Fleckhaus in mehreren Redaktionen in unterschiedlichen Positionen, bis er 1953 die gestalterische Leitung der Zeitschrift *Aufwärts* übernahm. Über zwanzig Jahre lang arbeitete er zudem eng mit der Fotografiemesse Photokina zusammen, war ein Mitbegründer der Zeitschrift *twen* und diente 1972/73 als Präsident des deutschen Art Directors Club.

Willy Fleckhaus (1925, Velbert, Allemagne – 1983, Castelfranco di Sopra, Italie) fut un des graphistes allemands les plus influents des années 1950 aux années 1980, mais aussi journaliste et professeur de communication visuelle aux universités d'Essen et de Wuppertal. Après avoir servi dans l'armée pendant la Seconde Guerre mondiale, il occupa différents postes éditoriaux avant d'assurer la direction conceptuelle de la revue *Aufwärts* en 1953. Fleckhaus a collaboré étroitement avec la Photokina pendant plus de deux décennies, fut cofondateur du magazine *twen* et président de l'Art Directors Club allemand en 1972–73.

1959 · Willy Fleckhaus · DE · Magazine cover

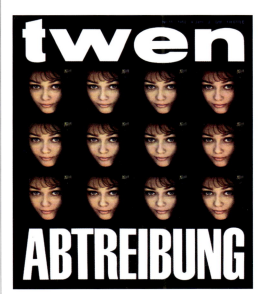

1962 · Willy Fleckhaus · DE · Magazine cover

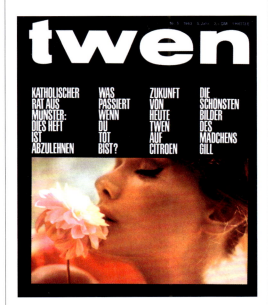

1963 · Willy Fleckhaus · DE · Magazine cover

Paul Rand (1914, New York – 1996, Norwalk, Connecticut) was an American designer who embraced the guidelines of modernism, and became renowned for his many corporate identities, including IBM, UPS, Westinghouse, and ABC. Educated at the Pratt Institute, and later a teacher at Yale University, Rand was initially influenced by the European graphic design pioneers of the 1920s and '30s. By his early 20s, Rand was already at the forefront of the graphic design field, and was art-directing several publications. In 1947, he published *Thoughts on Design*, a fundamental reference in visual communication.

Paul Rand (1914, New York – 1996, Norwalk, Connecticut) war ein amerikanischer Grafikdesigner, der sich die Leitlinien der Moderne zur Aufgabe machte und durch seine zahlreichen Logos für Unternehmen wie IBM, UPS, Westinghouse und ABC bekannt wurde. Rand, der seine Ausbildung am Pratt Institute erhielt und später an der Yale University unterrichtete, war ursprünglich von den Vorreitern des europäischen Grafikdesigns der 1920er- und 1930er-Jahre beeinflusst. Bereits als Anfang 20-Jähriger spielte er im Bereich des Grafikdesigns eine führende Rolle und fungierte bei mehreren Publikationen als Artdirector. 1947 veröffentlichte er sein Standardwerk zur visuellen Kommunikation *Thoughts on Design*.

Paul Rand (1914, New York – 1996, Norwalk, Connecticut) fut un graphiste américain qui reprit à son compte les lignes directrices du modernisme et se rendit célèbre par ses nombreuses images de marque, parmi lesquelles IBM, UPS, Westinghouse et ABC. Après une formation à l'Institut Pratt, et devenu professeur à l'université Yale, Rand fut d'abord influencé par les pionniers européens du graphisme des années 1920 et 1930. Dès le début de sa vingtaine, Rand était déjà chef de file dans le domaine et le directeur artistique de plusieurs publications. En 1947, il publia *Thoughts on Design*, référence fondamentale en matière de communication visuelle.

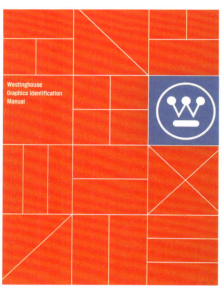

Westinghouse

abcdefghijklmnopqrstu
vwxyz st ABCDEFGHJKL
MNOPQRSTUVWXYZ&( )
1234567890$¢!?.,:;-‒―
abcdefghijklmnopqrstu
vwxyz st ABCDEFGHIJKL
MNOPQRSTUVWXYZ&( )
1234567890$¢!?.,:;-‒―

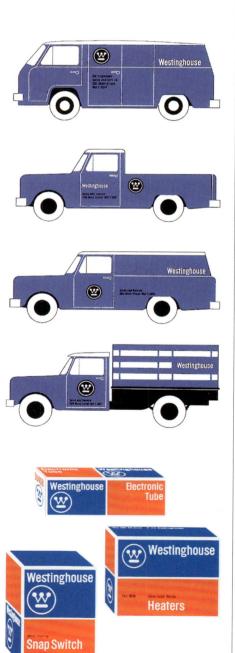

1960 · Paul Rand · US · Identity · Westinghouse

In the 1960s, Rand developed the corporate identities of both West-inghouse and IBM. With these two pioneering projects, he set the international standard of design in this newly burgeoning sector. A key part of Rand's approach was to seize upon the practice Peter Behrens had first employed in 1908, namely creating for a company its own individual corporate typeface.

In den 1960er-Jahren entwickelte Paul Rand die Firmenidentitäten für Westinghouse und IBM. Damit legte er zwei international weg-weisende Projekte dieses gerade aufblühenden Sektors vor. Rand griff dabei die um 1908 von Peter Behrens erstmals praktizierte Vor-gehensweise wieder auf, für ein Unternehmen eine eigene indivi-duelle Hausschrift zu entwickeln.

Dans les années 1960, Paul Rand développa les images de marque de Westinghouse et d'IBM. Il réalisa ainsi deux projets inter-nationaux révolutionnaires dans un secteur économique en plein boom. Pour ce faire, il reprit la démarche que Peter Behrens avait adoptée pour la première fois en 1908 lorsqu'il fut chargé de développer la signature visuelle spécifique d'une entreprise.

IBM *1401 Programming Systems*

P
PR
PRO SYSTEMS
PROG YSTEMS
PROGR STEMS
PROGRA TEMS
PROGRAM EMS
PROGRAMM MS
PROGRAMMI S
PROGRAMMIN
PROGRAMMING

1959 · Paul Rand · US · Brochure cover

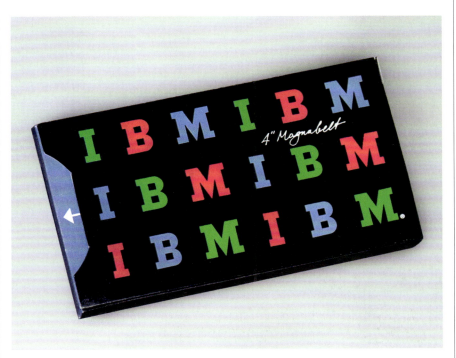

1974 · Paul Rand · US · Packaging

1962 · Paul Rand · US · Identity · IBM

1964 · Paul Rand · US · Brochure cover

1956 · Paul Rand · US · Logo · IBM

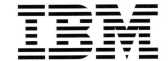

1967 · Paul Rand · US · Logo · IBM

1967 · Paul Rand · US · Logo · IBM

1960 · Sebastião Rodrigues · PT · Magazine cover

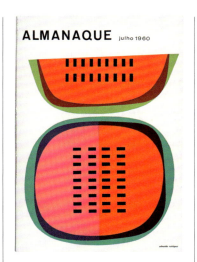

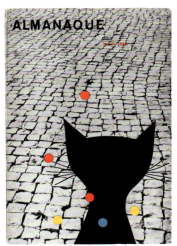

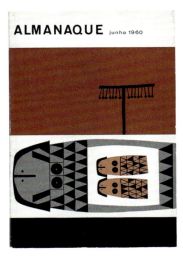

1960 · Sebastião Rodrigues · PT · Magazine covers

Sebastião Rodrigues (1929–1997, Lisbon) was a key protagonist in the development of graphic design in Portugal. Rodrigues began his career working for his father in the advertising department of the newspaper *A Voz*, before dedicating himself entirely to graphic arts from 1947. His numerous magazine and book covers, as well as editorial work, have informed a whole new generation of professionals in his country, while his tenure at the Calouste Gulbenkian Foundation in Lisbon allowed Rodrigues to give full voice to his modernist style. In 1991 he received the Excellence Award from Icograda.

Sebastião Rodrigues (1929–1997 Lissabon) spielte eine maßgebliche Rolle bei der Entwicklung des Grafikdesigns in Portugal. Seine berufliche Laufbahn begann Rodrigues als Mitarbeiter seines Vaters in der Werbeabteilung der Zeitung *A Voz*, ab 1947 widmete er sich dann ganz der Grafik. Mit seinen zahlreichen Zeitschriften- und Buchcovern sowie seiner redaktionellen Arbeit beeinflusste er eine ganze neue Generation portugiesischer Gebrauchsgrafiker. Die Stellung, die er bei der Stiftung Calouste Gulbenkian in Lissabon innehatte, ermöglichte es ihm, seinen modernen Stil voll zu entfalten. 1991 wurde er mit dem Excellence Award der Icograda ausgezeichnet.

Sebastião Rodrigues (1929–1997, Lisbonne) fut un acteur clé dans le développement du graphisme au Portugal. Rodrigues commença sa carrière en travaillant pour son père au service publicité du journal *A Voz*, avant de se consacrer entièrement au graphisme à partir de 1947. Ses nombreuses couvertures de magazines et de livres, ainsi que sa production éditoriale, ont favorisé l'émergence d'une nouvelle génération de professionnels dans son pays, tandis que son travail pour le compte de la Fondation Calouste Gulbenkian à Lisbonne lui a permis d'imposer son style moderniste. En 1991, l'Icograda (aujourd'hui Ico-D) lui décernait un Excellence Award.

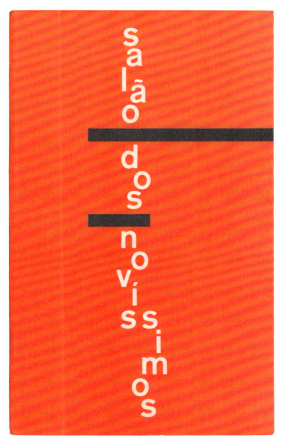

1959 · Sebastião Rodrigues · PT · Book cover

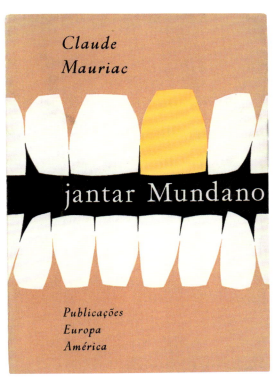

1962 · Sebastião Rodrigues · PT · Book cover

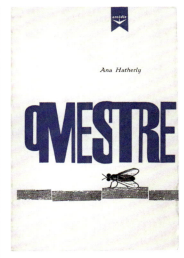

1963 · Sebastião Rodrigues · PT · Book cover

1963 · Sebastião Rodrigues · PT · Book cover

1964 · Sebastião Rodrigues · PT · Book cover

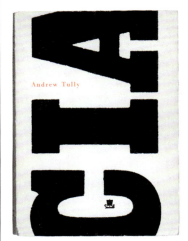

1960 · Sebastião Rodrigues · PT · Book cover

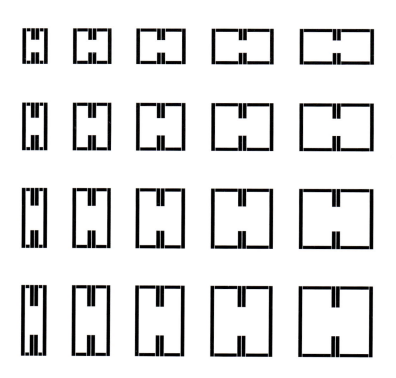

1960 · Karl Gerstner · CH · Logo · Holzäpfel Möbel

1960 · Karl Gerstner · CH · Packaging

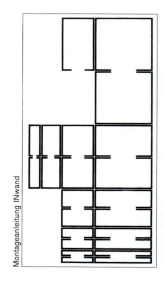

Montageanleitung INwand

1960 · Karl Gerstner · CH · Brochure cover

For the work he did for the furniture manufacturer Holzäpfel AG, Karl Gerstner produced a series of 20 modular logos which established the basis of the company's overall image. The idea was that each design could be applied flexibly and in a variety of ways to highlight different products. Such an array of functional motifs exemplifies Gerstner's systematic approach to design. Starting from basic principles, he would sketch a number of variations which were equally convincing as part of a series or as stand-alone elements.

Das Erscheinungsbild für die Holzäpfel AG stellt zwanzig modulare Logos bereit, durch ihren variablen Einsatz wird die Flexibilität der Produkte des Möbelherstellers hervorgehoben. Die Entwurfsreihe steht aber auch geradezu exemplarisch für Karl Gerstners systematisches Vorgehen in der Designarbeit. Ausgehend von einfachen Grundprinzipien der Gestaltung, erzeugte er Variationen, die gleichermaßen in der Serie wie als Einzelarbeit überzeugten.

L'image de marque d'Holzäpfel AG développée par Karl Gerstner s'appuyait sur vingt logos évolutifs dont les différents emplois soulignaient la modularité des produits du fabricant de meubles. Mais cette série est aussi une parfaite illustration de la démarche systématique du graphiste. Partant de principes simples, Gerstner savait produire des variantes convaincantes tant au sein d'une série que comme pièces singulières.

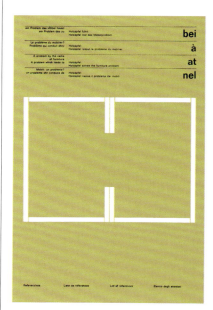

1960 · Karl Gerstner · CH · Brochure cover

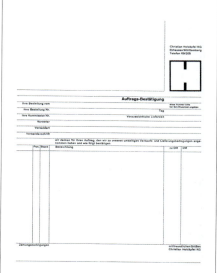

1960 · Karl Gerstner · CH · Letterhead

1960 · Karl Gerstner · CH · Brochure spread

Karl Gerstner (1930–2017, Basel) was a leading Swiss graphic designer and typographic innovator. He co-founded the design agency GGK with partners Paul Gredinger and Markus Kutter, which became a major design force in Switzerland. After studying design in Basel under Emil Ruder, Gerstner joined the pharmaceutical group Geigy, where he developed and implemented complex grids in print media, and applied text in unjustified columns. Gerstner created the morphological typogram program (1968), a new paradigm in the use of systematic design, listing basic parameters for type and their possible variations, which has been widely adopted in editorial, identity, and poster design.

Karl Gerstner (1930 – 2017 Basel) war ein maßgeblicher Schweizer Grafikdesigner und Typograf. Zusammen mit seinen Partnern Paul Gredinger und Markus Kutter gründete er die Agentur GGK, die zu einer in der Schweiz führenden Designinstitution wurde. Nach seinem Grafikstudium in Basel bei Emil Ruder ging Gerstner zum Pharmakonzern Geigy, wo er komplexe Raster in Printmedien entwickelte und umsetzte und mit Flattersatz in Kolumnentexten arbeitete. Gerstner kreierte das morphologische Typogramm-Programm (1968), ein neues Paradigma in der Anwendung systematischer Gestaltung, das grundlegende Parameter für Schrifttypen und ihre möglichen Variationen auflistete. Dieses Programm wurde im Zeitschriften-, Marken- und Plakatdesign vielfach aufgegriffen.

Karl Gerstner (1930–2017, Bâle) fut un graphiste suisse de renom et grand novateur dans le domaine de la typographie. Avec ses associés Paul Gredinger et Markus Kutter, il cofonda l'agence de design GGK, qui devint un acteur majeur du graphisme en suisse. Après des études de design à Bâle auprès d'Emil Ruder, Gerstner rejoignit le groupe pharmaceutique Geigy, pour lequel il conçut des grilles complexes dans la presse écrite, et inséra du texte dans des colonnes non justifiées. Gerstner créa le tableau morphologique du typogramme (1968), un nouveau paradigme dans l'application du design systématique, listant les paramètres fondamentaux des polices de caractères et leurs possibles variantes. Ce système a été largement adopté dans le monde de l'édition, de l'identité de marque et de la conception d'affiches.

1957 · Karl Gerstner · CH · Logo · Boîte à Musique

1958 · Karl Gerstner · CH · Logo · Niggli Verlag

1959 · Karl Gerstner · CH · Logo · Bech Electronic

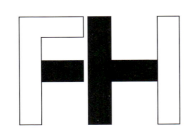

1960 · Karl Gerstner · CH · Logo · Felix Handschin

1961 · Karl Gerstner · CH · Logo · Fédération Horlogère

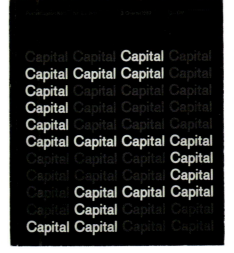

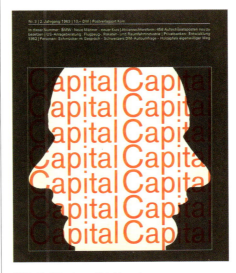

1963 · Karl Gerstner · CH · Magazine covers

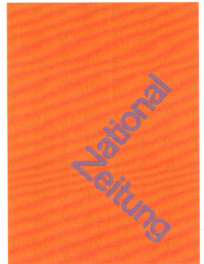

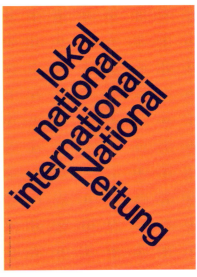

1960 · Karl Gerstner · CH · Posters

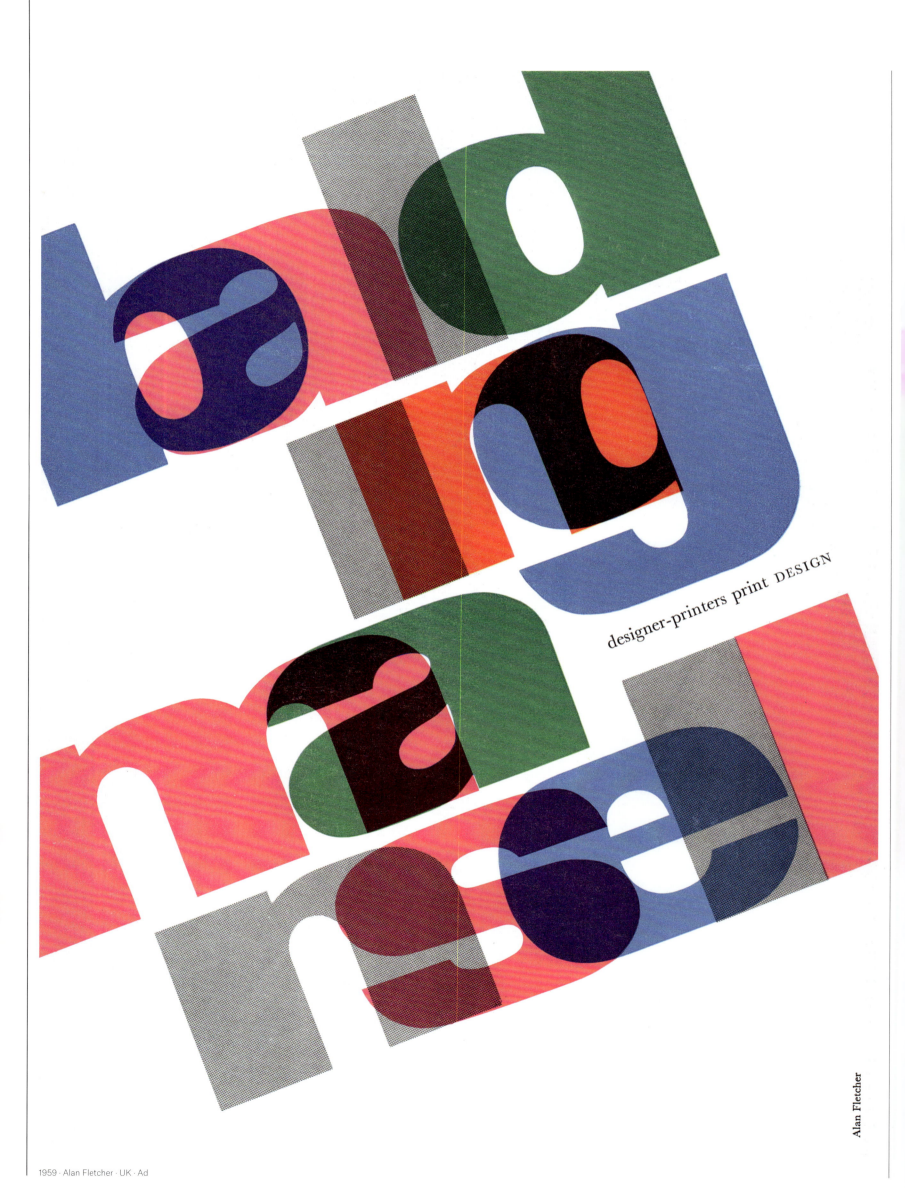

1959 · Alan Fletcher · UK · Ad

1965 · Crosby, Fletcher, Forbes, Gill · UK · Ad

92 graphic art; advertising art; applied art
freie graphik; gebrauchsgraphik; angewandte kunst
arts graphiques; arts appliqués; publicité

1960 · Alan Fletcher · UK · Magazine cover

Alan Fletcher (1931, Nairobi – 2006, London) was a prominent and very prolific British designer. After studying at the Royal College of Art and Yale School of Art and Architecture, in 1963 Fletcher co-published *Graphic Design: Visual Comparisons* with his design partners Colin Forbes and Bob Gill. Their clients included Pirelli, Penguin Books, and Olivetti, and after a reshuffle of partners, the studio became Pentagram in 1972, with the addition of Kenneth Grange and Theo Crosby, among others. Fletcher's influential work earned him multiple awards, including presidencies of the D&AD and AGI.

Alan Fletcher (1931, Nairobi – 2006, London) war ein renommierter und äußerst produktiver britischer Grafikdesigner. Nach dem Studium am Royal College of Art und an der Yale School of Art and Architecture brachte Fletcher 1963 mit seinen Partnern Colin Forbes und Bob Gill das Buch *Graphic Design: Visual Comparisons* heraus. Zu den Auftraggebern ihrer gemeinsamen Agentur gehörten Pirelli, Penguin Books und Olivetti. Nach einer personellen Umbesetzung entstand 1972 das neue Studio Pentagram, dem unter anderem auch Kenneth Grange und Theo Crosby angehörten. Fletchers einflussreiches Schaffen brachte ihm zahlreiche Auszeichnungen ein, darunter die Präsidentschaft von D&AD und der AGI.

Alan Fletcher (1931, Nairobi – 2006, Londres) fut un éminent et très prolifique graphiste britannique. Après des études au Royal College of Art et à la Yale School of Art and Architecture, Fletcher co-publia en 1963 *Graphic Design: Visual Comparisons* avec ses associés Colin Forbes et Bob Gill. Leurs clients ont compté Pirelli, Penguin Books et Olivetti. Après un remaniement des associés, le studio est devenu Pentagram en 1972 avec l'arrivée, notamment, de Kenneth Grange et Theo Crosby. Le travail influent de Fletcher lui a valu de nombreuses distinctions, notamment la présidence de la D&AD et de l'AGI.

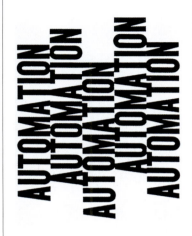

1959 · Alan Fletcher · UK · Brochure cover

1959 · Alan Fletcher · UK · Brochure cover

1962 · Alan Fletcher · UK · Ad

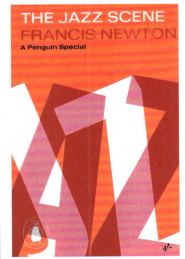

1961 · Alan Fletcher · UK · Book cover

1960–1969

1961

Former Bauhaus teacher Johannes Itten creates the **Farbkreis** (color wheel)

The **California Institute of the Arts** is established

Josef Müller-Brockmann's book **The Graphic Artist and his Design Problems** is published

Pierre Mendell and Klaus Oberer set up their design studio **Mendell & Oberer** in Munich

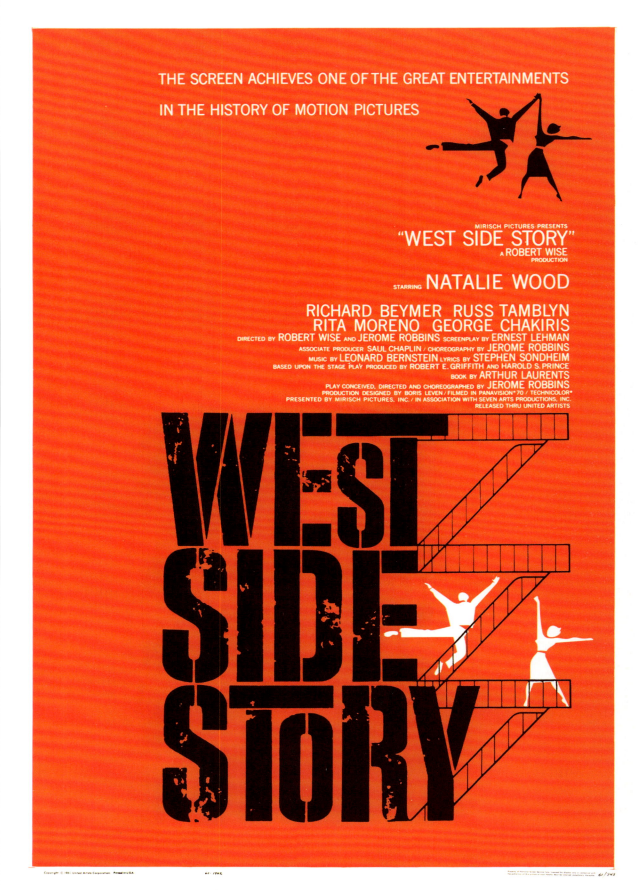

1961 · Joseph Caroff · US · Poster

1961 · A.M. Cassandre · FR · Logo · Yves Saint Laurent

1961 · Yasuo Kuroki · JP · Logo · Sony

1961 · Paul Rand · US · Logo · United Parcel Service

1961 · Ryuichi Yamashiro · JP · Poster

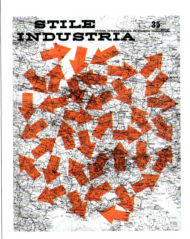

1961 · Enzo Mari · IT · Magazine cover

1961 · Józef Mroszczak · PL · Poster

1961 · Ruedi Külling · CH · Poster

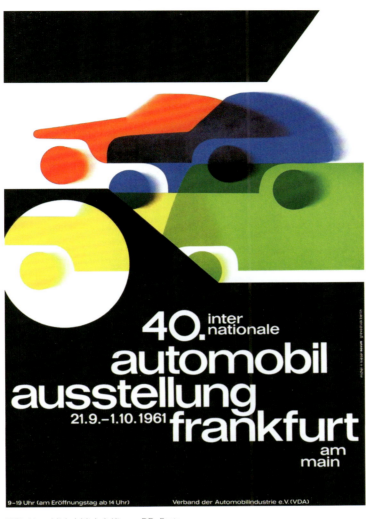

1961 · Hans Michel, Michel+Kieser · DE · Poster

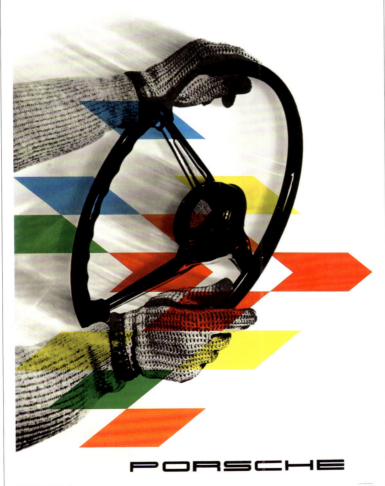

1961 · Erich Strenger · DE · Poster

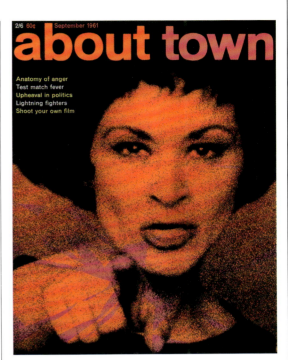

1961 · Tom Wolsey · UK · Magazine cover

1961 · Anonymous · US · Magazine cover

1961 · Kazumasa Nagai · JP · Poster

In 1961, the first edition of *Show—The Magazine of the Performing Arts* appeared in the United States. This innovative publication reflected America's flourishing cultural landscape of the period. The high standards demanded of contributors for articles and photo-spreads were echoed in the quality of the magazine's design, which was the responsibility of Austrian-born Henry Wolf, who had earlier made his mark as art director of the long-established *Harper's Bazaar*. Although *Show* did not manage lasting success, the magazine's extraordinary covers and timeless modern layouts set new benchmarks in international editorial design.

1961 erschien die erste Ausgabe der US-Zeitschrift *Show – The Magazine of the Performing Arts*. Das neuartige Medium war ein Spiegelbild der aufblühenden amerikanischen Kulturlandschaft jener Zeit. Der hohe Anspruch an Textbeiträge und Bildstrecken spiegelte sich auch im hohen Niveau der Magazingestaltung wider. Für diese zeichnete der gebürtige Österreicher Henry Wolf verantwortlich, der zuvor bereits als Artdirector des traditionsreichen *Harper's Bazaar* auf sich aufmerksam gemacht hatte. Obwohl *Show* wirtschaftlich kein langlebiger Erfolg wurde, setzte das Heft mit seinen außergewöhnlichen Covers und zeitlos-modernen Layouts neue Maßstäbe im internationalen Editorial Design.

Le premier numéro du magazine *Show – The Magazine of the Performing Arts* paraît aux États-Unis en 1961. Le nouveau média restitue à la perfection l'image du paysage culturel américain florissant de l'époque. Le niveau d'excellence imposé aux collaborateurs pour les textes et les photos se retrouve également dans le design éditorial. Le responsable est l'Autrichien d'origine Henry Wolf, qui s'est déjà fait remarquer comme directeur artistique du vétéran *Harper's Bazaar*. Si *Show* n'a pas connu un succès commercial durable, avec ses couvertures inhabituelles et sa mise en page intemporelle et moderne, le magazine a posé de nouveaux standards dans le domaine du design éditorial international.

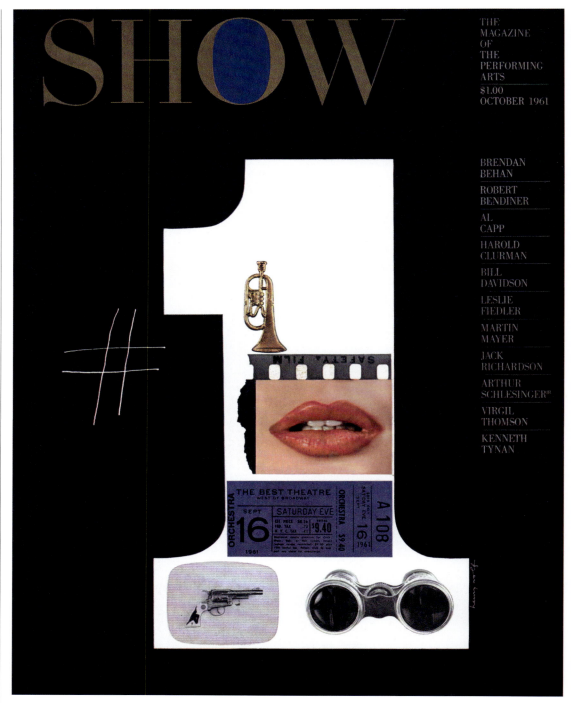

1961 · Henry Wolf · AT/US · Magazine cover

»When I started working, only a handful of magazines and two or three advertising agencies considered talent in design a real asset. The rest tolerated it. They kept a genius in a cage and watered down his production—'adapted' it for general use.«

Henry Wolf, *Graphic Designers in the USA*, vol. 1, 1971

1961 · Henry Wolf · AT/US · Magazine spreads

1962 · Henry Wolf · AT/US · Magazine cover

1963 · Henry Wolf · AT/US · Magazine cover

1963 · Henry Wolf · AT/US · Magazine cover

1964 · Henry Wolf · AT/US · Magazine cover

Henry Wolf (1925, Vienna – 2005, New York) was a prominent Austrian-American art director whose work for *Esquire* and *Harper's Bazaar* had a strong impact on editorial design. After the three-year ordeal that followed his family's escape from Nazi-controlled Vienna, Wolf studied art in Paris before emigrating to the United States in 1941, where he entered the army two years later. He then worked with Richard Avedon and other photographers before becoming *Esquire's* art director in 1952, and establishing its contemporary style. In 1965 he joined McCann Erickson, and started his own practice, Henry Wolf Productions, in 1971.

Henry Wolf (1925, Wien – 2005, New York) war ein prominenter austroamerikanischer Artdirector, dessen Arbeit für *Esquire* und *Harper's Bazaar* einen starken Einfluss auf die grafische Gestaltung von Zeitschriften ausübte. Nach einer dreijährigen Odyssee mit seiner Familie, die dem Anschluss Österreichs an Nazideutschland folgte, studierte Wolf zunächst Kunst in Paris und emigrierte 1941 in die Vereinigten Staaten, wo er zwei Jahre später in die Armee eintrat. Nach dem Krieg arbeitete er mit Richard Avedon und anderen Fotografen zusammen und wurde 1952 Artdirector der Zeitschrift *Esquire*, deren heutigen Stil er entwickelte. 1965 trat er in die Werbeagentur McCann Erickson ein und gründete 1971 mit Henry Wolf Productions sein eigenes Studio.

Henry Wolf (1925, Vienne – 2005, New York) fut un éminent directeur artistique austro-américain dont le travail pour *Esquire* et *Harper's Bazaar* a eu un impact durable sur le graphisme éditorial. Après les trois années de calvaire qui suivirent la fuite de sa famille de Vienne contrôlée par les nazis, Wolf fit ses études à Paris, avant d'émigrer aux États-Unis en 1941, où il servit dans l'armée deux ans plus tard. Il travailla ensuite avec Richard Avedon et d'autres photographes avant de devenir directeur artistique d'*Esquire* en 1952 et d'affirmer son style contemporain. En 1965, il rejoignit McCann Erickson, et en 1971, il ouvrit son propre studio, Henry Wolf Productions.

1960 · F.H.K. Henrion · UK · Logo · Associated Industrial Consultants

1960 · F.H.K. Henrion · UK · Logo · Cox of Watford

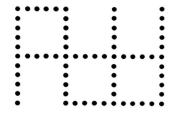

1964 · F.H.K. Henrion · UK · Logo · P.W. Partners

1967 · F.H.K. Henrion · UK · Logo · Tate & Lyle

1969 · F.H.K. Henrion · UK · Logo · British European Airways

1970 · F.H.K. Henrion · UK · Identity · The National Giro

1960 · F.H.K. Henrion · UK · Identity · London Electricity Board

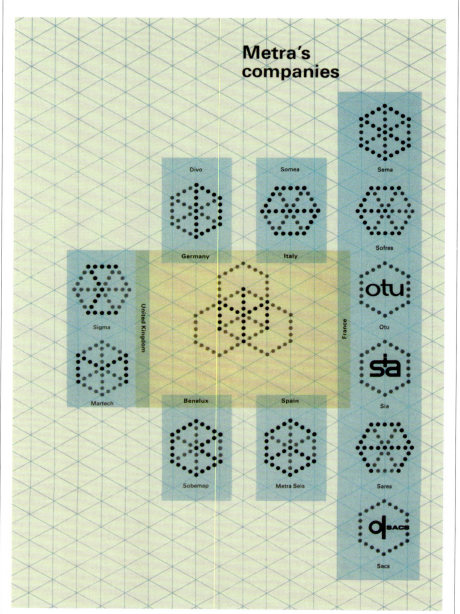

1960 · F.H.K. Henrion · UK · Identity · Metra Corporation

F.H.K. Henrion, Frederick Henri Kay Henrion (1914, Nuremberg – 1990, London) was a German-born graphic designer, and one of the early pioneers of corporate identity. After working in textiles in Paris he studied under the poster artist Paul Colin, before moving to London in 1936, where he established his own practice. His notable identity work for KLM Royal Dutch Airlines would become an icon of graphic design work. In addition to working in exhibition, packaging, and editorial design for books and magazines, Henrion also taught at the Royal College of Art and the London College of Printing.

F.H.K. Henrion, Frederick Henri Kay Henrion (1914, Nürnberg – 1990, London) war ein in Deutschland geborener Gebrauchsgrafiker und einer der frühen Pioniere von Corporate Identity. Nachdem er in Paris in der Textilbranche gearbeitet hatte, studierte er bei dem Plakatkünstler Paul Colin und ging 1936 nach London, wo er sein eigenes Studio eröffnete. Seine bemerkenswerte CI-Gestaltung für die KLM Royal Dutch Airlines sollte zu einer Ikone des Grafikdesigns werden. Neben seinen Arbeiten für Ausstellungen und Verpackungen und der Gestaltung von Büchern und Zeitschriften unterrichtete Henrion auch am Royal College of Art und am London College of Printing.

F.H.K. Henrion, Frederick Henri Kay Henrion (1914, Nuremberg – 1990, Londres) fut un graphiste d'origine allemande et l'un des pionniers en image de marque. Après avoir travaillé dans le textile à Paris, il étudia auprès de l'affichiste Paul Colin puis s'installa à Londres en 1936, où il ouvrit son propre studio. Son remarquable travail pour l'identité de la compagnie aérienne KLM Royal Dutch Airlines deviendra plus tard une icône du graphisme. À côté de sa production pour des expositions, des emballages et le graphisme éditorial pour des livres et des magazines, Henrion enseigna aussi au Royal College of Art et au London College of Printing.

F.H.K. Henrion was commissioned in 1961 to produce a new corporate identity for the Dutch airline KLM. He and his team developed a comprehensive design manual in the course of working on this commission which documented the whole process of brand development.

F.H.K. Henrion erhielt 1961 den Auftrag, ein neues einheitliches Erscheinungsbild für die niederländische Airline KLM zu realisieren. Gemeinsam mit seinem Team entwickelte er ein umfassendes Designmanual, das die neu erarbeitete Systematik des Branding dokumentierte.

En 1961, F.H.K Henrion fut chargé de développer une nouvelle image de marque pour la compagnie aérienne néerlandaise KLM. Avec son équipe, il conçut un manuel de graphisme complet qui documentait l'ensemble du processus de branding.

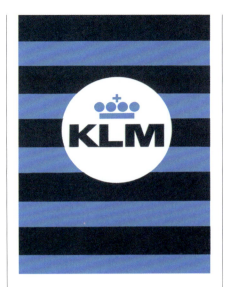
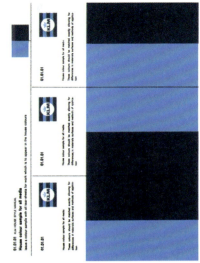
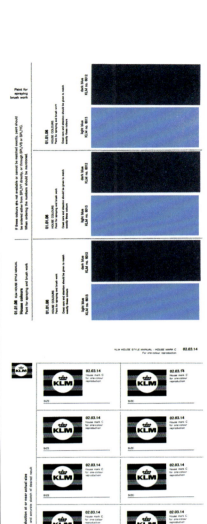

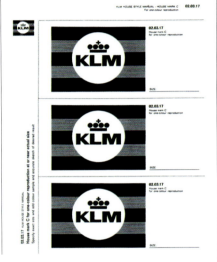
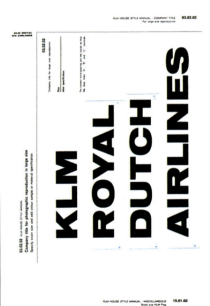

1961 · F.H.K. Henrion · UK · Identity · KLM

1961 · F.H.K. Henrion · UK · Design manual

Conflict and Creativity
Control of the Mind, Part 2
edited by
Seymour M. Farber
and
Roger H. L. Wilson

McGraw-Hill PAPERBACKS

1963 · Rudolph de Harak · US · Book cover

Personality and Psychotherapy
An Analysis in Terms of Learning, Thinking, and Culture
John Dollard
Neal E. Miller $3.25

McGraw-Hill Paperbacks

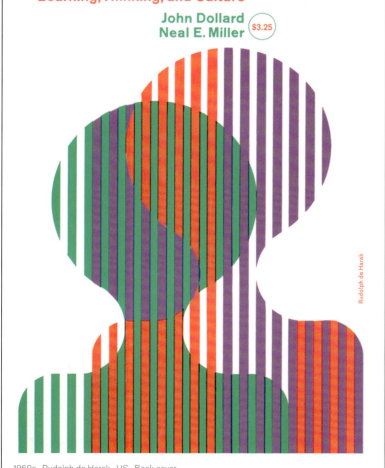

1960s · Rudolph de Harak · US · Book cover

A Moral Philosophy for Management

Benjamin M. Selekman $2.25

McGraw-Hill PAPERBACKS

1960s · Rudolph de Harak · US · Book cover

An Introduction to Scientific Research
E. Bright Wilson, Jr. $4.95

McGRAW-HILL PAPERBACKS

1960 · Rudolph de Harak · US · Book cover

Techniques of Leadership
Auren Uris $5.95

McGraw-Hill Paperbacks

1963 · Rudolph de Harak · US · Book cover

The Siege of Leningrad
Leon Goure
Foreword by Merle Fainsod $2.95

McGraw-Hill Paperbacks
Stanford University Press

1964 · Rudolph de Harak · US · Book cover

The Uncommon Man
Crawford H. Greenewalt $1.45

McGRAW-HILL PAPERBACKS

1960s · Rudolph de Harak · US · Book cover

Man and Civilization
The Family's Search for Survival
edited by
Seymour M. Farber
Piero Mustacchi
Roger H. L. Wilson $3.25

McGraw-Hill Paperbacks

1965 · Rudolph de Harak · US · Book cover

Between 1959 and 1965, the American graphic designer Rudolph de Harak worked for the scientific publisher McGraw-Hill, and during that period he produced about 350 book covers, sometimes at the extraordinary rate of 20 a month. Despite this massive workload, de Harak still managed to turn out many small masterpieces of modernist design.

Zwischen 1959 und 1965 arbeitete der amerikanische Gestalter Rudolph de Harak für den wissenschaftlichen Verlag McGraw-Hill. In dieser Zeit entstanden etwa 350 Umschläge für unterschiedlichste Sachbücher – teilweise realisierte de Harak bis zu 20 Cover im Monat. Trotz des immensen Arbeitsaufkommens gelangen ihm viele kleine Meisterwerke modernistischer Gestaltung.

Le graphiste américain Rudolph de Harak travailla pour l'éditeur scientifique McGraw-Hill de 1959 à 1965. Pendant ces années, il créa quelque 350 couvertures pour différents ouvrages pratiques – parfois au rythme effréné de 20 par mois. Malgré cette immense charge de travail, il parvint souvent à signer de petits chefs-d'œuvre du graphisme moderniste.

Modern Physics for the Engineer

edited by Louis N. Ridenour

McGRAW-HILL PAPERBACKS

$3.95

1960 · Rudolph de Harak · US · Book cover

Rudolph de Harak (1924, Culver City, California – 2002, Ellsworth, Maine) was an avant-garde American graphic artist and environmental designer who, together with Saul Bass, Alvin Lustig, and others, founded the Los Angeles Society for Contemporary Designers. After serving in WWII, de Harak turned to visual communication, working mostly in editorial design in New York. He also produced museum installations and taught widely at schools including the Cooper Union, Parsons School of Design, the Pratt Institute, and Yale.

Rudolph de Harak (1924, Culver City, Kalifornien – 2002, Ellsworth, Maine) war ein amerikanischer Avantgardegrafikdesigner und Vertreter des Umweltdesigns, der mit Saul Bass, Alvin Lustig und anderen die Los Angeles Society for Contemporary Designers begründete. Nach seinem Einsatz im Zweiten Weltkrieg wandte sich de Harak der visuellen Kommunikation zu und arbeitete hauptsächlich als Buchgestalter in New York. Zudem schuf de Harak Museumsinstallationen und widmete sich einer umfangreichen Lehrtätigkeit, unter anderem an der Cooper Union School of Art, der Parsons School of Design, dem Pratt Institute und der Yale University.

Rudolph de Harak (1924, Culver City, Californie – 2002, Ellsworth, Maine) fut un graphiste avant-gardiste américain, pionnier du design environnemental et cofondateur de la Los Angeles Society for Contemporary Designers, notamment avec Saul Bass et Alvin Lustig. Après avoir servi dans l'armée pendant la Seconde Guerre mondiale, de Harak se lança dans la communication visuelle, travaillant principalement dans le graphisme éditorial à New York. Il conçut aussi des scénographies pour des musées et fut très actif en tant qu'enseignant dans des écoles comme la Cooper Union, la Parsons School of Design, l'Institut Pratt et l'université Yale.

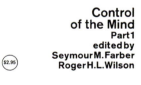

Control of the Mind
Part 1
edited by
Seymour M. Farber
Roger H. L. Wilson

$2.95

McGraw-Hill PAPERBACKS

1961 · Rudolph de Harak · US · Book cover

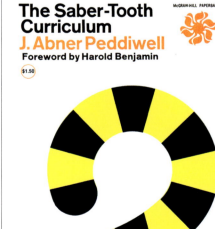

The Saber-Tooth Curriculum
J. Abner Peddiwell
Foreword by Harold Benjamin

$1.50

McGraw-Hill PAPERBACKS

1960s · Rudolph de Harak · US · Book cover

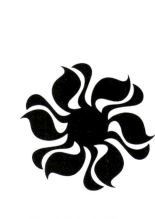

1959 · Rudolph de Harak · US · Logo

Adrian Frutiger (1928, Unterseen, Switzerland – 2015, Bern) was a major Swiss typeface designer, whose professional career and influence spread from the analog through to the digital age. His three sanserif font families, Univers, Frutiger, and Avenir, while considered his greatest contribution to design, actually constitute only a small part of his legacy, which includes a total of 76 different typefaces. From 1962 he also ran an influential graphic design studio in Paris and produced, together with Bruno Pfäffli and André Gürtler, many brand identities; this work also included creating wayfinding systems, such as the one for Charles de Gaulle Airport near Paris.

Adrian Frutiger (1928, Unterseen, Schweiz – 2015, Bern) war ein maßgeblicher Schweizer Schriftgestalter, dessen Wirken und Einfluss sich vom analogen bis zum digitalen Zeitalter erstreckten. Die drei von ihm entwickelten serifenlosen Schriften – Univers, Frutiger und Avenir – gelten zwar als sein bedeutendster Beitrag zum zeitgenössischen Grafikdesign, tatsächlich aber machen sie nur einen geringen Teil seines Vermächtnisses aus, das insgesamt 76 Schrifttypen umfasst. Ab 1962 leitete er ein einflussreiches Grafikdesignstudio in Paris und entwarf zusammen mit Bruno Pfäffli und André Gürtler zahlreiche Firmenlogos; zu dieser Arbeit gehört auch die Gestaltung von Orientierungssystemen etwa am Pariser Flughafen Charles de Gaulle.

Adrian Frutiger (1928, Unterseen, Suisse – 2015, Berne) fut un grand créateur de caractères suisse dont la carrière professionnelle et l'influence s'étendit de l'ère analogique à l'ère numérique. Bien qu'elles soient considérées comme sa contribution majeure au graphisme, ses trois familles de polices sans serif (Univers, Frutiger et Avenir) ne représentent en fait qu'une petite partie de son héritage typographique, qui compte au total 76 polices de caractères distinctes. À partir de 1962, Frutiger dirigea un important studio de design à Paris et fut le créateur de nombreuses images de marque avec Bruno Pfäffli et André Gürtler. Son travail comprend aussi la création de signalétiques comme celle de l'aéroport de Paris-Charles-de-Gaulle.

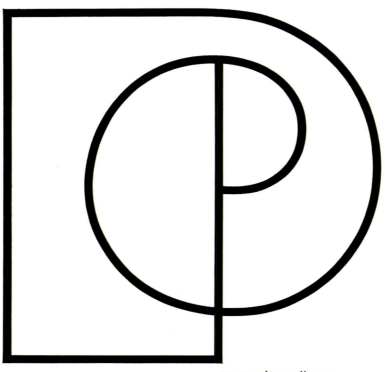

toutes les reliures
toute la reliure

Prache Auger de Franclieu
23 avenue Anatole France
Choisy-le-Roi
Téléphone Bel 20-40

1961 · Adrian Frutiger · CH/FR · Brochure cover

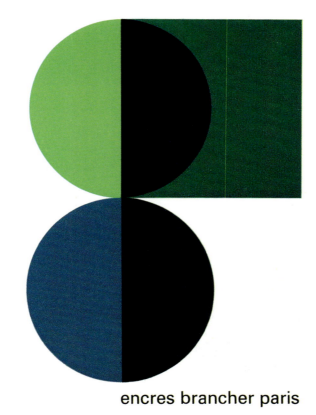

couleur attirante
couleur puissante
couleur brillante
couleur transparente

encres brancher paris

1961 · Adrian Frutiger · CH/FR · Brochure cover

1960s · Adrian Frutiger · CH/FR · Letterhead

1960s · Adrian Frutiger · CH/FR · Letterhead

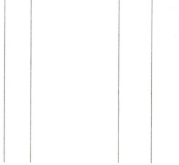

1960s · Adrian Frutiger · CH/FR · Letterhead

programme de vente · éditions scientifiques hermann

1961 · Adrian Frutiger · CH/FR · Brochure cover

sciences
scien
sciences
ces
sciences
scien
sciences
ces
sciences

revue française des sciences et des techniques

1960 · Adrian Frutiger · CH/FR · Magazine cover

1961 · Adrian Frutiger · CH/FR · Logo · IPREIG

1967 · Adrian Frutiger, Bruno Pfäffli · CH/FR · Logo · Druckerei Winterthur

1964 · Adrian Frutiger · CH/FR · Logo · Melpomene

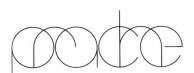

1967 · Adrian Frutiger, Bruno Pfäffli · CH/FR · Logo · Pierre Disderot

1970s · Adrian Frutiger · CH/FR · Logo · Autoroute Rhône-Alpes

1971 · Adrian Frutiger · CH/FR · Logo · Paris Airport

1974 · Adrian Frutiger · CH/FR · Logo · Musées Nationaux de France

1980 · Adrian Frutiger · CH/FR · Logo · Musée Rodin

1970s · Adrian Frutiger · CH/FR · Logo · Reliures à Spirales Prache

1980s · Adrian Frutiger · CH/FR · Logo · Europe

1962

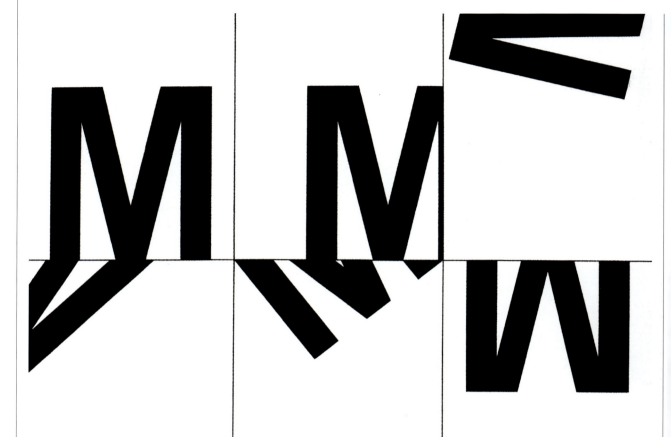

1962 · Herb Lubalin · US · Logo · Sudler, Hennessey & Lubalin Advertising

Moderna Museet
Alla dagar 12-17 onsdagar 12-21

1962 · John Melin, Anders Österlin · SE · Poster

1962 · Marcel Wyss · CH · Logo · Electrolux

1962 · Lippincott & Margulies · US · Logo · Chrysler

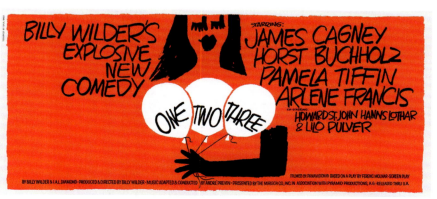

1962 · Saul Bass · US · Poster

Otl Aicher and his students create a new identity for **Lufthansa** airlines

Roger Excoffon creates the **Antique Olive** typeface

Sketchpad, a software prototype for graphic interfaces, is created by Ivan Sutherland at MIT

The **D&AD** organization is founded in London

The **Graphic Design Association of Taiwan** is founded

The **Letter Gothic** typeface by Roger Roberson is released after six years' work

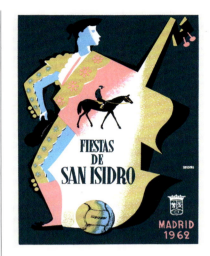

1962 · "Teodoro" · ES · Poster

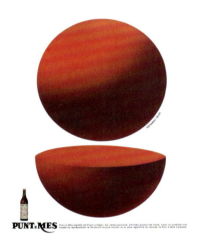

1962 · Armando Testa · IT · Ad

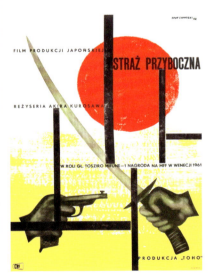

1962 · Eryk Lipiński · PL · Poster

1962 · Marcel Wyss · CH · Poster

1962 · "Joselito" · BR · Record cover

1962 · Jörg Hamburger · CH · Poster

1962 · Novum · DE · New year's card

1962 · Bea Feitler · BR · Book cover

1962 · Herbert W. Kapitzki · DE · Poster

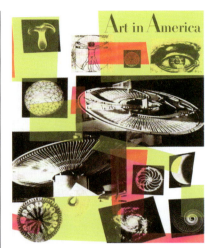

1962 · Alexey Brodovitch · RU/US · Magazine cover

1962 · Anonymous · CZ · Poster

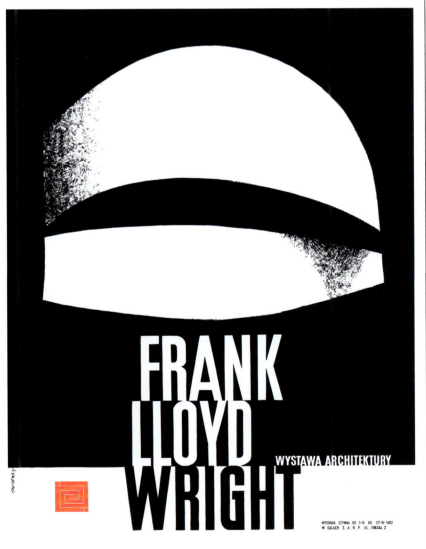

1962 · Waldemar Świerzy · PL · Poster

51

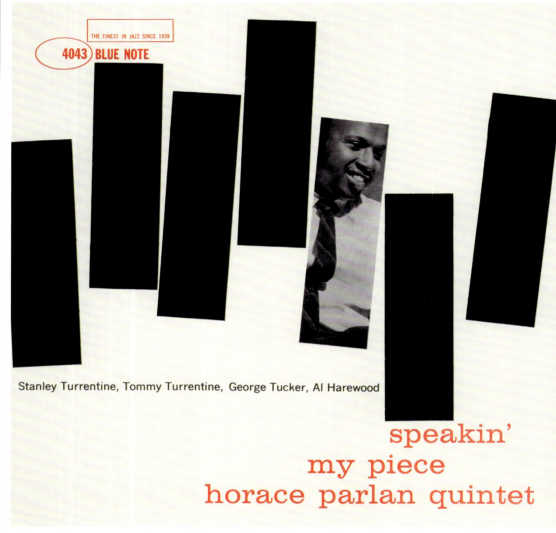

1960 · Reid Miles, Francis Wolff (PH) · US · Record cover

1962 · Reid Miles, Francis Wolff (PH) · US · Record cover

1967 · Reid Miles (AD & PH) · US · Record cover

1961 · Reid Miles, Francis Wolff (PH) · US · Record cover

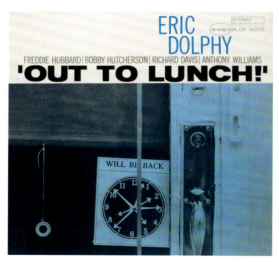

1964 · Reid Miles (AD & PH) · US · Record cover

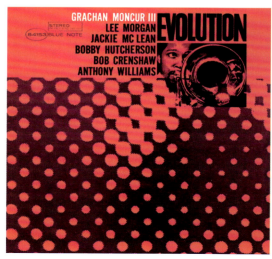

1963 · Reid Miles, Francis Wolff (PH) · US · Record cover

Beginning in 1956, Reid Miles designed nearly 500 album covers for the New York label Blue Note. Contemporary jazz records offered an ideal field of application for new visual concepts in graphic design. Many of the visuals created by Miles are now regarded as typical of 1960s aesthetics. Along with the record sleeves featuring purely graphic art, many others were developed in collaboration with Francis Wolff, a photographer with a passion who often took pictures of musicians in rehearsal, so providing Miles with suitable artworks.

Nahezu 500 Plattencover entwarf Reid Miles ab 1956 für das New Yorker Label Blue Note. Die zeitgenössischen Jazzaufnahmen waren ein ideales Anwendungsfeld für neue visuelle Konzepte im Grafikdesign. Viele von Miles entwickelten Visuals gelten heute als typisch für die Ästhetik der 1960er-Jahre. Neben rein grafischen Arbeiten entstanden zahlreiche Cover in Zusammenarbeit mit dem Fotografen Francis Wolff, der mit großer Vorliebe zum Experiment oft bei Probesessions der Musiker fotografierte und damit das passende Bildmaterial für Miles lieferte.

À partir de 1956, Reid Miles devait concevoir quelque 500 pochettes de disques pour la maison de disques new-yorkaise Blue Note. Les enregistrements de jazz contemporain étaient un champ d'application parfait pour les concepts graphiques. Nombre de visuels développés par Miles sont aujourd'hui considérés comme iconiques de l'esthétique des années 1960. À côté de travaux purement graphiques, il devait réaliser de nombreuses pochettes de disques en collaboration avec le photographe Francis Wolff, qui photographiait pendant les répétitions des musiciens avec une prédilection particulière pour l'expérimentation, et qui pouvait ainsi livrer à Miles le matériel visuel approprié.

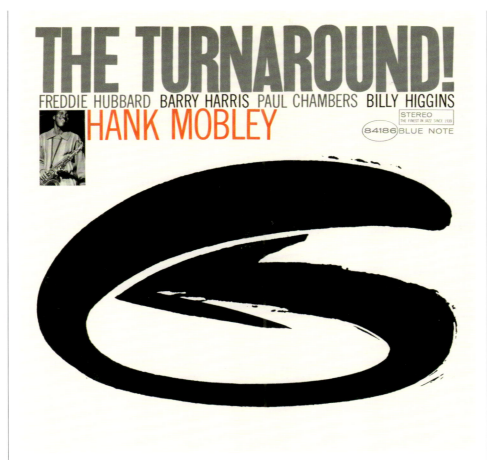

1965 · Reid Miles, Francis Wolff (PH) · US · Record cover

1966 · Reid Miles, Francis Wolff (PH) · US · Record cover

Reid Miles (1927, Chicago – 1993, Los Angeles) was an American designer and photographer whose contribution to the music industry heavily influenced the field of album cover design. After serving in the navy and enrolling at the Chouinard Art Institute in Los Angeles, Miles moved to New York, where he worked for *Esquire* magazine. In 1956 he moved to the Blue Note music label, where his striking sleeve designs for various jazz legends quickly stood out. His versatile use of typography and photography established a new school in graphic design for album art.

Reid Miles (1927, Chicago – 1993, Los Angeles) war ein amerikanischer Designer und Fotograf, der mit seiner Arbeit für die Musikindustrie stark beeinflusste. Nach seinem Militärdienst bei der Marine und seiner Ausbildung am Chouinard Art Institute in Los Angeles ging Miles nach New York und arbeitete für die Zeitschrift *Esquire*. 1956 wechselte er zum Musiklabel Blue Note, wo er Plattenhüllen für verschiedene Jazzlegenden gestaltete und mit seinen verblüffenden Entwürfen bald Aufmerksamkeit erregte. Durch seine vielseitige Verwendung von Typografie und Fotografie begründete er eine neue Schule der Gebrauchsgrafik für künstlerisches Albumdesign.

Reid Miles (1927, Chicago – 1993, Los Angeles) fut un graphiste et photographe américain dont la contribution à l'industrie musicale a fortement influencé la création de pochettes d'albums. Après avoir servi dans la Navy et être entré au Chouinard Art Institute à Los Angeles, Miles s'installa à New York, où il travailla pour le magazine *Esquire*. En 1956, il fut engagé par le label Blue Note, au sein duquel ses conceptions de pochettes d'albums pour différentes légendes du jazz se distinguèrent rapidement. Son utilisation versatile de la typographie et de la photographie instaura une nouvelle école de graphisme dans le domaine de l'art de l'album.

The James Bond franchise has always been at the forefront of a number of design fields, ranging from fashion to the various gadgets and specialized vehicles that appear in the films, but equally importantly in the area of logo design. Created in 1953 by author Ian Fleming, the 007 character made his screen debut in *Dr. No* (1962) and immediately the opening title sequence by Maurice Binder declared the smart, independent, and adventurous credentials of Bond and of the film itself. With over 25 movie releases spanning five decades, the 007 title sequences have continued to set standards for brand identity and motion-picture design.

Das James-Bond-Medienfranchise hat von Anfang an auf die Arbeit unterschiedlichster Designsparten zurückgegriffen, von Mode bis hin zu den diversen Accessoires und Spezialfahrzeugen, die in den Filmen vorkommen. Nicht minder bedeutend ist allerdings das Logodesign. Die 1953 vom Autor Ian Fleming geschaffene Figur des 007 debütierte 1962 als *Dr. No* auf der Leinwand, und bereits mit der Titelsequenz Maurice Binders wurde das smarte, unabhängige und abenteuerliche Image von Bond und dem Film selbst festgelegt. Mit über 25 Filmen, die im Lauf von fünfzig Jahren starteten, haben die 007-Titelsequenzen unweigerlich einen Standard für Markenidentität und Filmdesign gesetzt.

La franchise James Bond a toujours été à la pointe d'un certain nombre d'aspects de design, de la mode aux gadgets et véhicules spécialisés qui apparaissent dans les films, en passant, non moins importante, par la conception de logos. Créé en 1953 par l'écrivain Ian Fleming, le personnage de l'agent 007 fait ses débuts en 1962 dans *Dr. No*, et le générique réalisé par Maurice Binder annonce alors d'emblée les références de James Bond et du film – intelligence, indépendance, aventure. Avec plus de 25 films en cinq décennies, les génériques des James Bond ont continué de poser des standards dans le domaine de l'identité de marque et du graphisme de cinéma.

1962 · Anonymous · US · Poster

1964 · Robert Brownjohn · UK · Poster

1962 · Joseph Caroff · US · Logo

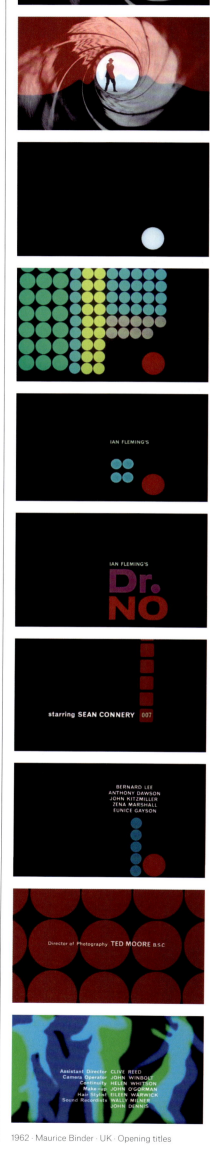

1962 · Maurice Binder · UK · Opening titles

Like Olivetti, Pirelli was an Italian company with a long-standing tradition to take into account when it came to reviewing its design strategy in the late 1950s. The tire manufacturer worked with some of the finest European designers of the day, including Alan Fletcher, Massimo Vignelli, and Michael Engelmann, using the most up-do-date stylistic devices for its advertising campaigns.

Neben Olivetti etablierte sich mit Pirelli Ende der 1950er-Jahre ein weiteres italienisches Traditions-unternehmen als Designinnovator. Der Reifenhersteller arbeitete zu der Zeit mit einigen der besten europäischen Gestalter wie Alan Fletcher, Massimo Vignelli und Michael Engelmann zusammen und setzte aktuellste Stil-mittel des Grafikdesigns für seine Werbekampagnen ein.

À côté d'Olivetti, à la fin des années 1950, une autre entreprise italienne héritière d'une longue tradition devient innovatrice dans le domaine du graphisme: Pirelli. Le fabricant de pneumatiques travaille alors avec certains des meilleurs graphistes de l'époque comme Alan Fletcher, Massimo Vignelli et Michael Engelmann et introduit les moyens stylistiques les plus récents dans la conception de ses campagnes publicitaires.

1961 · Bob Noorda · NL/IT · Logo

1961 · Bob Noorda · NL/IT · Logo

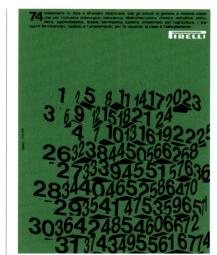

1963 · Pino Milas · IT · Ad

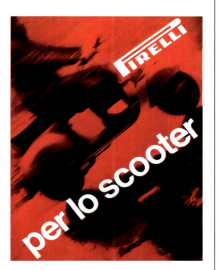

1963 · Anonymous · IT · Ad

1964 · Massimo Vignelli · IT · Poster

1962 · Confalonieri & Negri · IT · Ad

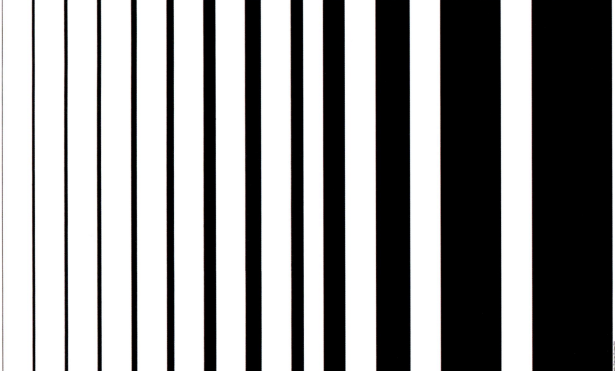

1965 · Crosby Fletcher Forbes · UK · Ad

1965 · Studio Boggeri · IT · Ad

1963

The design studio **Total Design** is founded by Wim Crouwel, Benno Wissing, and Friso Kramer in Amsterdam

The **Icograda** (International Council of Graphic Design Associations) is founded in London

Josef Albers's color theory **Interaction of Color** is published

Karl Gerstner publishes his book **Programme entwerfen** (Designing Programs)

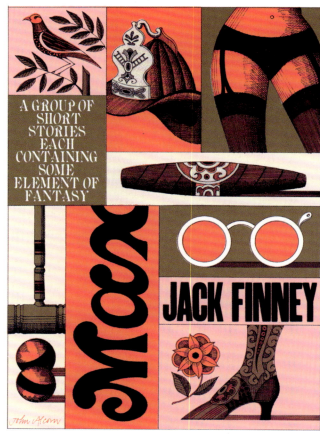

1963 · John Alcorn · US · Book cover

1963 · Wojciech Zamecznik · PL · Poster

1963 · Eero Syvänoja · FI · Poster

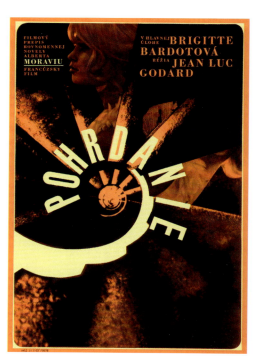

1963 · Anonymous · US · Record cover

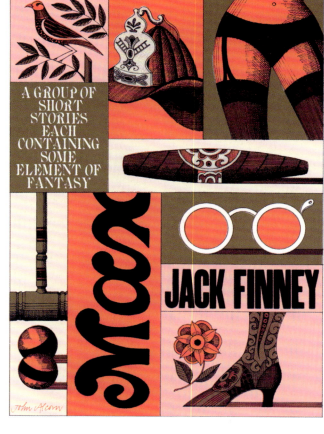

1963 · Anonymous · CZ · Poster

1963 · Bob Noorda · NL/IT · Logo · Metropolitana Milanese

1963 · Otto Treumann · NL/IL · Logo · El Al Airlines

1963 · Fletcher Forbes Gill · UK · Logo · D&AD

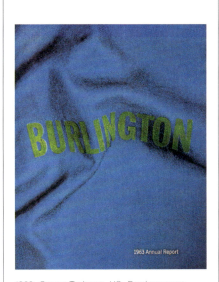

1963 · George Tscherny · US · Brochure cover

Colombi

1963 · Studio Boggeri · IT · Ad

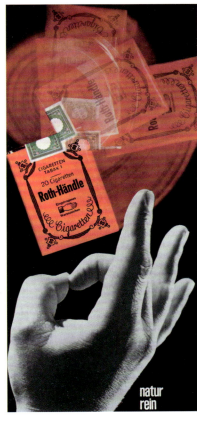

1963 · Michael Engelmann · DE · Poster

Basler Freilichtspiele
beim Letziturm im St. Albantal
15.–31. VIII 1963

Wilhelm Tell

1963 · Armin Hofmann · CH · Poster

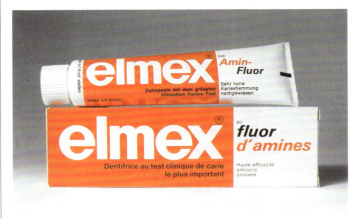

1963 · Roger Mayer · CH · Packaging

1963 · Yusaku Kamekura · JP · Packaging

Wolfgang Schmidt (1929, Fulda –
1995, Witzenhausen, Germany)
was a visual artist and one of
the most important commercial
designers in post-war Germany.
He studied at the Academy of
Fine Arts in Stuttgart and the
University of Kassel, later exhi-
biting at documenta III in 1964.
Schmidt's design projects included the wayfinding system for
Frankfurt's subway network,
poster work for the Atlas film
corporation, and the visual identity
of Vitsœ furniture.

Wolfgang Schmidt (1929, Fulda –
1995, Witzenhausen) war ein
bildender Künstler und einer der
bedeutendsten Gebrauchsgrafiker
im Deutschland der Nachkriegs-
zeit. Er studierte an der Kunstakademie Stuttgart und an der
Kunsthochschule Kassel und war
1964 mit einigen Arbeiten auf
der documenta III vertreten. Als
eines seiner bedeutendsten Projekte gilt die grafische Konzeption
des Orientierungssystems in
der Frankfurter U-Bahn. Außer-
dem gestaltete Schmidt Plakate
für den Atlas-Filmverleih sowie
das Erscheinungsbild der Möbel-
firma Vitsœ.

Wolfgang Schmidt (1929, Fulda –
1995, Witzenhausen, Allemagne)
fut un artiste visuel et graphiste
commercial majeur dans l'Allemagne d'après-guerre. Après des
études à Académie des arts de
Stuttgart et à l'université de
Cassel, il exposa à la documenta 3
en 1964. Les projets de Schmidt
dans le domaine du design
comptent des systèmes signalétiques pour le réseau métropo-
litain de Francfort, des affiches
pour la société de cinéma Atlas et
l'identité visuelle du fabricant de
meubles Vitsœ.

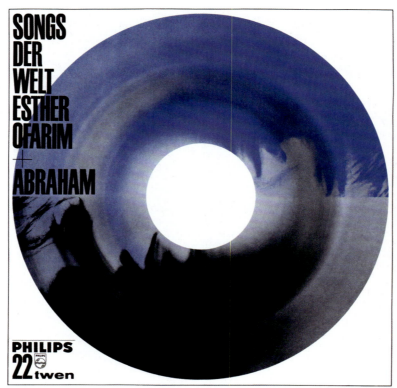

1963 · Wolfgang Schmidt · DE · Record cover

1963 · Wolfgang Schmidt · DE · Poster

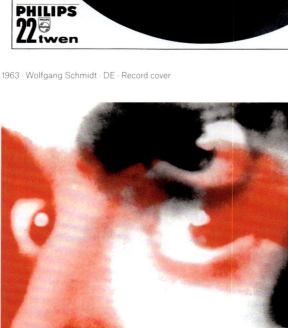

1965 · Wolfgang Schmidt · DE · Poster

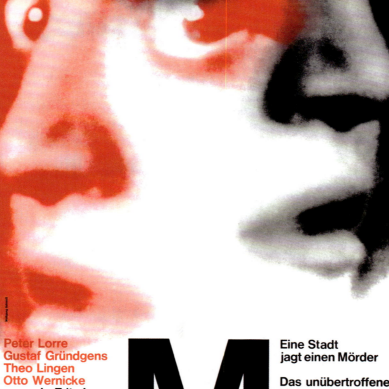

1966 · Wolfgang Schmidt · DE · Poster

Galerie Rudolf Zwirner

Essen Kahrstraße 54
Telefon 7915 05
am Folkwangmuseum

werktags 10 bis 18.30
samstags 10 bis 14

Januar Februar 1961
Skulpturen und Bilder
von

Takis
Takis
und
Soto

1961 · Wolfgang Schmidt · DE · Poster

1963 · Wolfgang Schmidt · DE · Poster

Distorted Typography

When taking a retrospective look at many design trends, it is often impossible to determine with any certainty who came up with the idea in the first place. This is the situation with skewed typefaces, which function with the help of photographic means, and are a design feature first seen in the early 1960s including on the cover of the Italian magazine *domus* and in the opening credits of the second James Bond movie, *From Russia with Love*. Over the following decade, designers from all over the world used different techniques to produce this kind of arresting effect, and even today the same ideas are still being applied in a whole variety of ways.

Bei vielen gestalterischen Trends lässt sich rückblickend nicht mehr mit Sicherheit ermitteln, wer eine Idee tatsächlich zum allerersten Mal aufbrachte. So auch im Fall der mithilfe fotografischer Mittel verzerrten Typografie. Erstmalig lässt sich dieses Gestaltungsmittel Anfang der 1960er-Jahre ausmachen, unter anderem auf dem Cover der italienischen Zeitschrift *domus* oder im Vorspann des zweiten James-Bond-Films *Liebesgrüße aus Moskau*. In den folgenden zehn Jahren generierten Gestalter auf der ganzen Welt auf diese Weise Texte zu plakativen Bildmotiven, und bis heute taucht die Idee immer wieder in den unterschiedlichsten Anwendungsformen auf.

Bien des tendances du graphisme ne permettent pas de déterminer à coup sûr qui fut la première personne à en avoir l'idée. Tel est le cas pour les distorsions typographiques réalisées à l'aide de moyens photographiques. Elles apparaissent pour la première fois au début des années 1960, notamment en couverture de la revue italienne *domus*, ou encore dans le générique du deuxième James Bond *Bons baisers de Russie*. Au cours des dix années suivantes, des graphistes du monde entier ont employé des techniques pour obtenir des motifs visuels accrocheurs, et encore aujourd'hui, cette idée réapparaît régulièrement sous diverses formes.

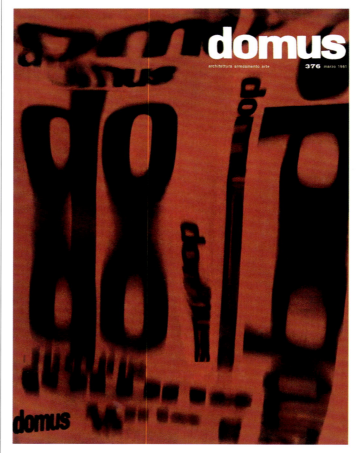

1961 · William Klein · US/IT · Magazine cover

1963 · Heinz Edelmann · DE · Poster

1963 · Gérard Miedinger · CH · Poster

1967 · Gilbert Lesser · US · Magazine cover

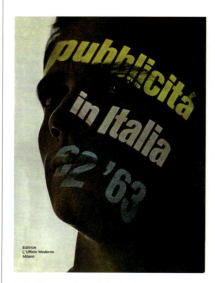

1963 · Franco Grignani · IT · Book cover

1963 · John Murello · US · Record cover

1967 · Mendell & Oberer · DE · Poster

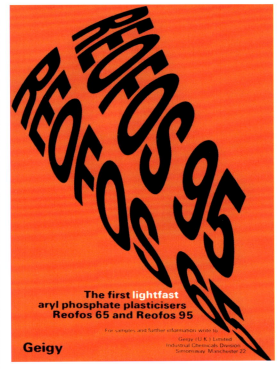

1969 · Brian Stones · UK · Ad

1965 · Robert Massin · FR · Book spread

1965 · Zdeněk Ziegler · CZ · Poster

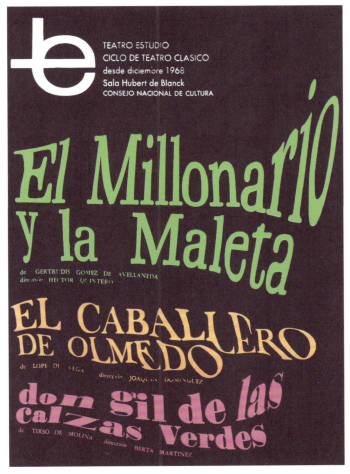

1968 · Anonymous · ES · Poster

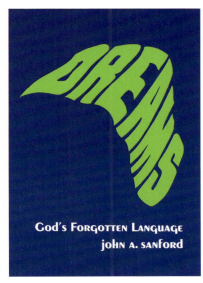

1968 · Don Bender · US · Book cover

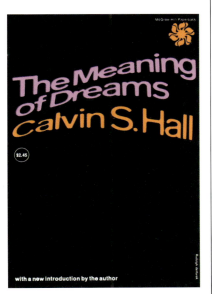

1966 · Rudolph de Harak · US · Book cover

1965 · Daniel Gil · ES · Book cover

1968 · Michael Tucker · UK · Logo · Achille Serre

Hans Hillmann · Germany

Founded in 1953, Neue Filmkunst Walter Kirchner was an arthouse film distributor that brought modern, independently produced movies and famous classics to German cinema screens. Until 1975, most of the responsibility for the company's extraordinary posters lay with Hans Hillmann. Given almost total freedom in his visual interpretation of the films' subjects, he created striking designs for more than 100 movie posters.

Neue Filmkunst Walter Kirchner war ein 1953 gegründeter Arthouse-Filmverleih, der aktuelle Independent-Produktionen und berühmte Filmklassiker in die deutschen Kinos brachte. Für die außergewöhnlichen Filmplakate des Unternehmens war bis 1975 vor allem Hans Hillmann verantwortlich. Er hatte nahezu völlige Freiheit bei der visuellen Interpretation der Filme und schuf mehr als 100 ikonografische Plakate.

Fondé en 1953, le distrbuteur de films d'art et d'essai Neue Filmkunst Walter Kirchner fit entrer des productions indépendantes récentes et des classiques du cinéma dans les salles allemandes. Jusqu'en 1975, les affiches inhabituelles de la firme furent signées pour l'essentiel par Hans Hillmann, qui bénéficia d'une liberté presque illimitée dans l'interprétation visuelle des œuvres cinématographiques et qui créa ainsi plus de 100 affiches iconiques.

1965 · Hans Hillmann · DE · Poster

1966 · Hans Hillmann · DE · Poster

1961 · Hans Hillmann · DE · Poster

1961 · Hans Hillmann · DE · Poster

1964 · Hans Hillmann · DE · Poster

Hans Hillmann (1925, Ujazd Dolny, Poland – 2014, Frankfurt am Main) was a designer and illustrator, generally regarded as the originator of the modern German movie poster. His work appeared on posters for films by such celebrated directors as Akira Kurosawa, Jean-Luc Godard, Federico Fellini, Luis Buñuel, and Jean Cocteau. Hillmann's flexible use of typography, photography, and illustration, often produced entirely by himself, strove to convey a direct message to the audience through its simplicity, whilst at the same time capturing each film's essence.

Hans Hillmann (1925, Nieder Mois, Schlesien, heute Polen – 2014, Frankfurt am Main) war ein Grafikdesigner und Illustrator, der allgemein als Urheber des modernen deutschen Filmplakats gilt. Er schuf Plakate für Filme berühmter Regisseure wie Akira Kurosawa, Jean-Luc Godard, Federico Fellini, Luis Buñuel und Jean Cocteau. Mit seiner flexiblen Verwendung von Typografie, Fotografie und Illustration, die er oft vollständig selbst gestaltete, bemühte Hillmann sich darum, dem Publikum durch Schlichtheit eine direkte Botschaft zu vermitteln und gleichzeitig das Wesentliche eines jeweiligen Films zu erfassen.

Hans Hillmann (1925, Ujazd Dolny, Pologne – 2014, Francfort-sur-le-Main) fut un graphiste et illustrateur généralement considéré comme le père de l'affiche de cinéma allemande moderne. Son travail apparaît dans des affiches de films de réalisateurs aussi célèbres qu'Akira Kurosawa, Jean-Luc Godard, Federico Fellini, Luis Buñuel et Jean Cocteau. Son utilisation très souple de la typographie, de la photographie et de l'illustration, souvent intégralement produites par lui-même, visait à faire passer au public un message direct par sa simplicité, tout en captant l'essence de chaque film.

1962 · Hans Hillmann · DE · Poster

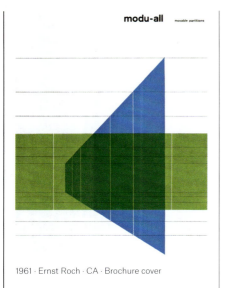

modu-all · movable partitions

1961 · Ernst Roch · CA · Brochure cover

Cuprophenyl-Informationen   Geigy

1964 · Toshihiro Katayama · JP · Brochure cover

The use of geometric forms in graphic design that began with the Swiss Style became one of the most commonly encountered basic approaches in the design work of the 1960s. Overlapping multicolored circles, triangles, and other shapes were to be seen as often on the labels of discs released by Brazilian record producers as on Japanese packaging design.

Ausgehend vom „Swiss Style", wurde die Arbeit mit geometrischen Formen zu einem der populärsten Gestaltungsansätze der 1960er-Jahre. Sich überlagernde mehrfarbige Kreise, Dreiecke und dergleichen fanden sich auf Schallplatten brasilianischer Musikhersteller ebenso wie im japanischen Verpackungsdesign.

Partant du style suisse, le travail avec des formes géométriques devint une des approches graphiques les plus populaires des années 1960. Superpositions de cercles, triangles et autres formes multicolores du même ordre se retrouvaient alors aussi bien sur les pochettes de disques de labels musicaux brésiliens que dans du packaging japonais.

"AO VIVO". NO TEATRO RECORD   P 632 780 L PHILIPS

o fino do fino elis regina e zimbo trio

PHILIPS

1965 · Carlos Prósperi · BR · Record cover

23.6.bis 30.6.1963 **KIELER WOCHE**

1960 · Otaka Takeshi · JP · Packaging

1963 · Hans Michel · DE · Poster

1964 · Karl Gerstner · CH · Ad

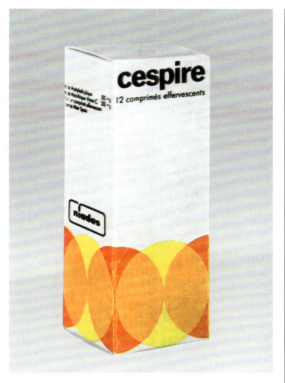

1970 · J. Angelopoulos, Frederick V. Carabott (AD) · GR · Packaging

Buchdruckerei A. Schöb Zürich 11|50 Birchstrasse 106 Telefon 051 48 52 53

1962 · Harry Boller · CH · Ad

1964 · Karl Gerstner · CH · Ad

AMORE SI SCRIVE COME SI VUOLE
SI PRONUNCIA ROSSANA

ROSSANA RB UN AMORE DI CUCINA RB CUCINE ROSSANA STEZZANO (BG)

1971 · Giancarlo Iliprandi · IT · Poster

LANCO

Swiss made

1956 · Bob Noorda · NL/IT · Poster

In the early 1960s, the German national airline Lufthansa's brand image was looking somewhat tired and outdated. The corporation took the unusual step of going straight to the Ulm School of Design and the designer Otl Aicher, one of the school's co-founders and who was then teaching there. Aicher and his students carried out a comprehensive preparatory study for the redesign of the brand image, and although Lufthansa rejected certain radical ideas—including a proposal to revamp the long-established crane logo, which dated back to 1919—the updated logo designed in Ulm had by 1963 largely been implemented. To this day, the brand concept created in the 1960s is recognized and respected worldwide.

Anfang der 1960er-Jahre wirkte der visuelle Auftritt der deutschen Fluggesellschaft Lufthansa uneinheitlich und altbacken. Das Unternehmen wählte einen ungewöhnlichen Schritt und wandte sich direkt an die Hochschule für Gestaltung in Ulm und den dort unterrichtenden Designer Otl Aicher. Gemeinsam mit seinen Studierenden entwickelte Aicher eine umfassende Studie zur Neugestaltung des visuellen Auftritts. Auch wenn Lufthansa einige radikale Vorschläge – darunter die Aktualisierung des seit 1919 etablierten Kranich-Logos – ablehnte, wurde das in Ulm erarbeitete Erscheinungsbild ab 1963 in wesentlichen Teilen realisiert. Bis heute bildet das damals entwickelte Konzept die Grundlage der weltweit bekannten und geschätzten Marke.

Au début des années 1960, la compagnie aérienne allemande Lufthansa affichait une image de marque plutôt vieillotte. L'entreprise prit une décision inhabituelle en s'adressant directement au Collège de design d'Ulm et au professeur de graphisme Otl Aicher, graphiste de métier et cofondateur de l'établissement. Avec ses étudiants, il mena une vaste étude pour redéfinir l'identité visuelle de la compagnie. Si Lufthansa rejeta quelques propositions jugées trop radicales – notamment l'actualisation du logo de la grue utilisé depuis 1919 – l'image développée à Ulm à partir de 1963 fut largement appliquée. À ce jour, le concept développé à l'époque est mondialement connu et apprécié.

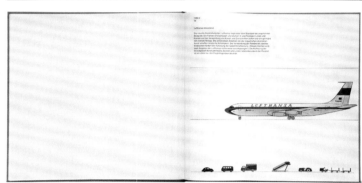

1962 · Otl Aicher, E5 · DE · Design study

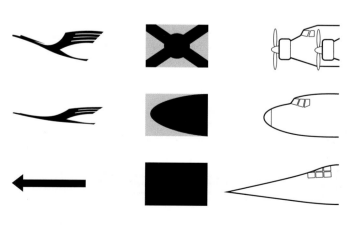

1962 · Otl Aicher, E5 · DE · Identity

Otl Aicher (1922, Ulm – 1991, Günzburg, Germany) was a German designer and typographer known for his structural visual systems. Before attending the Academy of Fine Arts in Munich he was drafted into the German army but deserted shortly before the end of the war, later setting up his own studio in Ulm in 1947. Aicher's most famous works include the identity systems for the Lufthansa airline and the 1972 Summer Olympics in Munich. Together with Max Bill he co-founded the Ulm School of Design (1953–68), which was a leading institution in the field.

Otl Aicher (1922, Ulm – 1991, Günzburg) war ein deutscher Grafikdesigner und Typograf, der sich vor allem mit seinem strukturellen System von Piktogrammen einen Namen machte. Als Rekrut zur Wehrmacht einberufen, desertierte er kurz vor Kriegsende, studierte später an der Akademie der Bildenden Künste in München und eröffnete schon 1947 sein eigenes Studio in Ulm. Zu Aichers bekanntesten Arbeiten gehören das visuelle Erscheinungsbild für die Lufthansa und für die Olympischen Sommerspiele 1972 in München. Zusammen mit Max Bill gründete er 1953 die Ulmer Hochschule für Gestaltung, die bis 1968 bestand und eine führende Institution auf ihrem Gebiet war.

Otl Aicher (1922, Ulm – 1991, Guntzbourg, Allemagne) fut un graphiste et typographe allemand qui se distingua pour ses systèmes visuels structurés. Avant de suivre des études à l'Académie des beaux-arts de Munich, il fut enrôlé de force dans l'armée, mais déserta pendant la Seconde Guerre mondiale et établit son propre studio à Ulm en 1947. Les travaux les plus célèbres d'Aicher comprennent des systèmes d'identité pour la compagnie aérienne Lufthansa et les jeux Olympiques d'été de Munich en 1972. Il fut avec Max Bill un des fondateurs du Collège de design d'Ulm (1953–68), qui devint une institution de premier plan dans ce domaine.

1963 · Otl Aicher, E5 · DE · Design manual

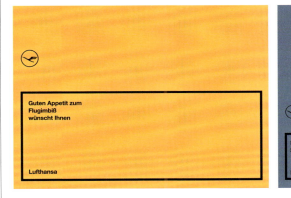

1963 · Otl Aicher · DE · Identity

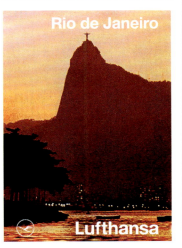

1964 · Otl Aicher (AD), Hans G. Conrad, Klaus Wille · DE · Posters

1963 · Otl Aicher · DE · Identity

1964

Herb Lubalin sets up his own studio in New York City

Josef Albers is honored as an AIGA medalist

Ken Garland publishes the **First Things First** manifesto on the values of graphic design which is backed by over 400 artists and graphic designers

Lou Dorfsman becomes director of design at CBS

1964 · François Dallegret · CA · Logo · Sofinco Drugstores

1964 · Kurt Wirth · CH · Logo · Buri

1964 · Jean-Marie Chourgnoz, Henry Chaney, Erich Brenzinger · FR · Logo · Elf Aquitaine

1965 · Anonymous · US · Record cover

1964 · Jacek Neugebauer · PL · Poster

1964 · Anonymous · UK · Magazine cover

Pablo Ferro Films is founded and produces the opening titles of the Kubrick film Dr. Strangelove

The first Czechoslovak Exhibition of Poster and Promotional Graphics is held, which later evolves to become the **Brno International Biennial of Graphic Design**

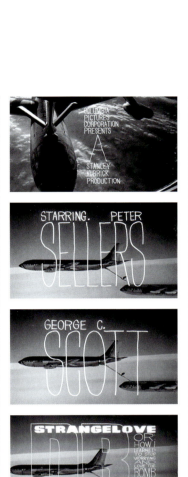

1964 · Pablo Ferro Films · US · Opening titles

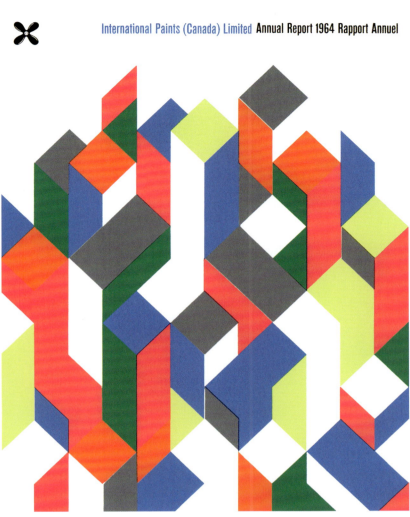

International Paints (Canada) Limited Annual Report 1964 Rapport Annuel

1964 · Rolf Harder · DE/CA · Brochure cover

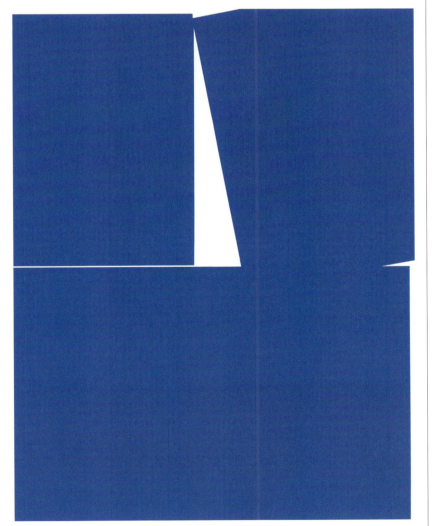

Kieler Woche 21.–28. Juni 1964

1964 · Hans Hillmann · DE · Poster

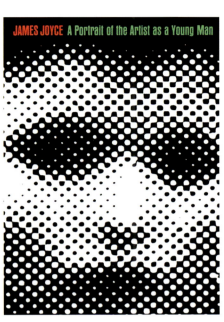

JAMES JOYCE A Portrait of the Artist as a Young Man

1964 · James Rosenzweig · US · Book cover

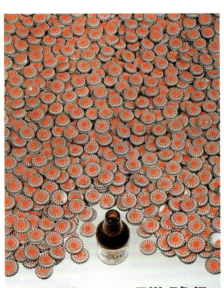

発売1年3億本 マイペースで飲もう アサヒスタイニー

1964 · Kazumasa Nagai · JP · Poster

copacabana filmes apresenta **deus e o diabo na terra do sol**
yoná magalhães
geraldo d'el rey
othon bastos um filme de glauber rocha
mauricio do valle produção: luiz augusto mendes

1964 · Rogério Duarte · BR · Poster

AIR FRANCE

1964 · Roger Excoffon · FR · Poster

69

In 1957, designers Jock Kinneir and Margaret Calvert started what would turn out to be a decade-long project to redesign the British road and motorway signage system, which up until then had been a patchwork of commissions by various different bodies. The result is probably the largest and most complex system of signs ever designed, and uses five main types (warning, regulatory, directional, motorway, and other) which are also subdivided into functional groups; road markings and traffic light signals are also covered. Typographically rigorous and methodologically impeccable, the standardization of this information system ranks among the most successful national design projects in history, and has gone on to serve as the basis for similar schemes in many other countries.

1957 begannen die Designer Jock Kinneir und Margaret Calvert ein Projekt, das sie zehn Jahre lang beschäftigen sollte und in dessen Verlauf sie die Beschilderung der britischen Straßen und Autobahnen neu gestalteten, die bis zu dem Zeitpunkt ein Durcheinander von beauftragten Entwürfen verschiedener Ämter gewesen war. In der Folge entstand das vermutlich größte und komplexeste Beschilderungssystem, das je entworfen wurde; es setzt sich zusammen aus fünf Hauptgruppen zusammen (Warnen, Regulieren, Richtungsweisen, Autobahn und Anderes), die in weitere Funktionsgruppen unterteilt sind. Auch Straßenmarkierungen und Ampelsignale sind abgedeckt. Mit ihrer typografischen Strenge und methodologischen Genauigkeit gehört die Standardisierung dieses Informationssystems zu den erfolgreichsten nationalen Designprojekten der Geschichte und dient mittlerweile vielen anderen Ländern als Bezugspunkt für ähnliche Vorhaben.

C'est en 1957 que les graphistes Jock Kinneir et Margaret Calvert commencèrent à travailler sur un projet d'une décennie consistant à la refonte de la signalisation routière et autoroutière britannique, jusqu'alors un patchwork de commandes exécutées par différents prestataires. Le résultat fut sans doute la plus vaste et complexe campagne de signalisation jamais réalisée – avec cinq catégories principales (avertissements, réglementation, directions, autoroutes et autres), elles-mêmes subdivisées en différents groupes fonctionnels. Les marquages au sol et les feux de signalisation étaient inclus dans le projet. D'une grand rigueur typographique et d'une méthodologie impeccable la standardisation de ce système d'information, un des projets de graphisme nationaux les plus réussis de l'histoire, a servi de base à des systèmes similaires dans de nombreux pays.

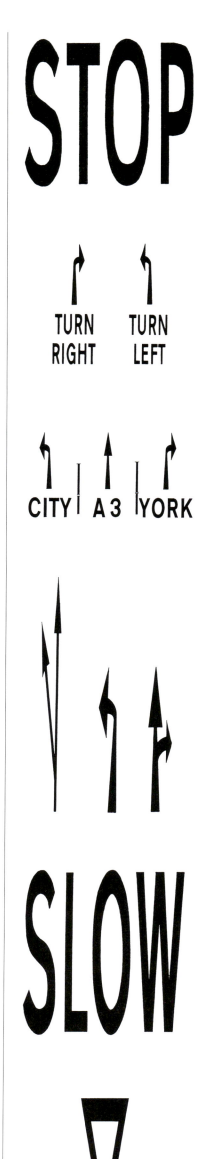

1964 · Jock Kinneir, Margaret Calvert · UK · Identity, Signage

1964 · Anonymous · JP · Poster

1951 · Franco Grignani · IT · Magazine cover

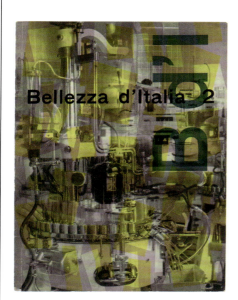

1953 · Franco Grignani · IT · Magazine cover

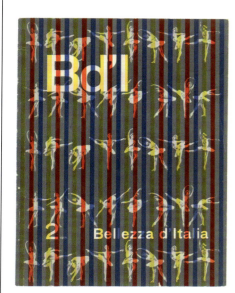

1954 · Franco Grignani · IT · Magazine cover

1968 · Franco Grignani · IT · Poster

1968 · Franco Grignani · IT · Poster

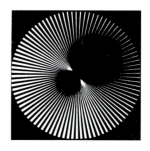

1960s · Franco Grignani · IT · Logo · Foto Grafica

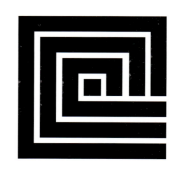

1969 · Franco Grignani · IT · Logo · Galleria d'Arte San Fedele

1969 · Franco Grignani · IT · Logo · Centro di Cultura G. Puecher

1973 · Franco Grignani · IT · Logo · Ceramiche Falcinelli

1973 · Franco Grignani · IT · Logo · Cremona Nuova

Franco Grignani (1908, Pieve Porto Morone, Italy – 1999, Milan) was an award-winning Italian artist and designer. Educated as an architect, Grignani soon became involved with the Futurism of the 1920s and '30s, and in the course of his career he experimented widely with geometry, Optical Art, and other styles. While his designs appeared in several exhibitions, he worked for the advertising review *Pubblicità in Italia,* as well as big corporations such as Montecatini, Pirelli, Dompé, and the printers Alfieri & Lacroix. Grignani is also the real designer of the world-famous Woolmark logo (1964), which for many years was attributed to the fictitious Francesco Saroglia.

Franco Grignani (1908, Pieve Porto Morone, Italien – 1999, Mailand) war ein preisgekrönter italienischer Künstler und Grafikdesigner, der sich schon bald nach seiner Ausbildung zum Architekten dem Futurismus der 1920er- und 1930er-Jahre anschloss. Im Verlauf seiner Karriere experimentierte Grignani ausgiebig mit Geometrie, Op-Art und anderen Stilen. Er hatte zahlreiche Ausstellungen und arbeitete für die Werbezeitschrift *Pubblicità in Italia* sowie für große Firmen wie Montecatini, Pirelli, Dompé und die Druckerei Alfieri & Lacroix. Grignani entwarf auch das weltberühmte Woolmark-Logo (1964), das jahrelang einem fiktiven Grafikdesigner namens Francesco Saroglia zugeschrieben wurde.

Franco Grignani (1908, Pieve Porto Morone, Italie – 1999, Milan) fut un artiste et graphiste italien primé. Après une formation d'architecte, Grignani rejoignit le mouvement futuriste dans les années 1920 et 1930; au cours de sa carrière, il expérimenta ensuite largement avec la géométrie, l'Op Art et d'autres styles. Il fit de nombreuses expositions et travailla pour la revue *Pubblicità in Italia,* mais aussi pour de grandes entreprises comme Montecatini, Pirelli, Dompé et l'imprimeur Alfieri & Lacroix. Grignani est aussi le créateur du logo mondialement célèbre de Woolmark (1964), attribué pendant de nombreuses années à un fictif Francesco Saroglia.

1964 · Franco Grignani · IT · Logo · Woolmark International

1969 · Franco Grignani · IT · Logo · Alfieri & Lacroix

1968 · Franco Grignani · IT · Logo · Aerhotel

1960 · Franco Grignani · IT · Poster

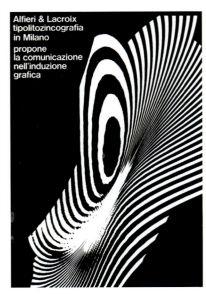

1964 · Franco Grignani · IT · Poster

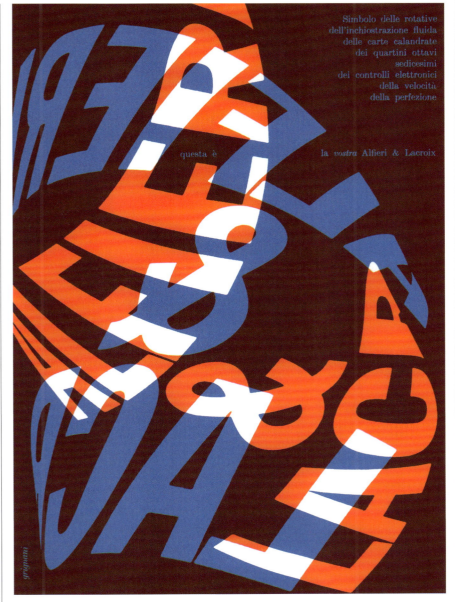

1960 · Franco Grignani · IT · Ad

Instituto di Tella · Argentina

The relatively late development of graphic design in Latin America was mostly due to the variable pace of socio-economic change within the different countries in the region. Many of the design schools and early studios were founded by immigrants, many of whom had arrived from the best institutions in Europe. In 1958 in Argentina, a rising economic power in the early 20th century, the Di Tella Foundation was set up to foster a range of cultural activities. A pioneering center for creative talent, including such designers as Juan Carlos Distéfano, Rubén Fontana, and Juan Andralis, its visual arts department was a defining force in graphic design throughout the 1960s until its closure in 1970. With a strong focus on typography, the department's artists constantly innovated in poster design, always offering a fresh alternative to the traditional schools in the country.

Die Geschichte des Grafikdesigns begann in Lateinamerika erst relativ spät, was vor allem mit dem unterschiedlichen Tempo zusammenhing, mit dem sich die sozioökonomischen Verhältnisse in den einzelnen Ländern der Region veränderten. Zahlreiche Designschulen und viele der ersten Studios wurden von Immigranten gegründet, die häufig von den besten Institutionen in Europa kamen. 1958 wurde in Argentinien – zu Anfang des 20. Jahrhunderts eine aufstrebende Wirtschaftsmacht – die Di Tella Foundation ins Leben gerufen zu dem Zweck, eine große Bandbreite kultureller Vorhaben zu fördern. Die Stiftung war bahnbrechend als Zentrum für kreative Talente, etwa für Designer wie Juan Carlos Distéfano, Rubén Fontana und Juan Andralis, und ihre Abteilung für bildende Kunst hatte die ganzen 1960er-Jahre hindurch bis zu ihrer Schließung 1970 einen maßgeblichen Einfluss im Grafikdesign. Typografie war einer ihrer Schwerpunkte, die dort tätigen Künstler entwickelten ständig innovative Ideen in der Plakatgestaltung und boten unweigerlich erfrischende Alternativen zu den traditionellen argentinischen Schulen.

Le développement plutôt tardif du graphisme en Amérique latine est surtout lié aux rythmes variables de l'évolution socio-économique dans les pays de la région. Les écoles de graphisme et les premiers studios furent souvent fondés par des immigrants formés dans les meilleures institutions européennes. En Argentine, puissance économique montante au début du XXᵉ siècle, l'Instituto Di Tella fut créé en 1958 pour promouvoir toute une série d'activités culturelles. Centre pionnier pour les talents créatifs – avec des graphistes comme Juan Carlos Distéfano, Rubén Fontana et Juan Andralis –, son département d'arts visuels fut une force déterminante du graphisme tout au long des années 1960 jusqu'à la fermeture de l'institut en 1970. Avec l'accent mis sur la typographie, les artistes du département innovèrent constamment en matière d'affiches, offrant toujours une approche nouvelle face aux écoles traditionnelles du pays.

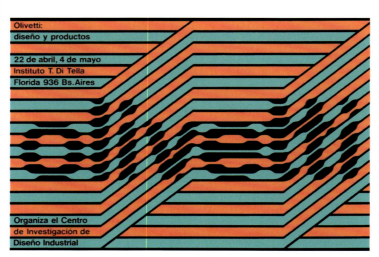

1964 · Juan Carlos Distéfano, Rubén Fontana, Carlos Soler · AR · Poster

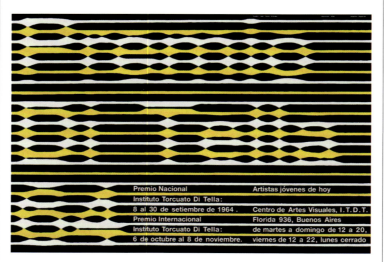

1964 · Juan Carlos Distéfano · AR · Poster

1966 · Juan Carlos Distéfano, Rubén Fontana · AR · Poster

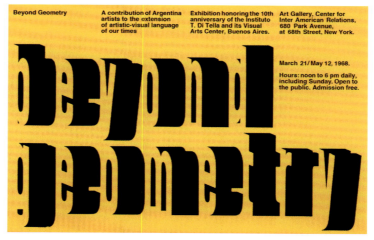

1968 · Juan Carlos Distéfano, Rubén Fontana · AR · Poster

1963 · Juan Carlos Distéfano, Rubén Fontana · AR · Brochure cover

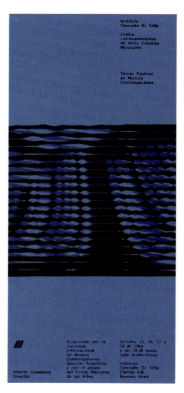

1964 · Juan Carlos Distéfano · AR · Brochure cover

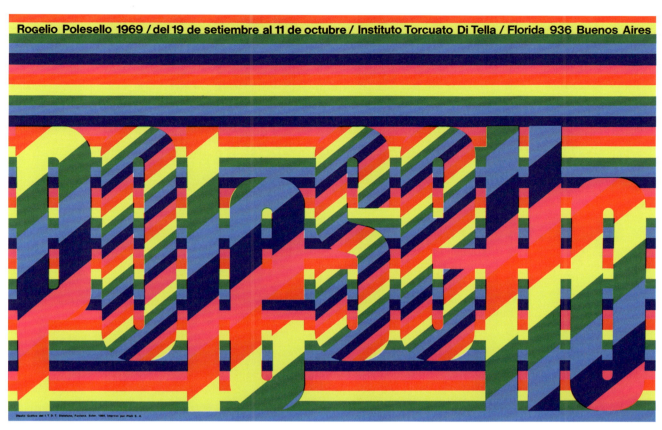

1969 · Juan Carlos Distéfano, Rubén Fontana, Carlos Soler · AR · Poster

Juan Carlos Distéfano (1933, Buenos Aires) is an Argentinean artist and graphic designer who introduced modern graphic design in his homeland during the 1960s. After studying painting at the Escuela de Artes Gráficas in Buenos Aires, in 1955 Distéfano joined an advertising agency but was soon recalled to his former college to take on a teaching post. From 1959 onwards he continued to lecture while also working as a freelance artist. Around this time he began to collaborate with the Di Tella Institute. However, from 1976 onwards he focused entirely on sculpture and a year later moved to Spain following the military coup in Argentina.

Juan Carlos Distéfano (1933, Buenos Aires) ist ein argentinischer Künstler und Grafiker, der in den 1960er-Jahren modernes Grafikdesign in seinem Heimatland etablierte. Nach einem Studium der Malerei an der Escuela de Artes Gráficas arbeitete er ab 1955 zunächst in einer Werbeagentur, wurde bald jedoch durch seine ehemalige Hochschule zum Professor berufen und arbeitete neben der Lehre ab 1959 freischaffend. Zur gleichen Zeit begann die Zusammenarbeit mit dem Kulturforschungsinstitut Di Tella. Dennoch wandte er sich ab 1976 vollständig der Bildhauerei zu und wanderte ein Jahr später als Reaktion auf den argentinischen Militärputsch nach Spanien aus.

Juan Carlos Distéfano (1933, Buenos Aires) est un artiste et graphiste argentin qui a introduit le graphisme moderne dans son pays natal dans les années 1960. Après des études de peinture à la Escuela de Artes Gráficas, il a d'abord travaillé dans une agence publicitaire à partir de 1955, pour être bientôt nommé professeur dans son ancienne école. À partir de 1959, il travaille alors en freelance à côté de son activité d'enseignant. À la même époque débute sa collaboration avec l'institut de recherche culturelle Di Tella. À partir de 1976, il se tourne entièrement vers la sculpture et émigre l'année suivante en Espagne à la suite du coup d'État militaire en Argentine.

1965 · Juan Carlos Distéfano, Rubén Fontana · AR · Brochure cover

1968 · Juan Carlos Distéfano · AR · Poster

1963 · Juan Carlos Distéfano · AR · Poster

1973 · Juan Carlos Distéfano · AR · Poster

The mid-1960s saw the birth of the Spaghetti Western, a sub-genre of the Western movie typically made cheaply in Europe and with Italian directors. Movie-goers continue to be fascinated by their inventive title sequences, created with great technical skill and dramatic effect, which had little in common with the uncluttered severity of the graphics of their time.

Mit dem Italowestern entstand Mitte der 1960er-Jahre ein Sub-genre der Westernkultur, oft günstig in Europa von italienischen Regisseuren produziert. Noch heute faszinieren die mit großem handwerklichen Aufwand produzierten expressiven Titelsequenzen, die so gar nichts mit der an-sonsten oft aufgeräumt-strengen Grafik ihrer Zeit gemein haben.

Au milieu des années 1960 apparaît le western dit «spaghetti», un sous-genre très populaire tourné à petit budget en Europe par des réalisateurs italiens. Même s'ils n'ont rien de commun avec le graphisme des plus épurés de leur époque, les génériques inventifs produits à grands renforts de moyens artisanaux n'ont rien perdu de leur pouvoir de fascination auprès des cinéphiles.

1966 · Iginio Lardani · IT · Opening titles

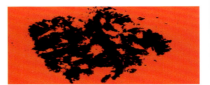

1966 · Iginio Lardani · IT · Opening titles

1967 · Iginio Lardani · IT · Opening titles

1964 · Iginio Lardani · IT · Opening titles

September 1964 Vol 17 No. 9 2s. 6d.

1964 · Carl Swann, Stevens & Swann · UK · Magazine cover

Ivan Chermayeff & Tom Geismar · United States

1964 · Chermayeff & Geismar · US · Logo · Mobil

1964 · Chermayeff & Geismar · US · Design manual

1960s · Chermayeff & Geismar · US · Packaging

1964 · Chermayeff & Geismar · US · Identity · Mobil

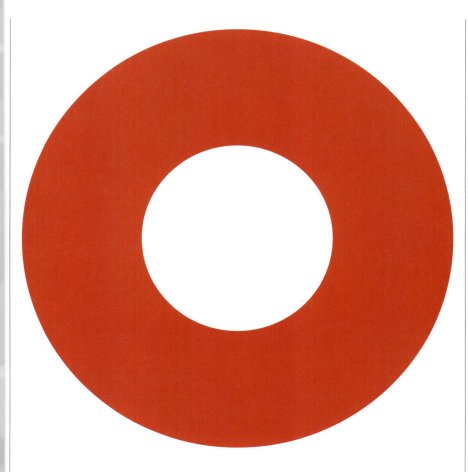

1964 · Chermayeff & Geismar · US · Identity · Mobil

Chermayeff & Geismar is a New York-based design firm founded in 1957 by Ivan Chermayeff (1932, London – 2017, New York) and Tom Geismar (1931, Glen Ridge, New Jersey), who built a global reputation based on their work for such brands as Chase Bank, *National Geographic,* Merck, Mobil, Pan Am, and PBS, among many others. After graduating from Yale, the two joined forces to work primarily on corporate identity and its collaterals, producing over 100 identities for big institutions. In 2006, graphic designer Sagi Haviv (1974, Israel) became the third partner in the business.

Chermayeff & Geismar ist ein New Yorker Designstudio, 1957 gegründet von Ivan Chermayeff (1932, London – 2017, New York) und Tom Geismar (Glen Ridge, 1931, New Jersey). Internationales Renommee erlangten die beiden durch ihre Arbeit für Unternehmen wie die Chase Bank, *National Geographic,* Merck, Mobil, Pan Am, PBS und andere. Nach dem Studium in Yale schlossen sie sich zusammen, um hauptsächlich im weiteren Bereich Corporate Identity zu arbeiten, wobei sie über 100 Identities für große Institutionen schufen. 2006 wurde der Grafikdesigner Sagi Haviv (1974, Israel) der dritte Partner in dem Unternehmen.

Chermayeff & Geismar, firme de design basée à New York et fondée en 1957 par Ivan Chermayeff (1932, Londres – 2017, New York) et Tom Geismar (1931, Glen Ridge, New Jersey), s'est gagné une notoriété internationale avec ses réalisations pour des clients comme Chase Bank, *National Geographic,* Merck, Mobil, Pan Am et PBS, parmi beaucoup d'autres. Diplômés de l'université Yale, les deux designers associèrent leurs forces pour travailler principalement sur des images de marque et leurs aspects dérivés, produisant plus de cent identités pour de grandes institutions. En 2006, le graphiste Sagi Haviv (1974, Israël) est devenu le troisième associé de la firme.

1960s · Chermayeff & Geismar · US · Logo · Chase Manhattan Bank

1965 · Chermayeff & Geismar · US · Logo · Screen Gems

1964 · Chermayeff & Geismar · US · Logo · Seatrain Lines

1964 · Chermayeff & Geismar · US · Logo · Burlington

1972 · Chermayeff & Geismar · US · Logo · Owens-Illinois

Aloísio Magalhães · Brazil

1964 · Aloísio Magalhães · BR · Logo · Petrobras

Aloísio Magalhães (1927, Recife, Brazil – 1982, Padua, Italy) is considered the founder of modern graphic design in Brazil. After first studying law, Magalhães was instrumental in professionalizing the design field, co-founding the first dedicated school in the country, the Escola Superior de Desenho Industrial in Rio de Janeiro. He served as Culture Secretary for the Ministry of Education, and in 1960 founded his own practice, PVDI, producing hundreds of corporate identities for big institutions. Magalhães died of a heart attack while lecturing in Padua.

Aloísio Magalhães (1927, Recife, Brasilien – 1982, Padua, Italien) gilt als Begründer der modernen Gebrauchsgrafik in Brasilien. Nachdem er ursprünglich Jura studiert hatte, wurde Magalhães zum Wegbereiter der Professionalisierung im Bereich Design und gehörte als solcher zu den Gründern der ersten Grafikerschule des Landes, der Escola Superior de Desenho Industrial in Rio de Janeiro. Er diente als Kulturstaatssekretär im Erziehungsministerium und eröffnete 1960 seine eigene Firma PVDI, die Hunderte von Corporate Identities für große Institutionen entwarf. Magalhães starb an einem Herzinfarkt während einer Vorlesung in Padua.

Aloísio Magalhães (1927, Recife, Brésil – 1982, Padoue, Italie) est considéré comme le père fondateur du graphisme moderne au Brésil. Après des études de droit, Magalhães devint un acteur clé de la professionnalisation du secteur en tant que cofondateur de la première école spécialisée dans son pays, la Escola Superior de Desenho Industrial à Rio de Janeiro. Il fut secrétaire à la Culture au sein du ministère de l'Éducation, et en 1960, il ouvrit son propre studio PVDI, produisant des centaines d'identités pour de grandes institutions. Magalhães est mort d'une crise cardiaque pendant une conférence à Padoue.

In 1970, the Rio de Janeiro-based design firm PVDI started work on renewing the identity for Petrobras in what would come to be regarded as the standard model for branding large, and notably state-run companies in Brazil. Given the scale of the multinational petroleum corporation, and all its subsidiaries, the project took over two decades to be fully implemented, the result as well of Petrobras being severely hit by the 1973 oil crisis.

1970 machte sich das in Rio de Janeiro ansässige Designstudio PVDI daran, die Identität von Petrobras zu erneuern, und sollte damit ein Modell schaffen, dem künftig die CI-Entwicklung aller großen Firmen, insbesondere von Staatsbetrieben, in Brasilien folgte. Angesichts der Größe des multinationalen Mineralölunternehmens mit seinen zahlreichen Tochterfirmen dauerte es über zwanzig Jahre, bis das Projekt zur Gänze umgesetzt war. Mit ein Grund dafür war die Ölkrise 1973, von der Petrobras stark betroffen war.

En 1970, la firme de graphisme PVDI basée à Rio de Janeiro commence à travailler au renouvellement de l'identité de Petrobras, dans le cadre de ce qui sera considéré comme le modèle de base pour l'image des grandes entreprises nationales brésiliennes. Étant donnée la taille de la multinationale pétrolière comptant de nombreuses filiales, le projet dut être mené sur deux décennies pour une complète application, mais aussi en raison du choc pétrolier de 1973, qui affecta également Petrobras.

1969 · Aloísio Magalhães · BR · Logo · Banco do Estado do São Paulo

1965 · Aloísio Magalhães · BR · Logo · Brafor

1965 · Aloísio Magalhães · BR · Logo · Banco Itaú América

1960s · Aloísio Magalhães · BR · Logo · Companhia de Cigarros Souza Cruz

1960s · Aloísio Magalhães · BR · Logo · Docenave

1964 · Aloísio Magalhães · BR · Identity · Petrobras

1960s · Aloísio Magalhães · BR · Logo · Editora Delta

1960s · Aloísio Magalhães · BR · Logo · Companhia Sol de Seguros

1960s · Aloísio Magalhães · BR · Logo · Laboratório Maurício Villela

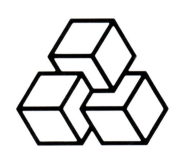

1965 · Aloísio Magalhães · BR · Logo · Banco do Estado do Rio Grande do Sul

1970 · Aloísio Magalhães · BR · Logo · Banco Nacional de Minas Gerais

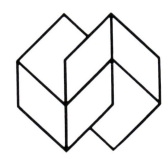

1969 · Aloísio Magalhães · BR · Logo · Banco Mercantil do Brasil

1972 · Aloísio Magalhães · BR · Logo · Indústrias Zillo

1960s · Aloísio Magalhães · BR · Logo · Policlínica Geral do Rio de Janeiro

1960s · Aloísio Magalhães · BR · Logo · ICOMI

1960s · Aloísio Magalhães · BR · Logo · Instituto Brasileiro de Geografia e Estatística

1957 · Aloísio Magalhães · BR · Book cover

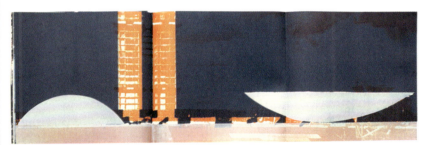

1959 · Aloísio Magalhães · BR · Book spread

1970s · Aloísio Magalhães · BR · Banknotes

1960–1969

ARBEITSBERICHT DER WERKKUNSTSCHULE DÜSSELDORF 1963

1963 · Heinz Edelmann · DE · Brochure cover

Gebrauchsgraphik
International
Advertising Art
B 3149 E   Juli 1965

1965 · Heinz Edelmann · DE · Magazine cover

1964 · Heinz Edelmann · DE · Poster

1964 · Heinz Edelmann · DE · Poster

1966 · Heinz Edelmann · DE · Poster

Heinz Edelmann (1934, Ústí nad Labem, Czech Republic – 2009, Stuttgart) was a German illustrator and designer best known for his work as art director for the Beatles' psychedelic animated film *Yellow Submarine* (1968). Edelmann's colorful and organic visual language has exerted a widespread influence on illustration. He studied at the Dusseldorf Arts Academy and remained active into his later years, designing the mascot for the World's Fair in Seville in 1992 as well as book covers for the German edition of Tolkien's *Lord of the Rings*, and Kenneth Grahame's *Wind in the Willows*.

Heinz Edelmann (1934, Ústí nad Labem [Aussig], heute Tschechien – 2009, Stuttgart) war ein deutscher Illustrator und Grafikdesigner, der vor allem durch seine Arbeit als Artdirector für den psychedelischen Beatles-Zeichentrickfilm *Yellow Submarine* (1968) bekannt wurde. Edelmanns farbenfrohe, organische Bildsprache übte einen starken Einfluss auf die Illustration aus. Er hatte an der Düsseldorfer Kunstakademie studiert und blieb sein Leben lang aktiv: So entwarf er nicht nur das Maskottchen für die Weltausstellung von Sevilla 1992, sondern gestaltete auch den Buchumschlag der deutschen Ausgabe von Tolkiens *Herr der Ringe* und Kenneth Grahames Kinderbuch *Der Wind in den Weiden*.

Heinz Edelmann (1934, Ústí nad Labem, République tchèque – 2009, Stuttgart) fut un illustrateur et graphiste allemand connu surtout pour son travail comme directeur artistique de *Yellow Submarine* (1968), le film animé psychédélique des Beatles. Le langage visuel haut en couleur et organique d'Edelmann exerça une forte influence sur l'illustration. Il étudia à l'Académie des beaux-arts de Düsseldorf et resta actif jusqu'à un âge avancé, dessinant notamment la mascotte de l'Exposition universelle de Séville en 1992, ainsi que des couvertures de livres pour l'édition allemande du *Seigneur des anneaux* de Tolkien et du *Vent dans les saules* de Kenneth Grahame.

Kammerspiele   Düsseldorf   **BÜRGER SCHIPPEL**

Theater am Wilhelm Marx
Haus, Alleestraße 49/51
Telefon 2 44 08
Karten von DM 2,60 bis
DM 10,60 täglich (außer
sonntags) 10.00 bis 13.00 und
15.00 bis 17.00 Uhr.
Vorstellungen:
jeweils donnerstags 20.00
freitags 20.00 sonnabends
19.30 und sonntags 20.00

Bürger Schippel
Komödie von Carl Sternheim
Inszenierung:
Hansjörg Utzerath
Bühnenbild: Heinz Balthes
Musikalische Einstudierung:
Emil Schuchardt.
Lore Schubert, Renate Woldt,
Walter Gottschow, Hermann
Hartmann, Walter Hoor,
Gerhard Kauffmann, Werner
Meyer. Regie-Assistenz:
Ursula Fentsch
Technische Leitung:
Klaus Bendgens

K

1960 · Heinz Edelmann · DE · Poster

1964 · Jan Lenica · PL · Poster

Jan Lenica (1928, Poznań, Poland – 2001, Berlin) was an influential Polish designer and cartoonist. After studying architecture in Warsaw, Lenica worked as a poster artist and animator, collaborating on the early films of Walerian Borowczyk. He lived and worked for 20 years in France before moving to Berlin in 1987, where he taught and continued to work in animation. His distinctive cut-out stop-motion technique, together with his poster designs, are key references in 20th-century Polish visual art. Lenica also worked on postage stamps, costumes, and children's books, and was an art critic.

Jan Lenica (1928, Poznań, Polen – 2001, Berlin) war ein einflussreicher polnischer Designer und Cartoonist. Nach seinem Architekturstudium in Warschau war Lenica als Plakatkünstler und Trickfilmzeichner tätig, unter anderem bei den frühen Zeichentrickfilmen von Walerian Borowczyk. Er lebte und arbeitete zwanzig Jahre lang in Frankreich und ging 1987 nach Berlin, wo er Animation unterrichtete, aber auch in diesem Bereich weiterarbeitete. Seiner charakteristischen Technik der Cut-out- und Stop-Motion-Animation sowie seinen Plakatentwürfen kommt in der bildenden Kunst Polens des 20. Jahrhunderts eine Schlüsselstellung zu. Lenica gestaltete auch Briefmarken, Kostüme und Kinderbücher und betätigte sich zudem als Kunstkritiker.

Jan Lenica (1928, Poznań, Pologne – 2001, Berlin) fut un influent graphiste et dessinateur de presse polonais. Après des études d'architecture à Varsovie, Lenica travailla comme affichiste et artiste animateur et collabora aux premiers films de Walerian Borowczyk. Il vécut et travailla pendant vingt ans en France avant de s'installer à Berlin en 1987, où il enseigna et continua d'exercer dans l'animation. Sa technique très particulière d'animation image par image en papier découpé et ses affiches, sont des références dans l'art visuel polonais du XXe siècle. Lenica créa aussi des timbres, des costumes et des livres pour enfants, et fut également critique d'art.

1958 · Jan Lenica · PL · Poster

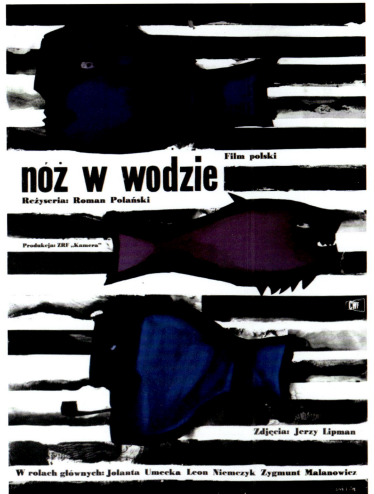

1962 · Jan Lenica · PL · Poster

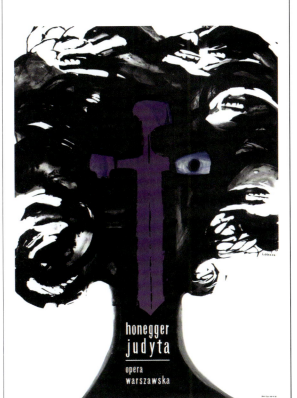

1962 · Jan Lenica · PL · Poster

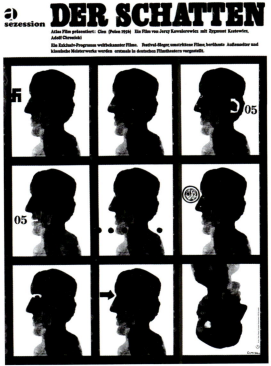

1966 · Jan Lenica · PL · Poster

1965

Armin Hofmann's **Graphic Design Manual** is published

International brand consultancy **Wolff Olins** is founded in London by Michael Wolff and Wally Olins

The **Unimark International** branding corporation is founded by Massimo Vignelli, Bob Noorda, and four other partners with offices in Chicago, Milan, and New York

1965 · Peter von Arx · CH · Poster

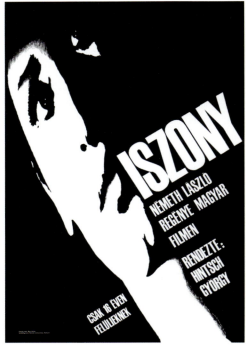

1965 · Anonymous · HU · Poster

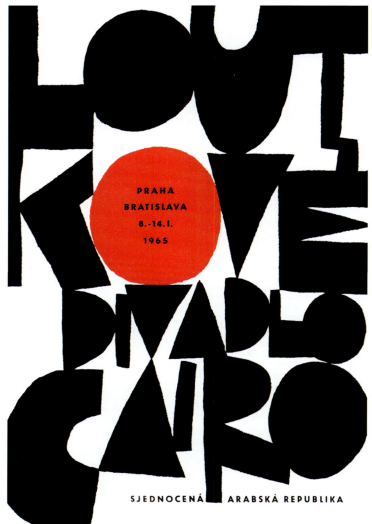

1965 · Bronislaw Zelek · PL · Poster

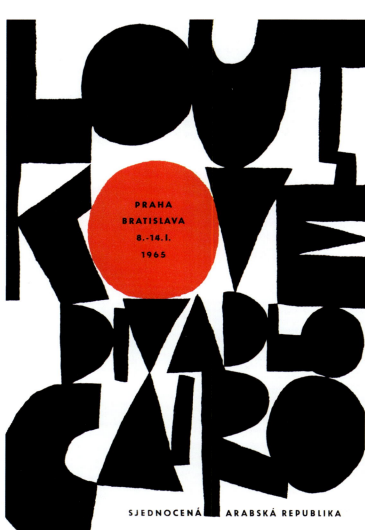

1965 · Anonymous · CZ · Poster

1965 · Raymond Loewy, CEI · FR/UK · Logo · British Petroleum

1965 · James Pilditch, John Harris, Allied International Designers · UK · Logo · Albert Heijn

1965 · Kinneir, Calvert & Associates · UK · Logo · Glasgow Airport

1965 · Zdeněk Ziegler · CZ · Poster

1965 · Anonymous · UK · Poster

1965 · Peter Megert · CH · Poster

1965 · Juan Carlos Distéfano, Design Department,
Instituto Torcuato di Tella · AR · Poster

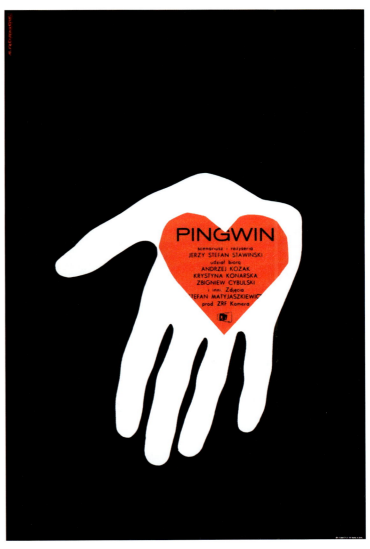

1965 · Marek Freudenreich · PL · Poster

1965 · Chermayeff & Geismar · US · Magazine cover

1965 · Anonymous · JP · Poster

1965 · Bruno Munari · IT · Poster

1965 · Hiroshi Tanaka · JP · Poster

Edgardo Giménez · Argentina

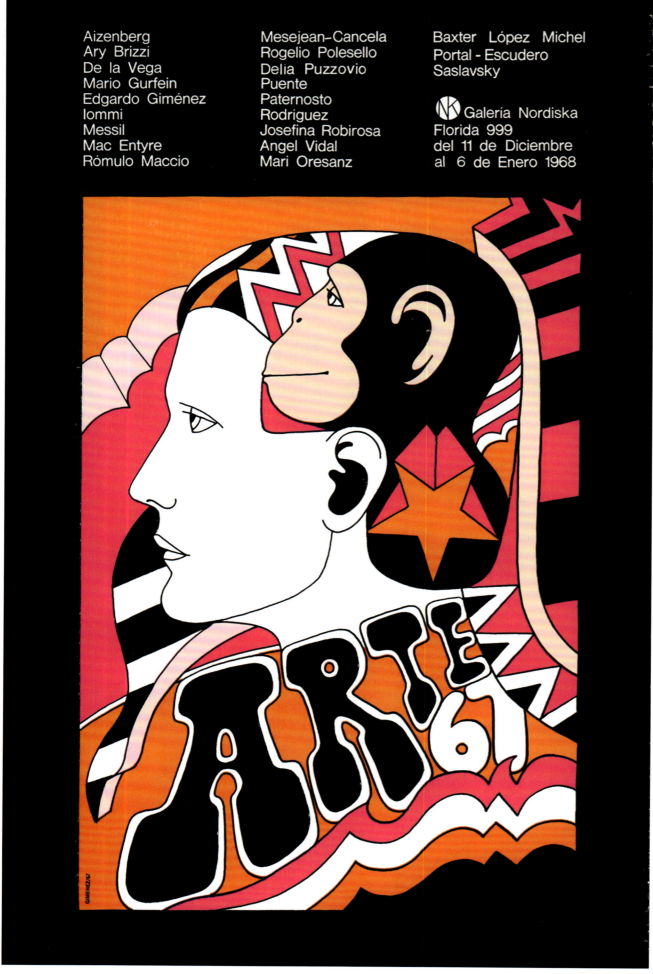

Aizenberg
Ary Brizzi
De la Vega
Mario Gurfein
Edgardo Giménez
Iommi
Messil
Mac Entyre
Rómulo Maccio

Mesejean–Cancela
Rogelio Polesello
Delia Puzzovio
Puente
Paternosto
Rodriguez
Josefina Robirosa
Angel Vidal
Mari Oresanz

Baxter López Michel
Portal - Escudero
Saslavsky

Galeria Nordiska
Florida 999
del 11 de Diciembre
al 6 de Enero 1968

1967 · Edgardo Giménez · AR · Poster

Edgardo Giménez (1942, Santo Tomé, Argentina) is an Argentinean visual artist and was a key figure at the Instituto Torcuato di Tella in Buenos Aires in the late 1960s. Self-taught, Giménez started in advertising at the age of 13, and went on to design sets for theater and movies, while also working as an artist. In 1980, he spent two years designing a number of popular posters for the Teatro San Martín, one of the most important theaters in the Argentinean capital. Giménez has exhibited in Europe and the United States, and continues to live and work in Buenos Aires.

Edgardo Giménez (1942, Santo Tomé, Argentinien) ist ein bildender Künstler, der in den späten 1960er-Jahren zu den prominenten Figuren am Instituto Torcuato di Tella in Buenos Aires gehörte. Der Autodidakt begann seine berufliche Laufbahn bereits als 13-Jähriger in der Werbebranche, später entwarf er Bühnen- und Filmausstattungen, während er gleichzeitig auch als Künstler tätig war. Ab 1980 gestaltete Giménez zwei Jahre lang zahlreiche populäre Plakate für das Teatro San Martín, eine der bedeutendsten Bühnen in der argentinischen Hauptstadt. Giménez, der in Europa und in den Vereinigten Staaten ausgestellt hat, lebt und arbeitet nach wie vor in Buenos Aires.

Edgardo Giménez (1942, Santo Tomé, Argentine) est un artiste visuel argentin qui fut une figure éminente de l'Instituto Torcuato di Tella à Buenos Aires à la fin des années 1960. Autodidacte, Giménez a travaillé dans la publicité dès l'âge de 13 ans avant de se lancer dans le décor de théâtre et de cinéma, tout en travaillant comme artiste. En 1980, il passe deux ans à concevoir de nombreuses affiches célèbres pour le Teatro San Martín, un des grands théâtres de la capitale argentine. Giménez a exposé en Europe et aux États-Unis et vit et travaille aujourd'hui encore à Buenos Aires.

1964 · Edgardo Giménez · AR · Poster

1964 · Edgardo Giménez · AR · Poster

1964 · Edgardo Giménez · AR · Poster

1965 · Edgardo Giménez · AR · Poster

1965 · Edgardo Giménez · AR · Poster

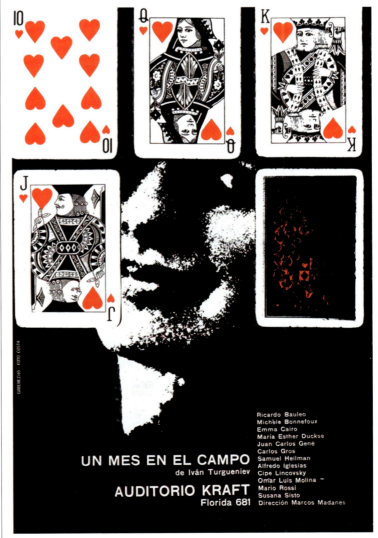

1965 · Edgardo Giménez · AR · Poster

1966

The first **International Poster Biennale** is held in Warsaw

Bruno Munari's book **Design as Art** is published

The design studio **Gottschalk+Ash** is founded in Montreal by Stuart Ash and Fritz Gottschalk

Günter Gerhard Lange begins his work on an update of the **Akzidenz Grotesk** typeface

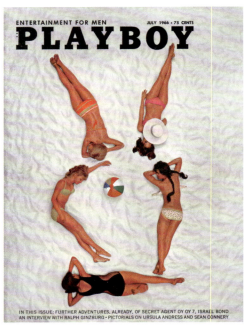

1966 · Dave Chaston · UK · Magazine cover

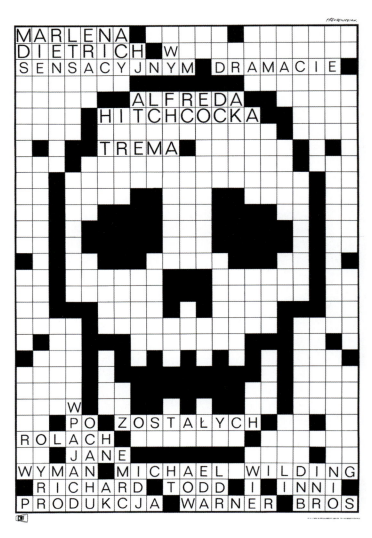

1966 · Marek Freudenreich · PL · Poster

1966 · Bob Noorda · NL/IT · Logo · Venice Biennial

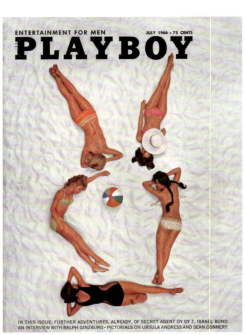

1966 · Art Paul (AD), Larry Gordon (PH) · US · Magazine cover

1966 · Yvon Laroche · CA · Logo · Cinema

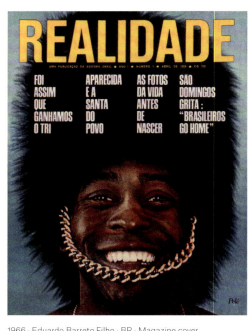

1966 · Eduardo Barreto Filho · BR · Magazine cover

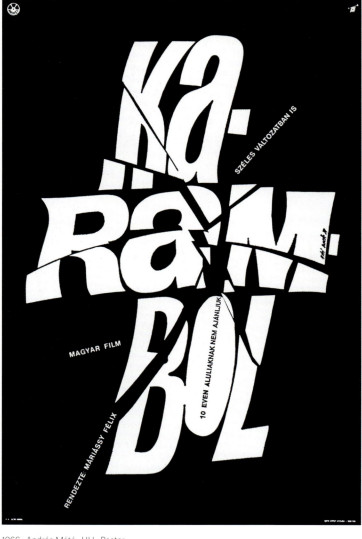

1966 · Anonymous · SE · Logo · Ikea

1966 · András Máté · HU · Poster

1966 · Jaroslav Sura · YU · Poster

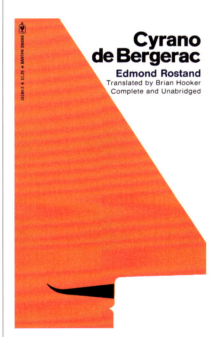

Cyrano de Bergerac

Edmond Rostand
Translated by Brian Hooker
Complete and Unabridged

1966 · Gips & Danne · US · Book Cover

randstad wenst u
prettige dagen en een best

1966 · Ben Bos, Total Design · NL · Brochure cover

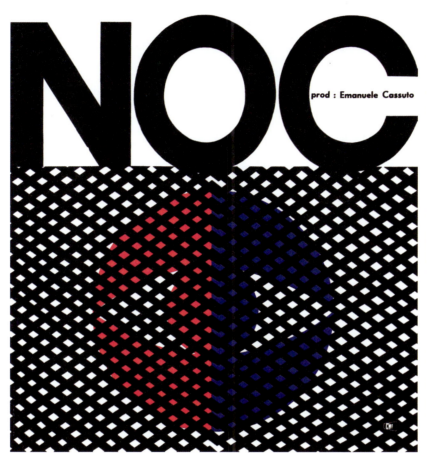

JEANNE MOREAU
MONICA VITTI
MARCELLO MASTROIANNI
MICHELANGELO ANTONIONIEGO

w wielkim dramacie psychologicznym

NOC

prod : Emanuele Cassuto

1966 · Andrzej Onegin Dabrowski · PL · Poster

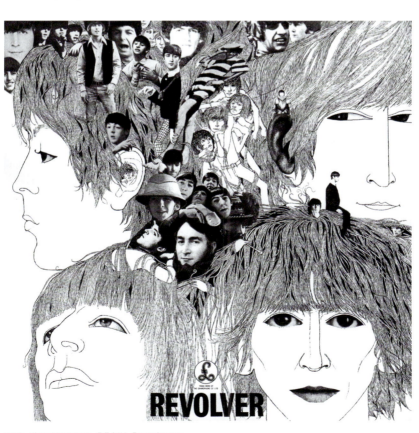

REVOLVER

1966 · Klaus Voormann · DE/UK · Record cover

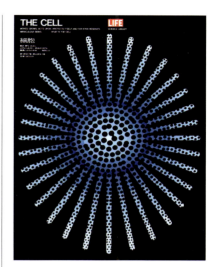

THE CELL · LIFE

1966 · Kazumasa Nagai · JP · Poster

FELKELÉS

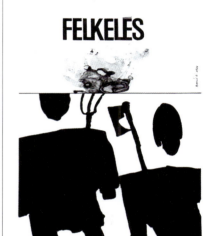

1966 · Árpád Bognár · HU · Poster

1966 · Mostafa Assadollahi · IR · Poster

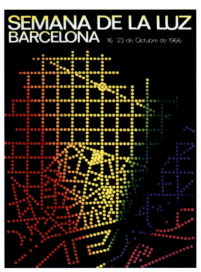

SEMANA DE LA LUZ
BARCELONA 16 · 23 de Octubre de 1966

1966 · Armand Domènech · ES · Poster

With the launch in 1957 of *The Push Pin Monthly Graphic*, the team of illustrators at Push Pin Studios in New York introduced a series of their own publications, which served both as a representation service for artists and at the same time as a place for graphic experimentation. Over a period of 23 years, a total of 86 issues were published in which Seymour Chwast and his colleagues revealed and extended the possibilities of contemporary illustration.

Die Illustratoren des New Yorker Push Pin Studios gründeten 1957 mit *The Push Pin Monthly Graphic* eine eigene Publikationsreihe – ein Repräsentationsmedium wie Experimentierfeld zugleich. Über einen Zeitraum von 23 Jahren erschienen insgesamt 86 Ausgaben, in denen Seymour Chwast und seine Kollegen die Möglichkeiten zeitgenössischer Illustration aufzeigten und vorantrieben.

En 1957, les illustrateurs de Push Pin Studios à New York lançaient la revue *The Push Pin Monthly Graphic*, une série de publications maison qui visaient la promotion des artistes et se voulait un lieu d'expérimentation. En l'espace de 23 ans parurent au total 86 numéros dans lesquels Seymour Chwast et ses collègues présentèrent et firent progresser les possibilités de l'illustration contemporaine.

1957 · Seymour Chwast · US · Magazine cover

1980 · Seymour Chwast · US · Magazine cover

1960 · Seymour Chwast · US · Magazine cover

Seymour Chwast (1931, New York) is an American designer and illustrator. In 1954, he co-founded Push Pin Studios together with Milton Glaser and others, resulting in the freeform publication *The Push Pin Monthly Graphic*. After attending Cooper Union, Chwast embarked on a prolific career working on posters, magazine and book covers, advertising, and packaging, including designing the first box for a McDonald's Happy Meal in 1979. An AIGA medalist and member of the Art Directors Hall of Fame, Chwast's diverse and innovative portfolio has had a lasting impact on American visual culture.

Seymour Chwast (1931, New York) ist ein amerikanischer Grafikdesigner und Illustrator. 1954 gründete er mit Milton Glaser und anderen die Push Pin Studios, die mit dem selbstpublizierten Magazin *The Push Pin Monthly Graphic* auf sich aufmerksam machte. Nach dem Besuch der Cooper Union School of Art begann für Chwast eine produktive Karriere: Er gestaltete Plakate, Zeitschriften- und Buchcover und entwarf als Werbe- und Verpackungsgrafikdesigner unter anderem 1979 die erste Box für ein McDonald's Happy Meal. Er wurde mit der Medaille des AIGA ausgezeichnet und war Mitglied der Art Directors Hall of Fame. Chwasts vielseitiges und innovatives Schaffen hatte einen nachhaltigen Einfluss auf die visuelle Kultur Amerikas.

Seymour Chwast (1931, New York) est un graphiste et illustrateur américain. En 1954, il fut un des fondateurs – notamment avec Milton Glaser – de Push Pin Studios, qui publia la revue *The Push Pin Monthly Graphic*. Après des études à la Cooper Union, Chwast se lance dans une carrière prolifique, travaillant sur des affiches, des magazines et des couvertures de livres, mais aussi dans la publicité et le packaging; il conçoit la première boîte du Happy Meal de McDonald's en 1979. Médaillé de l'AIGA et membre de l'Art Directors Hall of Fame, son travail éclectique et innovant a eu un impact durable sur la culture visuelle américaine.

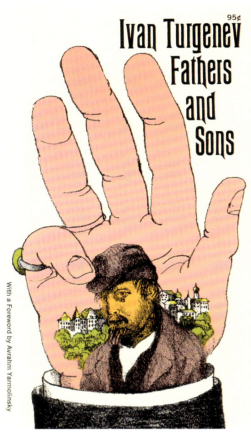

1966 · Seymour Chwast · US · Book cover

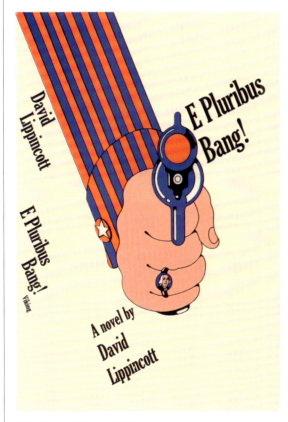

1970 · Seymour Chwast · US · Book cover

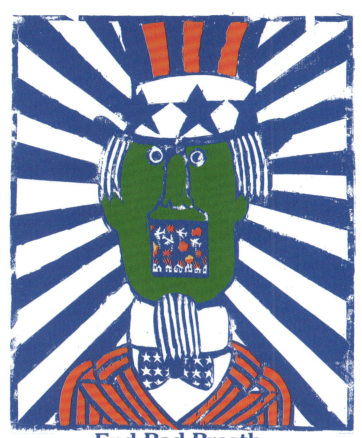

End Bad Breath.

1967 · Seymour Chwast · US · Poster

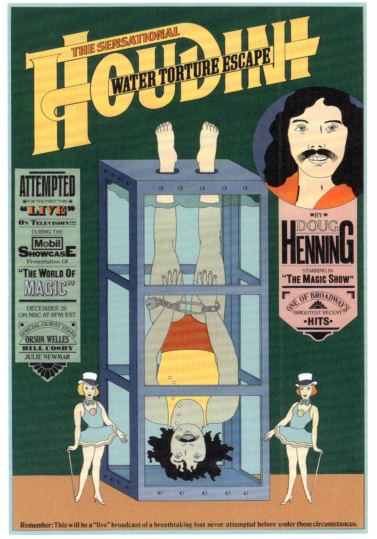

1975 · Seymour Chwast · US · Poster

1968 · Vignelli Associates · US · Brochure cover

1970 · Vignelli Associates · US · Brochure cover

1960s · Vignelli Associates · US · Packaging

1972 · Vignelli Associates · US · Brochures

Bertoia Florence Knoll, Saarinen, Mies van der Rohe, Noguchi have designed for Knoll. Aulenti Albinson, Cafiero, Christen, Colombo, Mangiarotti, Pearson, Pettit, Platner, Pollock, Schultz and Stephens still do. Knoll International, in 28 countries, has all these furniture and textile designs.

Knoll International

320 Park Avenue, New York

1967 · Vignelli Associates · US · Poster

Massimo Vignelli (1931, Milan – 2014, New York) was an Italian-American designer whose multidisciplinary practice encompassed almost all areas of design. After studying in Milan and Venice, Vignelli moved to the United States in 1966 to work for Unimark International, which rapidly became the largest design firm of its time. Fully embracing modernism, and holding to a steadfast vision to simplify visual communication, in 1971 he founded Vignelli Associates with his wife Lella. Vignelli's legacy includes identities for the New York subway, American Airlines, Knoll, and Bloomingdale's.

Massimo Vignelli (1931, Mailand – 2014, New York) war ein aus Italien stammender amerikanischer Grafikdesigner, dessen multidisziplinäre Praxis sämtliche Bereiche des Designs umfasste. Nach seinem Studium in Mailand und Venedig ging Vignelli 1966 in die Vereinigten Staaten, um für die Firma Unimark International zu arbeiten, die sich sehr schnell zum größten Designunternehmen ihrer Zeit entwickelte. Ganz der Moderne verpflichtet und konsequent auf eine Vereinfachung der visuellen Kommunikation bedacht, gründete er 1971 mit seiner Frau Lella die Firma Vignelli Associates. Zu seinem Vermächtnis gehören Corporate Identities für die New Yorker U-Bahn, American Airlines, Knoll und Bloomingdale's.

Massimo Vignelli (1931, Milan – 2014, New York) fut un graphiste italo-américain dont la pratique multidisciplinaire s'étendit à presque tous les domaines du design. En 1966, après des études à Milan et à Venise, Vignelli s'installa aux États-Unis, où il travailla pour Unimark International, qui devint rapidement la plus grande firme de design de son époque. Adoptant pleinement le modernisme et visant constamment à simplifier la communication visuelle, il fonda Vignelli Associates avec sa femme Lella en 1971. L'héritage de Vignelli compte des identités pour le métro de New York, American Airlines, Knoll et Bloomingdale's.

American Airlines **Annual Report** 1969

1969 · Vignelli Associates · US · Brochure cover

1966 · Vignelli Associates · US · Identity · American Airlines

1984 · Vignelli Associates · US · Packaging

1978 · Vignelli Associates · US · Packaging

1972 · Vignelli Associates · US · Identity · Bloomingdale's

bloomingdale's
bloomingdale's
bloomingdale's

1972 · Vignelli Associates · US · Logo · Bloomingdale's

Roman Cieślewicz · Poland/France

1966 · Roman Cieślewicz · PL · Magazine cover

»I consume magazines, books, and pictures. I cut, crop, and stick.«

Roman Cieślewicz, *HQ* #1, 1985

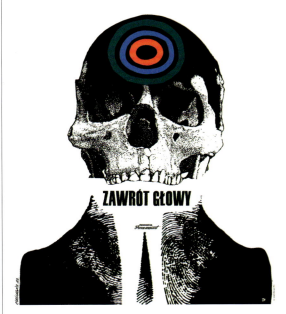

1963 · Roman Cieślewicz · PL · Poster

1966 · Roman Cieślewicz · PL · Poster

Roman Cieślewicz (1930, Lviv, Ukraine – 1996, Paris) was a Polish-French graphic artist and a key player in developing the Polish Poster School, as distinguished by its use of poetic metaphors and simple graphic solutions. Cieślewicz attended art school at the Krakow Academy of Fine Arts, before moving to France in 1963, where he gained French citizenship in 1971. In Paris, he art-directed both *Vogue* and *Elle* magazines, and worked at the advertising agency Mafia from 1969–72. Cieślewicz was a member of both the Association of Polish Artists and Designers, and the AGI.

Roman Cieślewicz (1930, Lemberg, heute Ukraine – 1996, Paris) war ein polnisch-französischer Grafikdesigner. Er spielte eine führende Rolle bei der Entwicklung der polnischen Plakatschule, die sich durch die Verwendung poetischer Metaphern und schlichte grafische Lösungen auszeichnet. Nach seinem Studium an der Kunsthochschule in Krakau ging Cieślewicz 1963 nach Frankreich, wo er 1971 die französische Staatsbürgerschaft annahm. In Paris war er als Artdirector für die Zeitschriften *Vogue* und *Elle* tätig und arbeitete von 1969 bis 1972 in der Werbeagentur Mafia. Cieślewicz war Mitglied des Verbandes der Polnischen Bildenden Künstler und der AGI.

Roman Cieślewicz (1930, Lviv, Ukraine – 1996, Paris) fut un artiste graphique polono-français et acteur clé du développement de l'école polonaise de l'affiche, caractérisée par l'emploi de métaphores poétiques et de solutions graphiques simples. Cieślewicz fit ses études à l'Académie des beaux-arts de Cracovie avant de s'installer en France en 1963 et d'acquérir la nationalité française en 1971. À Paris, il fut le directeur artistique tout à la fois des magazines *Vogue* et *Elle*, et travailla dans l'agence de publicité Mafia de 1969 à 1972. Cieślewicz fut aussi membre de l'Union des artistes plasticiens polonais et de l'AGI.

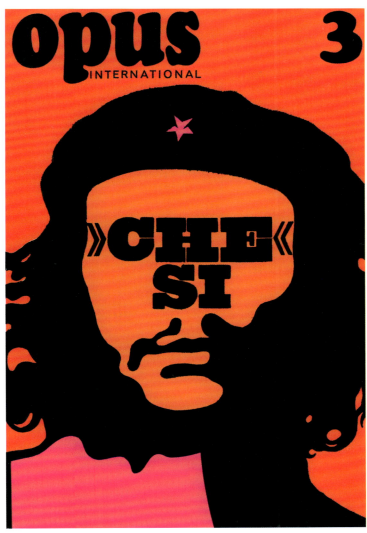

1967 · Roman Cieślewicz · PL/FR · Magazine cover

1967 · Roman Cieślewicz · PL/FR · Magazine cover

97

1967

Armin Hofmann becomes head of the design department at the Allgemeine Gewerbeschule Basel

Emil Ruder's influential book **Typographie** is first published

German illustrator **Heinz Edelmann** moves to London to work on the animated Beatles movie *Yellow Submarine*

Marshall McLuhan's book **The Medium is the Massage** is published

1967 · Wim Crouwel · NL · Brochure cover

1967 · Rafał Jasionowicz · PL · Poster

1967 · Till Neuburg · CH/IT · Logo · Bit magazine

1967 · Herb Lubalin · US · Logo · Mother & Child

1967 · Robert McGinnis · US/UK · Poster

1967 · Tadashi Masuda Design Institute · JP · Poster

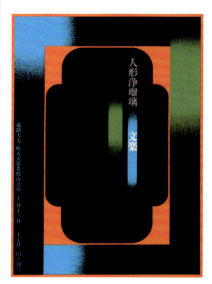

1967 · Hiromu Hara · JP · Poster

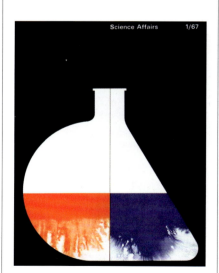

1967 · Stuart Ash · CA · Magazine cover

1967 · Victor Moscoso · US · Record cover

Bob Gill logo AGM hand image:

1967 · Bob Gill · UK · Logo · AGM

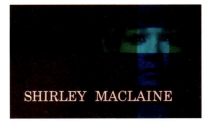

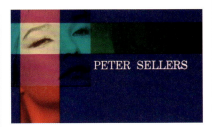

1967 · Jean Fouchet · FR · Opening titles

1967 · Tomi Ungerer · FR · Poster

1967 · Chermayeff & Geismar · US · Poster

1967 · Albrecht Ade · DE · Poster

1967 · Anonymous · HU · Poster

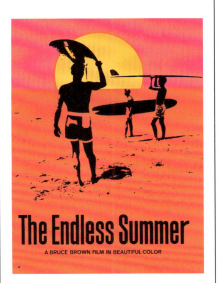

1967 · John Van Hamersveld · US · Poster

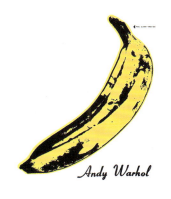

1967 · Andy Warhol · US · Record cover

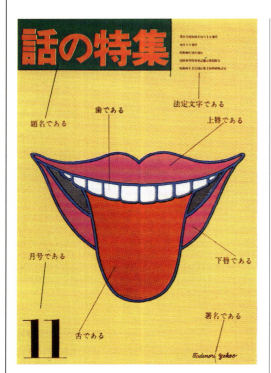

1967 · Tadanori Yokoo · JP · Magazine cover

1967 · Tadanori Yokoo · JP · Magazine cover

1968 · Tadanori Yokoo · JP · Magazine cover

1967 · Tadanori Yokoo · JP · Poster

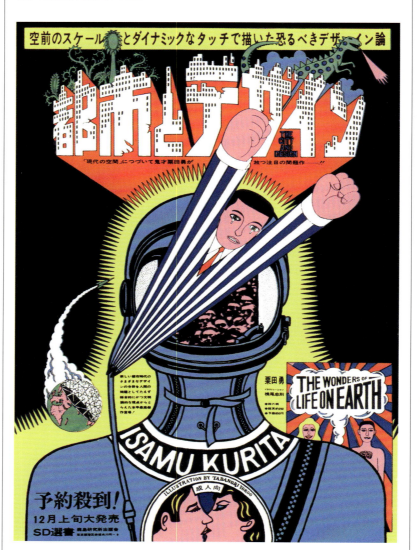

1967 · Tadanori Yokoo · JP · Poster

Tadanori Yokoo (1936, Nishiwaki, Japan) is a Japanese visual artist whose characteristic style of psychedelic montage has become a prominent symbol of contemporary Japanese visual culture. Yokoo started off as a stage designer in Tokyo before becoming a member of the Japan Advertising Artists Club at the age of 20 and developing his influences from film and illustration. After achieving international recognition, particularly for his posters, he has exhibited widely, including at MoMA in New York. Yokoo gave up commercial work in 1981 to dedicate himself exclusively to painting as a fine artist.

Tadanori Yokoo (1936, Nishiwaki, Japan) ist ein japanischer visueller Künstler, dessen charakteristischer Stil der psychedelischen Montage ein markantes Symbol zeitgenössischer visueller Kultur in Japan geworden ist. Yokoo begann seine Laufbahn als Bühnenbildner in Tokio, wurde im Alter von 20 Jahren Mitglied des Japan Advertising Artists Club und ließ sich dabei zunehmend von Einflüssen aus Film und Illustration inspirieren. Er gewann internationale Anerkennung, namentlich für seine Plakate, und hatte zahlreiche Ausstellungen, unter anderem im MoMA in New York. 1981 beendete Yokoo seine kommerzielle Tätigkeit, um sich als bildender Künstler ausschließlich der Malerei zu widmen.

Tadanori Yokoo (1936, Nishiwaki, Japon) est un artiste visuel japonais dont le style très caractéristique est devenu un emblème éminent de la culture visuelle japonaise contemporaine. Yokoo a débuté comme décorateur de théâtre à Tokyo avant de devenir membre du Japan Advertising Artists Club à l'âge de 20 ans et de développer ses influences à partir du cinéma et de l'illustration. Après avoir atteint une renommée internationale, en particulier pour ses affiches, il a beaucoup exposé, notamment au MoMA de New York. En 1981, Yokoo a abandonné les projets commerciaux pour se consacrer exclusivement à la peinture en tant qu'artiste indépendant.

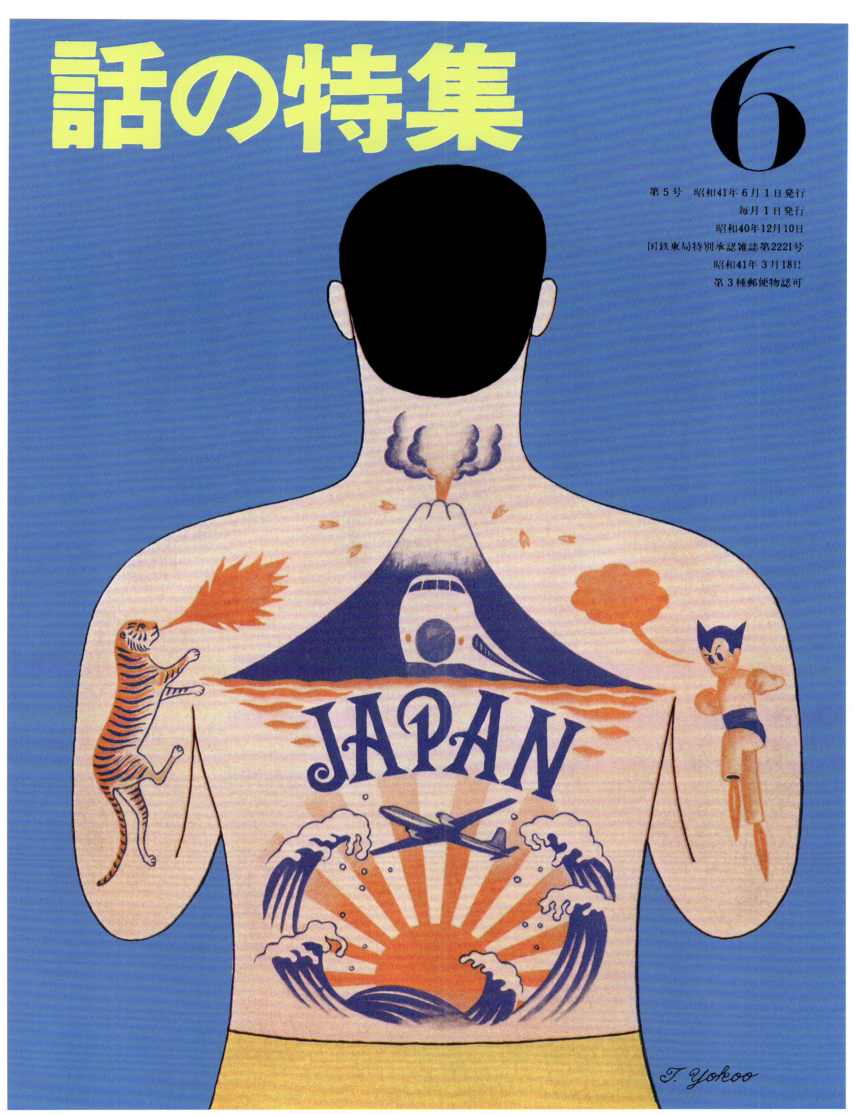

1967 · Tadanori Yokoo · JP · Magazine cover

Milton Glaser · United States

With his poster which accompanied Bob Dylan's 1967 *Greatest Hits* album, Milton Glaser created not only a classic of graphic design, but at the same time took a big step forward in consolidating the connection between music and graphics. Glaser created several concert posters for other big names in American music, such as Stevie Wonder and Simon & Garfunkel.

Mit einem beigelegten Poster im *Greatest-Hits*-Album von 1967 von Bob Dylan schuf Milton Glaser nicht nur eine Ikone des Grafikdesigns, sondern bereitete gleichzeitig den Weg für die damals noch nicht selbstverständliche Verbindung von Musik und Grafik. Glaser gestaltete zahlreiche Konzertplakate für andere Größen der US-Musik wie Stevie Wonder oder Simon & Garfunkel.

Avec le poster joint à l'album de Bob Dylan *Greatest Hits* en 1967, Milton Glaser créa non seulement une icône du graphisme, mais contribua aussi à affirmer la relation entre musique et illustration. Glaser créa de nombreuses affiches de concert pour d'autres grands noms de la musique américaine comme Stevie Wonder et Simon & Garfunkel.

1967 · Milton Glaser · US · Poster

1969 · Milton Glaser · US · Poster

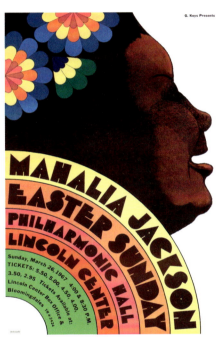

1967 · Milton Glaser · US · Poster

1967 · Milton Glaser · US · Poster

Milton Glaser (1929, New York) is one of the most important American designers of the modern age. A graduate of Cooper Union, Glaser studied at the Academy of Fine Arts in Bologna before returning to New York to co-found in 1954 the groundbreaking Push Pin Studios. In 1977 he designed the "I Love New York" logo, which has become one of the most recognizable marks in history and also earns the state $30 million each year. Glaser has taught and exhibited widely, and during his career has designed in excess of 300 posters; he was also awarded the National Medal of Arts by Barack Obama in 2009.

Milton Glaser (1929, New York) ist einer der bedeutendsten amerikanischen Grafikdesigner der Gegenwart. Als Absolvent der Cooper Union School of Art studierte er anschließend an der Accademia di Belle Arti in Bologna, ehe er nach New York zurückkehrte und 1954 die wegweisenden Push Pin Studios mitbegründete. 1977 entwarf er das Logo „I Love New York", das zu einem der markantesten Logos in der Geschichte wurde und um den Staat jährlich 30 Millionen US-Dollar einbringt. Glaser hat vielfach unterrichtet und ausgestellt und im Laufe seiner Karriere mehr als 300 Plakate entworfen; 2009 wurde er von Barack Obama mit der National Medal of Arts ausgezeichnet.

Milton Glaser (1929, New York) est un des grands designers américains de l'époque moderne. Diplômé de la Cooper Union, Glaser étudie ensuite à l'Académie des beaux-arts de Bologne avant de rentrer à New York, où il cofonde le révolutionnaire Push Pin Studios en 1954. En 1977, il dessine le logo «I Love New York», qui est devenu une des marques les plus reconnaissables de l'histoire, et qui rapporte chaque année 30 millions de dollars à l'État. Glaser a enseigné et exposé dans de multiples lieux et il a conçu plus de 300 affiches au fil de sa carrière. En 2009, il a reçu la National Medal of Arts des mains de Barack Obama.

1967 · Milton Glaser · US · Poster

1968 · Milton Glaser · US · Poster

Promoter Bill Graham was a visionary when it came to hiring designers to create the posters for his concerts. From the mid-1960s right through until his death in 1991, Graham commissioned a considerable roster of designers and artists, including Wes Wilson, Bonnie MacLean, Alton Kelley, Stanley Mouse, and Rick Griffin, amongst several others. By marrying Art Nouveau elements with the hippie aesthetic, these vibrant and evocative images not only encapsulated the essence of psychedelia, but have become synonymous with Graham's concerts, the venues where they were held, and the bands that played, such as the Rolling Stones, Jimi Hendrix, the Grateful Dead, and the Velvet Underground. Understanding the production value and the artistic importance of these graphic works, Graham also released numbered prints of his posters, postcards, and handbills, which are still highly sought after today.

Der Konzertveranstalter Bill Graham war ein Visionär, was die Wahl der Grafikdesigner für seine Konzertplakate betraf, und ab Mitte der 60er-Jahre bis zu seinem Tod 1991 beauftragte er eine Vielzahl von Grafikdesignern und Künstlern, darunter Wes Wilson, Bonnie MacLean, Alton Kelley, Stanley Mouse und Rick Griffin. Die ebenso kraftvollen wie beschwörenden Bilderwelten, in denen sich Jugendstilelemente mit Hippieästhetik verbinden, können als Inbegriff für alles Psychedelische gelten, sie sind aber auch zum Synonym für Grahams Konzerte selbst geworden, für die Orte, an denen sie stattfanden, und für die Bands, die dabei auftraten, ob nun die Rolling Stones, Jimi Hendrix, Grateful Dead oder Velvet Underground. Graham wusste um den Produktionswert und die künstlerische Bedeutung dieser Grafiken und verlegte eine limitierte Anzahl seiner Plakate, Postkarten und Handzettel, die heute als Sammlerstücke gelten.

Le producteur Bill Graham s'avéra être un visionnaire en recourant à des graphistes pour concevoir les affiches de ses concerts. Du milieu des années 1960 à sa mort en 1991, il engagea d'innombrables graphistes et artistes, dont Wes Wilson, Bonnie MacLean, Alton Kelley, Stanley Mouse et Rick Griffin, parmi bien d'autres. Mélangeant éléments Art nouveau et esthétique hippie, leurs images vibrantes et évocatrices ne se contentaient pas d'inclure l'essence du psychédélisme : elles devinrent emblématiques des concerts de Graham, des salles où ils se tinrent et des groupes qui y jouèrent – Rolling Stones, Jimi Hendrix, Grateful Dead, Velvet Underground. Conscient de la valeur de production et de l'importance artistique de ces œuvres graphiques, Graham sortit des tirages numérotés de ses affiches, cartes postales et prospectus, encore très recherchés à l'heure actuelle.

1968 · Lee Conklin · US · Poster

»Psychedelic artists required the people who looked at their art to take their time. This also tended to mean they themselves were opposed to the pressures of deadlines and time constraints imposed in the bourgeois world of conservative society, and took a stand against the credo that 'Time is money'.«

Lutz Hieber, *San Francisco 1967: Plakat im Summer of Love*, 2017

1967 · Tom Wilkes · US · Poster

1968 · Lee Conklin · US · Poster

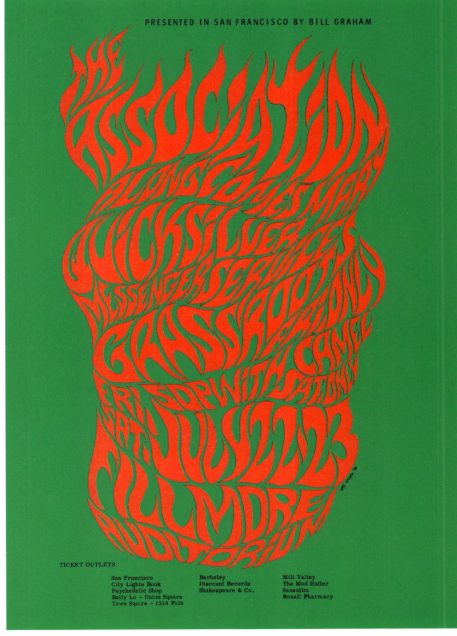

1966 · Wes Wilson · US · Poster

1967 · Joe Gomez · US · Poster

1969 · Landor · US · Logo · Bank of America

1972 · Landor · US · Logo · Royal Viking Line

1970s · Landor · US · Logo · San Francisco Municipal Railway

1970s · Landor · US · Logo · Dynic Corporation

1970 · Landor · US · Logo · Cotton

1970s · Landor · US · Logo · Alabama Bancorp

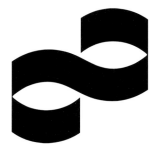

1970s · Landor · US · Logo · Golden Gate Transit

1970s · Landor · US · Logo · Liberty National Bank

1971 · Landor · US · Logo · Consolidated Foods

1970s · Landor · US · Logo · Alfa Corporation

1973 · Landor · US · Logo · First Wisconsin Bank

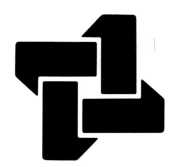

1970s · Landor · US · Logo · First National Bank

1971 · Landor · US/SG · Logo · Singapore Airlines

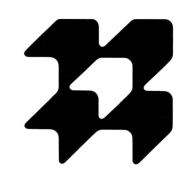

1972 · Landor · US/IT · Logo · Montedison Chemicals

1970s · Landor · US · Logo · State National Bank

1977 · Landor · US · Logo · Wacoal Corporation

1970s · Landor · US/TH · Logo · Thai Airways

1970s · Landor · US · Logo · Hawaiian Air

1979 · Landor · US/IN · Logo · Mahavir Hospital

1978 · Landor · US · Logo · Squirt

1967 · Landor · US/IT · Identity · Alitalia

1968 · Landor · US · Logo · Levi's

1983 · Landor · US · Logo · Dole

Walter Landor (1913, Munich – 1995, Tiburon, California) was a German-born brand designer and founder of Landor Associates in San Francisco in 1941. After moving to the United Kingdom for an internship, and studying at Goldsmiths College in London, he became the youngest Fellow of the Royal Society of Industrial Artists. Landor's design portfolio for big brands, such as Marlboro, Bank of America, Fujifilm, and several airlines, helped expand his company to become one of the biggest design firms in the world. The Smithsonian Institution honored Landor's design legacy with a permanent collection in 1994.

Walter Landor (1913, München – 1995, Tiburon, Kalifornien) war ein aus Deutschland gebürtiger Markendesigner, der 1941 in San Francisco die Firma Landor Associates gründete. Nachdem er für ein Praktikum nach Großbritannien gegangen war und am Goldsmiths College in London studiert hatte, wurde er der jüngste Fellow der Royal Society of Industrial Artists. Landors Arbeiten für Konzerne wie Marlboro, Bank of America, Fujifilm und verschiedene Fluggesellschaften trugen dazu bei, dass sein Unternehmen zu einer der größten Designfirmen der Welt wurde. Die Smithsonian Institution ehrte Landors Designvermächtnis 1994 mit der Einrichtung einer ständigen Sammlung.

Walter Landor (1913, Munich – 1995, Tiburon, Californie) fut un designer de marque d'origine allemande qui fonda Landor Associates en 1941 à San Francisco. Après s'être installé en Angleterre pour un stage en entreprise et avoir étudié au Goldsmiths College à Londres, il devint le plus jeune *Fellow* de la Royal Society of Industrial Artists. Le travail de Landor pour des grandes marques, comme Marlboro, Bank of America, Fujifilm et plusieurs compagnies aériennes, a aidé son entreprise à devenir une des plus grandes firmes de design au monde. Depuis 1994, la Smithsonian Institution honore son héritage par une collection permanente.

1976 · Landor · US/MX · Identity · Banamex

1967 · Keiichi Tanaami · JP · Poster

Keiichi Tanaami (1936, Tokyo) is a multifaceted visual artist whose work in design, illustration, and other forms of art has never been limited to one particular medium. A graduate of the Musashino University, Tanaami was closely associated with the Neo-dada artists in his native Japan, later embracing psychedelic culture and Pop Art. He has worked with film, silkscreen printing, painting, and sculpture, while his interests have always been broad—as indicated by his thematic concerns with art and design, merchandise and art, and the connections between beauty and daily life.

Keiichi Tanaami (1936, Tokio) ist ein vielseitiger visueller Künstler, der sich ebenso mit Grafikdesign beschäftigte wie mit Illustration und Kunst und dessen Werk sich nie auf ein spezifisches Medium beschränkte. Nach dem Studium an der Universität Musashino stand Tanaami in enger Verbindung mit den Neo-Dada-Künstlern seiner japanischen Heimat, später wandte er sich der psychedelischen Kultur und der Pop-Art zu. Er hat in den Medien Film, Siebdruck, Malerei und Skulptur gearbeitet, und seine Interessen sind nach wie vor weit gestreut; so beteiligt er sich an den Diskussionen über Kunst und Design, Ware und Kunst und die Verbindung von Alltag und Schönheit.

Keiichi Tanaami (Tokyo, 1936) est un plasticien aux multiples talents connu pour ses incursions dans les domaines du graphisme, de l'illustration et de l'art, et dont le travail ne s'est jamais limité à un support spécifique. Diplômé de la Musashino University, il a été étroitement associé au mouvement Néo-Dada dans son Japon natal avant d'adopter la culture psychédélique et le Pop Art. Il a travaillé dans les domaines du cinéma, de la sérigraphie, de la peinture et de la sculpture tout en conservant une vaste palette d'intérêts. Sa thématique porte sur art et graphisme, art et produits, ainsi que sur le rapport entre la vie quotidienne et la beauté.

1966 · Keiichi Tanaami · JP · Magazine cover

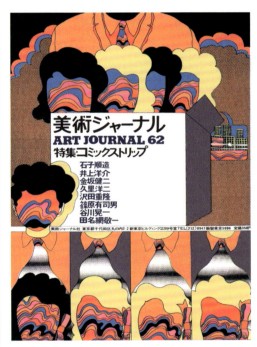

1967 · Keiichi Tanaami · JP · Poster

1967 · Keiichi Tanaami · JP · Poster

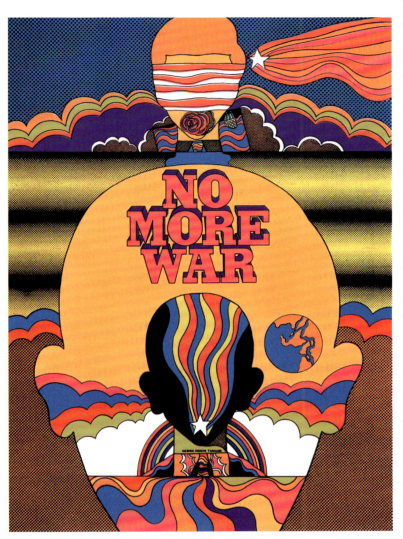

1967 · Keiichi Tanaami · JP · Poster

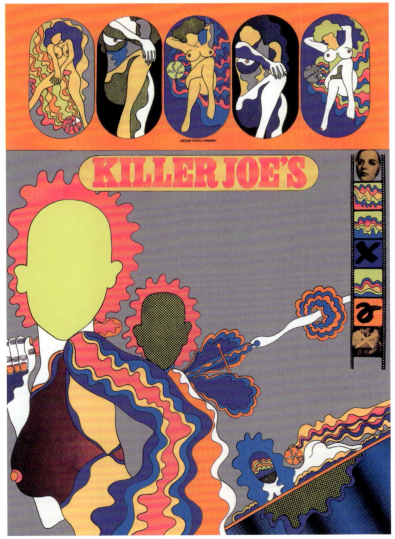

1968 · Keiichi Tanaami · JP · Poster

1968

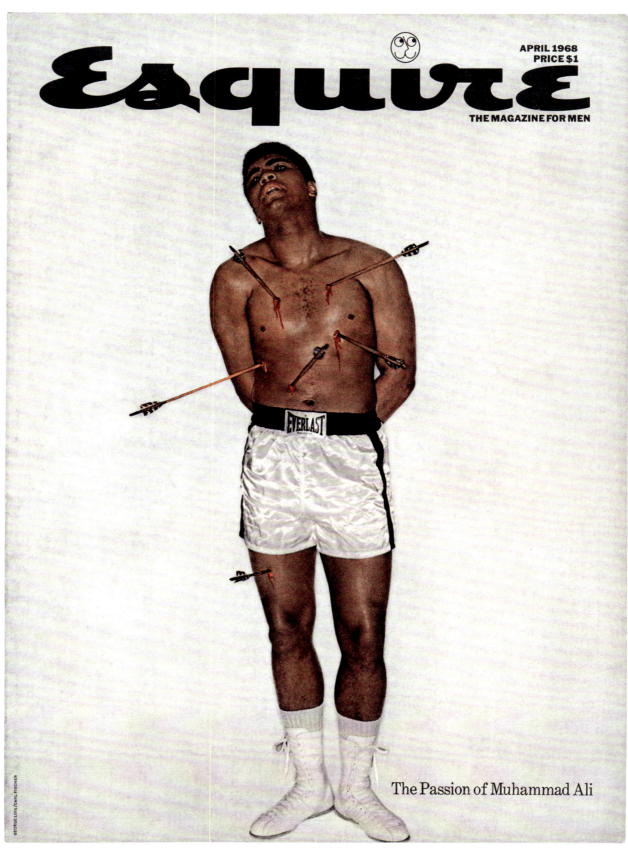

1968 · George Lois, Carl Fischer (PH) · US · Magazine cover

1968 · Stewart K. Widdess · US · Logo · Target

1968 · Robert Noyce, Gordon Moore · US · Logo · Intel

1968 · Heinz Schwabe · DE · Logo · Eurocheque

1968 · Raymond Loewy, CEI · FR · Logo · New Man

Adrian Frutiger designs **OCR-B**, a font
computers could recognize and which was
accepted as a worldwide standard in 1973

Wolfgang Weingart starts teaching
typography at the Allgemeine
Kunstgewerbeschule Basel

The first issue of **Avant Garde**
magazine is published under the
art direction of Herb Lubalin

1968 · Fernando Lemos · BR · Poster

1968 · Kazumasa Nagai · JP · Poster

1968 · Anonymous · US · Magazine cover

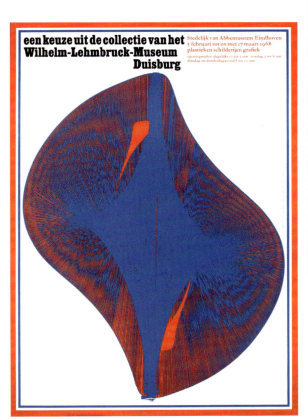

1968 · Jan van Toorn · NL · Poster

1968 · Steve Frankfurt · US · Poster

1968 · Gunter Rambow · DE · Poster

1968 · Antonio Reboiro · CU · Poster

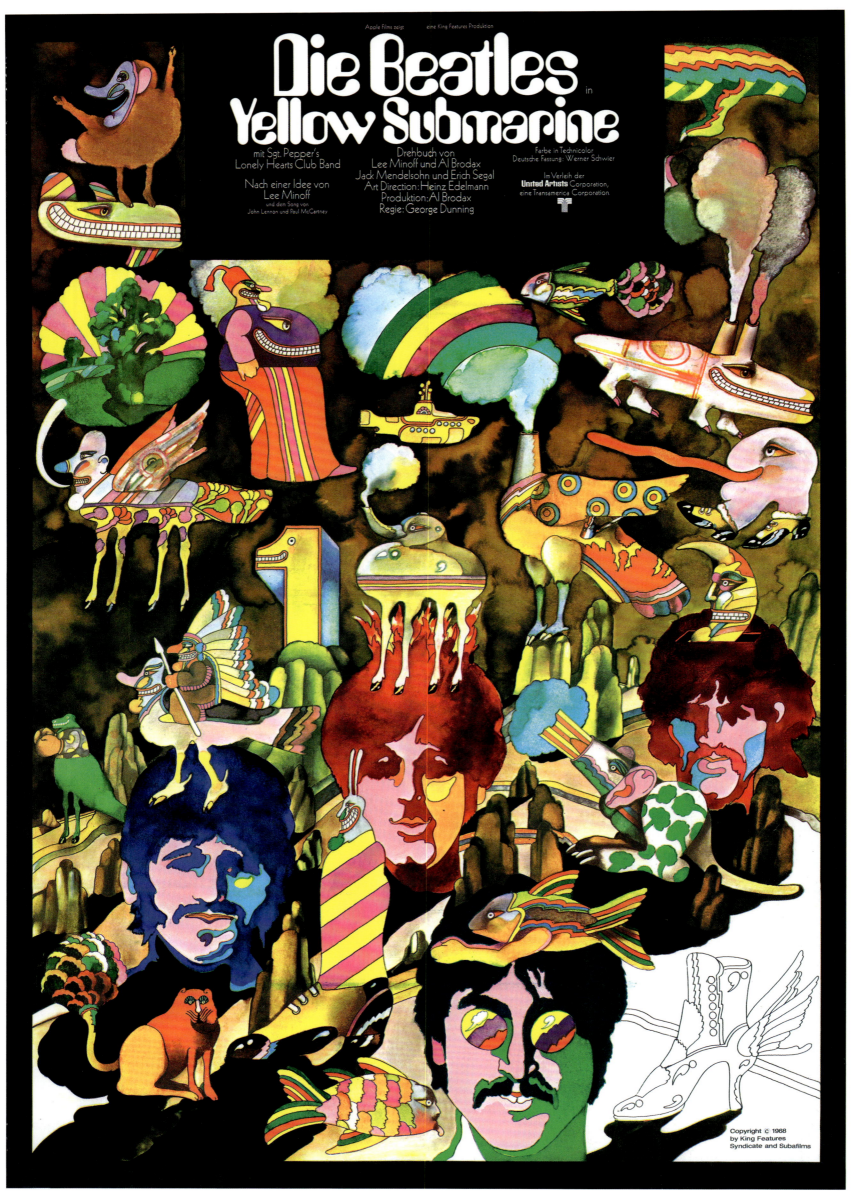

1968 · Heinz Edelmann · DE · Poster

Released in 1968, the Beatles' animated movie *Yellow Submarine* became an instant classic, perfectly capturing how it felt to be alive at that particular moment in history. The film was produced under art director Heinz Edelmann, and its Pop Art fairy-tale was one of many international projects to present the zeitgeist of the late 1960s, achieved amongst other things by deploying almost identical types of graphics to those that appeared in happening contexts in the wider world at the time.

Der 1968 veröffentlichte Beatles-Zeichentrickfilm *Yellow Submarine* wurde sofort nach seinem Erscheinen zu einem Klassiker, der punktgenau das Lebensgefühl einer bestimmten Zeit konservierte. Das unter der Art-direction von Heinz Edelmann entstandene Pop-Art-Märchen war eine von vielen internationalen Arbeiten, die den Zeitgeist mit nahezu identischen grafischen Mitteln visualisierten.

Le film d'animation *Yellow Submarine* sorti en 1968 autour des Beatles devint immédiatement un classique du genre qui capturait au détail près l'air du temps. Ce conte Pop Art créé sous la direction artistique de Heinz Edelmann a toutefois été une des nombreuses réalisations internationales qui ont illustré l'esprit de l'époque avec des moyens graphiques plus ou moins identiques à ceux qui émergeaient dans le reste du monde.

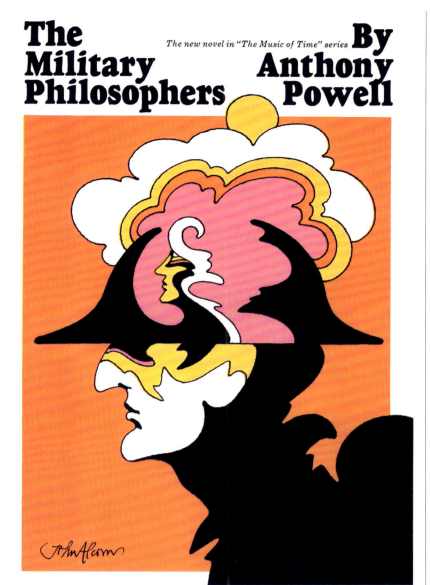

1968 · John Alcorn · US · Book cover

1968 · Tadanori Yokoo · JP · Poster

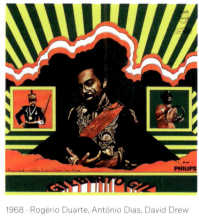

1968 · Rogério Duarte, Antônio Dias, David Drew Zingg · BR · Record cover

1968 · Robert & Barbara Flynn · US · Record cover

1968 · John Van Hamersveld (ILL), George Osaki (AD) · US · Record cover

1969 · E. Pomorska · PL · Record cover

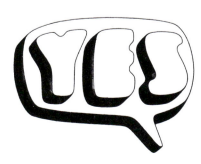

1968 · Crosby Fletcher Forbes · UK · Logo · Yes

Lance Wyman · United States/Mexico

In partnership with the British industrial designer Peter Murdoch, the young American Lance Wyman won the bid to design the graphics for the 1968 Mexico City Olympics. Wyman came up with an original and wide-ranging program that embraced the application of color, typography, pictograms, and other designs to be used for the event. The project was a quantum leap forward in terms of its overall approach, and for a long time afterwards this edition of the games influenced the whole perception of design used for later Olympic venues.

Im Team mit dem britischen Industriedesigner Peter Murdoch gewann der junge Amerikaner Lance Wyman die Ausschreibung zur visuellen Gestaltung der Olympischen Spiele 1968 von Mexico City. Wyman realisierte ein ausführliches visuelles Programm, das die Farbgebung, Typografie, Piktogramme und Muster der Veranstaltung vorgab und in dieser umfassenden konzeptionellen Form neu war. Das Projekt war ein Quantensprung und prägte noch lange nach den Spielen die visuelle Wahrnehmung des Austragungsortes.

En collaboration avec le designer industriel britannique Peter Murdoch, le jeune Américain Lance Wyman remporta l'appel d'offres lancé pour l'identité graphique des jeux Olympiques de Mexico de 1968. Wyman réalisa un programme original et détaillé prescrivant couleurs, typographie, pictogrammes et autres motifs pour l'événement sportif. Le projet supposa un saut quantique quant à l'approche conceptuelle globale et marqua encore longtemps après ces jeux le design des équipements olympiques d'éditions suivantes.

1968 · Lance Wyman · US/MX · Logo

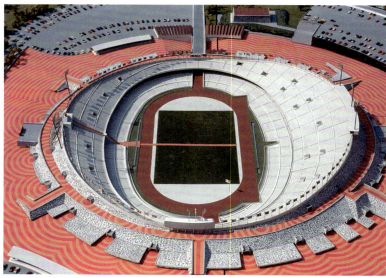

1968 · Lance Wyman · US/MX · Identity

1968 · Lance Wyman · US/MX · Identity

Lance Wyman (1937, Newark, New Jersey) is an American designer and leader in the field of environmental graphic design. After studying industrial design at the Pratt Institute, Wyman began his career in 1960, designing packaging systems for General Motors in Detroit; he later moved to New York and joined the office of designer George Nelson. From 1966–71 he established his own practice in Mexico, producing the logos for the 1968 Summer Olympics and 1970 FIFA World Cup. Wyman went on to set up his own studio in New York, where he also taught at the Parsons School of Design from 1973 to 2013.

Lance Wyman (1937, Newark, New Jersey) ist ein amerikanischer Grafikdesigner, der auf dem Gebiet des Umweltdesigns eine führende Rolle spielt. Nachdem er am Pratt Institute Industriedesign studiert hatte, begann er seine Berufslaufbahn 1960 mit dem Entwerfen von Verpackungssystemen für General Motors in Detroit. Später ging er nach New York und trat ins Grafikbüro von George Nelson ein. In den Jahren 1966–1971 war er selbstständig in Mexiko tätig, wo er die Logos für die Olympischen Sommerspiele von 1968 und für die Fußballweltmeisterschaft von 1970 entwarf. Nach seiner Rückkehr nach New York eröffnete Wyman dort sein eigenes Studio und unterrichtete von 1973 bis 2013 auch an der Parsons School of Design.

Lance Wyman (1937, Newark, New Jersey) est un designer américain, leader dans le domaine du design de environnemental. En 1960, après des études de design industriel à l'Institut Pratt, Wyman débute sa carrière en concevant des systèmes de packaging pour General Motors à Detroit. Il s'installe ensuite à New York, où il rejoint le cabinet du designer George Nelson. De 1966 à 1971, il transfère son activité à Mexico, où il produit des logos pour les jeux Olympiques d'été de 1968, et en 1970 pour la coupe du monde de la FIFA. Wyman poursuit son activité en ouvrant son propre studio à New York, où il a enseigné à la Parsons School of Design de 1973 à 2013.

1968 · Lance Wyman · US/MX · Brochure cover

1968 · Lance Wyman · US/MX · Stamps

1968 · Lance Wyman, Julia Murdoch · US/MX · Identity

With the seismic socio-political shifts that took place across the world in 1968, many designers and artists saw the opportunity to use their skills to amplify the messages of discontent amid rising oppression. In France, a group of artists from the distinguished École des Beaux-Arts became part of this movement when on May 16 they took over the school and formed the Atelier Populaire (Popular Workshop). Making use of very simple iconography, they responded to the strikes of May 1968, producing over 200 different posters, printed up in quantities from hundreds to thousands using a one-color silkscreen process. With their messages of resistance, anti-colonialism, pro-immigration, and workers' rights, Atelier Populaire became part of the collective visual consciousness of the wider student movement. Noted for its historical importance, the group's work has subsequently been exhibited in several countries.

Aufgrund der seismischen soziopolitischen Veränderungen, die sich 1968 in aller Welt ereigneten, brachten sich auch viele Designer und Maler ein, um inmitten zunehmender Repressionen die Botschaft der Unzufriedenen zu verbreiten. In Frankreich schloss sich eine Gruppe Künstler von der angesehenen École des Beaux-Arts der Bewegung an, übernahm die Schule am 16. Mai und gründete das Atelier Populaire (Volkswerkstatt). Ihre Reaktion auf die Streiks vom Mai 1968 kam in einer sehr schlichten Ikonografie zum Ausdruck, die Künstler gestalteten über 200 Plakate, von denen in einfarbiger Siebdrucktechnik Hunderte, bisweilen auch Tausende gedruckt wurden. Mit seiner Botschaft von Widerstand, Antikolonialismus, Immigrationsfreundlichkeit und Arbeiterrechten ging das Atelier Populaire in das kollektive visuelle Bewusstsein der allgemeinen Studentenbewegung ein. Aufgrund der historischen Bedeutung wurden die Arbeiten der Gruppe in der Folge in mehreren Ländern ausgestellt.

Dans le cadre des bouleversements socio-politiques qui se produisent un peu partout dans le monde en 1968, nombre de graphistes et d'artistes saisissent l'occasion pour mettre leur talent au service des messages d'exaspération liés à une répression croissante. En France, un groupe d'artistes de la vénérable École nationale supérieure des beaux-arts de Paris participe au mouvement en occupant l'école le 16 mai et en proclamant l'Atelier populaire des Beaux-Arts. Avec une iconographie des plus simples, ils font écho aux grèves de mai 1968 en produisant plus de 200 affiches distinctes tirées à des centaines et parfois des milliers d'exemplaires à l'aide d'un procédé sérigraphique monochrome. Par ses appels à la résistance anticolonialiste, pro-immigration et sa défense des droits des travailleurs, l'Atelier populaire devient un acteur important de la conscience visuelle collective du mouvement étudiant. Reconnu pour son importance historique, le travail du groupe sera exposé plus tard dans plusieurs pays.

1968 · Atelier Populaire · FR · Poster

1968 · Atelier Populaire · FR · Poster

1968 · Atelier Populaire · FR · Poster

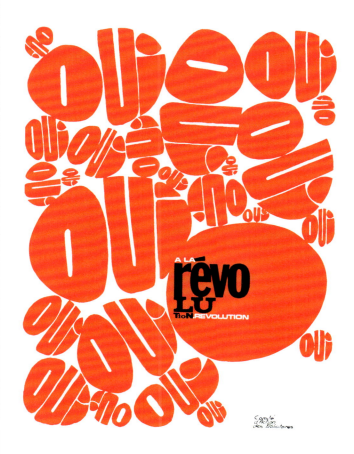

1968 · Atelier Populaire · FR · Poster

1968 · Atelier Populaire · FR · Poster

1968 · Atelier Populaire · FR · Poster

1968 · Atelier Populaire · FR · Poster

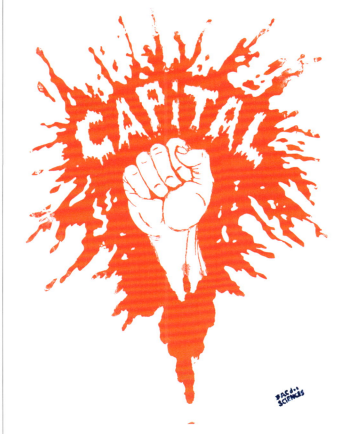

1968 · Atelier Populaire · FR · Poster

The corporate identity designed
for the Dutch passenger rail oper-
ator Nederlandse Spoorwegen is
an early example of the development of a modern, professional
image for a state-run institution.
Straightforward pictograms, easy-
to-read timetables, and, above all,
the eye-catching logo that is still
in use today, were all among the
tasks for which the design studio
Tel Design was commissioned.

Das Erscheinungsbild der niederländischen Eisenbahngesellschaft
ist ein frühes Beispiel für die Entwicklung eines modernen, profes-
sionellen Auftretens einer staatlichen Institution. Eindeutige
Piktogramme, leicht verständliche
Fahrpläne und vor allem das bis
heute verwendete markante Logo
gehörten zur komplexen Arbeit
des Designbüros Tel Design.

L'identité visuelle de la société de
chemins de fer néerlandaise est
un des premiers cas de développement d'une image moderne et
professionnelle pour le compte
d'une institution publique. Des
pictogrammes clairs, des horaires
faciles à lire, et surtout le logo at-
trayant, encore utilisé aujourd'hui
par la compagnie, composaient
la commande livrée par le studio
de design Tel Design.

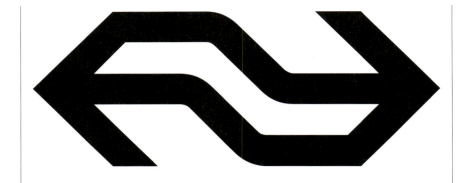

1968 · Gert Dumbar, Tel Design · NL · Logo · Nederlandse Spoorwegen

1968 · Gert Dumbar, Tel Design · NL · Identity · Nederlandse Spoorwegen

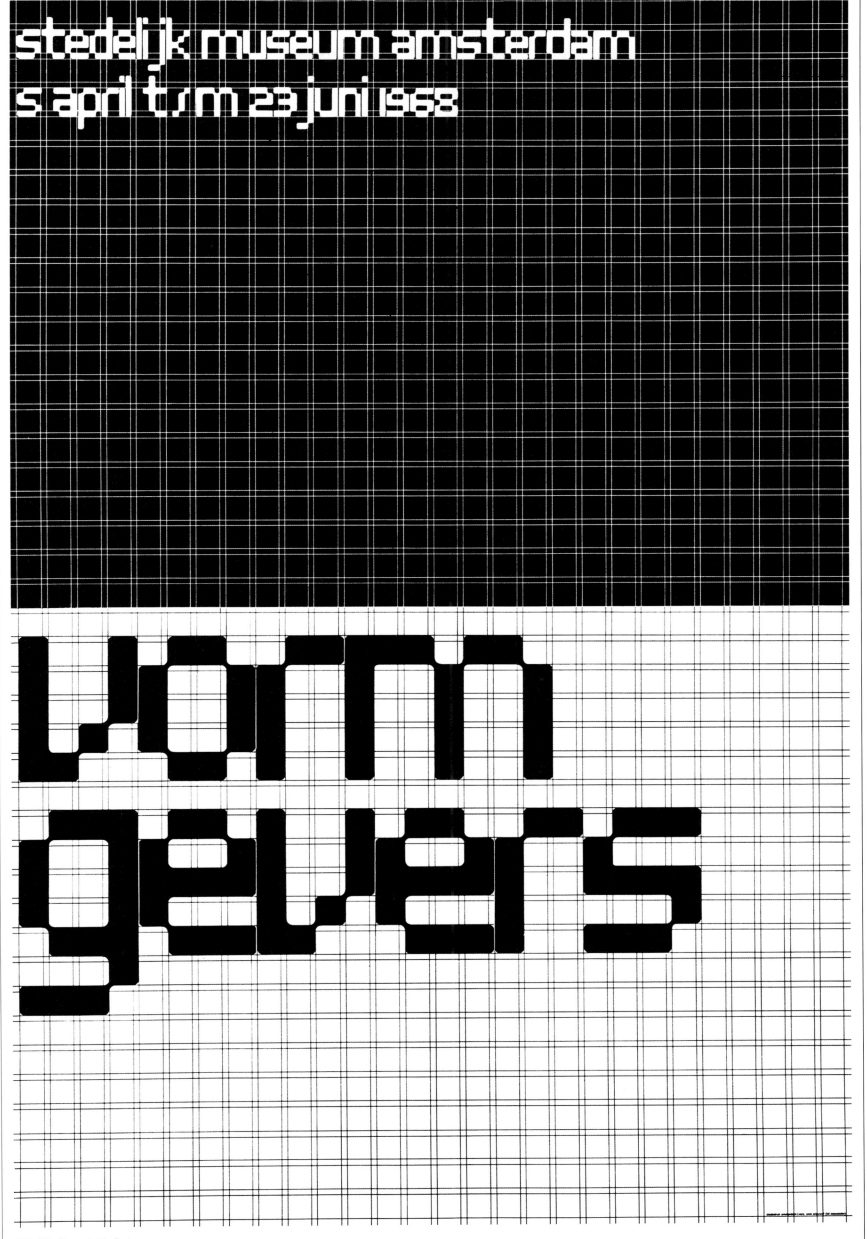

1968 · Wim Crouwel · NL · Poster

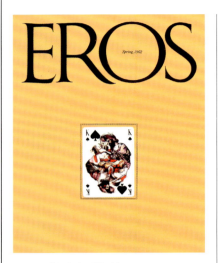

1962 · Herb Lubalin · US · Magazine cover

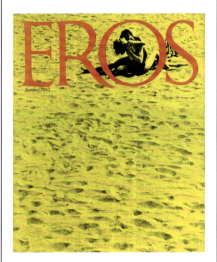

1962 · Herb Lubalin · US · Magazine cover

1962 · Herb Lubalin · US · Magazine cover

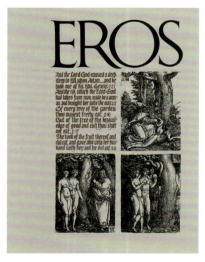

1962 · Herb Lubalin · US · Magazine cover

1964 · Herb Lubalin · US · Magazine cover

1966 · Herb Lubalin · US · Magazine cover

1966 · Herb Lubalin · US · Magazine cover

fact: A professor of ophthalmology says, "Everybody who puts on contact lenses will experience eye damage, and in many cases the damage will be permanent."

1966 · Herb Lubalin · US · Magazine cover

fact:
VOLUME ONE, ISSUE FOUR $1.25

"Bobby Kennedy is the most vicious, evil _ _ _ _ in American politics today," says lawyer Melvin Belli.

1964 · Herb Lubalin · US · Magazine cover

Herb Lubalin (1918–1981, New York) was a notable American graphic designer whose use of typography shaped editorial and corporate identity design for decades. Lubalin devised the original Avant Garde typeface, which was quickly adopted by designers around the world. After attending Cooper Union he worked at the healthcare communications firm Sudler & Hennessey, where he stayed for nearly two decades before opening his own practice in 1964. Lubalin co-founded the International Typeface Corporation (ITC) in 1970, and together with Ralph Ginzburg published the groundbreaking cultural magazines *Eros, Fact,* and *Avant Garde.*

Herb Lubalin (1918–1981, New York) war ein berühmter amerikanischer Grafikdesigner, dessen Typografien das Zeitschriften- und Firmendesign jahrzehntelang beeinflussten. Lubalin entwarf die ursprüngliche Schrifttype Avant Garde, die sehr bald von Grafikdesignern auf der ganzen Welt übernommen wurde. Nach seiner Ausbildung an der Cooper Union School of Art arbeitete er fast zwanzig Jahre lang für die auf Gesundheitskommunikation spezialisierte Firma Sudler & Hennessey, ehe er 1964 seine eigene Agentur eröffnete. Lubalin gehörte 1970 zu den Begründern der International Typeface Corporation (ITC) und publizierte gemeinsam mit Ralph Ginzburg die wegweisenden Kulturzeitschriften *Eros, Fact* und *Avant Garde.*

Herb Lubalin (1918–1981, New York) fut un grand graphiste qui modela des identités éditoriales et d'entreprise pendant des décennies par son utilisation particulière de la typographie. Lubalin conçut la police de caractères Avant Garde, qui fut rapidement adoptée par des designers du monde entier. Après des études à la Cooper Union, il travailla deux décennies pour la firme de communication Sudler & Hennessey avant d'ouvrir son propre studio en 1964. En 1970, Lubalin fut cofondateur de l'International Typeface Corporation (ITC). Il co-publia avec Ralph Ginzburg des magazines culturels aussi révolutionnaires qu'*Eros, Fact* et *Avant Garde.*

1968 · Herb Lubalin · US · Magazine cover

PORTRAITS OF THE AMERICAN PEOPLE A MONUMENTAL PORTFOLIO OF PHOTOGRAPHS

1971 · Herb Lubalin · US · Magazine cover

Out of a fruitful collaboration between the author and publisher Ralph Ginzburg and the New York designer Herb Lubalin came the magazines *Eros* (1962), *Fact* (1964–67), and *Avant Garde* (1968–71). In equal measure, all three became icons of the journalism and graphic design of the period, while even today they are still seen as examples of the perfect interaction between content and design.

Die Zusammenarbeit des Autors und Verlegers Ralph Ginzburg mit dem New Yorker Designer Herb Lubalin brachte die Magazine *Eros* (1962), *Fact* (1964–1967) und *Avant Garde* (1968–1971) hervor. Die Hefte wurden gleichermaßen Ikonen des Journalismus wie des Grafikdesigns ihrer Zeit. Bis heute stehen sie geradezu idealtypisch für die Verbindung von Inhalt und Gestaltung.

La fructueuse collaboration entre l'auteur et éditeur Ralph Ginzburg et le graphiste new-yorkais Herb Lubalin a produit les magazines *Eros* (1962), *Fact* (1964–1967) et *Avant Garde* (1968–1971). Ces revues sont devenues des icônes du journalisme et du graphisme de leur époque. Aujourd'hui encore, elles illustrent l'interaction parfaite entre graphisme et contenu.

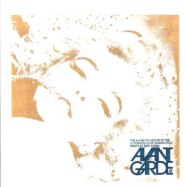

1968 · Herb Lubalin · US · Magazine cover

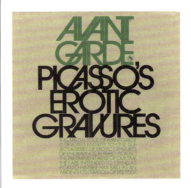

1968 · Herb Lubalin · US · Magazine cover

1969 · Herb Lubalin · US · Magazine cover

1960–1969

1969

Saul Bass receives an
Academy Award for his short
film **Why Man Creates**

The **Japan Institute of Design
Promotion** is founded

The **KECD** (Korean Ensemble of
Contemporary Design) design
association is founded in South Korea

1969 · Fred Troller · US · Poster

1969 · Milton Glaser · US · Poster

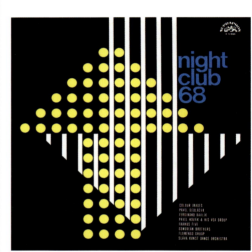

1969 · Josef Kalousek · CZ · Record cover

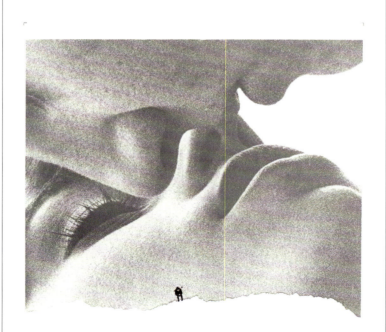

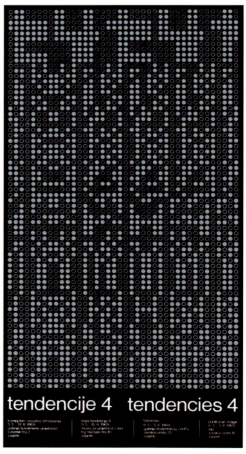

1969 · Alan Siegel, Siegel+Gale · US · Logo · NBA

1969 · Anonymous · US · Logo · DHL

1969 · Lippincott · UK/IT · Logo · Barilla

1969 · Steve Frankfurt · US · Poster

1969 · Ivan Picelj · HR · Poster

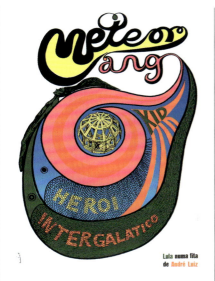

1969 · Rogério Duarte · BR · Poster

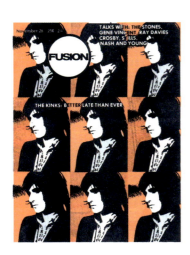

1969 · Anonymous · UK · Magazine cover

1969 · Kálmánchey Zoltán · HU · Record cover

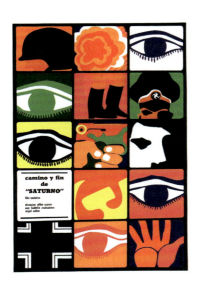

1969 · Eduardo Muñoz Bachs · CU · Poster

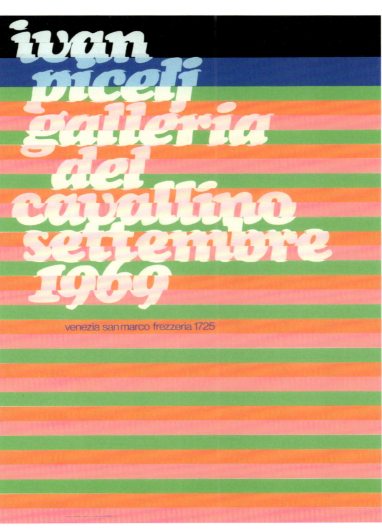

1969 · Mihajlo Arsovski · HR · Poster

1969 · Hubert Hilscher · PL · Poster

1969 · "SPN" · IT · Packaging

1969 · G. Lusso, L. Ricci, G. Vittori · IT · Poster

1969 · Gary Viskupic · US · Poster

Wim Crouwel/Total Design · Netherlands

Wim Crouwel (1928, Groningen, The Netherlands) is a Dutch designer and typographer. After studying fine arts in Groningen and typography in Amsterdam, Crouwel co-founded the studio Total Design in 1963. He created several distinctive typefaces, including New Alphabet (1967) which was inspired by early computer graphics and has been used on stamps as well as record covers. Through Total Design, Crouwel has created numerous identities, often employing grid systems and geometric wordmarks. He has also taught at the universities of Rotterdam and Delft, and at the predecessor of the Gerrit Rietveld Academie in Amsterdam.

Wim Crouwel (1928, Groningen, Niederlande) ist ein niederländischer Grafikdesigner und Typograf. Nachdem er in Groningen Kunst und in Amsterdam Typografie studiert hatte, gründete er 1963 mit anderen das Studio Total Design. Crouwel entwarf unverwechselbare Schriften, darunter New Alphabet (1967), die sich an früher Computergrafik orientierten und verwendete sie bei seinen Entwürfen für Plakate und Briefmarken. Mit Total Design schuf Crouwel zahlreiche Corporate Identities, wobei er oft Rastersysteme und geometrische Wortmarken verwendete. Zudem lehrte er an den Universitäten von Rotterdam und Delft sowie am Vorläufer der Gerrit Rietveld Academie in Amsterdam.

Wim Crouwel (1928, Groningen, Pays-Bas) est un graphiste et typographe néerlandais. Après ses études d'art à Groningen et de typographie à Amsterdam, Crouwel a été un des fondateurs du studio Total Design en 1963. Il est l'auteur de diverses polices de caractères connues, comme New Alphabet (1967), inspirée des premiers graphiques informatiques et employée sur des timbres et des pochettes d'albums. Au travers de Total Design, Crouwel a créé de nombreuses images de marque, souvent à l'aide de systèmes de grilles et de logotypes géométriques. Il a aussi enseigné aux universités de Rotterdam et de Delft, ainsi qu'à l'école qui a précédé l'Académie Gerrit Rietveld à Amsterdam.

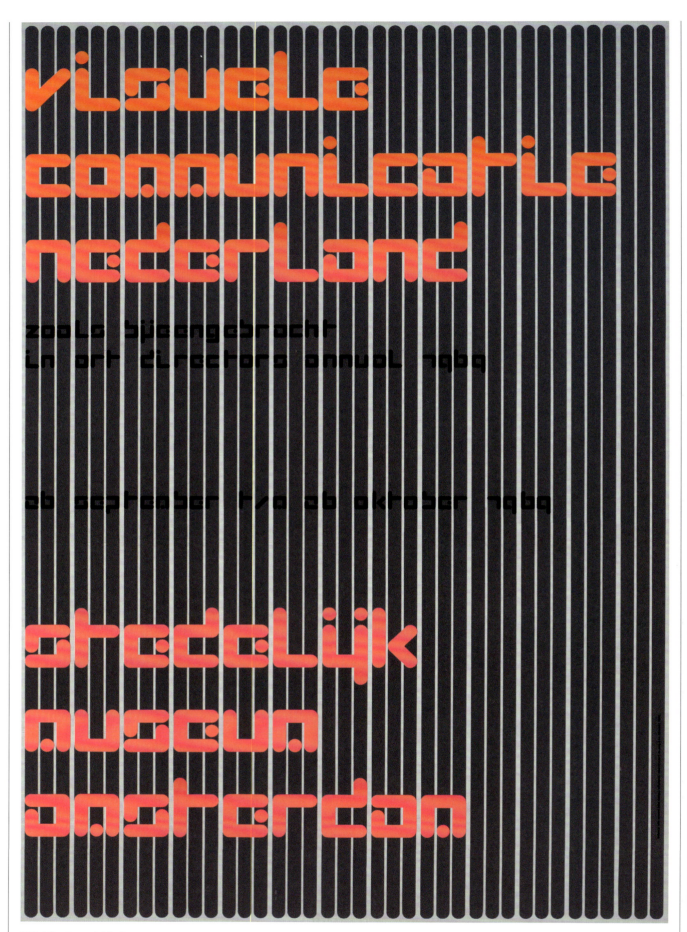

1969 · Wim Crouwel · NL · Poster

During the period from 1963 until 1985, Wim Crouwel and his studio Total Design were responsible for the corporate identity of Amsterdam's Stedelijk Museum. Along with systematically designed printed matter, including catalogs and advertising, Crouwel and his team created many individual posters for specific exhibitions, setting new standards in graphic design.

Zwischen 1963 und 1985 waren Wim Crouwel und sein Büro Total Design für das visuelle Erscheinungsbild des Amsterdamer Stedelijk Museum verantwortlich. Neben systematisch konzipierten Drucksachen entstanden zahlreiche individuelle Plakate für einzelne Ausstellungen, die neue Maßstäbe im Grafikdesign setzten.

Wim Crouwel et son studio Total Design ont été chargés de l'image visuelle du Stedelijk Museum d'Amsterdam de 1963 à 1985. À côté d'imprimés conçus selon une ligne systématique, de nombreuses affiches individuelles créées pour des expositions temporaires ont établi de nouveaux standards dans le domaine du graphisme.

1966 · Wim Crouwel · NL · Poster

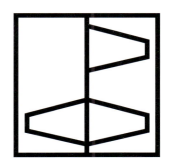

1966 · Wim Crouwel · NL · Poster

1958 · Wim Crouwel · NL · Logo · Pliege

1961 · Wim Crouwel · NL · Logo · Omniscreen

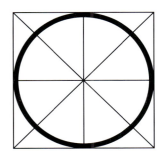

1963 · Wim Crouwel · NL · Logo · Teleac

1957 · Wim Crouwel · NL · Poster

jonge engelse beeldhouwers

stedelijk museum amsterdam
22 april t m 4 juni '67

1967 · Wim Crouwel · NL · Poster

vormen van de kleur

1967 · Wim Crouwel · NL · Poster

1968 · Wim Crouwel · NL · Logo · Packaging

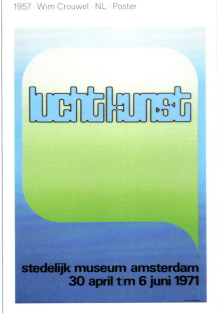

luchtkunst

stedelijk museum amsterdam
30 april t m 6 juni 1971

1971 · Wim Crouwel · NL · Poster

het nederlandse affiche 1890-1968

museum fodor amsterdam
keizersgracht 609
12 oktober t m 10 november 1968
zonnehof amersfoort
16 november t m 15 december 1968

1968 · Wim Crouwel · NL · Poster

RAUSCHENBERG

1968 · Wim Crouwel · NL · Poster

1973 · Wim Crouwel · NL · Logo · Friesland Bank

125

1973 · Christoph Ehbets · GDR · Record cover

1971 · Hamid Samandarian · IR · Poster

1970 —

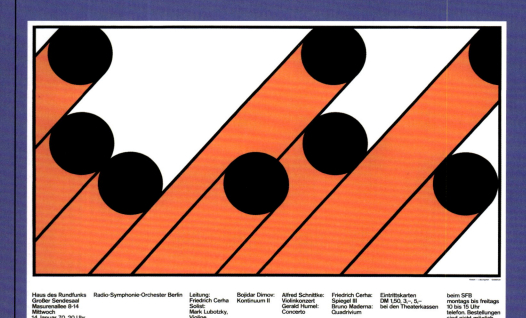

Haus des Rundfunks
Großer Sendesaal
Masurenallee 8-14
Mittwoch
14. Januar 70, 20 Uhr

Radio-Symphonie-Orchester Berlin

Leitung:
Friedrich Cerha
Solist:
Mark Lubotzky,
Violine

Bojidar Dimov:
Kontinuum II

Alfred Schnittke:
Violinkonzert
Gerald Humel:
Concerto

Friedrich Cerha:
Spiegel III
Bruno Maderna:
Quadrivium

Eintrittskarten
DM 1,50, 3,–, 5,–
bei den Theaterkassen

beim SFB
montags bis freitags
10 bis 15 Uhr
telefon. Bestellungen
sind nicht möglich

SFB|WDR   MUSIK DER GEGENWART

1970 · Hans Förtsch, Sigrid von Baumgarten · DE · Poster

1970 · Asela M. Perez · CU · Poster

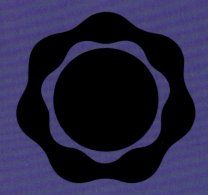

1977 · Mitsuo Katsui · JP · Logo · National Museum of Ethnology

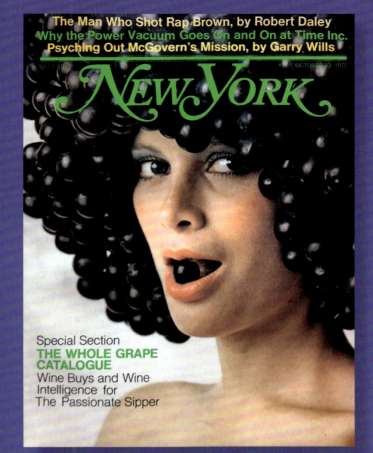

1972 · Walter Bernard (AD), Milton Glaser (AD), Henry Wolf (PH) · US · Magazine cover

1979

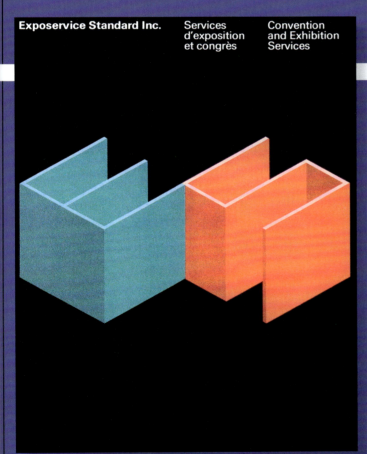

1979 · Ernst Roch · CA · Brochure cover

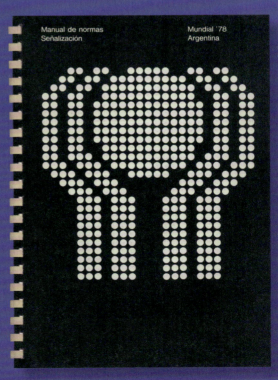

1978 · Gustavo Pedroza, Estudio MMB · AR · Design manual

The continuation and consolidation of the paths laid down in the previous decade, when modernism and the International Style finally broke through into the mainstream, was the template for the 1970s, as this became the age of strong corporate identities and a time when experimental design thrived throughout the cultural sector. To some degree, this new set of priorities forced commercial and cultural design to strike out in different directions. As a result of the professionalization of the visual arts by large corporations, outstanding pieces of work by individual designers became increasingly rare, especially in consumer advertising. Now, new imagery and the continuing revolution in the visual arts mostly appeared in the context of theater, music, and film, and it was in these environments that commissioning clients could often try out experimental photomontages or eye-catching illustrations with few, if any restrictions. So it was with punk, a spur-of-the-moment, unpredictable, and bloody-minded form of visual communication, and a totally distinctive stylistic trope that creatives regularly refer back to even today.

Die 1970er-Jahre setzen die im Jahrzehnt zuvor eingeschlagenen Pfade fort – die Moderne und der „International Style" etablieren sich im Mainstream. Es ist die Zeit der konsequenten Erscheinungsbilder ebenso wie der erblühenden experimentellen Kulturgrafik. In gewisser Weise forcierte diese Schwerpunktsetzung, dass kommerzielle und kulturelle Grafik unterschiedliche Richtungen einschlugen. Die visuelle Professionalisierung großer Unternehmen führte dazu, dass vor allem im Bereich der Konsumwerbung herausragende grafische Einzelarbeiten seltener entstehen konnten. Neue Bildsprachen und visuelle Fortentwicklungen zeigten sich nun vor allem im Kontext von Theater, Musik oder Film. Experimentelle Fotomontagen oder expressive Illustration konnten hier oftmals ohne nennenswerte Einschränkungen durch die Auftraggeber ausprobiert werden. So entstand etwa mit dem Punk eine improvisiert, imperfekt und rotzig wirkende visuelle Ausdrucksform, auf die seither als Stilmittel immer wieder einmal zurückgegriffen wird.

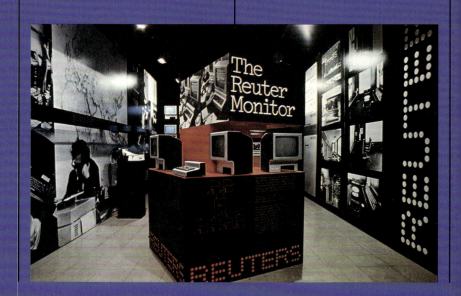

Les années 1970 développent les acquis de la décennie précédente, quand se sont imposés le modernisme et le style international, et leur donnent largement droit de cité. C'est l'époque des images de marque fortes, aussi bien que d'un graphisme expérimental florissant dans la sphère culturelle. D'une certaine manière, ce nouvel accent fait prendre au graphisme commercial et culturel des directions différentes. Avec la professionnalisation des grandes entreprises en matière d'arts visuels, les excellentes créations de designers individuels se font rares, surtout dans le domaine de la publicité de consommation. Dès lors, les progrès en termes d'images et de languages visuels s'apprécient principalement dans les domaines du théâtre, de la musique ou du cinéma, où les commanditaires se permettent des photomontages expérimentaux et des illustrations expressives souvent sans grandes restrictions. Ainsi, le mouvement punk donne naissance à une forme d'expression visuelle d'apparence improvisée, imprévisible et hargneuse, créant une figure stylistique caractéristique que les créateurs actuels emploient encore.

top left: A poster by the design collective Grapus advertising festivities to mark Bastille Day, July 14, 1978.

left: View of an exhibition staged by Pentagram at the London Design Centre in 1973. On show was the new monitor-based messaging system designed for the Reuters news agency.

---

links oben: Ein Plakat des Designerkollektivs Grapus, das für Feierlichkeiten rund um den französischen Nationalfeiertag am 14. Juli 1978 wirbt.

links: Blick in eine 1973 von Pentagram gestaltete Ausstellung im London Design Centre. Präsentiert wurde ein neues monitorbasiertes Nachrichtensystem der Presseagentur Reuters.

---

en haut à gauche: une affiche du collectif de graphistes Grapus annonce les festivités organisées en marge de la fête nationale du 14 juillet 1978.

à gauche: vue d'une exposition conçue en 1973 par Pentagram au Design Centre de Londres. L'exposition présentait un nouveau système de messagerie conçu pour l'agence de presse Reuters à partir de moniteurs.

below: Signs along the road leading into Munich, host city for the 1972 Olympic Games. These were part of the visual identity designed for this major event by Otl Aicher.

unten: Schilder an der Münchner Stadteinfahrt weisen auf die 1972 dort ausgetragenen Olympischen Spiele hin. Sie sind Teil der von Otl Aicher realisierten visuellen Identität dieser Großveranstaltung.

en bas: en 1972, à l'entrée de la ville de Munich, des panneaux évoquent les jeux Olympiques qui s'y tiennent. Ils font partie de l'identité visuelle créée par Otl Aicher pour le grand événement sportif.

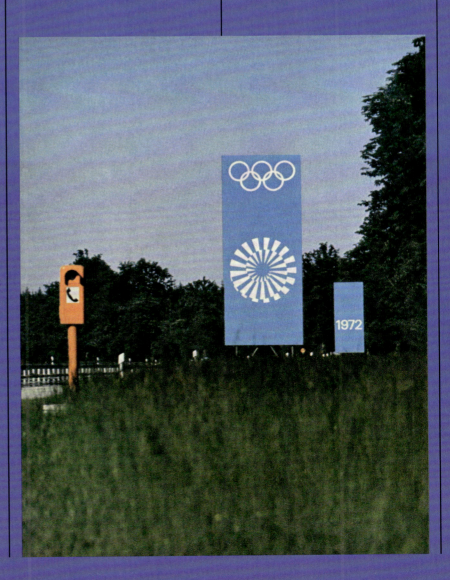

1970

Jimi Hendrix dies in London

The German terror organization the Red Army Faction is formed, also known as the Baader-Meinhof gang

Apollo 13 returns to Earth after an oxygen tank explosion destroyed its service module

Robert Altman's satirical military comedy *M.A.S.H.* is released

The Chevrolet Vega is introduced and goes on to sell in huge numbers, despite various reliability issues

The first annual New York City Marathon is held

The first Golden State Comic Book Convention takes place in San Diego

In the United States, the first Earth Day is celebrated

The Treaty on the Non-Proliferation of Nuclear Weapons comes into effect

The Beatles' last studio album, *Let it Be*, is released

1971

Bangladesh becomes an independent nation

Cigarette commercials on television and radio are banned in the United States

Daimler-Benz patents the airbag

Frederick Forsyth's novel *The Day of the Jackal* is published

The Nasdaq Stock Market begins trading in New York City

Jim Morrison dies in Paris

The environmental organization Greenpeace is founded

John Lennon records and releases his song "Imagine"

Stanley Kubrick's film *A Clockwork Orange* premieres

Intel releases the first commercially available microprocessor

1972

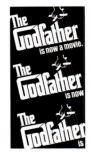
Francis Ford Coppola's movie adaptation of *The Godfather* is released in cinemas

HBO launches in the United States as the first subscription cable TV service

Kadir Nurman introduces a sandwich made with doner kebab meat as a fast-food item in Berlin

U.S. President Richard Nixon is re-elected

With Pong, Atari kicks off the first generation of video arcade games

Members of the Israeli team are kidnapped and killed during the Munich Olympics

Shirley Chisholm, the first African-American Congresswoman, announces her bid to become U.S. President

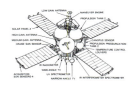
The space probe *Mariner 9* sends back images from Mars

American domestic politics is consumed by the Watergate scandal

1973

The rock band AC/DC forms in Sydney

Bruce Lee dies a week before the release of his last movie, *Enter the Dragon*

The bar code system is created by engineer George J. Laurer of IBM

Elvis Presley's *Aloha from Hawaii* is the first concert to be broadcast live by satellite

The Sydney Opera House opens

THE ROCKY HORROR SHOW
The musical of *The Rocky Horror Show* premieres in London

The first episode of *Kojak* starring Telly Savalas is aired on CBS

An embargo by OPEC causes an oil crisis in several countries worldwide

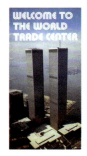
The Twin Towers of New York's World Trade Center are opened, at the time the tallest buildings in the world

The Bosphorus Bridge opens, the first to connect Europe and Asia since 480 BC

1974

Hungarian architect Ernő Rubik invents the Rubik's Cube

ABBA's hit "Waterloo" is released and wins the Eurovision Song Contest

Hewlett-Packard's HP-65, the first programmable pocket calculator, is put on the market

Derrick
The German crime television series *Derrick* premieres

Nixon resigns as U.S. president

Kraftwerk's album *Autobahn* is released

Stephen King's first novel *Carrie* is published

Uri Geller stuns people with his feats of metal-bending on international television

Punk begins to emerge with bands such as the Ramones, Television, and Patti Smith

The first issue of the American weekly society magazine *People* is published

1975

Available in kit form or ready assembled, the release of the Altair 8800 sparks the microcomputer revolution

International Women's Day is adopted by the United Nations

The death of General Franco leads to the restoration of the monarchy in Spain

The Soviet space probe *Venera 9* transmits the first images of the surface of Venus

The U.K. European Communities membership referendum is the first to be held nationwide throughout the whole United Kingdom

Angola becomes an independent country

The Microsoft Corporation is founded by Bill Gates and Paul Allen

Punk band the Sex Pistols form in London

The Vietnam War ends

1976

The Apple Computer Company is founded by Steve Jobs, Steve Wozniak, and Ronald Wayne

The Muppet Show premieres on ATV in the United Kingdom

The movie *One Flew Over the Cuckoo's Nest* wins all five major Academy Awards

More than two decades of Communist dictatorship under Mao Zedong come to an end with his death

NASA's *Viking 1* becomes the first spacecraft to land on Mars

High-speed InterCity 125 trains are introduced in the United Kingdom

Isabel Perón is deposed as President of Argentina by a right-wing coup and a military junta is installed to replace her

Construction of the CN Tower in Toronto is completed

The first commercial laser printer is introduced by IBM

1977

Australian author Colleen McCullough's novel *The Thorn Birds* is published

David Bowie's album *Heroes* is released

Elvis Presley dies in his mansion at Graceland in Memphis, Tennessee

World-famous nightclub and disco Studio 54 opens in New York City

Snow falls in Miami for the first time in its history

The Soviet icebreaker *Arktika* becomes the first surface vessel to reach the North Pole

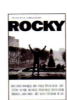

The Sylvester Stallone movie *Rocky* wins Oscars for Best Picture and Best Director

The world's first all-in-one home computer, the Commodore PET, is introduced

Spain enjoys its first free elections since 1936

The Centre Georges Pompidou in Paris officially opens

1978

Christopher Reeve stars in the first *Superman* movie

Double Eagle II becomes the first piloted balloon to cross the Atlantic Ocean

The American artist Gilbert Baker designs the Rainbow Flag as a symbol for the gay community

John Irving's novel *The World According to Garp* is published

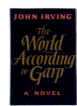

The film musical *Grease* is released, starring John Travolta and Olivia Newton-John

Reinhold Messner and Peter Habeler make the first ascent of Mount Everest without supplemental oxygen

Comic character Garfield is created by Jim Davis

The world's first test-tube baby, Louise Brown, is born in Oldham, England

The first episode of *Dallas* is aired on CBS

1979

Donna Summer's worldwide disco hit "Bad Girls" is released

Demonstrations force the Shah of Iran into exile and the Islamic Revolution appoints Ayatollah Khomeini as Supreme Leader

The Sony Walkman goes on sale in Japan

Margaret Thatcher is elected the first woman Prime Minister of the United Kingdom

The 3M corporation brings out its sticky notes under the name Post-it

Michael Jackson releases his breakthrough album *Off the Wall*

Saddam Hussein becomes President of Iraq

German writer Michael Ende's fantasy novel *The Neverending Story* is first published

Nickelodeon, a television network for young people, launches in the United States

In China, the one-child policy is introduced

1970

Adrian Frutiger creates a standard typeface for the signage for Paris airport, later expanded to become the **Frutiger** typeface, released in 1975

The French design collective **Grapus** is established

The type foundry **ITC** (International Typeface Corporation) is formed by Herb Lubalin and Aaron Burns

26 DE JULIO·XVII ANIVERSARIO

1970 · Alfonso Prieto · CU · Poster

BESOS ROBADOS

FILM FRANCES EN COLORES   DIRECCION: FRANCOIS TRUFFAUT   CON: JEAN-PIERRE LEAUD

1970 · René Azcuy · CU · Poster

1970 · Miroslav Pechánek · CZ · Poster

1970 · Minale, Tattersfield, Provinciali · UK · Logo · Baric Computing Services

IN COLD BLOOD
TRUMAN CAPOTE

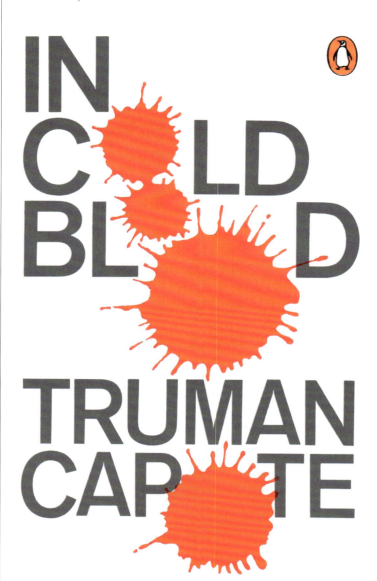

1970 · Bass & Associates · US · Logo · Avery

1970 · Gary Anderson · US · Logo · Recycling Symbol

1970 · David Pelham · UK · Book cover

1970 · Rafał Jasionowicz · PL · Poster

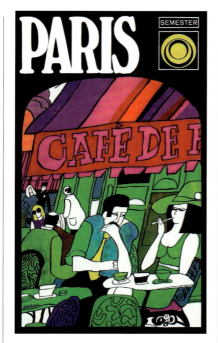

1970 · Stellan Kristenson · SE · Book cover

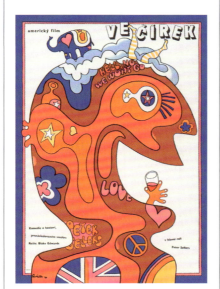

1970 · Jaroslav Fišer · CZ · Poster

1970 · Anonymous · US · Record cover

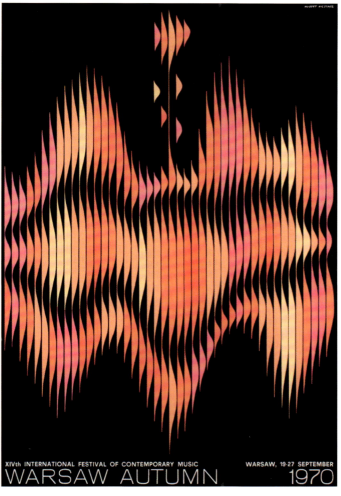

1970 · Hubert Hilscher · PL · Poster

1970 · Anonymous · JP · Poster

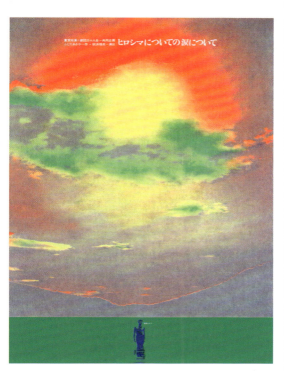

1970 · Keisuke Nagatomo · JP · Poster

1970 · Alfredo Rostgaard · CU · Poster

1970 · Woody Woodward · US · Record cover

Since Harry Beck and Bob Noorda developed their respective maps of the London Underground and the Milan Metro, many public transportation systems have adopted their schematic visual approach. In 1970, Unimark International was commissioned by the Metropolitan Transportation Authority (MTA) to improve the map of the New York City Subway, which had been in operation since 1904. Under the direction of Massimo Vignelli and Bob Noorda, the project was approved by the MTA that same year, although Vignelli then left Unimark in 1971 to start his own practice. The new signage system was launched on August 4, 1972, and is considered one of Vignelli's masterpieces; the project is still revered today as an artistic work, and one of the best examples of extensive use of the Helvetica typeface. The design has subsequently gone through a series of modifications.

Seit Harry Beck und Bob Noorda ihre Pläne der U-Bahn in London bzw. Mailand entwarfen, haben zahlreiche Verkehrsbetriebe deren schematische Darstellungsweise übernommen. 1970 erhielt Unimark International von der Metropolitan Transportation Authority (MTA) den Auftrag, den Plan der 1904 in Betrieb genommenen New Yorker U-Bahn zu verbessern. Unter der Leitung von Massimo Vignelli und Bob Noorda wurde das Projekt im selben Jahr von der MTA gebilligt, obwohl Vignelli 1971 Unimark verließ, um sein eigenes Büro zu gründen. Das neue System der Ausschilderung wurde am 4. August 1972 eingeführt und gilt als eines der Meisterwerke Vignellis. Das Projekt wird heute noch als Kunstwerk betrachtet und ist eines der besten Beispiele für den durchgängigen Gebrauch der Schrifttype Helvetica. Der Entwurf wurde seitdem mehrmals angepasst.

Depuis que Harry Beck et Bob Noorda ont développé leurs plans respectifs des métros de Londres et de Milan, nombre de systèmes de transports ont adopté leur approche visuelle schématique. En 1970, Unimark International fut chargée par la Metropolitan Transportation Authority (MTA) d'améliorer le plan de métro de la ville de New York en usage depuis 1904. Le projet dirigé par Massimo Vignelli et Bob Noorda reçut l'approbation de la MTA la même année, bien que Vignelli eut quitté Unimark en 1971 pour ouvrir son propre studio. La nouvelle signalétique lancée le 4 août 1972 est considérée comme un des chef-d'œuvres de Vignelli. Le projet est encore acclamé aujourd'hui comme une véritable création artistique et un des meilleurs exemples d'utilisation intensive de la police de caractères Helvetica. Plus tard, le graphisme a subi toute une série de modifications.

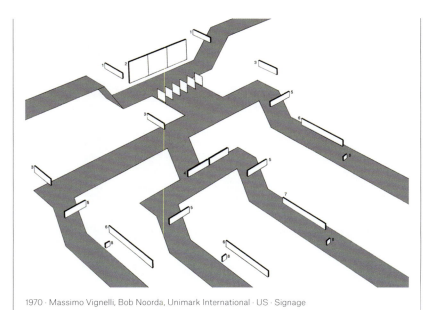

1970 · Massimo Vignelli, Bob Noorda, Unimark International · US · Signage

1970 · Massimo Vignelli, Bob Noorda, Unimark International · US · Identity

1970 · Massimo Vignelli, Bob Noorda, Unimark International · US · Signage

1970 · Massimo Vignelli, Bob Noorda, Unimark International · US · Signage

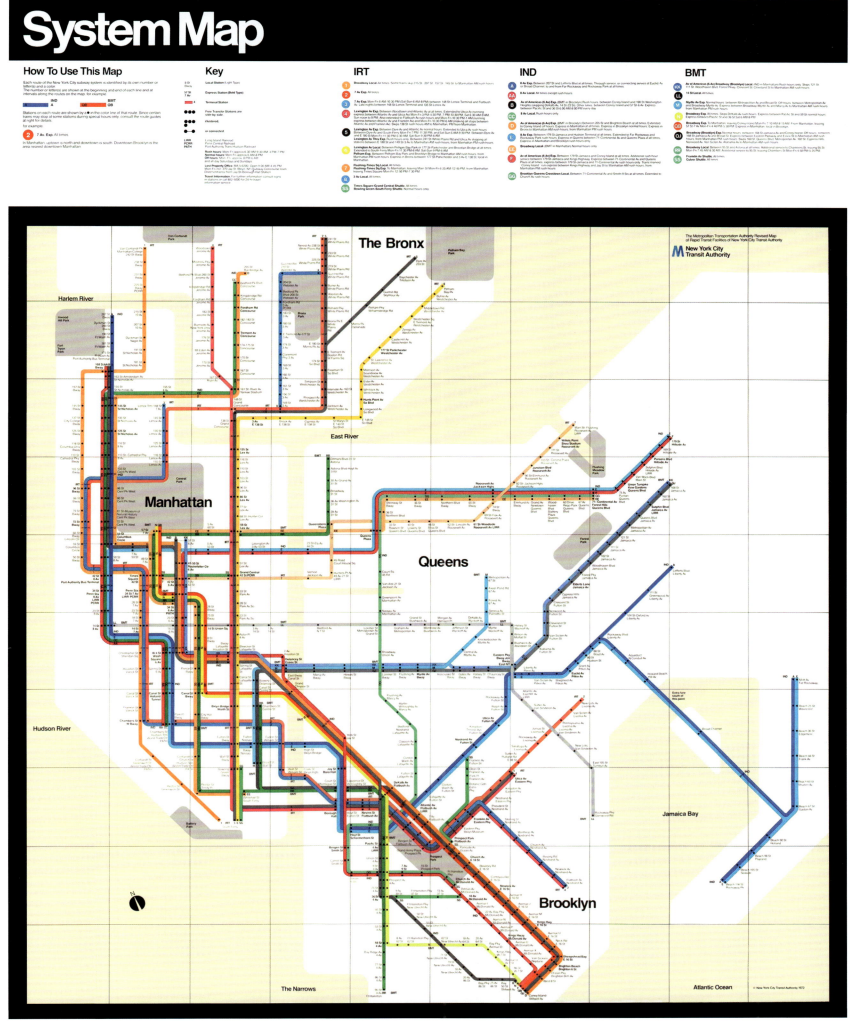

1970-72 · Massimo Vignelli, Joan Charysyn, Unimark International · US · Information graphic

1969 · Dan Reisinger · IL · Poster

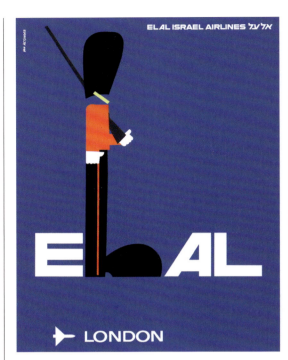

1970 · Dan Reisinger · IL · Poster

1970 · Dan Reisinger · IL · Poster

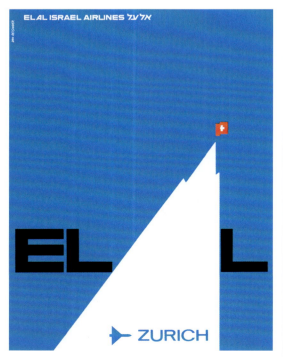

1970 · Dan Reisinger · IL · Poster

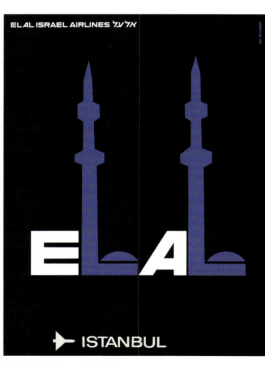

1970 · Dan Reisinger · IL · Poster

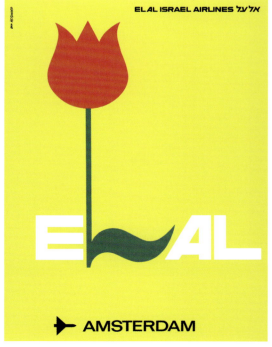

1970 · Dan Reisinger · IL · Poster

In 1970 Dan Reisinger was put in charge of reworking the Israeli airline El Al's corporate identity. Within the framework he set up for this he also produced a series of posters advertising the destinations the airline served. The combination of the company name with attention-grabbing visuals proved to be an effective international solution with a strong likeability factor.

Ab 1970 war Dan Reisinger für die Überarbeitung des Erscheinungsbilds der israelischen Fluggesellschaft El Al verantwortlich. In diesem Rahmen entstand auch eine Plakatserie, die für die Destinationen der Airline warb. Die Verbindung des Firmennamens mit markanten Bildikonen erwies sich als international funktionierende Lösung mit großem Sympathiefaktor.

À partir de 1970, Dan Reisinger fut chargé de redéfinir l'image visuelle de la compagnie aérienne israélienne El Al. C'est dans ce cadre que vit aussi le jour une série d'affiches illustrant les grandes destinations desservies par la compagnie. L'association graphique d'emblèmes touristiques et du nom «El Al» s'avéra être une solution fonctionnant partout dans le monde et porteuse d'un fort effet de sympathie.

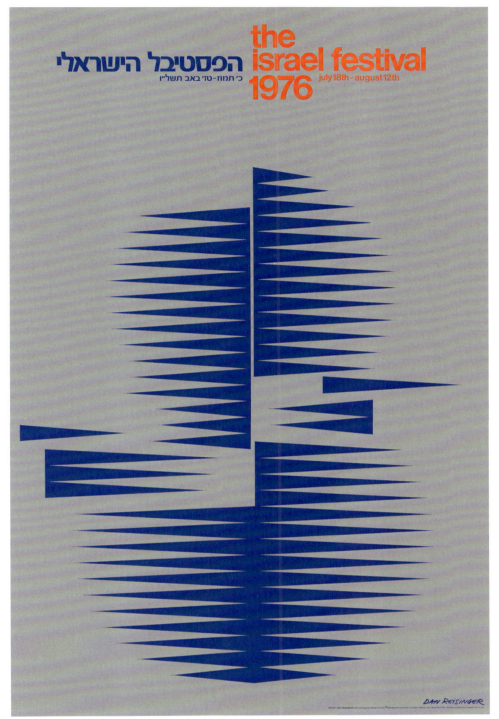

1976 · Dan Reisinger · IL · Poster

Dan Reisinger (1934, Kanjiza, Serbia) is an Israeli graphic designer, born to Jewish parents in the former Yugoslavia, who escaped the Holocaust and later emigrated to Israel in 1949. After attending the Bezalel Academy of Arts and Design in Jerusalem, Reisinger did his mandatory service in the Israeli Air Force working as art director of publications. He then went to Brussels and London, where he studied at the Central School of Art and Design. In 1966 Reisinger returned to Israel and opened his own agency in Givatayim. He became famous for his posters on social, political, and cultural topics and also designed over 150 logos and corporate identity systems for various companies in Israel.

Dan Reisinger (1934, Kanjiža, Serbien) ist ein israelischer Grafikdesigner. Geboren wurde er als Sohn jüdischer Eltern aus dem ehemaligen Jugoslawien, die dem Holocaust entkamen und 1949 nach Israel auswanderten. Nach dem Besuch der Bezalel Academy of Arts and Design in Jerusalem absolvierte Reisinger seinen Militärdienst bei der israelischen Luftwaffe, deren Publikationen er als Artdirector betreute. Anschließend ging er nach Brüssel und London, wo er an der Central School of Art and Design studierte. 1966 kehrte Reisinger nach Israel zurück und eröffnete in Giv'atajim seine eigene Agentur. Er wurde bekannt für seine Plakate zu sozialen, politischen und kulturellen Themen. Darüber hinaus entwarf er über 150 Logos und Corporate-Identity-Systeme für verschiedene Firmen in Israel.

Dan Reisinger (1934, Kanjiza, Serbie) est un graphiste israélien né de parents juifs dans l'ancienne Yougoslavie et rescapé de l'Holocauste, qui émigra en Israël en 1949. Après des études à la l'École des beaux-arts de Bezalel, à, Jérusalem, Reisinger fit son service militaire obligatoire dans l'armée de l'air israélienne, au sein de laquelle il assura la direction artistique de diverses publications. Il s'installa ensuite à Bruxelles et à Londres, où il étudia à la Central School of Art and Design. En 1966, Reisinger est retourné en Israël pour y ouvrir son studio à Givatayim. Il est devenu célèbre pour ses affiches sur des sujets sociaux, politiques et culturels. Il a également signé plus de 150 logos et systèmes d'identité pour diverses compagnies en Israël.

1973 · Dan Reisinger · IL · Logo · Maccabi Sport Festival

1968 · Dan Reisinger · IL · Logo · Habima National Theatre

1971 · Dan Reisinger · IL · Logo · El Al Airlines

1968 · Félix Beltrán · CU · Logo · Revista Unión
Letra B

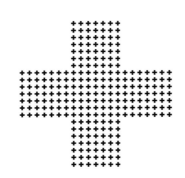

1964 · Félix Beltrán · CU · Logo · Cruz Roja
Internacional

1971 · Félix Beltrán · CU · Logo · Instituto Cubano
del Libro

1960 · Félix Beltrán · CU · Logo · Victoria Eletricity

1984 · Félix Beltrán · CU/MX · Logo · Nuñez
Architecture

1967 · Félix Beltrán · CU · Logo · New Year 1968

1972 · Félix Beltrán · CU · Logo · Hormicuba

1968 · Félix Beltrán · CU · Logo · Consejo Nacional
de Cultura

1969 · Félix Beltrán · CU/JP · Logo · Asociación
para la Solidaridad con Cuba

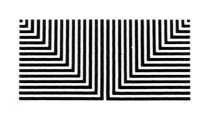

1985 · Félix Beltrán · CU/MX · Logo · Apple México

1973 · Félix Beltrán · CU · Logo · Mincex Havana

1970 · Félix Beltrán · CU · Logo · Galeria Uneac

1965 · Félix Beltrán · CU · Logo · Nacional Importadora

1956 · Félix Beltrán · CU · Logo · Hotel Habana

1978 · Félix Beltrán · CU · Logo · Encuentro de
Escultores

1972 · Félix Beltrán · CU · Logo · Televisión
Universitaria Havana

1971 · Félix Beltrán · CU · Logo · Unival Havana

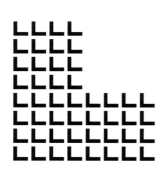

1982 · Félix Beltrán · CU/MX · Logo · Letra y Linea

1983 · Félix Beltrán · CU · Logo · Interexport

1965 · Félix Beltrán · CU/ES · Logo · Fábrica de Plásticos

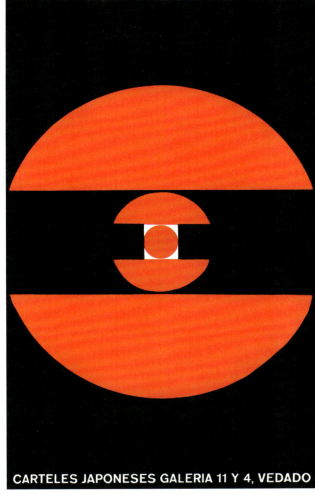

CARTELES JAPONESES GALERIA 11 Y 4, VEDADO

1970 · Félix Beltrán · CU · Poster

LIBERTAD PARA ANGELA DAVIS

1971 · Félix Beltrán · CU · Poster

SOLIDARIDAD CON CUBA, SOLIDARIDAD

1970 · Félix Beltrán · CU · Poster

ENRIQUE LAGUERRE
THE LABYRINTH

1958 · Félix Beltrán · CU/US · Book cover

Félix Beltrán (1938, Havana) is a Cuban visual artist who studied in New York, Paris, and Madrid, before becoming one of the most important poster artists in Latin America. Starting off in advertising at McCann Erickson in the years 1953–56, Beltrán later produced numerous posters for cultural events in Cuba, where he also taught at the Instituto Superior de Arte from 1976–82. In the mid-1980s he moved to Mexico City and became curator of the Archivo Gráfico Internacional at the Universidad Autónoma Metropolitana, a historical visual archive.

Félix Beltrán (1938, Havanna) ist ein kubanischer Künstler, der in New York, Paris und Madrid studierte und zu einem der bedeutendsten Plakatkünstler Lateinamerikas werden sollte. Seine Berufslaufbahn begann Beltrán in den Jahren 1953–1956 als Werbegrafiker bei McCann Erickson und entwarf später zahlreiche Plakate für Kulturveranstaltungen in Kuba, wo er von 1976 bis 1982 auch am Instituto Superior de Arte unterrichtete. Mitte der 1980er-Jahre zog er nach Mexico City und wurde Kurator des Archivo Gráfico Internacional an der Universidad Autónoma Metropolitana.

Félix Beltrán (1938, La Havane) est un artiste visuel cubain qui a étudié à New York, Paris et Madrid avant de devenir un des plus importants affichistes d'Amérique latine. Après des débuts dans la publicité chez McCann Erickson dans les années 1953–1956, Beltrán a produit de nombreuses affiches pour des événements culturels organisés à Cuba, où il a aussi enseigné à l'Instituto Superior de Arte de 1976 à 1982. Au milieu des années 1980, il s'installe à Mexico et devient conservateur de l'Archivo Gráfico Internacional, une archive visuelle historique de l'université autonome métropolitaine.

1971

Design student Carolyn Davidson creates the **Nike** swoosh for $35

Victor Papanek's book **Design for the Real World** is published

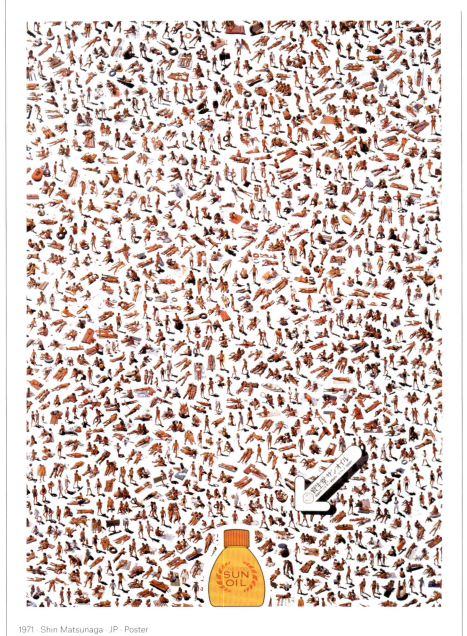

1971 · Shin Matsunaga · JP · Poster

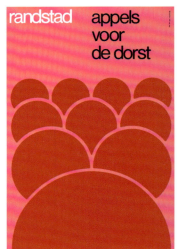

1971 · Ida van Bladel · BE · Poster

randstad appels voor de dorst

1971 · Ben Bos, Total Design · NL · Poster

1971 · Ricardo Blanco · AR · Logo · Equipamento de Hoy

1971 · Salvatore Gregorietti, Unimark International · IT · Logo · Agip

1971 · Carolyn Davidson · US · Logo · Nike

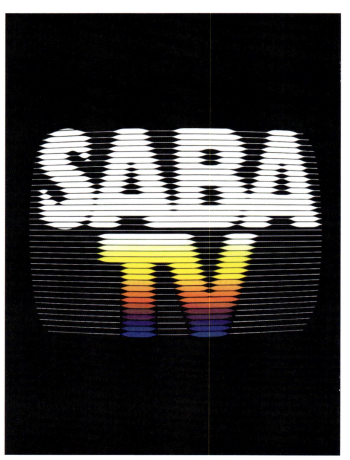

1971 · Neukomm+Pinschewer · CH · Poster

1971 · Gilbert Lesser · UK · Poster

1971 · Louis Danziger · US · Record cover

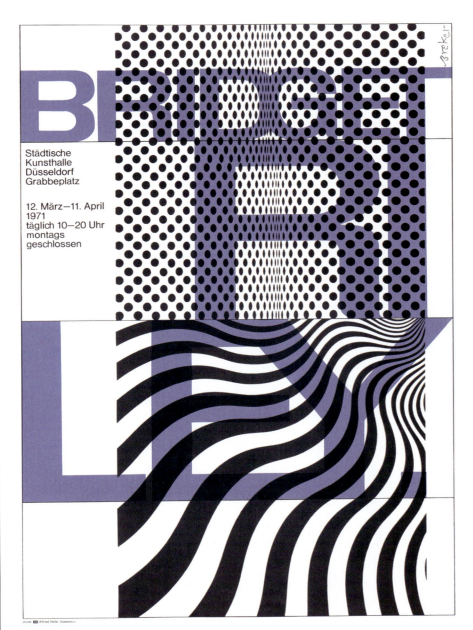

1971 · Walter Breker · DE · Poster

1971 · Anonymous · GDR · Packaging

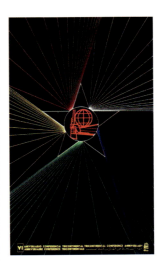

1971 · Lázaro Abreu · CU · Poster

1971 · Jerzy Flisak · PL · Poster

1971 · John Pasche · UK · Record cover

1971 · Herb Lubalin · US · Logo · PBS

1971 · Helmut Lortz · DE · Poster

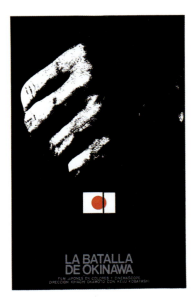

1971 · Anonymous · CU · Poster

Les Mason (1924, Fresno, California – 2009, Istanbul) was an American graphic designer who helped establish the industry in Australia. After emigrating from the United States in 1961, Mason began a 13-year association with *Epicurean*, one of the country's first and most influential food and wine magazines. Together with Garry Emery and others, in the early 1970s he formed a graphic designers' group, intended to promote its benefits amongst potential clients. Mason spent most of his later years painting and experimenting in his own print studio.

Les Mason (1924, Fresno, Kalifornien – 2009, Istanbul) war ein amerikanischer Grafikdesigner, der dazu beitrug, die Branche in Australien zu etablieren. Nachdem er 1961 aus den Vereinigten Staaten ausgewandert war, begann Mason eine 13-jährige Zusammenarbeit mit *Epicurean*, einem der ersten und einflussreichsten Food- und Weinmagazine Australiens. Zusammen mit Garry Emery und anderen gründete er Anfang der 1970er-Jahre eine Gruppe von Grafikdesignern mit dem Zweck, potenzielle Auftraggeber anzusprechen. In seinen späteren Jahren widmete sich Mason größtenteils der Malerei und Experimenten in seinem eigenen Druckstudio.

Les Mason (1924, Fresno, Californie – 2009, Istanbul) fut un graphiste américain qui contribua à asseoir cette profession en Australie. Après y avoir émigré des États-Unis en 1961, Mason entama une collaboration de 13 ans avec *Epicurean*, une des revues de gastronomie et d'œnologie les plus influentes du pays. Au début des années 1970, il forma avec Garry Emery et d'autres un groupe de designers graphiques en vue de vanter ses mérites à des clients potentiels. Mason passa la plupart de ses années tardives à peindre et à expérimenter dans son atelier d'imprimerie.

1971 · Les Mason · AU · Magazine cover

1973 · Les Mason · AU · Magazine cover

The Australian magazine *Epicurean*, launched in 1966, was the first such publication in the country to focus entirely on food and drink. Under its art director, the graphic designer Les Mason, every issue of the magazine featured a whole new layout, each time picking up on the very latest visual trends.

Mit dem australischen Magazin *Epicurean* erschien ab 1966 das erste Medium seiner Art, das sich vollständig auf Essen und Trinken fokussierte. Unter der Artdirection des Grafikdesigners Les Mason zeigte sich jede Ausgabe in völlig veränderter Aufmachung, die jeweils die aktuellsten visuellen Trends aufgriff.

Le magazine australien *Epicurean*, qui parut en 1966, fut le premier support du genre entièrement dédié à la gastronomie. Sous la direction artistique du graphiste Les Mason, chaque numéro présentait une mise en page nouvelle en intégrant chaque fois les tendances visuelles les plus récentes.

»Les Mason is the type of successful graphic artist we find today in nearly every country with a developed economy. His success is above all the result of his unceasing quest for artistic perfection which distinguishes even the smallest details of his designs.« Hans Kuh, *Gebrauchsgraphik*, 1967

1970s · Les Mason · AU · Magazine spreads

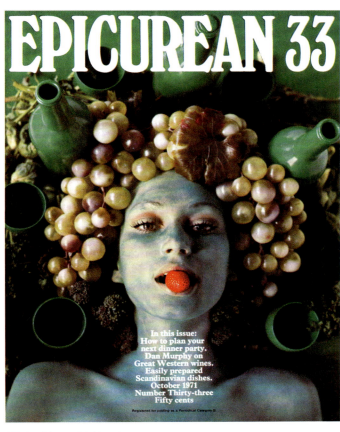

1971 · Les Mason · AU · Magazine cover

1972 · Les Mason · AU · Magazine cover

1966 · Les Mason · AU · Magazine cover

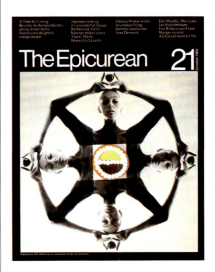

1969 · Les Mason · AU · Magazine cover

1969 · Les Mason · AU · Magazine cover

1969 · Les Mason · AU · Magazine cover

Jean Widmer (1929, Frauenfeld, Switzerland) is a Swiss designer whose work has had a considerable influence on visual communication in France since his arrival there in the 1950s. After studying in Zurich and Paris, Widmer introduced modernist design concepts in France from 1959 to the late 1960s, through his work as art director at the Galeries Lafayette, and then the fashion magazine *Jardin des Modes*. He subsequently changed to using much simpler forms, producing innovative posters and pictograms, including the French motorway signage system completed in 1978. Since 1970, he has run Visuel Design, working for such clients as the Centre Georges Pompidou and the Musée d'Orsay.

Jean Widmer (1929, Frauenfeld, Schweiz) ist ein Schweizer Grafikdesigner, der in den 1950er-Jahren nach Frankreich ging und seitdem die französische visuelle Kommunikation nachhaltig beeinflusst hat. Nach seinem Studium in Zürich und Paris führte Widmer zwischen Ende der 1950er-und der 1960er-Jahre moderne Designkonzepte in Frankreich ein, zunächst durch seine Arbeit als Artdirector bei den Galeries Lafayette, dann bei dem Modejournal *Jardin des Modes*. Später gestaltete er unter Verwendung sehr viel einfacherer Formen innovative Plakate und Piktogramme, unter anderem das Beschilderungssystem auf französischen Autobahnen, das 1978 fertiggestellt wurde. Seit 1970 leitet er die Agentur Visuel Design mit Auftraggebern wie dem Centre Georges Pompidou und dem Musée d'Orsay.

Jean Widmer (1929, Frauenfeld, Suisse) est un designer suisse dont le travail a exercé une influence considérable sur la communication visuelle en France quand il s'y installe dans les années 1950. Après des études à Zurich et à Paris, Widmer a introduit les concepts du design moderniste en France de 1959 à la fin des années 1960 par le truchement de son poste de directeur artistique des Galeries Lafayette, puis du magazine de mode *Les Jardin des Modes*. Plus tard, il a évolué vers des formes beaucoup plus simples, produisant des affiches et des pictogrammes innovants, notamment le système signalétique autoroutier français, qu'il a achevé en 1978. Il a dirigé Visuel Design à partir de 1970 et travaillé pour des clients comme le Centre Georges Pompidou et le Musée d'Orsay.

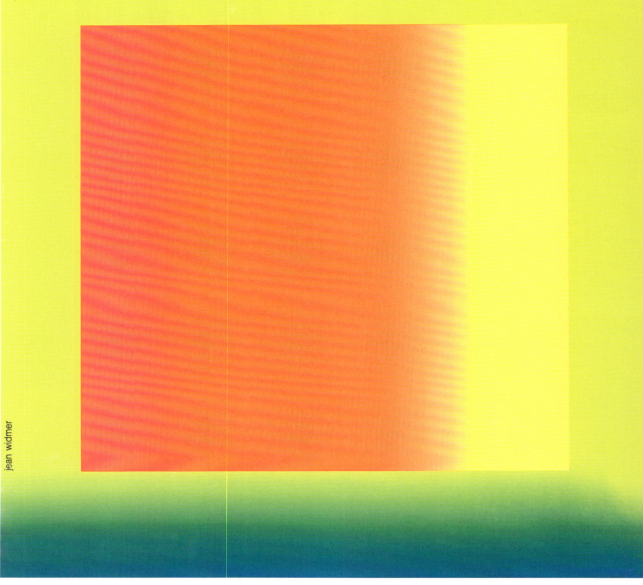

1972 · Jean Widmer · CH/FR · Poster

The series of posters Widmer created for France's Centre de Création Industrielle inevitably ask the question of where art becomes design, and *vice versa*. For a number of years, his captivating, instantly recognizable silkscreen posters were used to advertise a wide range of exhibitions staged by the French design center. At the same time though they were themselves works of abstract art.

Jean Widmers Plakatserie für das Centre de création industrielle führt unweigerlich zu der Frage, wann Kunst zu Design wird und umgekehrt. Die faszinierenden mit leuchtenden Sonderfarben hergestellten Siebdruckplakate warben mit hoher Wiedererkennbarkeit über mehrere Jahre für wechselnde Ausstellungen des französischen Designzentrums. Gleichzeitig waren sie abstrakte Kunstwerke für sich.

La série d'affiches réalisées par Jean Widmer pour le Centre de création industrielle soulève invariablement la question de savoir à quel moment l'art devient design et inversement. Ses fascinantes affiches sérigraphiées, immédiatement reconnaissables, ont annoncé pendant plusieurs années les expositions temporaires de l'organisme culturel français. Elles étaient en même temps des œuvres d'art abstraites à part entière.

1971 · Jean Widmer · CH/FR · Poster

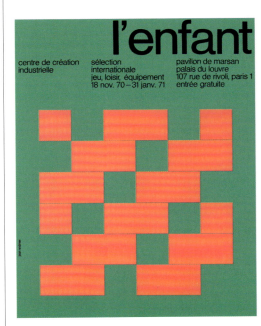

1970s · Jean Widmer · CH/FR · Poster

1971 · Jean Widmer · CH/FR · Poster

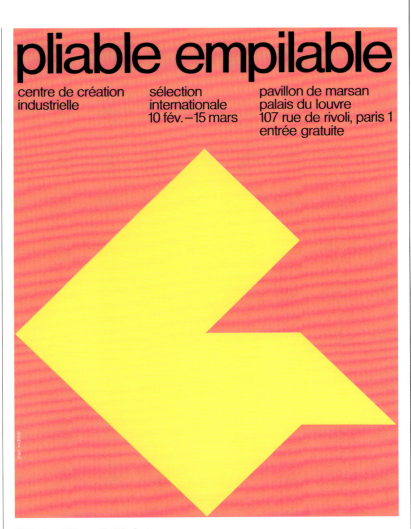

1970s · Jean Widmer · CH/FR · Poster

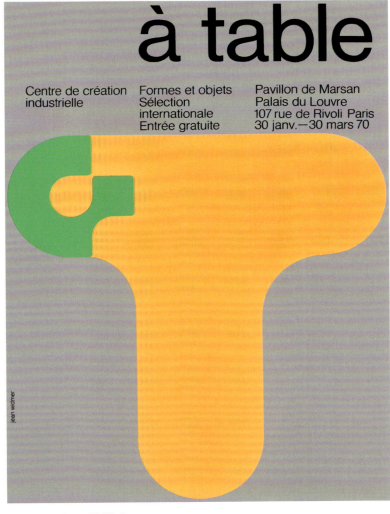

1970 · Jean Widmer · CH/FR · Poster

145

1972

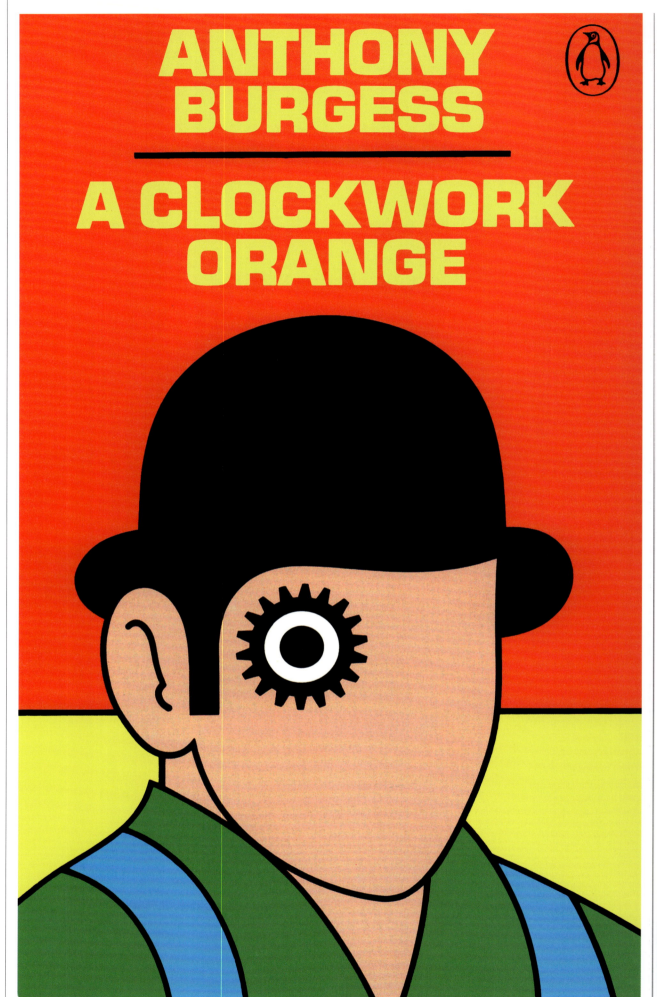

1972 · David Pelham · UK · Book cover

1972 · Victor Vasarely · HU/FR · Logo · Renault

1972 · George Opperman, Opperman-Harrington · US · Logo · Atari

1972 · Anonymous · DE · Logo · Adidas

1972 · Jerome Gould, James Camperos, Kent Maxson · US · Packaging

1972 · Isaac Diaz Pardo · ES · Poster

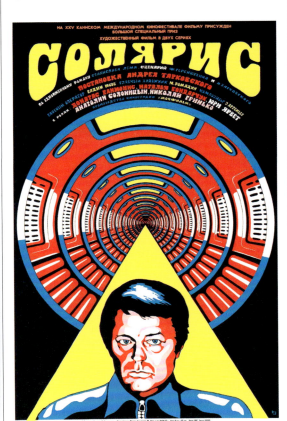

1972 · Anonymous · RU · Poster

Bernard Shaw
Der Katechismus des
Umstürzlers

edition suhrkamp
SV

Martin Walser
Der Schwarze Schwan

›im Dialog‹
edition suhrkamp
SV

Bernard Shaw
Die heilige Johanna
Deutsch von
Wolfgang Hildesheimer

edition suhrkamp
SV

Zbigniew Herbert
Ein Barbar in einem Garten

edition suhrkamp
SV

1972 · Willy Fleckhaus · DE · Book covers

THE GODS THEMSELVES A NOVEL BY ISAAC ASIMOV

1972 · David November · US · Book cover

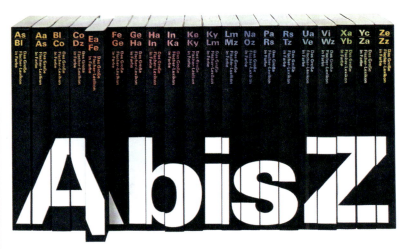

1972 · Pierre Mendell, Mendell & Oberer · DE · Book covers

INSTITUTO NACIONAL
DE INVESTIGAÇÃO
INDUSTRIAL

DIVISÃO DE FORMAÇÃO
E APERFEIÇOAMENTO

PLANO GERAL
DE ACTIVIDADES

formação 72·73

1972 · Alda Rosa · PT · Poster

1970–1979

?entagram

Colin Forbes will show work and answer questions about the new Pentagram Design Partnership on Wed 15 Nov at 7.30pm at Byggecentrum, Gyldenløvesgade 19. Entrance fee Kr 10.00, SIF members free Arrangement SIF Selskabet for Industriel Formgiving, Nikolaj Plads 9, 1067 København K, 01-152285

1972 · Colin Forbes, Pentagram · UK · Invitation card

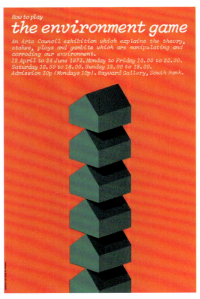

1973 · Alan Fletcher, Pentagram · UK · Poster

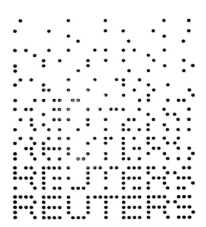

1979 · Mervyn Kurlansky, Pentagram · UK · Brochure

1982 · Alan Fletcher, Pentagram · UK · Poster

1985 · David Hillman, Pentagram · UK · Packaging

1988 · Kit Hinrichs, Pentagram · US · Magazine cover

1988 · Mervyn Kurlansky, Patrick O'Sullivan, Pentagram · UK · Poster

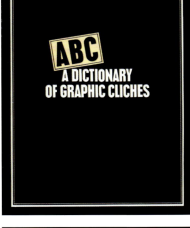

1975 · Pentagram · UK/US · Brochure covers

1972 · Mervyn Kurlansky, Pentagram · UK · Logo · Nobrium

1981 · John McConnell, Pentagram · UK · Logo · Faber & Faber

1985 · Peter Harrison, Kaspar Schmid, Pentagram · UK · Logo · Science Management Corporation

1987 · Alan Fletcher, Pentagram · UK · Logo · Asea Brown Boveri

1991 · John Rushworth, Pentagram · UK · Logo · Crafts Council

Pentagram (1972, London) is a full-service design firm begun by Alan Fletcher (1931, Nairobi – 2006, London), Theo Crosby (1925, Mafeking, South Africa – 1994, London), Colin Forbes (1928, London), Mervyn Kurlansky (1936, Johannesburg), and Kenneth Grange (1929, London). They established a unique form of partnership and interdisciplinary work and the company has since managed to remain independent with more than 40 partners throughout its history. Pentagram's copious work has produced hundreds of identities for many of the world's most famous brands, campaigns, and exhibitions, as well as countless books, magazines, and packaging designs, as a result of their many long-term client relationships.

Pentagram (1972, London) ist ein Fullservice-Designbüro der Gründer Alan Fletcher (1931, Nairobi – 2006, London), Theo Crosby (1925, Mafeking, Südafrika – 1994, London), Colin Forbes (1928, London), Mervyn Kurlansky (1936, Johannesburg) und Kenneth Grange (1929, London). Sie bildeten eine einzigartige Form der Partnerschaft mit einer interdisziplinären Arbeitsweise. Das Studio ist nach wie vor unabhängig und hatte im Lauf seiner Geschichte bislang über vierzig Partner. Zu den unzähligen Arbeiten des Studios gehören aufgrund der langjährigen Kundenbeziehungen Hunderte Identitäten für viele weltberühmte Marken, Kampagnen und Ausstellungen sowie zahllose Bücher, Zeitschriften und Verpackungsdesigns.

Pentagram (1972, Londres) est un studio de design polyvalent fondé par Alan Fletcher (1931, Nairobi – 2006, Londres), Theo Crosby (1925, Mahikeng, Afrique du Sud – 1994, Londres), Colin Forbes (1928, Londres), Mervyn Kurlansky (1936, Johannesbourg) et Kenneth Grange (1929, Londres). Ensemble, ils élaborèrent un type de partenariat et de travail interdisciplinaire entièrement inédit. Depuis, la firme a su préserver son indépendance avec plus de 40 associés tout au long de son histoire. L'énorme production de Pentagram compte des centaines d'identités, campagnes et expositions pour une foule de marques les plus célèbres au monde, ainsi que d'innombrables livres, magazines et emballages, tous fruits des relations à long terme avec leurs clients.

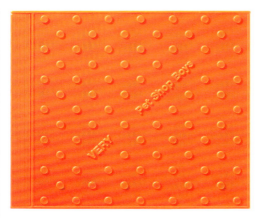

1993 · Daniel Weil, Pentagram · UK · Record cover

2001 · Woody Pirtle, Pentagram · US · Poster

2002 · Angus Hyland, Pentagram · UK · Identity · Eat

2004 · Michael Gericke, Pentagram · US/CA · Signage

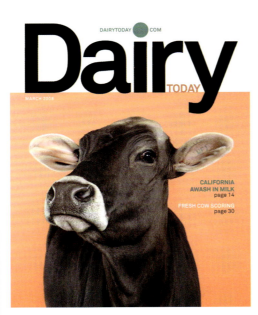

2008 · D.J. Stout, Pentagram · US · Magazine cover

2013 · Marina Willer, Brian Boylan, Pentagram · UK · Identity · Serpentine Galleries

2017 · Abbott Miller, Pentagram · US · Magazine

2017 · Natasha Jen, Pentagram · US · Packaging

2017 · Eddie Opara, Pentagram · US/TH · Environmental graphics

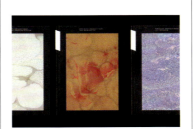

2017 · Harry Pearce, Pentagram · UK · Packaging

2018 · Luke Powell, Jody Hudson-Powell, Pentagram · UK · Identity · London Fashion Week

2018 · Abbott Miller, Naresh Ramchandani, Pentagram · US · Identity · American Express

1997 · Justus Oehler, Pentagram · DE/US · Logo · Star Alliance

2004 · John Rushworth, Pentagram · UK · Logo · Mothercare

2016 · Emily Oberman, Pentagram · US · Logo · DC Entertainment

2016 · Michael Bierut, Luke Hayman, Pentagram · US · Logo · Mastercard

2018 · Paula Scher, Pentagram · US · Logo · Expedia Group

When Munich won the bid to host the Summer Olympics of 1972, the organizers were determined to create a program in complete contrast to that of the 1936 Munich games, which were hijacked by the Nazis as a vehicle for their political ends. Otl Aicher, a pacifist and deserter from the Wehrmacht, was chosen in 1967 to design the identity system for this major sporting event. He put together a team with whom he firstly developed a systematic corporate image on which to base all printed matter, merchandise, and uniforms for the games. For all the simplicity of their designs, the overall effect was dynamic as well as easy on the eye, with a visual rigor that set new standards.

Als München den Zuschlag zur Ausrichtung der Olympischen Sommerspiele 1972 erhielt, wollten die Organisatoren ein Gegenprogramm zu den von den Nationalsozialisten missbrauchten Spielen von 1936 präsentieren. Der Pazifist und Kriegsdeserteur Otl Aicher wurde 1967 ausgewählt, um die visuelle Identität des Sportevents zu entwickeln. Er stellte ein Team zusammen, mit dem er zunächst ein systematisches Erscheinungsbild entwickelte und auf dieser Basis sämtliche Drucksachen, Merchandisingartikel und Uniformen der Spiele ausarbeitete. Bei aller gestalterischen Strenge entstand ein höchst lebendiger und freundlicher Gesamtauftritt, dessen visuelle Stringenz neue Standards setzte.

Lorsque Munich fut retenue pour organiser les jeux Olympiques d'été de 1972, les organisateurs voulurent se démarquer totalement du programme des jeux de 1936, qui avaient été politiquement détournés par les nazis. En 1967, le pacifiste et déserteur de la Wehrmacht Otl Aicher fut chargé de concevoir l'identité visuelle de l'événement. Il constitua une équipe et commença par élaborer une image systématique comme base de travail pour tous les imprimés, articles de merchandising et uniformes des jeux. Malgré la simplicité de la conception visuelle, il en résulta globalement une image extrêmement vivante et chaleureuse dont la cohérence établit de nouveaux standards.

1972 · Coordt von Mannstein (symbol), Otl Aicher · DE · Logo

1972 · Otl Aicher · DE · Identity

1972 · Otl Aicher, Rolf Müller · DE · Brochure spread

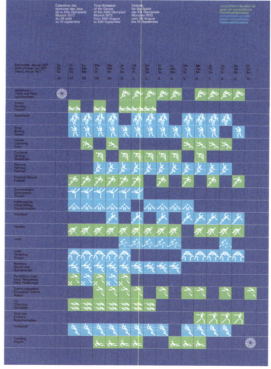

1972 · Otl Aicher · DE · Poster

1972 · Otl Aicher · DE · Poster

1972 · Otl Aicher · DE · Identity

DOCUMENTAL CUBANO   DIRECCION OCTAVIO CORTAZAR

sobre un primer combate

bachs 72

1972 · Eduardo Muñoz Bachs · CU · Poster

Eduardo Muñoz Bachs (1937, Valencia – 2001, Havana) was a Spanish-born visual artist whose family emigrated to Cuba in 1941. He is considered the most important film poster artist of the Caribbean island, and frequently employed handmade typography. Muñoz Bachs was a self-taught painter, illustrator, and draftsman whose prolific body of work included over 2,000 film posters. After the 1959 revolution, he became a leading artist at the new Instituto Cubano de Arte e Industria Cinematográficos (ICAIC), founded to promote the country's film industry.

Eduardo Muñoz Bachs (1937, Valencia – 2001, Havanna) war ein bildender Künstler spanischer Abstammung, dessen Familie 1941 nach Kuba auswanderte. Er gilt als bedeutendster Filmplakatkünstler der karibischen Insel und arbeitete häufig mit handgemachten Typografien. Das umfangreiche Schaffen des autodidaktisch geschulten Malers, Illustrators und Zeichners umfasste über 2000 Filmplakate. Nach der Revolution von 1959 wurde Muñoz Bachs zum maßgeblichen Künstler am neuen Instituto Cubano de Arte e Industria Cinematográficos (ICAIC), das zur Förderung der kubanischen Filmindustrie gegründet worden war.

Eduardo Muñoz Bachs (1937, Valence – 2001, La Havane) fut un artiste visuel d'origine espagnole dont la famille émigra à Cuba en 1941. Il est considéré comme le plus important concepteur d'affiches de cinéma de l'île caribéenne et il se servait souvent de typographies de son cru. Muñoz Bachs fut un peintre, illustrateur et dessinateur autodidacte dont le vaste héritage compte plus de 2000 affiches de films. Après la révolution cubaine de 1959, il devint un artiste majeur au nouvel Institut cubain des arts et de l'industrie cinématographiques (ICAIC), fondé pour promouvoir l'industrie cinématographique du pays.

1972 · Eduardo Muñoz Bachs · CU · Poster

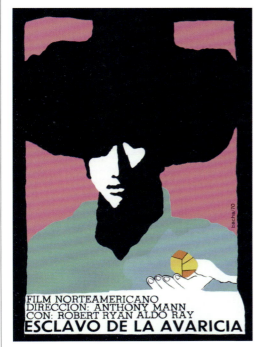

1970 · Eduardo Muñoz Bachs · CU · Poster

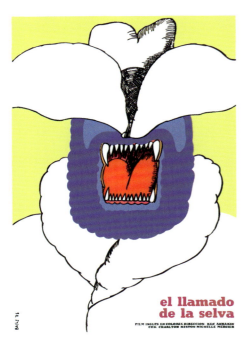

1975 · Eduardo Muñoz Bachs · CU · Poster

1969 · Eduardo Muñoz Bachs · CU · Poster

1977 · Eduardo Muñoz Bachs · CU · Poster

1977 · Eduardo Muñoz Bachs · CU · Poster

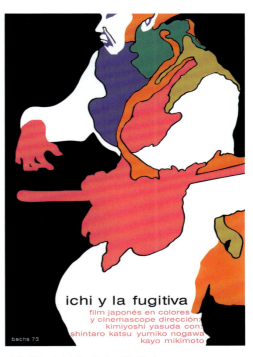

1973 · Eduardo Muñoz Bachs · CU · Poster

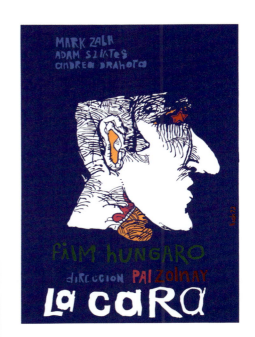

1972 · Eduardo Muñoz Bachs · CU · Poster

In Poland under Communist rule, the country's circuses were all administered by a government agency, and in 1962, the first Cyrk posters were duly commissioned. One by one, all the leading Polish designers then working were given contracts to contribute to this special series of images based on the general theme of circuses. The inclusion of the word "Cyrk" was the only recurring element in these designs, and hundreds of images were produced, well into the 1980s, which quickly became coveted collectors' items. They still provide impressive proof of the powerful visual impact of Polish poster design.

Unter der kommunistischen Regierung in Polen war eine staatliche Agentur für das gesamte nationale Zirkuswesen zuständig. 1962 gab sie die ersten „Cyrk"-Plakate in Auftrag. Nach und nach erhielten alle wichtigen polnischen Gestalter einen Auftrag, in dieser besonderen Serie Visualisierungen rund um das Thema Zirkus zu finden. Die Unterbringung des Wortes „Cyrk" war dabei die einzige gestalterische Konstante. Bis in die 1980er-Jahre entstanden so Hunderte von Motiven, die schnell zu begehrten Sammelobjekten wurden und bis heute ein eindrucksvoller Beweis für die visuelle Kraft des polnischen Plakats sind.

Dans la Pologne communiste, une agence gouvernementale chapeautait l'ensemble des cirques du pays. En 1962, elle commanda les premières affiches «Cyrk». Peu à peu, tous les graphistes polonais importants furent chargés de concevoir des solutions visuelles sur le thème du cirque, la présence du mot «Cyrk» étant la seule contrainte graphique imposée. Jusque dans les années 1980, des centaines de créations virent ainsi le jour et devinrent rapidement des objets de collection très prisés. Aujourd'hui encore, elles symbolisent toute la puissance visuelle de l'affiche polonaise.

1970s · Wiktor Górka · PL · Poster

»The modernized circus naturally calls for modernizing advertising and in particular for a new approach to the poster. [...] It was not easy to overcome the initial resistance to this change. It came in part from the general public, but in an even stronger form from circus people themselves.« Jerzy Wasniewski, *Graphis* #128, 1966

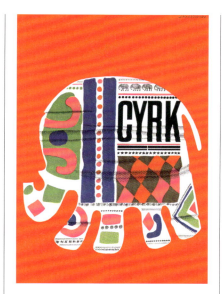

1967 · Jan Młodożeniec · PL · Poster

1972 · Waldemar Świerzy · PL · Poster

1974 · Romuald Socha · PL · Poster

1970 · Hubert Hilscher · PL · Poster

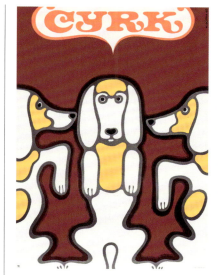

1969 · Wiktor Górka · PL · Poster

1974 · Janowski · PL · Poster

1970 · Hubert Hilscher · PL · Poster

1973

Graphis magazine publishes a first feature on computer-generated graphics

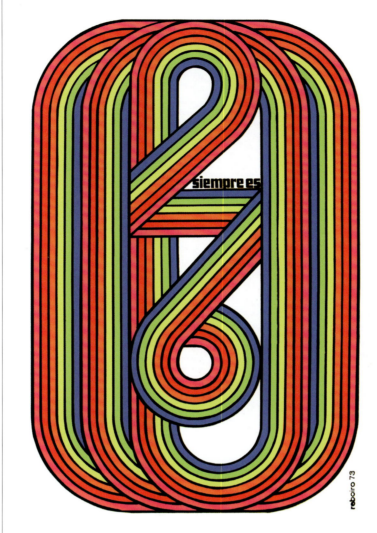

1973 · Antonio Reboiro · CU · Poster

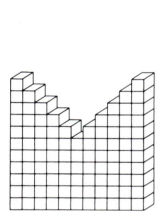

1973 · Angelo Sganzerla · IT · Logo · Multhipla

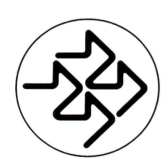

1973 · Peter Seitz · US · Logo · Jefferson Buslines

1973 · Benoy Sarkar · IN · Logo · Indian Airlines

41-a INTERNACIA
FOIRO DE BARCELONO
2-a 12-a JUNIO 1973

1973 · Anonymous · ES · Poster

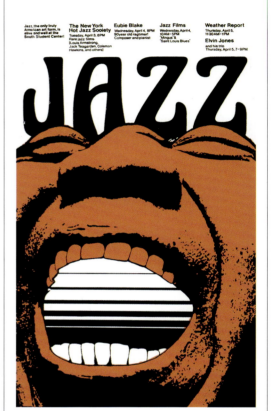

1973 · Gary Viskupic · US · Poster

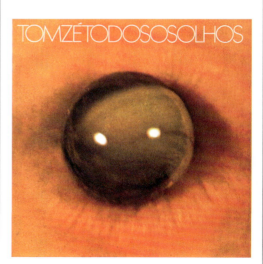

1973 · Décio Pignatari, Marcos Pedro Ferreira, Francisco Eduardo de Andrade · BR · Record cover

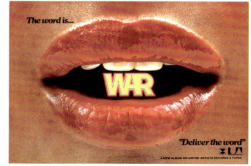

1973 · Anonymous · US · Ad

1973 · Guillermo González Ruíz, Ronald Shakespear · AR · Identity, Signage · City of Buenos Aires

1973 · Franco Maria Ricci · IT · Poster

1973 · Wiktor Górka · PL · Poster

1973 · Ettore Vitale · IT · Poster

1973 · Giulio Confalonieri · IT · Poster

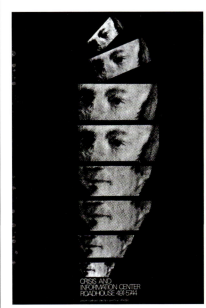

1973 · John J. Sorbie · US · Poster

1973 · Hipgnosis, George Hardie (ILL) · UK · Record cover

1973 · Jurriaan Schrofer · NL · Brochure cover

1973 · Morteza Momayez · IR · Poster

1990 · Morteza Momayez · IR · Poster

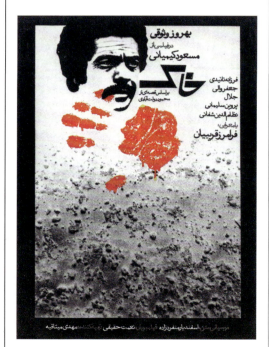

1975 · Morteza Momayez · IR · Poster

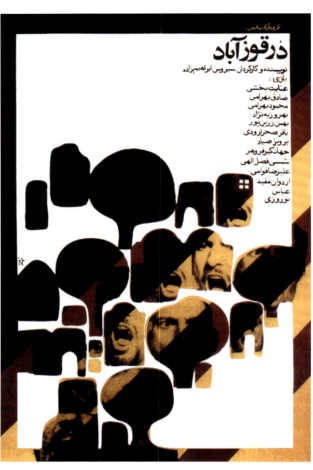

1973 · Morteza Momayez · IR · Poster

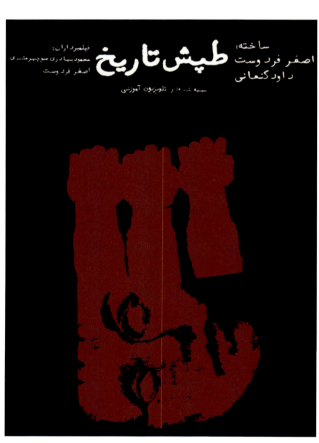

1980 · Morteza Momayez · IR · Poster

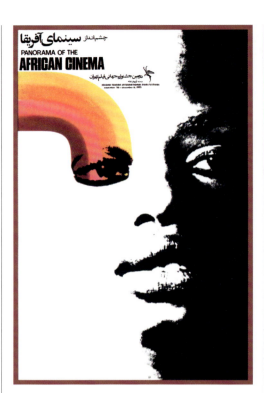

1973 · Morteza Momayez · IR · Poster

1974 · Morteza Momayez · IR · Poster

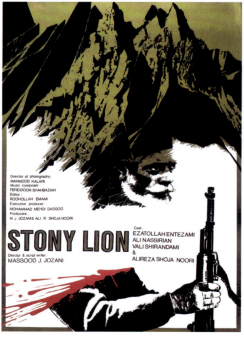

1987 · Morteza Momayez · IR · Poster

Morteza Momayez (1935–2002, Tehran) was an Iranian visual artist and co-founder of the Iranian Graphic Design Society (IGDS). A catalyst for design in the country, Momayez was the force behind a number of cultural institutes, publications, and graphic design exhibitions, including the Tehran International Poster Biennial. He attended the School of Fine Art at the University of Tehran, and the École Nationale Supérieure des Arts Décoratifs in Paris. One of the few designers in the region to gain international recognition, Momayez produced posters, logos, and book covers, for which he received several awards.

Morteza Momayez (1935–2002, Teheran) war ein iranischer Künstler und Mitbegründer der Iranian Graphic Design Society (IGDS). Momayez spielte im einheimischen Design die Rolle eines Katalysators und initiierte als solcher eine Reihe von Kulturinstitutionen, Publikationen und Grafikausstellungen wie etwa die Tehran International Poster Biennial. Er studierte an der Kunsthochschule der Universität Teheran und an der École Nationale Supérieure des Arts Décoratifs in Paris. Momayez, einer der wenigen Grafikdesigner in der Region, die auch international Anerkennung fanden, entwarf Plakate, Logos und Buchumschläge, die ihm mehrere Auszeichnungen eintrugen.

Morteza Momayez (1935–2002, Téhéran) fut un artiste visuel iranien et un des fondateurs de l'IGDS (Iranian Graphic Designers Society). Momayez joua un rôle de catalyseur pour le design dans son pays et fut le moteur de nombreux instituts culturels, publications et expositions de graphisme, notamment la Biennale internationale de l'affiche de Téhéran. Après des études à l'École des beaux-arts de l'université de Téhéran et à l'École nationale supérieure des Arts Décoratifs à Paris, il devint un des rares designers locaux à bénéficier d'une reconnaissance internationale. Momayez a produit des affiches, des logos et des couvertures de livres qui lui ont valu plusieurs prix.

1973 · Morteza Momayez · IR · Poster

159

The first issue of *Ms* appeared in the summer of 1972, and with the comic-book heroine Wonder Woman gracing the cover it was a clear statement that *Ms* had nothing in common with traditional women's magazines. This was the first time a publication designed to have popular appeal would focus on feminism and the women's movement, and in support of that aim Bea Feitler developed a uniquely personal style for the magazine's illustrations.

Im Sommer 1972 erschien die Erstausgabe von *Ms*. Das Cover zeigt die Comicheldin Wonder Woman und unterstreicht so, dass das Magazin mit traditionellen Frauenzeitschriften nichts gemein hat. Erstmals beschäftigte sich ein populär aufgemachtes Heft mit Themen der Frauenbewegung und des Feminismus. Bea Feitler entwickelte dafür einen ganz eigenen visuellen Stil.

C'est à l'été 1972 que parut le premier numéro de *Ms*. La couverture montrait l'héroïne de bande dessinée Wonder Woman, soulignant le fait que le magazine n'avait rien à voir avec ceux de la presse féminine traditionnelle. Pour la première fois, une revue à vocation populaire abordait des thèmes du mouvement féministe. Bea Feitler développa pour ces illustrations un style visuel tout à fait personnel qui servait la cause.

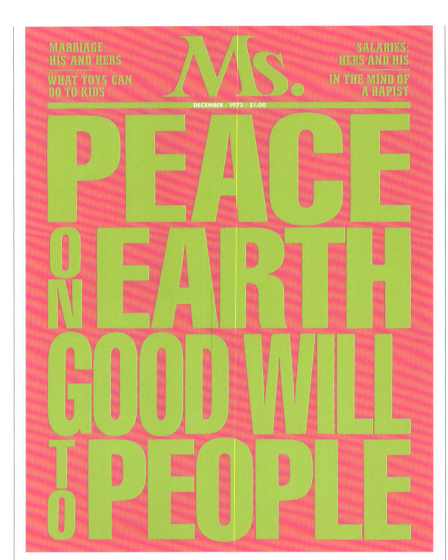

1972 · Bea Feitler · BR/US · Magazine cover

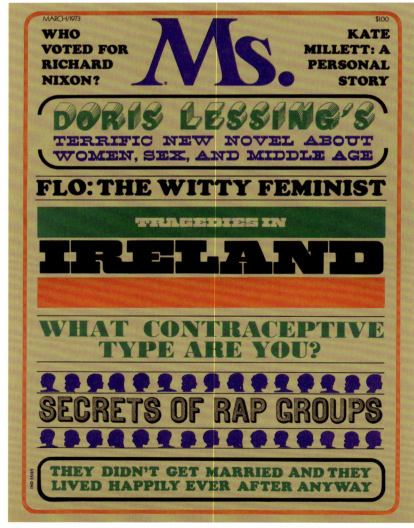

1973 · Bea Feitler · BR/US · Magazine cover

1972 · Bea Feitler · BR/US · Magazine cover

1972 · Bea Feitler · BR/US · Magazine cover

1974 · Bea Feitler · BR/US · Magazine cover

Bea Feitler (1938–1982, Rio de Janeiro) was a visionary Brazilian art director who greatly pushed the boundaries of editorial design. Feitler studied at Parsons School of Design where her use of photography and her experimental approach soon made her name on the New York design scene, securing commissions for books, record sleeves, and fashion brands. Her extensive work on magazines, notably for *Harper's Bazaar* and *Rolling Stone,* sealed her reputation. In 1982, Feitler redesigned the new *Vanity Fair,* though died of cancer before it was published at the age of only 44.

Bea Feitler (1938–1982, Rio de Janeiro) war eine visionäre brasilianische Artdirectorin, die die Grenzen des Zeitschriftendesigns radikal erweiterte. Feitler studierte an der Parsons School of Design in New York, wo sie sich mit ihrer Verwendung von Fotografie und ihrem experimentellen Ansatz schon bald einen Namen in der dortigen Designszene machte, was ihr Aufträge für Bücher, Plattencover und Modemarken einbrachte. Ihr umfangreiches Schaffen im Zeitschriftensektor, namentlich für *Harper's Bazaar* und *Rolling Stone,* trug zur Festigung ihres Rufs bei. 1982 gestaltete Feitler das neue Erscheinungsbild von *Vanity Fair,* starb aber schon vor der Veröffentlichung mit nur 44 Jahren an Krebs.

Bea Feitler (1938–1982, Rio de Janeiro) fut une directrice artistique brésilienne visionnaire qui repoussa fortement les limites du graphisme éditorial. Feitler suivit des études à la Parsons School of Design, où son utilisation de la photographie et son approche expérimentale lui permirent de se faire un nom sur la scène du design new-yorkais. S'ensuivirent des commandes pour des livres, des pochettes d'albums et des marques de mode. Son travail de grande envergure pour des magazines, particulièrement pour *Harper's Bazaar* et *Rolling Stone,* assurèrent sa réputation. En 1982, Feitler redessina le nouveau *Vanity Fair,* mais succomba à un cancer avant sa publication, à l'âge de seulement 44 ans.

1968 · Bea Feitler, Richard Avedon (PH) · BR/US · Magazine cover

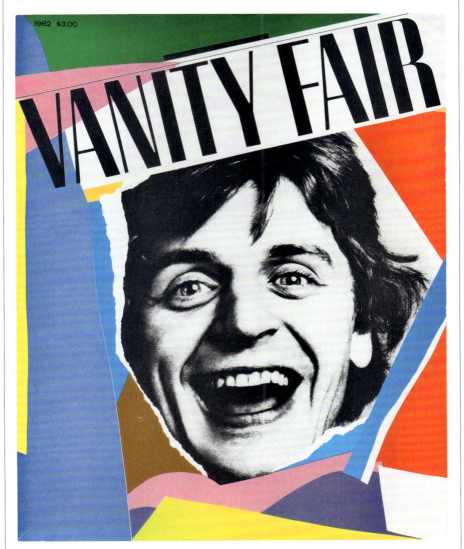

1982 · Bea Feitler · BR/US · Magazine cover

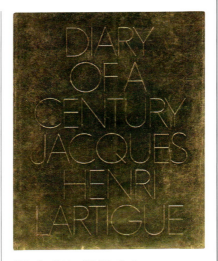

1970 · Bea Feitler · BR/US · Book cover

1976 · Bea Feitler · BR/US · Book cover

1976 · Bea Feitler, Helmut Newton (PH) · BR/US · Book cover

1980 · Bea Feitler · BR/US · Book cover

Gerd Leufert · Venezuela

1952 · Gerd Leufert · VE · Logo · Venezuelan Supply

1960s · Gerd Leufert · VE · Logo · Control Center

1968 · Gerd Leufert · VE · Logo · Imposibilia

1970 · Gerd Leufert · VE · Logo · Museo Jesús Soto

1957 · Gerd Leufert · VE · Logo · Pierre Denis

1964 · Gerd Leufert · VE · Logo · Instituto de Diseño

1968 · Gerd Leufert · VE · Logo · Visibilia Caracas

1971 · Gerd Leufert · VE · Logo · Del Libro sin Arco

1967 · Gerd Leufert · VE · Logo · Teatro Estable de Maracay

1967 · Gerd Leufert · VE · Logo · Cafetin Cafeteria

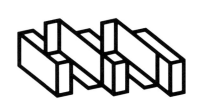

1969 · Gerd Leufert · VE · Logo · Architecture 70

1974 · Gerd Leufert · VE · Logo · Instituto Autónomo Aeropuerto Internacional de Maiquetía Simón

1965 · Gerd Leufert · VE · Logo · Consejo de Artesanías

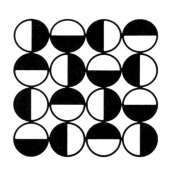

1969 · Gerd Leufert · VE · Logo · Color, Línea, Luz

1971 · Gerd Leufert · VE · Logo · Biblioteca Nacional

1978 · Gerd Leufert · VE · Logo · Escuela de Arte

1970 · Gerd Leufert · VE · Logo · Refolit

1970 · Gerd Leufert · VE · Logo · Conicit

1971 · Gerd Leufert · VE · Logo · Del Libro sin Arco

1979 · Gerd Leufert · VE · Logo · Estudio Uno

Gerd Leufert (1914, Klaipèda, Lithuania – 1998, Caracas) was a German-Venezuelan designer and a visual communication pioneer in South America. Leufert studied at the Academy of Fine Arts in Munich in 1939, and in the same city took over as head of the studio Bayerisches Bild in 1947. Emigrating to Venezuela in 1952, he built his reputation by producing striking corporate identities, infusing modernist concepts from Europe into South American design. Later in life, Leufert dedicated a great part of his time to teaching, painting, and sculpture.

Gerd Leufert (1914, Klaipèda [Memel], Litauen – 1998, Caracas) war ein deutsch-venezolanischer Grafikdesigner und Wegbereiter der visuellen Kommunikation in Südamerika. Leufert studierte 1939 an der Akademie der Bildenden Künste in München und übernahm dort 1947 die Leitung des Studios Bayerisches Bild. 1952 wanderte er nach Venezuela aus, wo er sich mit seinen Entwürfen prägnanter Corporate Identities einen Namen machte; gleichzeitig führte er damit moderne europäische Konzepte in das südamerikanische Design ein. In den späteren Jahren widmete Leufert einen großen Teil seiner Zeit dem Unterrichten, der Malerei und der Skulptur.

Gerd Leufert (1914, Klaipèda, Lituanie – 1998, Caracas) fut un designer germano-vénézuélien et pionnier de la communication visuelle en Amérique du Sud. Après des études à l'Académie des beaux-arts de Munich en 1939, Leufert prit dans cette même ville la tête du studio Bayerisches Bild en 1947. Après son émigration au Venezuela en 1952, il bâtit sa réputation en produisant de remarquables images de marque introduisant les concepts modernistes européens dans le graphisme d'Amérique du Sud. Plus tard dans sa vie, Leufert consacra une grande partie de son temps à l'enseignement, à la peinture et à la sculpture.

1968 · Gerd Leufert · VE · Identity · Caracas Hilton

1968 · Gerd Leufert · VE · Poster

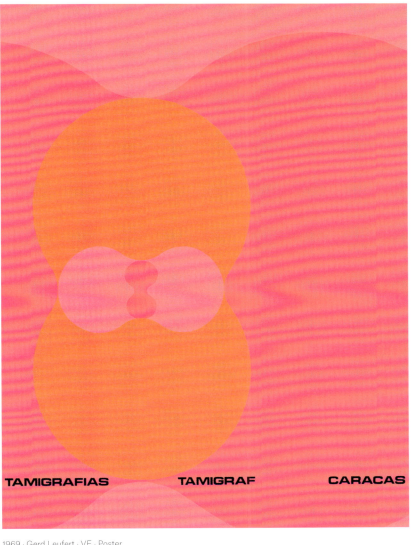

1969 · Gerd Leufert · VE · Poster

1965 · Gerd Leufert · VE · Magazine cover

1973 · Gerd Leufert · VE · Brochure cover

1973 · Gerd Leufert · VE · Poster

1974

John Murphy and his wife open the branding consultancy Novamark, which evolves to become **Interbrand** in 1979

The first issue of the typography magazine **Upper and Lower Case** is published

1974 · Italo Lupi, Liliana Collavo · IT · Magazine cover

1974 · Helmut Schmidt-Rhen · DE · Poster

NASA

1974 · Danne & Blackburn · US · Logo · NASA

ERCO

1974 · Otl Aicher · DE · Logo · Erco

1974 · Anton Stankowski · DE · Logo · Deutsche Bank

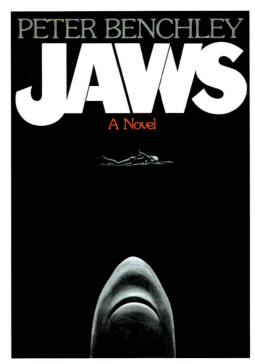

1974 · Paul Bacon · US · Book cover

1974 · Peter Geitner · DE · Record cover

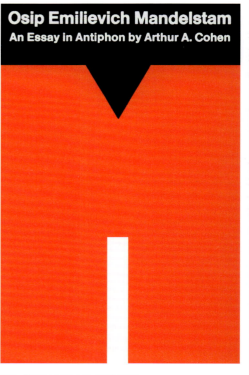

1974 · Elaine Lustig · US · Book cover

To be war not to be?

1974 · Mieczysław Wasilewski · PL · Poster

Mieczyslaw Wasilewski – Poland

Poster from an international competition organised in Poland

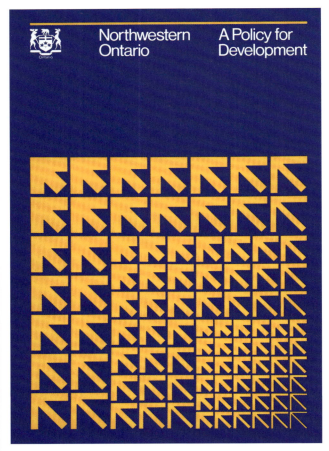

1972 · Burton Kramer · CA · Brochure cover

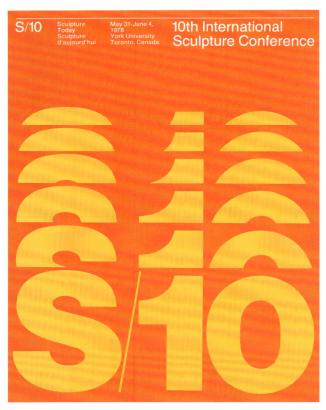

1978 · Burton Kramer · CA · Brochure cover

Burton Kramer (1932, New York) is a Canadian graphic designer and artist who studied visual communication at Yale and the Institute of Design in Chicago. Kramer first worked as an assistant to Will Burtin in New York, then at the Geigy Chemical Corp. before becoming art director at the Erwin Halpern advertising agency in Zurich. He moved to Toronto in 1965, where he designed graphics, signage, and the map system for Expo 67 in Montreal, then was design director at Clairtone Sound Corp. In the same year he founded Kramer Design Associates, and went on to create the logo for the Canadian Broadcasting Corp. in 1974. Kramer was a professor at the Ontario College of Art and Design for over 20 years.

Burton Kramer (1932, New York) ist ein kanadischer Künstler und Grafikdesigner, der in Yale und am Institute of Design in Chicago visuelle Kommunikation studierte. Kramer arbeitete zunächst als Assistent von Will Burtin in New York, dann bei Geigy Chemical, und später wurde er Artdirector in der Zürcher Werbeagentur Erwin Halpern. Er zog 1965 nach Toronto, wo er die Grafik für die Expo 67 in Montreal gestaltete, darunter auch das Wegeleitsystem, dann wurde er Designdirector bei Clairtone Sound Corp. Im selben Jahr gründete er die Agentur Kramer Design Associates, mit der er unter anderem 1974 das Logo für die Canadian Broadcasting Corp. entwarf. Kramer lehrte über 20 Jahre lang als Professor am Ontario College of Art and Design.

Burton Kramer (1932, New York) est un artiste et graphiste canadien formé en communication visuelle à l'université Yale et à l'Institute of Design à Chicago. Kramer a d'abord travaillé à New York en qualité d'assistant de Will Burtin, puis pour Geigy Chemical Corp., avant de devenir directeur artistique de l'agence de publicité Erwin Halpern à Zurich. À son installation à Toronto en 1965, il a produit le graphisme, la signalétique et les plans de l'Exposition universelle de Montréal (1967), puis a été engagé chez Clairtone Sound Corp. comme directeur du design. La même année, il a fondé Kramer Design Associates et en 1974, il a créé le logo de la Canadian Broadcasting Corp. Kramer a enseigné à l'Université de l'École d'art et de design de l'Ontario pendant plus de vingt ans.

Version 1/Grid   Version 1 Quadrillage

The grid shown below will clearly indicate the exact relationships of all elements comprising symbol Version 1. Although this version should, whenever possible, be reproduced from master copies contained in this manual, the occasion may arise when, for display, exhibition, interiors, etc., there will be a need to construct a symbol drawing. In such an event, the grid shown here is to be followed accurately to ensure proper relationships.

Le quadrillage ci-dessous indique clairement les proportions exactes de tous les éléments formant la version 1 de l'emblème. Bien que cette version de l'emblème doive être reproduite d'après des modèles figurant dans ce manuel, il peut arriver que pour une présentation, une exposition, des intérieurs, etc., on ait besoin de reconstituer un dessin de l'emblème. Dans ces cas-là, il faudra minutieusement suivre ce quadrillage pour garantir les proportions exactes.

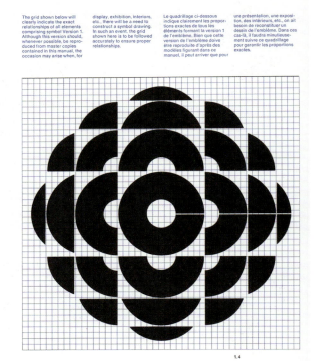

1.4

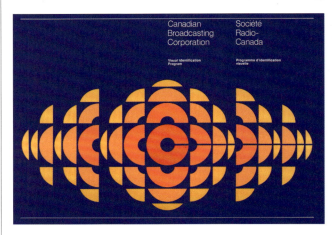

1974 · Burton Kramer · CA · Identity · Canadian Broadcasting Corporation

1961 · Burton Kramer · CA · Logo · Ytong Construction

1968 · Burton Kramer · CA · Logo · Student Action for International Dialogue

1971 · Burton Kramer · CA · Logo · Kuypers Adamson Norton

1975 · Burton Kramer · CA · Logo · Pinestone Inn Hotel

1965 · Burton Kramer · CA · Logo · Canadian Society & Anthropology Association

1969 · Burton Kramer · CA · Logo · Children's Playgrounds

1972 · Burton Kramer · CA · Logo · Canada Systems Group

1977 · Burton Kramer · CA · Logo · Hallmark Hotels

1967 · Burton Kramer · CA · Logo · BBR Canada

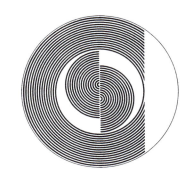

1969 · Burton Kramer · CA · Logo · Craft Dimensions Canada

1972 · Burton Kramer · CA · Logo · York Construction

1980 · Burton Kramer · CA · Logo · Copps Coliseum

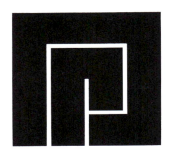

1967 · Burton Kramer · CA · Logo · Peter Robinson Industrial Design

1969 · Burton Kramer · CA · Logo · Gentil Plastics

1973 · Burton Kramer · CA · Logo · Anglo-Canadian Pulp & Paper

1980 · Burton Kramer · CA · Logo · Glassworks Toronto

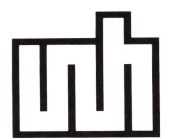

1967 · Burton Kramer · CA · Logo · Werner Herterich Associates

1969 · Burton Kramer · CA · Logo · Hamilton Hastings

1974 · Burton Kramer · CA · Logo · Reed Paper

1978 · Burton Kramer · CA · Logo · Trade Typesetting

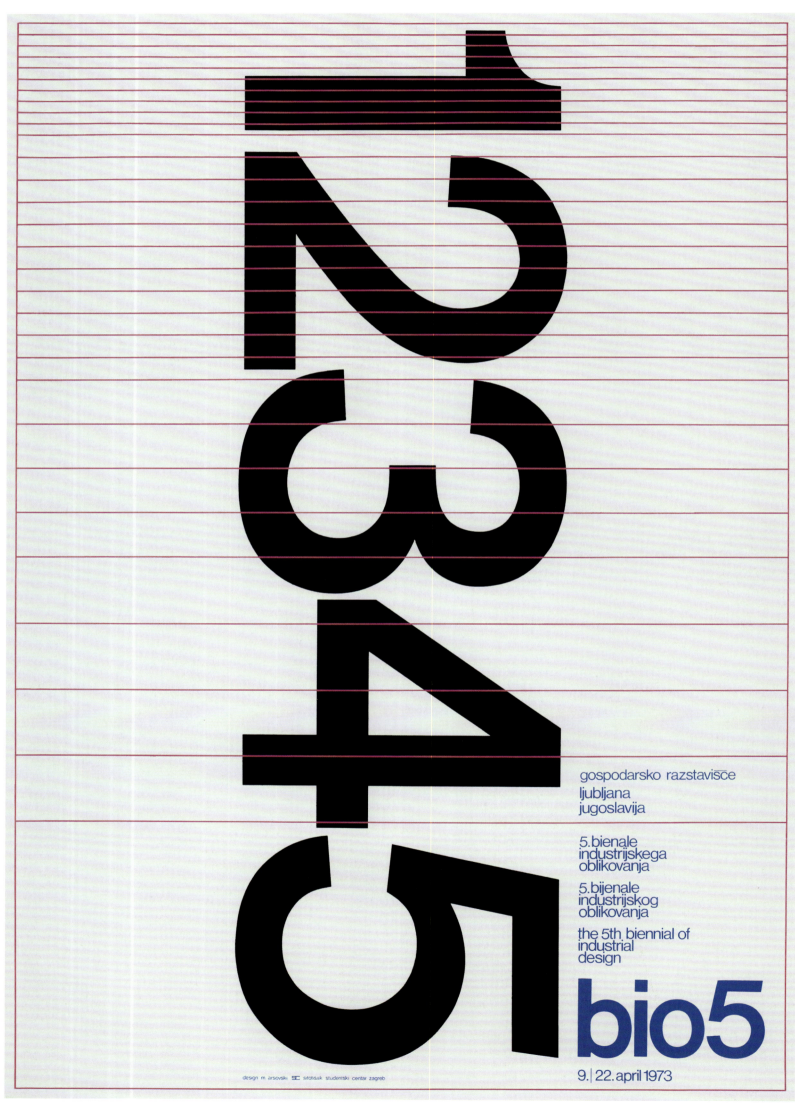

1973 · Mihajlo Arsovski · HR · Poster

1966 · Mihajlo Arsovski · HR · Poster

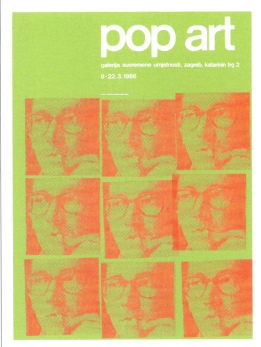

1966 · Mihajlo Arsovski · HR · Poster

1968 · Mihajlo Arsovski · HR · Poster

Mihajlo Arsovski (1937, Skopje, Macedonia) is a Croatian graphic artist. Arsovski studied art history and architecture in Zagreb, before discovering his talent as a poster artist; his work during the 1960s often featured a subtle critique of the Soviet-supported regime of Yugoslavian dictator Josip Tito. Managing to avoid becoming a propaganda artist for the state, he developed into one of the most prominent design figures in the region, in company with Boris Bućan. Combining smart typography, photomontage, and collage, Arsovski is especially noted for his poster work for the ITD Theater in Zagreb.

Mihajlo Arsovski (1937, Skopje, heute Mazedonien) ist ein kroatischer Grafikdesigner, der in Zagreb Kunstgeschichte und Architektur studierte, um später sein Talent als Plakatkünstler zu entdecken. Sein Schaffen der 1960er-Jahre enthielt oft eine subtile Kritik an dem von den Sowjets unterstützten Regime des jugoslawischen Diktators Josip Tito. Er konnte es vermeiden, zu einem Künstler für Staatspropaganda zu werden, und entwickelte sich neben Boris Bućan zu einem der prominentesten Designer in der Region. Arsovski, der intelligente Typografie mit Collage und Fotomontage kombiniert, ist vor allem für seine Plakate für das ITD Theater in Zagreb bekannt.

Mihajlo Arsovski (1937, Skopje, Macédoine) est un artiste graphiste croate. C'est seulement après des études d'histoire de l'art et d'architecture qu'il découvre son talent d'affichiste. Ses œuvres des années 1960 dénotent souvent une critique subtile du régime du dictateur yougoslave Josip Tito soutenu par l'Union soviétique. Il réussit toutefois à ne pas devenir un artiste de propagande au service de l'État et s'impose comme une des plus éminentes figures locales avec Boris Bućan. Associant savamment la typographie, le collage et le photomontage, Arsovski s'est fait particulièrement remarquer par ses affiches pour le théâtre ITD à Zagreb.

1971 · Mihajlo Arsovski · HR · Poster

1974 · Mihajlo Arsovski · HR · Poster

David Hillman · United Kingdom

David Hillman (1943, Oxford, England) is a British designer with a vast portfolio, ranging from editorial design and identities to stamps and web design. A partner at Pentagram in London since 1978, Hillman worked at the agency for clients across the world for nearly three decades before opening his own practice in 2006, Studio David Hillman. He attended the London School of Printing, and was later made a Fellow at the Royal College of Art. Hillman redesigned the *Guardian* newspaper in 1988, and is also D&AD's most awarded designer of all time.

David Hillman (1943, Oxford, England) ist ein britischer Grafikdesigner, dessen breit gefächertes Schaffen von Zeitschriftengestaltung und Corporate Identities bis zu Briefmarken und Webdesign reicht. Als Partner von Pentagram in London seit 1978 arbeitete Hillman fast drei Jahrzehnte lang für Auftraggeber auf der ganzen Welt, ehe er 2006 mit Studio David Hillman sein eigenes Büro eröffnete. Er besuchte die London School of Printing und wurde später zum Fellow am Royal College of Art ernannt. Hillman gestaltete 1988 die Tageszeitung *The Guardian* neu und ist bei der D&AD derjenige Grafikdesigner, der die meisten Auszeichnungen aller Zeiten erhielt.

David Hillman (1943, Oxford, Angleterre) est un designer britannique dont le vaste portefeuille s'étend du design éditorial et des identités visuelles à des timbres et à la conception de sites Web. Collaborateur du studio londonien Pentagram depuis 1978, Hillman a travaillé pour des clients du monde entier pendant trois décennies avant d'ouvrir en 2006 sa propre agence, Studio David Hillman. Après des études à la London School of Printing, il a reçu plus tard le titre de *Fellow* du Royal College of Art. Hillman a fait une refonte totale du journal *The Guardian* en 1988 et il est aussi le designer le plus primé de tous les temps de la D&AD.

1972 · David Hillman, Harri Peccinotti (PH) · UK · Magazine cover

1971 · David Hillman, Hans Feurer (PH) · UK · Magazine cover

From 1969 to 1975 the British designer David Hillman was responsible for the art direction of *Nova* magazine, which Hillman himself referred to as the "women's magazine for everyone." An unusual way of presenting contemporary photography, exciting layouts, and an innovative editorial policy all made *Nova* an exhilarating lifestyle publication in the era of Swinging London.

Zwischen 1969 und 1975 war der britische Designer David Hillman für die Gestaltung der Zeitschrift *Nova* verantwortlich, die sich als „women's magazine for everyone" positionierte. Ein ungewöhnlicher Umgang mit zeitgenössischer Fotografie, anregende Layouts und innovative redaktionelle Ideen machten die Hefte zu aufregenden Lifestyleobjekten in den Zeiten von „Swinging London".

De 1969 à 1975, le graphiste britannique David Hillman fut chargé du design éditorial de la revue *Nova*, que lui-même qualifiait de «magazine féminin pour tout le monde». Grâce à un maniement inhabituel de la photographie contemporaine, aux mises en pages attirantes et aux idées rédactionnelles innovantes, *Nova* s'est vu comme un passionnant magazine d'art de vivre à l'époque du «Swinging London».

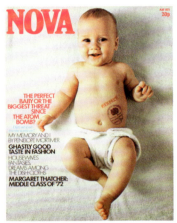

1972 · David Hillman, Tony Evans (PH) · UK · Magazine cover

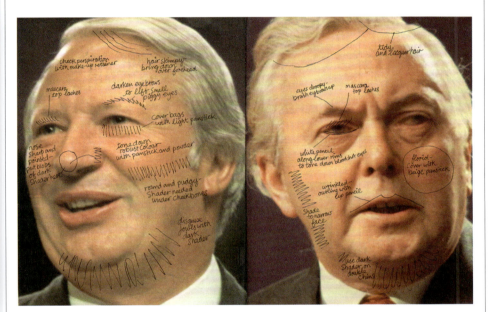

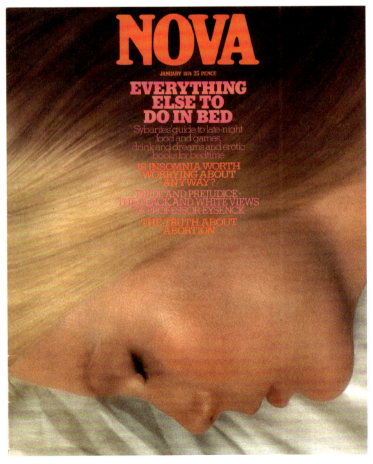

1974 · David Hillman · UK · Magazine spreads

1974 · David Hillman, Harri Peccinotti (PH) · UK · Magazine cover

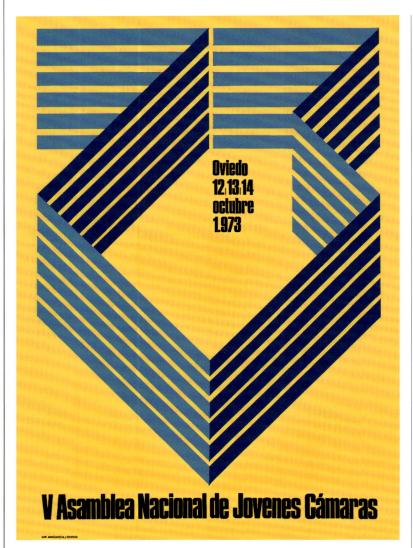

1973 · José Santamarina · ES · Poster

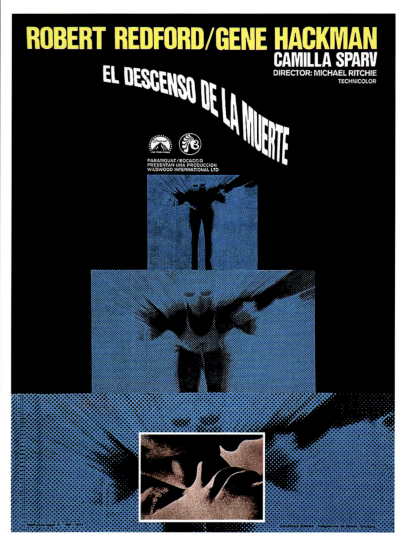

1974 · José Santamarina · ES · Poster

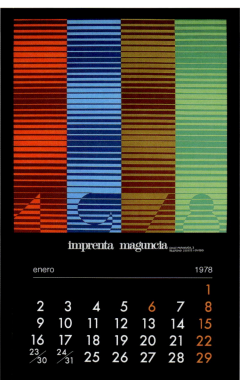

1974 · José Santamarina · ES · Calendar

José Santamarina (1941, Oviedo) is a Spanish designer and educator who taught at the Escuela de Artes Aplicadas y Oficios Artisticos in Zaragoza. After initially working in advertising he founded the design studio Elías & Santamarina in 1969 with Elías García Benavides, before moving into a shared studio with his children Carmen and Miguel in 1997, Santamarina Disenadores. His approach to design has had a great influence in Spain through its combination of national heritage with modern visual interpretations, and his work has been widely exhibited at home and abroad.

José Santamarina (1941, Oviedo) ist ein spanischer Grafikdesigner und Dozent, der an der Escuela de Artes Aplicadas y Oficios Artísticos in Zaragoza lehrte. Santamarina war zunächst in der Werbung tätig, 1969 dann gründete er mit seinem Partner Elías García Benavides das Studio Elías+Santamarina; später arbeitete er gemeinsam mit seinen Kindern Carmen und Miguel in seinem Studio Santamarina Diseñadores. In seinen einflussreichen Ideen für Grafikdesign in Spanien verband er moderne visuelle Interpretationen mit landestypischen Wurzeln. Sein Werk kam vielfach zur Ausstellung, sowohl in Spanien als auch weltweit.

José Santamarina (1941, Oviedo) est un graphiste et professeur espagnol qui a enseigné à la Escuela de Artes Aplicadas y Oficios Artísticos de Saragosse. Santamarina a d'abord travaillé dans le domaine publicitaire avant de fonder Elías+Santamarina en 1969 en partenariat avec Elías García Benavides. En 1997, il partage son studio avec ses enfants Carmen et Miguel sous l'appellation Santamarina Diseñadores. Son approche influente du graphisme en Espagne associe des racines nationales et des interprétations visuelles modernes. Son travail a été abondamment exposé dans son pays et à l'étranger.

1983 · José Santamarina · ES · Logo · Promusel Cargo

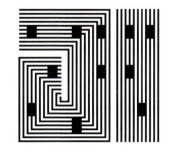

1967 · José Santamarina · ES · Logo · Asturiana de Informática

1970 · José Santamarina · ES · Logo · Ébano Boutique

1978 · José Santamarina · ES · Logo · Macias

1978 · José Santamarina · ES · Logo · Balbuena

1969 · José Santamarina · ES · Logo · Madin

1973 · José Santamarina · ES · Logo · Progression

1978 · José Santamarina · ES · Logo · F. Guardado

1970 · José Santamarina · ES · Logo · Estavisol

1970 · José Santamarina · ES · Logo · Muebles Arias

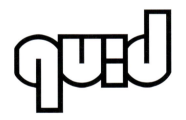

1984 · José Santamarina · ES · Logo · Quid

1979 · José Santamarina · ES · Logo · Rotur

1975 · José Santamarina · ES · Logo · Asociación de Peluqueros de Asturias

1973 · José Santamarina · ES · Logo · Asociación de Diseñadores Gráficos de Asturias

1979 · José Santamarina · ES · Logo · Grisetto Boutique

1978 · José Santamarina · ES · Logo · Tavola Art

1981 · José Santamarina · ES · Logo · Optica Piñile

1974 · José Santamarina · ES · Logo · S. Claudio

1977 · José Santamarina · ES · Logo · Odan

1974 · José Santamarina · ES · Logo · Cofer TV

1972 · Kazumasa Nagai · JP · Logo · Plus

1973 · Kazumasa Nagai · JP · Logo · Saitama Bank

1973 · Kazumasa Nagai · JP · Logo · Kawakichi

1974 · Kazumasa Nagai · JP · Logo · Japan
Amateur Sports

1983 · Kazumasa Nagai · JP · Logo ·
Minami-nihon TV

1974 · Kazumasa Nagai · JP · Poster

Kazumasa Nagai (1929, Osaka) is a pioneering graphic artist and printmaker, and co-founder of the Nippon Design Center in Tokyo (1960). Combining an abstract modernist approach with traditional Japanese styles, Nagai has created his own particular visual language and has employed it in work for cultural institutions as well as Japanese brands, such as Asahi Beer, Nikon, and Toshiba. He first studied art in Tokyo in the 1950s before co-founding the A-Club in Osaka, a meeting space for local designers, and subsequently joining the 21 Association, a creative group in Tokyo that met on the 21st day of each month to discuss new ideas in design. Nagai also designed the identity for the 1972 Winter Olympics in Sapporo.

Kazumasa Nagai (1929, Osaka) gilt als Pionier unter den Grafikdesignern und ist ein Mitbegründer des Nippon Design Center in Tokio (1960). Nagai verbindet die abstrakte Sprache der Moderne mit traditionellen japanischen Stilen, wodurch er eine ganz eigene visuelle Sprache schafft. Damit gestaltet er Arbeiten für Kulturinstitutionen ebenso wie für japanische Firmen wie Asahi Beer, Nikon und Toshiba. Nach dem Kunststudium in Tokio in den 1950er-Jahren rief er mit anderen den A-Club in Osaka ins Leben, einen Treffpunkt für die dortigen Designer, und wurde später Mitglied der 21 Association, einer Gruppe von Kreativen in Tokio, die sich am 21. eines jeden Monats traf, um über neue Ideen in der Gestaltung zu diskutieren. Nagai entwarf auch den grafischen Auftritt der Winterolympiade 1972 in Sapporo.

Kazumasa Nagai (1929, Osaka) est un graphiste et graveur pionnier dans son domaine, ainsi qu'un des fondateurs du Nippon Design Center à Tokyo (1960). En associant une approche moderniste abstraite aux styles japonais traditionnels, Nagai a créé un langage visuel personnel qu'il a appliqué dans ses créations pour des institutions culturelles et des marques japonaises, comme Asahi Beer, Nikon et Toshiba. Après des études d'art à Tokyo dans les années 1950, il devient un des fondateurs de l'A-Club à Osaka, un forum pour des designers locaux, avant de rejoindre la 21 Association, un groupe créatif de Tokyo qui se réunit le 21 de chaque mois pour débattre de nouvelles idées dans le domaine du design. Nagai a aussi conçu l'identité des jeux Olympiques d'hiver de 1972 à Sapporo.

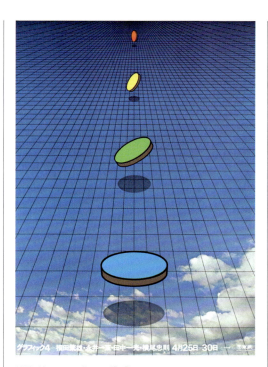

1979 · Kazumasa Nagai · JP · Poster

1984 · Kazumasa Nagai · JP · Poster

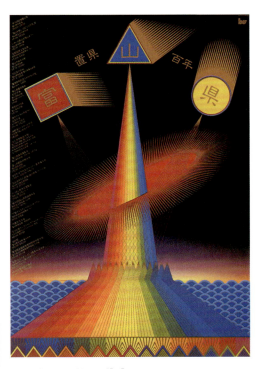

1985 · Kazumasa Nagai · JP · Poster

1988 · Kazumasa Nagai · JP · Poster

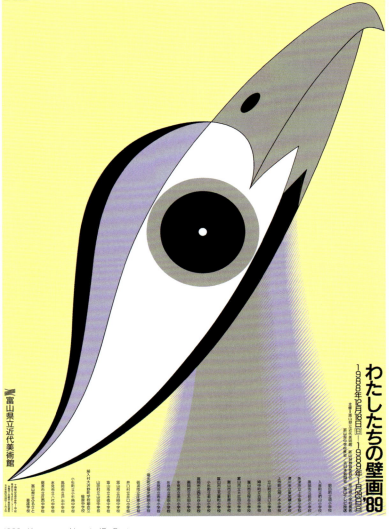

1989 · Kazumasa Nagai · JP · Poster

1975

Austrian designer Othmar Motter creates **Motter Tektura**, a typeface later used in the identities of Apple and Reebok

1975 · Mario Lovergine · IT · Poster

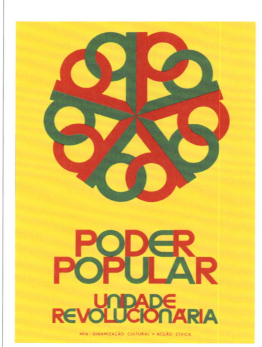

1975 · Marcelino Vespeira · PT · Poster

1975 · George Tscherny · US · Poster

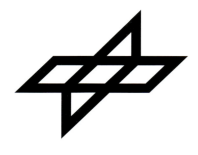

1975 · Bruno K. Wiese · DE · Logo · German Aerospace Center

1975 · Anne Lund · DK · Logo · The Smiling Sun

1975 · Hans Donner · DE/BR · Logo · Rede Globo

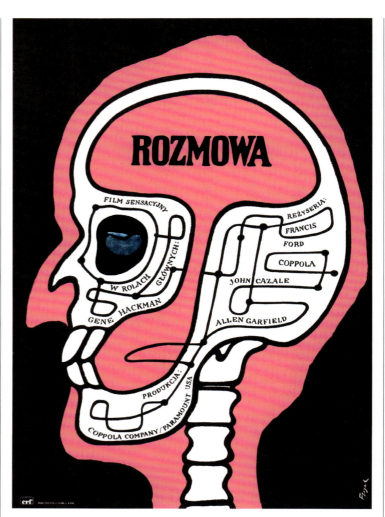

1975 · Jerzy Flisak · PL · Poster

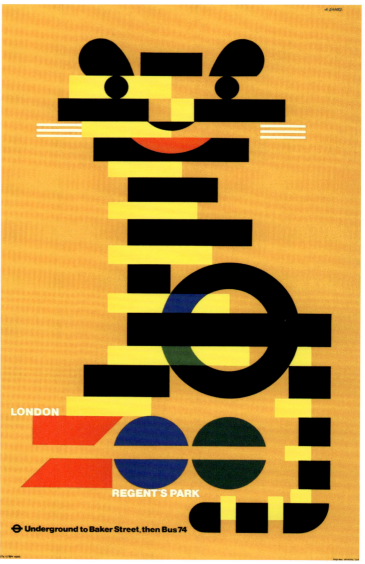

1975 · Abram Games · UK · Poster

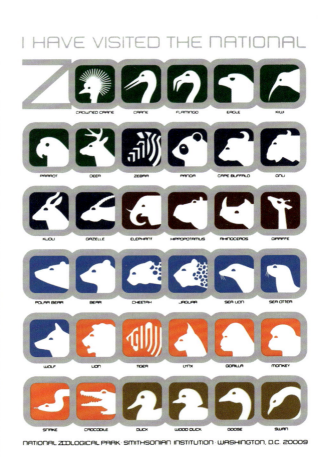

1975 · Lance Wyman · US · Identity · Washington Zoo

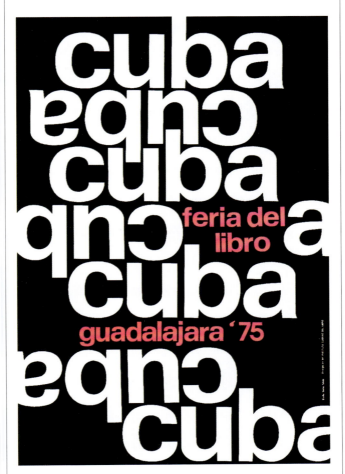

1975 · Santos Toledo · CU · Poster

1975 · Heinz Waibl · IT · Poster

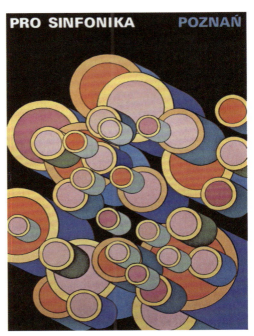

1975 · Tadeusz Piskorski · PL · Poster

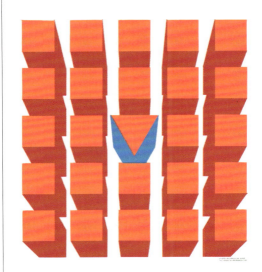

1975 · Rolando de Oraá · CU · Poster

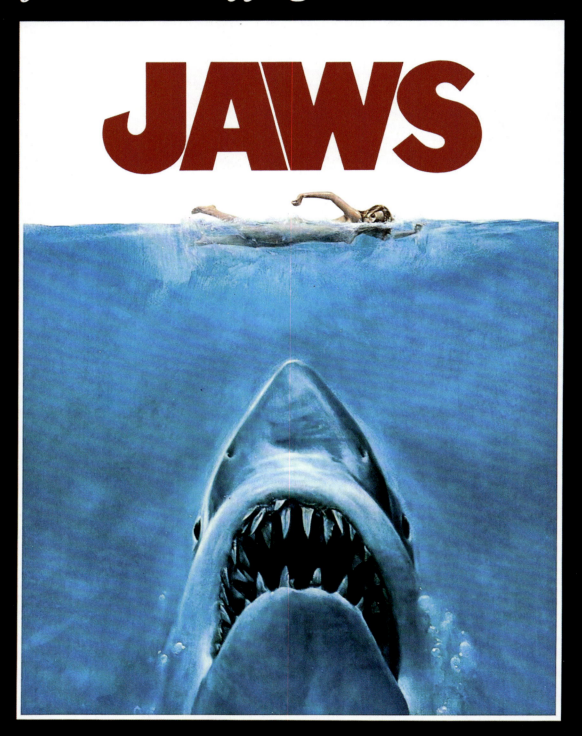

The terrifying motion picture
from the terrifying No. 1 best seller.

JAWS

**ROY
SCHEIDER** **ROBERT
SHAW** **RICHARD
DREYFUSS**

JAWS

Co-starring LORRAINE GARY · MURRAY HAMILTON · A ZANUCK/BROWN PRODUCTION
Screenplay by PETER BENCHLEY and CARL GOTTLIEB · Based on the novel by PETER BENCHLEY · Music by JOHN WILLIAMS
Directed by STEVEN SPIELBERG · Produced by RICHARD D. ZANUCK and DAVID BROWN · A UNIVERSAL PICTURE
TECHNICOLOR® PANAVISION® **PG** PARENTAL GUIDANCE SUGGESTED ⊙⊙   ORIGINAL SOUNDTRACK AVAILABLE ON MCA RECORDS & TAPES
SOME MATERIAL MAY NOT BE
SUITABLE FOR PRE-TEENAGERS   ...MAY BE TOO INTENSE FOR YOUNGER CHILDREN

COPYRIGHT © 1975 BY UNIVERSAL PICTURES COUNTRY OF ORIGIN U.S.A.   75/155

"JAWS"

1975 · Roger Kastel · US · Poster

The relaunch in 1975 of the revamped 7Up brand, designed by Morton Goldsholl and his Chicago-based studio, delivered a colorful, illuminated image that is now seen to exemplify the spirit of the 1970s. The new way of advertising the soft drink struck exactly the right note in the heyday of the disco and funk movements.

Der von Morton Goldsholl und seinem Chicagoer Designbüro 1975 umgesetzte Markenrelaunch von 7Up zeigte eine bunte und strahlende Ästhetik, die heute beispielhaft für die 1970er-Jahre steht. Die neue Werbeinszenierung des Softdrinks traf genau den richtigen Ton am Höhepunkt der Disco- und Funkbewegung.

Après sa refonte en 1975 par Morton Goldsholl et son agence de graphisme basée à Chicago, la marque 7Up affichait une esthétique radieuse et colorée qui est aujourd'hui encore emblématique des années 1970. La nouvelle approche publicitaire de la boisson gazeuse trouva le ton juste au plus fort des mouvements funk et disco.

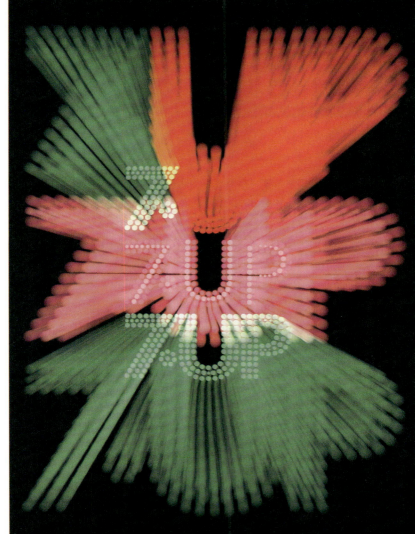

1975 · Morton Goldsholl · US · Identity

1975 · Morton Goldsholl · US · Packaging

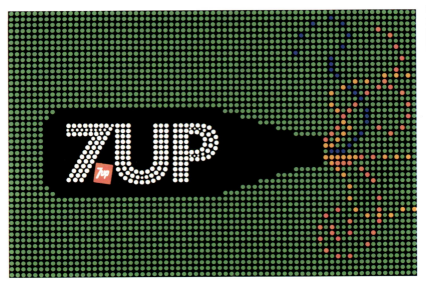

1975 · Morton Goldsholl · US · Identity

1975 · Morton Goldsholl · US · Logo

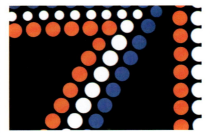

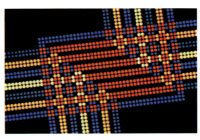
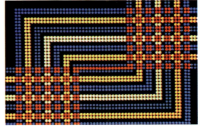

1975 · Morton Goldsholl · US · TV commercial

Whilst its main areas of research lie in the humanities, technology, and engineering, MIT had already set up a graphic design program as early as the 1950s. One offshoot of the new degree course in this subject was the establishment of the institute's own design department, which was responsible for university publications and campus announcements. In the 1970s, Jacqueline Casey, Ralph Coburn, and Dietmar Winkler were the team who created MIT's graphic identity, with their fascinating, modernist designs taking inspiration from the Swiss Style. Originally only intended for display around the Boston campus of MIT, the posters and brochures soon found international recognition from experts in the field, who were full of enthusiasm for the graphics produced at the university, which showed a dazzling modernity that is still impressive today.

Bereits in den 1950er-Jahren etablierte das eigentlich auf Geisteswissenschaften, Technik und Maschinenbau spezialisierte MIT ein Grafikdesignprogramm. Ein Ableger des neuen Studiengangs war eine eigene Designabteilung, die für Hochschulpublikationen und Campusankündigungen zuständig war. In den 1970er-Jahren prägten Jacqueline Casey, Ralph Coburn und Dietmar Winkler den grafischen Auftritt des MIT. Inspiriert vom „Swiss Style", realisierten sie faszinierende modernistische Arbeiten. Ursprünglich nur für den Aushang am Bostoner Campus gedacht, fanden die Plakate und Broschüren schnell auch internationale Beachtung in der Fachwelt, die von der bis heute bestechenden Modernität der universitären Grafik begeistert war.

Dès les années 1950, le MIT, spécialisé dans les sciences humaines, la technologie et l'ingénierie, développa un programme de graphisme. Un des aspects de ce nouveau cursus était la création du département de graphisme de l'établissement, chargé des publications de l'école et des annonces du campus. Dans les années 1970, Jacqueline Casey, Ralph Coburn et Dietmar Winkler définirent l'identité visuelle du MIT. Inspirés par le style suisse, ils réalisèrent des travaux modernistes passionnants. Conçues à l'origine pour le seul campus de Boston, leurs affiches et brochures attirèrent rapidement l'attention des experts en la matière, enthousiasmés par la modernité du graphisme des universitaires, qui a conservé tout son attrait jusqu'à aujourd'hui.

1975 · Jacqueline S. Casey · US · Poster

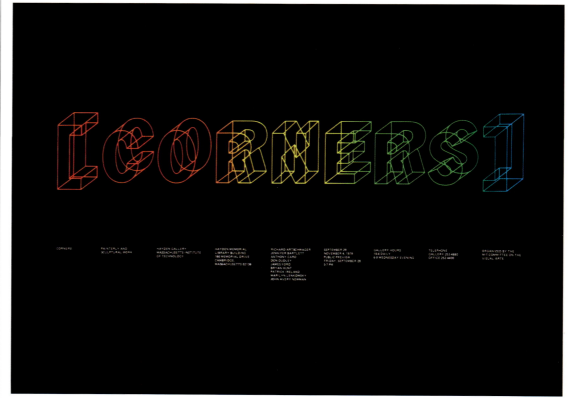

1979 · Jacqueline S. Casey · US · Poster

1969 · Dietmar R. Winkler · US · Poster

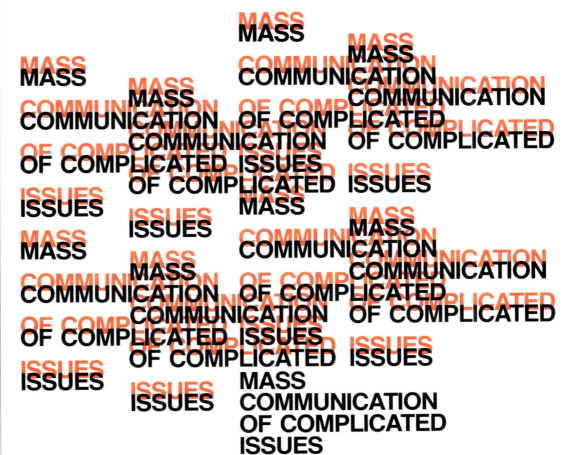

1970 · Dietmar R. Winkler · US · Poster

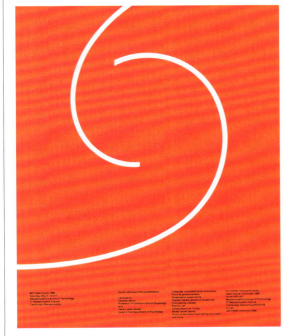

1973 · Jacqueline S. Casey · US · Poster

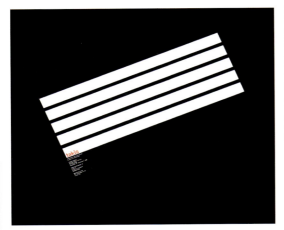

1973 · Jacqueline S. Casey · US · Poster

1973 · Ralph Coburn · US · Brochure cover

1973 · Jacqueline S. Casey · US · Poster

When similar design solutions appear at the same time it's often hard to say whether this is down to the zeitgeist, or to simple chance, or to the influence of comparable (or contrasting) imagery. One particularly interesting example of this situation is the rainbow symbol, which was used for the first time by Polaroid in the early 1970s, then in the Apple logo created in 1976, and in the LGBT (lesbian, gay, bisexual, and transgender) community's rainbow flag introduced in 1978.

Es ist schwer zu sagen, ob zur gleichen Zeit entstandene ähnliche Gestaltungslösungen dem Zeitgeist, dem Zufall, gleichen oder gegenseitigen Einflüssen geschuldet sind. Ein besonders interessantes Beispiel sind das Anfang der 1970er-Jahre erstmals verwendete Regenbogenmotiv von Polaroid, das 1976 eingeführte Design von Apple und die 1978 etablierte Regenbogenflagge der LGBT-Community.

Il est difficile de déterminer si la similarité de certaines solutions graphiques apparues à une même époque se doit à l'esprit du temps, au hasard, ou encore à des influences comparables ou opposées. Un exemple particulièrement intéressant en est le motif arc-en-ciel utilisé pour la première fois au début des années 1970 par Polaroid, puis pour le logo d'Apple créé en 1976 et pour drapeau de la communauté LGBT (lesbiennes, gays, bisexuels et transgenres) établi en 1978.

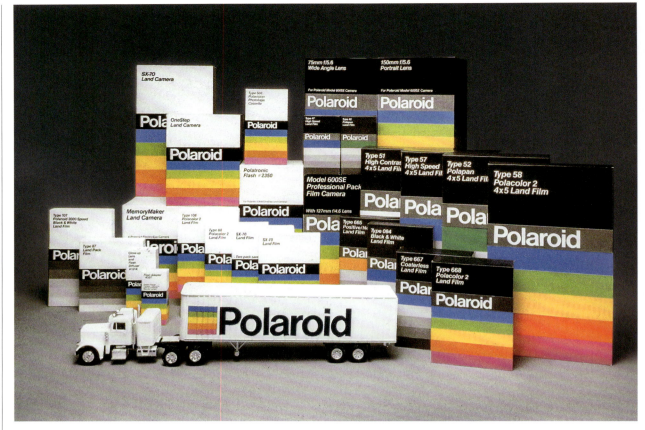

1980 · Roy Alan Hughes (AD) · US · Packaging

1976 · Rob Janoff · US · Logo

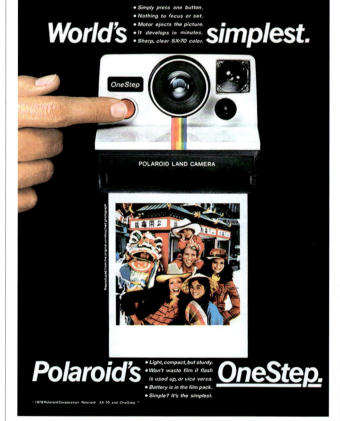

1977 · Anonymous · US · Ad

1978 · Anonymous · US · Flag

1976 · Anonymous · US · Packaging

Luova Espoo Esbo skapar
26.10.-2.11.75
Espoon kaupungin kulttuurilautakunta
Esbo stads kulturnämnd

1975 · Tapani Aartomaa · FI · Poster

1976

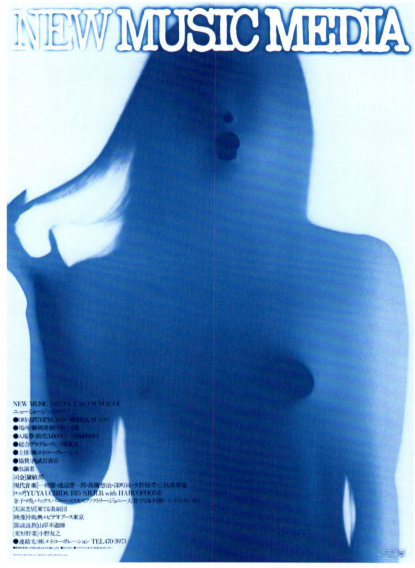

1976 · Shin Matsunaga · JP · Poster

1976 · Dan Reisinger · IL · Poster

1976 · Félix Beltrán · CU · Poster

1976 · Mieczysław Wasilewski · PL · Poster

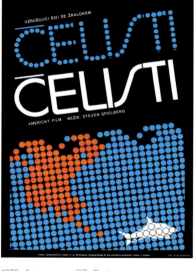

1976 · Anonymous · CZ · Poster

1976 · Georges Huel, Yvon Laroche, Pierre-Yves Pelletier · CA · Poster

1976 · Milton Glaser · US · Logo · New York City

1976 · Chermayeff & Geismar · US · Identity · American Revolution Bicentennial

1976 · Piero Gratton · IT · Logo · Rai 2 Television

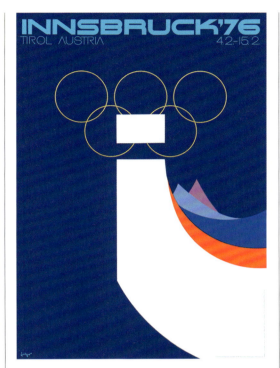

1976 · Anton Zelger · AT · Poster

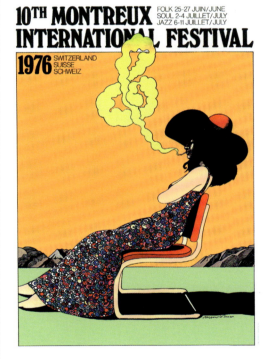

1976 · Milton Glaser · US · Poster

1976 · David Alexander (PH) · US · Record cover

1976 · Wim Crouwel · NL · Stamps

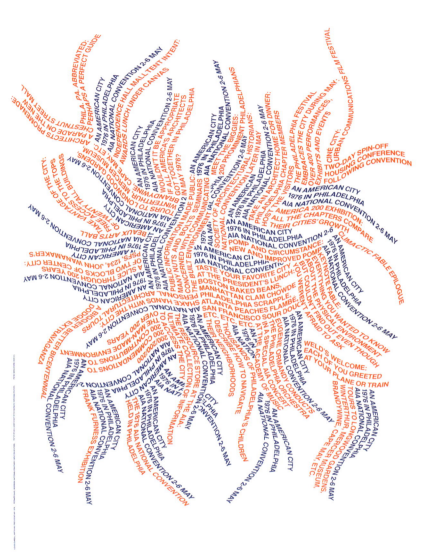

1976 · Peter Bradford · US · Poster

1976 · Wolfgang Weingart · CH/US · Poster

Sudarshan Dheer · India

In the 1970s, the adult literacy rate in India stood at a mere 30 percent. In conjunction with this, hundreds of different dialects were spoken across the country, and there were 14 different written languages. Clearly, here was a situation where the advantages of universally understandable graphic design could prove to be especially important. Sudarshan Dheer became one of modern India's pioneers of graphic design by applying just this approach, and was also one of the first designers to take western visual concepts and adapt them to the needs of domestic corporations and institutions across India.

In den 1970er-Jahren lag in Indien der Alphabetisierungsgrad bei knapp 30 Prozent. Dazu wurden Hunderte Dialekte gesprochen und 14 Sprachen geschrieben. Die Vorteile universell verständlichen Grafikdesigns waren hier von besonderer Bedeutung. Sudarshan Dheer wurde zu einem Pionier des modernen indischen Grafikdesigns, indem er modernistische Bildkonzepte des Westens als einer der ersten Grafikdesigner für zahlreiche heimische Unternehmen und Institutionen umsetzte.

Dans l'Inde des années 1970, le taux d'alphabétisation ne dépassait pas 30 pour cent, et des centaines de dialectes étaient parlés dans tout le pays et déclinés en 14 écritures. Les avantages d'un graphisme universellement intelligible y revêtaient donc une importance particulière. Fidèle à cette approche, Sudarshan Dheer devint un pionnier du graphisme de l'Inde moderne. Il fut l'un des premiers designers à importer certains concepts visuels du monde occidental et à les adapter pour créer l'identité de nombreuses entreprises et institutions nationales.

1971 · Sudarshan Dheer · IN · Logo · Ross Murarka

1972 · Sudarshan Dheer · IN · Logo · Ropan Film

1976 · Sudarshan Dheer · IN · Logo · Photoquip India

1973 · Sudarshan Dheer · IN · Logo · Poonam Hotels

1970s · Sudarshan Dheer · IN · Logo · Good Value Products

1970s · Sudarshan Dheer · IN · Logo · Communicaid

1974 · Sudarshan Dheer · IN · Logo · Hindusthan Petroleum

1970s · Sudarshan Dheer · IN · Logo · Mahavir Refractories

1970s · Sudarshan Dheer · IN · Logo · Spectrum Tricolor Laboratory

1970s · Sudarshan Dheer · IN · Logo · Alfred Allan Advertising

1976 · Sudarshan Dheer · IN · Logo · Shrenuj & Co. Jewelry

1970s · Sudarshan Dheer · IN · Logo · Unitel Communications

1970s · Sudarshan Dheer · IN · Logo · Triveni Print

1979 · Sudarshan Dheer · IN · Logo · Mahavir Hospital

1980 · Sudarshan Dheer · IN · Logo · Style Asia

»Every project for me has been a new learning. Even today it happens. And I have always tried not to work on the same path.«

Sudarshan Dheer, *designinindia.net*, 2007

Sudarshan Dheer (1937, Bassi Kalan, Punjab, India – 2018, Mumbai) was an Indian graphic designer and one of his country's leading design industry figures, who also made a huge contribution to the campaign for modern graphic design gaining acceptance in India. In the early 1960s, Dheer first studied fine and then applied art at the Sir J.J. School of Arts in Bombay (now Mumbai), before going on to work for various advertising agencies and then founding Graphic Communication Concepts in 1974. In 1989, Dheer published his book *The World of Symbols*, in which he presented modern corporate identities created in India, including many of his own designs. He was the winner of many international prizes.

Sudarshan Dheer (1937, Bassi Kalan, Punjab, Indien – 2018, Mumbai) war ein indischer Grafikdesigner, der zu den wichtigsten Gestaltern seines Landes gehört und maßgeblich dazu beitrug, modernes Grafikdesign in Indien durchzusetzen. Anfang der 1960er-Jahre studierte er zunächst Kunst, dann angewandte Kunst an der Sir J.J. School of Arts Bombay (heute Mumbai). Dheer war für verschiedene Werbeagenturen in Bombay tätig, bevor er 1974 das Studio Graphic Communication Concepts gründete. 1989 veröffentlichte er das Buch *The World of Symbols*, in dem er moderne Markenzeichen aus Indien präsentierte. Für sein gestalterisches Schaffen wurde er mit zahlreichen internationalen Preisen bedacht.

Sudarshan Dheer (1937, Bassi Kalan, Pendjab, Inde – 2018, Mumbai) fut un des grands graphistes indiens, véritable figure de proue dans son pays où il contribua largement à l'acceptation du graphisme moderne. Au début des années 1960, il étudia d'abord les beaux-arts, puis les arts appliqués à la Sir J.J. School of Arts de Bombay (rebaptisée Mumbai), où il travailla ensuite pour plusieurs agences publicitaires avant de fonder en 1964 le studio Graphic Communication Concepts. En 1989, il publia le livre *The World of Symbols*, qui présente des images de marque créées en Inde. Son travail a été récompensé par de nombreux prix internationaux.

1970s · Sudarshan Dheer · IN · Identity · Kissan Products

1970s · Sudarshan Dheer · IN · Logo · Associated Capsules

17th All India Printers Conference & Exhibition of Printed Material

Mezzanine Floor

26,27,28th March '76 10 AM to 7PM

1976 · Sudarshan Dheer · IN · Poster

1970s · Sudarshan Dheer · IN · Logo · Vilaza Hotels

1970s · Sudarshan Dheer · IN · Logo · HOEC

1970s · Sudarshan Dheer · IN · Logo · Good Value Products

1977 · Sudarshan Dheer · IN · Logo · Tantrik

Shigeo Fukuda · Japan

Shigeo Fukuda (1932–2009, Tokyo) was a significant Japanese designer and visual artist, known for his use of optical illusions. Employing extreme simplicity in his posters, Fukuda captivated his audience's attention with powerful messages conveyed with graphic wit. He was born into a family of toymakers, and studied fine arts in Tokyo until graduating in 1956; in 1987 he became the first Japanese designer to be inducted into the New York Art Directors Club Hall of Fame. With limited commercial work, Fukuda excelled in designing for social and cultural institutions, including Amnesty International, and also illustrated a column for *Asahi Shimbun* newspaper entitled "Ryu Mita Ka?" (Have You Seen the Dragon?).

Shigeo Fukuda (1932–2009, Tokio) war ein bedeutender japanischer Grafikdesigner und Künstler, der durch die Verwendung optischer Täuschungen bekannt wurde. Dank der äußersten Schlichtheit seiner Plakaten erregte Fukuda die Aufmerksamkeit der Betrachter mit prägnanten, durch grafischen Witz vermittelten Botschaften. Der Sohn einer Familie von Spielzeugherstellern absolvierte ein Kunststudium in Tokio, das er 1956 abschloss; 1987 wurde er als erster japanischer Grafikdesigner in die New Yorker Art Directors Club Hall of Fame aufgenommen. Fukuda, dessen kommerzielle Arbeit eher beschränkt war, brillierte mit Entwürfen für soziale und kulturelle Institutionen – unter anderem für Amnesty International – und illustrierte auch eine Kolumne für die Tageszeitung *Asahi Shimbun* mit dem Titel „Ryu Mita Ka?" (Hast du den Drachen gesehen?).

Shigeo Fukuda (1932–2009, Tokyo) fut un important designer et artiste visuel japonais qui se distingua par son utilisation des illusions d'optique. Appliquant la plus grande simplicité dans ses affiches, Fukuda attirait l'attention du public par des messages puissants doublés d'une grande intelligence graphique. Issu d'une famille de fabricants de jouets, il étudia les beaux-arts à Tokyo et obtint son diplôme en 1956. En 1987, il fut le premier designer japonais accueilli au sein du New York Art Directors Club Hall of Fame. Avec un travail commercial limité, Fukuda excella dans le design pour des institutions sociales et culturelles, notamment pour Amnesty International. Il illustra aussi une colonne du journal *Asahi Shimbun* intitulée «Ryu Mita Ka?» (Avez-vous vu le dragon?).

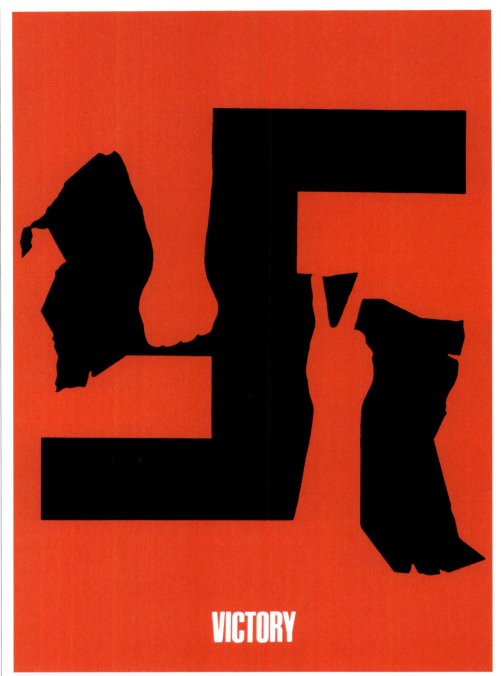

1976 · Shigeo Fukuda · JP · Poster

1974 · Shigeo Fukuda · JP · Ad

1971 · Shigeo Fukuda · JP · Poster

1981 · Shigeo Fukuda · JP · Poster

1985 · Shigeo Fukuda · JP · Poster

1993 · Shigeo Fukuda · JP · Poster

1976 · Shigeo Fukuda · JP · Poster

1968 · Gunter Rambow · DE · Poster

1970s · Gunter Rambow · DE · Poster

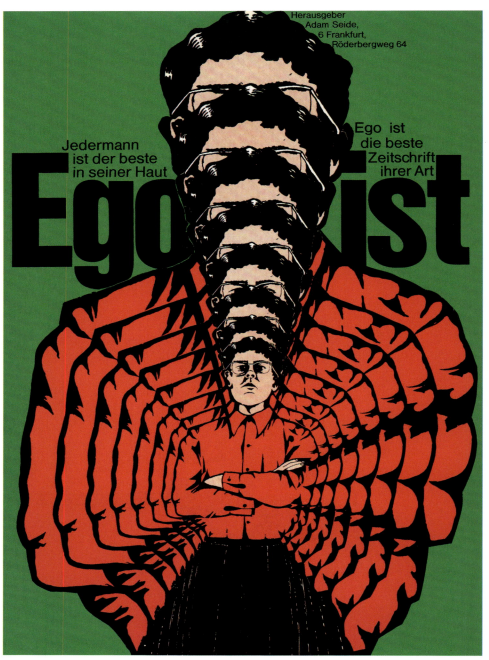

1968 · Gunter Rambow · DE · Poster

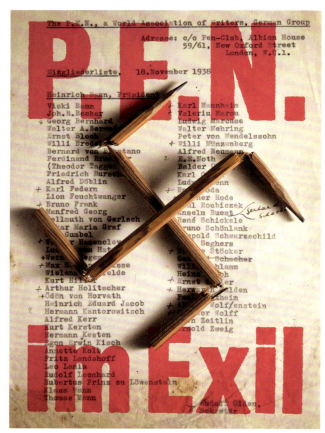

1983 · Gunter Rambow · DE · Poster

1976 · Gunter Rambow · DE · Poster

1976 · Gunter Rambow · DE · Poster

1979 · Gunter Rambow · DE · Poster

1976 · Gunter Rambow · DE · Poster

1980 · Gunter Rambow · DE · Poster

Gunter Rambow (1938, Neustrelitz, Germany) is a German designer and photographer. While still studying graphics in Kassel under Hans Hillmann, he formed the studio Rambow+Lienemeyer in 1960. His work for cultural institutions such as the Frankfurt Opera and the municipal theaters of Wiesbaden and Karlsruhe summarize the innovative use of photography and collage he has brought to design, notably in books and political posters. Rambow has taught in Germany since the 1970s and has also been a guest lecturer in China.

Gunter Rambow (1938, Neustrelitz) ist ein deutscher Grafikdesigner und Fotograf. Noch während seines Grafikstudiums in Kassel bei Hans Hillmann gründete er 1960 das Studio Rambow+Lienemeyer. Die innovativen Elemente – Fotografie und Collage –, die er bereits bei der Gestaltung von Büchern und politischen Plakaten eingeführt hatte, zeigen sich exemplarisch auch in seinen Arbeiten für Kulturinstitutionen wie die Frankfurter Oper oder die Stadttheater von Wiesbaden und Karlsruhe. Rambow unterrichtet in Deutschland seit den 1970er-Jahren und war auch Gastdozent in China.

Gunter Rambow (1938, Neustrelitz, Allemagne) est un designer et photographe allemand. En 1960, pendant ses études de graphisme à Cassel auprès de Hans Hillmann, il ouvre le studio Rambow+Lienemeyer. Son travail pour des institutions culturelles comme l'opéra de Francfort et les théâtres municipaux de Wiesbaden et de Karlsruhe résume son recours innovant dans ses créations à la photographie et au collage, particulièrement dans des livres et des affiches politiques. Rambow enseigne en Allemagne depuis les années 1970, et il est intervenu en Chine en qualité de professeur invité.

1977

The **R/GA** design studio is established in New York City by brothers Richard and Robert Greenberg

Studio Dumbar is founded in The Hague by Gert Dumbar

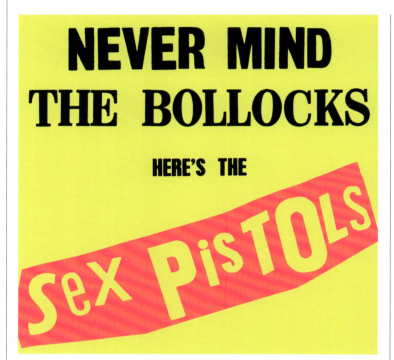

1977 · Jamie Reid · UK · Record cover

ARTES VISUALES 2
REVISTA TRIMESTRAL ☐ MUSEO DE ARTE MODERNO / CHAPULTEPEC ☐ MEXICO

1977 · Vicente Rojo · MX · Magazine cover

1977 · Herb Lubalin, PAOS · US/JP · Logo · Asics

1977 · Richard Bird · UK · Poster

1977 · Jamie Reid · UK · Record cover

1977 · Anton Stankowski · DE · Logo · Silit

1977 · Siegfried Odermatt, Odermatt+Tissi · CH · Logo · Datalink

1977 · Dennis Leigh (concept), Bloomfield-Travis · UK · Record cover

1977 · Erhard Grüttner · GDR · Poster

1977 · Dan Reisinger · IL · Poster

□ Svaz českých
výtvarných umělců
□ Svaz výtvarných
umělců Rumunské
socialistické
republiky

současná rumunská tapisérie

k 100. výročí nezávislosti
Rumunska
□ Srpen–září 1977
Galerie Václava Špály
Národní třída 30
Praha 1

1977 · Rostislav Vaněk · CZ · Poster

1977 · R. Tuten, W. Bostedt · US · Poster

1977 · Hipgnosis · UK · Record cover

1977 · Stan Martin, Tom Nikosey · US · Record cover

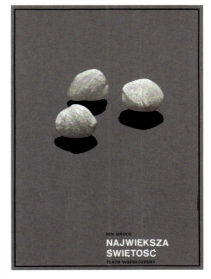

1977 · Marek Lewandowski · PL · Poster

1977 · Jarosław Jasiński · PL · Poster

1977 · Thomas Schleusing · GDR · Brochure cover

In the 1970s there was a short-lived trend for adapting the attention-grabbing effects of neon signs to create similarly eye-catching graphic design. At the time, the music world's emerging craze for disco provided the perfect opportunity for trying out these glitzy, sometimes over-the-top forms of visual imagery.

In den 1970er-Jahren machte sich ein kurzzeitiger Trend breit, bei dem man die plakative Wirkung von Neonschriftzügen für das Printdesign adaptierte. Die gerade bahnbrechende Discowelle in der Popmusik jener Zeit war ein ideales Anwendungsfeld für die schwungvollen und oft übertrieben ausgestalteten Wortbilder.

Au début des années 1970 s'est répandue une tendance éphémère qui adaptait l'effet tape-à-l'œil des enseignes au néon au domaine du design graphique. La vague disco qui déferlait alors dans la sphère musicale de l'époque fut un champ d'application idéal pour ces créations visuelles clinquantes et parfois excessives.

Catch it.

Opens December 16th at a theatre near you!

1977 · Diener Hauser Bates Advertising · US · Poster

1972 · John Casado · US · Logo · Joyce Jacobsen

1970s · Rod Dyer · US · Logo · Mama Lion

1970s · John LePrevost · US · Logo · The Big Broadcast

1974 · Michael McMahon · US · Logo · Mike McMahon

1978 · Jean Larcher · FR · Logo · Karen Cheryl

1970s · Rod Dyer · US · Logo · Smokey

1975 · Michael McMahon · US · Logo · Letter Express

1977 · Sergio Liuzzi · BR · Logo · Dancin' Days

1978 · Jean Larcher · FR · Logo · Contacts

1980 · Jay Vigon · US · Logo · Super Funtastic

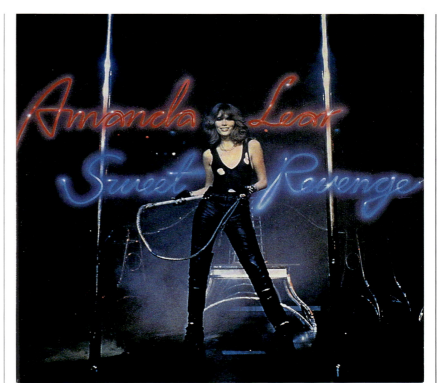

1978 · Ariola-Eurodisc Studio, Denis Taranto (PH) · DE · Record cover

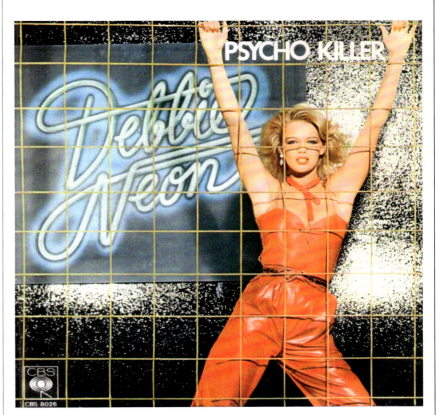

1979 · Anonymous · DE · Record cover

1978 · John Georgopoulos · US · Record cover

The special stamps issued in the mid-1970s by the Venezuelan post office are an especially exciting example of how modern design ideas can spread worldwide, even in essentially traditional fields. Creatives working in the country, such as Gerd Leufert, Alvaro Sotillo, and Nedo Mion Ferrario, did not just replicate the Swiss or American approach but instead found their own, absolutely individual solutions. Even though the typical portrait image had to feature as part of the content of some of the stamps, their creators still managed to defy convention by using symmetrical motifs, white spaces, and state-of-the-art typography, all of which had little in common with traditional stamp design.

Die ab Mitte der 1970er-Jahre herausgegebenen Sonderbriefmarken der venezolanischen Post sind ein besonders spannendes Beispiel für die internationale Ausbreitung modernistischer Gestaltungsideen – auch in eigentlich konservative Bereiche des Designs. Gestalter wie Gerd Leufert, Alvaro Sotillo oder Nedo Mion Ferrario kopierten dabei nicht etwa die Ansätze aus der Schweiz oder den USA, sondern fanden höchst eigenständige Lösungen. Selbst solche Briefmarken, die nicht auf ein klassisches Porträt verzichten konnten, wurden mit reichlich Asymmetrie, Weißraum und aktueller Typografie zu unkonventionellen Entwürfen, die mit traditioneller Briefmarkengestaltung nur noch wenig gemein hatten.

Les tirages spéciaux réalisés à partir du milieu des années 1970 par la poste vénézuélienne sont un exemple particulièrement passionnant de la diffusion mondiale de concepts graphiques modernes, y compris dans des domaines conservateurs. Des graphistes comme Gerd Leufert, Alvaro Sotillo ou Nedo Mion Ferrario n'ont nullement copié les approches suisse ou américaines et ont su trouver leurs propres expressions individuelles. Même les timbres qui ne pouvaient se passer du traditionnel portrait devinrent des projets anticonformistes par l'utilisation abondante de la symétrie, des espaces vides et de la typographie contemporaine: ils n'avaient plus grand-chose à voir avec la philatélie traditionnelle.

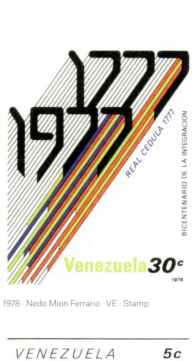

1978 · Nedo Mion Ferrario · VE · Stamp

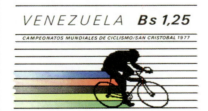

1977 · Anonymous · VE · Stamps

1979 · Anonymous · VE · Stamp

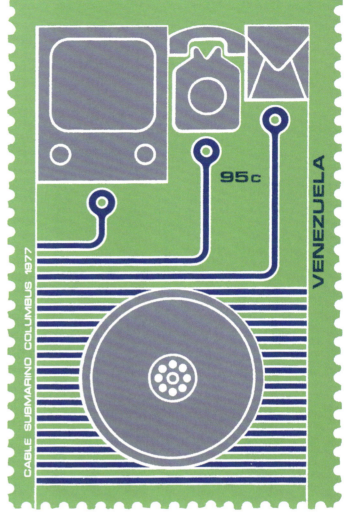

1977 · Alvaro Sotillo · VE · Stamp

1978 · Anonymous · VE · Stamp

1978 · Anonymous · VE · Stamp

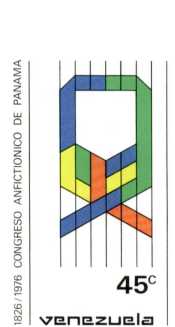

1826/1976 CONGRESO ANFICTIONICO DE PANAMA · 45ᶜ · venezuela · SETELIPAINO. 1976

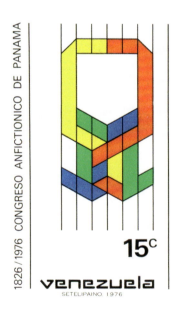

1826/1976 CONGRESO ANFICTIONICO DE PANAMA · 15ᶜ · venezuela · SETELIPAINO. 1976

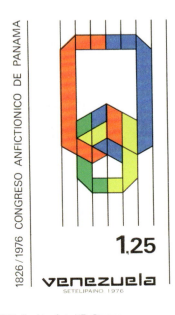

1826/1976 CONGRESO ANFICTIONICO DE PANAMA · 1.25 · venezuela · SETELIPAINO. 1976

1976 · Gerd Leufert · VE · Stamps

RAFAEL RANGEL ★ 1877 · venezuela 50c

1977 · Anonymous · VE · Stamp

70c · DIA DEL IDIOMA · VENEZUELA

1977 · Anonymous · VE · Stamp

VENEZUELA Bs.1 · DIRECCION DE CARTOGRAFIA NACIONAL · 1935 1975

1975 · Anonymous · VE · Stamp

75 · JUAN PABLO DUARTE 1976 CENTENARIO DE SU MUERTE · VENEZUELA

1976 · Anonymous · VE · Stamp

1966/1976 DECLARACION DE BOGOTA · VENEZUELA · 60c

1976 · Anonymous · VE · Stamp

30c · VENEZUELA NAVIDAD'79

1979 · Anonymous · VE · Stamp

VENEZUELA · 80c

1976 · Anonymous · VE · Stamp

VENEZUELA 30c · 1976 PRIMER ANIVERSARIO DE LA NACIONALIZACION DE LA EXPLOTACION DEL HIERRO

50c VENEZUELA · 1976 PRIMER ANIVERSARIO DE LA NACIONALIZACION DE LA EXPLOTACION DEL HIERRO

VENEZUELA 80c · 1976 PRIMER ANIVERSARIO DE LA NACIONALIZACION DE LA EXPLOTACION DEL HIERRO

VENEZUELA 1.05 · 1976 PRIMER ANIVERSARIO DE LA NACIONALIZACION DE LA EXPLOTACION DEL HIERRO

1.50 VENEZUELA · 1976 PRIMER ANIVERSARIO DE LA NACIONALIZACION DE LA EXPLOTACION DEL HIERRO

1976 PRIMER ANIVERSARIO DE LA NACIONALIZACION DE LA EXPLOTACION DEL HIERRO · 1.25 VENEZUELA

1977 · Nedo Mion Ferrario · VE · Stamps

1978

The **Bell Centennial** typeface by Matthew Carter is released on the occasion of AT&T's 100th anniversary

The **Japan Graphic Designers Association** is established

The Turkish design association **Grafik Tasarımcılar Meslek Kuruluşu** is founded

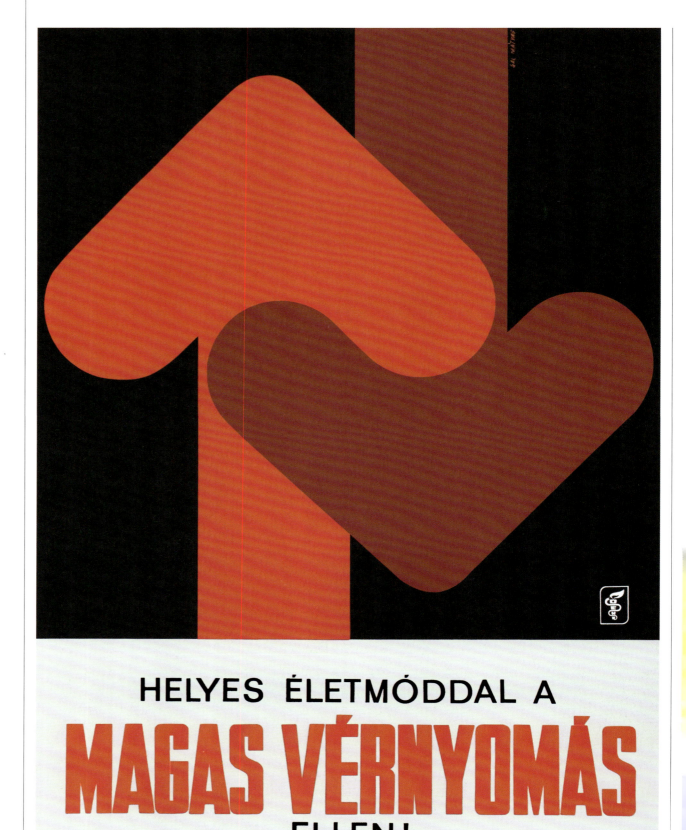

1978 · Mátyás Gál · HU · Poster

1978 · Anonymous · US · Logo · Life magazine

BDF ●●●●
Beiersdorf

1978 · Henrion & Associates · UK · Logo · Beiersdorf

3M

1978 · Siegel+Gale · US · Logo · 3M

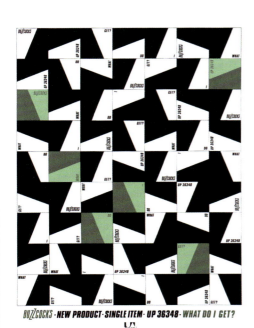

1978 · Malcolm Garrett · UK · Poster

1978 · Antal Gunda · HU · Poster

1978 · Yoshihiro Yoshida · JP · Poster

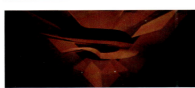

1978 · Richard Greenberg, R/GA · US · Opening titles

1978 · Emil Schult · DE · Record cover

This is a RECORD COVER. This writing is the DESIGN upon the record cover. The DESIGN is to help SELL the record. We hope to draw your attention to it and encourage you to pick it up. When you have done that maybe you'll be persuaded to listen to the music – in this case XTC's Go 2 album. Then we want you to BUY it. The idea being that the more of you that buy this record the more money Virgin Records, the manager Ian Reid and XTC themselves will make. To the aforementioned this is known as PLEASURE. A good cover DESIGN is one that attracts more buyers and gives more pleasure. This writing is trying to pull you in much like an eye-catching picture. It is designed to get you to READ IT. This is called luring the VICTIM, and you are the VICTIM. But if you have a free mind you should STOP READING NOW! because all we are attempting to do is to get you to read on. Yet this is a DOUBLE BIND because if you indeed stop you'll be doing what we tell you, and if you read on you'll be doing what we've wanted all along. And the more you read on the more you're falling for this simple device of telling you exactly how a good commercial design works. They're TRICKS and this is the worst TRICK of all since it's describing the TRICK whilst trying to TRICK you, and if you've read this far then you're TRICKED but you wouldn't have known this unless you'd read this far. At least we're telling you directly instead of seducing you with a beautiful or haunting visual that may never tell you. We're letting you know that you ought to buy this record because in essence it's a PRODUCT and PRODUCTS are to be consumed and you are a consumer and this is a good PRODUCT. We could have written the band's name in special lettering so that it stood out and you'd see it before you'd read any of this writing and possibly have bought it anyway. What we are really suggesting is that you are FOOLISH to buy or not buy an album merely as a consequence of the design on its cover. This is a con because if you agree then you'll probably like this writing – which is the cover design – and hence the album inside. But we've just warned you against that. The con is a con. A good cover design could be considered as one that gets you to buy the record, but that never actually happens to YOU because YOU know it's just a design for the cover. And this is the RECORD COVER.

1978 · Hipgnosis · UK · Record cover

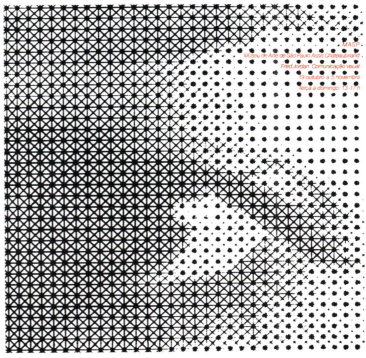

1978 · Fred Jordan · BR · Poster

Chinese Propaganda Posters

The Chinese had already established a strong tradition of poster design during the early 20th century, with themes such as looking to the future and oppression by the oligarchy having great appeal. Following the Chinese Communist Revolution of 1949, propaganda became the most powerful weapon in the arsenal of the newly installed government of the People's Republic. Led by Mao Zedong, the supreme leader of the country until 1976, the Communists saw the poster as the perfect medium to spread the Party message, and for the next two decades more than 1,000 artists produced several thousand examples. Whilst they were produced in an abundance of colorful styles, the posters adhered closely to a determined ideology which often focused on recurring motifs, notably using images of Mao himself, together with famous heroes and martyrs, and representations of strong women, workers, the People's Liberation Army, and the Cultural Revolution.

In China hatte sich bereits zu Anfang des 20. Jahrhunderts eine Tradition der Plakatgestaltung herausgebildet, wobei Themen wie der Blick in die Zukunft und die Unterdrückung durch die Oligarchie großen Anklang fanden. Nach der kommunistischen Revolution 1949 wurde Propaganda zur mächtigsten Waffe im Arsenal der neuen Regierung der Volksrepublik. Den Kommunisten unter der Leitung Mao Zedongs, bis 1976 der führende Politiker des Landes, galt das Plakat als das ideale Medium, um die Botschaft der Partei unters Volk zu bringen, und im Lauf der nächsten zwanzig Jahre entwarfen über eintausend Künstler mehrere tausend Poster. Auch wenn sie in unterschiedlichsten farbenfrohen Stilen gehalten waren, folgten sie alle ein und derselben Ideologie, die vielfach auf sich wiederholende Motive zurückgriff. Bevorzugt wurden dabei Porträts von Mao selbst verwendet, dazu Bilder berühmter Helden und Märtyrer sowie Darstellungen von kräftigen Frauen, Arbeitern, der Volksbefreiungsarmee und der Kulturrevolution.

Dès la première partie du XXᵉ siècle, les Chinois établirent une solide tradition de design d'affiches autour de thèmes aussi populaires que la confiance en l'avenir et l'oppression de l'oligarchie. Dans le sillage de la révolution communiste de 1949, la propagande devint l'arme la plus puissante dans l'arsenal du nouveau gouvernement de la République populaire de Chine. Sous la conduite de Mao Zedong, guide suprême du pays jusqu'en 1976, les communistes considérèrent l'affiche comme le support parfait pour diffuser le message du parti, et pendant les deux décennies suivantes, plus de 1000 artistes en produisirent des exemples par milliers. Créées dans une pléthore de styles hauts en couleur, les affiches suivirent à la lettre une idéologie tournant souvent autour de motifs récurrents, avec notamment des images du propre Mao, d'autres héros et martyrs célèbres, de femmes fortes, de travailleurs, de l'Armée populaire de libération et de la révolution culturelle.

1959 · Anonymous · CN · Poster

1967 · Anonymous · CN · Poster

1982 · Anonymous · CN · Poster

1979 · Anonymous · CN · Poster

»The image that used to prevail in the People's Republic of China was defined by the political images that were provided by propaganda art. Through all of its long history, the Chinese political system has used the arts to propagate correct behavior and thought.« Stefan R. Landsberger, *Chinese Propaganda Posters*, 2003

伟大的领袖毛主席万岁
热烈欢呼第四届全国人民代表大会的胜利召开

1975 · Anonymous · CN · Poster

1978 · Anonymous · CN · Poster

1978 · Anonymous · CN · Poster

1979

The first issue of the typography magazine **Baseline** is published as a corporate publication of Letraset

MetaDesign is founded in West Berlin by Gerhard Doerrié, Florian Fischer, Dieter Heil, and Erik Spiekermann

Tibor Kalman, Carol Bokuniewicz, and Liz Trovato start the design firm **M & Co.** in New York City

Steven Heller's first book on graphic design is published, **Artists' Christmas Cards**

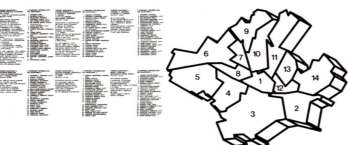
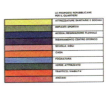

1979 · Michele Spera · IT · Poster

1979 · George Tscherny · US · Logo · Fidelity Group of Funds

1979 · Tomás Vellvé · ES · Logo · Instituto Nacional de Industria Barcelona

1979 · Rolf Müller · DE · Logo · IHK (Industrie- und Handelskammer)

1979 · Jill Mumford · UK · Record cover

1979 · Mike Wade · UK · Record cover

1979 · Tony Lane, Gary Meyer · US · Record cover

1979 · Petar Petrov · BG · Poster

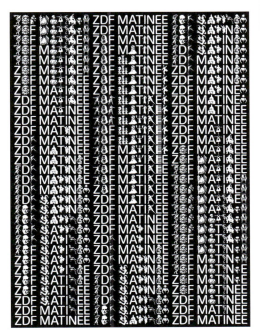

1979 · Christof Gassner · CH/DE · Poster

1979 · Anonymous · NL · Record cover

1979 · April Greiman, Jayme Odgers · US · Magazine cover

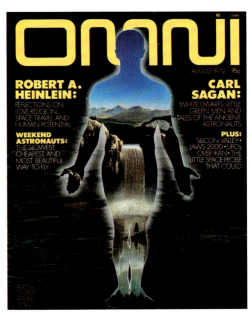

1979 · Frank Devino · US · Magazine cover

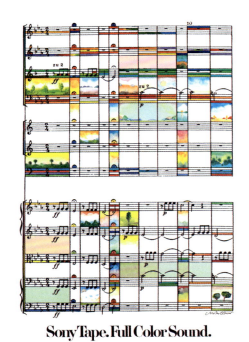

1979 · Milton Glaser · US · Poster

1970s · Stefan Kanchev · BG · On Air Design

1970s · Stefan Kanchev · BG · On Air Design

1970s · Stefan Kanchev · BG · On Air Design

1970s · Stefan Kanchev · BG · On Air Design

1965 · Stefan Kanchev · BG · Stamp

1979 · Stefan Kanchev · BG · Stamp

1978 · Stefan Kanchev · BG · Stamp

1976 · Stefan Kanchev · BG · Stamp

1979 · Stefan Kanchev · BG · Stamp

1979 · Stefan Kanchev · BG · Stamp

1971 · Stefan Kanchev · BG · Stamp

1965 · Stefan Kanchev · BG · Stamp

1971 · Stefan Kanchev · BG · Stamp

Stefan Kanchev (1915, Kalofer, Bulgaria – 2001, Sofia) was a Bulgarian graphic artist best known for his wide-ranging work on corporate identities. Widely regarded as the founding father of modern graphic design in his country, Kanchev's huge body of work comprises over 1,500 trademarks, from state-run companies to cultural institutions, and individual products. The son of an icon painter, he attended the National Academy of Arts in the capital Sofia, where he studied mural painting until 1945, and soon after he was taking part in design exhibitions and biennials in Bulgaria and many countries abroad. Kanchev's readily identifiable modernist approach to logo design became celebrated in publications worldwide.

Stefan Kantschew (1915, Kalofer, Bulgarien – 2001, Sofia) war ein bulgarischer Grafikdesigner, der vor allem für die zahlreichen von ihm gestalteten Corporate Identities bekannt ist. Kantschew, der allgemein als Gründungsvater des modernen Grafikdesigns in seiner Heimat gilt, hinterließ ein gewaltiges Œuvre, das über 1500 Markenzeichen umfasst, von staatlichen Gesellschaften bis zu Kulturinstitutionen und einzelnen Produkten. Der Sohn eines Ikonenmalers besuchte die Nationale Kunstakademie in der Hauptstadt Sofia, wo er bis 1945 Wandmalerei studierte; schon bald danach beteiligte er sich an Designausstellungen und Biennalen in Bulgarien und vielen anderen Ländern. Kantschews unverkennbar modernes Logodesign wurde in Publikationen weltweit gefeiert.

Stefan Kanchev (1915, Kalofer, Bulgarie – 2001, Sofia) fut un artiste graphiste bulgare connu surtout pour son travail de grande envergure sur des identités d'entreprises. Amplement considéré comme le père du graphisme moderne dans son pays, Kanchev laissa un immense héritage qui compte plus de 1500 marques – d'entreprises publiques à des institutions culturelles en passant par des produits. Fils d'un peintre d'icônes, il fit des études à l'Académie nationale des beaux-arts dans la capitale Sofia, où il étudia la peinture murale jusqu'en 1945 avant de prendre rapidement part à des expositions de graphisme et des biennales en Bulgarie et dans bien d'autres pays. L'approche moderniste du logo qui le caractérise de manière très distinctive a été célébrée dans des publications du monde entier.

»The time we live in is defined by the pictures which satisfy our artistic taste. For this reason, I am for everything that is new. For modern art. For all sorts of trends into which our times breathe life.« Stefan Kanchev, *Fatherland Front*, 1988

1957 · Stefan Kanchev · BG · Logo · Center for Applied Arts, Sofia

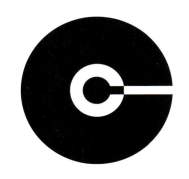

1963 · Stefan Kanchev · BG · Logo · Stomana

1968 · Stefan Kanchev · BG · Logo · Sofia Opera

1972 · Stefan Kanchev · BG · Logo · Ludogorska Slava Industrial

1957 · Stefan Kanchev · BG · Logo · Kino Studio

1963 · Stefan Kanchev · BG · Logo · Vinsavod

1970 · Stefan Kanchev · BG · Logo · Bulgarian Center for Graphic Design

1972 · Stefan Kanchev · BG · Logo · Bulgarian State Committee for Print

1959 · Stefan Kanchev · BG · Logo · National Art Gallery, Sofia

1964 · Stefan Kanchev · BG · Logo · Center for Industrial Design, Sofia

1970 · Stefan Kanchev · BG · Logo · DDD

1972 · Stefan Kanchev · BG · Logo · Puppet Theater

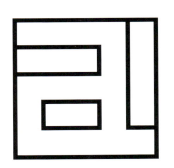

1961 · Stefan Kanchev · BG · Logo · Architectura

1964 · Stefan Kanchev · BG · Logo · Petrol

1971 · Stefan Kanchev · BG · Logo · Exhibition of Bulgarian Trademarks

1976 · Stefan Kanchev · BG · Logo · Bulgarian Television

1963 · Stefan Kanchev · BG · Logo · Central Puppet Theater, Sofia

1964 · Stefan Kanchev · BG · Logo · Zement Kombinat Wratza

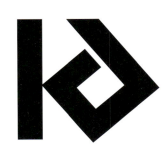

1972 · Stefan Kanchev · BG · Logo · Komsomolgz

1979 · Stefan Kanchev · BG · Logo · International Trademark Biennial

Waldemar Świerzy · Poland

Waldemar Świerzy (1931, Katowice, Poland – 2013, Warsaw) was a Polish graphic designer who numbered amongst the leading players in his country's famous poster scene. Having graduated from the Kracow Academy of Fine Arts, in 1952 Świerzy moved to Warsaw, where he worked as a designer for the publishing house WAG and the movie distributors CWF. In 1965 he was appointed to head the design department of the University of Fine Arts in Poznań, and between 1979 and 1994 he was president of the International Poster Biennale in Warsaw. During his long career, Świerzy created more than 2,500 posters, including many for Polish premieres of international classics, such as Apocalypse Now.

Waldemar Świerzy (1931, Kattowitz, Polen – 2013, Warschau) war ein polnischer Grafikdesigner, der zu den wichtigen Protagonisten der berühmten Plakatszene seines Landes zählte. Nach seinem Abschluss an der Staatlichen Kunstschule Krakau zog er 1952 nach Warschau, wo er für den Verlag WAG sowie für den Filmverleih CWF als Gestalter tätig war. Von 1965 an leitete er die Designabteilung der Staatlichen Schule für Kunst in Posen, und zwischen 1979 und 1994 war er der Vorsitzende der Internationalen Plakatbiennale Warschau. In seiner langen Karriere schuf er insgesamt über 2500 Plakate, darunter viele Filmplakate für die polnischen Kinoaufführungen internationaler Klassiker wie Apocalypse Now.

Waldemar Świerzy (1931, Katowice, Pologne – 2013, Varsovie) fut un graphiste polonais qui compta parmi les plus grands acteurs de la célèbre scène de l'affiche de son pays. En 1952, une fois diplômé de l'Académie des beaux-arts de Cracovie, il s'installa à Varsovie, où il travailla pour le compte de la maison d'édition WAG et du distributeur de films CWF. Après 1965, il dirigea le département de design de l'université des arts de Poznań, avant de présider la Biennale internationale de l'affiche de Varsovie de 1979 à 1994. Au cours de sa longue carrière, Świerzy créa plus de 2500 affiches, notamment pour les premières en polonais de classiques internationaux comme Apocalypse Now.

1974 · Waldemar Świerzy · PL · Poster

1984 · Waldemar Świerzy · PL · Poster

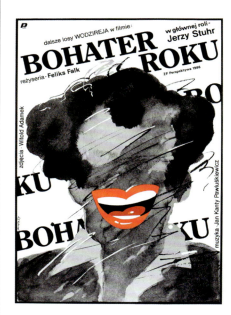

1987 · Waldemar Świerzy · PL · Poster

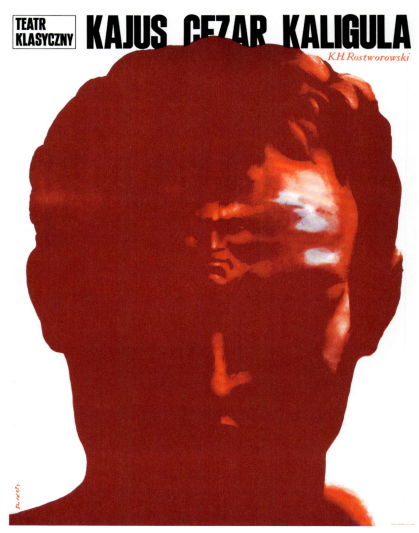

1966 · Waldemar Świerzy · PL · Poster

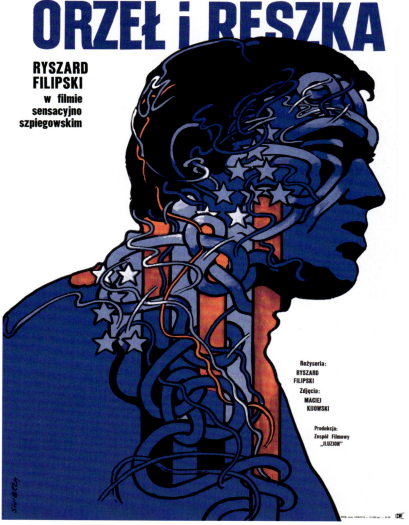

1974 · Waldemar Świerzy · PL · Poster

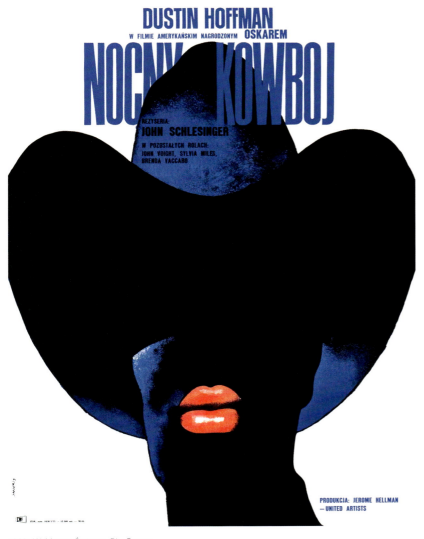

1969 · Waldemar Świerzy · PL · Poster

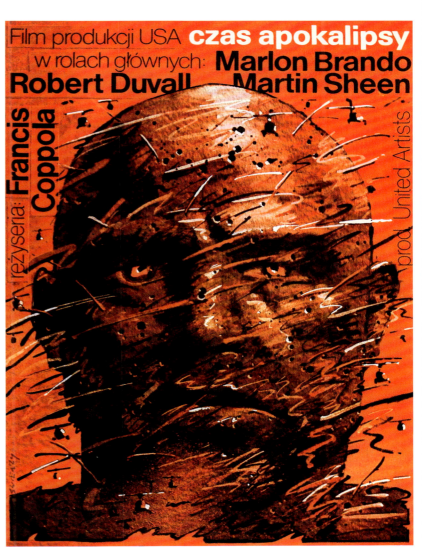

1979 · Waldemar Świerzy · PL · Poster

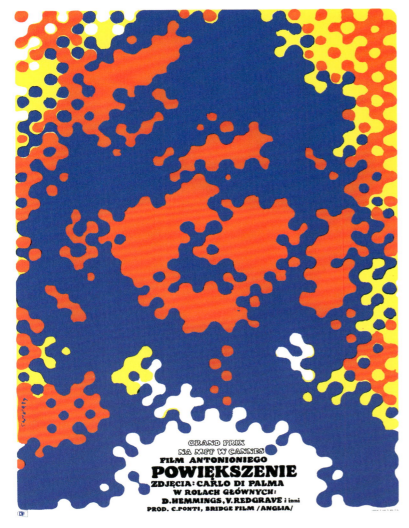

1968 · Waldemar Świerzy · PL · Poster

1971 · Waldemar Świerzy · PL · Poster

1982 · Max Kisman, Ronald Timmermans · NL · Poster

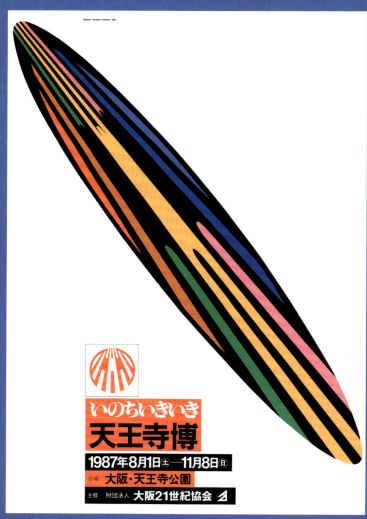

1989 · Anton Furst · UK/US · Poster

1980

1987 · Anonymous · UK · Magazine cover

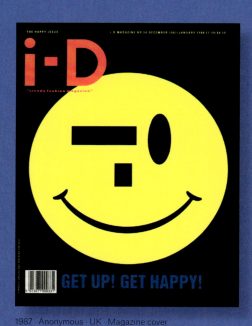

1986 · Shigeo Fukuda · JP · Poster

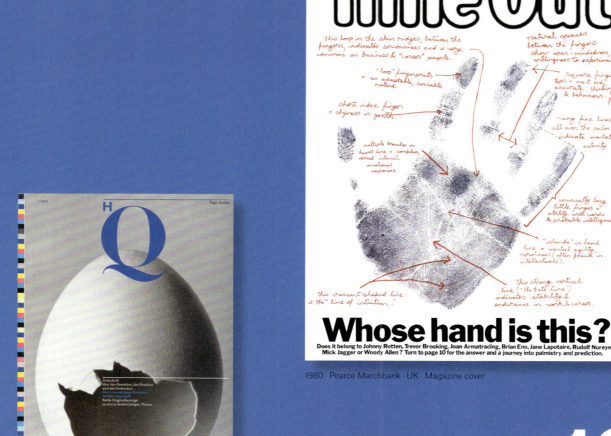

1980 · Pearce Marchbank · UK · Magazine cover

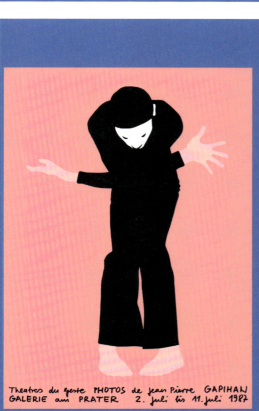

1985 · Rolf Müller · DE · Magazine cover

1989

1987 · Shimokochi-Reeves Design · US · Packaging

1987 · Hubert Riedel · GDR · Poster

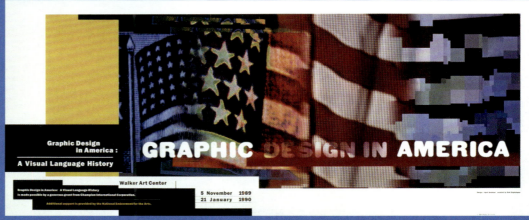

1989 · April Greiman · US · Poster

The new generation of young designers who appeared in the 1980s found that the modernist developments of the post-war decades now seemed largely antiquated. In their search for fresh approaches to design, they rebelled in a variety of ways against the basic notion that graphics must be spare and sober. Technological innovation, including the rapid rise of desktop publishing, came at just the right moment, and in 1984 Apple Macintosh brought out the first graphics-oriented computer. Page-Maker, which appeared a year later, was the first software to enable people to design and set up whole magazines and books in digital form. Programs for processing graphics and photos followed and immediately changed the entire face of the creative industry. Although it initially seemed that only the tools of the trade had disappeared, this first digital revolution found expression in an array of new works, many of them characterized by the sheer joy of trying out fresh possibilities.

In den 1980er-Jahren trat eine junge Generation von Gestalterinnen und Gestaltern in Erscheinung, denen die modernistische Entwicklung der Nachkriegsjahrzehnte als veraltet erschien. Auf der Suche nach neuen Ansätzen im Grafikdesign rebellierten sie auf unterschiedliche Art und Weise gegen die Maxime der aufgeräumten und sachlichen Grafik. Die technischen Innovationen, die das aufkommende Desktop-Publishing mit sich brachte, kamen da gerade zur rechten Zeit. 1984 wurde der Apple Macintosh als erster grafikorientierter Computer auf den Markt gebracht. Ein Jahr später erschien mit PageMaker eine Softwarelösung, die es erstmals ermöglichte, komplette Magazine und Bücher in digitaler Form zu realisieren. Programme zur Grafik- und Fotobearbeitung folgten und veränderten innerhalb kürzester Zeit die gesamte Kreativbranche. Auch wenn scheinbar nur das Handwerkszeug verändert wurde, schlug sich diese erste digitale Revolution auch in den realisierten Arbeiten nieder, die in vielen Fällen von der Experimentierfreude mit den neuen Möglichkeiten geprägt waren.

La nouvelle génération de jeunes graphistes qui émerge dans les années 1980 juge désuète l'évolution moderniste des décennies d'après-guerre. À la recherche de nouvelles approches, ils se rebellent de différentes manières contre la maxime d'un graphisme sobre et épuré. Dans ce contexte, des innovations technologiques comme le développement de la PAO arrivent à point nommé. Avec son Macintosh, Apple met sur le marché en 1984 le premier ordinateur à interface graphique. Un an plus tard, PageMaker devient le premier logiciel permettant de composer des magazines ou des livres complets sous forme numérique. Des programmes de traitement graphique et de retouche photo suivent et transforment l'ensemble du secteur créatif en un temps record. Même si seuls les outils de travail semblent avoir changé, cette révolution numérique se traduit aussi dans les réalisations, qui dénotent souvent le plaisir de l'expérimentation offert par les nouvelles technologies.

1980

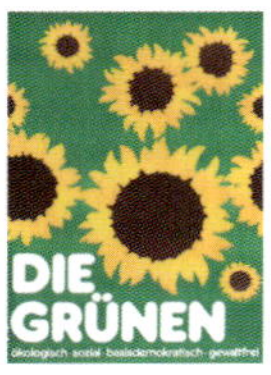

Green political parties become more actively engaged in Europe, Canada, and elsewhere

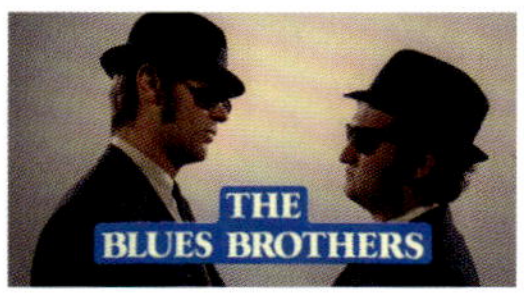

John Belushi and Dan Aykroyd star in *The Blues Brothers*

John Lennon is shot dead outside his house in New York

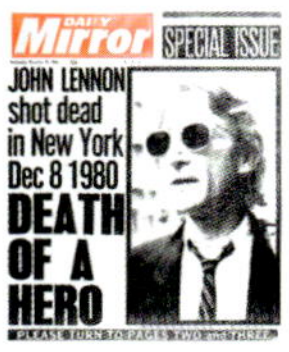

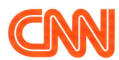

Cable Network News (CNN) is launched in the United States

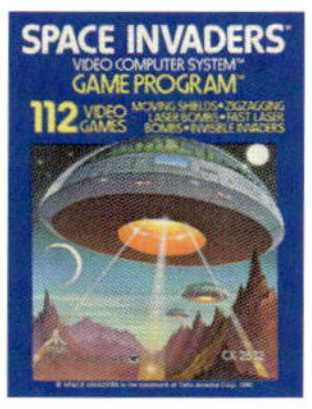

The Atari 2600 gaming console doubles its sales when the *Space Invaders* game is released

Ronald Reagan is elected president of the United States

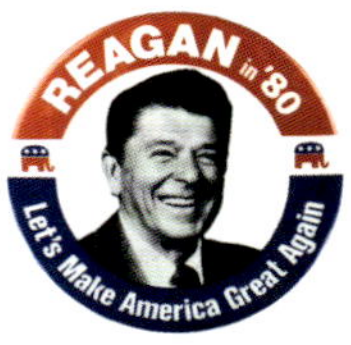

MUJI
無印良品

The Japanese retail company Muji is founded

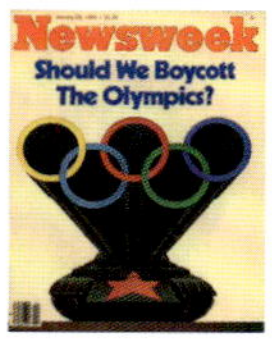

Several countries boycott the Summer Olympics in Moscow in protest at the Soviet invasion of Afghanistan

The Yugoslav Communist leader Marshal Josip Tito dies after 27 years of authoritarian presidency

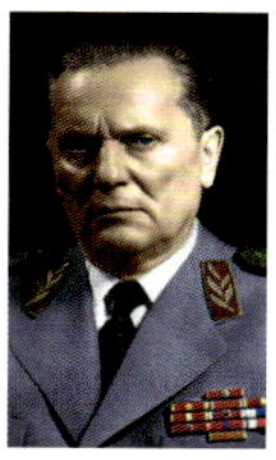

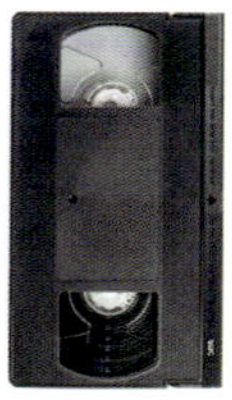

In the war over videotape formats VHS triumphs over Betamax

1981

Thrash metal arrives with new bands Metallica, Anthrax, and Slayer

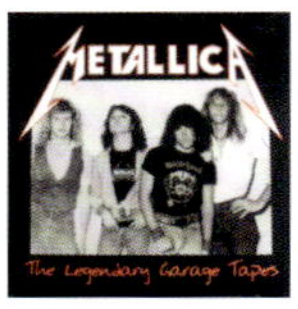

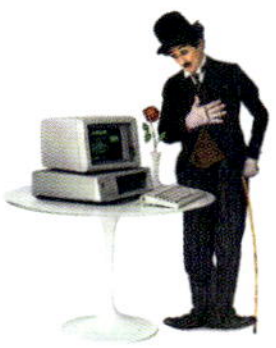

IBM enters the home personal computer market

The American music video channel MTV begins broadcasting

MUSIC TELEVISION®

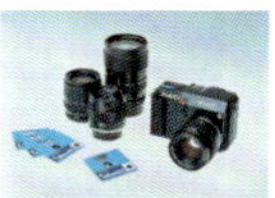

Sony unveils a prototype of its Mavica, the first still video camera, that used removable disks as the main recording medium

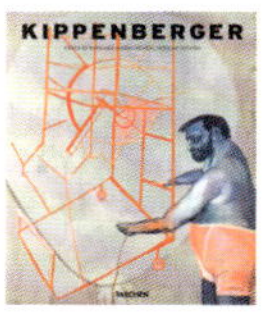

In Germany the free expressionistic art of the Neue Wilde movement features in a major exhibition

In the first attempted assassination of Pope John Paul II he is shot and wounded in St. Peter's Square

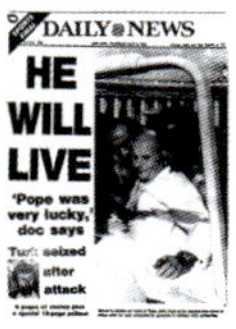

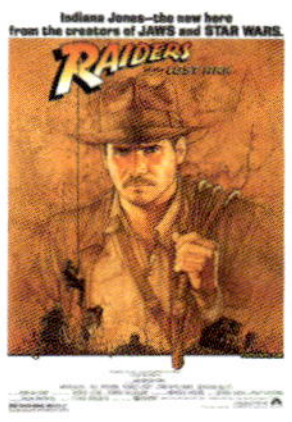

Raiders of the Lost Ark is released, the first Indiana Jones film

Columbia
YOUNG · CRIPPEN

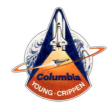

NASA's Space Shuttle program begins with the first flight of the orbiter *Columbia*

Colombian writer Gabriel García Márquez's novel *Chronicle of a Death Foretold* is published

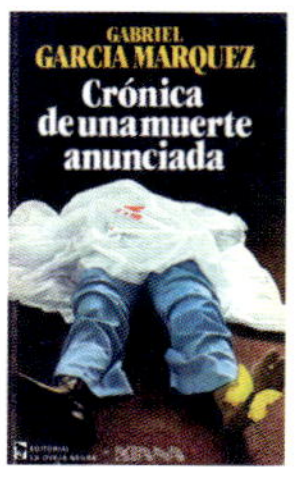

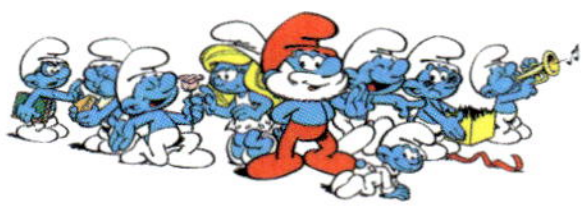

The animated television version of *The Smurfs* airs on NBC

1982

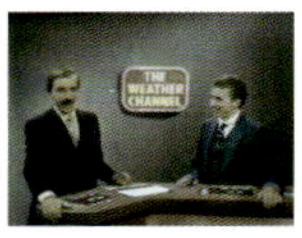

The Weather Channel starts broadcasting in the United States

ADOBE SYSTEMS INCORPORATED

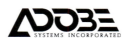

In California, Adobe Systems is founded by John Warnock and Charles Geschke

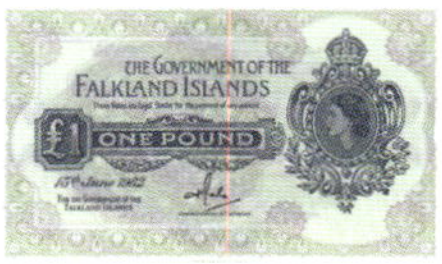

Argentina invades the Falkland Islands and starts a 10-week war with the United Kingdom

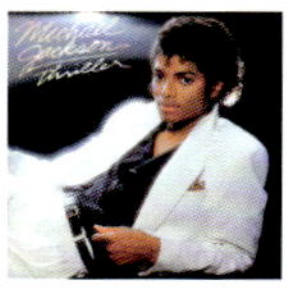

Michael Jackson's *Thriller* is released and becomes the best-selling album in recording history

The Commodore 64 home computer system is introduced

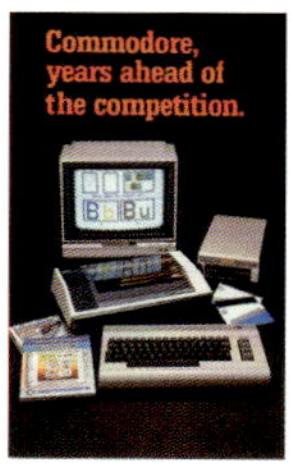

:-)

The first emoticons are posted by computer scientist Scott Fahlman

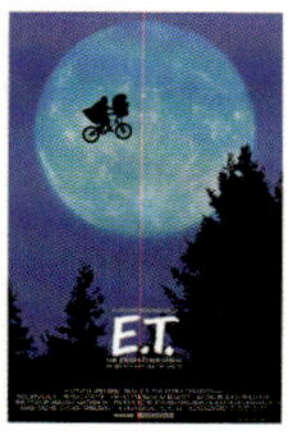

Steven Spielberg's movie *E.T. the Extra-Terrestrial* is released

Late Night with David Letterman

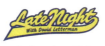

The talk show *Late Night with David Letterman* premieres on U.S. television

Isabel Allende's debut novel *The House of the Spirits* is published

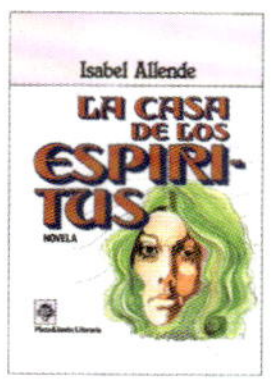

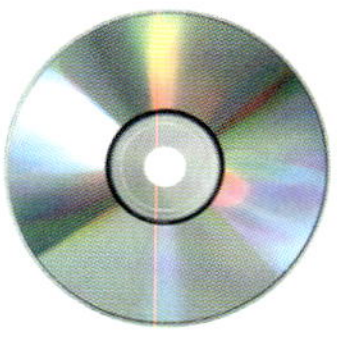

The CD is introduced as a new medium for the music industry

1983

Federal elections in West Germany confirm Helmut Kohl as Chancellor

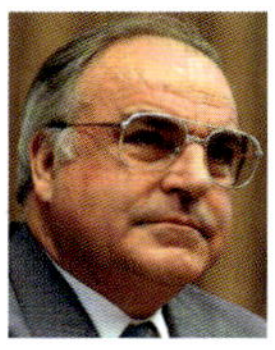

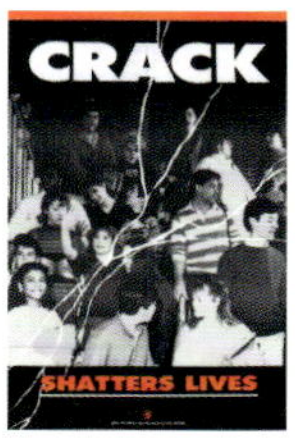

The first outbreak of crack cocaine use is recorded in the Bahamas

Madonna's self-titled debut album makes an initially slow start on the charts

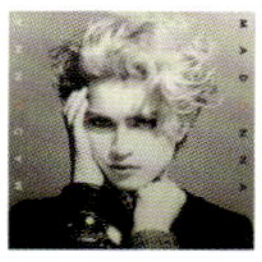

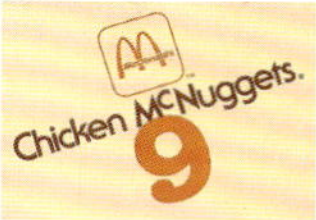

McDonald's introduces Chicken McNuggets

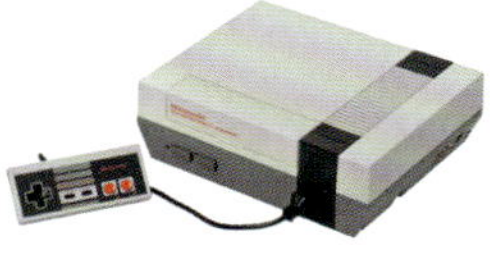

Nintendo releases its NES, the best-selling gaming console of its time

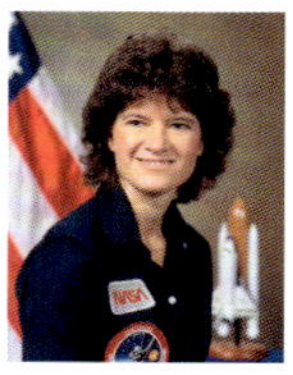

Sally Ride becomes the first American woman in space, on the Space Shuttle *Challenger's* STS-7 mission

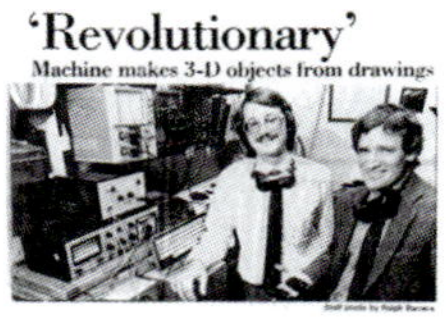

Chuck Hull develops the process behind stereolithography (3D printing)

The Monty Python film *The Meaning of Life* premieres in the United Kingdom, but is banned in Ireland

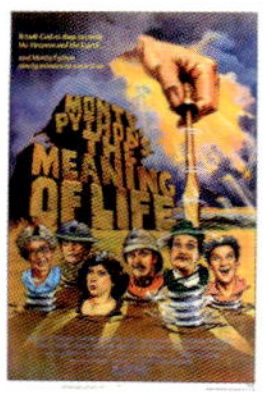

HOOTERS

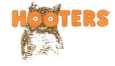

The first Hooters restaurant opens in Clearwater, Florida

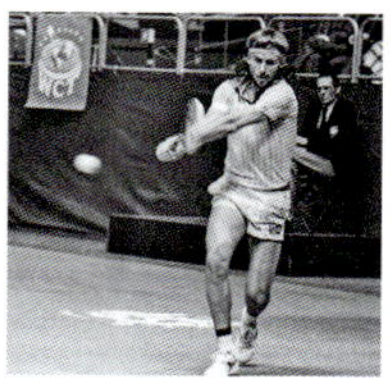

Björn Borg announces his retirement from tennis at the age of 26

1984

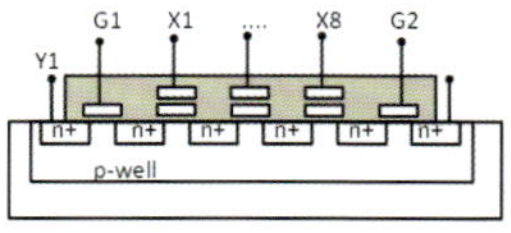

Toshiba introduces flash memory, invented by Fujio Masuoka

Arnold Schwarzenegger stars as the cyborg assassin in the sci-fi movie *The Terminator*

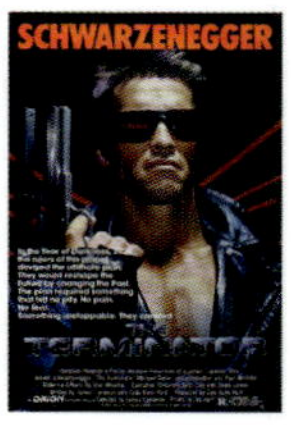

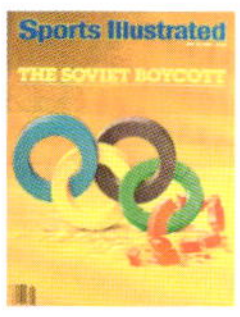

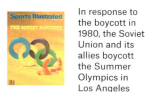

In response to the boycott in 1980, the Soviet Union and its allies boycott the Summer Olympics in Los Angeles

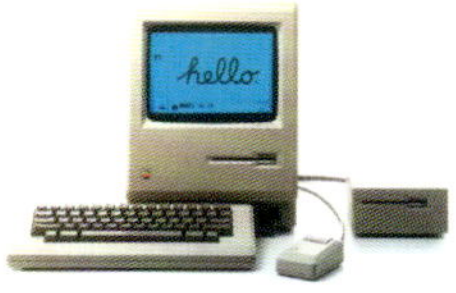

The Apple Macintosh is introduced

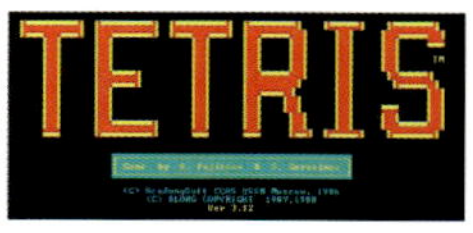

Russian game designer Alexey Pajitnov creates *Tetris*

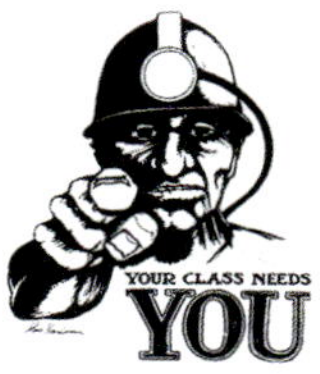

British coal-miners go on strike in March, and a bitter stand-off with the government lasts almost a year

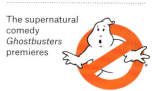

The supernatural comedy *Ghostbusters* premieres

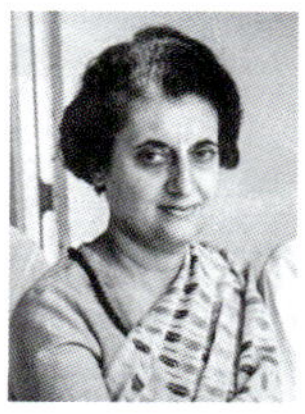

Indian Prime Minister Indira Gandhi is assassinated at home in New Delhi

CIRQUE DU SOLEIL.

The Cirque du Soleil performing group is founded in Canada

The title song "Purple Rain" is released from the album by Prince and the Revolution

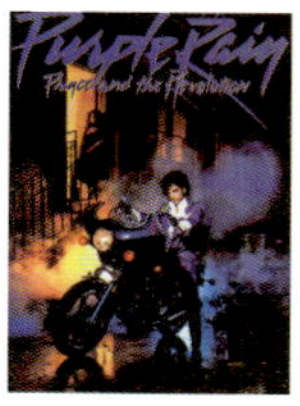

1985

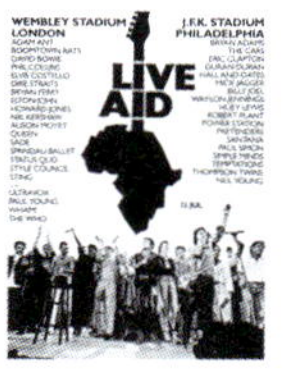
The multi-venue benefit concert Live Aid is held in response to the Ethiopian famine

The World Health Organization hosts the first conference on AIDS in response to the disease spreading worldwide

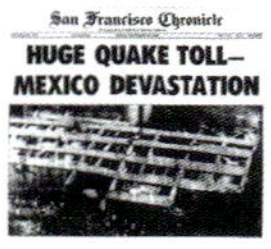
HUGE QUAKE TOLL–
MEXICO DEVASTATION
A huge earthquake hits Mexico City, killing at least 5,000 people and injuring 30,000

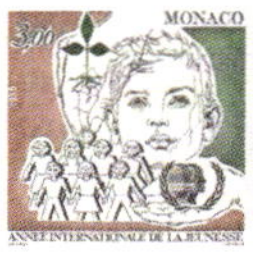
International Youth Year is proclaimed by the United Nations

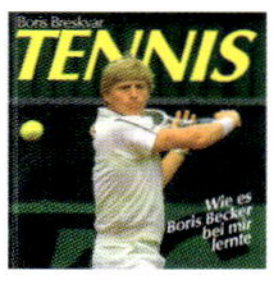
Boris Becker wins the tennis singles title at Wimbledon at the age of only 17

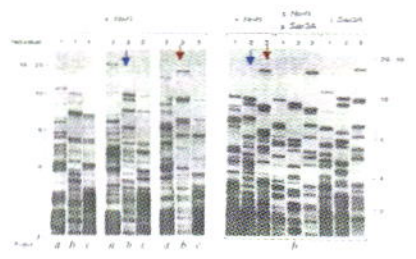
DNA is first used to assist in a criminal investigation

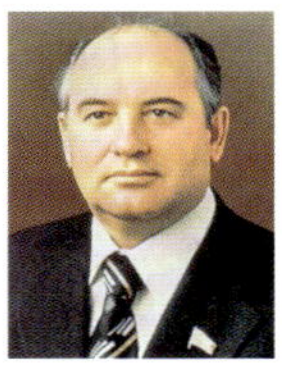
Mikhail Gorbachev becomes General Secretary of the Communist Party of the Soviet Union

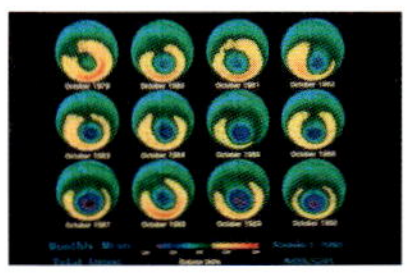
Discovery of the Ozone Hole is announced by scientists of the British Antarctic Survey

The NeXT computer company is founded by Steve Jobs

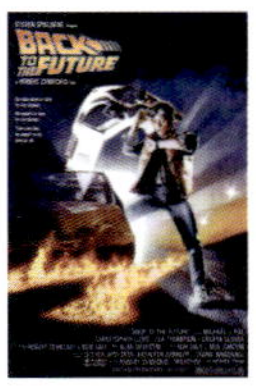
The first film in the *Back to the Future* series is released

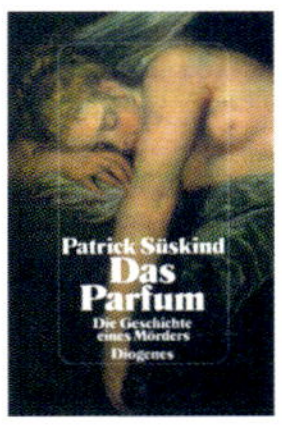
German author Patrick Süskind's novel *Perfume* is published

1986

ALF first appears on U.S. television

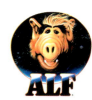

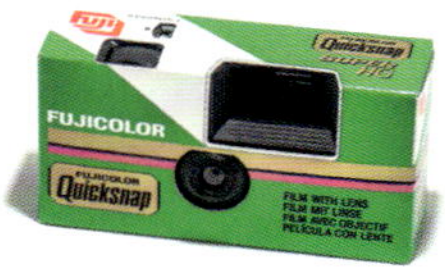
Fuji introduces the disposable camera

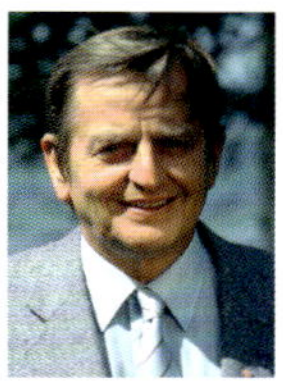
Swedish Prime Minister Olof Palme is assassinated in Stockholm

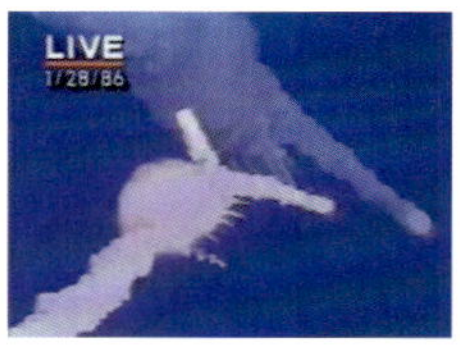
The Space Shuttle *Challenger* breaks up killing all seven crew members

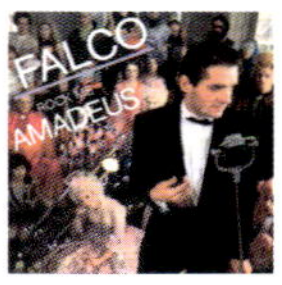
Austrian singer Falco's "Rock Me Amadeus" finds international success

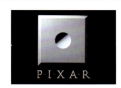

Pixar Animation Studios is founded in California

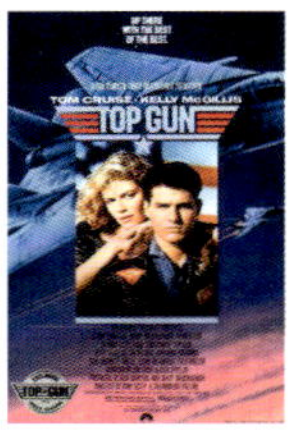
Tom Cruise stars in Tony Scott's *Top Gun* which becomes a huge success worldwide

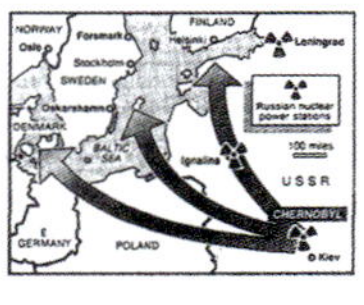
A catastrophic accident occurs at the Chernobyl nuclear power plant

The Treaty of Canterbury is signed, allowing work to proceed on the Channel Tunnel

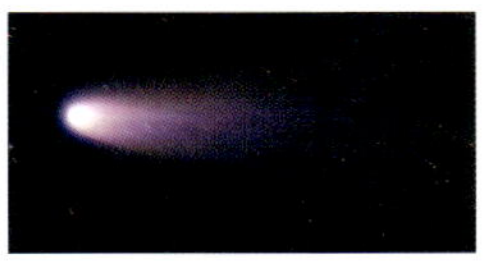
Halley's Comet is seen for the first time since 1910

1987

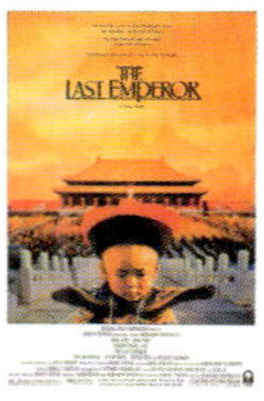
The British-Italian epic film *The Last Emperor* by Bernardo Bertolucci is released, winning nine Oscars the following year

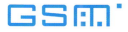

The first GSM technical specifications are agreed in Europe for mobile phone use and text messages

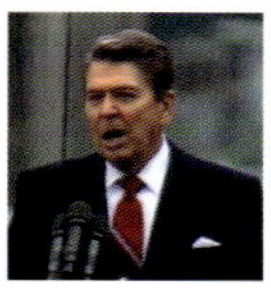
In a speech at the Brandenburg Gate in West Berlin, Reagan asks Gorbachev to "Tear down this wall!"

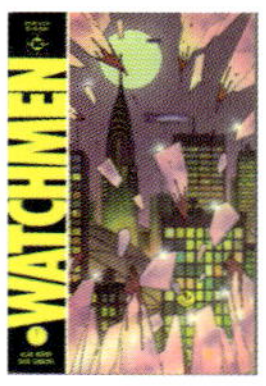
Watchmen is first published as a single-volume graphic novel

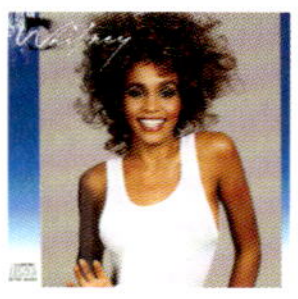
Whitney Houston's second album is the first by a female artist to top the Billboard charts on debut

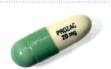

Prozac becomes available on prescription

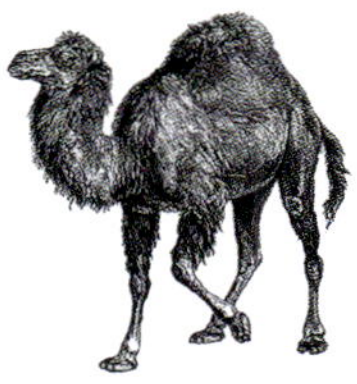
The Perl programming language is created by Larry Wall

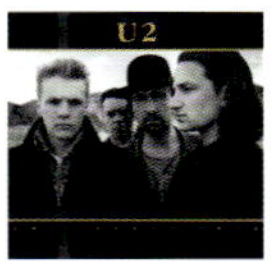
The Irish rock band U2 release their breakthrough album *The Joshua Tree*

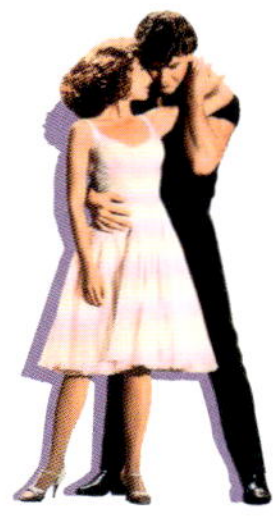
Patrick Swayze and Jennifer Grey star in *Dirty Dancing*

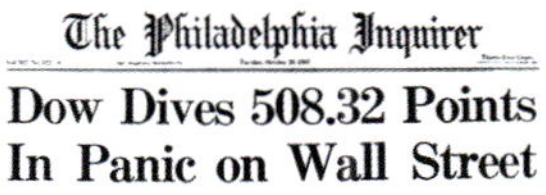
The Philadelphia Inquirer
Dow Dives 508.32 Points
In Panic on Wall Street
On Black Monday stock markets around the world crash in a way not seen since 1929

1988

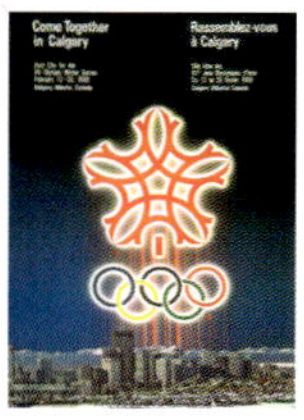
The Winter Olympics are held in Calgary, Canada

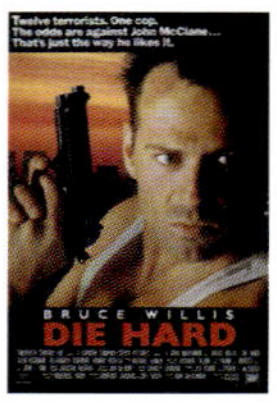
Bruce Willis stars in the first of the *Die Hard* movies

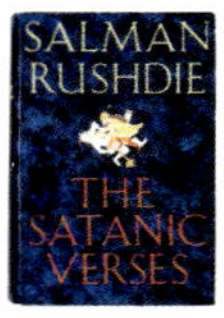
Salman Rushdie's novel *The Satanic Verses* is published, resulting in a *fatwa* being issued by Khomeini calling for his death

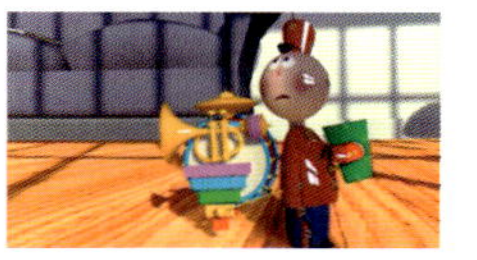
Pixar's *Tin Toy* becomes the first computer-animated film to win an Academy Award

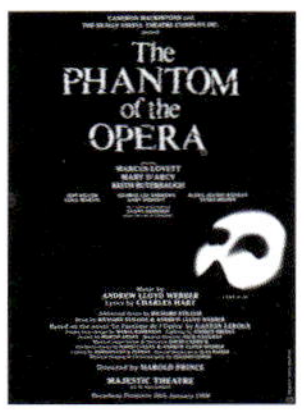
The Phantom of the Opera transfers from London's West End to Broadway, becoming its longest-running musical ever

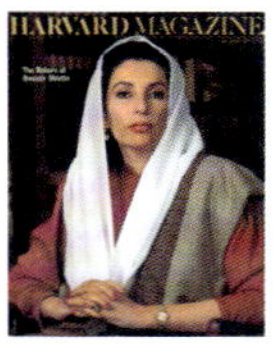
Benazir Bhutto becomes the Prime Minister of Pakistan and the first woman ever to lead a Muslim nation

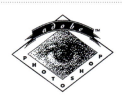

Adobe Photoshop is created by American Thomas Knoll

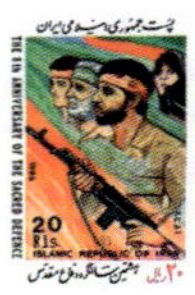
A ceasefire ends the eight-year Iran-Iraq War in which at least half a million people are estimated to have died

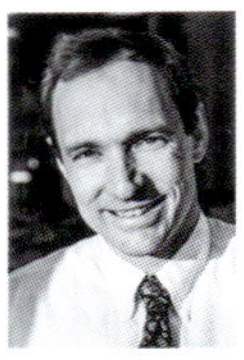
The first direct IP connection links Europe with North America and Tim Berners-Lee discusses a possible web-like system

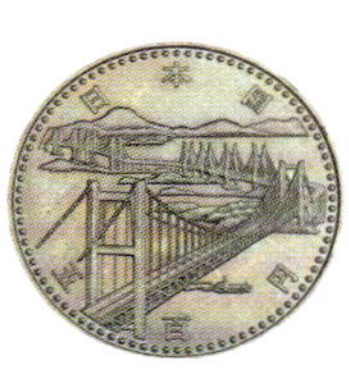
In Japan the Great Seto Bridge opens

1989

George H.W. Bush becomes president of the United States

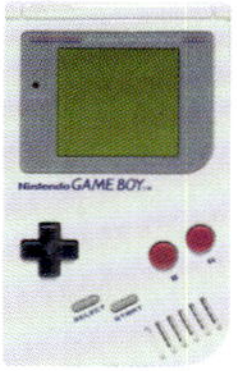
The Game Boy handheld gaming console is released by Nintendo

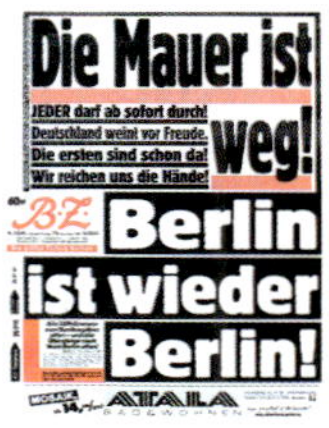
Die Mauer ist weg!
Berlin ist wieder Berlin!
The Berlin Wall falls and is officially demolished the following year

Burma changes its name to Myanmar

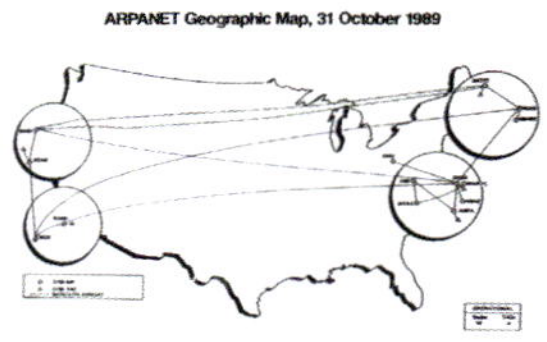
ARPANET Geographic Map, 31 October 1989
The packet-switching ARPANET system is replaced by the internet

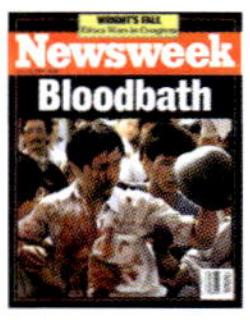
Newsweek
Bloodbath
Pro-democracy student protests in Beijing are forcibly suppressed, leading to the Tiananmen Square Massacre

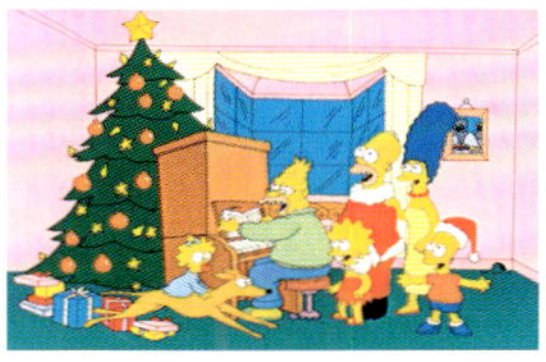
The first episode of *The Simpsons* is broadcast in the United States

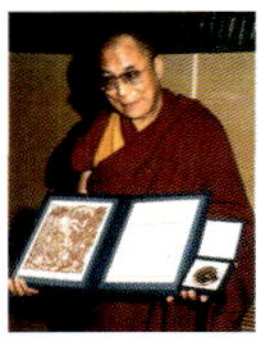
The 14th Dalai Lama wins the Nobel Peace Prize

The first Love Parade is held in West Berlin

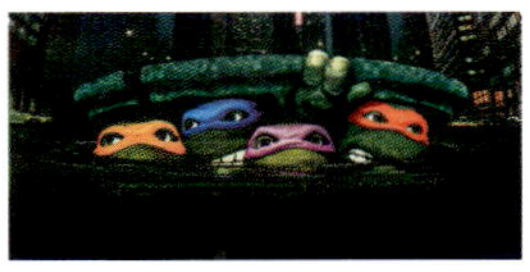
The Teenage Mutant Ninja Turtle craze sweeps the world

1980

The first issue of the British graphic design magazine **Creative Review** is published

The **Union des Designers en Belgique** (UDB) is founded, for graphic designers based in Belgium

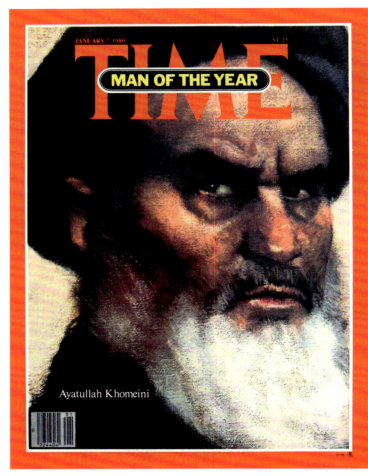

1980 · Walter Bernard (AD), Brad Holland (ILL) · US · Magazine cover

1980 · Pearce Marchbank · UK · Magazine cover

1980 · Karl Gerstner · CH · Logo · Ringier

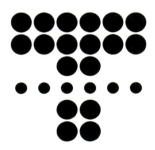

1980 · Stefan Kanchev · BG · Logo · Technica Books

1980 · Shawn Stüssy · US · Logo · Stüssy

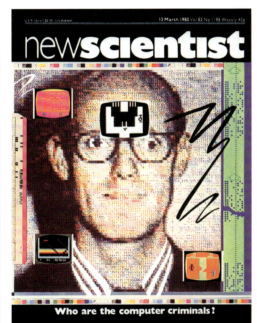

1980 · Anonymous · YU · Magazine cover

1980 · Christine Jones, Edward Bell · UK · Magazine cover

1980 · Fuki Ito · JP · Poster

1980 · Jean Widmer · CH/FR/DE · Poster

1980 · Jerzy Janiszewski · PL · Poster

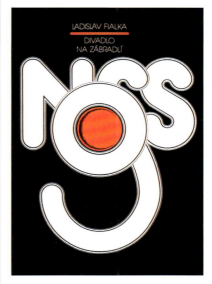

1980 · Jan Solpera · CZ · Poster

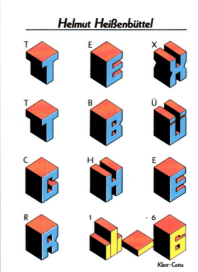

1980 · Heinz Edelmann · DE · Book cover

1980 · Anonymous · RU · Poster

1985 · Helmut Schmid · DE/JP · Packaging

1988 · Helmut Schmid · DE/JP · Packaging

1980 · Helmut Schmid · DE/JP · Packaging

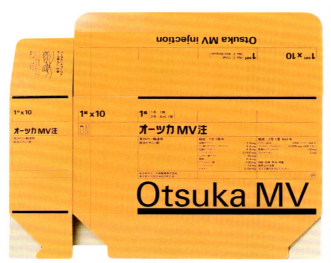

1980 · Helmut Schmid · DE/JP · Packaging

1980 · Helmut Schmid · DE/JP · Packaging

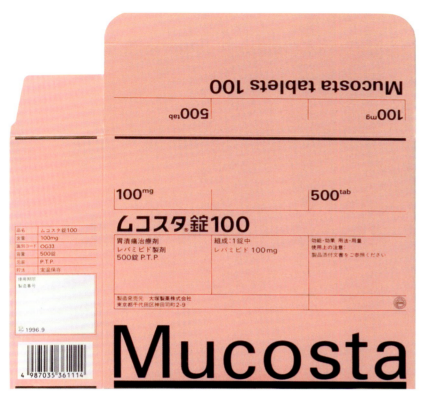

1988 · Helmut Schmid · DE/JP · Packaging

Helmut Schmid (1942, Ferlach, Austria – 2018, Osaka) was a German typographer (he was born a German citizen) and vital figure in the development of his field. Initially training as a typesetter in Germany, Schmid moved to Basel to study under Emil Ruder. During his international career he worked in Dusseldorf, Berlin, Stockholm, Montreal, and Osaka, also teaching at Kobe Design University in Japan and Hongik University in South Korea. His influential book *Typography Today* was first published in 1980, and Schmid's broad body of work also included packaging design for some of the largest food, pharmaceutical, and cosmetic brands in Japan.

Helmut Schmid (1942, Ferlach, Österreich – 2018, Osaka) hat als deutscher Schriftsetzer (er war von Geburt deutscher Staatsbürger) maßgeblich Anteil an der Weiterentwicklung der Typografie. Zunächst absolvierte er in Deutschland eine Ausbildung zum Schriftsetzer und ging dann nach Basel, um bei Emil Ruder zu studieren. Im Lauf seiner internationalen Karriere hat er in Düsseldorf, Berlin, Stockholm, Montreal und Osaka gearbeitet, zudem unterrichtete er an der Kobe Design University in Japan und der Hongik University in Südkorea. Sein einflussreiches Buch *Typography Today* erschien 1980. Zu Schmids umfassendem Œuvre gehört auch Verpackungsdesign für einige der größten Nahrungs-, Pharma- und Kosmetikfirmen Japans.

Helmut Schmid (1942, Ferlach, Autriche – 2018, Osaka) fut un typographe né citoyen allemand en Autriche et fervent acteur du développement de son domaine. Formé d'abord comme compositeur en Allemagne, Schmid s'installe ensuite à Bâle pour suivre des études auprès d'Emil Ruder. Pendant sa carrière internationale, il a travaillé à Düsseldorf, Berlin, Stockholm, Montréal et Osaka, et il a enseigné à la Kobe Design University, au Japon, et l'université de Hongik, en Corée du Sud. Son livre influent *Typography Today* a été publié pour la première fois en 1980, et le vaste travail de Schmid compte aussi du design d'emballages pour quelques-unes des plus grandes marques alimentaires, pharmaceutiques et cosmétiques du Japon.

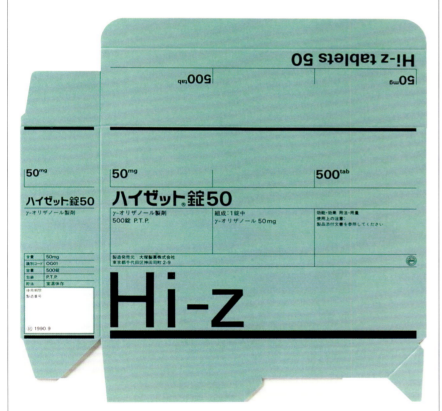

1988 · Helmut Schmid · DE/JP · Packaging

1980 · Helmut Schmid · DE/JP · Packaging

1981 · Wolfgang Weingart · CH · Poster

1981 · Wolfgang Weingart · CH · Poster

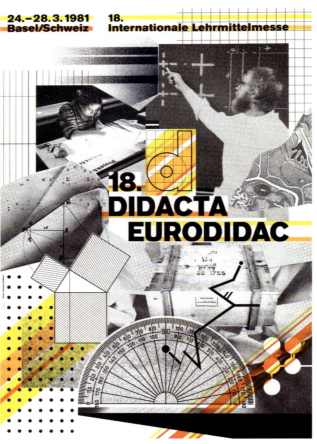

1981 · Wolfgang Weingart · CH · Poster

1984 · Wolfgang Weingart · CH · Poster

Wolfgang Weingart (1941, Constance, Germany) is a designer and typographer whose expressive work evolved out of the earlier Swiss Style. Following studies at the Merz Academy in Stuttgart, he trained as a typographer, then studied at the Basel School of Design under Emil Ruder and Armin Hofmann. With an insatiable appetite for experimentation, Weingart instigated a wholesale renewal of typography through his posters and radical cover designs for the *Typographische Monatsblätter* magazine, while teaching at the Basel School of Design. His courses at Yale and lectures around the world have earned him an international reputation. In 2014, the Museum of Design in Zurich presented a retrospective of Weingart's work.

Wolfgang Weingart (1941, Konstanz) ist ein Grafikdesigner und Typograf, dessen ausdrucksstarkes Werk aus dem früheren „Swiss Style" hervorgeht. Auf sein Studium an der Merz-Akademie in Stuttgart folgte zunächst eine Lehre als Schriftsetzer, dann studierte er in Basel an der Schule für Gestaltung bei Emil Ruder und Armin Hofmann. Mit leidenschaftlicher Experimentierfreudigkeit führte Weingart eine Rundumerneuerung der Typografie herbei, wie seine Plakate und die radikalen Entwürfe für die Titelseite der Zeitschrift *Typographische Monatsblätter* verdeutlichen. Gleichzeitig unterrichtete er an der Schule für Gestaltung in Basel. Durch seine Seminare in Yale und seine Vorträge in aller Welt ist er international anerkannt. 2014 richtete das Museum für Gestaltung Zürich eine Retrospektive seines Schaffens aus.

Wolfgang Weingart (1941, Constance, Allemagne) est un designer et typographe dont le style expressif s'est développé à partir du style suisse. Après des études à la Merz Akademie à Stuttgart, il suit une formation de typographe, puis étudie à l'école de design de Bâle auprès d'Emil Ruder et d'Armin Hofmann. Habité par un appétit insatiable pour l'expérimentation, Weingart a motivé un renouveau global de la typographie avec ses affiches et ses couvertures radicales pour la revue *Typographische Monatsblätter,* tout en enseignant à l'école de design de Bâle. Ses cours à l'université Yale et les conférences qu'il a données dans le monde entier lui ont valu une notoriété internationale. En 2014, le musée du design de Zurich a présenté une rétrospective du travail de Weingart.

1978 · Wolfgang Weingart · CH · Poster

As a founding member and art director of the legendary independent British label Factory Records, Peter Saville accessed a mass audience through pop music, best exemplified in the series of record sleeves he created for Joy Division and New Order between 1979 and 1993. His radical designs seemed to break all the rules, omitting information about artists or titles and fundamentally questioning modes of consumption and communication.

Als Gründungsmitglied und Artdirector des legendären britischen Independent-Labels Factory Records erreichte Peter Saville durch die Popmusik ein Millionenpublikum. Anschaulichstes Beispiel dafür sind die Plattencover, die er zwischen 1979 und 1993 für Joy Division und New Order gestaltete. Bei seinen radikalen Entwürfen brach er mit sämtlichen Regeln, verzichtete auf Informationen zu Musikern oder Titeln und stellte die Konsum- und Kommunikationskultur grundsätzlich infrage.

En tant que membre fondateur et directeur artistique du légendaire label de musique indépendant britannique Factory Records, Peter Saville a pu toucher un public de masse à travers la musique pop, comme l'illustrent le mieux les pochettes d'albums qu'il a créées entre 1979 et 1993 pour Joy Division et New Order. Ses graphismes absolus semblaient rompre avec toutes les règles établies, omettant une partie de l'information sur les artistes ou les titres, et questionnant fondamentalement les modes de consommation et de communication.

1983 · Peter Saville · UK · Record cover (front)

1983 · Peter Saville · UK · Record cover (back)

Section 25-Always now friendly fires dirty disco c.p. loose talk costs lives inside out melt close hit babies in the bardo be brave new horizon produced by martin hannett engineer john caffrey recorded at brittania row disegnatori : grafica industria e typografica berthold a factory records product fact 45

1981 · Peter Saville · UK · Record cover

1980 · Peter Saville, Ben Kelly · UK · Record cover

Peter Saville (1955, Manchester) is a British artist and designer whose contribution to culture has been unique. After graduating from Manchester Polytechnic in 1978 he founded his own studio in London. Saville is recognised for creating pioneering work in the fields of music, fashion, sport, and politics, and his achievements were celebrated in *The Peter Saville Show* at the Design Museum in London in 2003. His first major show in a contemporary art museum was at the Migros Museum in Zurich in 2005 and he continues to exhibit internationally. Saville is a Royal Designer for Industry and won the London Design Medal in 2013.

Peter Saville (1955, Manchester) ist ein britischer Künstler und Grafikdesigner, der einen einzigartigen Beitrag zur Kultur geleistet hat. Nach abgeschlossenem Studium am Manchester Polytechnic im Jahr 1978 gründete er in London sein eigenes Grafikbüro. Saville gilt als Schöpfer bahnbrechender Arbeiten in den Bereichen Musik, Mode, Sport und Politik, seine Leistungen wurden 2003 mit der *Peter Saville Show* im Design Museum in London gewürdigt. Seine erste große Ausstellung in einem Museum für zeitgenössische Kunst folgte 2005 im Migros Museum in Zürich, seitdem ist er immer wieder weltweit durch Ausstellungen vertreten. Saville ist ein Royal Designer for Industry und wurde 2013 mit der London Design Medal ausgezeichnet.

Peter Saville (1955, Manchester) est un artiste et graphiste britannique qui a apporté à la culture une contribution unique en son genre. Après avoir obtenu son diplôme de la Manchester Polytechnic en 1978, il ouvre son propre studio à Londres. Saville est connu pour son travail pionnier dans les domaines de la musique, de la mode, du sport et de la politique, et ses réalisations ont été célébrées en 2003 dans l'exposition «The Peter Saville Show» présentée au musée du design de Londres. Sa première grande exposition dans un musée d'art contemporain s'est tenue au Musée Migros à Zurich en 2005, et il continue d'exposer au niveau international. Saville a reçu la distinction de Royal Designer for Industry et a remporté la London Design Medal en 2013.

1998 · Peter Saville, John Currin, Horst Diekgerdes (PH) · UK · Record cover

1993 · Peter Saville, Brett Wickens · UK · Record cover

1989 · Peter Saville, Trevor Key · UK · Record cover

2006 · Peter Saville · UK · Sneaker

1978 · Peter Saville · UK · Poster

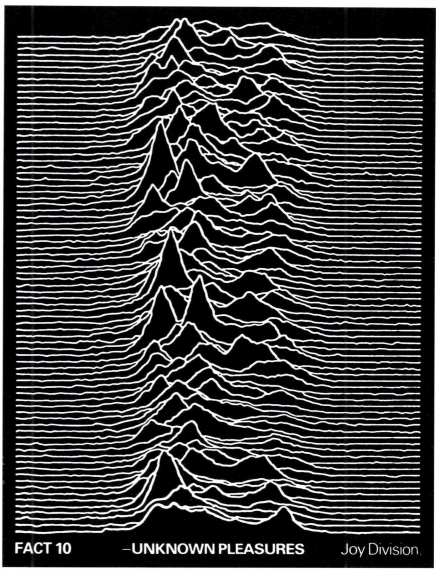

1979 · Peter Saville · UK · Promotional sticker

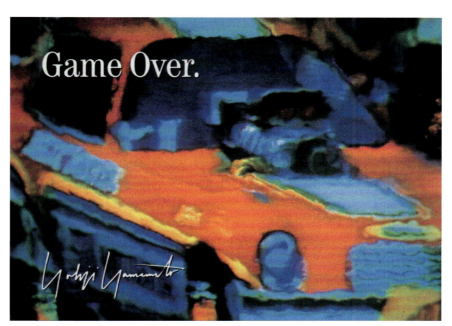

1991 · Peter Saville · UK · Ad

2013 · Peter Saville · UK/FR · Experimental logo · Lacoste

2016 · Peter Saville · UK · 3D graphic representation

221

1981

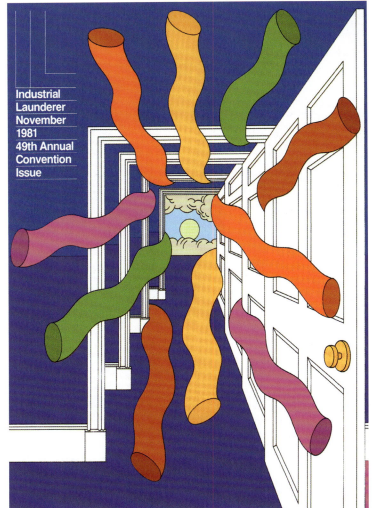

1981 · Jack Lefkowitz · US · Magazine cover

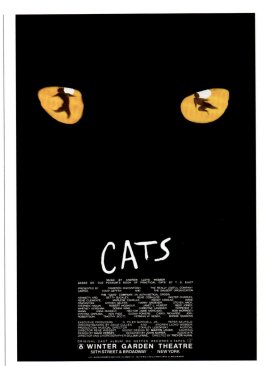

1981 · Anonymous · US · Poster

1981 · Paul Rand · US · Poster

1981 · Anonymous · YU · Magazine cover

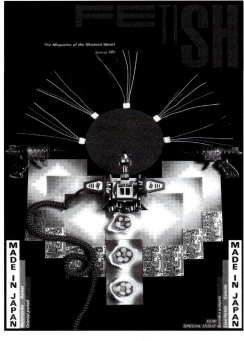

1981 · Jane Kosstrin, David Sterling · US · Magazine cover

Josef Müller-Brockmann's theoretical work **Rastersysteme für die visuelle Gestaltung** (Grid Systems in Graphic Design) is published

Neville Brody becomes art director of **The Face** magazine

The **Bitstream** corporation is founded to distribute digital typefaces

ERTOIL

1981 · Fernando Medina · ES · Logo · Ertoil

1981 · Asher Kalderon · IL · Logo · Jewish Youth Games

1981 · Thales Pereira · BR · Logo · BRB Engineering

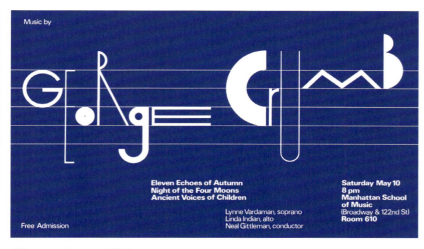

1981 · Lorraine Ferguson · US · Poster

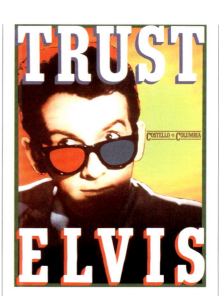

1981 · Paula Scher · US · Poster

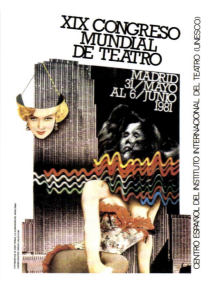

1981 · Miguel Calatayud · ES · Poster

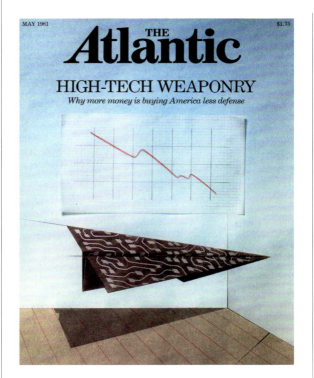

1981 · Walter Bernard (AD), André Thijssen (ILL) · US · Magazine cover

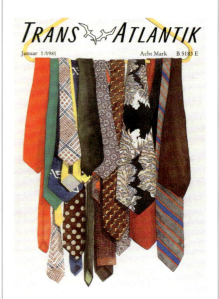

1981 · Isolde Monson-Baumgart · DE · Magazine cover

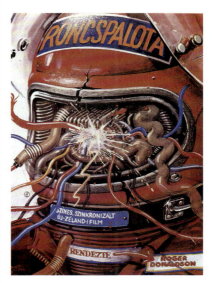

1981 · Eri J. Tamás · HU · Poster

1981 · Michael Doret · US · Poster

1981 · GGK München · DE · Poster

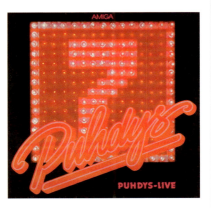

1981 · Anonymous · GDR · Record cover

Although the music channel MTV has lost some of the pulling power it could boast during its heyday in the 1980s, its logo has become a pop-cultural icon. Much of this is down to the introduction, a few years after broadcasting began, of animated versions of the logo, which were aired between music videos. These sequences, often lasting only seconds, turned the 1960s rule of "Don't play with the logo" completely on its head. Many artists, filmmakers, and graphic designers have done the craziest and most bizarre things with the MTV logo, thereby creating a vibrant brand identity which is made even more memorable because it breaks all the rules.

Obwohl der Musiksender MTV nicht mehr die Strahlkraft seiner Hochzeit in den 1980er-Jahren besitzt, ist sein Logo eine Ikone der Popkultur geworden. Maßgeblichen Anteil daran hatte das wenige Jahre nach dem Sendestart entwickelte Konzept animierter Logos, die zwischen jedem Musikvideo gezeigt wurden. In oft nur wenige Sekunden dauernden Sequenzen wurde die in den 1960er-Jahren formulierte Regel „Don't play with the logo" ins Gegenteil verkehrt. Zahlreiche Künstler, Filmemacher und Grafikdesigner stellten die verrücktesten und absurdesten Dinge mit dem MTV-Markenzeichen an und schufen dabei eine höchst lebendige Identität, die gerade durch ihre Nonkonformität einprägsam wurde.

Même si la chaîne musicale MTV a perdu de l'aura qui était la sienne à son apogée dans les années 1980, son logo est resté une icône de la culture populaire. L'introduction quelques années après les débuts de la chaîne de logos animés apparaissant entre chaque vidéoclip y a largement contribué. Ces séquences souvent limitées à quelques secondes déjouaient la règle «On ne joue pas avec le logo» formulée dans les années 1960. De nombreux artistes, réalisateurs et graphistes créèrent alors les choses les plus folles et absurdes à partir du logo MTV, donnant ainsi lieu à une identité des plus dynamiques qui frappa les esprits précisément par son anticonformisme.

1981 · Pat Gorman, Frank Olinsky, Patti Rogoff, Manhattan Design · US · Logo

»Probably the most revolutionary part of the story came when they were asked to come up with the 'corporate colors' for the logo. The decision was made that there weren't any, and that the logo should always change.« Frank Olinsky, 2008

1980s · Various · US · Television graphics

1975 · Takenobu Igarashi · JP · Magazine cover

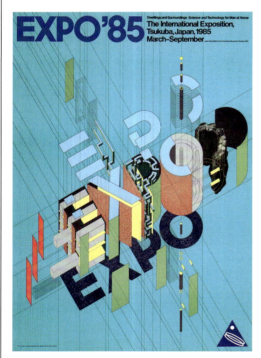

1985 · Takenobu Igarashi · JP · Poster

1987 · Takenobu Igarashi · JP · Brochure cover

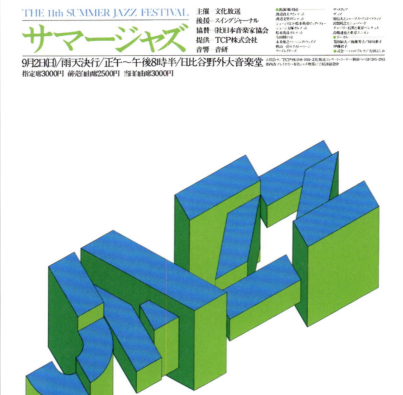

1983 · Takenobu Igarashi · JP · Poster

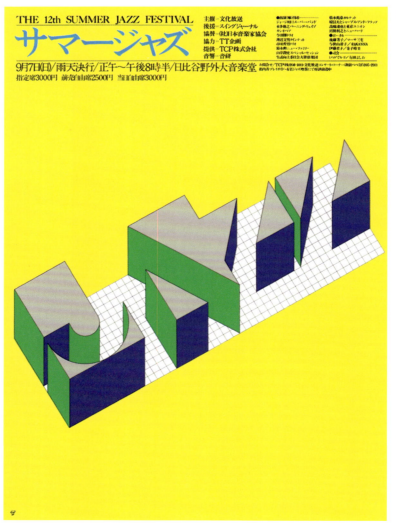

1980 · Takenobu Igarashi · JP · Poster

Takenobu Igarashi (1944, Tokyo) is a Japanese designer and sculptor. Gaining international recognition for his identity work and product design in the 1970s and '80s, he began developing groundbreaking 3D typographic experiments on axonometric grids, as showcased in his book *Igarashi Alphabets: From Graphics to Sculptures* (1987). Igarashi graduated from Tama Art University in Tokyo in 1968, before completing his postgraduate studies in California. Notable works include his Aluminum (1983) and Ori (Folded, 1985) alphabets, as well as the MoMA Calendar Series, for which he produced over 4,000 different hand-drawn axonometric numerals. Since 1994, Igarashi has focused on making art.

Takenobu Igarashi (1944, Tokio) ist ein japanischer Grafikdesigner und Bildhauer. International zu Ansehen gelangte er in den 1970er- und 1980er-Jahren durch seine CI-Projekte und sein Produktdesign. In der Folge entwickelte er seine bahnbrechenden typografischen 3-D-Experimente auf axonometrischen Rastern, wie man sie aus seinem Buch *Igarashi Alphabets: From Graphics to Sculptures* (1987) kennt. Igarashi machte 1968 an der Tama Art University in Tokio seinen Abschluss und schloss seine Ausbildung in Kalifornien ab. Zu seinen berühmten Arbeiten gehören seine Alphabete Aluminum (1983) und Ori (Folded, 1985) sowie die MoMA-Kalenderserie, für die er von Hand über 4.000 verschiedene axonometrische Ziffern schuf. Seit 1994 widmet Igarashi sich vorwiegend der Kunst.

Takenobu Igarashi (1944, Tokyo) est un designer et sculpteur japonais. Reconnu internationalement pour ses identités de marques et designs de produits dans les années 1970 et 1980, il commence à se livrer à des expériences révolutionnaires de typographie en 3D sur des grilles axonométriques, telles que celles dans son livre *Igarashi Alphabets: From Graphics to Sculptures* (1987). En 1968, Igarashi s'est diplômé de l'université des beaux-arts Tama à Tokyo, puis a poursuivi des études de troisième cycle en Californie. Ses œuvres les plus remarquables sont les alphabets Aluminum (1983) et Ori (Plié, 1985), ainsi que la série de calendriers réalisés pour le MoMA, pour lesquels il a produit à la main plus de 4000 chiffres axonométriques distincts. Depuis 1994, Igarashi se consacre essentiellement à la production artistique.

1981 · Takenobu Igarashi · JP · Magazine cover

1981 · Takenobu Igarashi · JP · Magazine cover

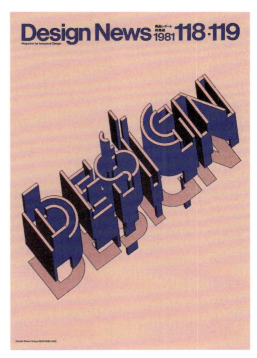

1981 · Takenobu Igarashi · JP · Magazine cover

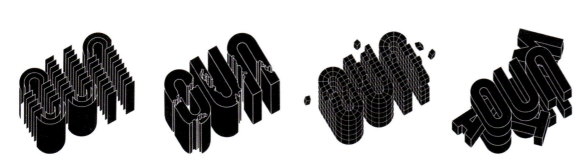

1986 · Takenobu Igarashi · JP · Logo/Identity · Oun

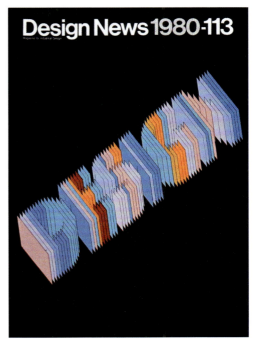

1980 · Takenobu Igarashi · JP · Magazine cover

1982

The **Adobe Corporation** is founded by John Warnock and Charles Geschke

The **Arial** typeface is designed by Robin Nicholas and Patricia Saunders for Monotype, for use on low-definition computer displays

1982 · Anonymous · DE · Record cover

ERICSSON

1982 · Terry Moore · UK · Logo · Ericsson

1982 · Félix Beltrán, Teresa Echartea · CU/MX · Tequila Mexicano

1982 · Paul Rand · US · Logo · AIGA

1982 · Oliviero Toscani · IT · Ad

1982 · Gerald Scarfe · UK · Poster

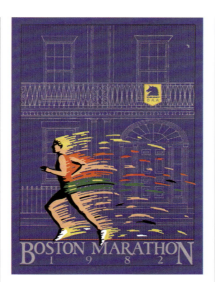

1982 · Hugh Ricks · US · Poster

The logotype shown below is the copyright of Channel Four Television and may not be reproduced or transformed in any form or by any means without the proper permission of Channel Four Television. The logotype consists of both the numeral 4 and the words Channel Four Television and must be used in it's entirety on all items relating to the company.
Application of the logotype must conform to one of the standard designs shown on the artwork supplied.
No other arrangement of the numeral and wording or typestyle or colour is permissable, nor may the logotype be linked to any typography or other graphic device.

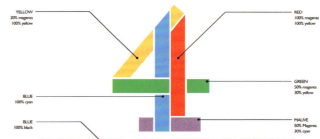

YELLOW
20% magenta
100% yellow

RED
100% magenta
100% yellow

GREEN
50% magenta
30% yellow

BLUE
100% cyan

MAUVE
50% magenta
30% cyan

BLUE
100% black

CHANNEL FOUR TELEVISION

1982 · Nancy Donald, Robert Peak · US · Record cover

COLOUR ON WHITE   COLOUR ON BLACK   WHITE ON BLACK OR COLOUR   BLACK ON WHITE

COLOUR SPECIFICATION
ARTWORK SHEET ONE
ARTWORK SHEET TWO

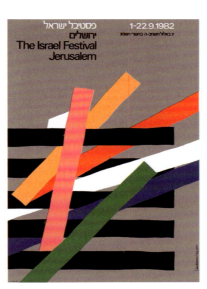

1982 · Yarom Vardimon · IL · Poster

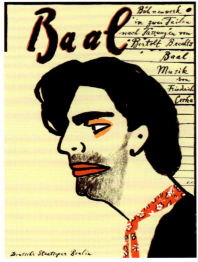

1982 · Volker Pfüller · GDR · Poster

1982 · Barney Bubbles · UK · Record cover

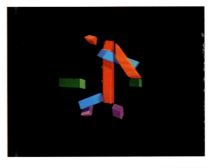
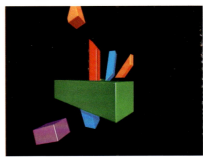

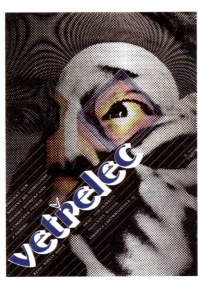

1982 · Zdeněk Ziegler · CZ · Poster

1982 · Anonymous · JP · Ad

1982 · Lambie-Nairn · UK · Identity · Channel Four Television

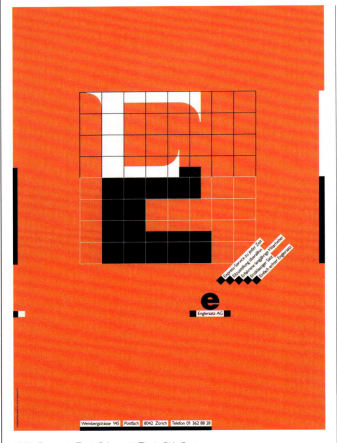

1983 · Rosmarie Tissi, Odermatt+Tissi · CH · Poster

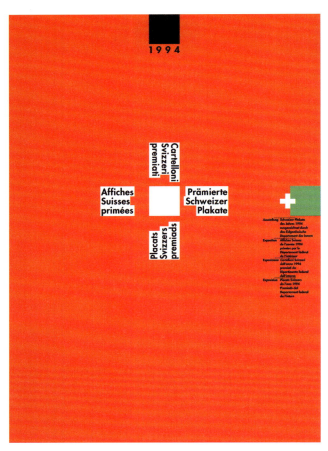

1994 · Rosmarie Tissi, Odermatt + Tissi · CH · Poster

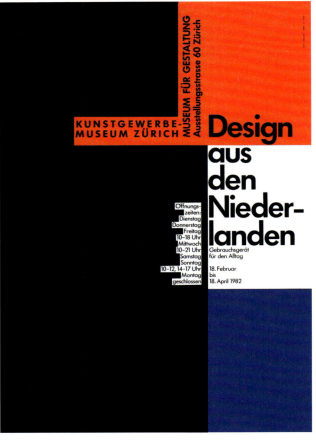

1982 · Siegfried Odermatt, Odermatt+Tissi · CH · Poster

1984 · Rosmarie Tissi, Odermatt + Tissi · CH · Poster

Odermatt & Tissi (1968, Switzerland) is the creative partnership of designers Siegfried Odermatt (1926–2017, Zurich) and Rosmarie Tissi (1937, Thayngen, Switzerland). After studying in Zurich at the School of Design, Tissi joined the self-taught Odermatt originally as a trainee. Their unique visual approach—with radical cropping of images, and distinctive use of typography and color—gained the duo a cult status. In 1992, the pair exhibited some of their poster work at the Reinhard-Brown Gallery in New York, and later had shows in Tokyo, Essen, and other locations. They also designed several books.

Odermatt & Tissi (1968, Schweiz) ist die Kreativpartnerschaft der Grafikdesigner Siegfried Odermatt (1926–2017, Zürich) und Rosmarie Tissi (1937, Thayngen, Schweiz). Nach dem Besuch der Schule für Gestaltung Zürich machte Tissi bei dem Autodidakten Odermatt zunächst eine Lehre. Das Duo hat mit seiner einzigartigen visuellen Sprache – radikales Anschneiden der Bilder, markante Verwendung von Typografie und Farbe – einen Kultstatus erreicht. 1992 stellten Odermatt & Tissi einen Teil ihrer Plakate in der Reinhard-Brown Gallery in New York aus, seitdem waren sie mit Ausstellungen in Tokio, Essen und anderen Städten vertreten. Darüber hinaus haben sie mehrere Bücher gestaltet.

Odermatt & Tissi (1968, Suisse) est le partenariat créatif des designers Siegfried Odermatt (1926–2017, Zurich) et Rosmarie Tissi (1937, Thayngen, Suisse). Après des études à l'école de design de Zurich, Tissi rejoint l'autodidacte Odermatt, d'abord en qualité de stagiaire. Leur approche visuelle tout à fait unique, avec un cadrage radical des images et une utilisation très particulière de la typographie et des couleurs, a conféré au duo un statut culte. En 1992, ils présentent quelques-unes de leurs affiches à la Reinhard-Brown Gallery à New York; depuis, ils ont exposé leur travail à Tokyo, Essen et dans d'autres endroits. Ils ont également signé plusieurs livres.

»I have always reduced my design to the essential, employed only a few elements, and played with the proportions and the empty spaces. I believe that this helped to develop a timeless design aesthetics, owing also to the fact that I hardly ever followed any popular trend.« Rosmarie Tissi, *designculture.it*, 2014

1981 · Rosmarie Tissi, Odermatt+Tissi · CH · Poster

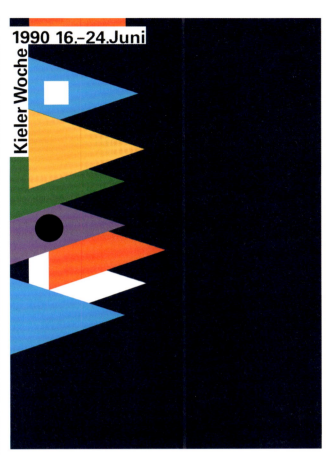

1990 · Rosmarie Tissi, Odermatt + Tissi · CH · Poster

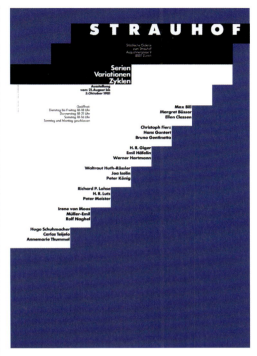

1981 · Siegfried Odermatt, Odermatt+Tissi · CH · Poster

1993 · Rosmarie Tissi, Odermatt + Tissi · CH · Poster

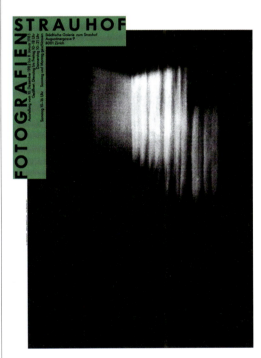

1983 · Odermatt + Tissi · CH · Poster

1997 · Rosmarie Tissi, Odermatt + Tissi · CH · Poster

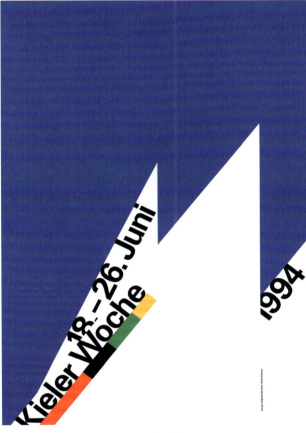

1994 · Sigi Odermatt, Odermatt + Tissi · CH · Poster

1993 · Rosmarie Tissi, Odermatt + Tissi · CH · Poster

PAOS (1968, Japan) is the creative studio of Motoo Nakanishi (1938, Kobe), which has gained international recognition for the design of over 100 corporate identities, with clients that include Kenwood, Mazda, and TDK. A fine arts graduate from Waseda University, Tokyo, Nakanishi was later instrumental in setting up the design faculty at the institution. In 1964 he co-published *Design Policy: Corporate Image Formation*, the first book to appear in Japan on corporate design strategy; he also taught in China. During the 1980s and '90s, PAOS opened satellite branches in New York, Boston, Beijing, and Shanghai.

PAOS (1968, Japan) ist das Kreativbüro von Motoo Nakanishi (1938, Kobe), das durch die Gestaltung von über 100 Firmensignets – u. a. für Kenwood, Mazda und TDK – international bekannt geworden ist. Nakanishi, der an der Waseda University in Tokio Kunst studierte, war maßgeblich daran beteiligt, die dortige Fakultät für Gestaltung zu gründen. 1964 gab er mit anderen *Design Policy: Corporate Image Formation* heraus, das erste in Japan verlegte Buch, das sich mit der Gestaltung von Firmenidentitäten beschäftigte. Nakanishi unterrichtet auch in China. In den 1980er- und 1990er-Jahren eröffnete PAOS Ableger in New York, Boston, Beijing und Schanghai.

PAOS (1968, Japon) est le studio créatif de Motoo Nakanishi (1938, Kobe), qui bénéficie d'une reconnaissance internationale grâce au design de plus de 100 identités d'entreprises pour des clients comme Kenwood, Mazda et TDK. Diplômé des beaux-arts à l'université Waseda de Tokyo, Nakanishi devient ensuite un acteur clé de la création de la faculté de design au sein de l'institution. En 1964, il publie avec d'autres auteurs *Design Policy: Corporate Image Formation*, premier livre paru au Japon sur la stratégie en matière de design d'entreprise. Nakanishi a par ailleurs enseigné en Chine. Pendant les années 1980 et 1990, PAOS a ouvert des bureaux à New York, Boston, Pékin et Shanghai.

1984 · PAOS · JP · Identity · Bridgestone

1982 · PAOS · JP · Identity · Sun Chain

1981 · PAOS · JP · Identity · Kirin Beer

1986 · PAOS · JP · Identity · Ricoh

1977 · Herb Lubalin, Yasaburo Kuwayama, PAOS · JP/US · Packaging

1975 · PAOS · JP · Identity · Daiei

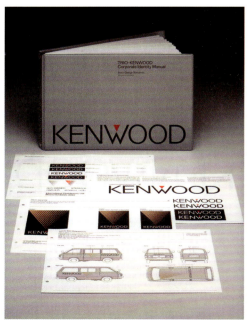

1982 · PAOS · JP · Identity · Kenwood

From the 1980s there was a marked increase in Japanese corporations trading on the global market, and in response to this the Japanese design studio PAOS prepared sets of sophisticated concepts on which to base internationally recognizable corporate identities for such companies. Alongside a detailed design manual, PAOS also produced so-called "design trees", which outlined the key elements of brand development in the form of an easy-to-read chart.

Von den 1980er-Jahren an operierten japanische Unternehmen zunehmend auf dem Weltmarkt. Das japanische Designbüro PAOS konzipierte für zahlreiche dieser Firmen komplexe Leitbilder für ein internationales Erscheinungsbild. Neben einem detaillierten Designmanual entstand das Format des „Brand Trees", der die wesentlichen Elemente des Branding auf einem übersichtlichen Schaubild verständlich zusammenfasste.

À partir des années 1980, les grandes entreprises nippones opèrent chaque fois plus au niveau mondial. Pour nombre d'entre elles, l'agence de graphisme japonaise PAOS a conçu des identités visuelles sophistiquées et identifiables partout dans le monde. Outre un manuel de design détaillé, PAOS a réalisé les fameux «arbres de création», qui reprennent les éléments essentiels du branding dans une présentation facile à comprendre.

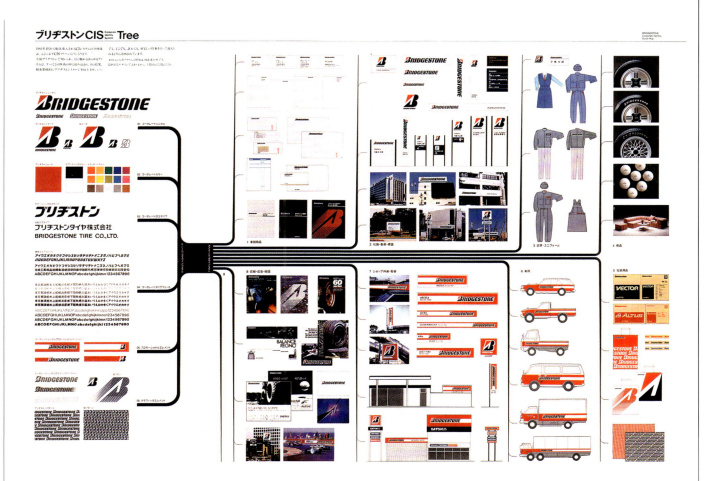

1984 · Masanori Umeda, PAOS · JP · Identity · Bridgestone

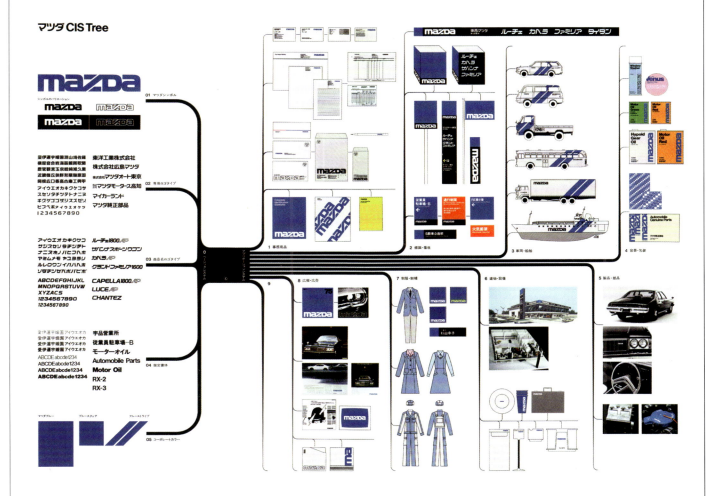

1975 · Masanori Umeda, PAOS · JP · Identity · Mazda

1982 · Grapus · FR · Poster

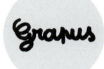

Grapus was a ground-breaking French design collective, founded in 1970 by Pierre Bernard (1942–2015, Paris), Gérard Paris-Clavel (1943, Paris), and François Miehe (1942, Paris). Their studio felt a strong commitment to issues of social responsibility and campaigned vigorously for improvements in the relationship between the state and its citizens. In the mid-1970s, Jean-Paul Bachollet (1931, Paris) and Alex Jordan (1947, Saarbrucken) joined the group. Grapus became renowned for the radical, experimental style of its posters, which dealt with subjects such as poverty, capitalism, and exploitation. The collective split up in 1991.

Grapus war ein innovatives französisches Designkollektiv, das 1970 von Pierre Bernard (1942–2015, Paris), Gérard Paris-Clavel (1943, Paris) und François Miehe (1942, Paris) gegründet wurde. Ihr Atelier fühlte sich dem Gedanken gesellschaftlicher Verantwortung verpflichtet und engagierte sich stark für die Verbesserung der Beziehungen zwischen dem Staat und den Bürgern. Jean-Paul Bachollet (1931, Paris) und Alex Jordan (1947, Saarbrücken) schlossen sich der Gruppe Mitte der 1970er-Jahre an. Legendär wurden Grapus und sein radikaler Experimentalstil durch Plakate zu Themen wie Armut, Kapitalismus und Ausbeutung. Das Kollektiv löste sich 1991 auf.

Grapus fut un collectif de design français novateur fondé en 1970 par Pierre Bernard (1942–2015, Paris), Gérard Paris-Clavel (1943, Paris) et François Miehe (1942, Paris). Leur studio travailla sous le signe d'une forte conscience sociale et lutta fermement pour l'amélioration du dialogue entre le gouvernement et les citoyens. Le groupe fut rejoint dans les années 1970 par Jean-Paul Bachollet (1931, Paris) et Alex Jordan (1947, Sarrebruck). Avec un style radicalement expérimental, Grapus s'est fait connaître par ses affiches sur des thèmes comme la pauvreté, le capitalisme et l'exploitation. Le collectif s'est séparé en 1991.

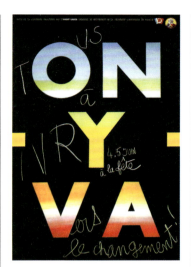

1977 · Grapus · FR · Poster

1986 · Grapus · FR · Poster

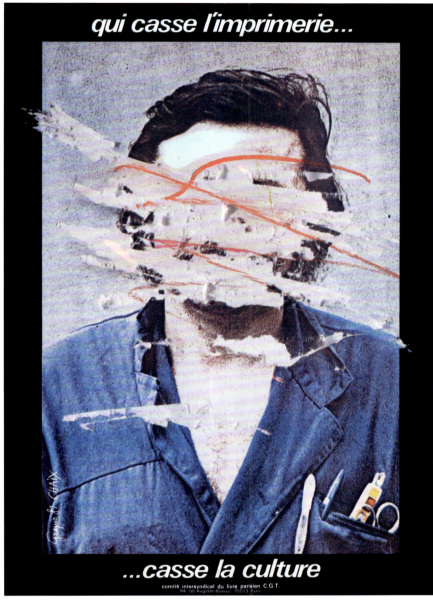

1981 · Grapus · FR · Poster

1984 · Grapus · FR · Logo · Centre National des Arts Plastiques

1986 · Grapus · FR · Logo · La Villette

1989 · Grapus · FR · Logo · Louvre

1980 · Grapus · FR · Poster

1989 · Grapus · FR · Logo · Clichy

1990 · Grapus · FR · Logo · Parcs Nationaux de France

1983

Designer **Lars Müller** founds a publishing company in Zurich for books on design, art, and architecture

Philip B. Meggs's book **A History of Graphic Design** is published

Lisa, the first personal computer with a Graphical User Interface (GUI), is introduced by Apple

1983 · Henryk Tomaszewski · PL · Poster

1983 · Martti Mykkänen · FI · Poster

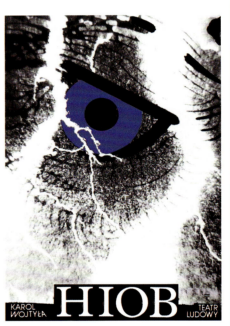

1983 · Władysław Puta · PL · Poster

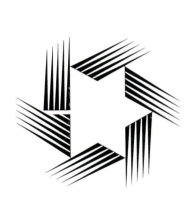

1983 · Ernst Roch · CA · Logo · Canadian Pacific

1983 · Peter Adam · CA · Logo · Security Trust

1983 · Félix Beltrán · CU · Logo · Oea Campaign

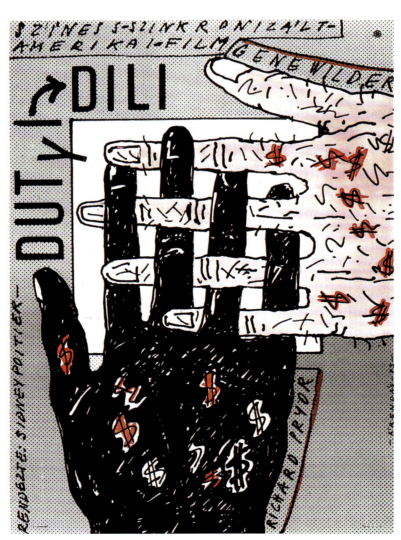

1983 · József Árendás · HU · Poster

1983 · Walter Bernard (AD), Milton Glaser (AD), Manuel Biderman (PH) · US/FR · Magazine cover

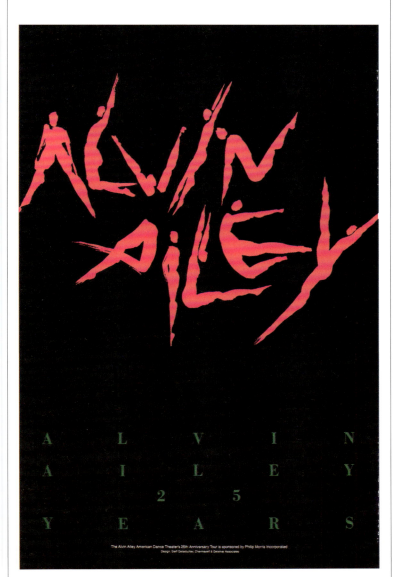

1983 · Steff Geissbuhler, Chermayeff & Geismar · US · Poster

1983 · Boris Bućan · HR · Poster

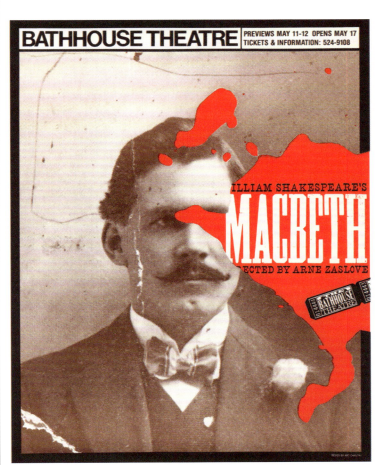

1983 · Art Chantry · US · Poster

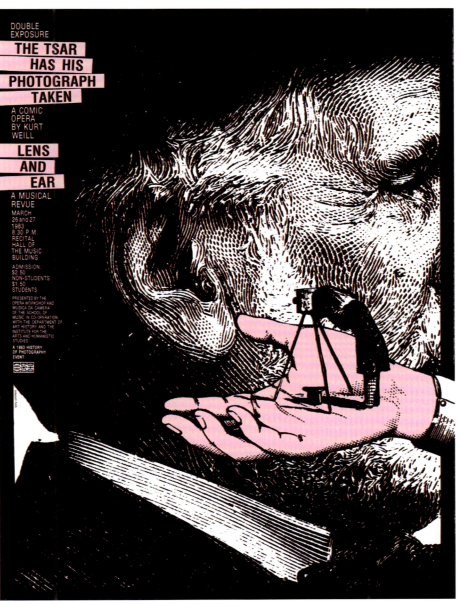

1983 · Lanny Sommese · US · Poster

Henry Steiner · Hong Kong

Henry Steiner (1934, Vienna) is an award-winning Austrian-born designer, renowned for his corporate identity work. Raised in New York, Steiner studied at Yale under Paul Rand, and at the Sorbonne in Paris. In 1964, he established Steiner & Co. in Hong Kong, which has since become one of the world's leading branding firms. Steiner's diverse list of clients has included HSBC, the Hong Kong Jockey Club, and Unilever. He has also designed coins for the Singapore Mint and, since 1975, has created banknotes for the Standard Chartered Bank in Hong Kong.

Henry Steiner (1934, Wien) ist ein preisgekrönter Grafikdesigner, der insbesondere wegen seiner Arbeiten im Bereich Corporate Identity bekannt ist. Der gebürtige Österreicher wuchs in New York auf und studierte in Yale bei Paul Rand sowie an der Sorbonne in Paris. 1964 gründete er in Hongkong Steiner & Co., das mittlerweile zu den weltweit führenden Brandingbüros gehört. Steiners zahlreiche Auftraggeber sind u. a. die HSBC, der Hong Kong Jockey Club und Unilever. Darüber hinaus hat er Münzen für die Münzanstalt Singapore entworfen und gestaltet seit 1975 Banknoten für die Standard Chartered Bank in Hongkong.

Henry Steiner (1934, Vienne) est un graphiste primé d'origine autrichienne, renommé pour son travail en matière d'identités d'entreprises. Après avoir grandi à New York, il étudie à Yale auprès de Paul Rand, puis à la Sorbonne. En 1964, il fonde Steiner & Co. à Hong Kong, une firme qui est aujourd'hui un des leaders mondiaux en branding. La liste très diverse de clients de Steiner compte notamment HSBC, le Hong Kong Jockey Club et Unilever. Steiner a aussi conçu des pièces pour The Singapore Mint et, à partir de 1975, des billets de banque pour la Standard Chartered Bank à Hong Kong.

1980 · Henry Steiner · HK · Logo · Taikoo Shing

1960s · Henry Steiner · HK · Logo · Hong Kong Hyatt

1960s · Henry Steiner · HK · Logo · Leela Boutique

1979 · Henry Steiner · HK · Logo · Patterson Plaza

1970 · Henry Steiner · HK · Logo · The Hong Kong Land Co.

1972 · Henry Steiner · HK · Logo · Jardine Fleming

1973 · Henry Steiner · HK · Logo · Classic Jewellers

1982 · Henry Steiner · HK · Logo · The I Club

1980 · Henry Steiner · HK · Logo · Peak Tower

1980 · Henry Steiner · HK · Logo · Hong Kong Girl Guides

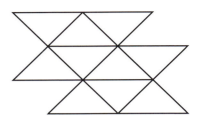

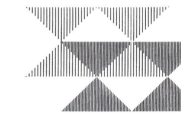

1960s · Henry Steiner · HK · Logo · The Hong Kong Hilton Hotel

»Graphic design isn't decoration and it's not just about aesthetics. It's first and foremost a form of communication and persuasion. The right logo can benefit a company by visually defining a coherent identity. You can attach brand values to a marque—it's like a flag that everyone can salute.« Henry Steiner, *Post Magazine*, 2014

1973 · Henry Steiner · HK · Banknote

1973 · Henry Steiner · HK · Banknote

1983 · Henry Steiner · HK · Identity · HSBC

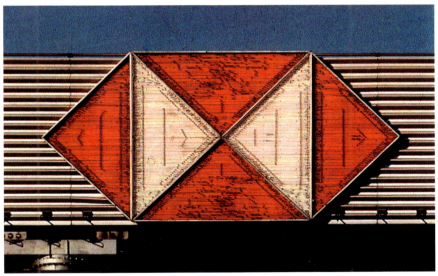

1977 · Henry Steiner · HK · Brochure cover

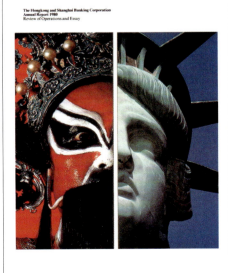

1977 · Henry Steiner · HK · Brochure cover

1981 · Mirko Ilić · BA · Poster

1980 · Mirko Ilić · BA · Poster

1985 · Mirko Ilić · BA · Poster

Mirko Ilić (1956, Bijeljina, Bosnia and Herzegovina) is a New York-based art director, designer, and illustrator. Ilić went to the School of Applied Arts in Zagreb before going on to work on comics and magazines, also designing popular record sleeves. In 1977 he launched his international career, publishing in Marvel's *Epic Illustrated* anthology and working for the Italian magazine *Panorama*. Moving to the United States in 1986, Ilić became an art director at *Time* magazine, and later for the op-ed pages of *The New York Times*. He teaches at the School of Visual Arts, and has co-authored several books.

Mirko Ilić (1956, Bijeljina, Bosnien und Herzegowina) ist ein in New York tätiger Artdirector, Grafikdesigner und Illustrator. Er besuchte die Kunstakademie in Zagreb, im Anschluss daran arbeitete er für Comics und Zeitschriften, gestaltete aber auch populäre Plattencover. Nach dem internationalen Durchbruch 1977 wurden seine Arbeiten in der Anthologie *Epic Illustrated* von Marvel Comics veröffentlicht, zudem arbeitete er für die italienische Zeitschrift *Panorama*. 1986 ging Ilić in die Vereinigten Staaten und wurde Artdirector des *Time*-Magazins und später für die Kommentarseiten der *New York Times*. Ilić unterrichtet an der School of Visual Arts und ist Co-Autor mehrerer Bücher.

Mirko Ilić (1956, Bijeljina, Bosnie-Herzégovine) est un directeur artistique, graphiste et illustrateur installé à New York. Ilić a étudié à l'École des arts appliqués de Zagreb avant de travailler sur des projets de bandes dessinées et de magazines, ainsi que des pochettes d'albums célèbres. En 1977, il lance sa carrière internationale en publiant son travail dans *Epic Illustrated*, de Marvel, et en travaillant pour le magazine italien *Panorama*. Il s'installe aux États-Unis en 1986, où il devient directeur artistique du magazine *Time*, et plus tard dirige les pages d'opinions du *New York Times*. Il enseigne à la School of Visual Arts et a cosigné plusieurs livres.

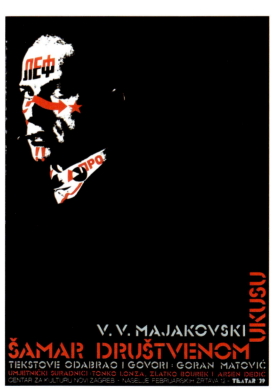

1982 · Mirko Ilić · BA · Poster

1978 · Mirko Ilić · BA · Poster

»If you're from Eastern Europe and you tell someone in the West that you design posters, they think that you must mean Polish posters. Unfortunately they have become a symbol of the whole of Eastern Europe. As if a hundred million people should design posters in the same way.« Mirko Ilić, *Fist to Face*, 2012

1979 · Mirko Ilić · BA · Record cover

1981 · Mirko Ilić · BA · Record cover

1984 · Mirko Ilić · BA · Record cover

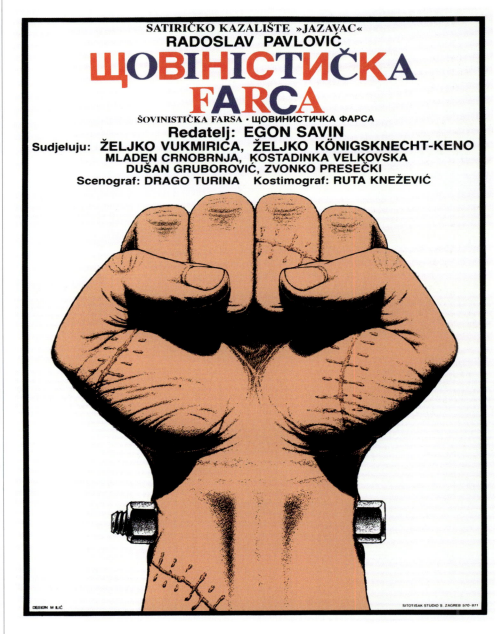

1983 · Mirko Ilić · BA · Poster

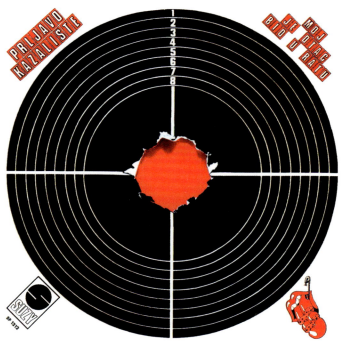

1979 · Mirko Ilić · BA · Record cover

1984

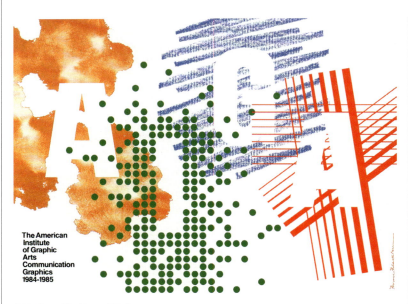

The American Institute of Graphic Arts Communication Graphics 1984-1985

1984 · Bruce Blackburn · US · Poster

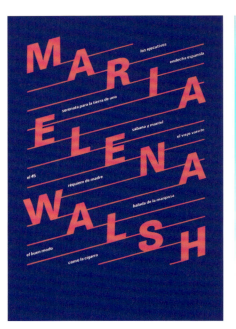

1984 · Rubén Fontana · AR · Brochure cover

Design '84
Design som konkurransemiddel
Rådet for Industridesign – RID

ID – Norske Industridesignere
ICSID – International Council of Societies of Industrial Design

1984 · Bruno Oldani · CH/NO · Poster

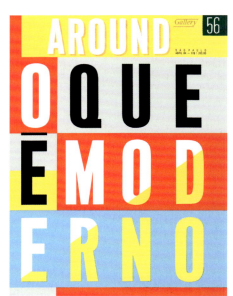

1984 · Rafic Farah · BR · Magazine cover

1984 · Paul Ibou · BE · Logo · Pittors video services

1984 · Mervyn Kurlansky · UK · Logo · Museum of Modern Art, Oxford

1984 · Steff Geissbuhler · US · Poster

1984 · Ott+Stein · DE · Poster

QANTAS

1984 · Tony Lunn · AU · Logo · Qantas Airways

1984 · Franciszek Starowieyski · PL · Poster

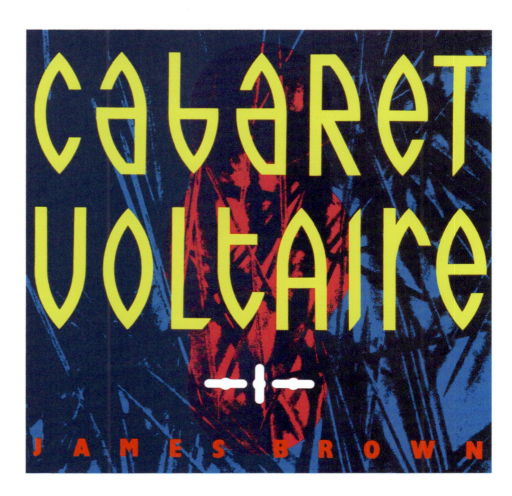

1984 · Neville Brody · UK · Record cover

1984 · Marisa Rizzato · IT · Poster

1984 · Hans-Rudolf Lutz · CH · Poster

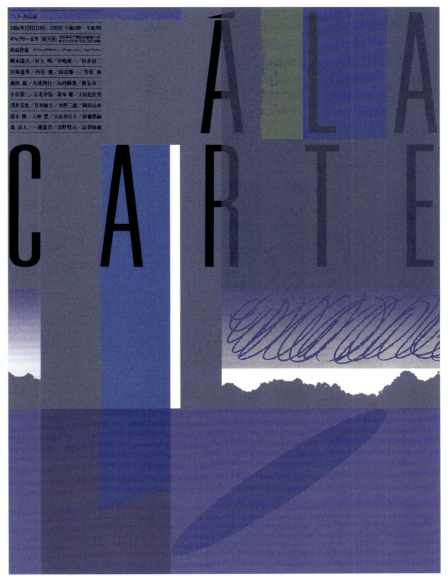

1984 · Shigeo Okamoto · JP · Poster

The launch of the Mac OS marked the beginning of a design revolution. After a few images were released to the press, Steve Jobs took the stage to present the new computer, starting it to show the screen with the little face and its smile, still in use today, followed by all the other familiar symbols such as crash, trash, and processing. They were created by American designer Susan Kare and have become the foundation of the screen icons which today are omnipresent in our digital application, from computers to smartphones to television sets.

Die Entwicklung des Mac-Betriebssystems war der Startschuss für eine Designrevolution. Nachdem die Presse einige Bilder erhalten hatte, trat Steve Jobs auf die Bühne, um den neuen Computer vorzustellen, und fuhr ihn hoch, um den Bildschirm mit dem kleinen Gesicht und dem Lächeln vorzuführen, wie es heute noch verwendet wird; dann folgten alle anderen bekannten Icons wie Bombe, Mülltonne und Armbanduhr. Die Symbole, die von der amerikanischen Designerin Susan Kare stammten, dienten als Ausgangspunkt für die Bildschirmicons, die in unseren digitalen Anwendungen heute allgegenwärtig sind, vom Computer über das Smartphone bis zum Fernseher.

Le lancement du système Mac OS a marqué le début d'une révolution dans le monde du design. Après la publication de quelques images dans la presse, Steve Jobs monta sur scène pour présenter le nouvel ordinateur: il le démarra pour montrer l'écran au visage souriant encore utilisé aujourd'hui, suivi de tous les symboles familiers comme la bombe, la corbeille et de traitement en cours. Ces symboles étaient l'œuvre de la graphiste américaine Susan Kare et sont les ancêtres des icônes aujourd'hui omniprésentes dans nos applications numériques, des ordinateurs aux smartphones en passant par les téléviseurs.

1984 · Susan Kare · US · Icons

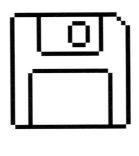

1984 · Susan Kare · US · Icons

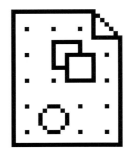

1984 · Susan Kare · US · Icons

1984 · Susan Kare · US · Interface design

1984 · Gábor Gyárfás · HU · Poster

The Face, founded in London by Nick Logan in 1980, focused on current developments in music, fashion, and similar cultural areas. A year after it was launched the designer Neville Brody joined the team at the monthly magazine, and it was his innovative layouts that challenged readers and raised the written content to an entirely different level. An unmistakable design vocabulary, coupled with specially designed typefaces, became The Face's unique selling point, while Brody became one of the first magazine designers to venture way beyond the usual range of design elements, creating in the process a periodical with what he referred to as "a core design DNA".

The Face, 1980 von Nick Logan in London gegründet, beschäftigte sich mit aktuellen Entwicklungen in Musik, Mode und Kultur. Ein Jahr nach der Gründung stieß Neville Brody als Gestalter zum Team des monatlich erscheinenden Magazins. Seine neuartigen Layouts stellten die Leser vor Herausforderungen und verliehen den Inhalten eine zusätzliche Ebene. Eine unverkennbare Formensprache in Verbindung mit seiner speziell entwickelten Typografie für die Headlines wurde zum Alleinstellungsmerkmal von The Face. Neville Brody war damit einer der ersten Magazingestalter, der, weit über wiederkehrende Gestaltungselemente hinausgehend, einem Heft eine integrale visuelle DNA verlieh.

The Face, fondé à Londres en 1980 par Nick Logan, traitait des nouveautés des mondes de la musique, de la mode et de la culture. Un an après le lancement du mensuel, le graphiste Neville Brody en rejoignait l'équipe. Ses mises en page inédites allaient régulièrement défier les habitudes du lecteur et ajouter un niveau supplémentaire aux contenus. Un langage conceptuel incomparable associé à une typographie spécialement conçue pour les gros titres devinrent l'argument de vente de The Face. Neville Brody fut ainsi un des premiers graphistes éditoriaux à conférer à un magazine un ADN visuel qui allait bien au-delà des aspects graphiques habituels.

1985 · Neville Brody, Jamie Morgan (PH) · UK · Magazine cover

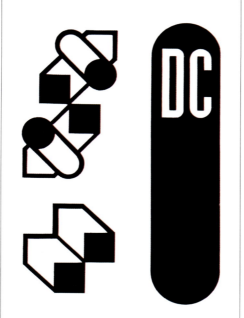

1985 · Neville Brody · UK · Magazine graphics

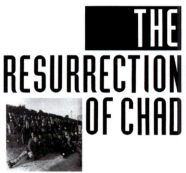

1985 · Neville Brody · UK · Magazine spreads

1984 · Neville Brody · UK · Magazine cover

1983 · Neville Brody · UK · Magazine cover

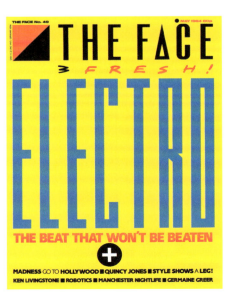

1984 · Neville Brody · UK · Magazine cover

Neville Brody (1957, London) is a leading British designer and dean of the School of Communication at the Royal College of Art in London. After attending the London College of Printing, Brody gained recognition in the early 1980s art-directing *The Face* magazine and designing record covers for acts such as Depeche Mode. He founded Research Studios in 1994 (rebranded as Brody Associates in 2014), producing groundbreaking work in the areas of editorial, identity, and typography; the *FUSE* project he established with Jon Wozencroft in 1991 became an exploratory ground for new typography. Brody's list of clients has included HSBC, Samsung, and *The Times*.

Neville Brody (1957, London) ist ein führender britischer Grafikdesigner und Dekan der School of Communication am Royal College of Art in London. Nach dem Besuch des London College of Printing wurde er Anfang der 1980er-Jahre durch seine Artdirection der Zeitschrift *The Face* bekannt, aber auch durch seine Plattencover für Bands wie Depeche Mode. 1994 gründete er die Research Studios (2014 zu Brody Associates umfirmiert) und legte bahnbrechende Arbeiten vor, ob im Bereich Editorial Design, CI oder Typografie: Das *FUSE*-Projekt, das er 1991 mit Jon Wozencroft ins Leben rief, wurde zur Versuchsanordnung für neue Typografie. Zu Brodys Auftraggebern zählen unter anderem HSBC, Samsung und *The Times*.

Neville Brody (1957, Londres) est un graphiste britannique chef de file et doyen del'école de communication du Royal College of Art à Londres. Après des études au London College of Printing, Brody s'est fait connaître au début des années 1980 avec la direction artistique du magazine *The Face* et par les pochettes d'albums qu'il a conçues notamment pour Depeche Mode. En 1994, il fonde Research Studios (rebaptisé Brody Associates en 2014) et produit des travaux révolutionnaires dans les domaines de l'édition, de l'identité et de la typographie. Le projet *FUSE* qu'il a lancé en 1991 avec Jon Wozencroft est devenu une base exploratoire pour une nouvelle typographie. Les clients de Brody incluent notamment HSBC, Samsung et *The Times*.

1986 · Louise Fili · US · Book cover

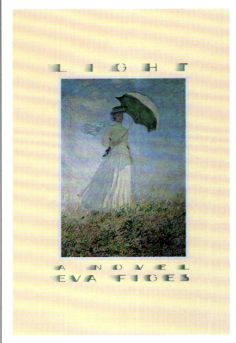

1983 · Louise Fili · US · Book cover

1986 · Louise Fili · US · Book cover

1984 · Louise Fili · US · Book cover

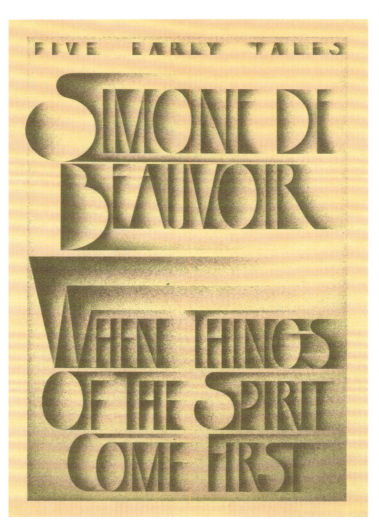

1982 · Louise Fili · US · Book cover

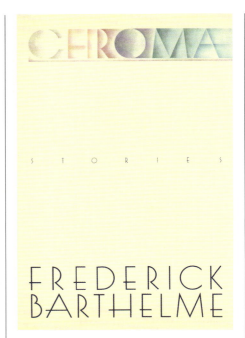

1987 · Louise Fili · US · Book cover

1987 · Louise Fili, Dugald Stermer (ILL) · US · Book cover

1986 · Louise Fili, Dugald Stermer (ILL) · US · Book cover

1999 · Louise Fili · US · Packaging

Louise Fili (1951, New Jersey) is an Italian-American graphic designer long admired for combining creativity with technical skills to produce work of exceptional brilliance. Fili graduated in art from Skidmore College in 1973 and moved to New York City for further studies at the School of Visual Arts. She worked in Herb Lubalin's studio before joining Pantheon Books in 1978 as art director. By the time Fili left in 1989 to set up her own studio, she had designed some 2,000 book jackets. Continuing since with book design, she has also focused on branding for many restaurants and designed packaging for high-end foodstuffs. Fili has taught at the School of Visual Arts, and in 2004 was admitted to the Art Directors Club Hall of Fame.

Louise Fili (1951, New Jersey) ist eine italienisch-amerikanische Grafikdesignerin, die seit Jahren mit Arbeiten begeistert, in denen sich gestalterisches wie handwerkliches Können exzellent verbinden. Sie studierte Kunst am Skidmore College und zog nach ihrem Abschluss 1973 nach New York City, wo sie an der School of Visual Arts einen weiteren Abschluss erwarb. Anschließend arbeitete sie im Atelier von Herb Lubalin und war ab 1978 als Artdirector für den Verlag Pantheon Books tätig. Als sie 1989 den Verlag verließ, um ihr eigenes Studio zu gründen, hatte sie nahezu 2000 Buchumschläge entworfen. Erscheinungsbilder für Restaurants sowie Verpackungsentwürfe wurden zu weiteren Schwerpunkten. Fili unterrichtet an der School of Visual Arts und wurde 2004 in die Hall of Fame des Art Directors Club aufgenommen.

Louise Fili (1951, New Jersey) est une graphiste italo-américaine dont le travail passionne depuis de nombreuses années par de splendides réalisations qui associent compétences créatives et techniques. Au terme de ses études d'art au Skidmore College en 1973, elle s'installe à New York, où elle obtient un second diplôme à la School of Visual Arts. Elle travaille ensuite au studio de Herb Lubalin, avant de devenir en 1978 la directrice artistique chez Pantheon Books. Quand elle arrête en 1989, elle a à son actif quelque 2000 couvertures de livres. Outre la conception d'ouvrages, Fili s'est livrée au branding pour nombre de restaurants, ainsi qu'au design d'emballages de produits alimentaires haut de gamme. Elle a enseigné à la School of Visual Arts et est entrée en 2004 au Hall of Fame de l'Art Directors Club.

1998 · Louise Fili · US · Packaging

1998 · Louise Fili, James Grashow (ILL) · US · Packaging

1999 · Louise Fili · US · Packaging

2008/2009 · Louise Fili · US · Packaging

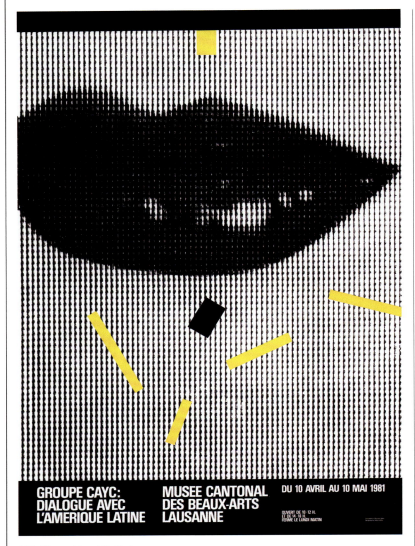

1981 · Werner Jeker · CH · Poster

1984 · Werner Jeker · CH · Poster

1984 · Werner Jeker · CH · Poster

1979 · Werner Jeker · CH · Poster

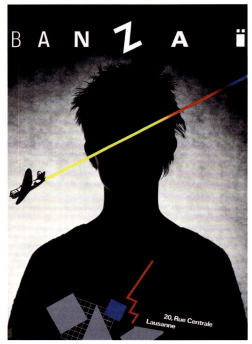

1982 · Werner Jeker · CH · Poster

Werner Jeker (1944, Mümliswil-Ramiswil, Switzerland) is a graphic designer best known for his asymmetric yet harmonious posters, which often combine photography with experimental typography. In 1983 he co-founded Les Ateliers du Nord, a studio in Lausanne specializing in book and poster design. From 1974–86 Jeker was head of graphic design at the School of Fine Arts in Lausanne, and has also taught at the Karlsruhe Academy of Art and Design, at the École Nationale Supérieure des Arts Décoratifs in Paris, and elsewhere. Jeker's clients have included the Théâtre de Vidy and the Musée de l'Elysée in Lausanne, the Swiss Foundation for Photography, and Magnum Photos.

Werner Jeker (1944, Mümliswil-Ramiswil, Schweiz) ist als Grafik-designer vor allem durch seine asymmetrischen und zugleich harmonischen Plakate bekannt geworden, in denen er häufig foto-grafische Elemente mit experimenteller Typografie verbindet. 1983 gründete er mit anderen in Lausanne das Studio Les Ateliers du Nord, das sich auf die Gestaltung von Büchern und Plakaten konzentrierte. Von 1974 bis 1986 leitete er die Grafikdesignabteilung an der Kunsthochschule in Lausanne, zudem unterrichtete er an der Hochschule für Gestaltung in Karlsruhe, an der École Nationale Supérieure des Arts Décoratifs in Paris und anderswo. Zu Jekers Auftraggebern gehören u. a. das Théâtre de Vidy und das Musée de l'Elysée in Lausanne, die Fotostiftung Schweiz sowie Magnum Photos.

Werner Jeker (1944, Mümliswil-Ramiswil, Suisse) est un graphiste connu surtout pour ses affiches asymétriques mais harmonieuses, qui associent souvent photographie et typographie expérimentale. En 1983, Jeker cofonde Les Ateliers du Nord, un studio lausannois spécia-lisé dans le design d'affiches et de livres. De 1974 à 1986, il est maître principal de la classe de graphisme à l'École des beaux-arts de Lausanne. Il enseigne aussi entre autres à l'Académie des beaux-arts de Karlsruhe et à l'École na-tionale supérieure des Arts Déco-ratifs de Paris. Parmis ses clients, Jeker compte le Théâtre de Vidy et le musée de l'Élysée à Lau-sanne, la Fondation suisse pour la photographie et Magnum Photos.

1984 · Werner Jeker · CH · Poster

Sussman/Prejza & Co. · United States

For the Los Angeles Olympics in 1984, a design team led by Deborah Sussman and Paul Prejza developed a visual master plan that set new standards in the combination of graphic design and architecture. Working around a series of colors, shapes, patterns, and symbols, they designed a large number of new buildings that transformed a typically monotonous Los Angeles into a colorful sports venue.

Für die Olympischen Spiele 1984 in Los Angeles entstand unter der Leitung von Deborah Sussman und Paul Prejza ein visuelles Gesamtkonzept, das neue Maßstäbe in der Verbindung von Grafikdesign und Architektur setzte. Basierend auf einem Katalog von Farben, Formen, Mustern und Symbolen, wurden zahlreiche Bauten entwickelt und verwandelten das eher graue Los Angeles in eine farbenfrohe Sportkulisse.

Pour les jeux Olympiques de Los Angeles en 1984, une équipe de graphistes dirigée par Deborah Sussman et Paul Prejza élabora un schéma directeur qui dictait de nouveaux standards pour associer graphisme et architecture. Travaillant autour d'une série clairement définie de formes, de couleurs, de motifs et de symboles, ils conçurent un grand nombre de constructions nouvelles qui transformèrent la monotone cité de Los Angeles en un site sportif haut en couleur.

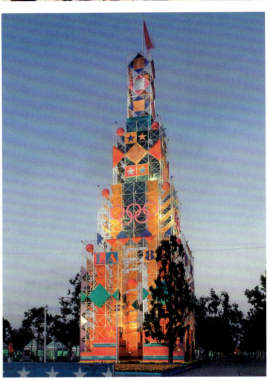

1984 · The Jerde Partnership, Sussman/Prejza & Co. · US · Identity, Environmental graphics

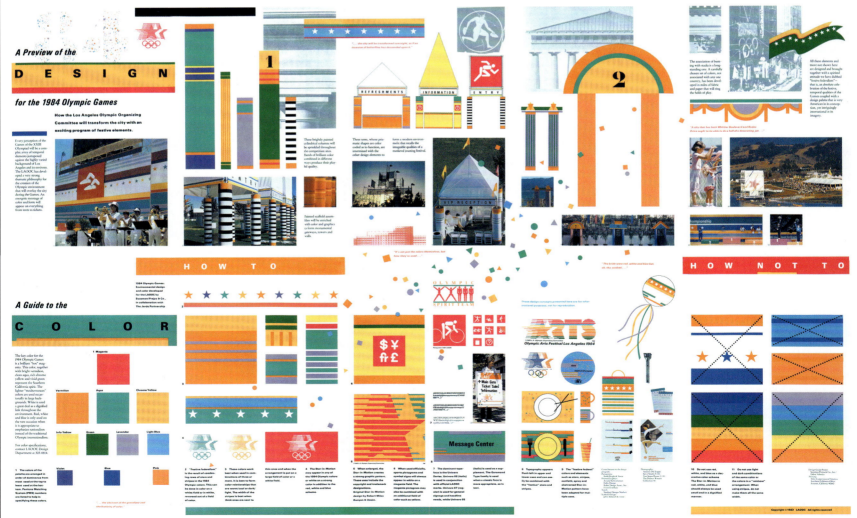

1984 · The Jerde Partnership, Sussman/Prejza & Co. · US · Identity, Environmental graphics

Deborah Sussman (1931, New York – 2014, Los Angeles) was a major figure in environmental graphic design and urban branding. Trained in multiple fields, including painting and acting at Bard College in New York, Sussman later graduated in graphic design from the Institute of Design in Chicago under László Moholy-Nagy. She spent over a decade working for the Eames office in California before going solo in 1968. Sussman later teamed up with her husband, the architect Paul Prejza, and focused on urban identity projects, such as that for the city of Philadelphia and the 1984 Los Angeles Olympics.

Deborah Sussman (1931, New York – 2014, Los Angeles) war eine führende Vertreterin des Orientierungsdesigns und Urban Branding. Nach einer vielfältigen Ausbildung, u. a. in Malerei und Schauspiel am Bard College in New York, studierte sie Grafikdesign am Institute of Design in Chicago bei László Moholy-Nagy. Mehr als zehn Jahre lang war sie beim Eames-Büro Kalifornien tätig, ehe sie sich 1968 selbstständig machte. Später tat sie sich mit ihrem Ehemann, dem Architekten Paul Prejza, zusammen und konzentrierte sich auf Projekte der Urban Identity wie jenes der Stadt Philadelphia und der Olympiade von Los Angeles 1984.

Deborah Sussman (1931, New York – 2014, Los Angeles) fut une figure majeure du graphisme d'environnement et de branding urbain. Formée dans différentes disciplines, notamment comme peintre et comédienne au Bard College à New York, Sussman décrocha ensuite son diplôme de graphisme à l'Institute of Design de Chicago, sous la direction de László Moholy-Nagy. Elle a passé plus d'une décennie à travailler chez Eames Office, en Californie, avant de voler de ses propres ailes en 1968. Sussman s'associa plus tard avec son époux et architecte Paul Prejza pour se consacrer à des projets d'identité urbaine, notamment celui pour la ville de Philadelphie et pour les jeux Olympiques de Los Angeles de 1984.

1992 · Sussman/Prejza & Co. · US · Identity · Euro Disney

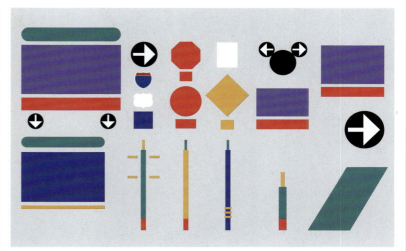

1992 · Sussman/Prejza & Co. · US · Environmental graphics

1985

The **8vo** design studio is set up in London by Simon Johnston, Mark Holt, and Hamish Muir

The **Herb Lubalin Study Center of Design and Typography** is established at Cooper Union school in New York City

The first desktop layout software **PageMaker** is released by Aldus

The first **Toyama Poster Triennial** is held in Japan

1985 · Anonymous · DE · Record cover

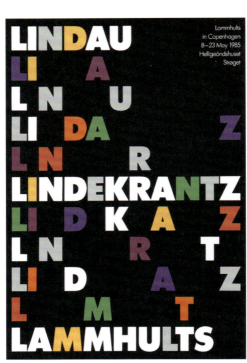

1985 · Hans-Christer Ericson · SE · Poster

1985 · Stipe Brčić, CIO Design · YU · Logo · SRCE

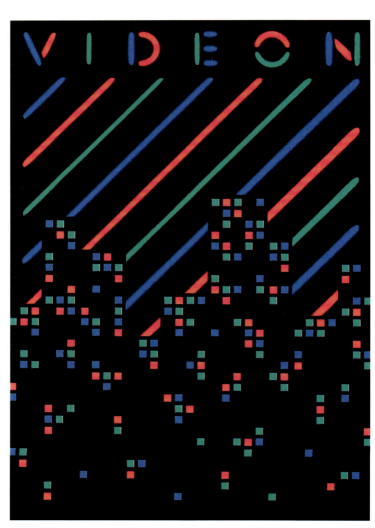

1985 · Pierre Mendell · DE · Identity · Videon

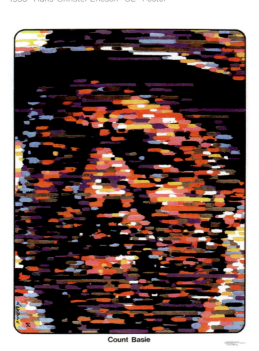

Count Basie

1985 · Waldemar Świerzy · PL · Poster

HEAT WAVE

1985 · Tim Girvin · US · Logo · Heat Wave

1985 · Phil Gips, Frankfurt Gips Balkind · US · Logo · ESPN Television

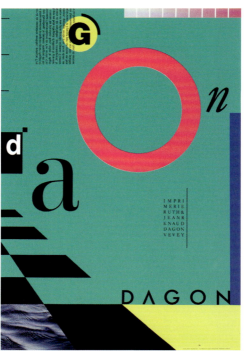

1985 · Pierre Neumann · CH · Poster

The first issue of **HQ** design
magazine is published, designed
and edited by Rolf Müller

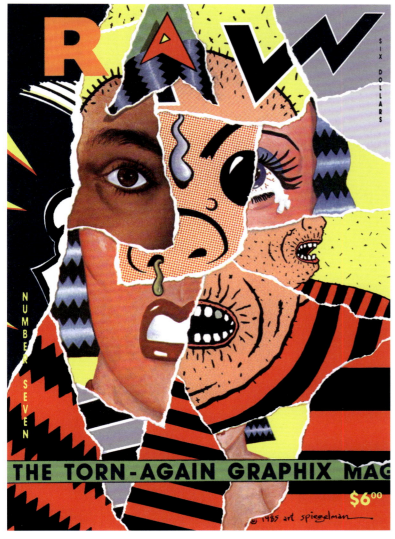

1985 · Art Spiegelman · US · Magazine cover

1985 · Shigeo Fukuda · JP · Poster

1985 · Drew Struzan (ILL) · US · Poster

1985 · Carol Thompson, Eamonn McCabe, Terry Jones · UK · Magazine cover

1985 · Erhard Grüttner · GDR · Poster

1985 · Leif Frimann Anisdahl · NO · Identity
Posten Norge

Ikko Tanaka · Japan

Ikko Tanaka (1930, Nara – 2002, Tokyo) was a renowned Japanese graphic designer whose notable work in posters blended a traditional Japanese aesthetic with bold shapes, vivid colors, and an incisive use of typography. After working for the *Sankei Shimbun* newspaper and at the Nippon Design Center, Tanaka started his first studio in 1963 in Tokyo. He created the logos for Osaka University and the World City Expo Tokyo '96, while he is also credited with co-developing the homeware brand Muji. Tanaka also worked for Issey Miyake, Mazda, and the V&A in London.

Ikko Tanaka (1930, Nara – 2002, Tokio) war ein angesehener japanischer Grafikdesigner, der in seinen Plakaten eine traditionelle japanische Ästhetik mit klaren Formen, lebhaften Farben und einer prägnanten Verwendung von Typografie verband. Nach ersten Arbeitserfahrungen bei der Zeitung *Sankei Shimbun* und beim Nippon Design Center gründete er 1963 in Tokio sein erstes Studio. Er entwarf die Logos für die Osaka University und die World City Expo Tokyo '96, zudem war er an der Gestaltung der Haushaltswarenmarke Muji beteiligt. Zu Tanakas weiteren Auftraggebern gehörten Issey Miyake, Mazda sowie das V&A in London.

Ikko Tanaka (1930, Nara – 2002, Tokio) fut un graphiste japonais renommé dont le travail remarqué dans le domaine de l'affiche mêle l'esthétique japonaise traditionnelle à des formes audacieuses, des couleurs vives et un emploi incisif de la typographie. Après sa collaboration pour le journal *Sankei Shimbun* et le Nippon Design Center, Tanaka ouvrit son premier studio en 1963 à Tokyo, créant des logos pour l'université d'Osaka et la World City Expo Tokyo '96. On lui doit aussi sa contribution au développement de la marque d'articles pour la maison Muji. Tanaka a travaillé pour Issey Miyake, Mazda et le V&A à Londres.

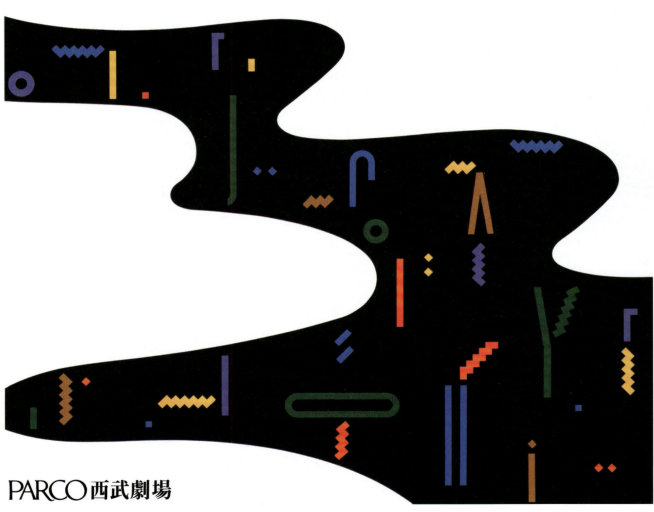

1985 · Ikko Tanaka · JP · Poster

1979 · Ikko Tanaka · JP · Logo · IM

1984 · Ikko Tanaka · JP · Logo · IBC

1981 · Ikko Tanaka · JP · Logo · Spiral

1986 · Ikko Tanaka · JP · Logo · Ginza Graphic Gallery

1984 · Ikko Tanaka · JP · Logo · JK Design Institute

1986 · Ikko Tanaka · JP · Poster

1974 · Ikko Tanaka · JP · Poster

1982 · Ikko Tanaka · JP · Poster

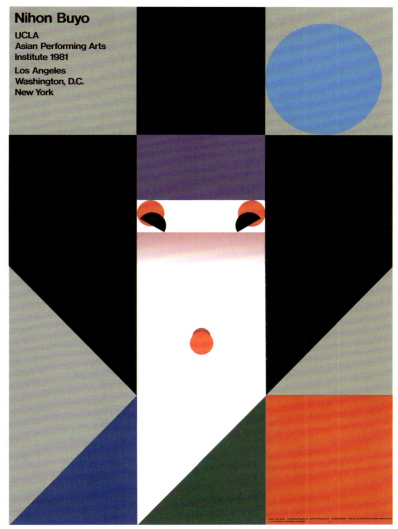

1981 · Ikko Tanaka · JP · Poster

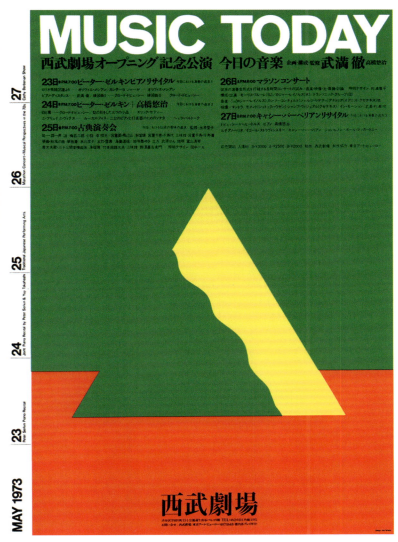

1973 · Ikko Tanaka · JP · Poster

Christof Gassner · Switzerland/Germany

In 1985, the innovative consumer magazine *Öko-Test*, published in support of the environmental movement, first appeared on the market in Germany. For the new publication Christof Gassner developed an unusual design concept, largely dispensing with photography, and instead turning to graphics in four primary colors—using natural printing inks on unbleached, recycled paper.

Unter dem Namen *Öko-Test* kam 1985 im Zuge der Umweltbewegung ein neuartiges Verbrauchermagazin auf den deutschen Markt. Christof Gassner entwickelte für das Heft ein ungewöhnliches Gestaltungskonzept. Es verzichtet weitgehend auf Fotografie und setzt stattdessen grafische Elemente aus vier Echtfarben ein – natürlich auf ungebleichtem Recyclingpapier gedruckt.

En 1985, le magazine de consommation *Öko-Test* d'un nouveau genre arrivait sur le marché allemand dans le sillage du mouvement écologiste. Pour ce mensuel, Christof Gassner élabora un concept graphique inédit qui renonçait largement à la photographie pour miser sur des éléments graphiques dans quatre couleurs primaires. L'impression se faisait évidemment sur papier recyclé non blanchi.

1985 · Christof Gassner · CH/DE · Poster

1986 · Christof Gassner, Monika Weiss · CH/DE · Poster

1985 · Christof Gassner · CH/DE · Identity

1985 · Christof Gassner · CH/DE · Magazine spreads

1980s · Christof Gassner · CH/DE · Magazine covers

Christof Gassner (1941, Zurich) is a Swiss-born designer and typographer. Originally studying in Zurich under Josef Müller-Brockmann and Walter Käch, Gassner then worked at the in-house design studio of Braun and started his own practice in Frankfurt in 1966, moving to Darmstadt in 1992. His work has included many corporate identity and editorial design projects, most notably his influential concept for Öko-Test magazine. Since the 1980s Gassner has designed several official German postage stamps; he has also lectured at Darmstadt University of Applied Sciences, and Kassel University School of Art.

Christof Gassner (1941, Zürich), ein Schweizer Grafikdesigner und Typograf, studierte zunächst in Zürich unter Josef Müller-Brockmann und Walter Käch, anschließend arbeitete er in der Designabteilung von Braun. 1966 eröffnete er sein eigenes Studio in Frankfurt und ging 1992 nach Darmstadt. In seinen Arbeiten finden sich viele Projekte in den Bereichen Corporate Identity und Editorial Design, insbesondere sein wegweisendes Konzept für die Zeitschrift Öko-Test. Seit den 1980er-Jahren hat Gassner mehrere Briefmarken der Deutschen Post entworfen. Er unterrichtet an der TU in Darmstadt sowie an der Kunsthochschule Kassel.

Christof Gassner (1941, Zurich) est un graphiste et typographe, d'origine suisse. Après avoir d'abord étudié à Zurich auprès de Josef Müller-Brockmann et Walter Käch, Gassner a travaillé dans le studio de design d'intérieur de Braun. En 1966, il ouvre sa propre agence à Francfort et en 1992, il s'installe à Darmstadt. Son travail compte de nombreux projets d'identités d'entreprises et de design éditorial, notamment son approche novatrice pour le magazine Öko-Test. Depuis les années 1980, Gassner a conçu plusieurs timbres pour la poste allemande. Il a aussi enseigné à l'université de sciences appliquées de Darmstadt, ainsi qu'à l'école des beaux-arts de l'université de Cassel.

1986

April Greiman designs an issue of the magazine **Design Quarterly** using only a computer

Omnicom Group, a global marketing and corporate communications holding controlling BBDO, TBWA, and other global advertising agencies, is established in New York City

The first issue of typography magazine **Octavo** is published in the United Kingdom

1986 · Anonymous · US · Record cover

1986 · Richard Rockwood, Autograph Design Partnership · UK · Logo · Jones

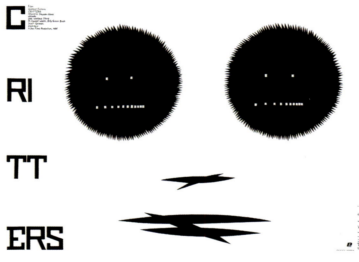

1986 · Mieczysław Wasilewski · PL · Poster

1986 · Lance Anderson · US · Logo · THX

1986 · Thales Pereira · BR · Invitation card

1986 · Paul Rand · US · Logo · Next

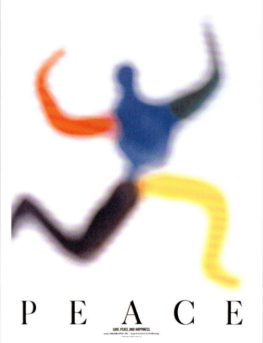

PEACE

1986 · Shin Matsunaga · JP · Poster

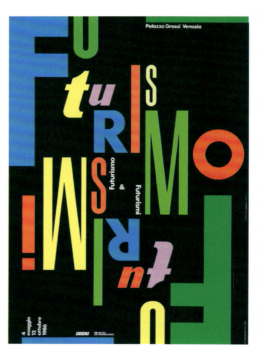

1986 · Pierluigi Cerri · IT · Poster

WHAM!

1986 · Peter Saville Associates · UK · Record cover

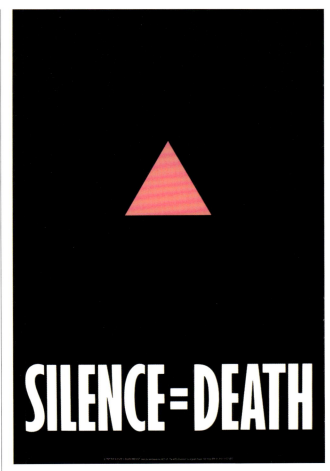

1986 · Act Up · US · Poster

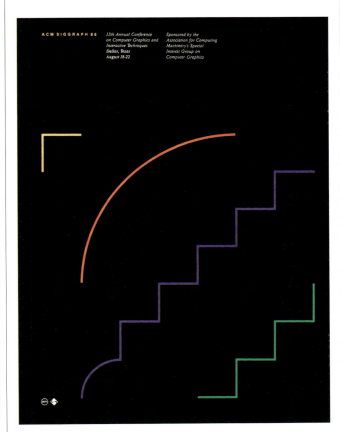

1986 · Woody Pirtle, Pirtle Design · US · Brochure cover

1986 · Yusaku Kamekura · JP · Poster

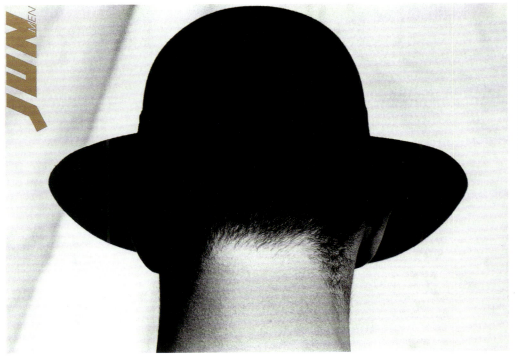

1986 · Makoto Saito · JP · Poster

261   **1980–1989**

April Greiman · United States

As soon as it became possible to work out her design ideas on an Apple Mac, the Californian designer April Greiman turned to this new technology with drive and enthusiasm. In a 1986 edition of *Design Quarterly* she presented one of the very first digitally produced layouts, while other new possibilities, such as the use of video stills, led to the creation of a comprehensive and completely independent visual language.

Sobald es möglich war, Gestaltungsideen auf einem Macintosh umzusetzen, wendete sich die kalifornische Grafikdesignerin April Greiman dieser neuen Technik zu. Mit einer Ausgabe von *Design Quarterly* legte sie 1986 eines der ersten vollständig digital erzeugten Layouts vor. Neue Möglichkeiten wie die Verwendung von Videostills führten zu einer ganz eigenständigen Bildsprache.

Dès qu'il fut possible d'élaborer des idées graphiques sur un Macintosh, la graphiste californienne April Greiman adopta avec enthousiasme cette nouvelle technologie. En 1986, elle présenta dans un numéro de *Design Quarterly* une des premières mises en page entièrement réalisées sur ordinateur. Des possibilités inédites comme l'utilisation d'images vidéo ouvrirent la voie à un langage visuel entièrement indépendant.

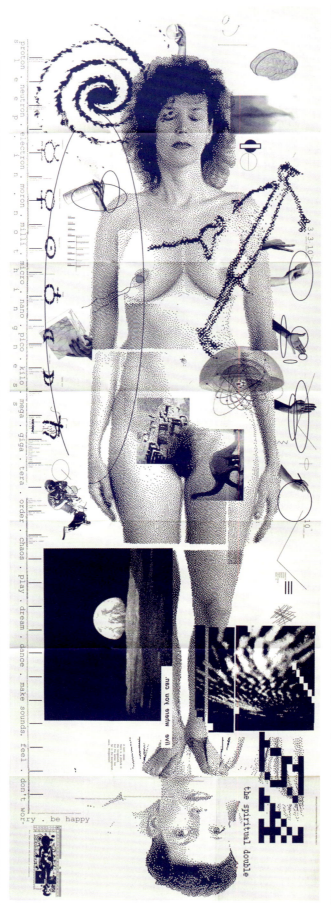

1986 · April Greiman · US · Magazine (outside)

1986 · April Greiman · US · Magazine (inside)

April Greiman (1948, New York) is an American designer based in Los Angeles, where she heads the design consultancy Made in Space. A pioneering advocate for the use of computer technology as a design tool, Greiman played a major role in developing New Wave design in the United States. After attending Kansas City Art Institute in Missouri, she studied at the Basel School of Design under Armin Hofmann and Wolfgang Weingart. Notable amongst her works are posters for CalArts (1977, with Jayme Odgers) and the 1984 Los Angeles Olympics. In 1982 Greiman became head of the design department at CalArts, two years later changing its name to Visual Communications and thus broadening its influence.

April Greiman (1948, New York) ist eine amerikanische Grafikdesignerin, die in Los Angeles die Design Consulting Agentur Made in Space leitet. Als Vorreiterin beim Einsatz von Computertechnik in der Gestaltung spielte sie in den Vereinigten Staaten eine maßgebliche Rolle bei der Entwicklung von New-Wave-Design. Nach dem Besuch des Kansas City Art Institute in Missouri studierte sie an der Schule für Gestaltung in Basel bei Armin Hofmann und Wolfgang Weingart. Am bekanntesten sind ihre Plakate für CalArts (1977, mit Jayme Odgers) und für die Olympischen Spiele 1984 in Los Angeles. 1982 übernahm Greiman die Leitung der Designabteilung an der CalArts, die sie zwei Jahre später in „Visuelle Kommunikation" umbenannte und damit deren Einflusssphäre vergrößerte.

April Greiman (1948, New York) est une graphiste américaine résidant à Los Angeles, où elle supervise le cabinet de conseil en design Made in Space. Pionnière et ardente promotrice des technologies numériques dans le domaine du design, Greiman a joué un rôle majeur dans le développement du design New Wave aux États-Unis. Après des études au Kansas City Art Institute (Missouri), elle étudie à l'école de design de Bâle auprès d'Armin Hofmann et de Wolfgang Weingart. Parmi ses travaux les plus remarqués figurent ses affiches pour le CalArts (1977, avec Jayme Odgers) et pour les jeux Olympiques de Los Angeles en 1984. En 1982, Greiman est devenue directrice du département de design du CalArts. Deux ans plus tard, elle l'a rebaptisé de communication visuelle, étendant ainsi son influence.

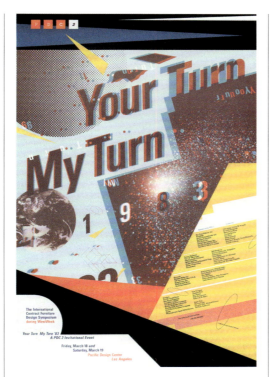

1983 · April Greiman · US · Poster

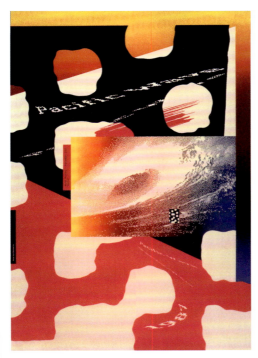

1981 · April Greiman · US · Poster

1981 · April Greiman · US · Magazine cover

1986 · April Greiman · US · Poster

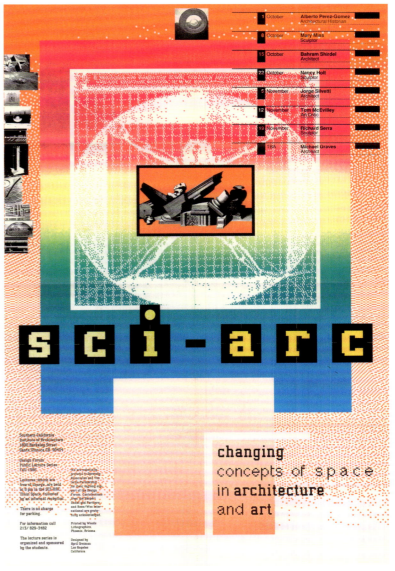

1985 · April Greiman · US · Poster

Drawn Graphics

While graphic design of the 1960s and '70s often sought to turn away from the home-spun styles of earlier times, 1980s designers made a conscious choice to revive them. Many works from the period confirmed the preference for using a minimal design vocabulary to create maximum emotional impact. Endless variations on what once seemed a contradictory connection have continued to be applied ever since.

Während die Grafik der 1960er- und 1970er-Jahre oftmals eine Abkehr von der handge-machten Stilistik früherer Epochen verfolgte, wurde genau diese in den 1980er-Jahren wieder ganz bewusst als Stilmittel einge-setzt. Viele der Arbeiten dieser Zeit ver-banden dabei die kommunikativen Vorzüge reduzierter Formensprache mit der emotio-nalen Anmutung des Gezeichneten. Seither wird diese zunächst widersprüchlich erschei-nende Verbindung immer wieder in den unterschiedlichsten Variationen im Grafik-design verwendet.

Alors que le graphisme des années 1960 et 1970 visait souvent à se démarquer de toute stylistique artisanale d'époques antérieures, c'est précisément cette esthétique que les designers des années 1980 réintroduisirent délibérément. Nombre des réalisations op-taient pour un langage réduit en vue d'avoir un impact émotionnel. Depuis, cette combi-naison à première vue contradictoire n'a cessé d'être appliquée.

1981 · Tony Lane · US · Record cover

1987 · Richard Greenberg · US · Logo · Dirty Dancing

1984 · Jay Vigon, Ed Thrasher (AD) · US · Logo · Purple Rain

1983 · Joan Miró · ES · Logo · España

1989 · John Hornall, Jack Anderson · US · Logo · Corbis

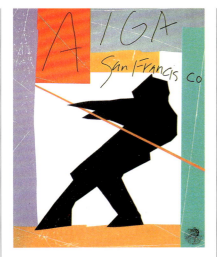

1984 · Michael Manwaring · US · Poster

1992 · Craig Frazier, Grant Peterson, Frazier Design · US · Logo · Lucas Arts

1980s · Derick Hudspith, John Sorrell, Newell & Sorrell · UK · Logo · Lumino

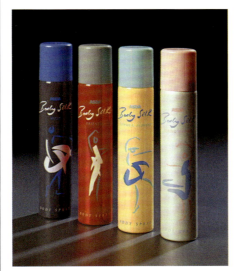

1987 · Lloyd Northover · UK · Packaging

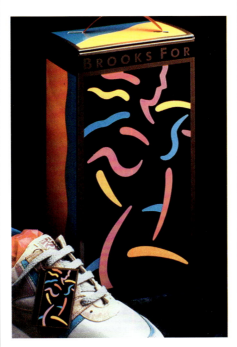

1986 · Duffy Design · US · Packaging

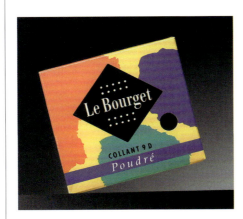

1994 · Béatrice Mariotti · FR · Packaging

1990 · George Tscherny · US · Poster

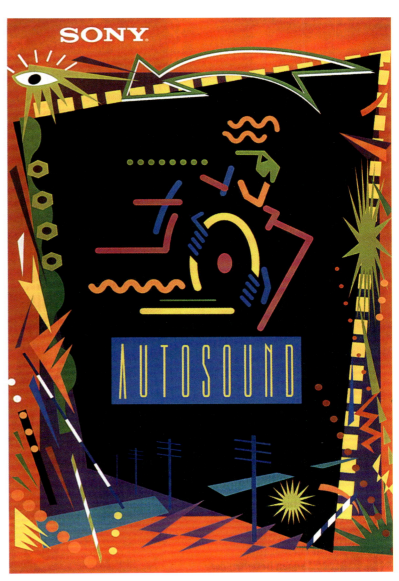

1994 · Javier Romero Design Group · US · Poster

1987

The first version of the layout software **QuarkXPress** is released

The **Random House-Knopf** publishing company establishes an in-house design group, including Barbara deWilde, Carol Devine Carson, Archie Ferguson, and Chip Kidd

The **Tokyo Type Directors Club** is established

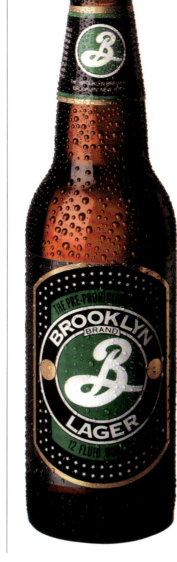

1987 · Bruno Suter · CH/FR · Logo · Galeries Lafayette

1987 · Pat Hansen · US · Logo · Chocolate & Co.

1987 · Milton Glaser · US · Identity/Packaging · Brooklyn Brewery

1987 · Michael Bierut · US · Poster

1987 · Anonymous · US · Record cover

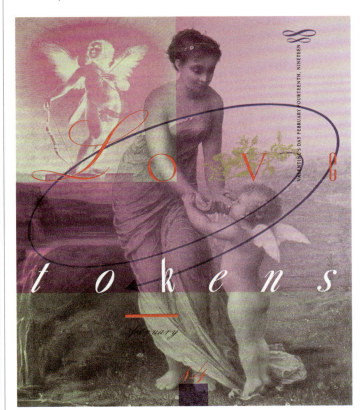

1987 · Robert Valentine · US · Poster

1987 · Rostislav Vaněk · CZ · Poster

1987 · Erhard Grüttner · GDR · Poster

1987 · Takenobu Igarashi · JP · Magazine cover

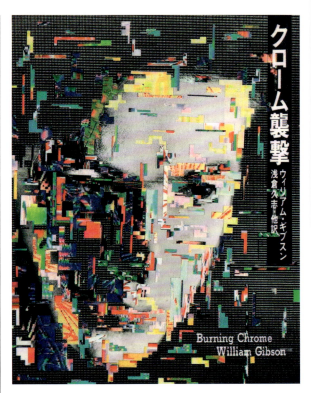

1987 · Yukimasa Okumura · JP · Book cover

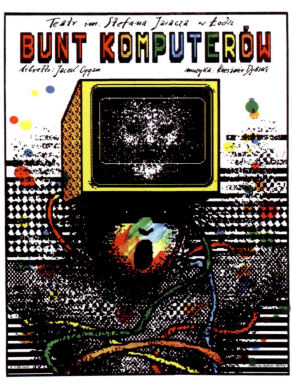

1987 · Andrzej Pągowski · PL · Poster

1987 · Henry Marquez, Gary Panter, Nels Israelson (PH) · US · Record cover

1974 · Peter Mussfeldt · DE/EC · Identity · Galapagos

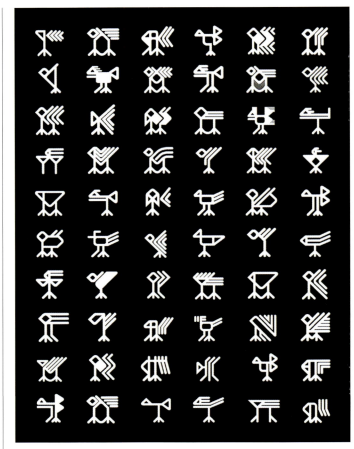

1975 · Peter Mussfeldt · DE/EC · Symbols

1985 · Peter Mussfeldt · DE/EC · Poster

Peter Mussfeldt (1938, Berlin) is a German-Ecuadorean artist and graphic designer, who pioneered the use of modern graphics in his adopted country. After studying art in Dresden, Mussfeldt escaped to West Germany and continued his studies at the Dusseldorf Arts Academy before moving in 1962 to Guayaquil in Ecuador. Here he founded a design practice, creating logos for shops, businesses, TV channels, and museums. He also produced a wide range of silk-screen prints, textiles, and etchings, some of which were purchased by MoMA in New York. Mussfeldt has for many years taught at the Universidad Casa Grande in Guayaquil, where he received an honorary doctorate in 2014.

Peter Mussfeldt (1938, Berlin) ist ein deutsch-ecuadorianischer Künstler und Grafikdesigner, der in seiner Wahlheimat Ecuador der bedeutendste Wegbereiter moderner Grafik war. Nach einem Kunststudium in Dresden, der Flucht nach Westdeutschland und einem weiteren Studium an der berühmten Kunstakademie Düsseldorf zog er 1962 nach Guayaquil, Ecuador. Hier gründete er ein Designbüro und schuf Logos für kleine und große Unternehmen, für Einkaufszentren, Museen oder TV-Sender. Parallel entstand ein umfangreiches freies Werk, bestehend aus Siebdrucken, Textilarbeiten und Radierungen, einige davon erwarb das Museum of Modern Art New York. Peter Mussfeldt lehrt seit vielen Jahren an der Universidad Casa Grande in Guayaquil, die ihm 2014 die Ehrendoktorwürde verliehen hat.

Peter Mussfeldt (1938, Berlin) est un artiste et graphiste germano-équatorien qui a instauré le graphisme moderne dans son pays d'adoption. Après des études d'art à Dresde et une fuite en Allemagne de l'Ouest, suivie de nouvelles études à la célèbre académie des beaux-arts de Düsseldorf, il se retire à Guayaquil, en Équateur, en 1962. Il y fonde un studio de graphisme et crée des logos pour des magasins, des entreprises, des centres commerciaux, des musées et des chaînes de télévision. Parallèlement, il produit une large éventail de sérigraphies, œuvres textiles et eaux-fortes, quelques-unes ayant été acquises par le Museum of Modern Art de New York. Mussfeldt enseigne depuis de nombreuses années à la Universidad Casa Grande de Guayaquil, qui lui a conféré le titre de docteur honoris causa en 2014.

1975 · Peter Mussfeldt · DE/EC · Logo · Cartram

1972 · Peter Mussfeldt · DE/EC · Logo · Banco del Pacífico

2000 · Peter Mussfeldt · DE/EC · Logo · MAAC

2009 · Peter Mussfeldt · DE/EC · Logo · Versus

1978 · Peter Mussfeldt · DE/EC · Logo · La Moneda

1985 · Peter Mussfeldt · DE/EC · Logo · Factorandina Financiera

2010 · Peter Mussfeldt · DE/EC · Logo · Democracia – Una convivencia de tolerancia

2010 · Peter Mussfeldt · DE/EC · Logo · Versus

20¯0 · Peter Mussfeldt · DE/EC · Logo · CONAH

2010 · Peter Mussfeldt · DE/EC · Logo · Cerveceria Nacional

1985 · Peter Mussfeldt · DE/EC · Logo · Banco Popular

2009 · Peter Mussfeldt · DE/EC · Logo · Oasis

2010 · Peter Mussfeldt · DE/EC · Logo · Empresa Nacional de Bebidas

1968 · Peter Mussfeldt · DE/EC · Logo · Arquitecto Xavier Quevedo

2017 · Peter Mussfeldt · DE/EC · Logo · Negocios Industriales Real (Nirsa)

1995 · Peter Mussfeldt · DE/EC · Logo · Golf Copa Los Andes

1990 · Peter Mussfeldt · DE/EC · Logo · Financapital

2005 · Peter Mussfeldt · DE/EC · Logo · Transoceania

2005 · Peter Mussfeldt · DE/EC · Logo · Grupo Berlin

2010 · Peter Mussfeldt · DE/EC · Logo · Adan y Eva

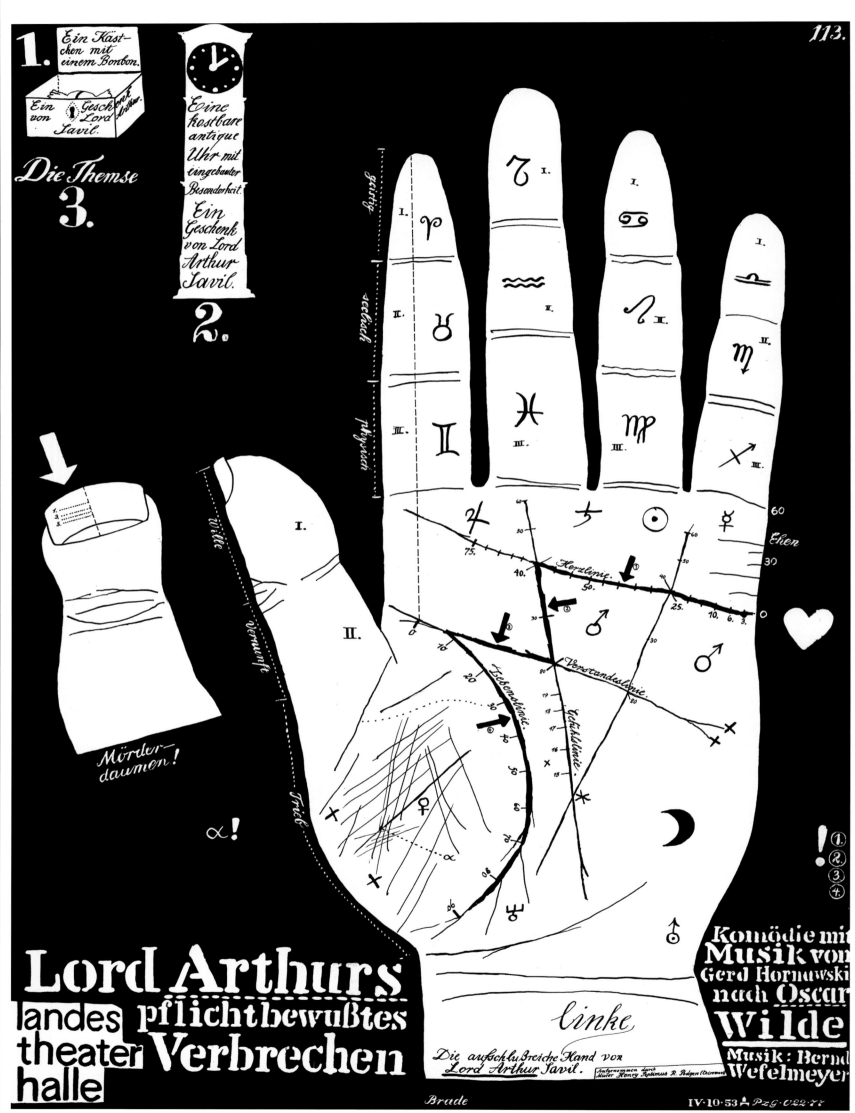

1977 · Helmut Brade · GDR · Poster

1981 · Helmut Brade · GDR · Poster

1986 · Helmut Brade · GDR · Poster

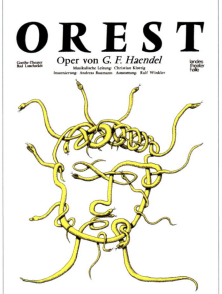

1988 · Helmut Brade · GDR · Poster

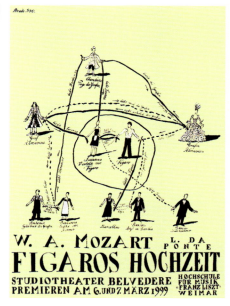

1999 · Helmut Brade · DE · Poster

1976 · Helmut Brade · GDR · Poster

1994 · Helmut Brade · DE · Poster

1988 · Helmut Brade · GDR · Poster

1990 · Helmut Brade · DE · Poster

1997 · Helmut Brade · DE · Poster

Helmut Brade (1937, Halle, Germany) is a graphic artist, designer, and educator, most famous for his poster designs. After studying architecture, ceramics, and graphic design at the Academy of Industrial Design in Halle, Brade began his career in 1972, designing sets for theaters and operas in Berlin, Budapest, Tokyo, Oslo, and many other cities. He began teaching in Halle in 1993, becoming professor of communication design a year later. From 1999–2004 Brade also served as president of the Free Academy of the Arts in Leipzig.

Helmut Brade (1937, Halle an der Saale) ist ein Grafiker, Designer und Dozent, am bekanntesten ist er allerdings aufgrund seiner Plakate. Er studierte Keramik, Architektur und Grafikdesign an der Hochschule für industrielle Formgestaltung Halle und arbeitete anschließend ab 1972 zunächst als Bühnenbildner für Theater- und Opernhäuser in Berlin, Budapest, Tokio, Oslo und vielen anderen Städten. Ab 1993 unterrichtete er in Halle, im Jahr darauf wurde er dort zum Professor für Kommunikationsdesign ernannt. Von 1999 bis 2004 wirkte Brade zudem als Präsident der Freien Akademie der Künste in Leipzig.

Helmut Brade (1937, Halle, Allemagne) est un artiste graphiste, designer et professeur, célèbre surtout pour ses conceptions d'affiches. Après des études d'architecture, de céramique et de graphisme à l'école de design industriel de Halle, Brade débute sa carrière en 1972 en concevant des décors de théâtre et d'opéra à Berlin, Budapest, Tokyo, Oslo et de nombreuses autres villes. En 1993, il commence à enseigner à Halle, où il est nommé professeur de design communicationnel un an plus tard. De 1999 à 2004, Brade a aussi été président de l'Académie libre des arts à Leipzig.

1988

The **Rotis** typeface is created by
Otl Aicher, becoming one of the
most widely used fonts of its time

The **Australian Graphic Design
Association** (AGDA) is founded

The Graphic Language of Neville Brody is published, and with
the combined sales of the follow-up volume in 1994 it becomes one
of the most successful titles on graphic design

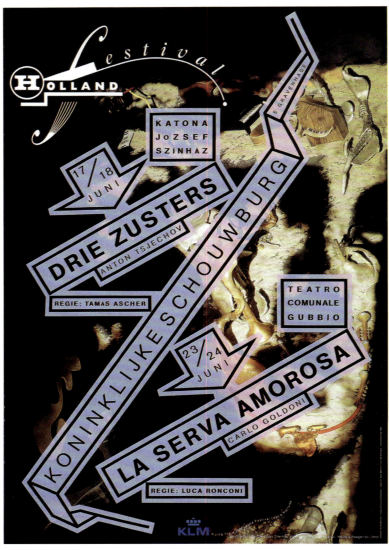

1988 · Studio Dumbar · NL · Poster

1988 · Sergio Liuzzi · BR · Identity · Cantão

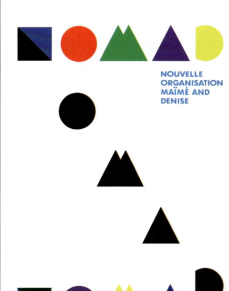

1988 · Ikko Tanaka · JP · Poster

The **Guardian**

1988 · David Hillman, Pentagram · UK · Logo ·
The Guardian

1988 · Scott Idleman · US · Logo · New Music

1988 · Evelyn Grumach · BR · Logo · AT2

1988 · Guto Lacaz, Carlos Baptistella · BR · Magazine cover

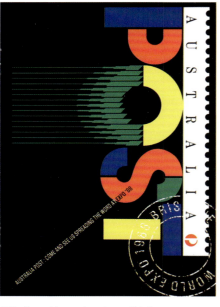

1988 · Emery Vincent Associates · AU · Poster

Adrian Frutiger's typeface
Avenir is released

The first version of the vector-based
graphic software **FreeHand** is released

The first **Tehran International Poster
Biennial** is held in Iran

1988 · Bruno Oldani · CH/NO · Poster

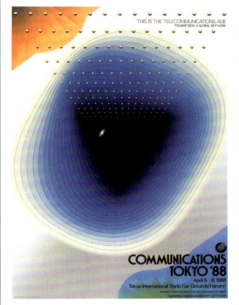

1983 · Mitsuo Katsui · JP · Poster

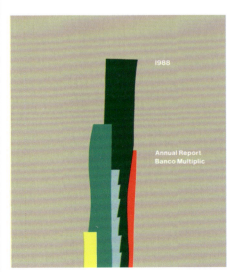

1983 · Kiko Farkas · BR · Brochure cover

1988 · Dusan Junek · SK · Poster

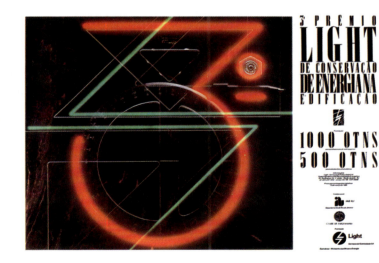

1988 · Helio Rosas · BR · Ad

1988 · Eugene Grossman · US/DE · Identity · DEA

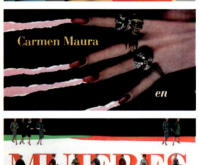

1988 · Juan Gatti · ES · Opening titles

In the 1980s, several European countries began to privatize what had previously been state-run services. PTT, the national postal service in the Netherlands, was one of the businesses most broadly affected by this change, and naturally enough, there was a need for eye-catching images to publicize the switch from government agency to independent service provider. Studio Dumbar was assigned the task of revamping the postal service's outdated and somewhat erratic brand image and giving it a completely new face. The result was a corporate identity that succeeded in redefining the organization's multifaceted functions. The focal point of the project was a lavish design manual which not only provided the rationale behind every detail but also clearly proclaimed the postal service's brand-new approach.

In den 1980er-Jahren begannen viele europäische Länder, bislang staatlich geführte Betriebe zu privatisieren. In den Niederlanden war die Post die größte davon betroffene Institution. Die Transformation von Behörde zum Dienstleister musste sich natürlich auch visuell bemerkbar machen, und so erhielt das Studio Dumbar den herausfordernden Auftrag, der uneinheitlich und altmodisch auftretenden PTT ein völlig neues Gesicht zu geben. Es entstand eine Corporate Identity, die sämtliche Aspekte des Unternehmens in zeitgemäßer Form neu definierte. Im Mittelpunkt der Arbeit stand ein aufwendig produziertes Designmanual, das die Designparameter nicht einfach rational für jedes Detail vermittelte, sondern aus dem der neue Ton des Unternehmens förmlich heraussprach.

Dans les années 1980, de nombreux pays européens commencèrent à privatiser des entreprises publiques. Aux Pays-Bas, la poste fut la plus grande institution touchée par cette tendance, et une telle transformation du service public en prestataire de services devait évidemment être reflétée visuellement. C'est ainsi que Studio Dumbar fut chargé par la poste néerlandaise de la refonte totale de son image plutôt incohérente et désuète. L'aspect central de ce travail fut l'élaboration d'un sompteux manuel de design qui ne se bornait pas à justifier chaque détail, mais qui défendait aussi la nouvelle tonalité de l'entreprise.

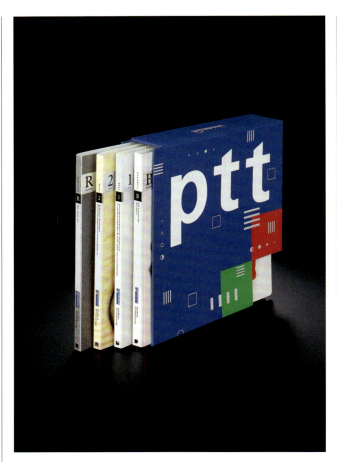

1988 · Studio Dumbar · NL · Design manual

1988 · Studio Dumbar · NL · Logos

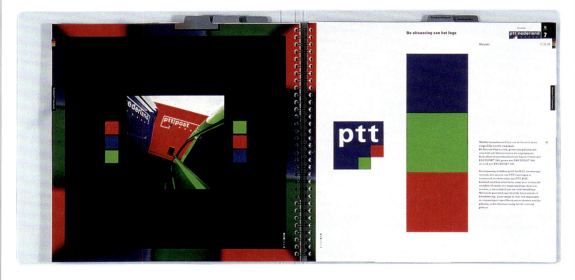

1988 · Studio Dumbar · NL · Design manual

Studio Dumbar (1977, The Netherlands) is an international design agency originally based in The Hague (later Rotterdam). Its comprehensive work in typography, corporate identity, and visual branding, led for three decades by Gert Dumbar (1940, Indonesia), has helped shape several aspects of contemporary graphic design. The studio's redesign of the road signage system in South Korea, as well as the completely new identity for the Dutch police, demonstrates the team's capability to undertake complex projects. Gert Dumbar retired in 2003, but his studio lives on with branches also in Shanghai and Seoul.

Studio Dumbar (1977, Niederlande) ist eine internationale Designagentur, ursprünglich mit Sitz in Den Haag (und später Rotterdam). Ihre vielfältigen Arbeiten in Typografie, Corporate Identity und Markenidentität, die dreißig Jahre lang unter der Leitung von Gert Dumbar (1940, Indonesien) entstanden, beeinflussten mehrere Aspekte des zeitgenössischen Grafikdesigns. Mit der Neugestaltung des südkoreanischen Systems der Straßenbeschilderung sowie mit dem völlig neuen Auftritt der niederländischen Polizei bewies das Dumbar-Team seine Fähigkeit, komplexe Projekte umzusetzen. Gert Dumbar ging 2003 in den Ruhestand, sein Studio existiert jedoch mit Ablegern in Schanghai und Seoul weiter.

Studio Dumbar (1977, Pays-Bas) est une agence de design internationale initialement basée à La Haye (et plus tard à Rotterdam). Son travail global intégrant typographie, image de marque et identité visuelle, a été supervisé pendant trois décennies par Gert Dumbar (1940, Indonésie) et a façonné différents aspects du graphisme contemporain. Le remaniement de la signalétique routière en Corée du Sud, ainsi que la redéfinition de l'identité de la police néerlandaise, montrent la capacité de l'équipe à traiter des projets complexes. Gert Dumbar a pris sa retraite en 2003, mais son studio perdure avec des bureaux à Shanghai et Séoul.

1988 · Studio Dumbar · NL · Identity · PTT

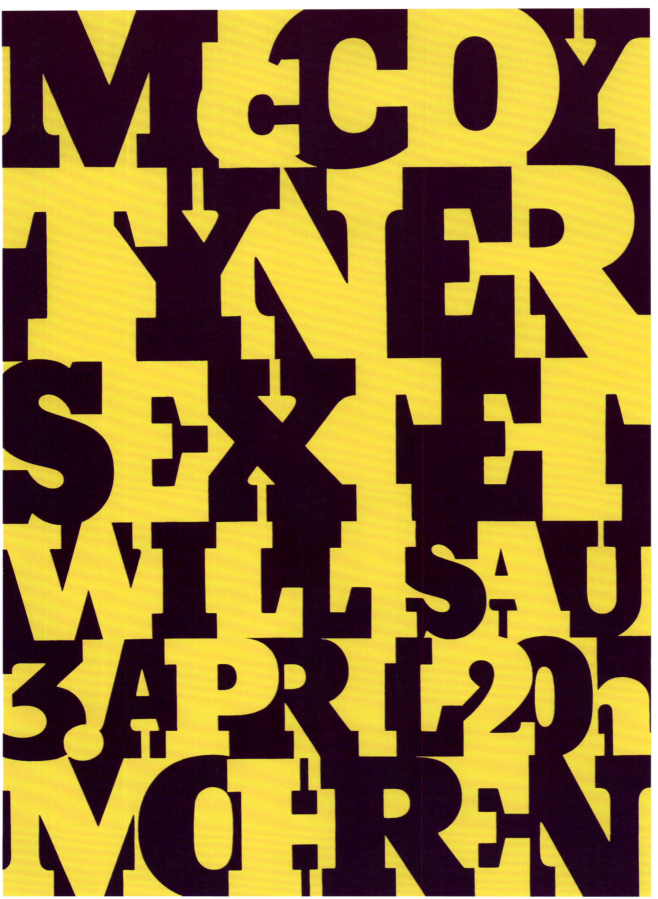

1980 · Niklaus Troxler · CH · Poster

Niklaus Troxler (1947, Willisau, Switzerland) is an award-winning graphic artist working in corporate identity and illustration, most notably in poster design, and mainly through the Willisau Jazz Festival, which he organized since 1975. Troxler studied graphic design at the School of Art and Design in Lucerne before briefly working in Paris as an art director in the early 1970s. He returned home to found his own studio, and run his music festival until 2009. Troxler makes little use of photography in his silkscreen and lithographic posters, preferring to explore typographic, figurative, and abstract narratives.

Niklaus Troxler (1947, Willisau, Schweiz) ist ein preisgekrönter Grafikdesigner, der durch seine Firmensignets und seine Illustrationen bekannt ist, insbesondere für Plakate, und zwar hauptsächlich durch das Willisau Jazz Festival, das er 1975 ins Leben rief. Troxler studierte Grafikdesign an der Schule für Gestaltung in Luzern und arbeitete anschließend, Anfang der 1970er-Jahre, kurzzeitig als Artdirector in Paris. Nach seiner Rückkehr in die Schweiz gründete er sein eigenes Büro und leitete bis 2009 sein Musikfestival. Troxler verwendet in seinen Siebdruck- und lithografischen Plakaten nur selten Fotografie, sondern arbeitet lieber mit typografischen, figurativen und abstrakten Elementen.

Niklaus Troxler (1947, Willisau, Suisse) est un artiste graphiste primé qui travaille dans les domaines de l'image de marque et de l'illustration, notamment la conception d'affiches à l'occasion du festival de jazz de Willisau qu'il organise à partir de 1975. Troxler a suivi des études de graphisme à la Haute école d'art et de design de Lucerne avant de travailler brièvement à Paris comme directeur artistique au début des années 1970. Il rentre ensuite en Suisse pour fonder son propre studio et s'occuper de son festival musical jusqu'en 2009. Dans ses affiches lithographiques et en sérigraphie, Troxler se sert très peu de la photographie, préférant explorer le mode de la narration typographique, figurative et abstraite.

It is safe to say that the most appreciative client is the one who gives the designer a completely free hand. Indeed, none more so than the case of Niklaus Troxler and his poster designs for the Willisau Jazz Festival in his native Switzerland, since Troxler was also the founder and organizer of the annual event, up until 2009. Since the 1970s, he came up with fascinating posters which, time and again, showed fresh visual interpretations of music, testifying to the endless opportunities that exist for visual variations.

Es heißt immer, die dankbarsten Auftraggeber seien diejenigen, die bei der Gestaltung völlig freie Hand lassen. Im Fall von Niklaus Troxler und seinen Plakaten für diverse Jazzveranstaltungen im schweizerischen Willisau trifft dies in ganz besonderem Maße zu, denn er persönlich war Initiator und Veranstalter dieser Events bis 2009. Seit den 1970er-Jahren faszinieren seine Plakate mit immer wieder neuen visuellen Interpretationen von Musik, die die unendlichen Möglichkeiten grafischer Variation aufzeigen.

On dit toujours que les clients les plus satisfaits sont ceux qui laissent toute liberté au graphiste. Ceci vaut tout particulièrement pour Niklaus Troxler et ses affiches pour le festival de jazz à Willisau, dans sa Suisse natale, un événement qu'il a fondé et organisé jusqu'en 2009. Depuis les années 1970, ses affiches frappent régulièrement par leurs interprétations toujours nouvelles de la musique, démontrant en même temps les possibilités infinies des variantes graphiques.

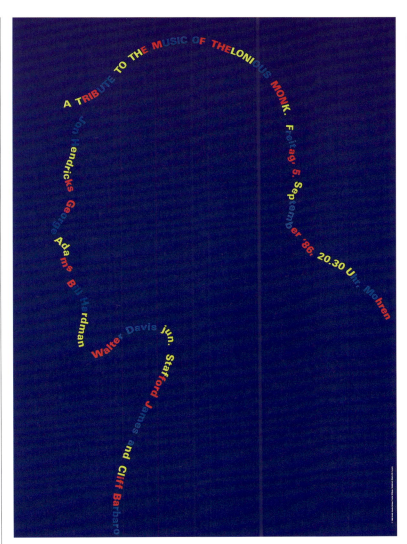

1986 · Niklaus Troxler · CH · Poster

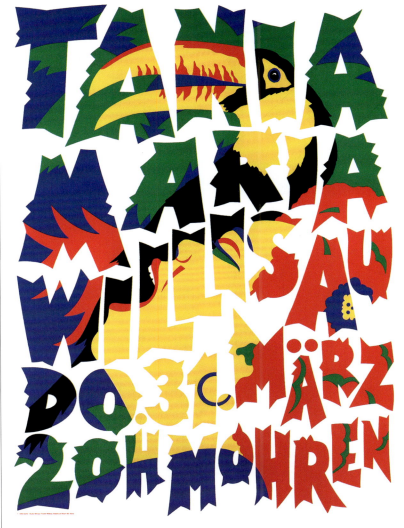

1988 · Niklaus Troxler · CH · Poster

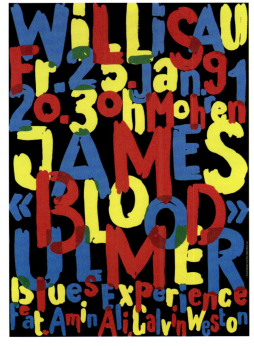

1991 · Niklaus Troxler · CH · Poster

2005 · Niklaus Troxler · CH · Poster

2016 · Niklaus Troxler · CH · Poster

Esprit was one of the first fashion labels to consider a consistent brand-staging strategy to be just as important as its product design. The Japanese designer Tamotsu Yagi took charge of the company's advertising campaigns, store design, and printed matter, for both the domestic and overseas markets, creating visuals with a distinctly 1980s feel.

Esprit gehörte zu den ersten Modelabels, bei denen die konsequente Markeninszenierung ebenso wichtig war wie das Design der Produkte selber. Der japanische Gestalter Tamotsu Yagi verantwortete Werbekampagnen, Storedesign und Drucksachen des international agierenden Unternehmens und visualisierte damit ein Stück des Lebensgefühls der 80er.

Esprit a été une des premières marques de mode à accorder autant d'importance à la mise en scène cohérente de son image qu'au design de ses articles. Le graphiste japonais Tamotsu Yagi signa les campagnes publicitaires, l'agencement des boutiques et le matériel imprimé de la marque, donnant lieu à des créations caractéristiques des années 80.

ESPRIT

1979 · John Casado · US · Logo

1988 · Tamotsu Yagi, Esprit graphic design team · JP/US · Identity

СОЮЗ ХУДОЖНИКОВ СССР,
СОЮЗ ХУДОЖНИКОВ РСФСР,
МОСКОВСКАЯ ОРГАНИЗАЦИЯ
СОЮЗА ХУДОЖНИКОВ,
ИЗДАТЕЛЬСТВО «ПЛАКАТ»

ВЫСТАВКА

КОМПЛЕКТ-ВЫСТАВКА

ПЛАКАТ – ПЕРЕСТРОЙКЕ

МОСКВА «ПЛАКАТ» 1988

1988 · Anonymous · RU · Poster

A **Design Museum** opens in a former banana warehouse in London

Erik Spiekermann and Just van Rossum create the **Officina** typeface

The anti-consumerist **Adbusters Media** is set up in Vancouver

Kurt Weidemann's Corporate **ASE** typeface is released, originally designed for Mercedes-Benz

SPECIAL ANNIVERSARY ISSUE
OMNI
OCTOBER 1989
TRENDS AND PREDICTIONS FOR THE YEAR 2000 AND BEYOND

$3.50

1989 · Anonymous · US · Magazine cover

1989 · Ron Dumas (AD), Gary Nolton (PH), Nike Inc. · US · Poster

1989 · Katherine McCoy · US · Poster

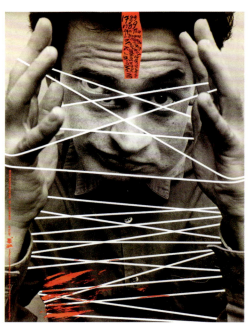

1989 · Rico Lins · BR · Poster

1989 · Mengü Ertel · TR · Logo · TRT Television

V&A

1989 · Alan Fletcher, Pentagram · UK · Logo · Victoria & Albert Museum

1989 · The Pushpin Group · US · Logo · Solo Editions

1989 · Ott+Stein · DE · Poster

1989 · Georgii N. Kamenskikh · RU · Poster

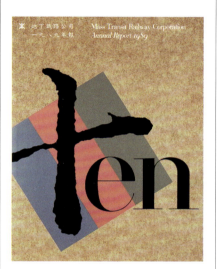

1989 · Henry Steiner · HK · Brochure cover

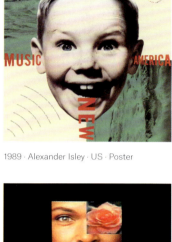

1989 · Alexander Isley · US · Poster

1989 · Tibor Kalman, Emily Oberman, M & Co. · US · Identity · Lifetime Television

1989 · Vaughan Oliver (AD), Simon Larbalestier (PH) · UK · Record cover

1989 · Edite Gornova · LV · Poster

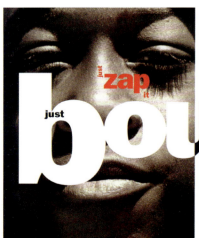

1989 · Neville Brody · UK · Ad

1979 · Shin Matsunaga · JP · Logo · Savas

1984 · Shin Matsunaga · JP · Logo · Select

1984 · Shin Matsunaga · JP · Logo · Daichi Tableware

1986 · Shin Matsunaga · JP · Logo · Fusosha

1983 · Shin Matsunaga · JP · Logo · Ban Dai

1988 · Shin Matsunaga · JP · Logo · Gachi

1989 · Shin Matsunaga · JP · Logo · Takenaka Works

1991 · Shin Matsunaga · JP · Logo · Tagawa Museum of Art

1988 · Shin Matsunaga · JP · Logo · Fukumitsuya

1986 · Shin Matsunaga · JP · Logo · Waltz

1990 · Shin Matsunaga · JP · Logo · RIHGA Royal Hotel

1991 · Shin Matsunaga · JP · Logo · Aiwa

1991 · Shin Matsunaga · JP · Logo · Miwa

1991 · Shin Matsunaga · JP · Logo · Hachijuni Bank

1991 · Shin Matsunaga · JP · Logo · Roam

1994 · Shin Matsunaga · JP · Logo · Calbee

1996 · Shin Matsunaga · JP · Logo · Bank of Tokyo-Mitsubishi

2004 · Shin Matsunaga · JP · Logo · Design Association

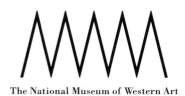

2004 · Shin Matsunaga · JP · Logo · National Museum of Western Art

2005 · Shin Matsunaga · JP · Logo · Mitsui Memorial Museum

Shin Matsunaga (1940, Tokyo) is a Japanese graphic designer who, as well as creating many superb posters, has also produced numerous corporate identities and packaging designs. Graduating in 1964 from the Tokyo National University of Fine Arts and Music, Matsunaga's first job was with the advertising department of the cosmetic manufacturer Shiseido. In 1971, he opened his own design studio in Tokyo and from then on worked for Japanese companies in various sectors. Matsunaga's works have featured in international solo exhibitions and are also to be found in the collections of leading museums, including the Museum of Modern Art in New York, the same city's Cooper Hewitt, Smithsonian Design Museum, and the Victoria & Albert Museum in London.

Shin Matsunaga (1940, Tokio) ist ein japanischer Grafikdesigner, der neben vielfach ausgezeichneten Plakaten auch unzählige Firmenidentitäten und Verpackungsentwürfe schuf. 1964 beendete er sein Studium an der Tokyo National University of Fine Arts and Music und arbeitete zunächst in der Werbeabteilung des Kosmetikherstellers Shiseido. 1971 eröffnete Matsunaga ein eigenes Designstudio in Tokio und war fortan für japanische Unternehmen unterschiedlicher Branchen tätig. Seine Arbeiten waren in internationalen Einzelausstellungen zu sehen und befinden sich in den Sammlungen bedeutender Museen wie dem Museum of Modern Art New York, dem Cooper Hewitt, Smithsonian Design Museum oder dem Victoria & Albert Museum London.

Shin Matsunaga (1940, Tokyo) est un graphiste japonais qui, outre de superbes affiches, a signé d'innombrables identités d'entreprises et projets d'emballages. Il termine en 1964 ses études à l'université des arts de Tokyo et travaille d'abord au sein du département de publicité du groupe de cosmétiques Shiseido. En 1971, Matsunaga ouvre son propre studio de graphisme à Tokyo et dès lors aura des clients de différents secteurs. Ses travaux ont été présentés dans des expositions individuelles internationales et figurent dans les collections de musées prestigieux comme le Museum of Modern Art et le Cooper Hewitt, Smithsonian Design Museum à New York, ou le Victoria & Albert Museum à Londres.

ISSEY MIYAKE

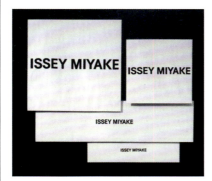

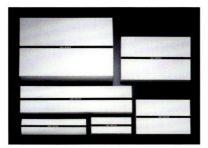

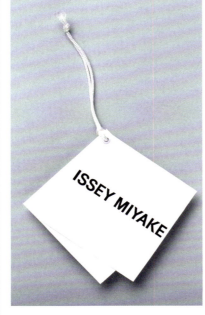

1989 · Shin Matsunaga · JP · Identity · Issey Miyake

1983 · Shin Matsunaga · JP · Packaging

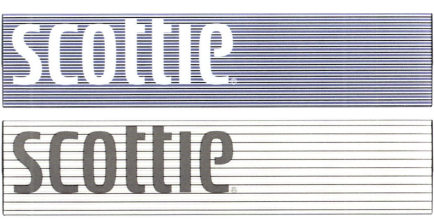

1986 · Shin Matsunaga · JP · Packaging

1984 · Shin Matsunaga · JP · Packaging

Uwe Loesch · Germany

Uwe Loesch (Dresden, 1943) is a German communication designer who studied from 1964–68 at the Peter Behrens Academy in Dusseldorf. Loesch is also one of the most important international designers of modern posters and in 1984 several of his posters became part of the permanent exhibition of MoMA in New York. From 1985–90 he was professor of mixed media at the University of Applied Sciences in Dusseldorf, then from 1990–2008 professor of communication design at the University of Wuppertal. Loesch became a member of the Alliance Graphique Internationale in 1988, and in 2013 was given the Lifetime Achievement Award of the Federal Republic of Germany.

Uwe Loesch (1943, Dresden) ist ein deutscher Kommunikationsdesigner und gehört zu den international bedeutendsten Plakatgestaltern der Gegenwart. Von 1964 bis 1968 studierte er an der Peter Behrens Werkkunstschule in Düsseldorf. Ab 1984 wurden seine Arbeiten über mehrere Jahre im MoMA New York gezeigt. Loesch unterrichtete als Professor für medienübergreifende Gestaltung von 1985 bis 1990 an der Fachhochschule Düsseldorf sowie zwischen 1990 und 2008 Kommunikationsdesign an der Bergischen Universität Wuppertal. Die Alliance Graphique Internationale nahm ihn 1988 auf. 2013 wurde er mit dem Designpreis der Bundesrepublik Deutschland für sein Lebenswerk ausgezeichnet.

Uwe Loesch (Dresde, 1943) est un designer allemand en communication visuelle qui s'inscrit parmi les plus grands affichistes internationaux de notre époque. Entre 1964 et 1968, il étudie à l'école d'art Peter Behrens à Düsseldorf. À partir de 1984, ses travaux ont été intégrés à la collection permanente du Museum of Modern Art de New York. De 1985 à 1990, il a enseigné la création multimédia à l'école technique de Düsseldorf. De 1990 à 2008, il a été professeur de design communicationnel à l'université de Wuppertal. En 1988, il est devenu membre de l'Alliance Graphique Internationale. En 2013, il a reçu de la République fédérale d'Allemagne le prix pour l'ensemble de son œuvre.

1984 · Uwe Loesch · DE · Poster

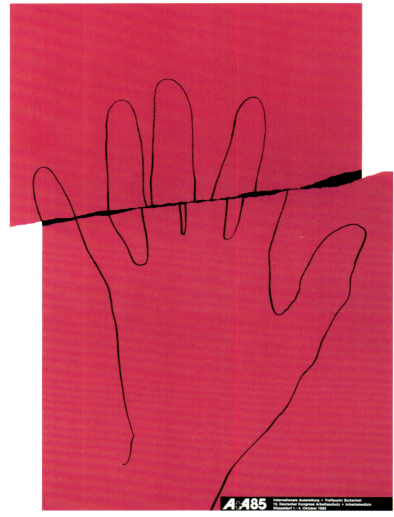

1985 · Uwe Loesch · DE · Poster

1991 · Uwe Loesch · DE · Poster

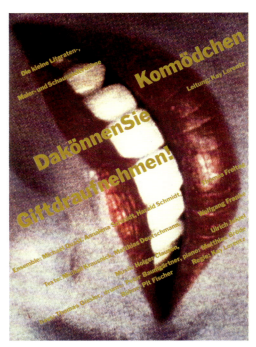

1984 · Uwe Loesch · DE · Poster

1992 · Uwe Loesch · DE · Poster

1991 · Uwe Loesch · DE · Poster

1992 · Uwe Loesch · DE · Poster

1996 · Uwe Loesch · DE · Poster

1989 · Uwe Loesch · DE · Poster

1998 · Norio Nakamura · JP · Record cover

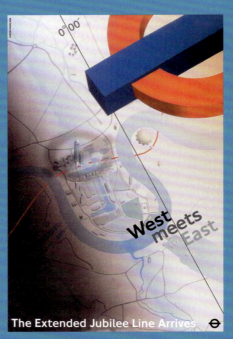

1999 · Keith Godard · UK · Poster

1990

1992 · José Carlos Lollo, Marcello Serpa · BR · Poster

1992 · Javier Mariscal · ES · Poster

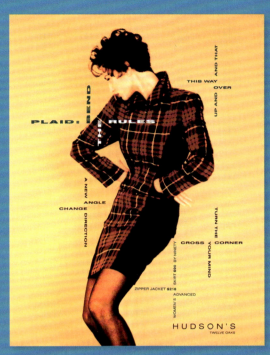

1992 · Nesnadny & Schwartz · US · Brochure cover

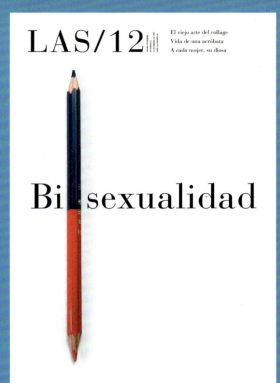

1999 · Alejandro Ros · AR · Magazine cover

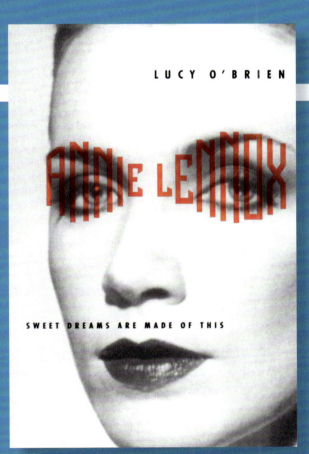

1993 · Angela Skouras · US · Book cover

1994 · Roberto Turégano · ES · Logo · Vallexe Jazz Festival

1998 · Ghobad Shiva · IR · Poster

1999

In the early 1990s, the Americans April Greiman and David Carson and Britain's Neville Brody became the design world's new heroes. Their computer-generated works delivered a wealth of uniquely stimulating ideas and new ways of seeing, while in the wider sphere the possibilities offered by computer-based design found favor not only with the new avant-garde but also quickly became part of general contemporary stylistics. The all-encompassing success of the internet, which became apparent as the decade wore on, and the mass-market breakthrough of home PCs, led to even greater progress. Digital media design was a completely new field of application for graphic design, and thanks to simple software applications computer users now had the wherewithal to create their own designs entirely from scratch. The result of this is that, even today, professionals continue to feel the challenge brought about by the knowledge that home users and part-timers may be equally competent and capable designers.

April Greiman und David Carson aus den USA sowie der Brite Neville Brody wurden Anfang der 1990er-Jahre die neuen Helden der Designszene. Ihre digital realisierten Arbeiten lieferten eine Reihe originärer Impulse und brachen mit Sehgewohnheiten des analogen Zeitalters. Die Möglichkeiten der computerbasierten Gestaltung hielten jedoch auch abseits dieser neuen Avantgarde schnell Einzug in die allgemeine Stilistik der Gegenwart. Mit der flächendeckenden Durchsetzung des Internets und dem Durchbruch von Home-PCs am Massenmarkt zur Mitte der Dekade wurde diese Entwicklung noch einmal befeuert. Die Gestaltung digitaler Medien war ein völlig neues Anwendungsfeld von Grafikdesign. Gleichzeitig hatte jeder Computeranwender dank einfach anzuwendender Software die Möglichkeit an der Hand, eigene Entwürfe umzusetzen. Bis heute bleibt diese Egalisierung für Gestalter immer wieder eine Herausforderung.

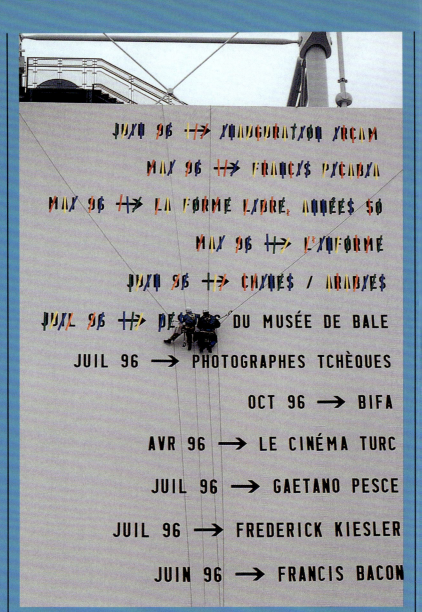

Pierre Bernard's large-format typographic installation displaying the events calendar for the Pompidou Center in Paris.

top right: Designs developed by Masaaki Hiromura for the MOO Market at the Fisherman's Wharf in Kushiro, Japan.

bottom right: Uniform of the Dutch police, part of the new visual identity designed by Studio Dumbar in 1993.

Großformatige Typoinstallation von Pierre Bernard, auf der Veranstaltungstermine des Pariser Centre Pompidou angekündigt werden.

rechts oben: Von Masaaki Hiromura entwickeltes Design für den MOO Market am Kushiro Fisherman's Wharf in Japan.

rechts unten: Uniform der niederländischen Polizei, die Teil der 1993 neu eingeführten visuellen Identität von Studio Dumbar war.

Installation typographique grand format de Pierre Bernard annonçant les dates d'événements du Centre Beaubourg, à Paris.

en haut à droite: graphisme développé par Masaaki Hiromura pour le MOO Market au Kushiro Fisherman's Wharf, au Japon.

en bas à droite: l'uniforme de la police néerlandaise, qui fait partie de la nouvelle identité visuelle conçue en 1993 par Studio Dumbar.

Au début des années 1990, les Américains April Greiman et David Carson ainsi que le Britannique Neville Brody deviennent les nouveaux héros de la scène du design. Leurs travaux réalisés sur ordinateur livrent une profusion d'idées stimulantes et d'approches inédites. Parallèlement à cette nouvelle avant-garde, les possibilités créatives offertes par le numérique entrent rapidement dans la stylistique générale de l'époque. Vers la fin de la décennie, l'indéniable succès global d'Internet et la percée massive de l'ordinateur personnel sur le marché accélèrent encore davantage cette évolution. La conception via des médias numériques devient un tout nouveau champ d'application du graphisme, et grâce à des solutions logicielles simples, les ordinateurs permettent désormais aux utilisateurs de réaliser de zéro leurs propres projets. C'est pourquoi aujourd'hui encore, les professionnels du graphisme sont conscients que le savoir-faire des amateurs et personnes s'y dédiant à temps partiel peur parfaitement le faire de l'ombre.

1990

Germany reunites

Nelson Mandela is freed

Child actor Macaulay Culkin helps *Home Alone* break box-office records

Co-founder of the Solidarity trade union Lech Walesa becomes president of Poland

Julia Roberts and Richard Gere star in the movie *Pretty Woman*

The Green Dot system is developed in Germany to indicate that packaging is recycled

The Hubble Space Telescope is launched into orbit

The prototype version of the World Wide Web is first demonstrated

English boy band Take That forms in Manchester

The first Nintendo World Championships take place in the United States

1991

The Bret Easton Ellis novel *American Psycho* is published to mixed acclaim and outrage

In the Philippines, Mount Pinatubo erupts in the second-largest eruption on Earth of the 20th century

Jodie Foster and Anthony Hopkins play the lead characters in *The Silence of the Lambs*

Nirvana's grunge anthem "Smells Like Teen Spirit" is released

Ötzi, the naturally preserved body of a man from 3300 BC, is found in the Alps

Queen's lead singer Freddie Mercury dies from AIDS

John Grisham's legal thriller *The Firm* is published

In Operation Desert Storm, coalition forces defeat Iraq and the Gulf War ends

The Soviet Union breaks up and Baltic and Central Asian states gain independence

Tupac Shakur's debut album is released

1992

Bill Clinton is elected president of the United States

The U.N. backs a peacekeeping intervention in the Somali Civil War

California's Anime Expo marks the rise of the Japanese animation style outside Asia

Euro Disney opens in France

Johnny Carson retires after 29 years of hosting *The Tonight Show* on U.S. television

English author Nick Hornby's novel *Fever Pitch* is published

In Bloomington, Minnesota, the Mall of America becomes the largest shopping mall in the country

American rock band Rage Against the Machine release their self-titled debut LP

Whitney Houston and Kevin Costner star in *The Bodyguard* and its soundtrack album becomes the best-selling of all time

The Summer Olympics are held in Barcelona

1993

The Maastricht Treaty comes into force

Apple introduces a handheld computer, the Newton MessagePad

Colombian drug baron Pablo Escobar is killed in a shootout as he tries to evade capture

The first-person shooter video game *Doom* is released

Intel releases its Pentium microprocessor

Yitzhak Rabin and Yasser Arafat sign the Oslo Accords

The first issue of *Wired* magazine is published

The mystery series *The X-Files* is first aired on U.S. television

A truckload of explosives is set off in an underground car-park beneath the World Trade Center

Steven Spielberg's film version of *Jurassic Park* becomes the highest-grossing film of the year

1994

Nelson Mandela becomes the first black president of South Africa

amazon

Jeff Bezos founds Amazon

Kenzaburo Oe wins the Nobel Prize in Literature

The Battle of Britpop sees Blur and Oasis competing in the charts

Nirvana frontman Kurt Cobain kills himself

Quentin Tarantino's cult movie *Pulp Fiction* premieres

The first passengers travel through the Eurotunnel from England to France

The Disney animated movie *The Lion King* is released

The first PlayStation goes on the market

Jupiter is hit by 21 large fragments of comet Shoemaker–Levy 9

Tom Hanks stars in *Forrest Gump*

1995

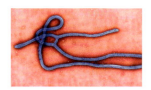

A major outbreak of Ebola in Zaire (now DRC) causes panic worldwide

Jacques Chirac is elected president of France

Yahoo! is founded

Pierce Brosnan is the new James Bond in *GoldenEye*

eBay is founded

The artist Christo transforms Berlin's Reichstag building into an artwork

UNESCO initiates World Book Day

Microsoft releases its Windows 95 operating system

The first version of the Java programming language is introduced by Sun Microsystems

The digital video disc is developed by Philips and Sony

1996

Destruction of the rainforest from logging reaches 38 million acres a year

Greenpeace designs its fuel-efficient SmILE, based on the Renault Twingo

The Tamagotchi handheld digital pet is introduced in Japan

The multinational pharmaceutical company Novartis is formed in Switzerland

Sci-fi movie *Independence Day* becomes a global blockbuster

The Al Jazeera television network is established in Doha, Qatar

The Spice Girls debut album sells two million copies in its first week

Chuck Palahniuk's novel *Fight Club* is published to critical acclaim

The movie adaption of *The English Patient* is released and the following year wins nine Oscars

Dolly the sheep becomes the first mammal to be cloned successfully from an adult cell

1997

The Kyoto Protocol on climate change is signed

The video game *Grand Theft Auto* is released

IBM's Deep Blue defeats the world chess champion Garry Kasparov

Netflix starts as a mail-order DVD sale and rental service

Princess Diana dies in a car accident in Paris

The first book in J.K. Rowling's Harry Potter series is published

Google's web search engine is launched

James Cameron's *Titanic* epic is the first movie to gross over a billion dollars

The first episode of *South Park* is aired

Hong Kong is returned to China

1998

Viagra goes on the market

Jim Carrey stars in *The Truman Show*

Expo 98 opens in Lisbon, the first world exhibition to be held in Portugal

Construction begins on the International Space Station

Apple launches the first iMac

News emerges of a sexual relationship between President Clinton and White House intern Monica Lewinsky

German manufacturer Smart introduces its first compact cars

Hurricane Mitch makes landfall in Central America and kills more than 11,000 people

In Japan, the world's longest suspension bridge opens across the Akashi Strait

The Three Tenors Concert in Paris is watched by 3 billion people worldwide

1999

Bertrand Piccard and Brian Jones become the first balloonists to circumnavigate the Earth without landing

Keanu Reeves stars in the sci-fi movie *The Matrix*

Sony presents the AIBO robotic pet dog

The Britney Spears single "...Baby One More Time" is released

The first Sumo book is published by TASCHEN

American animated sitcom *Family Guy* debuts on television

WiFi technology allows cable-free network connections at home

Vladimir Putin becomes president of Russia

The HBO television series *The Sopranos* debuts and becomes a major ratings success

1990

Eye design magazine
is launched in London
by Rick Poynor

Michael Bierut becomes a partner
at the New York office of **Pentagram**,
followed by Paula Scher in 1991

The **Caecilia** typeface is created by
Dutch designer Peter Matthias Noordzij

Robert Slimbach's **Minion**
typeface is released

1990 · Brunazzi & Associati · IT · Identity · Italia 90

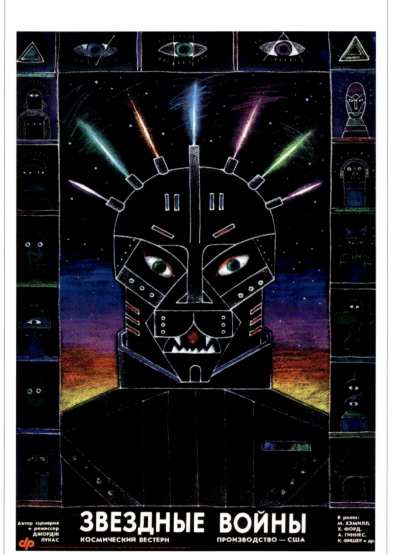

1990 · Anonymous · RU · Poster

1990 · Tel Design · NL · Logo · Gasunie

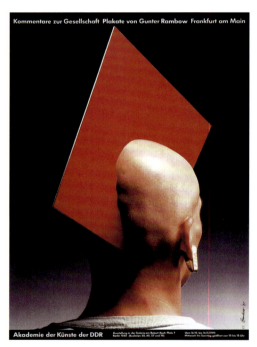

1990 · Gunter Rambow · DE · Poster

1990 · Karol Śliwka · PL · Logo · Alfa Chemicals

1990 · Jean Widmer, Bruno Monguzzi · FR · Logo ·
Musée d'Orsay

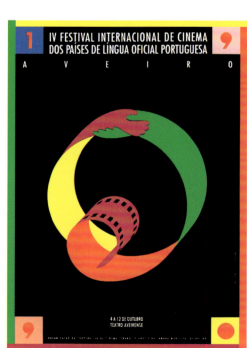

1990 · João Machado · PT · Poster

1990 · Shimokochi-Reeves Design · US · Packaging

1990 · Ogilvy & Mather · US · Ad

1990 · Koeweiden Postma · NL · Poster

1990 · Why Not Associates · UK · Brochure spread

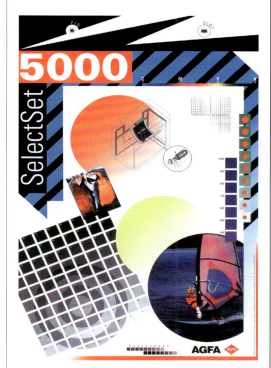

1990 · Burns, Connacher & Waldron Design · US · Poster

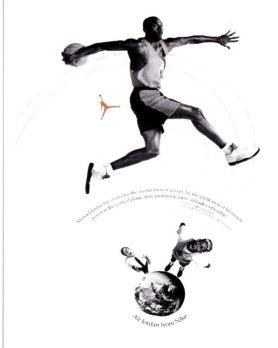

1990 · Michael Prieve, Wieden+Kennedy · US · Poster

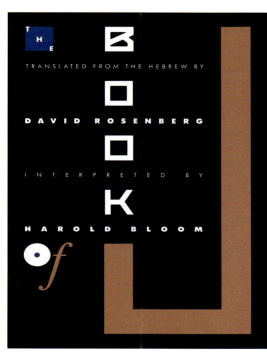

1990 · Carin Goldberg · US · Book cover

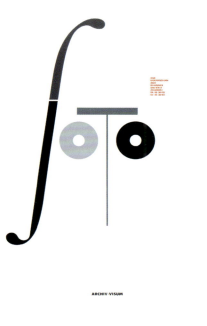

1990 · Ott+Stein · DE · Poster

293

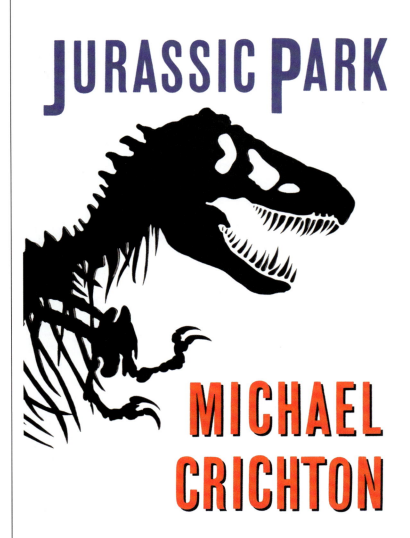

1990 · Chip Kidd · US · Book cover

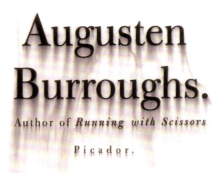

2004 · Chip Kidd · US · Book cover

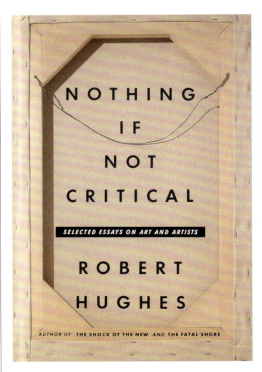

1990 · Chip Kidd · US · Book cover

1992 · Chip Kidd · US · Book cover

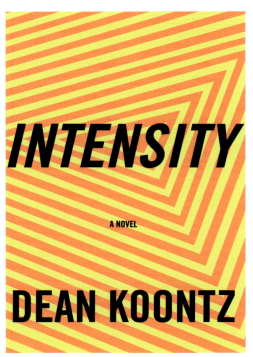

1996 · Chip Kidd · US · Book cover

Chip Kidd (1964, Reading, Pennsylvania) is a leading American designer specializing in book covers, with work extending to branding and film. Educated at Pennsylvania State University, Kidd started designing jackets for Random House imprint Knopf in 1986. His influence has been a fresh voice in the print industry, with his most acclaimed works including Michael Crichton's *Jurassic Park*, Haruki Murakami's *1Q84*, and *Time* magazine. His own novels, *The Cheese Monkeys* and *The Learners,* use typography as an integral part of the narrative.

Chip Kidd (1964, Reading, Pennsylvania) ist ein führender amerikanischer Grafikdesigner, der sich auf die Gestaltung von Büchern spezialisiert hat, aber auch Branding- und Filmprojekte umsetzt. Nach dem Studium an der Pennsylvania State University entwarf er ab 1986 zunächst Buchcover für das Random-House-Imprint Knopf. Sein Einfluss war für die Printmedien wie ein frischer Wind. Zu seinen bekanntesten Grafikprojekten gehören Michael Crichtons *Jurassic Park*, Haruki Murakamis *1Q84* und das *Time*-Magazin. In seinen eigenen Romanen *The Cheese Monkeys* und *The Learners* setzte er Typografie als integralen Bestandteil der Erzählung ein.

Chip Kidd (1964, Reading, Pennsylvanie) est un graphiste américain de premier plan spécialisé dans les couvertures de livres, et dont l'activité s'étend aussi au branding et au cinéma. En 1986, après des études à l'université d'État de Pennsylvanie, Kidd commence à concevoir des jaquettes pour la maison d'édition Knopf rachetée par Random House. Son influence a supposé un vent de fraîcheur dans le domaine de l'imprimerie grâce à ses travaux les plus acclamés, notamment pour *Jurassic Park* de Michael Crichton, *1Q84* de Haruki Murakami et le magazine *Time*. Ses propres romans *The Cheese Monkeys* et *The Learners* utilisent la typographie comme partie intégrante du récit.

2008 · Chip Kidd · US · Book cover

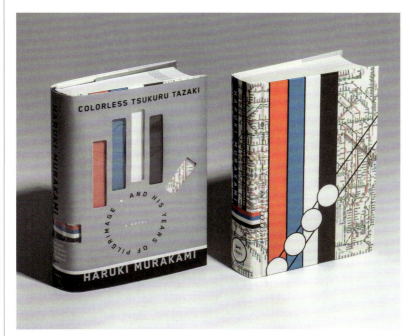

2014 · Chip Kidd · US · Book covers

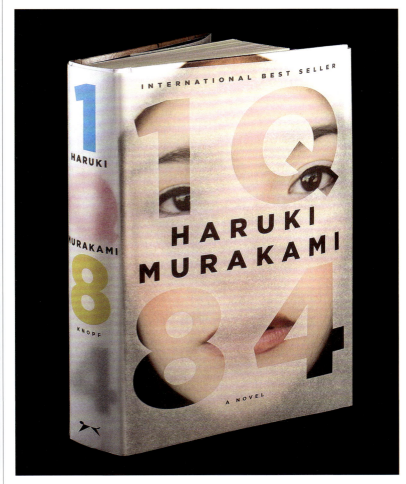

2011 · Chip Kidd · US · Book cover

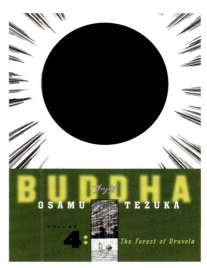

2005 · Chip Kidd · US · Book cover

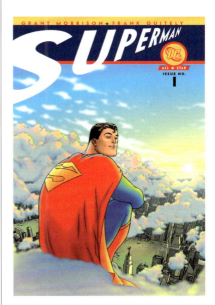

2007 · Chip Kidd · US · Book cover

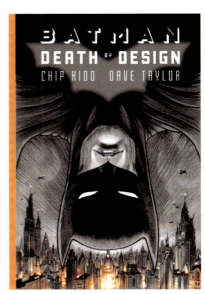

2012 · Chip Kidd · US · Book cover

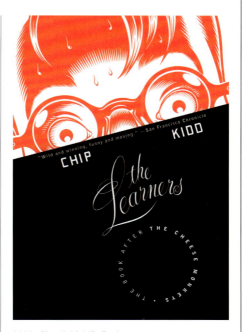

2008 · Chip Kidd · US · Book cover

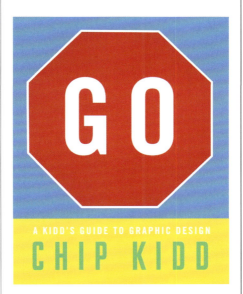

2013 · Chip Kidd · US · Book cover

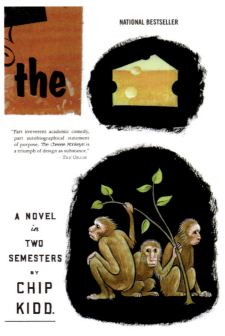

2001 · Chip Kidd · US · Book cover

Emigre Magazine · United States

In 1984, designers Rudy VanderLans and Zuzana Licko launched *Emigre* magazine, a quarterly publication devoted to different aspects of visual communication. Coinciding with the arrival of the Apple Mac, *Emigre* was an early adopter of the new technology and created some of the very first digital layouts and typeface designs, for which the duo received both worldwide acclaim and much criticism. The exposure of these typefaces in the magazine eventually led to the creation of Emigre Fonts, one of the first independent type foundries utilizing personal computer technology for design and distribution. Licko and VanderLans thus created the model for the hundreds of small foundries that followed in their footsteps.

Die Grafikdesigner Rudy VanderLans und Zuzana Licko gaben 1984 erstmals das mittlerweile berüchtigte Magazin *Emigre* heraus, eine vierteljährlich erscheinende Publikation zum Thema visuelle Kommunikation. Zur gleichen Zeit kam der Macintosh-Computer auf den Markt, und so gehörte *Emigre* zu den Ersten, die sich die neue Technik aneigneten und einige der allerersten digitalen Layouts und Schriften entwarfen. Dadurch fanden VanderLans und Licko weltweit Anerkennung, stießen aber auch auf nicht minder heftige Kritik. Der Gebrauch ihrer Schriften im Magazin *Emigre* führte schließlich zur Gründung von Emigre Fonts, einem der frühesten unabhängigen Schriftenhersteller, der die Technik des Personal Computer für die Gestaltung und Verbreitung von Schriften nutzte. Das Unternehmen bereitete den Boden für Hunderte kleiner Schriftenhersteller, die seinem Beispiel folgten.

En 1984, les graphistes Rudy VanderLans et Zuzana Licko fondaient le trimestriel *Emigre* consacré à divers aspects de la communication visuelle. Son lancement coïncida avec la naissance des ordinateurs Macintosh et il fut parmi les premiers à adopter la nouvelle technologie pour réaliser des mises en page entièrement numériques et créer des polices de caractères qui ont valu au duo à la fois un accueil enthousiaste dans le monde et un déluge de critiques. L'emploi de ces polices dans la revue *Emigre* conduisit finalement à la création d'Emigre Fonts, une des premières fonderies indépendantes à exploiter la technologie des PC pour concevoir et distribuer des polices de caractères, devenant ainsi un modèle pour les centaines de petites fonderies qui lui ont emboîté le pas.

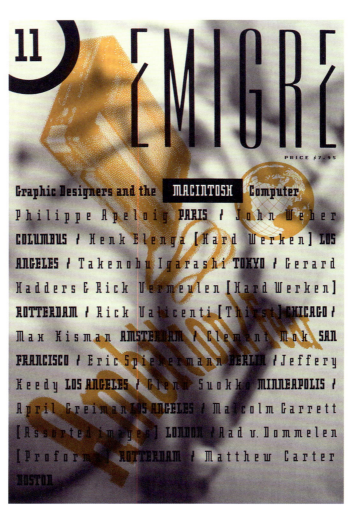

1989 · Rudy VanderLans, Zuzana Licko · US · Magazine cover

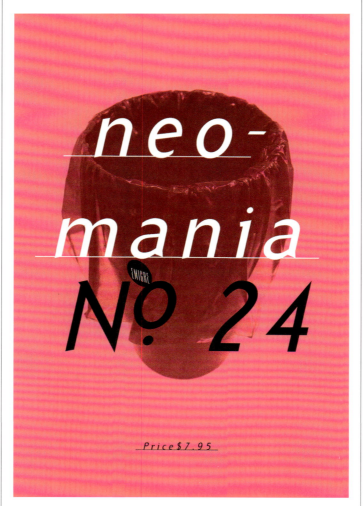

1992 · Rudy VanderLans, Zuzana Licko · US · Magazine cover

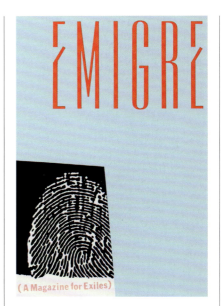

1984 · Rudy VanderLans, Zuzana Licko · US · Magazine cover

1986 · Rudy VanderLans, Zuzana Licko · US · Magazine cover

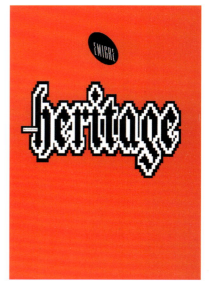

1992 · Rudy VanderLans, Zuzana Licko · US · Magazine cover

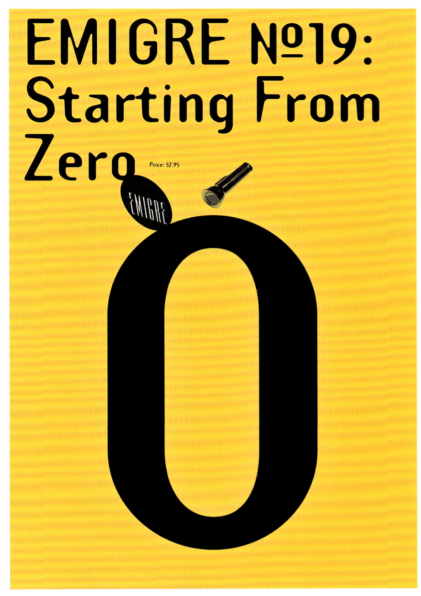

1991 · Rudy VanderLans, Zuzana Licko · US · Magazine cover

1990 · Rudy VanderLans, Zuzana Licko · US · Poster

1995 · Rudy VanderLans, Zuzana Licko · US · Magazine cover

1996 · Rudy VanderLans, Zuzana Licko · US · Magazine cover

1997 · Rudy VanderLans, Zuzana Licko · US · Magazine cover

1998 · Rudy VanderLans, Zuzana Licko · US · Magazine cover

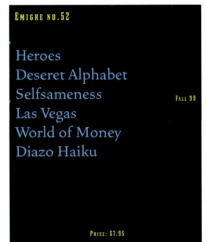

1999 · Rudy VanderLans, Zuzana Licko · US · Magazine cover

2000 · Rudy VanderLans, Zuzana Licko · US · Magazine cover

1991

Erik Spiekermann's **Meta** typeface is released

The **Association of Designers of Russia** (ADR) is founded

The experimental typography magazine **FUSE** is launched in London

Erik van Blokland's typeface **Trixie** is released

1991 · Lambie-Nairn · UK · Identity · BBC Two

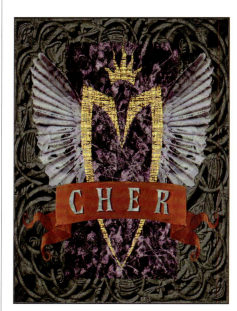

1991 · Margo Chase · US · Packaging

UFA

1991 · Lo Breier, Neville Brody, Johannes Erler, Büro X · DE · Logo · UFA

SBS

1991 · Ken Cato · AU · Logo · SBS Television

ENO

1991 · Mike Dempsey, CDT Design · UK · Logo · English National Opera

1991 · Michael Jensen · DK · Poster

1991 · Neville Brody · UK · Magazine/Poster

1991 · Robert Fisher, Kirk Weddle (PH) · US · Record cover

1991 · Why Not Associates · UK · Poster

1991 · Satoshi Saito · JP · Poster

1991 · Summa · ES · Magazine cover

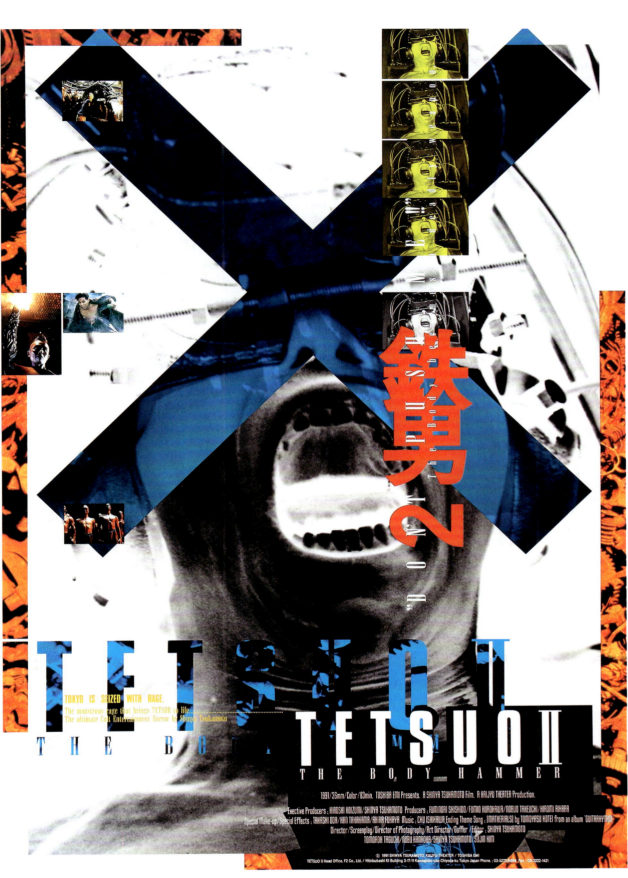

1991 · Anonymous · JP · Poster

1991 · Tsuguya Inoue, Humichika Kato, Seiai Hirota · JP · Ad

Oliviero Toscani, photographer and art director for the Italian fashion label Benetton, looked for a partner in New York to set up an innovative magazine that would be devoted to social issues. In the progressive designer Tibor Kalman he found the ideal person to collaborate with on the project, which appeared just one year later, in 1991, under the title of *Colors*. Funded by Benetton, a company which had become known in the 1980s for its controversial advertising campaigns, the magazine was free to publish issues concentrating entirely on subjects such as AIDS, racism, or religion, and in ways that bypassed the conventions of traditional print media. Challenging articles, flamboyant photography, and, not least, exceptional design made *Colors* a highly respected media phenomenon of the 1990s as the magazine's distribution reached more than 100 countries.

Oliviero Toscani, Fotograf und Artdirector des italienischen Modelabels Benetton, suchte in New York City einen Partner für ein neuartiges Gesellschaftsmagazin. In dem progressiven Designer Tibor Kalman fand er die perfekte Persönlichkeit für dieses Vorhaben, das bereits ein Jahr später, 1991, unter dem Namen *Colors* erschien. Finanziert durch Benetton, ein Unternehmen, das in den 1980er-Jahren mit einer kontroversen Werbekampagne bekannt geworden war, konnte das Magazin in monothematischen Ausgaben Themen wie „Aids", „Rassismus" oder „Religion" ohne die Konventionen traditioneller Printmedien behandeln. Ausgefallene Artikel, extravagante Fotografien und nicht zuletzt die ungewöhnliche Gestaltung machten die in mehr als 100 Ländern vertriebenen Hefte zum viel beachteten Medienphänomen der 1990er-Jahre.

Oliviero Toscani, photographe et directeur artistique de la marque de mode italienne Benetton, cherchait à New York un partenaire pour lancer un magazine d'un genre nouveau traitant de questions sociales. C'est avec le graphiste progressiste Tibor Kalman qu'il devait trouver la personne idéale pour réaliser ce projet apparu en 1991 sous le nom *Colors*. Financé par Benetton, qui s'était fait connaître dans les années 1980 par une campagne publicitaire controversée, le magazine put traiter dans ses numéros monothématiques des sujets de société comme le sida, le racisme ou la religion, sans devoir se plier aux conventions de la presse traditionnelle. Des articles ambitieux, des photographies extravagantes et en bonne partie aussi, un graphisme original, feront de cette revue distribuée dans plus de 100 pays un phénomène médiatique retentissant des années 1990.

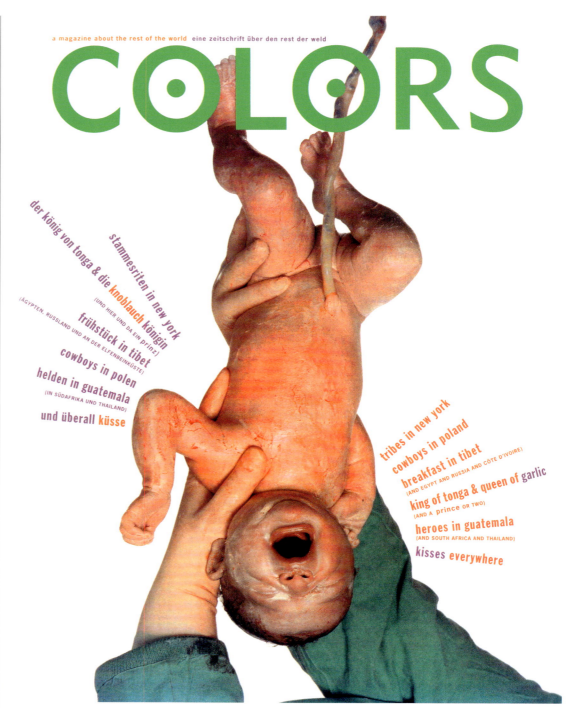

1991 · Tibor Kalman (AD), Oliviero Toscani (PH), Emily Oberman · US/IT · Magazine cover

1991 · Tibor Kalman (AD), Oliviero Toscani (PH), Emily Oberman · US/IT · Magazine spread

1993 · Tibor Kalman (AD) · US/IT · Magazine cover

1993 · Tibor Kalman (AD) · US/IT · Magazine cover

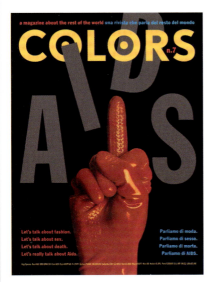

1994 · Tibor Kalman (AD) · US/IT · Magazine cover

1995 · Tibor Kalman (AD) · US/IT · Magazine cover

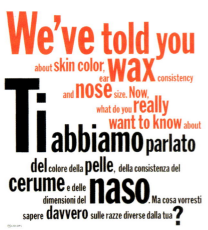

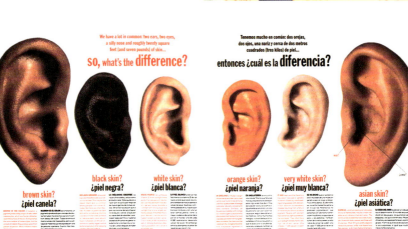

1990s · Tibor Kalman (AD) · US/IT · Magazine spreads

Tibor Kalman (1949, Budapest – 1999, Puerto Rico) was a Hungarian-born American art director, who moved to the United States in 1956. After dropping out from studying journalism, Kalman worked for Barnes & Noble (then a single bookstore in New York City), eventually becoming head of its in-house design team. In 1979 he co-founded the design studio M&Co., which became highly influential for its grounding in social activism. This paved the way for his most productive period in the early 1990s, when he moved to Italy to become editor-in-chief for the Benetton-sponsored magazine *Colors*, based at Fabrica, its creative lab in Treviso.

Tibor Kalman (1949, Budapest – 1999, Puerto Rico) war ein aus Ungarn gebürtiger amerikanischer Artdirector, der 1956 in die USA auswanderte. Nach einem abgebrochenen Journalismusstudium arbeitete er bei Barnes & Noble (damals ein einzelnes Buchgeschäft in New York), wo er schließlich zum Leiter der hausinternen Designabteilung aufstieg. 1979 gründete er mit anderen das Designbüro M&Co., das sich dem sozialen Engagement verpflichtete und dadurch großen Einfluss ausübte. Das führte zu Kalmans produktivster Phase Anfang der 90er-Jahre, als er nach Italien ging und Herausgeber des von Benetton gesponserten Magazins *Colors* wurde, das in Fabrica angesiedelt ist, dem Kreativlabor der Firma in Treviso.

Tibor Kalman (1949, Budapest – 1999, Porto Rico) fut un directeur artistique américain d'origine hongroise qui s'installa aux États-Unis en 1956. Après avoir abandonné des études de journalisme, Kalman travailla pour Barnes & Noble (qui n'était alors qu'une simple librairie à New York), avant d'y être engagé comme directeur de l'équipe interne de design. En 1979, il cofonda le studio de design M&Co., qui devint hautement influent du fait de son enracinement dans l'activisme social. Kalman connu alors sa période la plus productive au début des années 1990, quand il s'installa en Italie pour devenir rédacteur en chef du magazine *Colors*, sponsorisé par Benetton et installé au centre de recherche Fabrica, à Trévise.

1991 · Erik Spiekermann, MetaDesign · DE · Identity/Signage · Berliner Verkehrsbetriebe

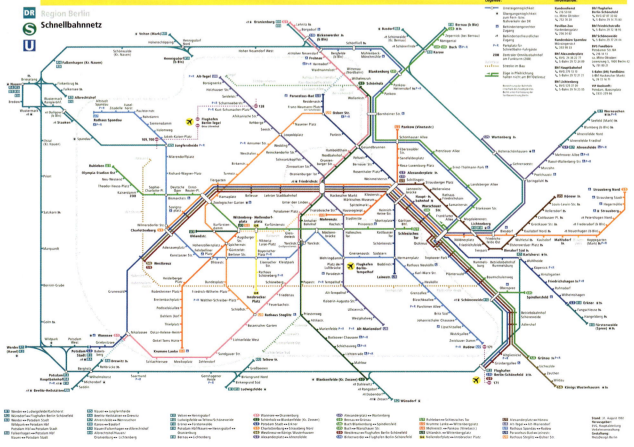

1991 · Erik Spiekermann, MetaDesign · DE · Information graphic

Erik Spiekermann (1947, Stadthagen, Germany) is one of the most respected figures in contemporary typography and graphic design. Having funded his art history degree in Berlin by running a letterpress printing studio in his basement, Spiekermann turned to design, first working in London before co-founding MetaDesign in 1979 in Berlin. In 1989, he co-founded FontShop—the first reseller of digital fonts—with his then-wife, Joan. Spiekermann's groundbreaking identity systems include those for Dusseldorf Airport, Audi, and Volkswagen. From 2009 he has led Edenspiekermann, with offices in Berlin, Stuttgart, Amsterdam, and San Francisco. Since 2014 he has been running the typographic workshop p98a in Berlin.

Erik Spiekermann (1947, Stadthagen) ist einer der angesehensten Vertreter der zeitgenössischen Typografie und des Grafikdesigns. Nach einem Kunststudium in Berlin, das er mit einer kleinen Druckerei im Keller finanzierte, wandte er sich der Gestaltung zu und arbeitete zunächst in London, ehe er 1979 in Berlin mit anderen MetaDesign gründete. 1989 rief er mit seiner damaligen Frau Joan FontShop ins Leben, den ersten Vertrieb für digitale Schriften. Wegweisende Identity-Systeme gestaltete Spiekermann u. a. für den Flughafen Düsseldorf, Audi und Volkswagen. Seit 2009 leitet er Edenspiekermann mit Büros in Berlin, Stuttgart, Amsterdam und San Francisco, seit 2014 betreibt er die typografische Werkstatt p98a in Berlin.

Erik Spiekermann (1947, Stadthagen, Allemagne) est une des figures les plus respectées de la typographie et du graphisme contemporains. Après avoir financé ses études en histoire de l'art à Berlin en faisant tourner un atelier de typographie dans sa cave, Spiekermann se lance dans le design, travaillant d'abord à Londres avant de cofonder Meta-Design en 1979 à Berlin. En 1989, il cofonde FontShop – premier revendeur de polices numériques – avec sa femme d'alors, Joan. Les systèmes d'identité révolutionnaires de Spiekermann incluent l'aéroport de Düsseldorf, Audi et Volkswagen. Depuis 2009, il dirige Edenspiekermann, avec des bureaux à Berlin, Stuttgart, Amsterdam et San Francisco. Il est aussi à la tête de l'atelier typographique p98a à Berlin depuis 2014.

»The page is the molecule and the atom is the word. You see, I read. I read before I design, and I write. I design outwards from words.« Erik Spiekermann, *Eye* #18, 1995

Die Bahn

DB **Head**

DB **Sans**

DB **Sans Condensed**

DB **Sans Compressed**

DB **Serif**

DB **News**

Niedersachsen-Ticket:
Von A zu jedem B. Für 22 Euro.

Bis 5 Personen. 1 Tag. 1 Preis.

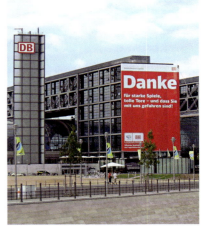

2001 · Erik Spiekermann, Edenspiekermann · DE/UK · Magazine

2006 · Erik Spiekermann, Edenspiekermann · DE · Identity · Deutsche Bahn

Fred Woodward (1953, Noxapater, Mississippi) is an American art director whose work for *Rolling Stone* helped win the magazine a record number of awards for editorial design. At Mississippi State, and later Memphis State University, Woodward started in journalism, moving to physical education and political science, before switching to graphic arts. His tenure at *Rolling Stone* also made Woodward the youngest person to be inducted into the Art Directors Club Hall of Fame in 1996. In 2001, Woodward became design director at *GQ* magazine.

Fred Woodward (1953, Noxapater, Mississippi) ist ein amerikanischer Artdirector, der mit seiner Arbeit für den *Rolling Stone* dazu beitrug, dass das Magazin eine rekord-verdächtige Anzahl von Auszeichnungen für grafische Gestaltung erhielt. Woodward studierte an der Mississippi State University und anschließend an der Memphis State University zunächst Journalismus, dann sattelte er auf Sport und Politikwissenschaft um und entschied sich schließlich für Grafik. Aufgrund seiner Arbeit für den *Rolling Stone* wurde Woodward 1996 auch als jüngstes Mitglied in die Art Directors Club Hall of Fame aufgenommen. 2001 trat er bei der Zeitschrift *GQ* die Stelle des Designdirectors an.

Fred Woodward (1953, Noxapater, Mississippi) est un directeur artistique américain dont le travail pour *Rolling Stone* a permis au magazine de remporter un nombre de prix record pour son design éditorial. Woodward a d'abord suivi des études de journalisme à l'université d'État du Mississippi, et plus tard à l'université d'État de Memphis, avant de passer à l'éducation physique et aux sciences politiques, et pour finir aux arts graphiques. Son rôle chez *Rolling Stone* a aussi fait de Woodward le plus jeune directeur artistique à entrer à l'Art Directors Club Hall of Fame en 1996. En 2001, Woodward est devenu directeur du design pour le magazine *GQ*.

1993 · Fred Woodward (AD), Andrew Macpherson (PH) · US · Magazine cover

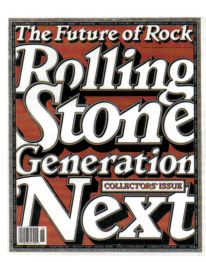

1994 · Fred Woodward (AD) · US · Magazine cover

1994 · Fred Woodward (AD), Herb Ritts (PH) · US · Magazine cover

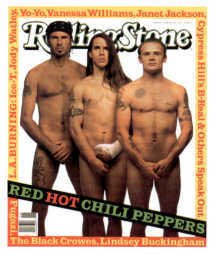

1992 · Fred Woodward (AD), Mark Seliger (PH) · US · Magazine cover

»I've always approached this magazine as a work-in-progress. The constant pressure of a bi-weekly deadline leaves little time for philosophical reflection.« Fred Woodward, *Graphis Magazine Design*, vol. 1, 1998

In 1987, as art director of *Rolling Stone*, Woodward was presented with the opportunity to reinvent the design of the music magazine. In the 14 years he was in the job, more than 300 editions were produced under his leadership. He introduced a bold and playful typographic style which was mainly used for lead stories and proved to be a major influence on 1990s magazine design.

1987 erhielt Woodward die Möglichkeit, als Artdirector die Gestaltung des Musikmagazins *Rolling Stone* zu erneuern. In den 14 Jahren seiner Tätigkeit entstanden über 300 Hefte unter seiner Leitung. Er führte eine spielerisch-plakative Typografie ein, die sich vor allem in den Aufmacherseiten großer Artikel zeigte und die Magazingestaltung der 1990er-Jahre stark beeinflusste.

Alors directeur artistique de *Rolling Stone* en 1987, Woodward s'est vu offrir l'opportunité de réinventer le graphisme du magazine musical. Pendant les quatorze années qu'il a passées à ce poste, plus de 300 éditions ont vu le jour sous sa direction. Woodward a infusé au magazine un style typographique ludique et osé principalement utilisé pour les articles à la une, et a ainsi exercé une influence majeure sur le graphisme de magazines dans les années 1990.

1991 · Fred Woodward (AD), Andrew Eccles (PH) · US · Magazine spread

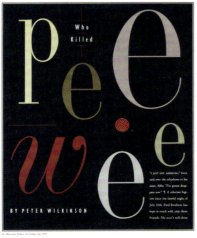 

1992 · Fred Woodward (AD), Matt Mahurin (ILL) · US · Magazine spread

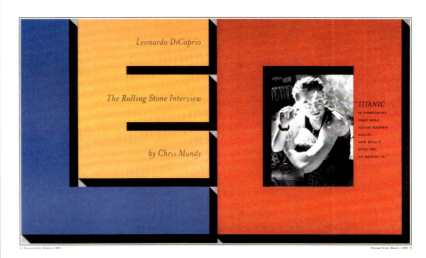

2000 · Fred Woodward (AD), Mark Seliger (PH) · US · Magazine spread

1991 · Fred Woodward (AD), Herb Ritts (PH) · US · Magazine spread

1992

The international design
magazine **IdN** is launched

David Carson becomes art
director of **Ray Gun** magazine

Jonathan Barnbrook's typeface
Mason is released

The first **Moscow Global Biennale
of Graphic Design** (Golden Bee) is held

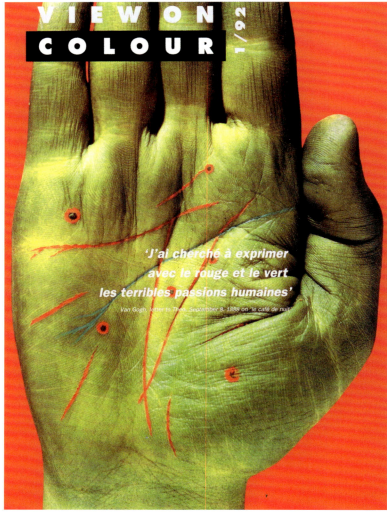

1992 · Anthon Beeke · NL · Magazine cover

1992 · Joe Duffy · US · Packaging

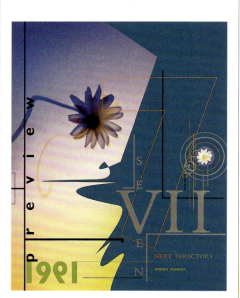

1992 · Why Not Associates · UK · Brochure cover

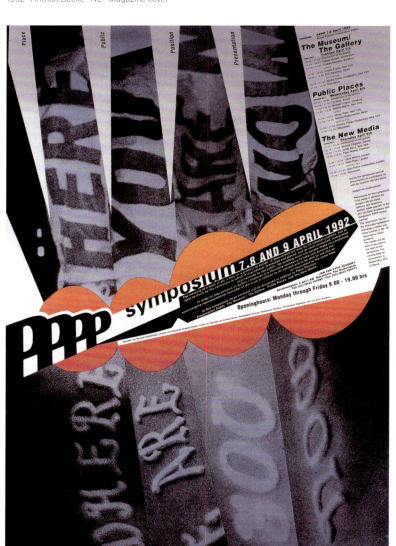

1992 · Mevis & Van Deursen · NL · Poster

1992 · Lloyd Ziff · US · Magazine cover

1992 · Holly Chasin · US · Logo · E Television

1992 · Mario Gemin · AR · Logo · Kinney Clothing

1992 · Josep M. Trias · ES · Logo · Barcelona 92

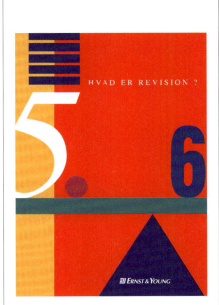

1992 · Peter Bysted · DK · Brochure cover

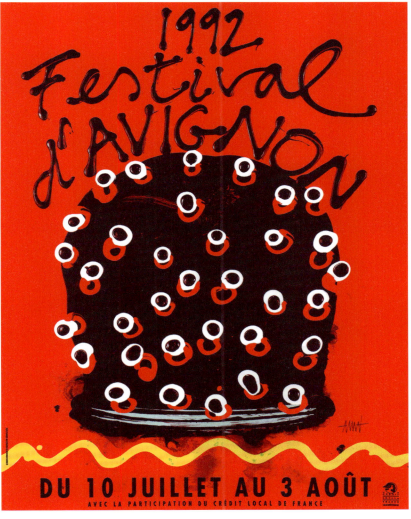

1992 · Ezio Frigerio · IT/FR · Poster

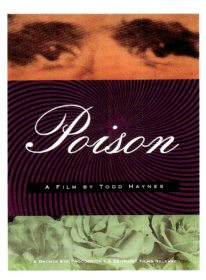

1992 · Bekka Lindstrom, Todd Haynes · US · Poster

1992 · The Mednick Group · US · Record cover

1992 · Martine Waltzer · FR · Poster

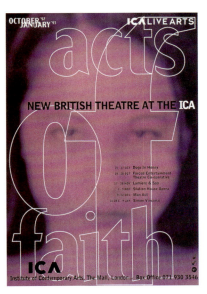

1992 · Tony Arefin · UK · Poster

1992 · Mostafa Assadollahi · IR · Poster

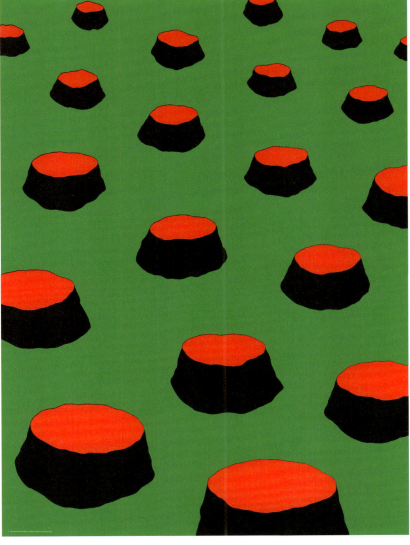

1992 · Niklaus Troxler · CH · Poster

Margo Chase (1958–2017, Los Angeles) was an American designer, noted for her work in the film and music industries. Originally trained as a biologist, Chase switched to visual communication after taking a course at California Polytechnic State University, later founding the Chase Design Group in 1986. From designing for such entertainment names as Madonna, Cher, *Buffy the Vampire Slayer*, and others, she also expanded into branding, working for Target, Disney, and Nestlé. Departing from a commonly advocated minimalism, Chase's distinctive illustrative style won her multiple awards. She was also a lecturer at CalArts, and Long Beach State University.

Margo Chase (1958–2017, Los Angeles) war eine amerikanische Designerin, die insbesondere durch ihre Arbeiten für die Film- und Musikindustrie bekannt wurde. Als studierte Biologin sattelte sie auf visuelle Kommunikation um, nachdem sie an der California Polytechnic State University einen Kurs besucht hatte. 1986 gründete sie die Chase Design Group. Zunächst gehörten Größen des Entertainments wie Madonna, Cher, *Buffy the Vampire Slayer* und andere zu ihren Auftraggebern, dann dehnte sie ihre Arbeit auch auf Branding aus, u. a. für Target, Disney und Nestlé. Für ihren unverkennbaren illustrativen Stil, der vom vielfach propagierten Minimalismus abweicht, erhielt sie zahlreiche Auszeichnungen. Close unterrichtete an der CalArts und an der Long Beach State University.

Margo Chase (1958–2017, Los Angeles) fut une graphiste américaine remarquée pour son travail dans l'industrie cinématographique et musicale. Après des études initiales de biologie, Chase passa à la communication visuelle suite à un cours à l'université d'État polytechnique de Californie, avant de fonder le Chase Design Group en 1986. Outre son travail pour des noms du spectacle comme Madonna, Cher, *Buffy contre les vampires* et d'autres, Chase étendit son activité au branding, notamment pour Target, Disney et Nestlé. S'écartant du minimalisme habituellement privilégié, son style illustratif distinctif lui valut de multiples récompenses. Chase enseigna au CalArts et à l'université d'État de Californie à Long Beach.

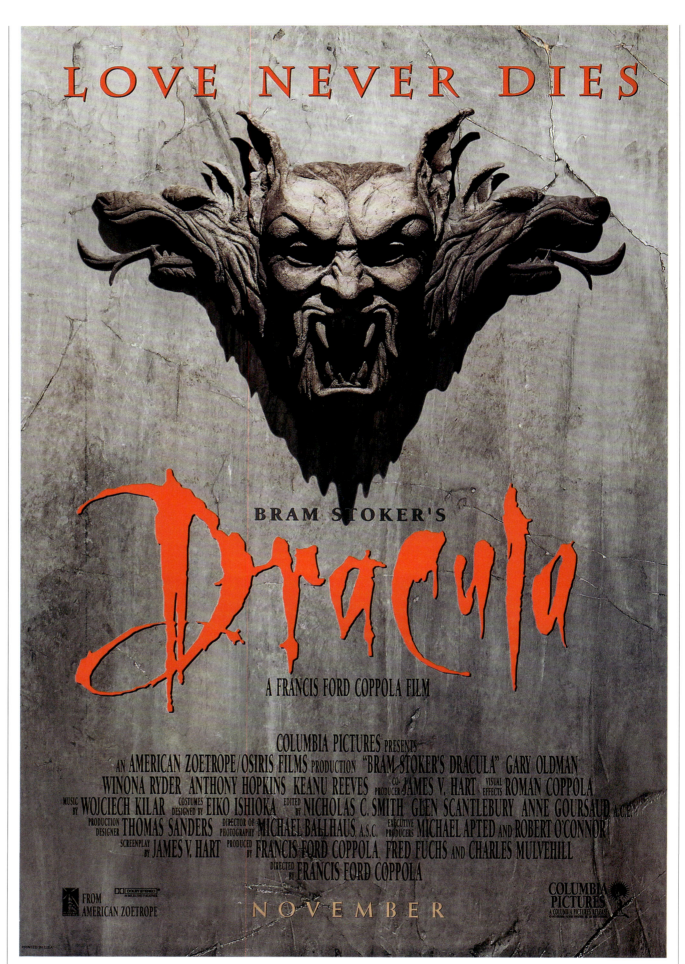

1992 · Margo Chase · US · Poster

1989 · Margo Chase · US · Logo · Madonna –
Like a Prayer

1990 · Margo Chase · US · Logo · Prince –
New Power Generation

1994 · Margo Chase · US · Logo · Four Weddings
and a Funeral

1997 · Margo Chase · US · Logo · Buffy the
Vampire Slayer

1998 · Margo Chase · US · Logo · Charmed

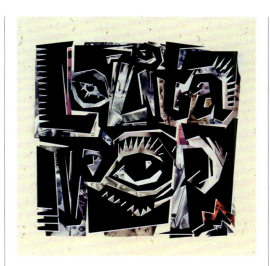

1987 · Margo Chase · US · Record cover

1991 · Margo Chase · US · Record cover

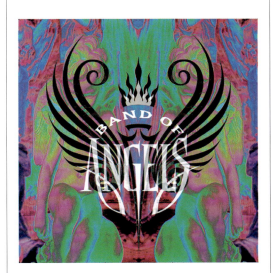

1992 · Margo Chase · US · Record cover

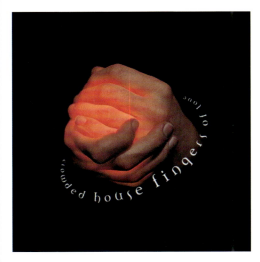

1994 · Margo Chase, Sidney Cooper (PH) · US · Record cover

1990 · Margo Chase, Sidney Cooper (PH) · US · Record cover

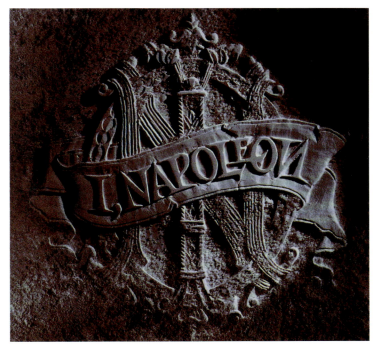

1991 · Margo Chase, Michele Clement (PH) · US · Record cover

1993 · Margo Chase, Merlyn Rosenberg (PH) · US · Record cover

In 1992, Rio de Janeiro hosted the United Nations Conference on Environment and Development. To mark the occasion, the Brazilian graphic designer Felipe Taborda put together a project for "30 Posters on Environment and Development". Some of the world's finest graphic designers were invited to create a design on the theme of environmental protection and the posters were then used as official gifts presented to visiting heads of state by the Brazilian government. The whole series was also displayed in a number of museums and galleries around the world.

Rio de Janeiro war 1992 Gastgeber der Konferenz der Vereinten Nationen über Umwelt und Entwicklung. Aus diesem Anlass entwickelte der brasilianische Grafikdesigner Felipe Taborda das Projekt „30 Plakate über Umwelt und Entwicklung". Einige der besten internationalen Grafikdesigner wurden eingeladen, ein Plakat zu Themen des Umweltschutzes zu entwerfen. Die Plakate wurden das offizielle Geschenk der brasilianischen Regierung für die an der Konferenz teilnehmenden Staatsoberhäupter, darüber hinaus wurde die Serie in vielen Museen und Galerien auf der ganzen Welt gezeigt.

En 1992, Rio de Janeiro accueillait la conférence des Nations unies sur l'environnement et le développement. C'est à cette occasion que le graphiste brésilien Felipe Taborda développa le projet «30 affiches sur l'environnement et le développement». Quelques-uns des meilleurs graphistes internationaux furent invités à réaliser une affiche sur des thèmes liés à la protection de l'environnement. Les affiches servirent de cadeau officiel du gouvernement brésilien aux chefs d'État participant au sommet. La série complète fut ensuite présentée dans de nombreux musées et galeries du monde entier.

1992 · Felipe Taborda · BR · Poster

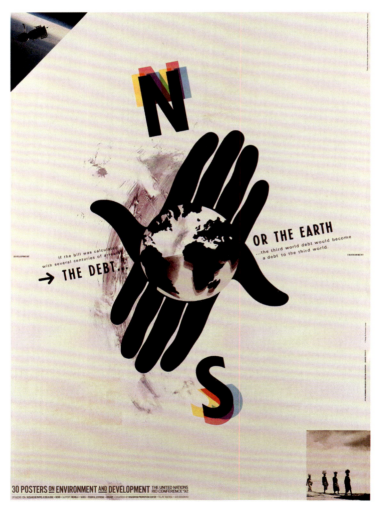

1992 · Pierre Bernard · FR/BR · Poster

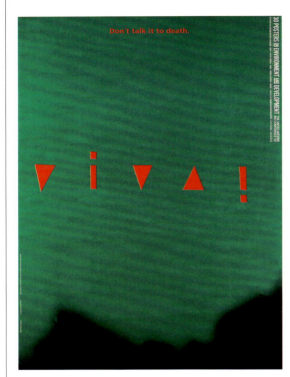

1992 · Uwe Loesch · DE/BR · Poster

1992 · Lech Majewski · PL/BR · Poster

1992 · Rico Lins · BR · Poster

1992 · István Orosz · HU/BR · Poster

1992 · Nancy Skolos, Thomas Wedell · US/BR · Poster

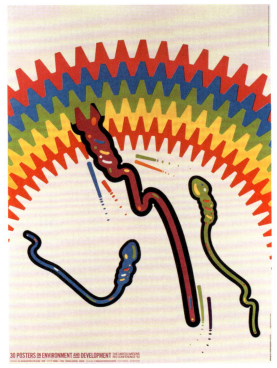

1992 · Santiago Pol · VE/BR · Poster

1992 · Neville Brody · UK/BR · Poster

1992 · Peret · ES/BR · Poster

1992 · Ken Cato · AU/BR · Poster

1992 · Rafic Farah · BR · Poster

1992 · Gert Dumbar, Studio Dumbar · NL/BR · Poster

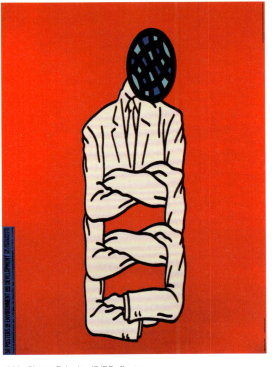

1992 · Shigeo Fukuda · JP/BR · Poster

1993

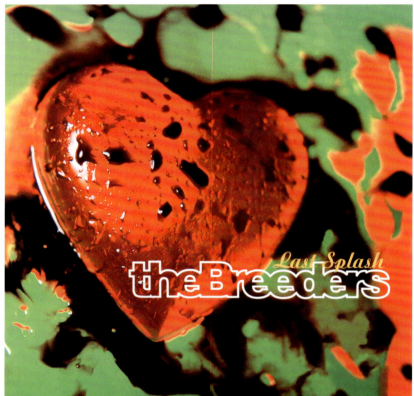

1993 · Vaughan Oliver (AD), Jason Love (PH) · UK · Record cover

1993 · Anonymous · KR · Logo · Samsung

1993 · Chermayeff & Geismar · US · Logo · Casa

1993 · Bart Crosby · US · Logo · Digital Composition

1993 · André Baldinger · FR · Poster

1993 · Mirko Ilić · BA/US · Newspaper spreads

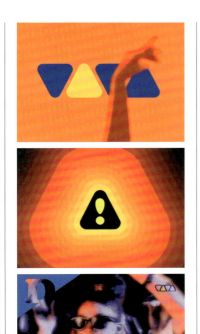

1993-98 · DMC · DE · Motion graphics

1993 · Bruce Mau Design · CA · Identity

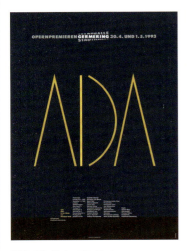

1993 · Ott+Stein · DE · Poster

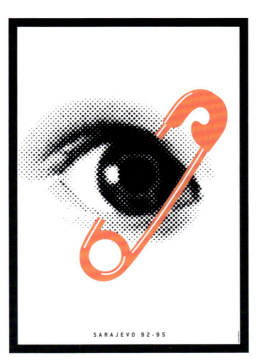

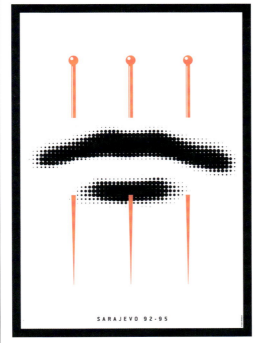

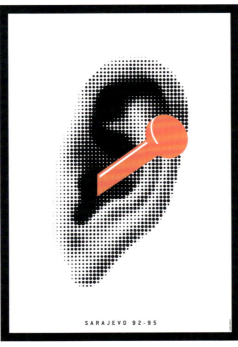

1993 · Sasha Vidakovic · BA · Poster series

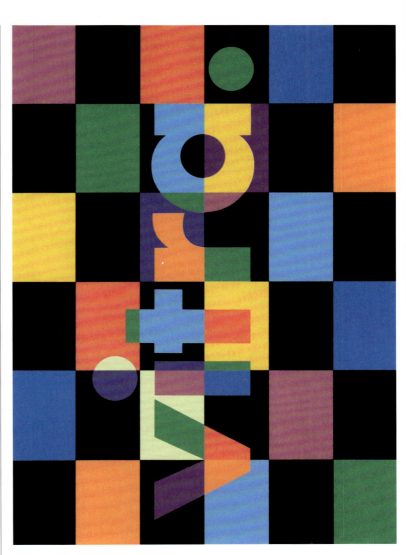

1993 · Pierre Mendell, Mendell & Oberer · DE · Identity · Vitra

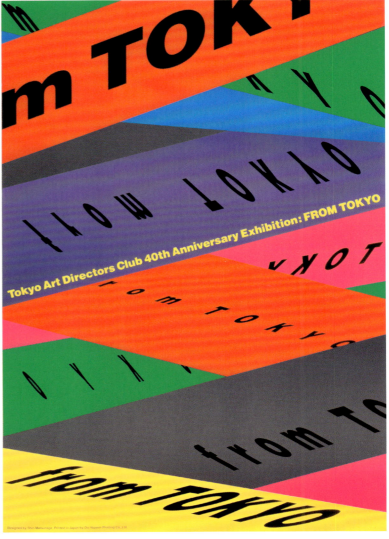

1993 · Shin Matsunaga · JP · Poster

David Carson · United States

Ray Gun, the American magazine devoted to the alternative rock scene, first appeared in 1992. With ex-professional surfer and designer David Carson as its art director, the magazine became the prototype for a new kind of non-conformism, while the new digital possibilities that were enabling a breakaway from the hard-and-fast rules of design became *Ray Gun*'s trademark. Carson's decision to set an interview with the musician Bryan Ferry, which he considered to be boring, in illegible Dingbat characters (although the text could be read in a supplement to the magazine), remains the stuff of legend. This sort of boundary-pushing earned the magazine cult status and made Carson one of the most important new voices in contemporary graphic design.

Das US-Magazin *Ray Gun* beschäftigte sich mit der alternativen Rockmusikszene, es erschien erstmals 1992. Unter der Artdirection von Exprofisurfer und Designer David Carson wurde das Magazin zum Prototypen eines neuen Nonkonformismus. Die neuen digitalen Möglichkeiten erlaubten den Bruch feststehender Gestaltungsregeln und wurden zum Charakteristikum von *Ray Gun*. Legendär ist bis heute ein der Redaktion langweilig erscheinendes Interview mit dem Musiker Bryan Ferry, das Carson in der Symbolschrift „Dingbat" umsetzte und damit unlesbar machte (wenngleich es im Anhang des Hefts noch einmal nachzulesen war). Derartige Grenzüberschreitungen verliehen dem Magazin einen Kultstatus und machten Carson zu einer der wichtigsten neuen Stimmen im Grafikdesign seiner Zeit.

Le magazine américain *Ray Gun*, dont le premier numéro parut en 1992, était consacré à la scène rock alternative. Sous la direction artistique de l'ex-surfer professionnel et graphiste David Carson, le magazine devint le prototype d'un nouvel anticonformisme. Les possibilités offertes par le numérique permirent à Carson de rompre avec des règles graphiques strictes et devinrent la marque de fabrique de *Ray Gun*. Jusqu'à ce jour, une interview avec le chanteur Bryan Ferry est restée légendaire : Carson la trouvant inintéressante, il la fit imprimer en dingbats, la rendant ainsi illisible (même si elle était disponible en annexe). Ce genre d'extravagance conféra au magazine un statut culte et fit de Carson une des grandes voix du graphisme de son époque.

1993 · David Carson · US · Magazine cover

1992 · David Carson · US · Magazine cover

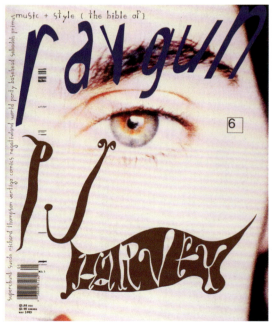

1993 · David Carson · US · Magazine cover

»I'm a big believer in the emotion of design, and the message that's sent before somebody begins to read, before they get the rest of the information; what is the emotional response they get to the product, to the story, to the painting—whatever it is.«

David Carson, *ted.com*, 2003

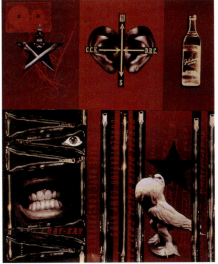

1992–94 · David Carson · US · Magazine spreads

David Carson (1954, Corpus Christi, Texas) is a trailblazing American art director, often cited as the godfather of "grunge typography". Carson revolutionized graphic design in the 1990s by defying the boundaries of the grid and challenging modernist logic. A sociology graduate from San Diego State University, he was also a professional surfer, at one point ranking ninth in the world. In 1984 he started working for *Transworld Skateboarding* magazine, but made his professional leap in 1992 when he became the first art director of the alternative music and lifestyle magazine *Ray Gun*.

David Carson (1954, Corpus Christi, Texas) ist ein bahnbrechender amerikanischer Artdirector, der häufig als Pate der „Grunge-Typografie" gilt. In den 1990er-Jahren revolutionierte er das Grafikdesign, indem er sich über die Grenzen des Rasters hinwegsetzte und die Logik der Moderne hinterfragte. Er hatte an der San Diego State University Soziologie studiert, war aber auch ein professioneller Surfer und hatte einmal auf Platz 9 der Weltrangliste gestanden. Ab 1984 arbeitete er für das Magazin *Transworld Skateboarding*, der Durchbruch gelang ihm 1992, als er zum ersten Artdirector der alternativen Musik- und Lifestylezeitschrift *Ray Gun* ernannt wurde.

David Carson (1954, Corpus Christi, Texas) est un directeur artistique américain précurseur, souvent désigné comme le parrain de la «grunge typography». Carson a révolutionné le graphisme dans les années 1990 en transcendant les limites de la grille et en contestant la logique moderniste. Diplômé en sociologie à l'université d'État de San Diego, il a aussi été surfer professionnel, se hissant jusqu'à la neuvième place mondiale. En 1984, il commence à travailler pour le magazine *Transworld Skateboarding*, mais sa carrière fait un bond en 1992 quand il devient le premier directeur artistique du magazine de musique et de société alternatif *Ray Gun*.

2014 · David Carson · US · Poster

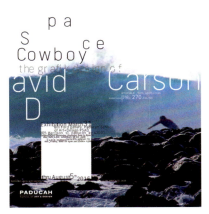

2015 · David Carson · US · Poster

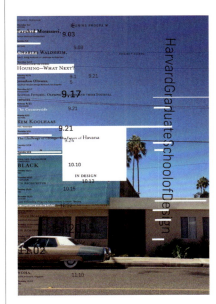

2015 · David Carson · US · Poster

1993 · Ralph Schraivogel · CH · Poster

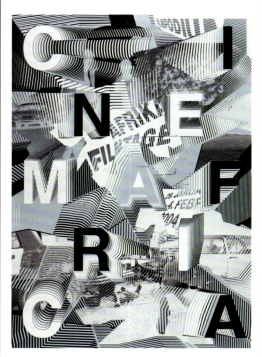

2004 · Ralph Schraivogel · CH · Poster

2006 · Ralph Schraivogel · CH · Poster

Ralph Schraivogel (1960, Lucerne) is a Swiss poster designer known for his meticulous approach. Schraivogel's longstanding collaborations with cultural organizations, such as Filmpodium, the Zurich Museum of Design, and the CinemAfrica film festival in Stockholm, showcase his influence on the poster as a thriving medium for communication. After finishing his studies in Zurich in 1982 he went on to develop his own visual language, often mixing handmade and computer-assisted designs, and won several accolades for his innovative processes. Schraivogel has lectured in Zurich, Lucerne, and Basel, and his body of work also encompasses editorial design and corporate identity.

Ralph Schraivogel (1960, Luzern) ist ein Schweizer Plakatgestalter, der sich insbesondere durch die große Präzision seiner Arbeiten auszeichnet. In den Entwürfen, die in seiner langjährigen Zusammenarbeit mit diversen Kultureinrichtungen wie etwa dem Filmpodium, dem Museum für Gestaltung Zurich und dem Filmfestival CinemAfrica in Stockholm entstanden, zeigt sich der Einfluss, den Schraivogel auf das Plakat als lebendiges Kommunikationsmedium hat. Nach dem Studium in Zürich 1982 entwickelte er eine eigene visuelle Sprache, wobei er vielfach von Hand angefertigte Entwürfe mit computergestützten mischte. Wegen seiner innovativen Arbeitsweise wurde er mehrfach ausgezeichnet. Schraivogel hat in Zürich, Luzern und Basel unterrichtet. Zu seinen Tätigkeitsfeldern gehören auch Editorial Design und Corporate Identity.

Ralph Schraivogel (1960, Lucerne) est un affichiste suisse connu pour son approche particulièrement méticuleuse. Ses collaborations au long cours avec des organisations culturelles comme Filmpodium, le musée du design de Zurich et le festival de cinéma CinemAfrica à Stockholm, illustrent son influence sur l'affiche en tant que support florissant pour la communication. Au terme de ses études à Zurich en 1982, il s'attache à développer son propre langage visuel, mélangeant souvent créations à la main et par ordinateur, et reçoit plusieurs distinctions pour ses procédés innovants. Schraivogel a enseigné à Zurich, à Lucerne et à Bâle, et le corpus de son œuvre comprend aussi du design éditorial et des identités d'entreprises.

1995 · Ralph Schraivogel · CH · Poster

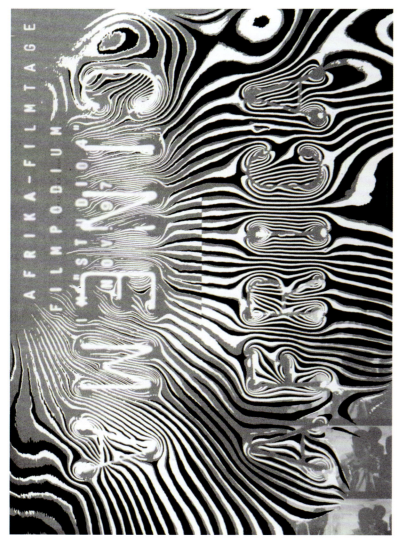

1997 · Ralph Schraivogel · CH · Poster

1991 · Ralph Schraivogel · CH · Poster

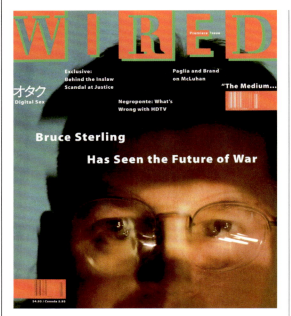

1993 · Plunkett+Kuhr · US · Magazine cover

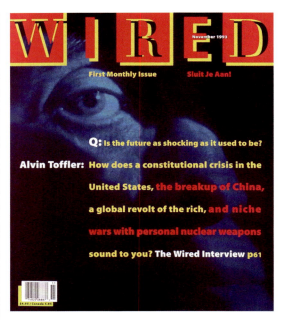

1993 · Plunkett+Kuhr · US · Magazine cover

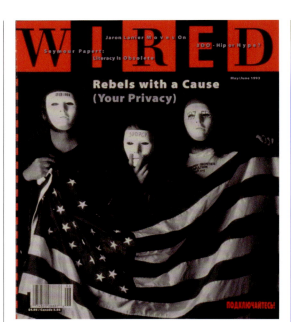

1993 · Plunkett+Kuhr · US · Magazine cover

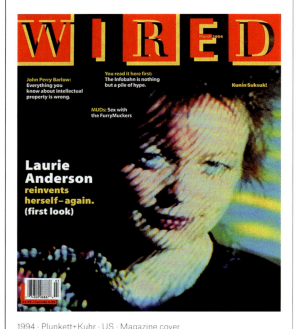

1994 · Plunkett+Kuhr · US · Magazine cover

1997 · Plunkett+Kuhr · US · Magazine cover

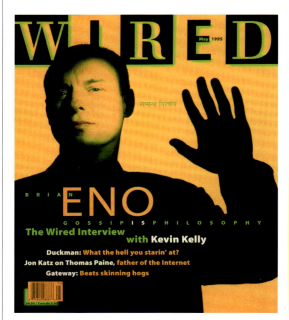

1995 · Plunkett+Kuhr · US · Magazine cover

1990s · Plunkett+Kuhr · US · Magazine spines

In the late 1980s, the American journalist Louis Rossetto became aware of the groundbreaking digital revolution that was then getting under way. In 1991, he and a small team that included the designers John Plunkett and Barbara Kuhr began developing the concept for *Wired*. In terms of both its content and visuals, the magazine, which first appeared in January 1993, documented the early years of PCs, cellphones, and of course the internet more authentically than any other similar publication. Then, in 1994, came the launch of hotwired.com that was originally intended simply as a sideline, but instead became the world's first commercial web magazine.

Der amerikanische Journalist Louis Rossetto wurde Ende der 1980er-Jahre auf die bahnbrechenden digitalen Revolutionen aufmerksam und entwickelte ab 1991 mit einem kleinen Team, darunter die Designer John Plunkett und Barbara Kuhr, das Konzept von *Wired*. Die ab Januar 1993 erschienenen Hefte dokumentierten das gerade anbrechende Zeitalter von PCs, Mobiltelefonen und natürlich des Internets inhaltlich wie visuell so authentisch wie kein anderes Heft. Ganz nebenbei entstand als Ableger der Zeitschrift 1994 unter hotwired.com das weltweit erste kommerzielle Webmagazin.

À la fin des années 1980, le journaliste américain Louis Rossetto comprit qu'une révolution fondamentale était en route avec l'avènement de l'ère numérique. En 1991, il développa en équipe avec les graphistes John Plunkett et Barbara Kuhr le concept de *Wired*. Tant par son contenu que son esthétique, le magazine lancé en janvier 1993 allait documenter les premières années du PC, des téléphones portables et bien sûr d'Internet de manière plus authentique que toute autre publication du même ordre. En 1994 fut lancé hotwired.com, qui ne se voulait à l'origine qu'une activité secondaire, mais qui devint en fait le premier magazine commercial en ligne au monde.

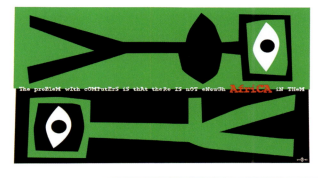

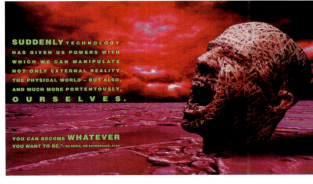

1990s · Plunkett+Kuhr · US · Magazine spreads

1990s · Plunkett+Kuhr · US · Magazine covers

Plunkett+Kuhr (1990, Park City, Utah) is a design studio partnership run by Barbara Kuhr (1954, Great Falls, Montana) and John Plunkett (1952, Chicago). Kuhr studied design at Montana State University and was later employed by a number of design studios, including Chermayeff & Geismar. Plunkett studied at Parsons School of Design and CalArts before going on to work for Saul Bass, Louis Danziger, Deborah Sussman, and Colin Forbes. As Plunkett+Kuhr they created designs for the Sundance Film Festival, a number of TED conferences, and for the Carnegie Hall Museum in New York. However, their most influential work has been the designs they developed between 1991 and 1998 for *Wired* magazine, the winner of three National Magazine Awards.

Plunkett+Kuhr (1990, Park City, Utah) ist das gemeinsame Designstudio von Barbara Kuhr (1954, Great Falls, Montana) und John Plunkett (1952, Chicago). Kuhr studierte Design an der Montana State University und war später unter anderem für Chermayeff & Geismar tätig. Plunkett studierte an der Parsons School of Design und an der CalArts. Anschließend arbeitete er für Saul Bass, Louis Danziger, Deborah Sussman und Colin Forbes. Als Plunkett+Kuhr waren sie für das Sundance Filmfestival, die TED-Konferenz und für das Carnegie Hall Museum in New York tätig. Den meisten Einfluss erlebte jedoch ihre Entwicklung des Magazins *Wired* zwischen 1991 und 1998, das mit drei National Magazine Awards prämiert wurde.

Plunkett+Kuhr (1990, Park City, Utah) est un studio de graphisme codirigé par Barbara Kuhr (1954, Great Falls, Montana) et John Plunkett (1952, Chicago). Kuhr a fait des études de graphisme à l'université d'État du Montana avant de travailler dans toute une série d'agences de graphisme parmi lesquelles figure notamment Chermayeff & Geismar. Plunkett a étudié à la Parsons School of Design et au CalArts avant de travailler pour Saul Bass, Louis Danziger, Deborah Sussman et Colin Forbes. Sous le nom Plunkett+Kuhr, les deux associés ont créé pour le festival du film de Sundance, plusieurs conférences TED et le Carnegie Hall Museum à New York. Leur travail le plus influent reste toutefois leurs créations entre 1991 et 1998 pour le magazine *Wired*, lauréat de trois National Magazine Awards.

1994

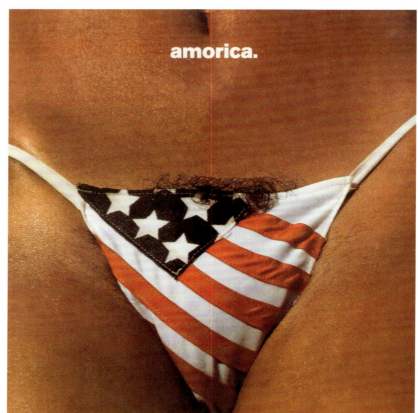

1994 · Janet Levinson, Chris Robinson · US · Record cover

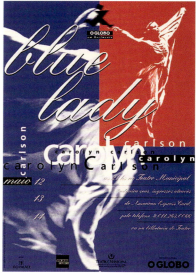

1994 · Sergio Liuzzi · BR · Poster

1994 · Vince Frost · UK/CA · Magazine cover

1994 · Lindon Leader, Landor · US · Logo · FedEx

1994 · Pentagram · US · Logo · World Cup '94

1994 · David High, High Design · US · Poster

1994 · Uwe Loesch · DE · Poster

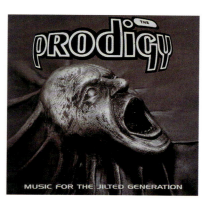

1994 · Stuart Haygarth · UK · Record cover

1994 · Manabu Sakamoto · JP · Logo · PlayStation

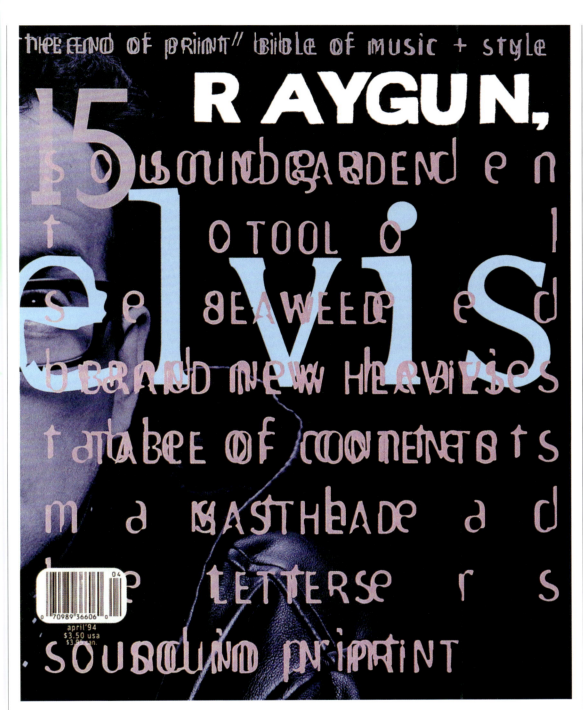

"the end of print" bible of music + style

R AYGUN,
15 soundgarden en
o tool o
seaweed e
brand new heavies
table of contents
a masthead ad
letters r s
sound imprint

elvis

1994 · David Carson, Davies + Starr (PH) · US · Magazine cover

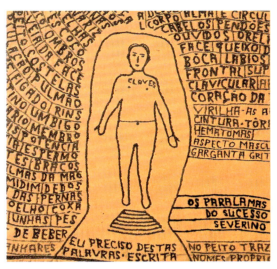

1994 · Gringo Cardia, Arthur Bispo do Rosário · BR · Record cover

GOT A DEAL FOR YOU. PUT THESE SHOES ON. GET A BALL. FIND A HOOP. LET'S SEE YOUR BEST 360° DOUBLE-PUMP SLAM DUNK. WHEN YOU COME DOWN — AND YOU WILL — YOU'LL FEEL THAT THE AIR MAX² UPTEMPO SHOES ARE THE MOST CUSHIONED, STABLE, AND COMFORTABLE BASKETBALL SHOES YOU'VE EVER WORN. IF YOU DON'T, WE'LL REFUND YOUR MONEY. OH YEAH, THEY WERE FREE. OK — WE'LL JUST CALL IT A DARE.

1994 · Dan Richards · US · Poster

Our customers
fel me
Häagen-Dazs is unique.
Between you and
there are no secrets to it. only the world's best ingredients.

Häagen-Dazs
Dedicated to Pleasure.

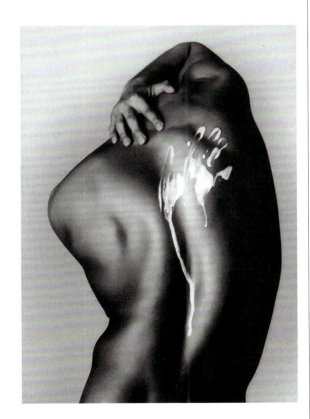

1994 · BBH · UK · Ad

1994 · Igor Maistrovsky · RU · Poster

The visual part of the web, including many aspects of the user interface, was initially put together by an army of curious nerds, very often engineers who saw the web as an opportunity to change the way we work, communicate, sell, and interact with one another. The first websites for today's multi-billion-dollar corporations such as Amazon and Adobe were built from scratch, one line of code at a time, and carefully designed to process data as quickly as was possible with the dial-up connections that were then all that was available. Templates were unknown, image resolution was low, but companies understood that the web needed designers to improve such things, from the logos of internet-based companies to the layouts of web pages. In an endless history of trial and error, standards in programming, structure, and usability were conceived and reworked in a huge collective effort.

Die visuellen Aspekte des Web, einschließlich vieler Elemente der Bildschirmoberfläche, wurden anfangs von einem Heer schräger Nerds entwickelt, häufig Techniker, die das Web als Möglichkeit begriffen, die Art zu verändern, wie wir arbeiten, kommunizieren, verkaufen und interagieren. Die ersten Websites für die heute Milliarden Dollar schweren Unternehmen wie Amazon und Adobe wurden von Grund auf aufgebaut, eine Codezeile nach der anderen, und umsichtig entworfen, damit Daten so schnell wie möglich über die damals verfügbaren Modemverbindungen per Telefonleitung verarbeitet werden konnten. Templates waren unbekannt, die Bildauflösung war schlecht, aber den Unternehmen war klar, dass das Web Designer brauchte, um diese Aspekte zu verbessern, von den Logos der Internetunternehmen bis zum Layout der Webseiten. In einer endlosen Abfolge von Trial and Error und durch eine gewaltige kollektive Anstrengung wurden die Standards bei der Programmierung, der Struktur und der Bedienungsfreundlichkeit konzipiert und überarbeitet.

La partie visuelle du web, notamment bien des aspects de l'interface utilisateur, fut d'abord compilée par une armée de curieux et de passionnés – souvent des ingénieurs qui considéraient le web comme une opportunité pour changer notre manière de travailler, de communiquer, de vendre et d'interagir. Les premiers sites réalisés pour des entreprises qui pèsent aujourd'hui des milliards de dollars comme Amazon et Adobe furent construits à partir de rien, ligne de code par ligne de code, et soigneusement conçus pour traiter les données le plus rapidement possible à travers les connexions téléphoniques, seules disponibles à l'époque. Les modèles étaient inconnus, la résolution des écrans faible, mais les entreprises avaient conscience que le web devait s'appuyer sur des graphistes pour améliorer des aspects comme les logos des entreprises en ligne ou la composition des pages web. Après maintes tentatives et erreurs, les standards de la programmation, de l'architecture numérique et de l'utilisabilité furent conçus et remaniés grâce à un immense effort collectif.

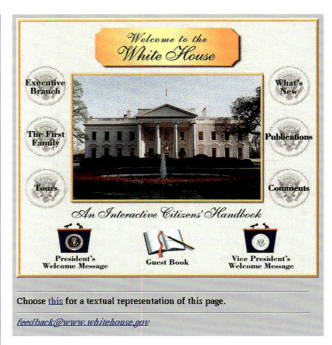

1994 · Anonymous · US · Website

1994 · Anonymous · US · Website

1994 · Plunkett+Kuhr, Max Kisman (ILL) · US · Website

1995 · Anonymous · US · Website

1995 · Anonymous · US · Website

1996 · Anonymous · US · Website

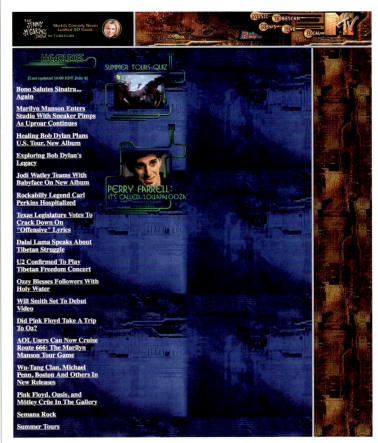

1996 · Anonymous · US · Website

1996 · Anonymous · US · Website

1996 · Anonymous · US · Website

1996 · Anonymous · US · Website

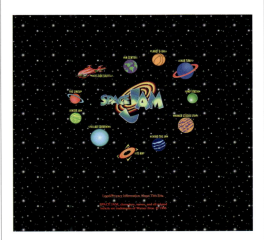

1996 · Anonymous · US · Website

1991 · Anonymous · US · Logo · America Online

1994 · Anonymous · US · Logo · Amazon.com

1996 · Kevin Farnham, Organic · US · Logo · Yahoo!

1996 · Anonymous · US · Logo · Hotbot

1996 · Rebeca Méndez · US · Logo · Go2net

Paula Scher (1948, Washington, DC) is one of the most important American graphic designers of modern times. After attending the Tyler School of Art in Pennsylvania, Scher went on to design advertising and record sleeves for CBS and Atlantic, later becoming the first female principal at Pentagram which she joined in 1991. Her most notable works include identities for Citibank, MoMA, the New York Philharmonic, and the Metropolitan Opera. Scher has taught at the School of Visual Arts, Cooper Union, and Yale University, having widely exhibited both her design and fine art work for over three decades.

Paula Scher (1948, Washington, D.C.) ist im Bereich Grafikdesign eine der bedeutendsten amerikanischen Persönlichkeiten unserer Zeit. Nach dem Besuch der Tyler School of Art in Pennsylvania gestaltete sie Werbung und Plattencover für CBS und Atlantic, 1991 ging sie zu Pentagram und wurde die erste Frau, die diese Designfirma leitete. Zu ihren bemerkenswertesten Arbeiten gehören das CI für die Citibank, das MoMA, das New York Philharmonic und die Metropolitan Opera. Scher unterrichtet an der School of Visual Arts, an der Cooper Union und der Yale University. Seit über dreißig Jahren kommen ihre Arbeiten – sowohl in der Grafik wie in der Malerei – vielfach zur Ausstellung.

Paula Scher (1948, Washington, D.C.) est une des grandes graphistes américaines contemporaines. Après des études à la Tyler School of Art, Pennsylvanie, Scher enchaîne avec la conception publicitaire et des pochettes d'albums pour CBS et Atlantic, devenant plus tard la première femme à intégrer Pentagram, qu'elle rejoint en 1991. Ses travaux les plus remarqués comptent notamment des identités pour Citibank, le MoMA, le New York Philharmonic et le Metropolitan Opera. Scher a enseigné à la School of Visual Arts, à la Cooper Union et à l'université Yale. Elle expose depuis plus de trois décennies ses œuvres de design et d'art.

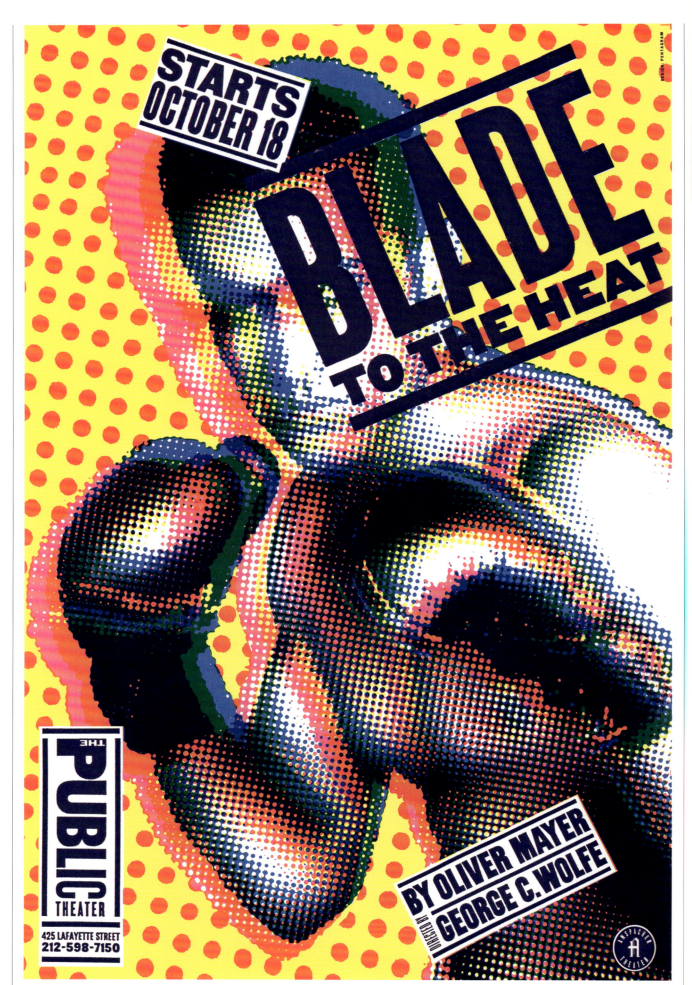

1994 · Paula Scher, Pentagram · US · Poster

1995 · Paula Scher, Pentagram · US · Poster

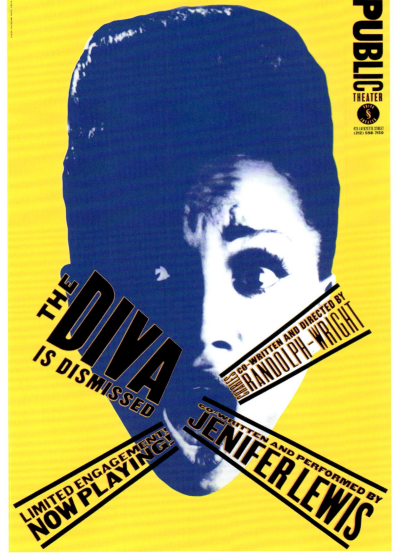

1994 · Paula Scher, Pentagram · US · Poster

In 1994, Scher was awarded the contract to develop a new visual identity for the Public Theater in New York City. With her unconventional visual vocabulary and playful use of typefaces, she managed to introduce an avant-garde aesthetic to a field which all too often tends towards the unadventurous. At the same time, her designs captured the imagination of potential new theater audiences.

Im Jahr 1994 erhielt Paula Scher den Auftrag zur Entwicklung einer neuen visuellen Identität für das Public Theater in New York City. Mit unkonventioneller Bildsprache und spielerisch eingesetzter Typografie gelang es ihr, eine neuartige Ästhetik in diesem ansonsten oft konservativ auftretenden Bereich zu etablieren. Damit ließen sich auch neue Zielgruppen für das Programm begeistern.

En 1994, Paula Scher fut chargée de développer la nouvelle identité visuelle du Public Theater à New York. Son langage visuel anticonformiste et son utilisation ludique de la typographie lui permirent de créer une esthétique d'un nouveau genre dans un secteur qui se donne volontiers une image conservatrice. Cette approche a aussi eu le mérite d'attirer et de passionner de nouvelles cibles pour le programme du théâtre.

1994 · Paula Scher, Pentagram · US · Identity

1990s · Paula Scher, Pentagram · US · Poster

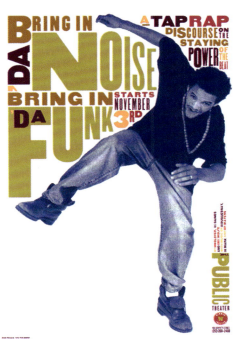

1995 · Paula Scher, Pentagram · US · Poster

1990s · Paula Scher, Pentagram · US · Poster

1995

Dutch designer Albert-Jan Pool creates a new digital version of the German standard typeface **DIN**, which becomes one of the most influential typefaces of the following years

The FUSE 95 design conference is held, later renamed **TYPO Berlin**

David Carson's book **The End of Print** is published

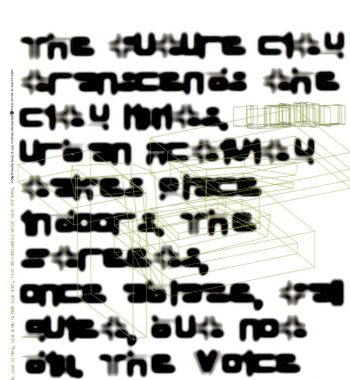

1995 · Neville Brody · UK · Poster

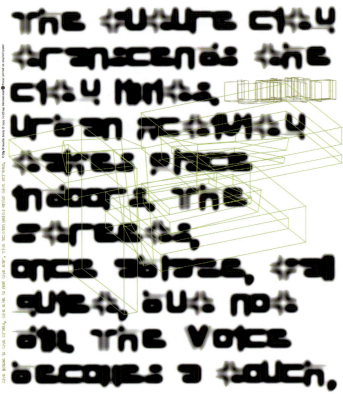

1995 · Yoshimaru Takahashi · JP · Magazine cover

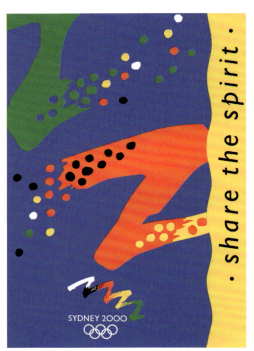

1995 · Michael Bryce · AU · Poster

1995 · Justus Oehler, Pentagram · DE/US · Logo · World Economic Forum

1995 · Vignelli Associates · US/IT · Logo · United Colors of Benetton

1995 · Zintzmeyer & Lux · CH/DE · Logo · Deutsche Telekom

1995 · P. Scott Makela, Billy Phelps (PH) · US · Magazine cover

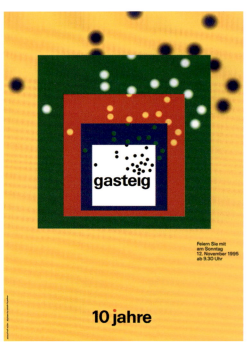

1995 · Rolf Müller · DE · Poster

1995 · Erik Spiekermann, MetaDesign · DE · Identity · Audi

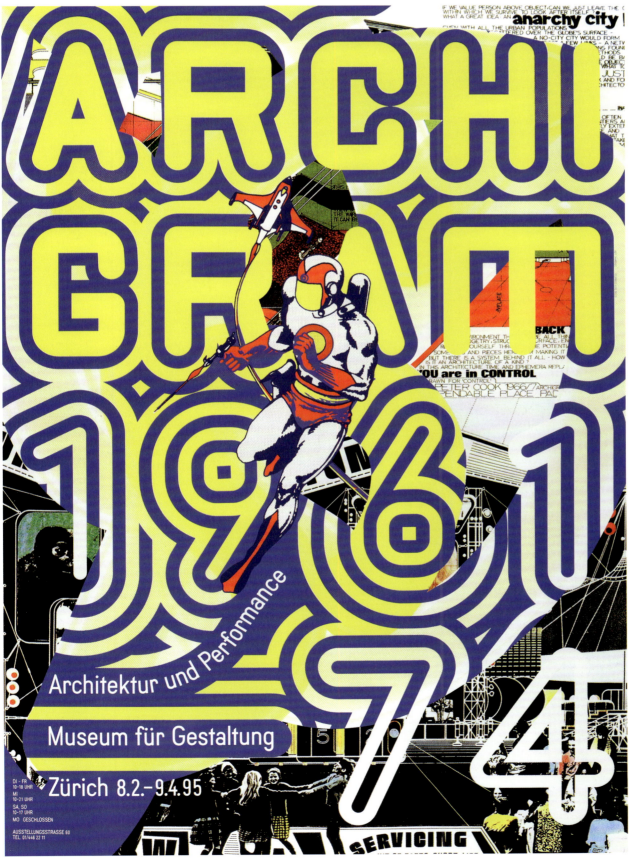

1995 · Ralph Schraivogel · CH · Poster

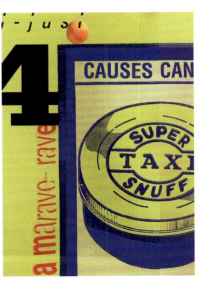

1995 · Garth Walker · ZA · Magazine covers

327

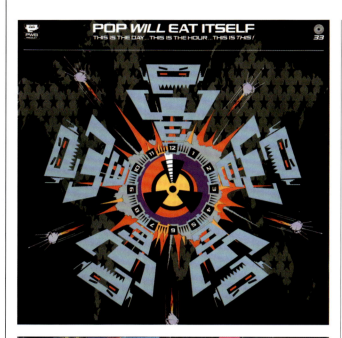

1989 · The Designers Republic™ · UK · Record cover

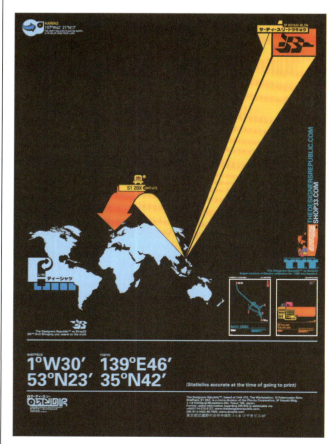

1990s · The Designers Republic™ · UK · Poster

1990s · The Designers Republic™ · UK · Poster

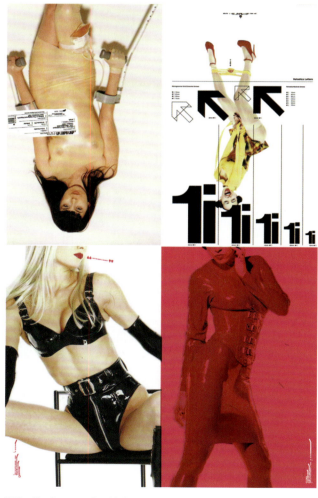

1990s · The Designers Republic™ · UK · Poster

The Designers Republic™ (tDR; 1986, Sheffield, England) was a British multimedia design studio formed by Ian Anderson (1961, London) and Nick Phillips (1962, London). With a subversive take on consumerism and corporate branding, the duo produced groundbreaking work for film festivals, computer games, Sony's AIBO robot pets, and Coca-Cola, while perhaps most notably designing album covers for cult UK electronica label Warp Records. The company closed its doors in 2009, with Anderson relaunching tDR as a slimmed-down enterprise. Their work is in the permanent collections of MoMA and the V&A.

The Designers Republic™ (tDR; 1986, Sheffield, England) war ein britisches Multimediadesignbüro, gegründet von Ian Anderson (1961, London) und Nick Phillips (1962, London). Mit seinem subversiven Blick auf Konsumdenken und Unternehmensbranding schuf das Duo bahnbrechende Arbeiten für Computerspiele, Filmfestivals, Sonys AIBO-Robotertiere und für Coca-Cola; am bekanntesten sind allerdings wohl ihre Albumcover für das britische Electronica-Kultlabel Warp Records. Das Büro wurde 2009 aufgelöst, Anderson eröffnete das Studio im kleineren Format neu. Arbeiten von tDR liegen in der ständigen Sammlung des MoMA und des V&A.

The Designers Republic™ (tDR; 1986, Sheffield, Angleterre) fut un studio de design multimédia britannique formé par Ian Anderson (1961, Londres) et Nick Phillips (1962, Londres). Avec une approche subversive du consumérisme et de l'image de marque, le duo a produit des projets révolutionnaires pour des jeux vidéo, des festivals de cinéma, les chiens robots AIBO de Sony et Coca-Cola. Mais leur travail le plus remarquable reste peut-être les pochettes d'albums pour Warp Records, le très culte label britannique de musique électronique. tDR a fermé ses portes en 2009, Anderson relançant une version réduite de la firme. Leur travail a sa place dans les collections permanentes du MoMA et du V&A.

1995 · The Designers Republic™ · UK · Poster

1989 · The Designers Republic™ · UK · Logo · Warp Records

1990s · The Designers Republic™ · UK · Poster

1994 · The Designers Republic™ · UK · Poster

1992 · The Designers Republic™ · UK · Poster

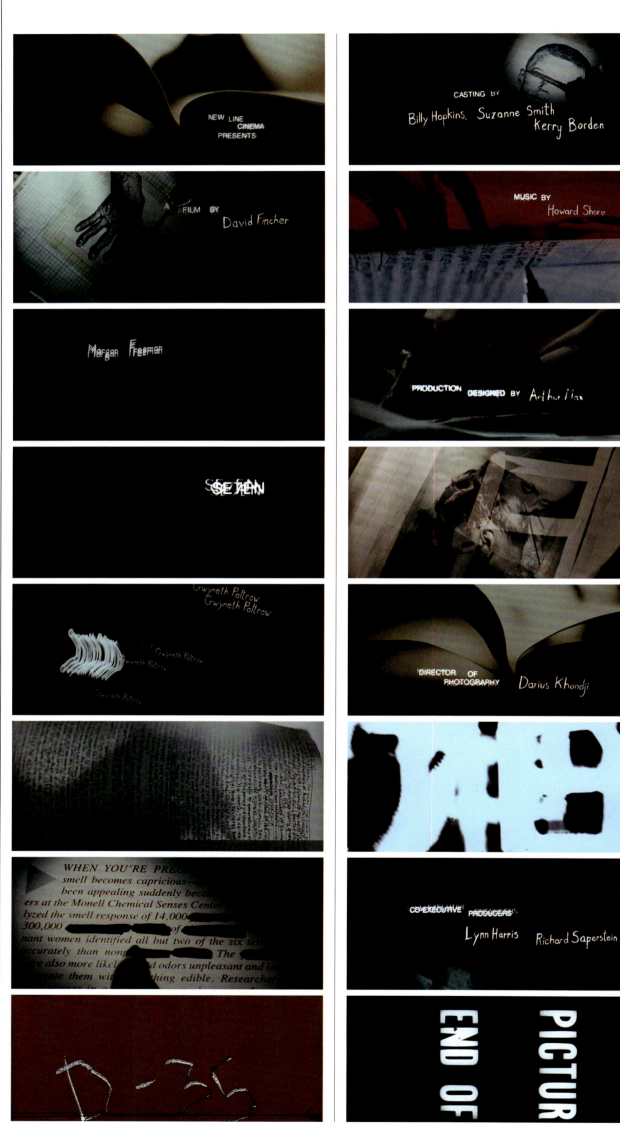

1995 · Kyle Cooper, R/GA · US · Opening titles

Kyle Cooper (1962, Salem, Massachusetts) is a leading Hollywood motion picture designer who specializes in film and TV title sequences. After taking architecture at UMass Amherst, Cooper studied graphic design under Paul Rand at Yale School of Art, gaining his Master's in 1988. Following in the footsteps of Saul Bass, his creative agencies Imaginary Forces (1996) and Prologue Films (2003) have revitalized the visual narrative of the title sequence, over 150 of which he has helped to produce, including for *Seven* (1995) and *Iron Man* (2008). Cooper received an AIGA medal in 2014.

Kyle Cooper (1962, Salem, Massachusetts) ist in Hollywood ein führender Filmdesigner, der sich auf Titelsequenzen von Kino- und Fernsehfilmen spezialisiert hat. Zunächst studierte er Architektur an der UMass Amherst und dann Gestaltung bei Paul Rand an der Yale School of Art; 1988 machte er seinen Magister. Dem Beispiel Saul Bass' folgend, hat Cooper mit seinen Kreativagenturen Imaginary Forces (1996) und Prologue Films (2003) dazu beigetragen, die bildliche Erzählung der Titelsequenz zu beleben. Bislang hat er an mehr als 150 derartigen Sequenzen mitgewirkt, u.a. für *Sieben* (1995) und *Iron Man* (2008). 2014 wurde Cooper mit einer AIGA-Medaille geehrt.

Kyle Cooper (1962, Salem, Massachusetts) est un graphiste de cinéma de premier plan à Hollywood, spécialisé dans les génériques de films et de télévision. Après des études d'architecture à l'université du Massachusetts à Amherst, Cooper étudie le graphisme auprès de Paul Rand à la Yale School of Art et décroche son master en 1988. Suivant les pas de Saul Bass, ses agences créatives Imaginary Forces (1996) et Prologue Films (2003) ont redynamisé le visuel des génériques de films, dont il a aidé à produire plus de 150, notamment *Seven* (1995) et *Iron Man* (2008). Cooper a reçu une médaille de l'AIGA en 2014.

As far back as the 1950s, Saul Bass had set about revolutionizing the art of the movie title sequence. With his groundbreaking computer-generated titles for the thriller *SE7EN*, Kyle Cooper renewed them once again, and made a lasting impact on the sector. Using the very latest techniques, he set new benchmarks in title design, in terms of both atmosphere and typographic effects.

Schon Saul Bass hatte in den 1950er- und 1960er-Jahren das Medium Filmvorspann revolutioniert. Mit seiner wegweisenden Titelsequenz für den Thriller *SE7EN* gelang Kyle Cooper eine nachhaltige Belebung des Sektors mittels digitaler Bearbeitung. Mit diesen modernen Möglichkeiten setzte er neue atmosphärische und typografische Maßstäbe.

Dès les années 1950, Saul Bass avait déjà révolutionné l'esthétique du générique de film. Avec celui résolument novateur qu'il créa pour le thriller *SE7EN*, Kyle Cooper a redynamisé de façon durable ce domaine grâce à la conception numérique. Les nouvelles technologies lui ont permis d'établir de nouveaux standards en termes d'ambiance et de typographie.

1996 · Kyle Cooper, R/GA · US · Opening titles

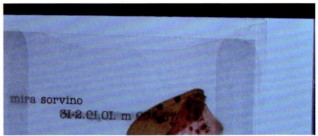

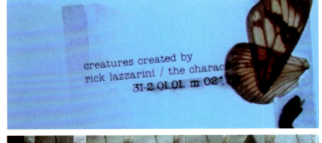
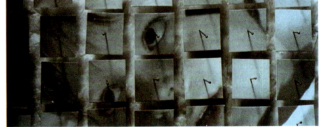
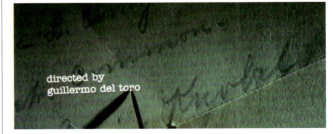

1997 · Kyle Cooper, Imaginary Forces · US · Opening titles

Trainspotting 18

THIS FILM IS EXPECTED TO ARRIVE...

23:02:96

From the team that brought you Shallow Grave

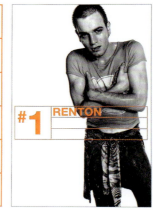

#1 RENTON

#2 BEGBIE

#3 DIANE

#4 SICK BOY

#5 SPUD

1996 · Mark Blamire, Rob O'Connor, Stylorouge, Lorenzo Agius (PH) · UK · Poster

L ^uX

1996 · April Greiman · US · Logo · Lux Pictures

miu miu

1996 · Italo Lupi · IT · Logo · Miu Miu

c i n e t e a m

1996 · Koeweiden Postma · NL · Logo · Cineteam

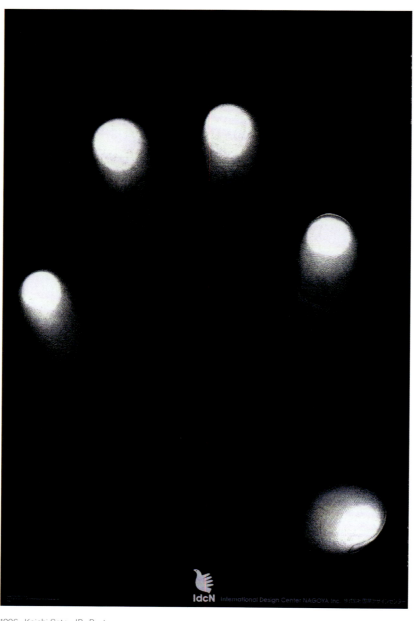

1996 · Koichi Sato · JP · Poster

1996 · Jin Sato · JP · Poster

1996 · Mostafa Assadollahi · IR · Poster

Imaginary Forces, a motion graphics studio based in Hollywood and New York, is founded by Kyle Cooper, Peter Frankfurt, and Chip Houghton

1996 · Chris Ashworth, Neil Fletcher · UK · Magazine covers

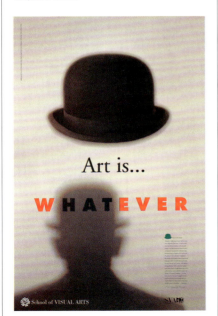

1996 · Milton Glaser · US · Poster

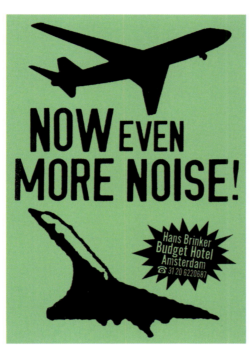

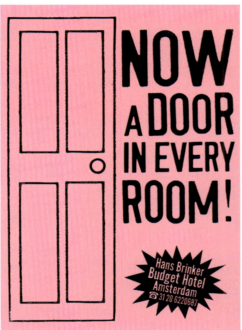

1996 · Anthony Burrill, KesselsKramer · NL · Ads

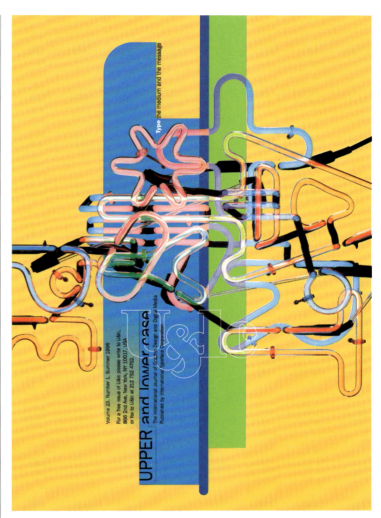

1996 · Why Not Associates · UK · Magazine cover

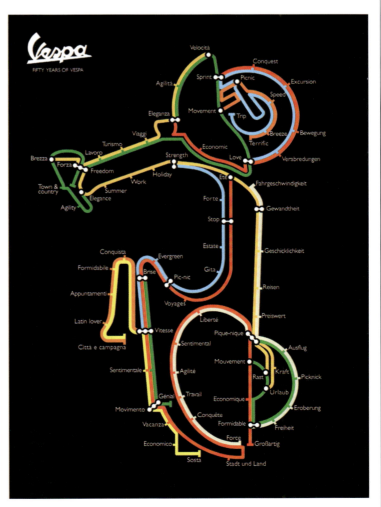

1996 · Italo Lupi · IT · Poster

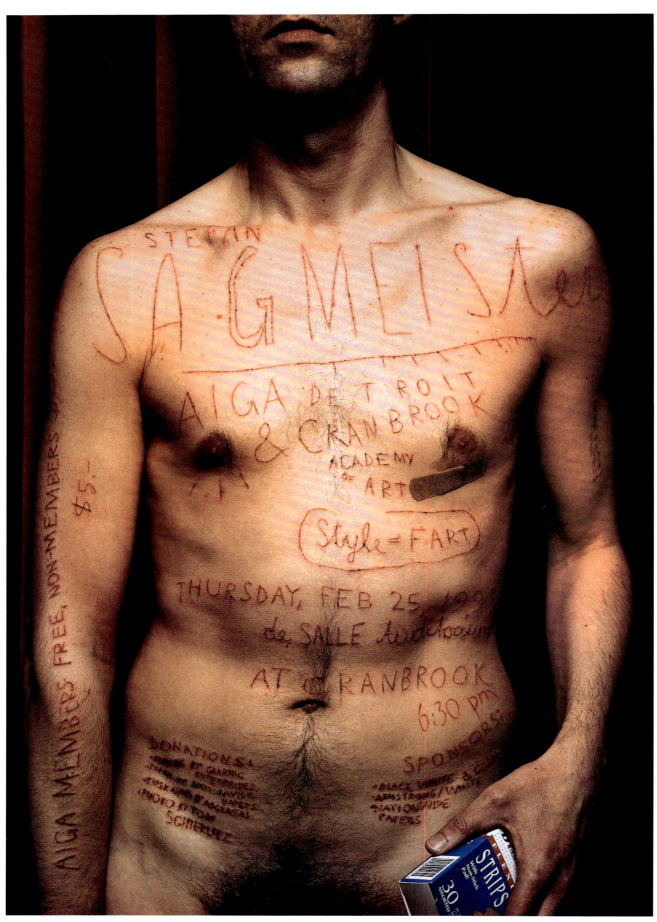

1999 · Stefan Sagmeister · AT/US · Poster

Stefan Sagmeister (1962, Bregenz, Austria) is an Austrian-American designer and typographer based in New York, where he runs Sagmeister & Walsh with Jessica Walsh (1986, New York). Always challenging visual conventions and the reach of a designer's influence, Sagmeister's design work ranges from record covers to software, besides creating new aesthetics and interactions. He has received Grammy Awards for packaging designs for Talking Heads, David Byrne, and Brian Eno. After originally studying in Vienna, and at New York's Pratt Institute, he worked in advertising in Hong Kong and then in New York with Tibor Kalman, before starting Sagmeister Inc. in 1993.

Stefan Sagmeister (1962, Bregenz, Österreich) ist ein österreichisch-amerikanischer Grafikdesigner und Typograf mit Sitz in New York, wo er gemeinsam mit Jessica Walsh (1986, New York) Sagmeister & Walsh leitet. In seiner Arbeit fordert er die visuellen Konventionen und den herkömmlichen Einflussbereich von Design heraus und gestaltet vor diesem Hintergrund Plattencover ebenso wie Software; zudem schafft er eine neue Ästhetik und neue Interaktionen. Für seine Packagingdesigns für Talking Heads, David Byrne und Brian Eno wurde Sagmeister jeweils mit einem Grammy Award ausgezeichnet. Er studierte in Wien und am Pratt Institute in New York, anschließend arbeitete er in Hongkong in der Werbebranche und dann in New York bei Tibor Kalman, ehe er 1993 Sagmeister Inc. gründete.

Stefan Sagmeister (1962, Bregenz, Autriche) est un designer et typographe austro-américain basé à New York, où il dirige Sagmeister & Walsh avec Jessica Walsh (1986, New York). Défiant toujours les conventions visuelles et le champ d'influence du designer, le travail de Sagmeister va de pochettes d'albums aux logiciels, sans compter la création de nouvelles esthétiques et interactions. Il a reçu des Grammy Awards récompensant ses designs d'emballages pour Talking Heads, David Byrne et Brian Eno. Après des études à Vienne et l'Institut Pratt de New York, Sagmeister a travaillé dans la publicité à Hong Kong, puis à New York avec Tibor Kalman, avant de lancer Sagmeister Inc. en 1993.

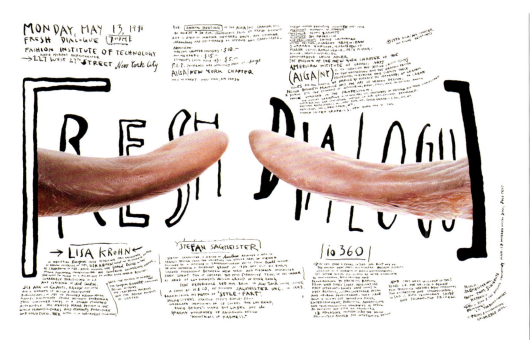

1996 · Stefan Sagmeister · AT/US · Poster

1996 · Stefan Sagmeister · AT/US · Poster

1998 · Stefan Sagmeister · AT/US · Business card

1994 · Stefan Sagmeister · US · Record cover

1997 · Stefan Sagmeister · AT/US · Record cover

2001 · Stefan Sagmeister · AT/US · Book covers

City Branding

After the idea of branding had taken over the product marketing departments of the world, it was time for cities to wake up to the concept and revamp their images, with the result that some of the most renowned creative minds in the industry were frequently hired for the jobs. For cities it became important to communicate what made them special individually and what they stood for, as changing times meant that they were about to become as relevant as countries in terms of geopolitics, as well as being the focus for the future of urban planning and a general base for democracy.

Nachdem der Gedanke der Markenbildung in die Marketingabteilungen weltweit Einzug gehalten hatte, war es an der Zeit, dass auch Städte das Konzept übernahmen und ihr Image aufwerteten. Zu dem Zweck wurden häufig die angesehensten kreativen Köpfe in dem Gewerbe engagiert. Für Städte wurde es wichtig zu vermitteln, wodurch sie sich jeweils auszeichneten und wofür sie standen, denn durch den Wandel der Zeiten wurden sie geopolitisch ebenso bedeutsam wie ganze Länder. Zudem sind sie nicht nur das Fundament der Demokratie, sondern auch der Dreh- und Angelpunkt der Stadtplanung.

Après que l'idée de branding eut conquis les services de marketing produit du monde entier, le temps était venu pour les villes de s'éveiller à ce concept et de repenser leur image. Elles firent alors souvent appel à quelques-uns des grands créatifs du secteur pour communiquer ce qui les rendait spéciales et ce qu'elles représentaient. La démarche était essentielle car l'évolution historique les transformait en acteurs géopolitiques aussi importants que les pays, en centres de la planification urbaine du futur et de bases universelles de la démocratie.

1998 · Peter Schmidt Group · DE · Logo · Hamburg

1998 · Erik Spiekermann, MetaDesign · DE · Logo · Berlin

1999 · Studio Dumbar · NL · Logo · Rotterdam

1998 · Euro RSCG · UK · Logo · London

2000 · Euro RSCG · UK · Logo · London

2009 · Landor · US/AU · Logo · Melbourne

2009 · Landor · US/AU · Identity · Melbourne

2014 · Anonymous · US · Logo · Mississauga

2004 · Landor · US/ES · Logo · Madrid

2010 · M&C Saatchi · UK/AE · Logo · Abu Dhabi

2008 · Lloyd Northover · UK · Logo · Belfast

2004 · Anonymous · PT · Logo · Lisbon

2009 · Peter Saville · UK · Logo · Manchester

2014 · Anonymous · AE · Logo · Dubai

2010 · AD Partners · AT · Logo · Innsbruck

2010 · Landor · US/HK · Logo · Hong Kong

2011 · Romulo Castilho · BR · Logo · São Paulo

2013 · Natalia Chobanu · RU · Logo · Kostroma

2015 · Landor · US · Logo · Covington

2002 · Eden, Thonik · NL · Logo · Amsterdam

2013 · Graphèmes · FR · Logo · Lille

2010 · BBH Asia-Pacific · UK/SG · Logo · Singapore

2012 · Anonymous · US · Logo · Dallas

2003 · Studio Najbrt · CZ · Logo · Prague

2012 · Anuncian Tormenta · ES · Logo · Burgos

2013 · MMAP · FR · Logo · Paris Region

2011 · Art. Lebedev Studio · RU · Logo · Kaluga

1997

1997 · Iris Utikal, Michael Gais, Qwer · DE · Logo · Expo 2000 Hannover

1997 · Landor · US · Logo · Fortis

1997 · Enterprise IG · US · Logo · Hilton Hotels

1997 · TBWA\Chiat\Day · US · Posters

1992 · David Carson · US/BR · Magazine cover

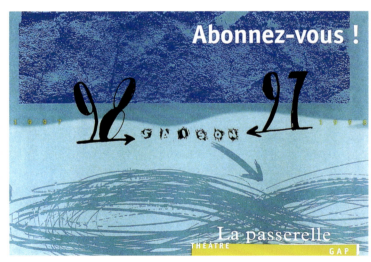

1997 · Thérèse Troika · FR · Poster

1997 · Vignelli Associates · US · Identity · Guggenheim Museum

1997 · Shin Matsunaga · JP · Packaging

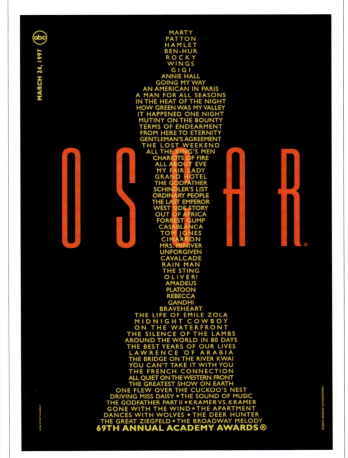

1997 · Arnold Schwartzman · UK/US · Poster

1997 · Stefan Sagmeister · AT/US · Poster

1997 · Felipe Taborda · BR · Poster

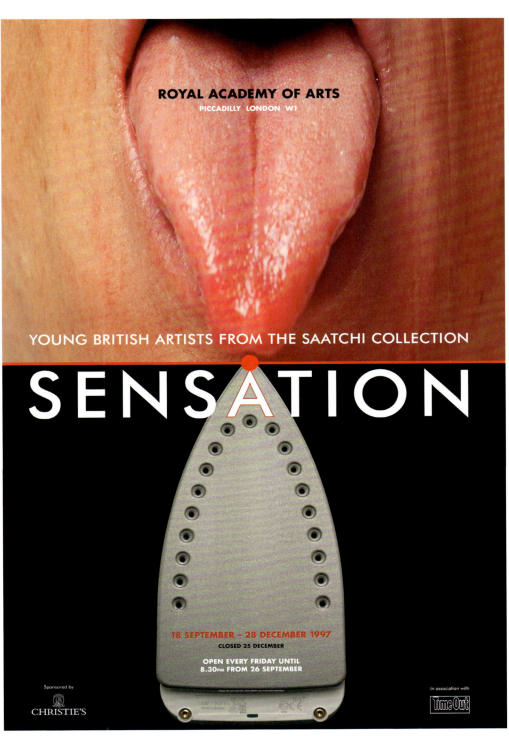

1997 · Why Not Associates · UK · Poster

Melchior Imboden · Switzerland

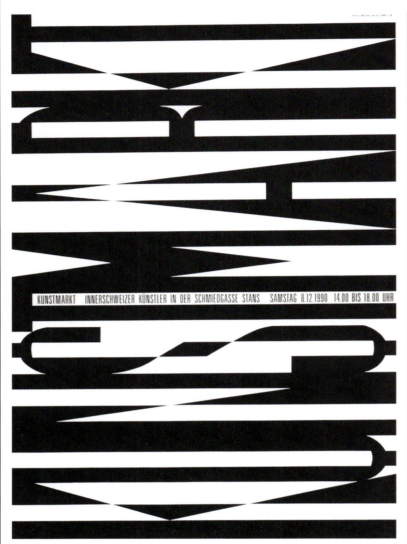

1990 · Melchior Imboden · CH · Poster

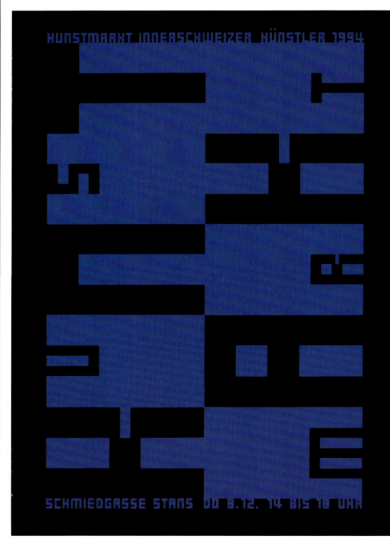

1994 · Melchior Imboden · CH · Poster

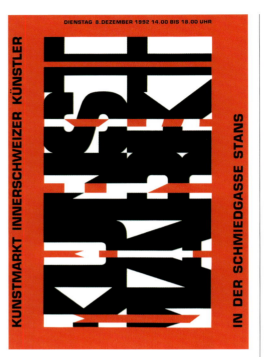

1992 · Melchior Imboden · CH · Poster

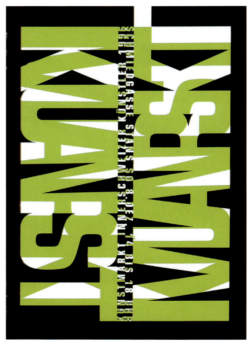

1996 · Melchior Imboden · CH · Poster

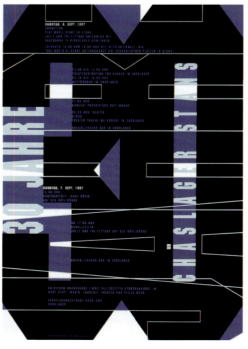

1997 · Melchior Imboden · CH · Poster

Melchior Imboden (1956, Stans, Switzerland) is a Swiss poster artist and photographer. After briefly studying interior design, Imboden enrolled at the School of Art and Design in Lucerne (1984–89) to study graphic design, during which time he worked in advertising, later starting his own practice in 1992. He has taught graphic design and photography in Karlsruhe, and poster design in Berlin. Imboden's landmark works include over 500 photographic portraits of designers, and his numerous posters, often using rural images to reflect his connection with his homeland. From 2006 to 2010 he was President of AGI Switzerland.

Melchior Imboden (1956, Stans, Schweiz) ist ein Schweizer Plakatkünstler und Fotograf. Nach einem kurzen Studium der Innenarchitektur besuchte er von 1984 bis 1989 die Grafikfachklasse der Hochschule Luzern Design & Kunst und arbeitete unterdessen als Werbegrafiker; seit 1992 ist er als selbstständiger Grafikdesigner tätig. Er hat Grafikdesign und Fotografie in Karlsruhe sowie Plakatdesign in Berlin unterrichtet. Zu Imbodens bedeutendsten Arbeiten zählen über 500 Fotoporträts von Designern sowie seine zahlreichen Plakate, die häufig ländliche Bilder zeigen und die Verbundenheit mit seiner Heimat verdeutlichen. Von 2006 bis 2010 war er Präsident der AGI Schweiz.

Melchior Imboden (1956, Stans, Suisse) est un affichiste et photographe suisse. Après de brèves études de design d'intérieur, Imboden se forme au graphisme à la Haute École de Lucerne (1984–89) tout en travaillant dans la publicité. Il ouvre son propre studio en 1992. Il a enseigné le graphisme et la photographie à Karlsruhe et la conception d'affiches à Berlin. Ses réalisations de référence comptent plus de 500 portraits photographiques de designers, et ses nombreuses affiches, qui utilisent souvent des images rurales, évoquent ses liens avec son pays natal. Imboden a été président de l'AGI Suisse de 2006 à 2010.

1997 · Melchior Imboden · CH · Poster

Pierre Mendell · Germany

1997 · Pierre Mendell · DE · Poster

2004 · Pierre Mendell · DE · Poster

2008 · Pierre Mendell · DE · Poster

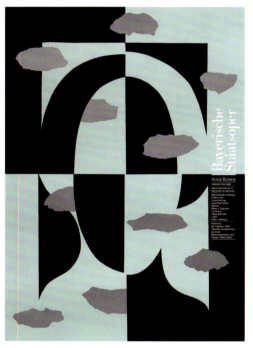

1995 · Pierre Mendell · DE · Poster

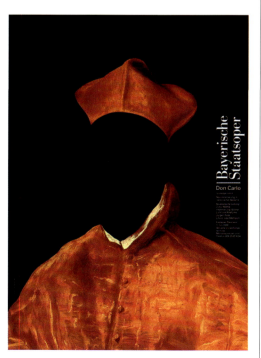

1999 · Pierre Mendell · DE · Poster

Pierre Mendell (1929, Essen – 2008, Munich) was a forward-looking designer, known for his minimalist approach to poster work. Mendell's family fled Nazi Germany in 1934 for the Netherlands and then France, before emigrating to America in 1945. On returning to Europe he began studying graphic design at the age of 29 in Basel, under Armin Hofmann. He later founded the Mendell & Oberer studio in Munich, with photographer Klaus Oberer (1937, Basel), eventually going solo in 2000. With a portfolio ranging from social causes to cultural institutions, Mendell's achievements included several pieces for the prestigious Neue Sammlung design museum and the Bayern Opera House, both in Munich.

Pierre Mendell (1929, Essen – 2008, München) war ein zukunftsweisender Grafikdesigner, der berühmt war wegen seiner minimalistisch geprägten Plakate. Seine Familie floh 1934 aus Deutschland in die Niederlande und weiter nach Frankreich, ehe sie 1945 in die Vereinigten Staaten auswanderte. Nach der Rückkehr nach Europa studierte Mendell im Alter von 29 Jahren in Basel Grafikdesign bei Armin Hofmann. In der Folge gründete er zusammen mit dem Fotografen Klaus Oberer (1937, Basel) in München das Studio Mendell & Oberer, ab 2000 schließlich arbeitete er alleine. Mendell übernahm Aufträge für gesellschaftsrelevante Anliegen ebenso wie für Kulturinstitutionen und gestaltete u. a. mehrere Entwürfe für die renommierte Neue Sammlung im Museum für angewandte Kunst, München, und für die Bayerische Staatsoper.

Pierre Mendell (1929, Essen – 2008, Munich) fut un graphiste allemand tourné vers l'avenir et connu pour son approche minimaliste de l'affiche. En 1934, fuyant le régime nazi, la famille de Mendell se réfugia aux Pays-Bas, puis en France, avant d'émigrer aux États-Unis en 1945. De retour en Europe, Mendell commença des études de graphisme à l'âge de 29 ans à Bâle auprès d'Armin Hofmann. Il fonda ensuite le studio Mendell & Oberer à Munich avec le photographe Klaus Oberer (1937, Bâle), avant de s'installer en indépendant en 2000. Avec un portefeuille de projets allant de causes sociales à des institutions culturelles, Mendell est l'auteur de réalisations pour le musée du design Die Neue Sammlung et l'opéra d'État de Bavière, tous deux situés à Munich.

In 1980, Mendell was appointed to create the brand image for Die Neue Sammlung, Munich's Design Museum. His poster designs transformed the subjects of the museum's various exhibitions into memorable images, whose minimalist virtuosity alone was enough to draw attention across the city. To this day they remain an impressive example of how design can itself be used to promote design.

Ab 1980 war Mendell für den visuellen Auftritt des Münchner Designmuseums Die Neue Sammlung verantwortlich. Seine Plakate übersetzten die unterschiedlichen Ausstellungsthemen in einprägsame Bilder, die im Stadtraum allein schon durch ihre geniale Reduktion auffielen. Bis heute sind sie eindrucksvolle Beispiele dafür, wie Design für Design werben kann.

En 1980, l'identité visuelle du Die Neue Sammlung, le musée du design de Munich, fut confiée à Mendell. Ses affiches traduisirent les thèmes des expositions en images frappantes dont le génial minimalisme les rendaient inratables dans l'espace urbain. Elles sont aujourd'hui encore un impressionnant exemple de promotion du graphisme par le graphisme.

1994 · Pierre Mendell · DE · Poster

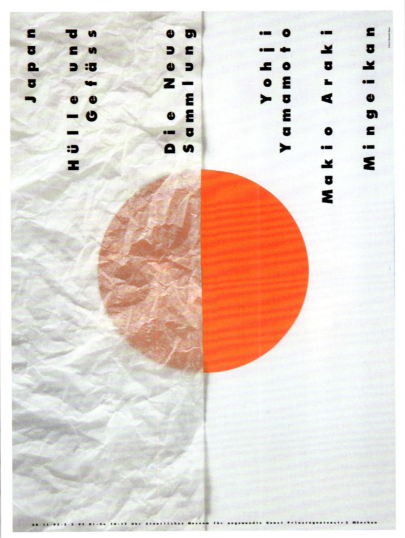

1992 · Pierre Mendell · DE · Poster

1985 · Pierre Mendell · DE · Poster

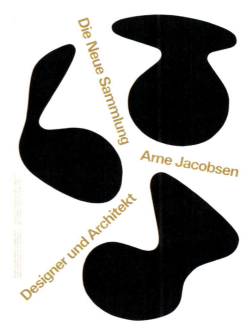

1994 · Pierre Mendell · DE · Poster

1986 · Pierre Mendell · DE · Poster

1998

Publication of the reference book
Typography: When Who How by Friedrich
Friedl, Nicolaus Ott, and Bernard Stein

The international branding corporation
Moving Brands is founded by graduates
of Central Saint Martins College in London

The **Werkplaats Typografie** Master's course
in typography is founded in Arnhem, Netherlands,
by Wigger Bierma and Karel Martens

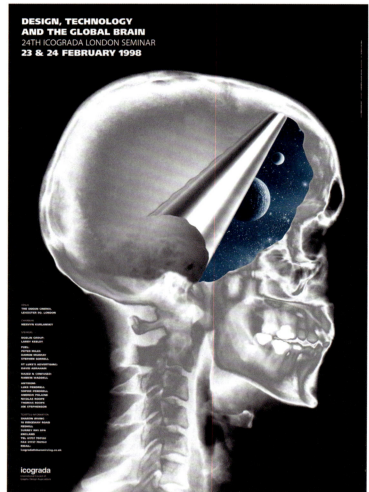

1998 · Mervyn Kurlansky · UK · Poster

1998 · Gunter Rambow, Rambow van de Sand · DE · Poster

1998 · Rosmarie Tissi, Odermatt+Tissi · CH/JP · Poster

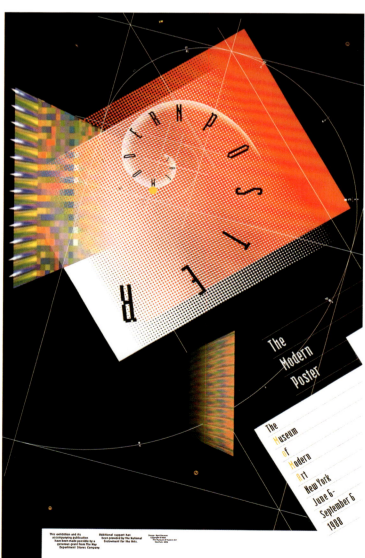

1998 · April Greiman · US · Poster

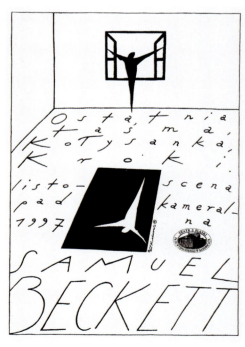

1997 · Roman Kalarus · PL · Poster

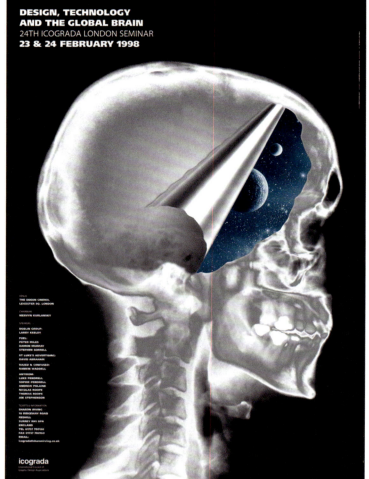

1998 · Turner Duckworth · US · Logo · SETI Institute

1998 · Stockholm Design Lab · SE · Logo · SAS
Scandinavian Airlines

1998 · FutureBrand · AU · Logo · Crown Melbourne

1998 · Kit Hinrichs, John Hersey (ILL) · US · Magazine cover

1998 · Jennifer Morla · US · Ad

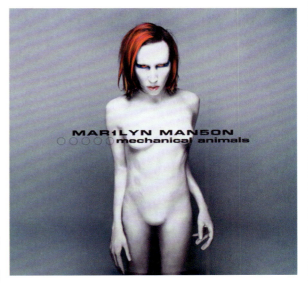

1998 · Paul R. Brown, Bau-Da Design Lab · US · Record cover

1998 · Helmut Schmid · DE/KR · Packaging

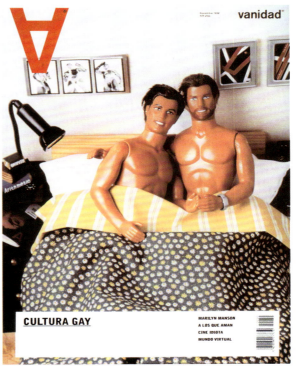

1998 · Fernando Gutiérrez · ES · Magazine cover

1989 · 8vo · UK · Poster

8vo (1985–2001) was a British design studio whose typographic and graphic design projects won worldwide acclaim. Between them, the founders, Mark Holt (1958, Leeds, England), Simon Johnston (1959, Leamington Spa, England), and Hamish Muir (1957, Paisley, Scotland), studied at various institutions including Basel School of Design under Wolfgang Weingart. They applied their distinctive typography to commissions from clients such as American Express, Christie's, and Scandinavian Airlines. In addition, between 1986 and 1992, 8vo published eight issues of Octavo, a typographic magazine which is still regarded as one of the most significant design publications of its time. In 1986, the designer Michael Burke (1944, Leicestershire, England) joined the studio as a partner.

8vo (1985–2001) war ein britisches Designstudio, das weltweit beachtete Projekte in Typografie und Grafikdesign realisierte. Die Gründer Mark Holt (1958, Leeds, England), Simon Johnston (1959, Leamington Spa, England) und Hamish Muir (1957, Paisley, Schottland), hatten unter anderem an der Allgemeinen Gewerbeschule in Basel bei Wolfgang Weingart studiert. Ihre markante Handschrift setzten sie für Auftraggeber wie American Express, Christie's oder Scandinavian Airlines ein. Zwischen 1986 und 1992 veröffentlichte 8vo zudem acht Ausgaben der Typografiezeitschrift Octavo, die bis heute als eine der wichtigen Designpublikationen ihrer Zeit gilt. 1986 wurde der Designer Michael Burke (1944, Leicestershire, England) weiterer Partner des Studios.

8vo (1985–2001) fut un studio de création graphique britannique qui signa des projets de reconnaissance mondiale dans les domaines typographique et du graphisme. Les fondateurs Mark Holt (1958, Leeds, Angleterre), Simon Johnston (1959, Leamington Spa, Angleterre) et Hamish Muir (1957, Paisley, Écosse) avaient notamment étudié dans diverses institutions, dont l'école de design de Bâle auprès de Wolfgang Weingart. Leurs typographies caractéristiques furent mises au service de clients comme American Express, Christie's ou Scandinavian Airlines. Entre 1986 et 1992, 8vo publia également huit numéros de la revue de typographie Octavo, considérée aujourd'hui encore comme une des plus importantes publications de design de l'époque. En 1986, le designer Michael Burke (1944, Leicestershire, Angleterre) rejoignit le studio en qualité d'associé.

1990 · 8vo · UK · Poster

1986 · 8vo · UK · Poster

b-vb

Museum Boymans-van Beuningen Rotterdam

17/6-30/7/89

Günther Förg:

Complete Grafiek

1/7-6/8/89

Moderne Duitse Schilderkunst:

Baselitz/Immendorf/Kiefer/ Knoebel/Lüpertz/ Penck/Polke/Richter

1989 · 8vo · UK/NL · Poster

1992 · 8vo · UK · Multimedia CD-Rom

1997 · 8vo · UK · Poster

1998 · 8vo · UK · Poster

1999 · 8vo · UK · Poster

Adbusters magazine updates the **First Things First** manifesto by Ken Garland from 1964, as signed by 33 international graphic designers

Jonathan Hoefler and Tobias Frere-Jones establish the **Hoefler & Frere-Jones** type foundry in New York City

The book **Radical Graphics/Graphic Radicals** presents an overview of recent developments in graphic design

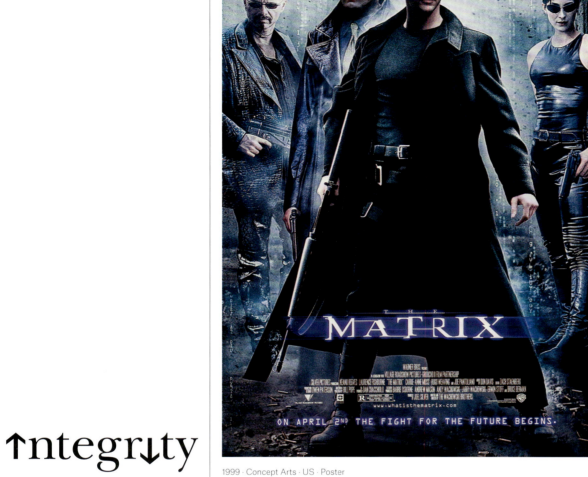

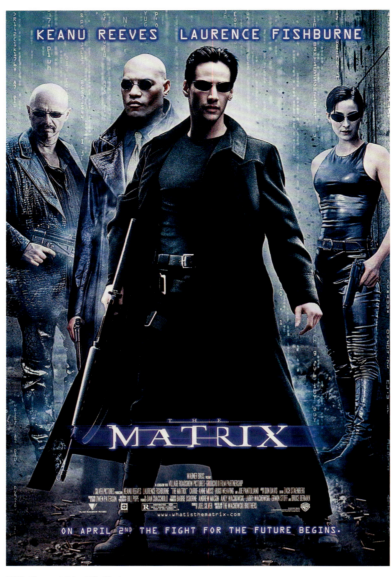

1999 · Concept Arts · US · Poster

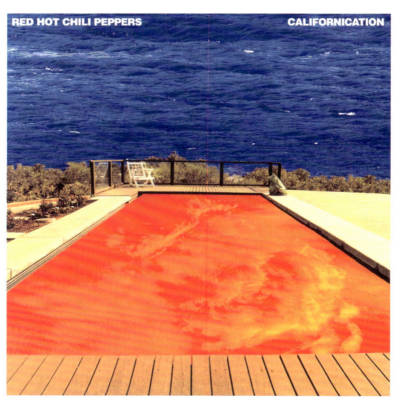

1999 · Lawrence Azerrad (AD), Sonya Koskoff (PH) · US · Record cover

1999 · Ian Chilvers, Atelier Works · UK · Logo · Integrity

1999 · April Greiman · US · Logo · Roto Architects

1999 · Paula Scher, Pentagram · US · Logo · Citibank

1999 · Daniel Kleinman · UK · Opening titles

The Dutch type foundry **Underware** is established

The Malaysian graphic design association **WREGA** is founded

1999 · Michael Bierut, Pentagram · US · Poster

1999 · Patrick Mitchell · US · Magazine cover

1999 · Andy Dreyfus, Apple Inc. · US · Packaging

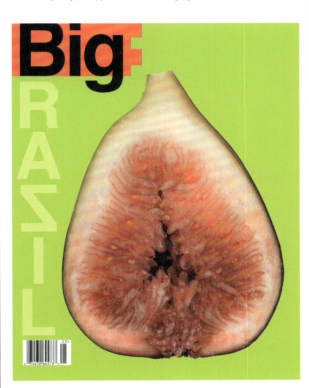

1999 · Rico Lins · BR · Magazine cover

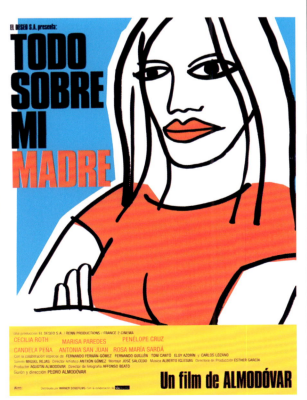

1999 · Oscar Mariné · ES · Poster

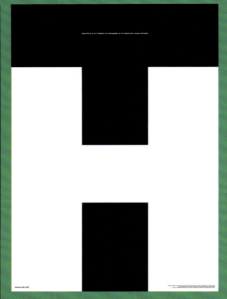

2007 · Melchior Imboden · CH · Poster

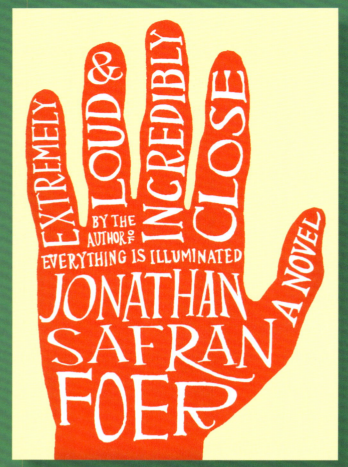

2005 · Jonathan Gray · UK · Book cover

2000 ——————

2006 · Karel Martens · NL · Magazine cover

2008 · "Obey" (Shepard Fairey) · US · Poster

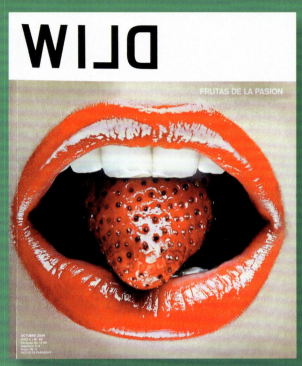

2004 · Victor Candia · PY · Magazine cover

2004 · Ostengruppe · RU · Poster

2009

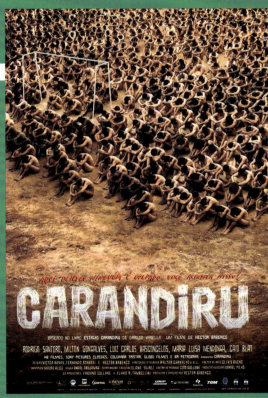

2003 · Marcelo Pallotta, Cassio Leitão (TY) · BR · Poster

2007 · Cato Brand Partners · AU · Identity · Pluna Airlines

Whether it could be attributed to the sometimes overwhelming surfeit of computer graphics, or was a reaction to the flood of digitally produced imagery, at the turn of the millennium there was a clear return to austere, minimalist solutions in graphic design. Following the initiative of a few innovative design studios in central Europe, 1960s modernism was rediscovered and reinvented in a new contemporary guise. The heroes of the Swiss Style and Dutch Design were celebrated in major retrospectives and even Helvetica, the typeface long regarded as no more than "reliable", enjoyed a revival, which included a highly respected film documentary made to mark its 50th birthday. Simultaneously, huge progress was made in media design. For example, it was now perfectly simple to animate a design or to make your own short movie. The internet and the increasing use of broadband also speeded up connections with designers working in other parts of the world, making the discovery of new visual trends and technological advances still quicker and easier.

Möglicherweise aus Überdruss an der teils überbordenden Menge an Computergrafik, vielleicht auch als Reaktion auf die Flut an visuellen Eindrücken durch digitale Medien: Etwas hat während der Jahrhundertwende zu einer Rückbesinnung auf strenge und reduzierte Lösungen im Bereich des Grafikdesigns geführt. Ausgehend von einigen innovativen Designbüros in Mitteleuropa, wurde der Modernismus der 1960er-Jahre wiederentdeckt und in einer neuen und zeitgemäßen Form wiederbelebt. Die Helden der Schweizer Grafik oder des niederländischen Designs wurden in großen Retrospektiven gefeiert, und selbst die lange als ausschließlich zweckmäßig angesehene Schrift Helvetica erlebte zu ihrem fünfzigsten Geburtstag ein Revival, inklusive einer viel beachteten Filmdokumentation. Gleichzeitig entwickelten sich die Möglichkeiten digitaler Gestaltung enorm weiter. Es war nun beispielsweise ganz einfach möglich, Entwürfe zu animieren oder eigene kleine Filme zu produzieren. Das Internet und der Ausbau der Breitbandkommunikation förderten zudem die Vernetzung der internationalen Designszene und sorgten für eine beschleunigte Wahrnehmung visueller Trends und neuer Entwicklungen.

Que ce soit en raison d'une saturation face à la masse d'infographies, ou en réaction au flot incessant d'images numériques, le changement de millénaire fut témoin d'un clair retour à des solutions austères et minimalistes en matière de graphisme. Des studios de design innovants d'Europe centrale eurent cette initiative et de là, on redécouvrit le modernisme des années 1960, qui connut un revival sous une forme contemporaine. Les héros du style suisse ou du design néerlandais furent célébrés dans de grandes rétrospectives, et même l'Helvetica, longtemps considérée comme une police de caractères purement utilitaire, fêta sa renaissance, notamment dans un documentaire très remarqué à l'occasion de son cinquantième anniversaire. En parallèle, les possibilités du graphisme numérique se multiplièrent et il était désormais facile d'animer un graphisme ou de produire de petits films. Internet et l'emploi croissant du haut débit favorisèrent en outre la mise en réseau de la scène internationale du design et la découverte de nouvelles tendances visuelles et évolutions technologiques.

2000

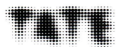

The Tate Modern opens in London

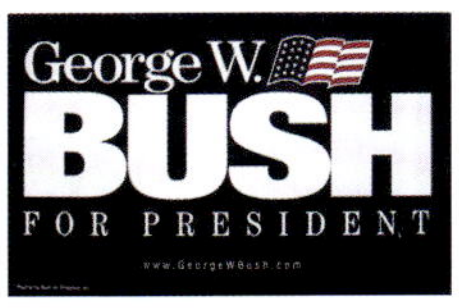

George W. Bush is elected president of the United States

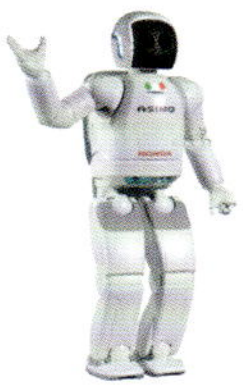

Honda unveils its walking humanoid robot, ASIMO

Dave Ulmer posts the location of the first geocached items, outside Beavercreek, Oregon

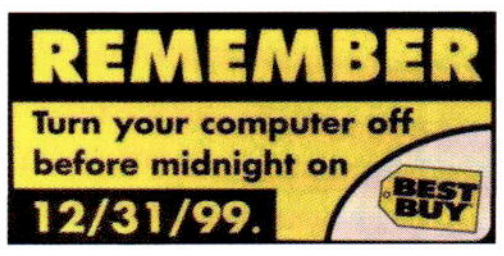

Fears about the so-called Y2K or Millennium Bug turn out to be almost completely unfounded

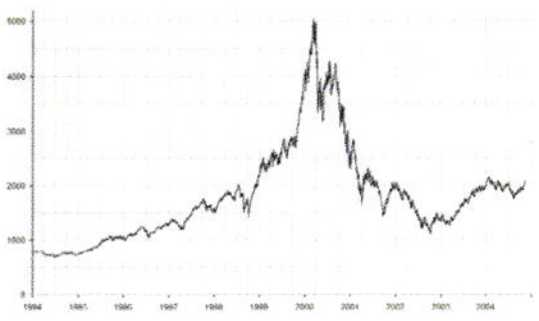

The dot-com bubble bursts

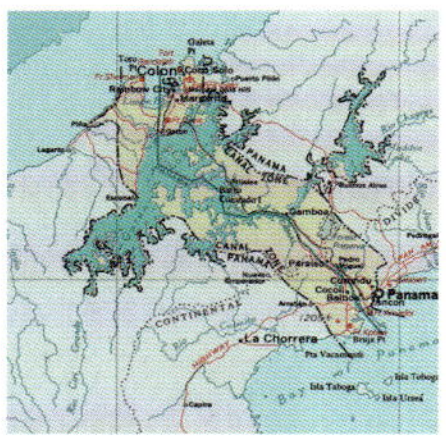

Control of the Panama Canal is handed over to Panama, on condition that its neutrality is guaranteed

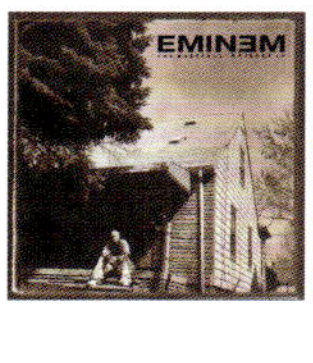

Eminem's *The Marshall Mathers LP* breaks all records for fastest-selling solo and hip hop albums

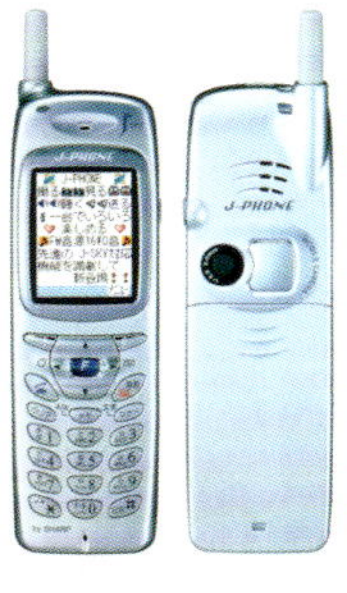

The first mobile phones with a built-in camera are introduced

2001

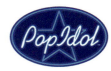

British TV show *Pop Idol* is first aired and the format quickly spreads worldwide

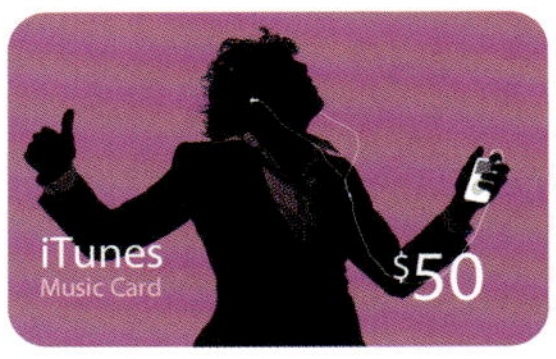

Apple launches the iPod and iTunes

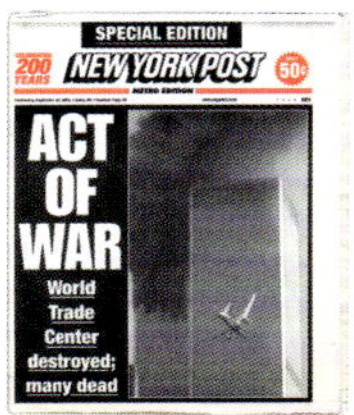
SPECIAL EDITION
NEW YORK POST
ACT OF WAR
World Trade Center destroyed; many dead

Aircraft hijacked by al Qaeda crash into the Pentagon and bring down the Twin Towers in New York

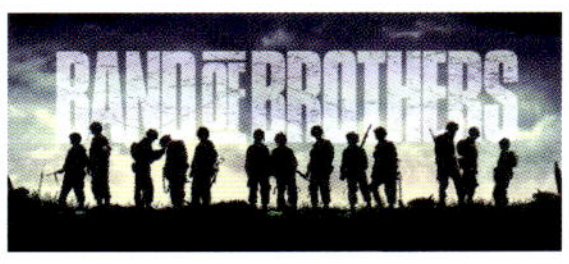

The TV series *Band of Brothers* premieres on HBO

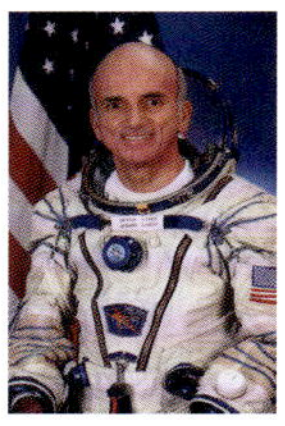

U.S. entrepreneur Dennis Tito is the first tourist to fund his own trip into space

Wikipedia
The Free Encyclopedia

Wikipedia goes online

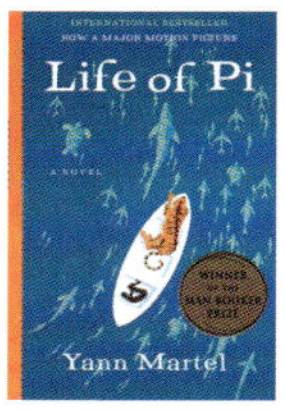

Yann Martel's novel *Life of Pi* becomes an international bestseller

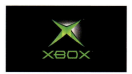

Microsoft's Xbox gaming console is released

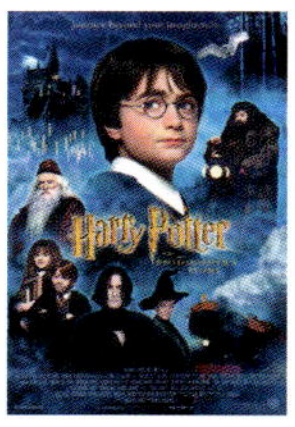

The first of the Harry Potter movies premieres

2002

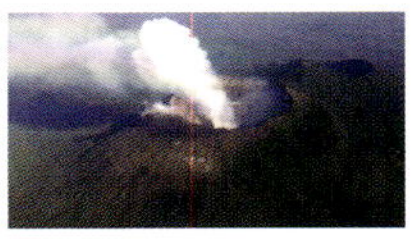

Called "the most dangerous volcano in the world", Nyiragongo erupts causing widespread destruction around Goma (DRC)

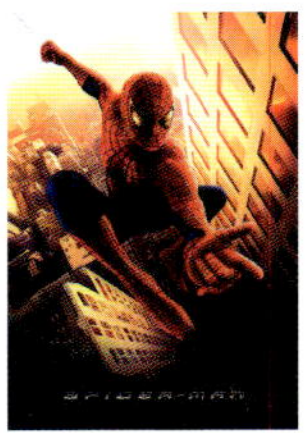

The hugely successful *Spider-Man* heralds a return for the superhero film genre

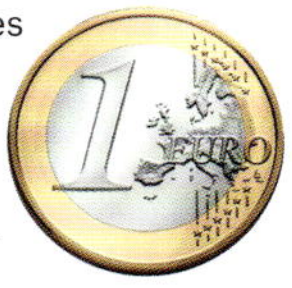

The Euro replaces old notes and coins in the Eurozone to become the only legal tender

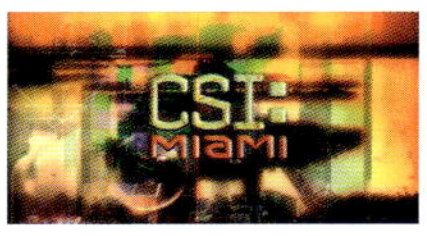

CSI Miami premieres, the first spin-off in the *CSI* crime TV shows

The International Criminal Court is established in The Hague in the Netherlands

Switzerland finally joins the United Nations

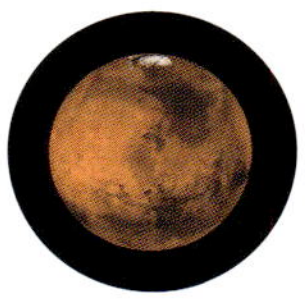

The 2001 *Mars Odyssey* orbiter finds large deposits of water ice beneath the planet's surface

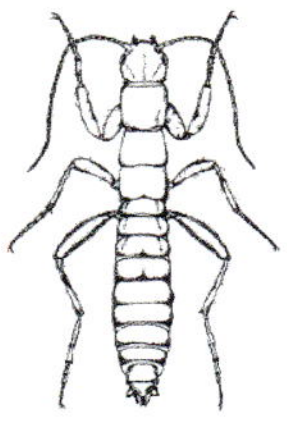

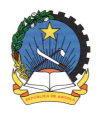

The discovery of *Mantophasmodea* is announced, the first new insect order since 1914

The Angolan Civil War comes to an end after 26 years of fighting that killed 500,000 people

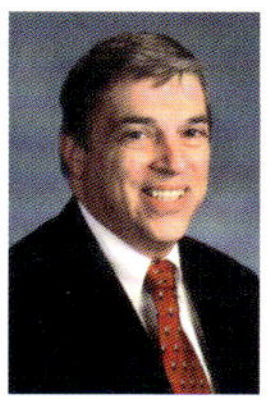

Former FBI agent Robert Hanssen is sentenced to life imprisonment for selling secrets to Soviet and Russian agents

2003

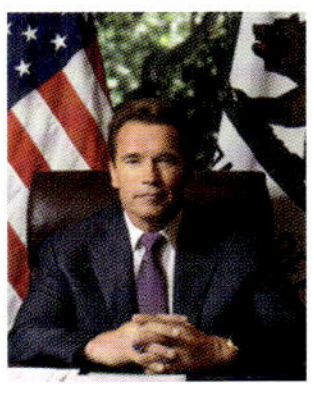

Action film star Arnold Schwarzenegger is elected governor of California

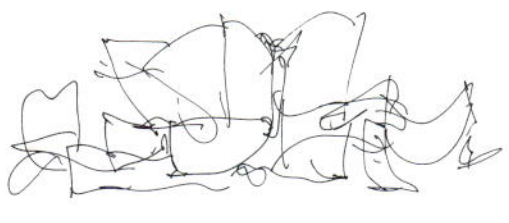

The Walt Disney Concert Hall opens in Los Angeles, designed by Frank Gehry

The electric vehicle manufacturer Tesla is founded in California

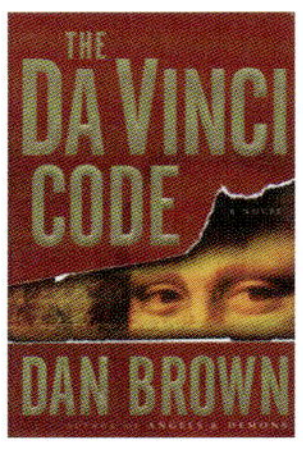

Dan Brown's *The Da Vinci Code* is published and becomes a bestseller despite many claims of factual inaccuracies

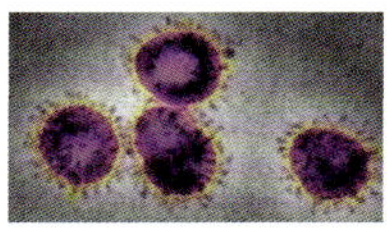

An outbreak of the respiratory disease SARS in southern China is contained but only after 774 people have died from it worldwide

The Iraq War begins when a U.S.-led coalition invades the country to overthrow Saddam Hussein

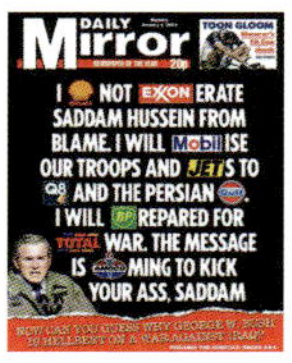
DAILY Mirror
TOON GLOOM
I NOT EXXON ERATE SADDAM HUSSEIN FROM BLAME. I WILL MOBIL ISE OUR TROOPS AND JETS TO Q8 AND THE PERSIAN GULF. I WILL BP REPARED FOR TOTAL WAR. THE MESSAGE IS COMING TO KICK YOUR ASS, SADDAM

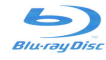

The Blu-ray disc is introduced

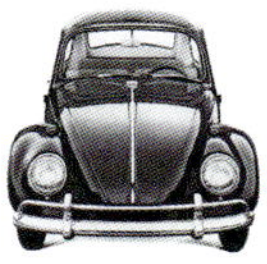

The last old-style Volkswagen Beetle rolls off the assembly line in Mexico

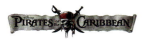

Johnny Depp stars in the first of the *Pirates of the Caribbean* movies

The musical *Wicked* premieres in San Francisco

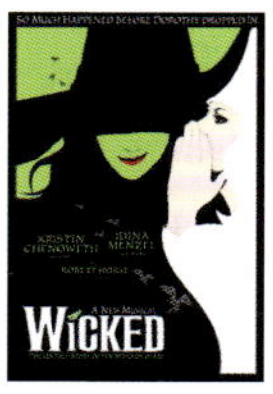

myspace
a place for friends

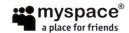

The social-networking website MySpace is founded

2004

The Summer Olympics are held in Athens

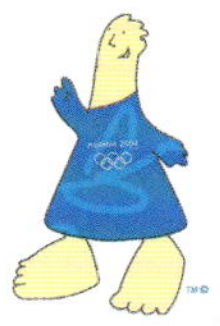

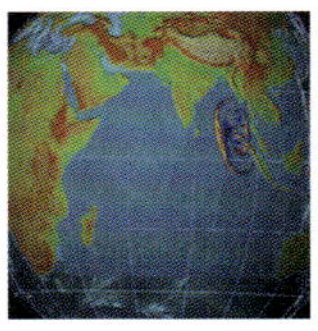

A tsunami in the Indian Ocean kills more than 230,000 people

facebook

Mark Zuckerberg launches Facebook from his dormitory room at Harvard University

Donald Trump hosts the first season of reality TV series *The Apprentice* in the United States

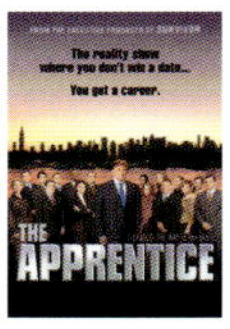

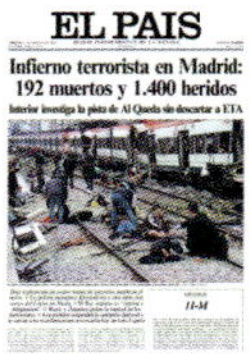
EL PAIS

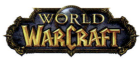

An Islamist terrorist attack in Madrid kills 192 and injures over 1,400 people, three days before general elections are held

World of Warcraft goes online

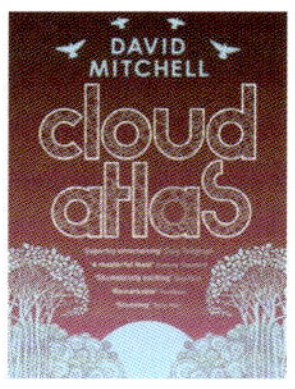

David Mitchell's award-winning *Cloud Atlas* is published

2M1207b is discovered, one of the first directly observed planets outside the Solar System

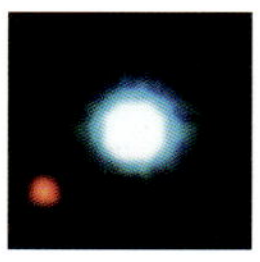

The hacker group Anonymous is formed when all its posts are signed with this name

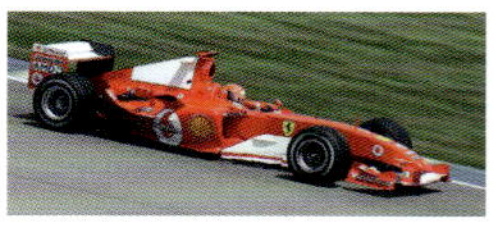

Michael Schumacher wins his seventh and final Formula One racing championship

The first episode of U.S. television series *Lost* is aired

2005

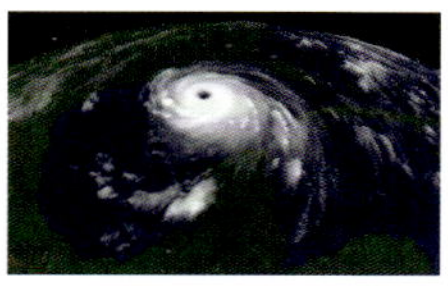

Hurricane Katrina and later flooding kill over 1,200 people and cause massive damage in New Orleans and along the Gulf coast

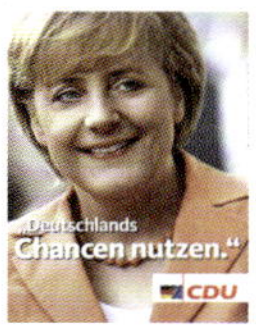

Angela Merkel is elected Chancellor of Germany, the first woman to occupy this post

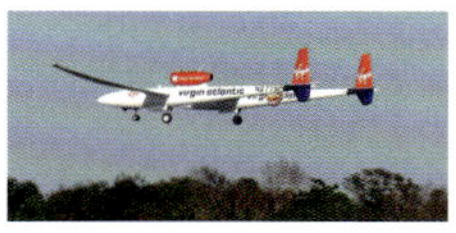

Steve Fossett completes the first non-stop, non-refueled, solo flight around the world

Rihanna's debut album *Music of the Sun* is released

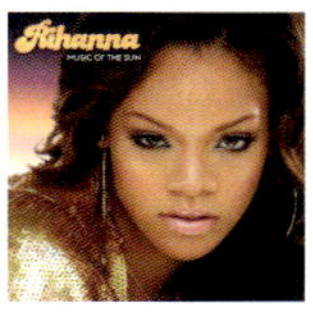

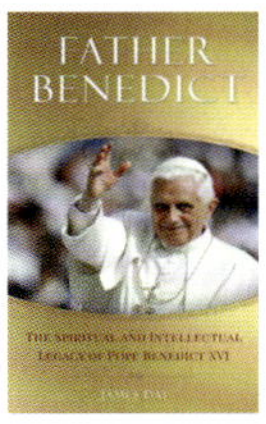

Following the death of Pope John Paul II, Cardinal Joseph Ratzinger becomes the 265th pope with the name Benedict XVI

The first book in Stephenie Meyer's *Twilight* series is published

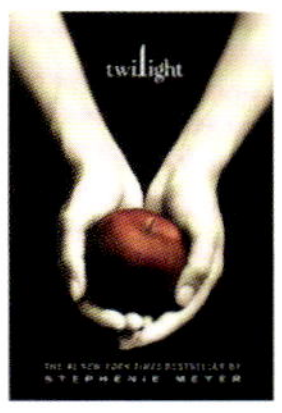

YouTube is launched

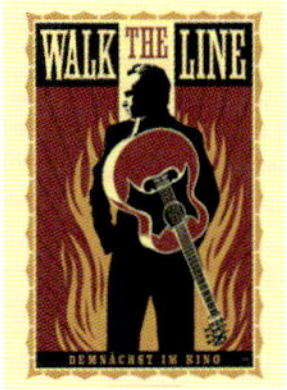

The Johnny Cash biopic *Walk the Line* premieres, starring Joaquin Phoenix

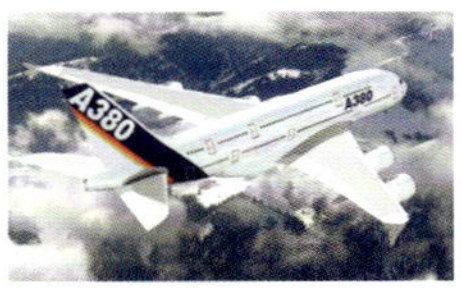

The Superjumbo jet airliner Airbus A380 makes its maiden flight from Toulouse

Elected president of Liberia, Ellen Johnson Sirleaf is the first woman to lead an African country

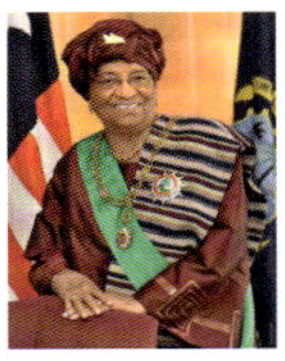

2006

Twitter is launched

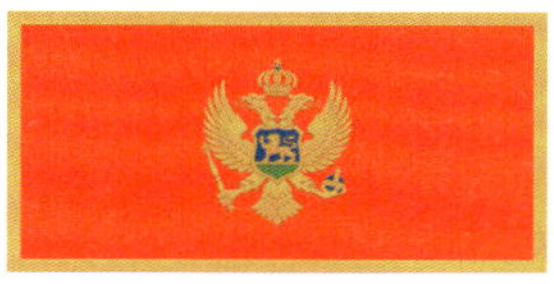

The state of Montenegro gains independence

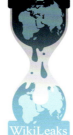

The WikiLeaks organization for publishing secret and classified information is founded in Iceland by Julian Assange

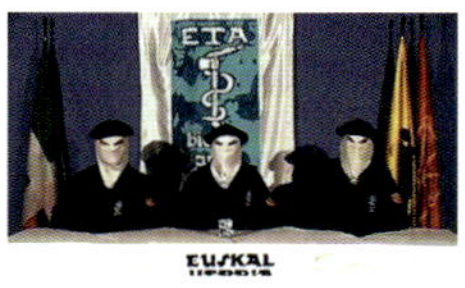

The Basque separatist group ETA announces a ceasefire

Nintendo's Wii gaming console is released

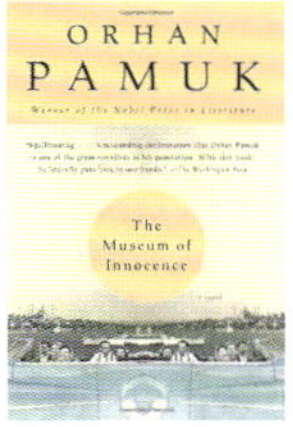

Turkish novelist Orhan Pamuk wins the Nobel Prize for Literature

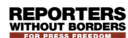

Reporters Without Borders publishes its fifth annual report on press freedom, listing 85 journalists killed worldwide this year

International music retailer Tower Records goes into liquidation

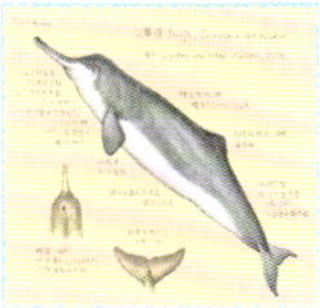

The Baiji or Chinese river dolphin is declared extinct

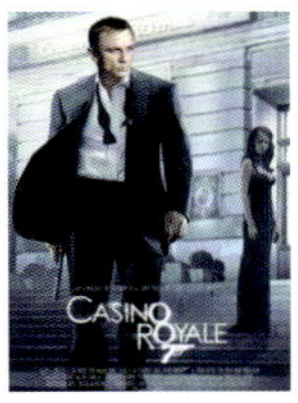

Daniel Craig is the new James Bond in *Casino Royale*

2007

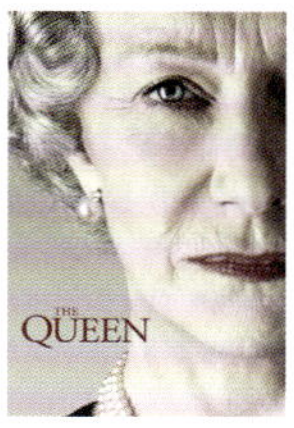

Helen Mirren wins an Oscar for her title role in *The Queen*

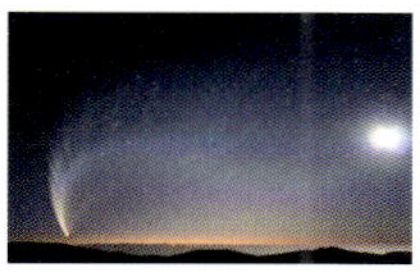

Comet McNaught, the brightest in more than 40 years, is visible by day worldwide

The first season of *Mad Men* is aired

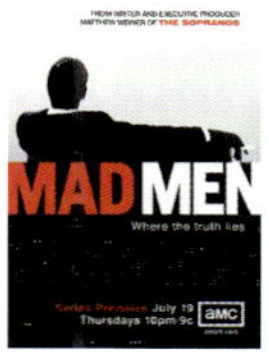

The new Wembley stadium in London opens

The Apple iPhone is released

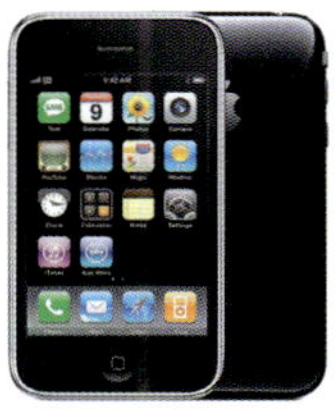

Smoking in enclosed public and work places is banned in the United Kingdom

American sitcom *The Big Bang Theory* premieres on CBS

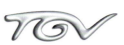

A high-speed TGV test train breaks the record in France for the fastest wheeled train

Nicolas Sarkozy is elected president of France

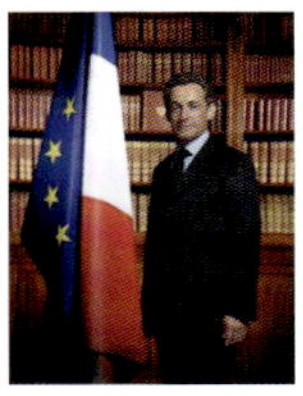

Live Earth benefit concerts are held in 12 locations around the world to highlight climate change

2008

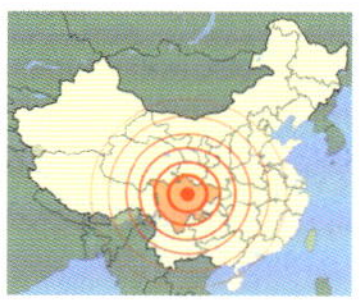

An earthquake in Sichuan, China, kills over 70,000 people

Lady Gaga's debut album *The Fame* is released

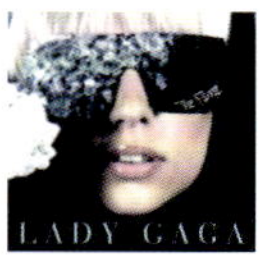

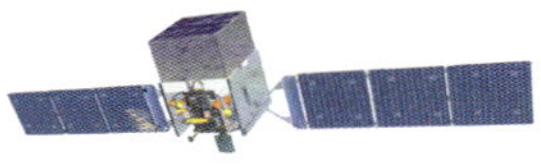

The Fermi Gamma-ray Space Telescope is launched

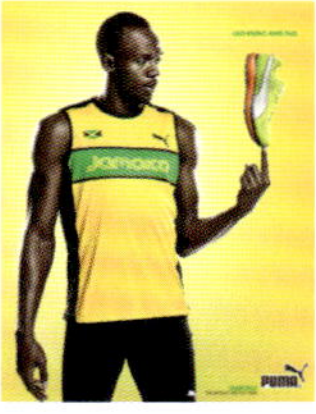

Jamaican Usain Bolt breaks the 100m world sprint record for the first time

The *Messenger* spacecraft sends back photographs of the unseen side of Mercury

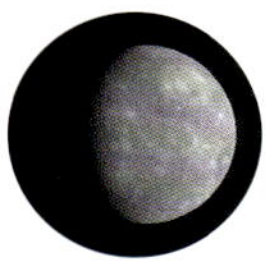

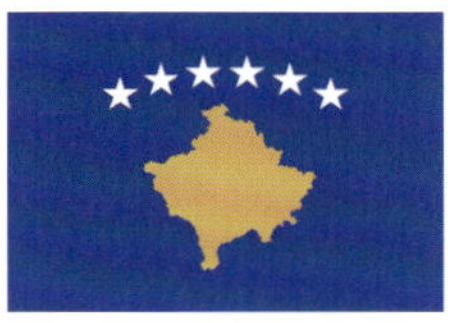

Kosovo becomes an independent nation

Fidel Castro steps down as president of Cuba after almost 50 years in power

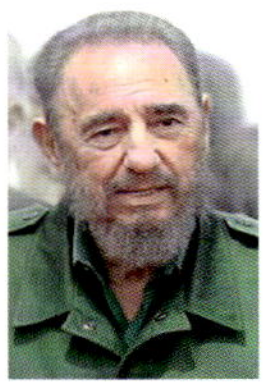

Apple's App Store opens and after three days downloads exceed 10 million

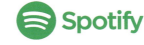

The Spotify music-streaming service is launched in Sweden

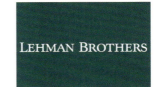

The U.S. investment bank Lehman Brothers goes bankrupt causing an international financial crisis

2009

The 3D movie *Avatar* becomes an international box-office smash

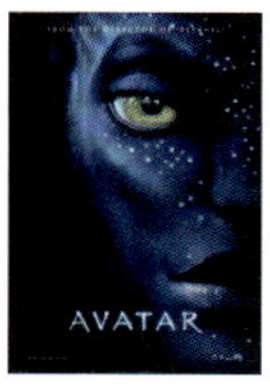

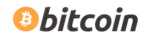

The virtual currency Bitcoin is created

Adele wins the Grammy for Best New Artist

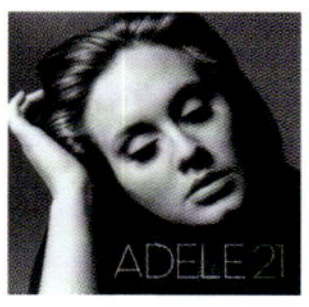

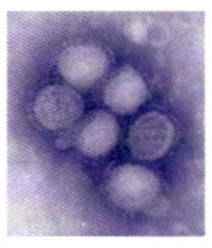

An outbreak of H1N1 swine flu kills some 300,000 people worldwide

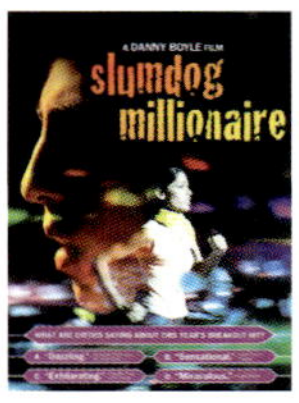

Filmed and set in India, Danny Boyle's film *Slumdog Millionaire* premieres

Michael Jackson dies

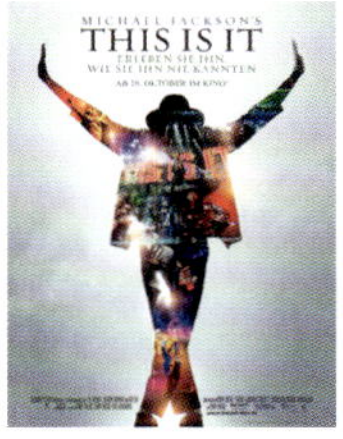

Barack Obama becomes the first African-American president of the United States

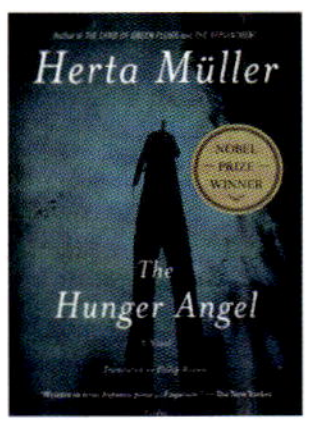

Romanian-German author Herta Müller wins the Nobel Prize for Literature

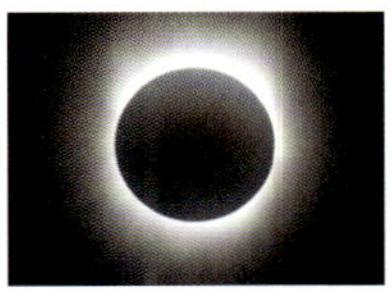

The longest total solar eclipse of the 21st century occurs over parts of Asia and the Pacific Ocean

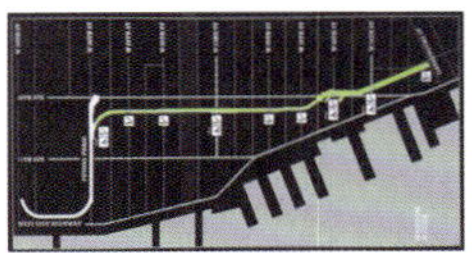

The first part of the High Line Park opens on the west side of Manhattan

2000

The visual culture magazine **Dot Dot Dot** is launched

Graphic designers Jan Wilker of Germany and Hjalti Karlsson of Iceland open the design firm **Karlssonwilker** in New York City

Steven Heller's monograph on Paul Rand is published

place
kobe design university ippanto, room 1225

special lecture
on typography on modern typography

speaker
helmut schmid typographer

date
2000 01 26 14:40

場所
神戸芸術工科大学
一般棟 1225教室

視覚情報デザイン特別講義C
タイポグラフィ について

講師
ヘルムート シュミット
タイポグラファー

日時
2000年**1**月**26**日（水）
14:40

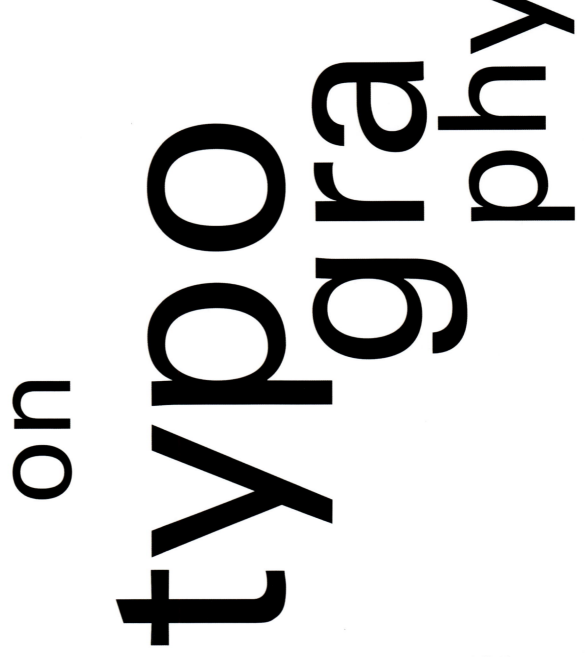

design by Helmut Schmid
typeface univers by Adrian Frutiger

2000 · FHA Image Design · AU · Logo · Sydney Olympic Games

2000 · Paula Scher, Pentagram · US · Logo · Whitney Museum of American Art

2000 · Helmut Schmid · DE/JP · Poster

2000 · Hiroshige Fukuhara · JP · Logo · Walkman

2000 · Germán Montalvo Aguilar · MX · Poster

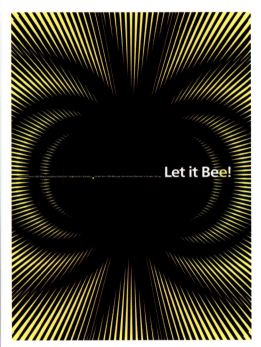

2000 · Yuri Surkov · RU · Poster

2000 · Anna Berkenbusch · DE · Poster

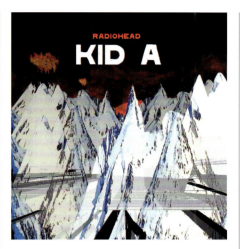

2000 · Stanley Donwood, Thom Yorke · UK · Record cover

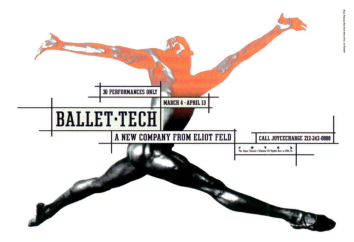

2000 · Paula Scher, Pentagram · US · Poster

2000 · NB Studio · UK · Poster

2000 · Michael Bierut, Pentagram · US · Poster

Michael Bierut (1957, Cleveland, Ohio) is a leading American designer who was vice-president of graphic design at Vignelli Associates before becoming a partner at Pentagram in 1990. Bierut has been a prolific educator and senior critic in design at Yale School of Art; the author of a number of books on design, his own works have been acquired by major institutions worldwide. Notable achievements have ranged from the redesign of *The Atlantic* magazine to the signage system for Lower Manhattan, while Bierut has also served as the president of AIGA, and was a founding member of the *Design Observer* blog.

Michael Bierut (1957, Cleveland, Ohio) ist ein führender amerikanischer Grafikdesigner, der als Vizepräsident bei Vignelli Associates tätig war, ehe er 1990 Partner bei Pentagram wurde. Bierut hat vielfach Lehrtätigkeiten ausgeübt und ist Senior Critic in Grafikdesign an der Yale School of Art. Zum Thema Design hat er zudem eine Reihe von Büchern verfasst; seine eigenen Arbeiten wurden von führenden Institutionen in aller Welt erworben. Zu seinen bedeutendsten Projekten gehören das Redesign der Zeitschrift *The Atlantic* ebenso wie das Beschilderungssystem in Lower Manhattan. Zudem ist Bierut Präsident des AIGA und ein Gründungsmitglied des Blogs *Design Observer*.

Michael Bierut (1957, Cleveland, Ohio) est un graphiste américain de premier plan qui a été vice-président du département de graphisme chez Vignelli Associates avant de s'associer à Pentagram en 1990. Bierut a été un enseignant prolifique et intervenant principal en design à la Yale School of Art. Auteur de nombreux livres sur le graphisme, ses propres œuvres ont été acquises par de grandes institutions du monde entier. Ses réalisations les plus remarquées vont de la refonte du magazine *The Atlantic* au système de signalisation dans Lower Manhattan. Bierut a aussi présidé l'AIGA et a été membre fondateur du blog *Design Observer*.

2007 · Michael Bierut, Pentagram, Marian Bantjes (TY) · US · Poster

2014 · Michael Bierut, Pentagram · US · Poster

The lecture series at the Yale School of Architecture have been notable for many reasons but their significance for graphic design dates back to 1998, when Michael Bierut started designing the posters. They quickly became collectible items in their own right for the detailed and inventive typographic work involved, and were all produced in black and white until 2015, after which another printed color was introduced for the backgrounds.

Die Vortragsreihen an der Yale School of Architecture sind aus vielen Gründen bemerkenswert, doch ihre Bedeutung für das Grafikdesign geht auf das Jahr 1998 zurück, als Michael Bierut erstmals die Plakate gestaltete. Wegen der detailreichen, fantasievollen Verwendung von Typografie wurden die Poster sehr bald zu Sammlerstücken. Bis Ende 2015 waren sie alle in Schwarz-Weiß gehalten, danach wurde eine weitere Druckfarbe für den Hintergrund eingeführt.

Si les cycles de conférences de la Yale School of Architecture ont été remarquables à bien des égards, leur importance dans le domaine du graphisme remonte à 1998, quand Michael Bierut commença à concevoir les affiches de l'école. Celles-ci devinrent rapidement des pièces de collection à part entière du fait de leur approche typographique détaillée et ingénieuse. Elles ont toutes été produites en noir et blanc jusqu'en 2015, après quoi une couleur fut adoptée pour l'arrière-plan.

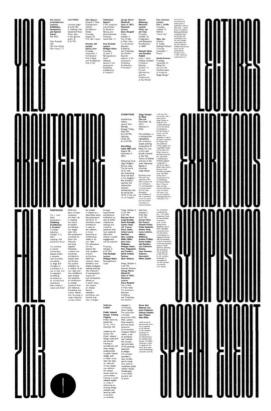

2013 · Michael Bierut, Pentagram · US · Poster

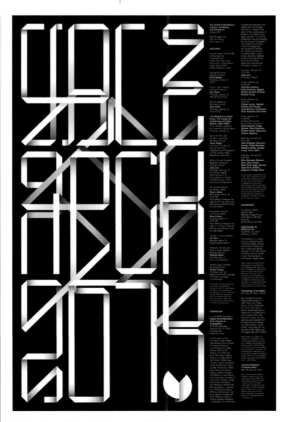

2014 · Michael Bierut, Pentagram · US · Poster

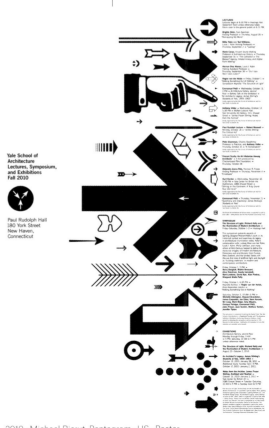

2010 · Michael Bierut, Pentagram · US · Poster

2001

The German **100 Best Posters** competition is extended to Austria and Switzerland

Peter Bilak starts the creation of the **Fedra** family of typefaces

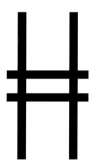

2001 · Paula Scher, Pentagram · US · Logo · The High Line, New York

2001 · Lambie-Nairn · UK · Logo · O2

2001 · Eden · NL · Logo · Furore

2001 · Milton Glaser · US · Poster

2001 · Michael Bierut, Pentagram · US · Identity · New York Jets

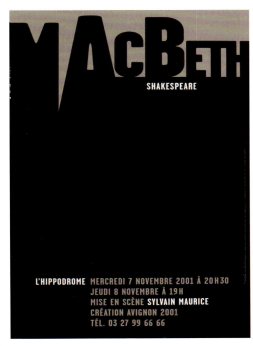

2001 · Catherine Zask · FR · Poster

2001 · Uwe Loesch · DE · Poster

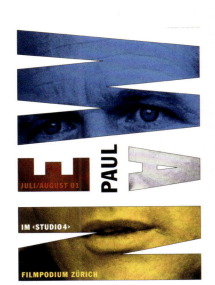

2001 · Ralph Schraivogel · CH · Poster

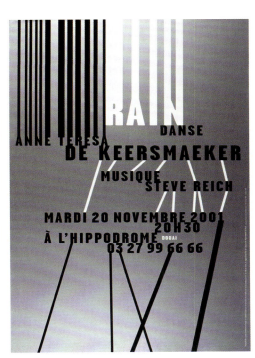

2001 · Catherine Zask · FR · Poster

2001 · Heine/Lenz/Zizka · DE · Packaging

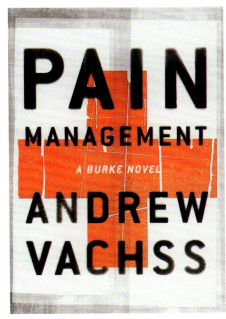

2001 · Evan Gaffney · US · Book cover

2001 · Andreas Uebele, Büro Uebele · DE · Poster

Environmental Graphics

As early as the 1970s, designers had begun to create the first examples of what became known as "supergraphics", whose typography and abstract graphics appeared on the broad faces of various public buildings. Whether intended simply as a way of catching the consumer's eye with logos that took up much more space, or as a more particular signposting system, by the turn of the 21st century this field of graphic design once again experienced a boom, which in turn generated a variety of outstanding results. The starting point for this special manifestation of the designer's art often alternates between aesthetic considerations and user-orientation.

Bereits in den 1970er-Jahren realisierten Gestalterinnen und Gestalter erstmals Arbeiten aus dem Bereich der sogenannten Supergraphics, bei dem öffentliche Gebäude zum Spielfeld von Typografie und abstrakter Grafik werden. Ob einfach nur als Blickfang, als räumliche Erweiterung des Brandings oder als Wegeleitsystem, erlebte dieses Feld in den 2000er-Jahren einen neuen Boom und brachte eine Vielzahl herausragender Lösungen hervor. Die Arbeiten dieser besonderen Ausprägung von Grafikdesign bewegen sich nicht selten zwischen ästhetischen und nutzungsorientierten Ansatzpunkten.

Dès les années 1970, des graphistes réalisaient les premiers travaux relevant de ce qui allait être baptisé «supergraphics», où les façades de bâtiments publics deviennent le terrain de jeu de la typographie et du graphisme abstrait. Simple accroche visuelle à l'aide de logos démesurés ou signalétiques plus ciblées, cette approche graphique connut dans les années 2000 un véritable essor et donna d'excellents résultats. Il n'est pas rare que ce type d'expression évolue aux confins de réflexions esthétiques et d'une volonté d'orientation.

2001 · Paula Scher, Pentagram · US · Environmental graphics

2011 · Andreas Uebele, Carolin Himmel, Büro Uebele · DE · Environmental graphics

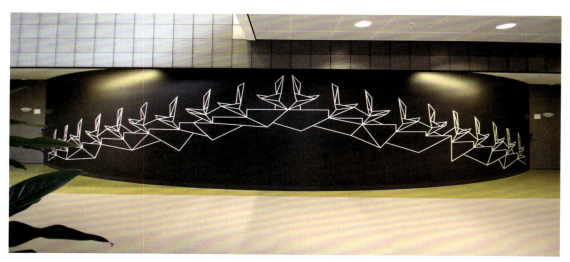

2016 · Lava · NL · Environmental graphics

> »Nowadays the term supergraphics is almost completely divorced from its origins in architectural theory; today, it means big graphics in an architectural setting, and is now more commonly referred to as environmental graphics.«
>
> Adrian Shaughnessy, *Supergraphics*, 2010

2004 · Andreas Uebele, Gerd Häußler, Büro Uebele · DE · Environmental graphics

2000s · Paula Scher, Pentagram · US · Environmental graphics

2007 · April Greiman · US · Environmental graphics

2009 · Mevis & Van Deursen · NL · Environmental graphics

1995 · April Greiman · US/JP · Environmental graphics

R2 (1995, Porto) is the design studio of Lizá Defossez Ramalho (1971, Troyes, France) and Artur Rebelo (1971, Porto). Both attended the Faculty of Fine Arts at the University of Porto and completed Master's degrees in Design Research in Barcelona. Members of the AGI since 2007, Ramalho and Rebelo have worked on identity, editorial, posters, and other projects, often also making excursions into the art world. R2's exploratory practice is well regarded for combining in-depth research and analysis with a highly conceptual approach to each subject. *Esquire* magazine and the Calouste Gulbenkian Foundation are among their clients.

R2 (1995, Porto) ist das Design-büro von Lizá Defossez Ramalho (1971, Troyes, Frankreich) und Artur Rebelo (1971, Porto). Beide besuchten die Fakultät der Schönen Künste der Universität Porto, darauf folgte in Barcelona ein Design-Research-Studium mit dem Abschluss Magister. Die beiden Grafikdesigner, seit 2007 Mitglieder des AGI, arbeiten an CI-Projekten ebenso wie im Bereich Editorial Design und Plakat-gestaltung, machen aber auch immer wieder Abstecher in die Kunst. Bekannt sind Ramalho und Rebelo wegen der gründlichen Recherchen und Analysen, die jedem ihrer Projekte vorausgehen, ergänzt von einer stark konzep-tuell ausgerichteten Sicht auf das jeweilige Thema. Zu ihren Auf-traggebern gehören das Magazin *Esquire* und die Stiftung Calouste Gulbenkian.

R2 (1995, Porto) est le studio de graphisme de Lizá Defossez Ramalho (1971, Troyes) et Artur Rebelo (1971, Porto). Ramalho et Rebelo ont fait leurs études à la faculté des beaux-arts de l'univer-sité de Porto et décroché un mas-ter de recherche en design à Bar-celone. Membres de l'AGI depuis 2007, ils ont notamment travaillé dans les domaines de l'identité, de l'édition et de l'affiche, avec des incursions fréquentes dans le monde de l'art. La pratique explo-ratoire de R2 est très appréciée pour son mélange de recherche et d'analyse approfondies, doublé d'une approche très conceptuelle de chaque sujet. Les clients du duo comptent notamment le magazine *Esquire* et la Fondation Calouste Gulbenkian.

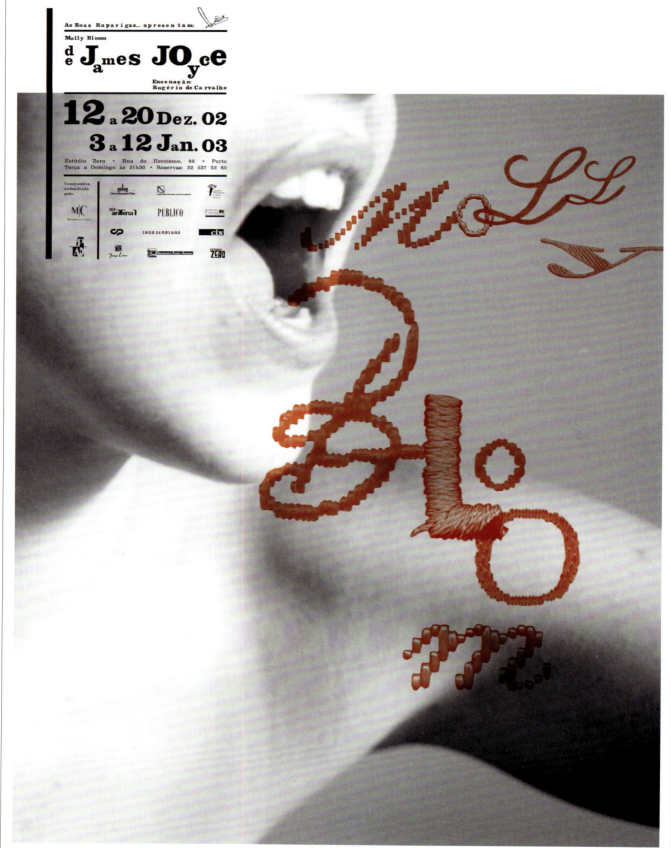

2002 · R2 · PT · Poster

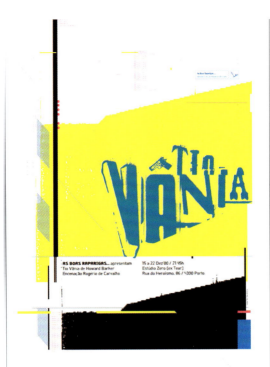

2000 · R2 · PT · Poster

2006 · R2 · PT · Poster

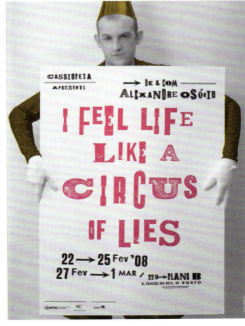

2008 · R2 · PT · Poster

2005 · R2 · PT · Poster

2009 · R2 · PT · Poster

2014 · R2 · PT · Poster

2016 · R2 · PT · Poster

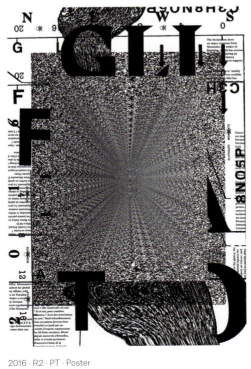

2016 · R2 · PT · Poster

2002

Christian Schwartz's **Neutraface** typeface is released, which has become one of the most popular fonts of the 2010s

Lars Müller's book **Helvetica: Homage to a Typeface** is published

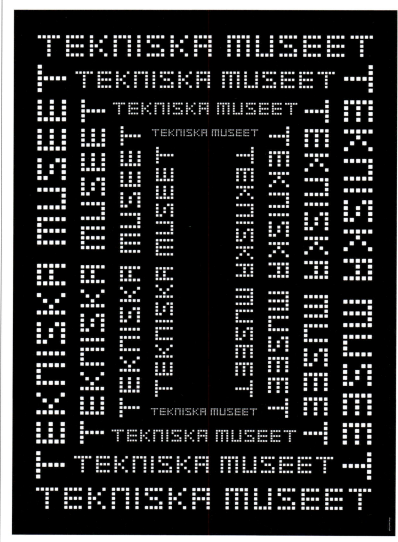

2002 · Gabor Palotai · SE · Poster/Identity

2002 · Angus Hyland, Pentagram · UK · Logo · EAT

2002 · Interbrand · UK · Logo · British Library

2002 · Graphic Thought Facility · UK · Logo · Habitat

2002 · Ostengruppe · RU · Poster

2002 · Ott+Stein · DE · Poster

2002 · Fritz Gottschalk · CH · Poster

2002 · Jonathan Gray · US · Book cover

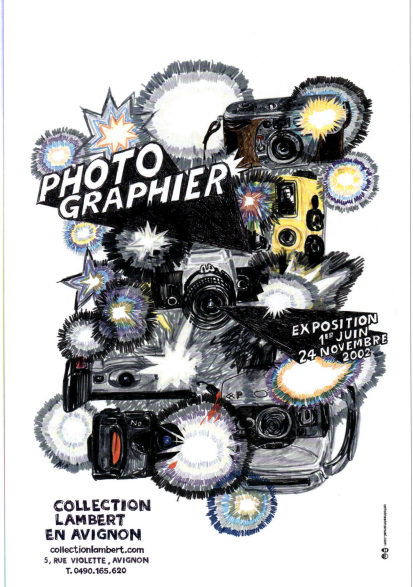

2002 · Antoine+Manuel · FR · Poster

2002 · Karlssonwilker · US · Record cover

2002 · Anette Lenz · FR · Posters

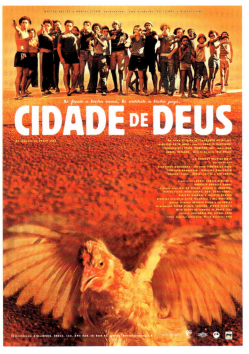

2002 · Marcelo Pallotta · BR · Poster

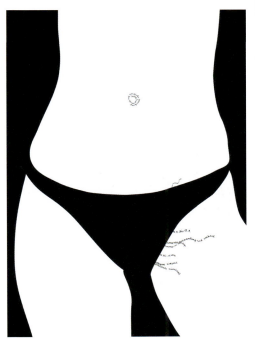

2002 · Fons Hickmann · DE · Poster

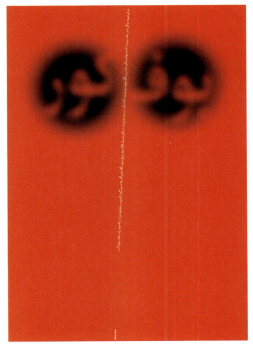

2002 · Majid Abbasi · IR · Poster

367

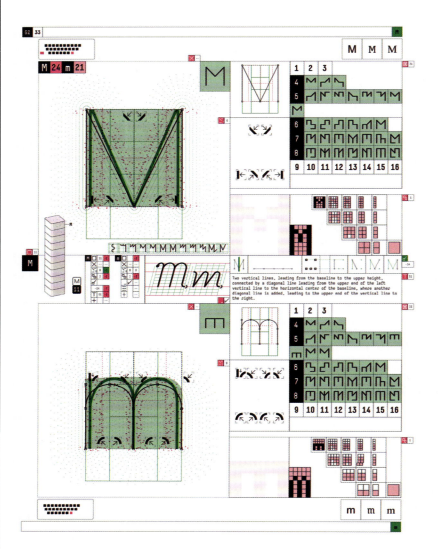

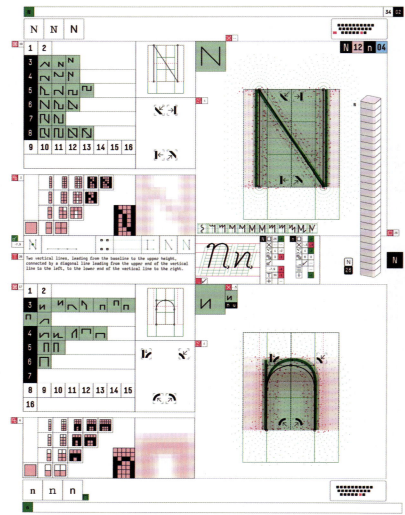

2002 · Norm · CH · Book spread

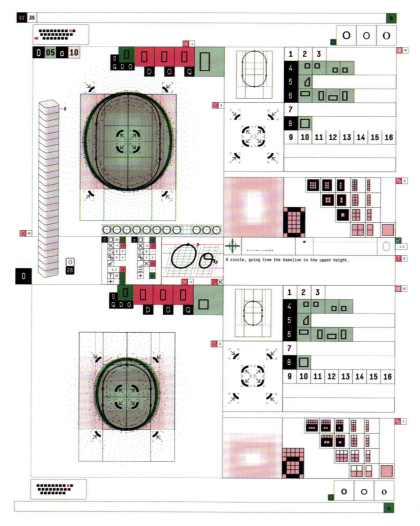

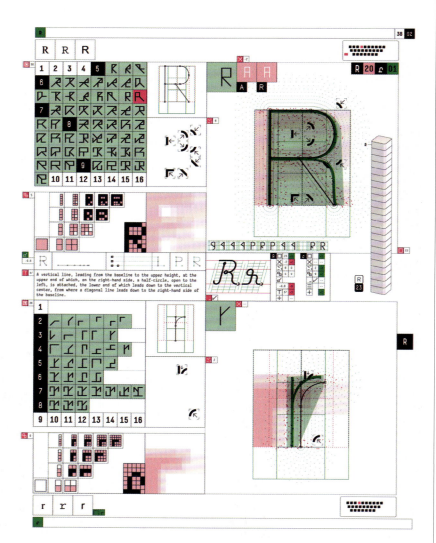

2002 · Norm · CH · Book spread

Norm (1999, Zurich) is the Swiss design studio of Dimitri Bruni (1970, Biel) and Manuel Krebs (1970, Bern), recognized for pushing the boundaries of typography in their work on corporate identity, posters, and editorial. The duo met at the design school in Biel in the 1990s, and have since cultivated a meticulous and critical approach to typeface design, employing grids and patterns to ensure both legibility and usability. Notable projects include developing the typography for Cologne Airport and Omega watches.

Norm (1999, Zürich) ist das Schweizer Grafikdesignbüro von Dimitri Bruni (1970, Biel) und Manuel Krebs (1970, Bern), deren Markenzeichen es ist, mit ihren Entwürfen – sei es im Bereich Corporate Identity, Plakat oder Print – ständig die Grenzen der Typografie zu sprengen. Die beiden Grafikdesigner lernten sich in den 1990er-Jahren an der Schule für Gestaltung in Biel kennen und haben seitdem einen präzisen und kritischen Ansatz in der Gestaltung von Schriften entwickelt. Raster und Muster sorgen dafür, dass die Schriften dabei sowohl lesbar als auch praktikabel bleiben. Zu ihren bedeutendsten Projekten bislang gehören die Schrift für den Flughafen Köln und für Omega-Uhren.

Norm (1999, Zurich) est le studio de design suisse de Dimitri Bruni (1970, Bienne) et Manuel Krebs (1970, Berne), célèbre pour avoir repoussé les limites de la typographie dans les domaines de l'identité d'entreprise, de l'affiche et du graphisme éditorial. Le duo s'est connu à l'École d'arts visuels de Bienne dans les années 1990 et cultive depuis une approche rigoureuse et critique de la conception de caractères, utilisant des grilles et des modèles pour concilier lisibilité et utilité. Leurs projets notoires comptent le développement de polices de caractères pour l'aéroport de Cologne et les montres Omega.

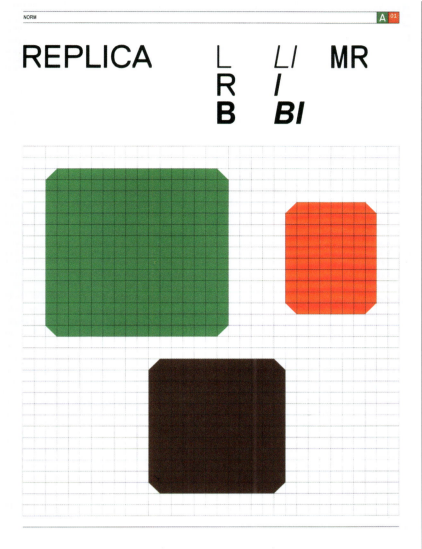

2008 · Norm · CH · Brochure cover

2010 · Norm · CH · Poster

2014 · Norm · CH · Poster

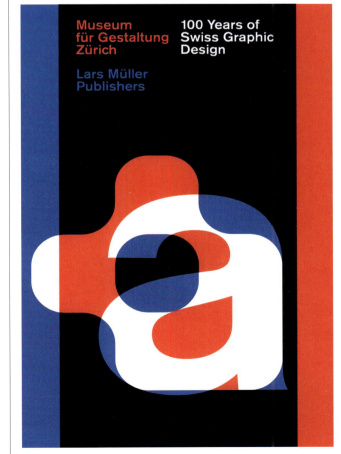

2012 · Norm · CH · Book cover

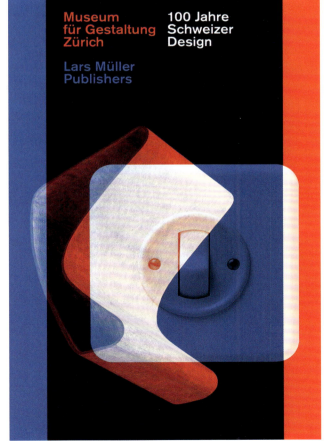

2012 · Norm · CH · Book cover

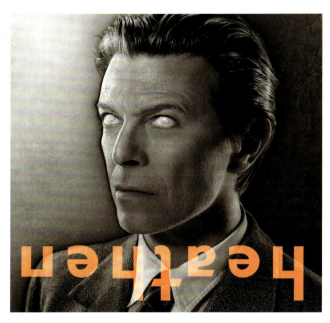

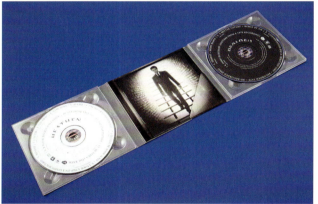

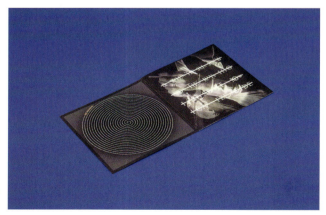

2002 · Jonathan Barnbrook · UK · Record cover and inside

2003 · Jonathan Barnbrook · UK · Record cover and inside

Jonathan Barnbrook (1966, Luton, England) is a British designer and typographer. After attending Central Saint Martins and the Royal College of Art in London, Barnbrook went on to develop several typefaces, collaborating with such artists as Damien Hirst and David Bowie. His work has always been associated with an anti-corporate critique, notably expressed in his 1999 billboard, "Designers, stay away from corporations that want you to lie for them" (a quote from Tibor Kalman), first displayed in Las Vegas in conjunction with a meeting there of the AIGA. Barnbrook's typographical oeuvre includes fonts such as Bastard, Exocet, and Mason (originally Manson).

Jonathan Barnbrook (1966, Luton, England) ist ein britischer Grafikdesigner und Typograf. Er besuchte das Central Saint Martins College of Art and Design und das Royal College of Art in London und entwickelte in der Folge nicht nur mehrere Schrifttypen, sondern arbeitete auch mit Künstlern wie Damien Hirst und David Bowie. In seinem Werk übt er Kritik am Konzerndenken, was insbesondere 1999 in seiner Plakatwand „Designers, stay away from corporations that want you to lie for them" (etwa „Designer, lasst euch nicht mit Konzernen ein, die von euch erwarten, für sie zu lügen", ein Zitat Tibor Kalmans) deutlichen Ausdruck fand. Das erste Mal war das Plakat im Rahmen einer Konferenz des AIGA in Las Vegas zu sehen. Barnbrook gestaltete u. a. die Schrifttypen Bastard, Exocet und Mason (ursprünglich Manson).

Jonathan Barnbrook (1966, Luton, Angleterre) est un designer et typographe britannique. Après des études au Central Saint Martins College of Art and Design et au Royal College of Art à Londres, Barnbrook commence à concevoir différentes polices de caractères, collaborant avec des artistes comme Damien Hirst et David Bowie. Son travail a toujours été lié à une critique anti-entreprises qu'il a notoirement exprimée dans le panneau d'affichage «Designers, restez à l'écart d'entreprises qui veulent que vous mentiez à leur place» (une citation de Tibor Kalman), révélé lors d'un colloque de l'AIGA à Las Vegas. L'œuvre typographique de Barnbrook compte des polices de caractères comme Bastard, Exocet et Mason (initialement Manson).

The collaboration between Barnbrook and David Bowie began in 2002 with the latter's album *Heathen*. In the years that followed, their working relationship produced a whole series of fascinating sleeve designs in an assortment of styles. The powerful visual impact of Bowie's final album *Blackstar*, released in 2016, attracted a lot of attention in both music and design circles and it went on to receive the 2017 Grammy Award for Best Recording Package.

Mit dem Album *Heathen* begann 2002 die Zusammenarbeit von David Bowie und Barnbrook. Die enge Kollaboration der beiden Kreativen brachte in den folgenden Jahren eine ganze Reihe faszinierender Coverentwürfe ganz unterschiedlichen Stils hervor. Das starke visuelle Konzept des 2016 veröffentlichten letzten Bowie-Albums *Blackstar* fand in der Musik- und Designszene besondere Beachtung und wurde 2017 mit einem Grammy in der Kategorie „Best Recording Package" ausgezeichnet.

La première coopération entre David Bowie et Barnbrook remonte à 2002 avec l'album *Heathen*. Au cours des années suivantes, cette collaboration a produit toute une série de pochettes attirantes présentant des styles extrêmement différents. L'énorme impact visuel de *Blackstar*, le dernier album de Bowie, sorti en 2016 et très remarqué dans le monde musical comme graphique, a été récompensé en 2017 par un Grammy Award à la meilleure pochette d'album.

2013 · Jonathan Barnbrook · UK · Record cover

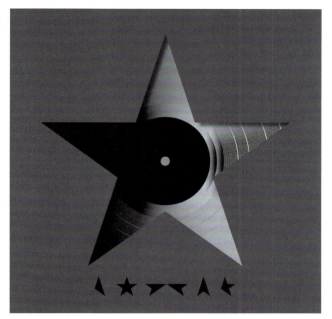

David Bowie. A: Valentine's Day. Valentine told me who's to go. Feelings he's treasured most of all. The teachers and the football star. It's in his tiny face. It's in his scrawny hand. Valentine told me so. He's got something to say. It's Valentine's Day. The rhythm of the crowd. Teddy and Judy down. Valentine sees it all. He's got something to say. It's Valentine's Day. Valentine told me how he'd feel. If all the world were under his heel. Or stumbling through the mall. It's in his tiny face. It's in his scrawny hand. Valentine knows it all. He's got something to say. It's Valentine's Day. It's in his scrawny hand. It's in his icy heart. It's happening today. Valentine valentine. B: Plan.

88883756667

2013 · Jonathan Barnbrook · UK · Record cover

2016 · Jonathan Barnbrook · UK · Record cover and inside

2016 · Jonathan Barnbrook · UK · Poster/Ad

2003

The first issue of Iranian design magazine **Neshan** is published

A group of prominent German designers initiate the **11 Designer** campaign in protest against the official FIFA logo for the 2006 Soccer World Cup in Germany

The widely acclaimed book **Tell Me Why** is published, on the first 24 months of New York-based graphic design studio Karlssonwilker

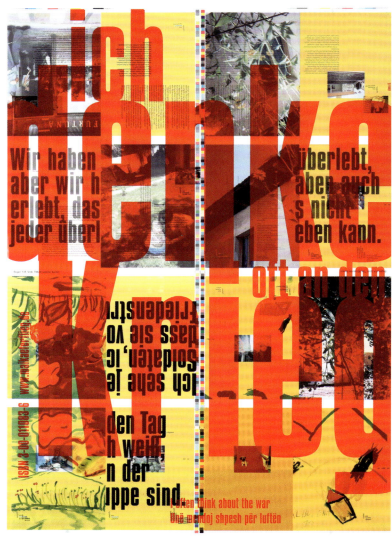

2003 · Anna Berkenbusch · DE · Poster

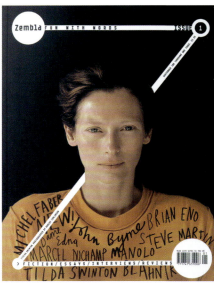

2003 · Frost* Design · AU · Magazine cover

2003 · TBWA · US · Poster

2003 · Skype design team · LU · Logo · Skype

2003 · FutureBrand · US · Logo · UPS

2003 · Suburbia · UK · Logo · Pop magazine

2003 · Goebel Weyne · BR · Poster

2003 · Ralph Schraivogel · CH · Poster

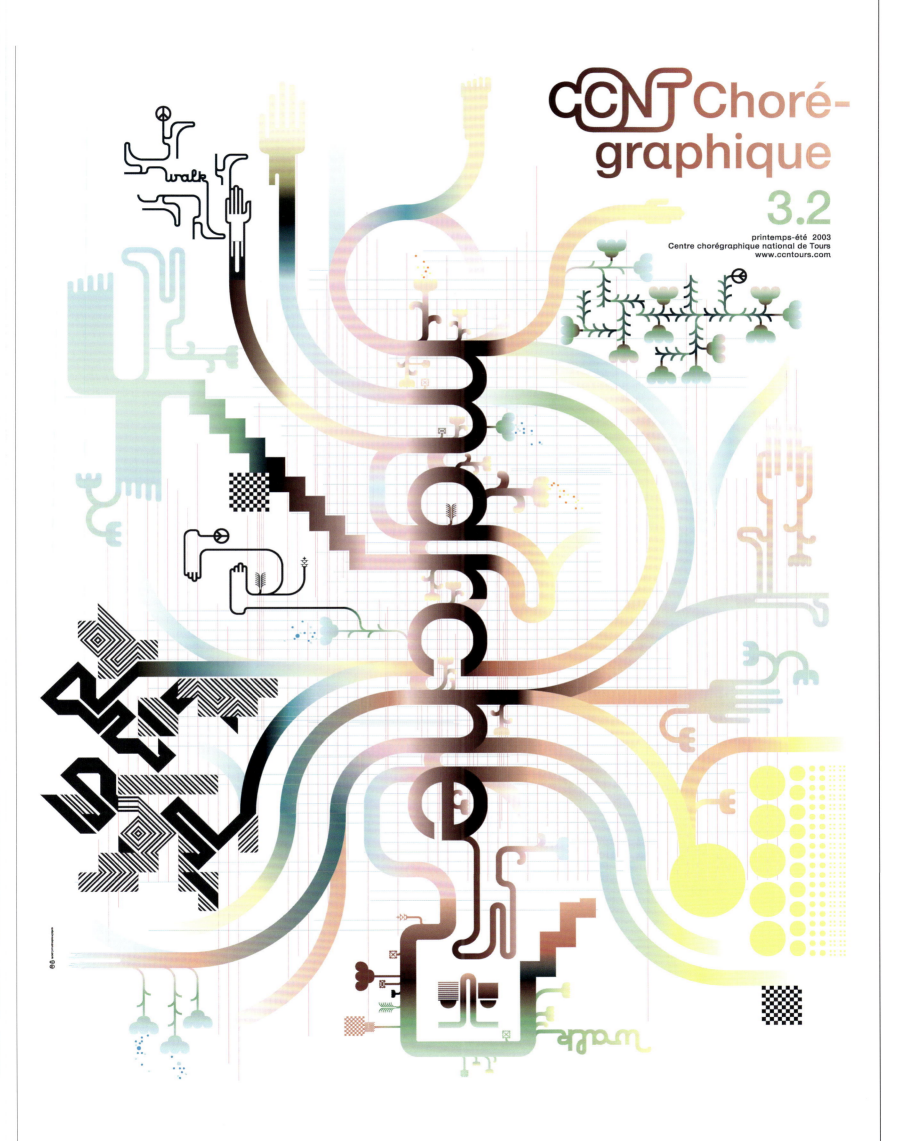

CCN Choré-
graphique

3.2

printemps-été 2003
Centre chorégraphique national de Tours
www.ccntours.com

2003 · Antoine+Manuel · FR · Poster

2004

Swiss designer Laurenz Brunner creates the **Akkurat** typeface

Ellen Lupton's book **Thinking with Type** is published

The type foundry **Commercial Type** is established by Paul Barnes and Christian Schwartz in New York and London

The first issue of Swiss graphic design magazine **Idpure** is published

47% OF PEOPLE BELIEVE THE IDEA OF WEATHER IN OUR SOCIETY IS BASED ON CULTURE

53% BELIEVE IT IS BASED ON NATURE

The Unilever Series:
OLAFUR ELIASSON

16 October 2003 – 21 March 2004
Free Admission
Open Daily 10.00 – 18.00
Late nights Friday and Saturday until 22.00
Visit www.tate.org.uk
Southwark/Blackfriars
The Unilever Series,
an annual art commission sponsored by

MODERN
TATE

2004 · James Goggin · UK · Poster

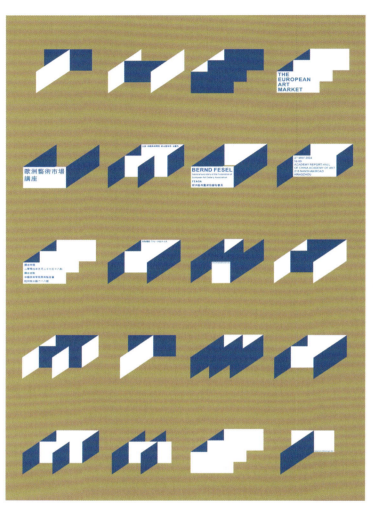

2004 · Chen Zhengda · CN · Poster

2004 · Chermayeff & Geismar · US · Logo · Opet

NEW YORK

2004 · Luke Hayman, Pentagram · US · Logo · New York magazine

Shelter

2004 · Michael Johnson · UK · Logo · Shelter

2004 · Kosuke Niwano, Shinmura Design Office · JP · Poster

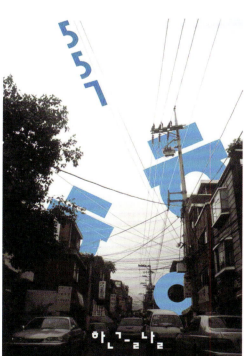

2004 · Ahn Sang-Soo · KR · Poster

2004 · Jürg Lehni · CH · Magazine cover

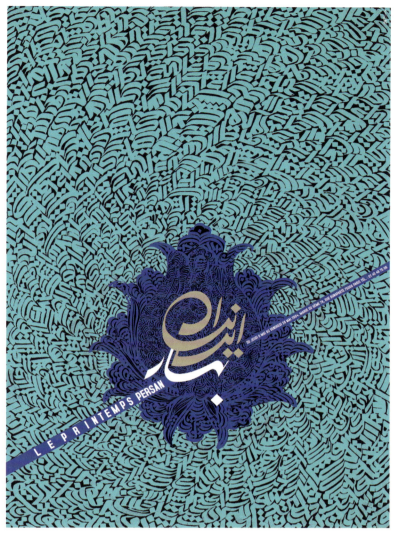

2004 · Mehdi Saeedi · IR · Poster

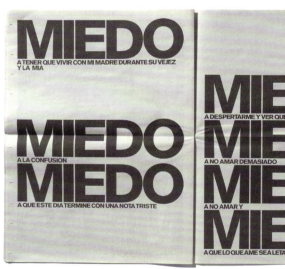

2004 · Atlas · ES · Brochure spreads

2004 · 2x4 · US · Identity · Brooklyn Museum

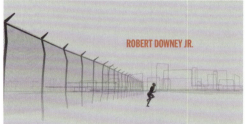

2004 · Danny Yount, Prologue Films · US · Opening titles

Wild Typography

Throughout the history of design there have always been phases in which attempts were made to break or bend the centuries-old basic rules of typography. Such experiments took place in the 1920s with the New Typography movement and in the 1990s, with the dawn of the computer age. Then, around 2000, the fresh possibilities offered by digital image manipulation, and by the ability to create completely computer-generated images with 3D-software, heralded another completely new era in offbeat typographic designs. Alongside obviously computer-generated solutions, many projects deliberately deployed an analog aesthetic, and several designers discovered exciting associations between type and nature. Among these was Stefan Sagmeister, who caused a major stir with the experimental typo-installations in his highly regarded book, *Things I Have Learned In My Life So Far*, published in 2008.

In der Designgeschichte gab es immer wieder einzelne Phasen, in denen das traditionelle und seit Jahrhunderten geprägte Regelwerk der Typografie zu überwinden oder zu erweitern versucht wurde – sei es durch die Bewegung der „Neuen Typografie" in den 1920er-Jahren oder durch die wilden Jahre der frühen Computerzeit in den 1990er-Jahren. Die neuen Möglichkeiten digitaler Bildmanipulation oder gar vollständig digitaler Bilderzeugung mit 3-D-Software läuteten um das Jahr 2000 noch einmal eine ganz neue Phase nonkonformistischer Gestaltung mittels Schriften an. Neben offensichtlich digital erzeugten Lösungen entstanden zahlreiche Arbeiten, die ganz bewusst analoge Ästhetik einsetzten. Viele Gestalter entdeckten die spannungsreiche Verbindung von Schrift und Natur, so auch Stefan Sagmeister, der die Designszene mit seinen experimentellen Typo-Installationen in dem viel beachteten Buch *Things I Have Learned In My Life So Far* von 2008 begeisterte.

L'histoire du graphisme a régulièrement été ponctuée de tentatives pour enfreindre ou contourner un corpus de règles typographiques marqué par une tradition séculaire. Ce fut notamment le cas au début des années 1920 avec le mouvement «La Nouvelle Typographie» et avec la folie des débuts de l'ère informatique dans les années 1990. Vers 2000, les nouvelles possibilités offertes par la manipulation d'images et les images entièrement générées à l'aide de logiciels de 3D ont proclamé une phase inédite de création typographique non conformiste. À côté de solutions entièrement numériques, de nombreux travaux faisaient délibérément appel à une esthétique analogique. Beaucoup de graphistes ont découvert la relation fascinante entre caractères et nature, comme Stefan Sagmeister, qui enthousiasma la scène du graphisme avec les installations typographiques expérimentales de son livre très remarqué *Things I Have Learned In My Life So Far*, paru en 2008.

2004 · Stefan Sagmeister · AT/US · Poster

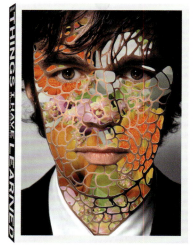

2006 · Stefan Sagmeister · AT/US · Book cover and spread

2006 · Stephen Doyle, Doyle Partners · US · Poster

2009 · Mirko Ilić · BA · Poster

2007 · Grandpeople · NO · Poster

2003 · Oded Ezer, Shaxaf Haber (PH) · IL · Poster

2008 · Stephen Doyle, Doyle Partners · US · Poster

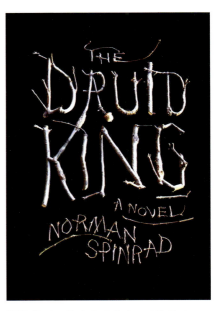

2006 · Stephen Doyle, Doyle Partners · US · Book cover

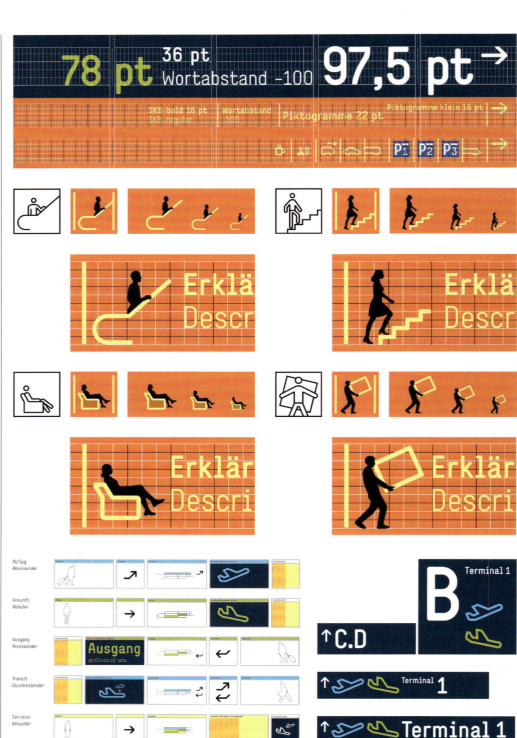

2004 · Intégral Ruedi Baur · CH/DE · Identity, Signage · Cologne Bonn Airport

Ruedi Baur (1956, Paris) is a Franco-Swiss designer and author best known for his work in identity and wayfinding systems. Baur's seven-concept approach—antici-pate, question, inscribe, perplex, orient, translate, and differen-tiate—has become his framework for numerous collaborations with architects, cultural institutions, and exhibition planners, among other outlets. After studying at the School of Art and Design in Zurich, under Michael Baviera, he spent six years transforming the fortunes of Atelier BBV in Milan, Lyon, and Zurich, before establishing the multi-partner practice Intégral in 1989.

Ruedi Baur (1956, Paris) ist ein Frankoschweizer Grafikdesigner und Autor, der insbesondere durch seine Arbeiten im Bereich CI sowie für Leit- und Orientierungssysteme bekannt ist. Baurs siebenstufiges Arbeitskonzept – antizipieren, hin-terfragen, einschreiben, irritieren, orientieren, übersetzen und unter-scheiden – wurde für ihn zum Grundgerüst zahlreicher Gemein-schaftsprojekte mit Architekten, Kulturinstitutionen, Ausstellungs-planern und Vertretern anderer Disziplinen. Nach dem Studium an der Hochschule für Kunst und Gestaltung in Zürich bei Michael Baviera gründete er im Dreieck Mailand, Lyon und Zürich das Atelier BBV, ehe er 1989 die inter-disziplinäre Agentur Intégral ins Leben rief.

Ruedi Baur (1956, Paris) est un graphiste et auteur franco-suisse connu surtout pour son travail sur l'identité et les systèmes de signalisation. L'approche de Baur, qui se décline en sept concepts – anticiper, questionner, inscrire, surprendre, orienter, traduire et différencier – a servi de grille de travail pour ses nombreuses colla-borations avec des architectes, institutions culturelles et organisa-teurs d'expositions, parmi d'autres branches professionnelles. Après des études à la Haute École d'art de Zurich auprès de Michael Baviera, Baur a passé six ans à la barre des ateliers BBV à Milan, Lyon et Zurich, avant d'ouvrir le studio coopératif Intégral en 1989 avec d'autres associés.

2014 · Intégral Ruedi Baur · CH/DE · Identity, Signage · New School, New York

2005

Adrian Shaughnessy's influential book **How to be a Graphic Designer, without Losing Your Soul** is published

The first issue of **Slanted** design magazine is published

2005 · Lava · NL · Poster

2005 · Reza Abedini · IR · Poster

2005 · Spin · UK · Logo · More4

2005 · Chad Hurley · US · Logo · YouTube

2005 · Joe Kral, Cuban Council, Test Pilot Collective · US · Logo · Facebook

2005 · Masayoshi Kodaira, Flame Design · JP · Poster

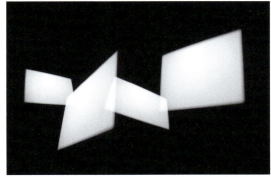

2005 · Intégral Ruedi Baur · FR · Identity · La Cinémathèque Française

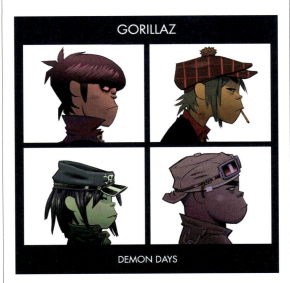

2005 · Jamie Hewlett · UK · Record cover

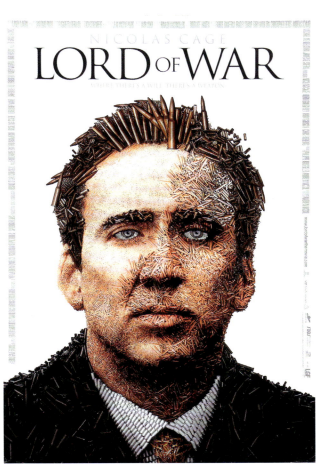

2005 · Art Machine · US · Poster

2005 · Radovan Jenko · SI · Poster

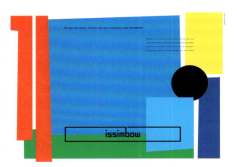

2005 · Shin Matsunaga · JP · Packaging

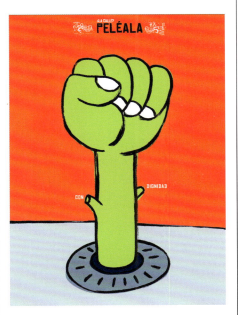

2005 · Frank Arbelo · CU/BO · Poster

2005 · Sascha Lobe, Ina Bauer · DE · Book series

381

de theater
compagnie
gilgamesj

de dood is blind

De Theatercompagnie
25 januari 2005
t/m 26 maart 2005

Regie: Theu Boermans
Tekst: Raoul Schrott
Vertaling: Tom Kleijn

Het Compagnietheater
Kloveniersburgwal 50
Amsterdam

reserveren 020 5205320
www.theatercompagnie.nl
info@theatercompagnie.nl

Spelers:
Anneke Blok
Theu Boermans
Stefaan Degand
Bracha van Doesburgh
Casper Gimbrère
Fedja van Huët

Myranda Jongeling
Jeroen van
Koningsbrugge
Hans Leendertse
Harry van Rijthoven
Lineke Rijsman

2005 · Experimental Jetset · NL · Poster

de theater
compagnie
gilgamesj

net zo blind als wij

De Theatercompagnie
25 januari t/m 26 maart 2005

Regie: Theu Boermans
Tekst: Raoul Schrott
Vertaling: Tom Kleijn

Het Compagnietheater
Kloveniersburgwal 50
Amsterdam

reserveren 020 5205320
www.theatercompagnie.nl
info@theatercompagnie.nl

Spelers:
Anneke Blok
Theu Boermans
Stefaan Degand
Bracha van Doesburgh
Casper Gimbrère
Fedja van Huët
Myranda Jongeling
Jeroen van Koningsbrugge
Hans Leendertse
Ruben Lürsen
Harry van Rijthoven
Lineke Rijsman

2005 · Experimental Jetset · NL · Poster

75 Helvetica Bold   65 Helvetica Medium   55 Helvetica Roman   45 Helvetica Light

The ABC DEFGHI JKLMNO PQRSTU VWXYZ of Mate rialist Dia lectics.

The 1234 567890 abcdefhij klmnopq stuvwxyz of Mate rialist Dia lectics.

"I will here attempt to sketch the substance of the problem in a very concise form. The Aristotelian logic of the simple syllogism starts from the proposition that 'A' is equal to 'A'. This postulate is accepted as an axiom for a multitude of practical human actions and elementary generalisations. But in reality, 'A' is not equal to 'A'. This is easy to prove if we observe these two letters under a lens – they are quite different from each other. But, one can object, the question is not of the size or the form of the letters, since they are only symbols for equal quantities, for instance, a pound of sugar. The objection is beside the point; in reality a pound of sugar is never equal to a pound of sugar – a more delicate scale always discloses a difference. Again one can object: but a pound of sugar is equal to itself. Neither is this true – all bodies change uninterruptedly in size, weight, colour, etc. They are never equal to themselves."
– From 'The ABC of Materialist Dialectics' (1939), Leon Trotsky.

Helvetica
A documentary film by
Gary Hustwit

2008 · Experimental Jetset · NL · Poster

Meet the cast:

ABCD EFGHIJK LMNOP QRSTUV WXYZ

Now see the movie:

Helvetica

A documentary film by Gary Hustwit

2007 · Experimental Jetset · NL · Poster

Experimental Jetset (1997, Amsterdam) is a Dutch graphic design studio (whose partners met at the Gerrit Rietveld Academie) with a strong focus on print work and site-specific installations. With their conceptual approach of "turning language into objects", the team quickly gained international recognition and a string of successful projects led to a major acquisition of their works by MoMA in New York in 2007. Studio members have taught at both the Rietveld and Werkplaats Typografie in the Netherlands.

Experimental Jetset (1997, Amsterdam) ist ein niederländisches Grafikdesignbüro, das sich insbesondere auf Arbeiten im Printbereich sowie mit standortspezifischen Installationen spezialisiert hat. Das Team – dessen Partner sich an der Gerrit Rietveld Academie kennenlernten – fand durch sein Arbeitskonzept, „Sprache in Objekte zu verwandeln", rasch internationale Anerkennung. Eine Reihe erfolgreicher Projekte hatte zur Folge, dass das MoMA in New York 2007 bedeutende Arbeiten des Studios erwarb. Mitglieder von Experimental Jetset haben in den Niederlanden sowohl an der Rietveld Academie als auch an der Academie Werkplaats Typografie unterrichtet.

Experimental Jetset (1997, Amsterdam) est un studio de graphisme néerlandais (ses associés se sont connus à l'académie Gerrit Rietveld) dont le travail porte principalement sur les travaux d'impression et les installations in situ. Avec leur approche conceptuelle visant à «transformer le langage en objets», l'équipe s'est rapidement fait connaître à l'échelle internationale. En 2007, une série de projets très remarqués a conduit à une acquisition substantielle de leurs œuvres par le MoMA de New York. Les membres du studio ont enseigné aux académies néerlandaises Gerrit Rietveld et Werkplaats Typografie.

Stedelijk Museum CS

16.05 31.12
**Tussenstand:
een keuze uit de
collectie**
Intermission:
a choice from the
collection

16.05 03.10
20/20 Vision
Yesim Akdeniz Graf,
Francis Alÿs, Marc
Bijl, Germaine Kruip,
De Rijke / De Rooij,
Mathias Poledna,
Steve McQueen,
Torbjørn Rødland

16.05 29.08
**Kramer vs. Rietveld
/Contrasten in
de meubelcollectie**
Kramer vs. Rietveld
/Contrasts in the
furniture collection

www.stedelijk.nl

Stedelijk Museum CS
Oosterdokskade 5
1011 AD Amsterdam

Dagelijks open: 10·18 uur
Donderdag: 10·21 uur
Open daily: 10 am·6 pm
Thursday: 10 am·9 pm

Verwacht: Best Verzorgde
Boeken, Prix de Rome,
Sandberg, Gemeente Kunst
Aankopen, Who If Not We,
Robert Smit & Gold, IDFA

Expected: Best Book Design,
Prix de Rome, Sandberg,
Municipal Art Acquisitions,
Who If Not We, Robert Smit
& Gold, IDFA

Meubelindustrie
Gelderland BV
Mondriaan Stichting

Gemeente
Amsterdam
Economische Zaken

2005 · Experimental Jetset · NL · Poster

Geel Metalliek   Metallic Yellow

Stedelijk Museum CS
Goud voor /
Gold for Robert Smit

05.11.2004
30.01.2005

2004 · Experimental Jetset · NL · Poster

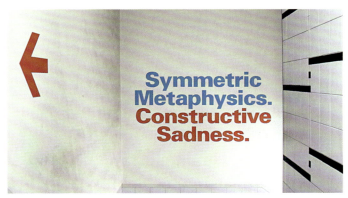

Stedelijk Museum CS   Stedelijk Museum CS

2004 · Experimental Jetset · NL · Identity · Stedelijk Museum

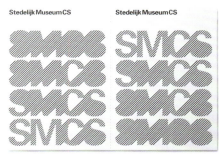

2004 · Experimental Jetset · NL · Signage

2006

The design blog **Brand New** begins, run by Texas-based design studio UnderConsideration

The magazine design blog **magCulture** is set up in London by creative director Jeremy Leslie

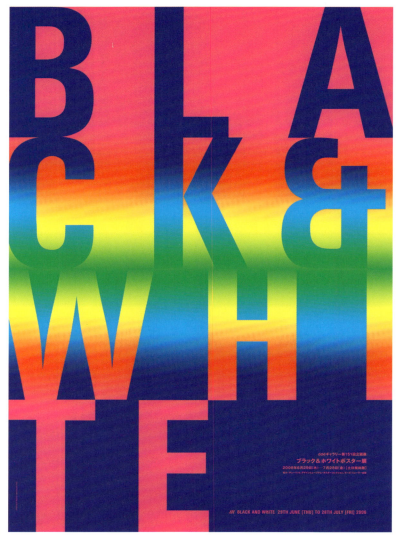

2006 · Melchior Imboden · CH · Poster

2006 · Mark Gowing Studio · AU · Poster

2006 · Paula Scher, Julia Hoffmann, Pentagram · US · Logo · Criterion Collection

2006 · Mark Gowing · AU · Logo · Title Music and Films

CISCO™

2006 · Joe Finocchiaro, Jerry Kuyper · US · Logo · Cisco

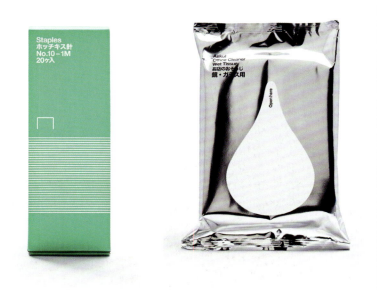

2006 · Stockholm Design Lab · SE · Packaging

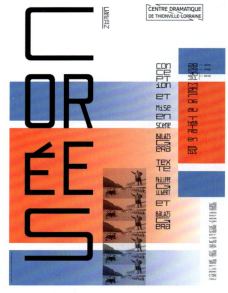

2006 · André Baldinger · FR · Poster

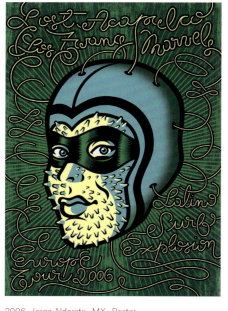

2006 · Jorge Alderete · MX · Poster

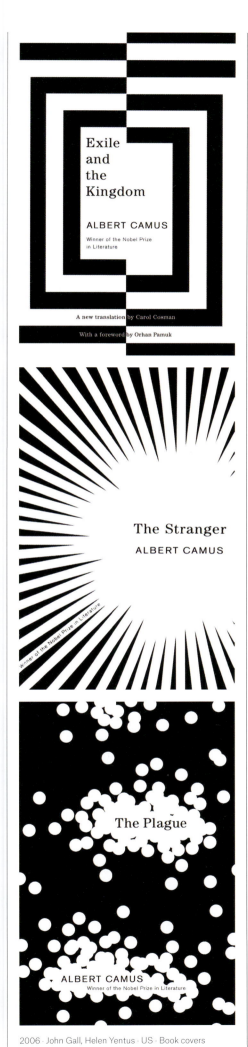

2006 · John Gall, Helen Yentus · US · Book covers

2006 · Richard Turley · UK · Magazine cover

2006 · Jianping He · CN · Poster

2006 · Saed Meshki · IR · Poster

Established in 1988, the brand name of Uniqlo (from the contraction of the words Unique and Clothing, followed by a mis-reading of C for Q) became a global phenomenon by offering fast fashion focused on basic clothing designs. In the 2000s, the retailer and manufacturer worked with renowned art director Kashiwa Sato to redesign its identity and roll out a national and international expansion. Choosing to retain the brand's Japanese identity, Sato designed a modular system in which both the Roman letters and the katakana alphabet could be employed. The company was used to the overlapping of two languages and scripts, and the new system made this more fluent by the use of simple typography in all printed material, as well as the almost-exclusive use of red and black.

Das Unternehmen mit dem 1988 geschaffenen Markennamen Uniqlo (zusammengesetzt aus den Worten „unique" [= einzigartig] und „clothing" [= Kleidung], wobei das „q" als „c" gelesen werden muss) wurde durch den Verkauf von alltagstauglicher Fast Fashion zu einem weltweiten Phänomen. In den 2000er-Jahren arbeitete der Einzelhändler und Hersteller mit dem angesehenen Art-director Kashiwa Sato zusammen, um die Firmenidentität neu zu gestalten und gleichzeitig national und international zu expandieren. Sato behielt die japanische Identität der Marke bei und entwickelte ein modulares System, in dem sowohl römische Buchstaben als auch das Katakana-Alphabet verwendet werden können. Die Firma war an das Überlappen von zwei Sprachen und Schriften gewöhnt, und das wurde durch das neue System noch flüssiger, denn für alles Gedruckte wird eine schlichte Typografie verwendet, zudem beschränkt man sich fast ausschließlich auf die Farben Rot und Schwarz.

Établie en 1988, la marque Uniqlo (contraction des mots «Unique» et «Clothing» en remplaçant le «c» par un «q») est devenue un phénomène mondial avec une mode éphémère reposant sur des designs vestimentaires basiques. Dans les années 2000, le détaillant et fabricant fit appel au célèbre directeur artistique Kashiwa Sato pour redéfinir son identité et assurer un déploiement national et international. Optant pour conserver l'identité japonaise de la marque, Sato élabora un système modulaire permettant d'utiliser les caractères romains aussi bien que l'alphabet katakana. Si l'entreprise était déjà habituée à passer d'une langue et d'une écriture à l'autre, le nouveau système rendit cette alternance plus fluide grâce à une typographie simplifiée pour tout le matériel imprimé et à l'emploi presque exclusif du rouge et du noir.

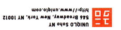
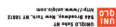

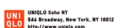

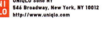

2006 · Kashiwa Sato · JP · Identity

2006 · Kashiwa Sato (AD) · JP · Identity

Kashiwa Sato (1965, Tokyo) is a Japanese designer and art director who for many years has crossed the boundaries between advertising, graphic design, architecture, and product design, finding equal success in all these fields. After his design degree at Tama Art University, Sato worked for 11 years at the long-established Japanese advertising agency Hakuhodo. In 2000 he set up his own design studio under the name of Samurai. The winner of many awards for his designs, Sato is also the author of several best-sellers, including his *Ultimate Method for Reaching the Essentials* (2007), and has been a visiting professor at Keio University and Tama Art University.

Kashiwa Sato (1965, Tokio) ist ein japanischer Designer und Art Director, der seit vielen Jahren als Grenzgänger in den Bereichen Werbung, Grafikdesign, Architektur und Produktdesign gleichermaßen erfolgreich ist. Nach einem Designstudium an der Tama Art University war er elf Jahre lang für die traditionsreiche japanische Werbeagentur Hakuhodo tätig. Ab 2000 baute er unter dem Namen Samurai ein eigenes Designstudio auf. Vielfach für seine Designarbeiten prämiert, ist Kashiwa Sato auch Autor mehrerer Bestseller wie *Ultimate Method for Reaching the Essentials* (2007). Als Gastprofessor lehrte er an der Keio University sowie an der Tama Art University.

Kashiwa Sato (1965, Tokyo) est un graphiste et directeur artistique japonais qui connaît un grand succès comme acteur interdisciplinaire dans les domaines de la publicité, du graphisme, de l'architecture et du design de produits. Après des études de graphisme à l'université des beaux-arts Tama, il a travaillé pendant onze ans pour l'agence publicitaire japonaise Hakuhodo, dépositaire d'une prestigieuse tradition. Il ouvre en 2000 son propre studio de design sous le nom de Samurai. Lauréat de nombreux prix pour son travail de designer, Kashiwa Sato est aussi l'auteur de plusieurs best-sellers comme *Ultimate Method for Reaching the Essentials* (2007). Il a enseigné comme professeur invité à l'université Keio, ainsi qu'à l'université des beaux-arts Tama.

UNIQLO

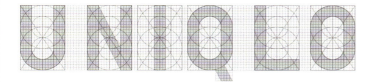

ABCDEFGHIJKLMNOPQRSTUVWXYZ

abcdefghijklmnopqrstuvwxyz

0123456789/@$%#!?&()[]""''".,:;-+_*

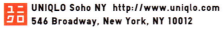

2006 · Kashiwa Sato (AD) · JP · Identity

2006 · Kashiwa Sato (AD) · JP · Poster

2006 · Kashiwa Sato (AD) · JP · Identity

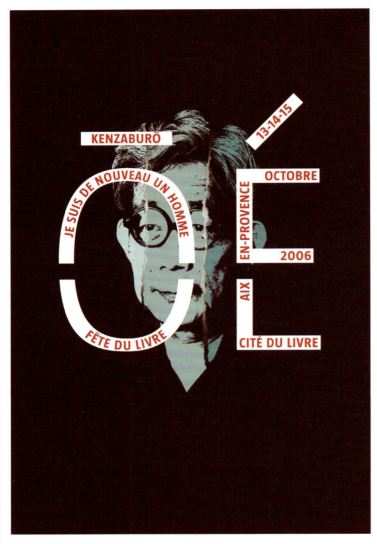

2006 · Philippe Apeloig · FR · Poster

2006 · Philippe Apeloig · FR · Poster

Philippe Apeloig (1962, Paris) is a leading French designer and typographer. After attending the École Nationale Supérieure des Arts Décoratifs in Paris, Apeloig worked as an intern at Total Design and the Musée d'Orsay before going to work with April Greiman in Los Angeles. In 1997 he became design consultant at the Louvre, a post he held until 2008. Apeloig's teaching posts have included Cooper Union, where he also served as curator of the Herb Lubalin Study Center of Design and Typography. He currently runs his own studio in Paris, and was made a Chevalier de l'Ordre des Arts et des Lettres in 2011.

Philippe Apeloig (1962, Paris) ist ein führender französischer Grafikdesigner und Typograf. Nach dem Besuch der École Nationale Supérieure des Arts Décoratifs in Paris machte er ein Praktikum bei Total Design sowie beim Musée d'Orsay, ehe er nach Los Angeles zu April Greiman ging. 1997 trat er beim Louvre die Stelle des Designconsultants an, die er bis 2008 innehatte. Apeloig hat u. a. an der Cooper Union unterrichtet, wo er auch als Kurator des Herb Lubalin Study Center of Design and Typography tätig war. Gegenwärtig hat er ein eigenes Grafikbüro in Paris. 2011 wurde er in den Stand eines Chevalier de l'Ordre des Arts et des Lettres erhoben.

Philippe Apeloig (1962, Paris) est un graphiste et typographe français de premier plan. Après des études à l'École nationale supérieure des Arts Décoratifs à Paris, Apeloig a été stagiaire chez Total Design et au musée d'Orsay avant de travailler aux côtés d'April Greiman à Los Angeles. En 1997, il devient conseiller en design au musée du Louvre, poste qu'il occupe jusqu'en 2008. Apeloig a notamment enseigné à la Cooper Union, où il a aussi été conservateur du Herb Lubalin Study Center of Design and Typography. Aujourd'hui, il dirige son propre studio à Paris et a été fait chevalier de l'ordre des Arts et des Lettres en 2011.

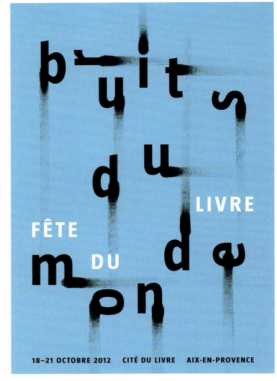

2012 · Philippe Apeloig · FR · Poster

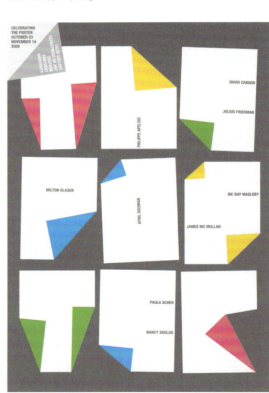

2000 · Philippe Apeloig · FR · Poster

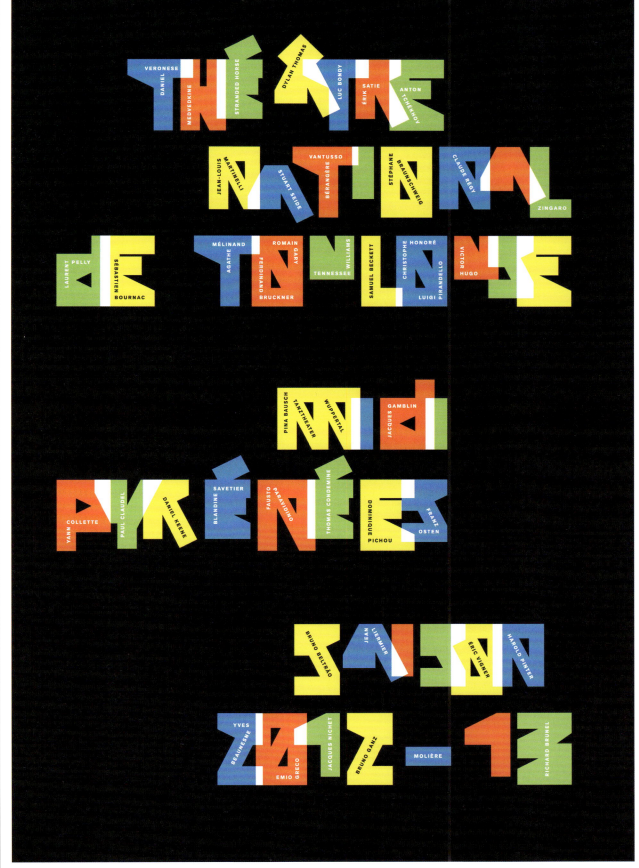

2012 · Philippe Apeloig · FR · Poster

2004 · Philippe Apeloig · FR · Logo · IUAV

2004 · Philippe Apeloig · FR · Logo · FIAF

2005 · Philippe Apeloig · FR · Logo · Musée de France

2006 · Philippe Apeloig · FR · Logo · Théâtre du Châtelet

2006 · Philippe Apeloig · FR · Logo · abF

Gary Hustwit's film documentary on the **Helvetica** typeface premieres

The first **European Design Awards** are held

The design blog **It's Nice That** is founded

2007 · Michael Bierut, Pentagram · US · Identity · Saks Fifth Avenue

2008 · Edmund Wee, Zann Wan, Epigram · SG · Identity · Simply Sandwich

2007 · Atlas · ES · Magazine spread

LACMA

LOS ANGELES COUNTY MUSEUM OF ART

2007 · 2x4 · US · Identity · LACMA

2007 · Holger Jacobs, Mind Design · UK · Logo · Tea

DELTA

2007 · Lippincott · US · Logo · Delta Air Lines

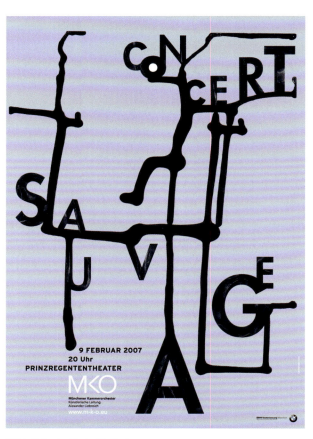

2007 · Catherine Zask · FR · Poster

2007 · Kyosuke Tsuji, Takashi Kamada, Romando · JP · Poster

2007 · Steve Fuller, Mark Gardner, Imaginary Forces · US · Opening titles

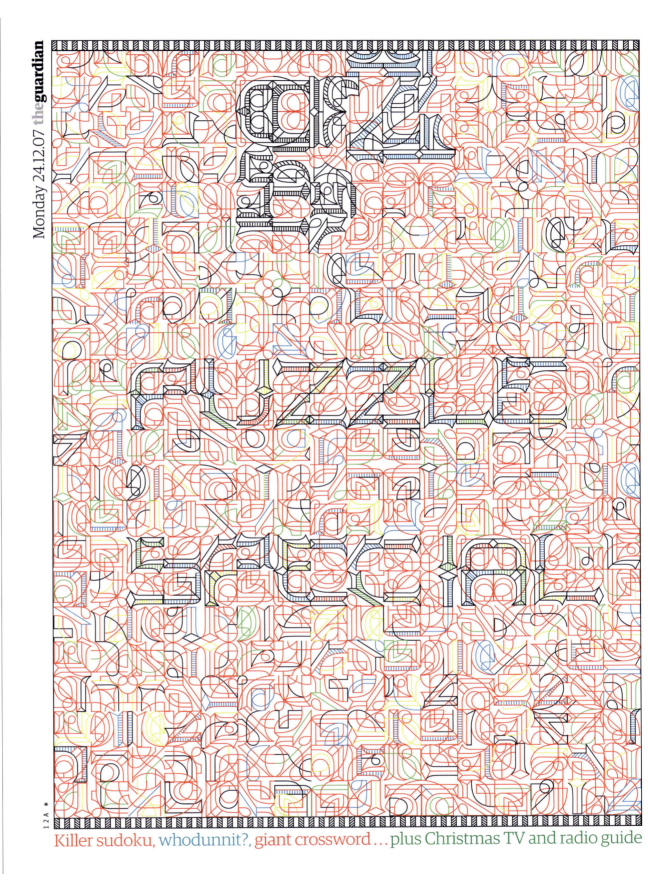

2007 · Marian Bantjes · CA/UK · Magazine cover

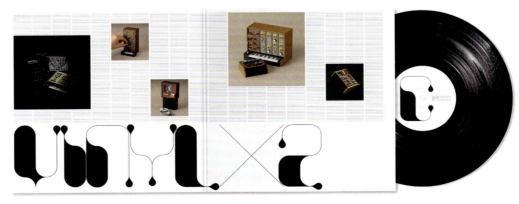

2007 · Non-Format · UK · Record cover

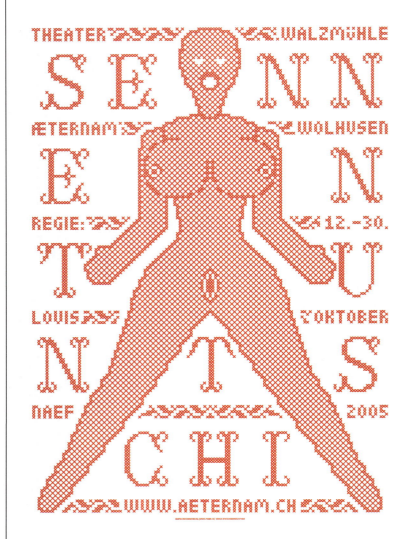

2005 · Erich Brechbühl · CH · Poster

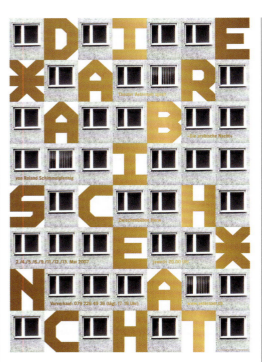

2007 · Erich Brechbühl · CH · Poster

Erich Brechbühl (1977, Sempach, Switzerland) is a Swiss graphic designer whose career started in film at the early age of 13 with Mix Pictures, an experimental cultural foundation. Brechbühl served as an apprentice typographer in Lucerne before working with Niklaus Troxler in Willisau from 1998–2002, later moving to Germany and working as an intern at MetaDesign in Berlin. He then returned to Lucerne to start his own graphic design practice, Mixer. In 2009, he co-founded the poster festival Weltformat in Lucerne, and the graphic design exchange group Show & Tell in 2012.

Erich Brechbühl (1977, Sempach, Schweiz) ist ein Schweizer Grafikdesigner, dessen Karriere bereits mit 13 Jahren bei der experimentalen Kulturstiftung Mix Pictures begann. Brechbühl absolvierte in Luzern eine Lehre als Schriftsetzer, ehe er von 1998 bis 2002 bei Niklaus Troxler in Willisau arbeitete. Später ging er nach Deutschland und machte ein Praktikum bei MetaDesign in Berlin, um dann nach Luzern zurückzukehren und sein eigenes Grafikbüro Mixer zu eröffnen. 2009 gründete er dort mit anderen das Plakatfestival Weltformat, 2012 dann Show & Tell, eine Austauschplattform für Grafikdesigner.

Erich Brechbühl (1977, Sempach, Suisse) est un graphiste suisse dont la carrière a débuté au cinéma à l'âge précoce de 13 ans avec Mix Pictures, une fondation culturelle expérimentale. Brechbühl a été apprenti typographe à Lucerne avant de travailler avec Niklaus Troxler à Willisau de 1998 à 2002, puis de s'installer à Berlin pour y travailler comme stagiaire chez MetaDesign. Il est retourné ensuite à Lucerne pour ouvrir sa propre agence de design, Mixer. En 2009, il est un des fondateurs du festival d'affiche Weltformat à Lucerne, puis du groupe de réflexion sur le graphisme Show & Tell en 2012.

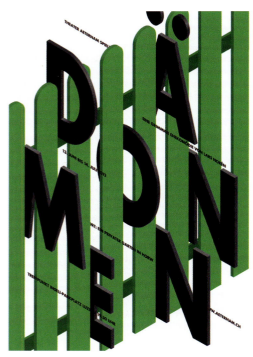

2012 · Erich Brechbühl · CH · Poster

2013 · Erich Brechbühl · CH · Poster

2014 · Erich Brechbühl · CH · Poster

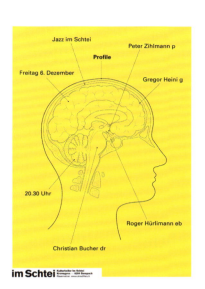

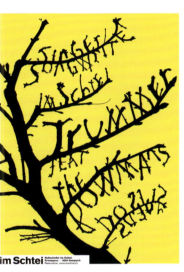

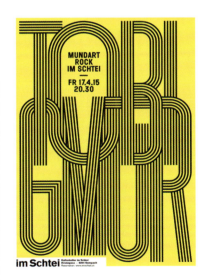

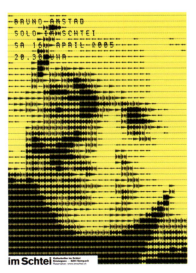

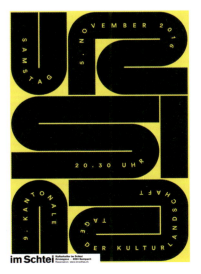

1999–2016 · Erich Brechbühl · CH · Posters

2008

A **Graphic Design Museum** (later renamed the Museum of the Image) opens in Breda, Netherlands

The **Replica** typeface is created by Norm

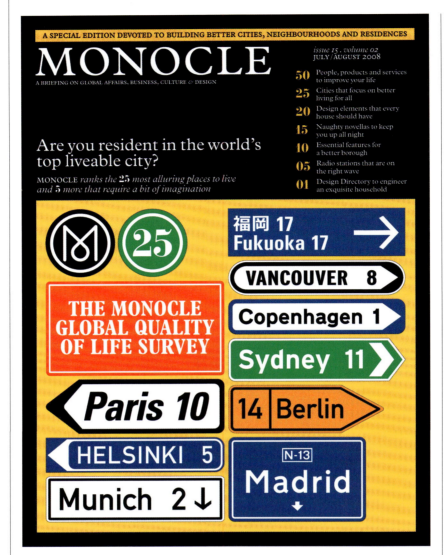

2008 · Tyler Brûlé · CA/UK · Editorial design

2008 · Karlssonwilker · US · Magazine cover

2008 · Neville Brody · UK · Newspaper design

2008 · Mark Gowing · AU · Poster

2008 · Jorge Silva, Silvadesigners · PT · Poster

2008 · Karel Martens · NL · Magazine cover

2008 · Summa, Tilman Solé, Rocío Martinavarro, Joern Oelsner · ES · Logo · Radiotelevisión Española

BREE

2008 · Andreas Uebele, Sabine Schönhaar, Büro Uebele · DE · Logo · Bree

2008 · Sol Sender · US · Logo · Obama Campaign

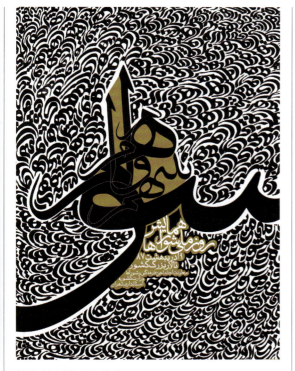

2008 · Mehdi Saeedi · IR · Poster

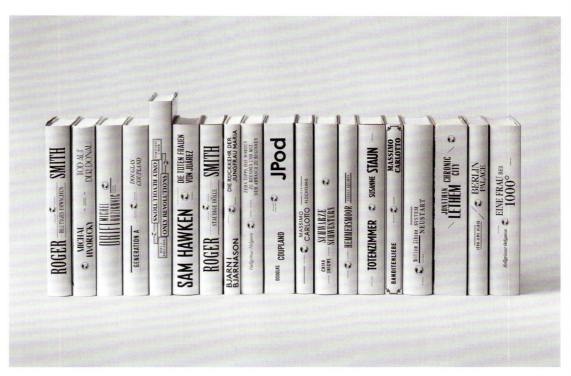

2008 · Herburg Weiland · DE · Book spines

2008 · Jianping He · CN · Poster

2008 · Oded Ezer · IL · Poster

2008 · Gavillet & Cie · CH · Poster

Three-Dimensional Logos

For many years, designing a logo meant coming up with a sign in just one color and measuring only a few centimeters across so that it would fit neatly on to a ballpoint pen. At the turn of the 21st century, the advances offered by digital design technology led to purely cosmetic improvements which simply added a third dimension to existing two-dimensional logos. This development was followed by a surge of completely three-dimensional designs, which only worked if they were in color and of a specific minimum size. International corporations, such as AT&T and DC Comics, were amongst the organizations to adopt this short-lived trend. After a few years though, many firms went back to using two-dimensional logos. Designed by computer and with the help of graphic reduction, these provided clear and simple brand recognition.

Über viele Jahre galt im Logodesign der Grundsatz, dass ein Zeichen auch einfarbig und wenige Zentimeter groß – beispielsweise auf einem Kugelschreiber – funktionieren muss. Fortschreitende Möglichkeiten der digitalen Entwurfstechnik führten Anfang der 2000er-Jahre zunächst zu rein kosmetischen Aktualisierungen, die zweidimensionalen Logos nachträglich einen räumlichen Effekt gaben. Auf diese Entwicklung folgte eine Welle vollständig dreidimensionaler Entwürfe, die nur in farbiger Anwendung und in einer gewissen Mindestgröße funktionierten. International agierende Unternehmen wie AT&T oder DC Comics folgten diesem Trend, der sich jedoch nur als kurzlebige Phase herausstellte. Nach wenigen Jahren kehrten viele Firmen zu zweidimensionalen Logos zurück, die auch im digitalen Anwendungsbereich dank grafischer Reduktion für eindeutige und einfache Wiedererkennung sorgen.

Pendant bien des années, le design de logos s'est cantonné à des symboles monochromes de quelques centimètres pour par exemple tenir sur un stylo à bille. Au début des années 2000, les possibilités accrues offertes par la conception numérique ont d'abord conduit à des actualisations purement cosmétiques qui dotaient les logos en 2D d'une troisième dimension. À cette évolution a succédé une vague de projets entièrement tridimensionnels, fonctionnant exclusivement en couleurs et avec une taille minimale déterminée. Des entreprises internationales comme AT&T ou DC Comics ont suivi cette tendance passagère. Après seulement quelques années, bien des compagnies sont revenues à des logos bidimensionnels conçus par ordinateur et dont la réduction graphique assure une reconnaissance sans équivoque.

2001 · Hiroshige Fukuhara, Takuya Kawagoi · JP · Logo · Sony Ericsson

2007 · Bruno Maag, Moving Brands · UK/CH · Logo · Swisscom

2010 · Kiko Farkas · BR · Logo · Brasil

2005 · Interbrand · US · Logo · AT&T

2012 · Landor · US · Logo · DC Comics

2012 · Thjnk · DE · Logo · Unitymedia

2013 · Happy F&B · SE/UK · Logo · Thomas Cook

2004 · Steven Garrity, Jon Hicks · UK · Logo · Firefox

2008 · Anonymous · US · Logo · Google Chrome

2013 · Wolff Olins · UK/US · Logo · Univision

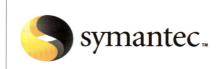

2008 · Anonymous · US · Logo · Symantec

2003 · Anonymous · AU · Logo · Cricket Australia

2009 · SDG · NO · Logo · Statoil

2009 · Moving Brands · UK · Logo · Mindshare

2001 · Anonymous · JP · Logo · Nintendo GameCube

2004 · Hulsbosch · AU · Logo · Hyundai A-League

2007 · Anonymous · US · Logo · Silverlight

2006 · Studio Dumbar · NL · Logo · KPN

2005 · Anonymous · US · Logo · Xbox

2008 · Anonymous · MY · Logo · Champions League

2008 · Interbrand · US · Logo · Xerox

2006 · Anonymous · SE · Logo · Malaco

2006 · Anonymous · DE · Logo · Schindler

2016 · Tátil · BR · Logo · Rio 2016

2007 · Anonymous · US · Logo · Lay's

2008 · The Brand Union · UK · Logo · Barclaycard

2014 · Liquid · US · Logo · Novvi

2010 · Anonymous · IT · Logo · Serie A

2011 · Irma Boom · NL · Book

1996 · Irma Boom · NL · Book

2008 · Irma Boom · NL · Book

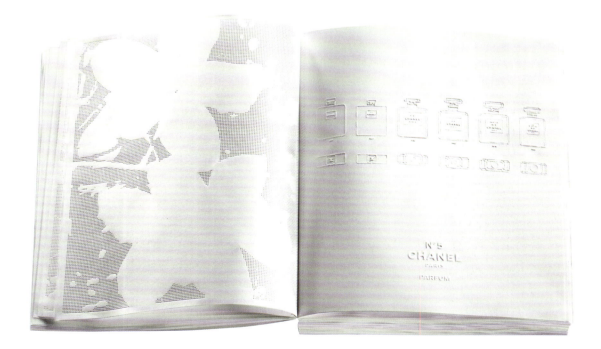

2013 · Irma Boom · NL · Book

2010 · Irma Boom · NL · Book

Irma Boom (1960, Lochem, Netherlands) is a world-renowned book designer based in Amsterdam. Boom's attention to detail and deep knowledge of production, typography, and composition have earned her a rare status among designers and publishers. More than 50 of her books are in the permanent collection of MoMA, and in 2001 she won the prestigious Gutenberg Prize (the youngest recipient to date); she has also won a gold medal at the Leipzig Book Fair, and the Johannes Vermeer Award in the Netherlands. Boom's clients have included Chanel, the architect Rem Koolhaas, and the Rijksmuseum in Amsterdam.

Irma Boom (1960, Lochem, Niederlande) ist eine weltbekannte Buchgestalterin mit Sitz in Amsterdam. Durch die Aufmerksamkeit, die sie auf Details richtet, und durch ihr immenses Wissen bezüglich Herstellung, Typografie und Komposition genießt sie unter Gestaltern und Verlegern einen ausgezeichneten Ruf. Über fünfzig ihrer Bücher liegen in der ständigen Sammlung des MoMA. 2001 wurde Boom als bislang jüngste Preisträgerin mit dem renommierten Gutenberg-Preis ausgezeichnet. Ferner erhielt sie die Goldmedaille der Leipziger Buchmesse sowie den niederländischen Johannes Vermeer Prijs. Zu Booms Auftraggebern gehören u.a. Chanel, der Architekt Rem Koolhaas und das Rijksmuseum in Amsterdam.

Irma Boom (1960, Lochem, Pays-Bas) est une conceptrice de livres de renommée internationale installée à Amsterdam. Son sens du détail et sa connaissance approfondie de la production, de la typographie et de la composition lui ont valu un statut d'exception parmi les designers et éditeurs. Plus de 50 de ses livres figurent dans les collections permanentes du MoMA et en 2001, elle a remporté le prestigieux prix Gutenberg (elle en reste à ce jour la plus jeune lauréate). Elle a aussi remporté une médaille d'or à la Foire du livre de Leipzig, et le prix Johannes Vermeer aux Pays-Bas. Les clients de Boom comptent notamment des marques comme Chanel, l'architecte Rem Koolhaas et le Rijksmuseum à Amsterdam.

2010 · Irma Boom · NL · Book

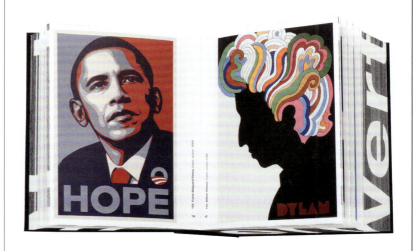

2013 · Irma Boom · NL · Book

2009 · Irma Boom · NL · Book

2003 · Reza Abedini · IR · Poster

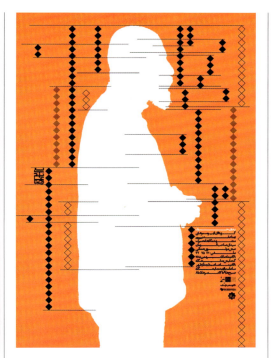

2006 · Reza Abedini · IR · Poster

2002 · Reza Abedini · IR · Poster

2005 · Reza Abedini · IR · Poster

2004 · Reza Abedini · IR · Poster

2015 · Reza Abedini · IR · Poster

Reza Abedini (1967, Tehran) is
a leading Iranian designer and
typographer, whose internationally
acclaimed work often blurs the
boundaries between art and design. Abedini's playful approach
to language and meaning through
letter forms and composition
has offered a contemporary interpretation of traditional Persian
design. An author, art critic, and
magazine editor, he has also
taught at the University of Tehran
since 1996, and been professor of
graphic design and visual culture
at the American University of
Beirut. In addition, Abedini is an
active member of both the Iranian Graphic Designers Society
(IGDS) and AGI, and has served
on numerous judging panels for
design awards.

Reza Abedini (1967, Teheran) ist
ein führender iranischer Grafikdesigner und Typograf, bei dessen
international anerkanntem Werk
die Grenzen zwischen Kunst und
Grafikdesign vielfach verschwim-
men. Abedini nähert sich der Sprache und der Bedeutung durch
Buchstabenformen und Kompo-
sitionen spielerisch an und gibt
damit der traditionellen persischen
Designgebung eine zeitgenössische Interpretation. Er ist nicht
nur als Autor, Kunstkritiker und
Zeitschriftenherausgeber tätig,
sondern unterrichtet seit 1996
auch an der Universität Teheran
und ist zudem Professor für Grafikdesign und visuelle Kultur an der
American University in Beirut.
Darüber hinaus ist Abedini aktives
Mitglied der Iranian Graphic Designers Society (IGDS) und des AGI
und saß bei zahlreichen Grafik-
designauszeichnungen in der Jury.

Reza Abedini (1967, Téhéran) est
un designer et typographe iranien
chef de file dont le travail mondialement reconnu brouille souvent
les frontières entre art et design.
Son approche ludique du langage
et du sens en jouant avec des
lettres et la composition a livré
une interprétation contemporaine
du graphisme perse traditionnel.
Auteur, critique d'art et rédacteur
de magazines, Abedini enseigne
à l'université de Téhéran depuis
1996 et a été professeur de graphisme et de culture visuelle
à l'université américaine de
Beyrouth. Il est en outre membre
actif de l'IGDS (Iranian Graphic
Designers Society) et de l'AGI,
et il a pris part à de nombreux
jurys de prix de design.

2009

2009 · Majid Abbasi · IR · Book cover

2009 · Proud Creative · US · Logo · Syfy Television

2009 · Landor · US · Logo · Hertz

2009 · Jean-Pierre Ploué, Landor · FR · Logo · Citroën

2009 · Antoine+Manuel · FR · Poster

2009 · Neil Kellerhouse, Kellerhouse Inc. · US · Poster

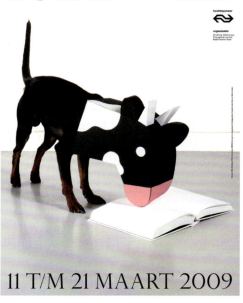

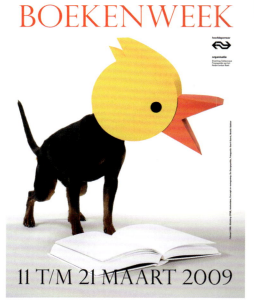

2009 · Designpolitie · NL · Posters

2009 · Erik Spiekermann (TY), Edenspiekermann · DE · Identity · ZDF Heute Journal

2009 · Holger Jacobs, Mind Design · UK · Identity

2009 · Gavillet & Cie · CH · Poster

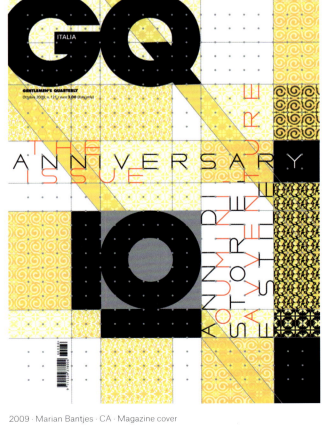

2009 · Marian Bantjes · CA · Magazine cover

2009 · Daniel Trench · BR · Magazine cover

Süddeutsche Zeitung Magazin

weniger ist mehr
Es wird Zeit, dass Gestalter und Architekten sich wieder auf das Wesentliche besinnen und den Menschen ins Zentrum ihrer Arbeit stellen. Zum 90. Jahrestag der Bauhaus-Gründung: ein Heft über die ethische Verantwortung des Designs

2009 · Heye & Partner · DE · Magazine cover

2009 · Poststudio · BG · Poster

2009 · Non-Format · UK/NO · Poster

Non-Format (2000) is the London-based creative studio of Kjell Ekhorn (1965, Narvik, Norway) and Jon Forss (1966, Pinvin, England), with offices in Oslo and the Twin Cities, USA. The firm's output, which ranges from art direction and design to illustration, initially focused on music and cultural sectors before gaining the attention of major clients, such as IBM, Coca-Cola, and Nike. Ekhorn and Forss studied at Central Saint Martins and Leicester Polytechnic respectively, before collaborating at independent label Leaf, for whom they have designed dozens of record sleeves.

Non-Format (2000) ist das in London ansässige Kreativbüro von Kjell Ekhorn (1965, Narvik, Norwegen) und Jon Forss (1966, Pinvin, England) mit Ablegern in Oslo und den Twin Cities, USA. Zunächst arbeiteten die beiden Grafikdesigner an Projekten im Musik- und Kulturbereich, wobei sie die Artdirection ebenso übernahmen wie Gestaltung und Illustration, doch dann wurden Großkunden wie IBM, Coca-Cola und Nike auf sie aufmerksam. Ekhorn und Forss studierten an der Central Saint Martins bzw. am Leicester Polytechnic, ehe sie bei dem Independent-Label Leaf zusammentrafen, für das sie Dutzende Plattencover gestaltet haben.

Non-Format (2000) est le studio de création de Kjell Ekhorn (1965, Narvik, Norvège) et Jon Forss (1966, Pinvin, Angleterre), basé à Londres avec des bureaux à Oslo et à Twin Cities, aux États-Unis. Leur travail, qui va de la direction artistique et du design à l'illustration, s'est d'abord exercé dans le monde de la musique et le secteur culturel avant d'attirer l'attention de grands clients comme IBM, Coca-Cola et Nike. Ekhorn et Forss ont étudié respectivement au Central Saint Martins et à l'Institut de technologie de Leicester avant de collaborer avec le label musical indépendant Leaf, pour lequel ils ont conçu des dizaines de pochettes d'albums.

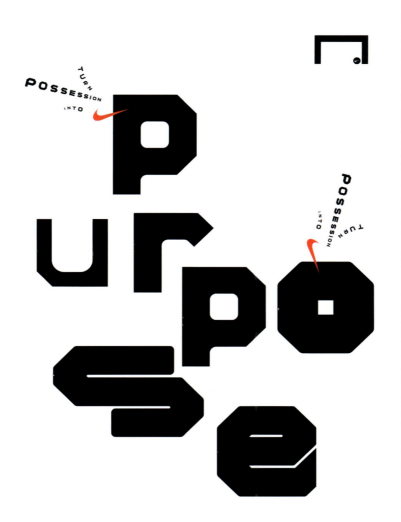

2009 · Non-Format · UK/NO · Poster

2007 · Non-Format · UK/NO · Record cover

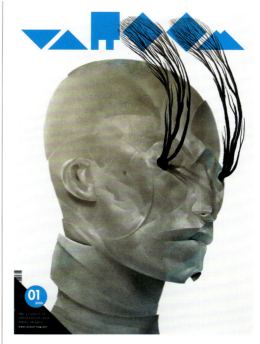

2006 · Non-Format · UK/NO · Magazine cover

2007 · Nor-Format · UK/NO · Magazine cover

2008 · Non-Format · UK/NO · Magazine cover

1991 · Cyan · DE · Poster

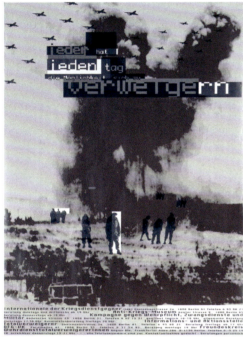

1991 · Cyan · DE · Poster

1998 · Cyan · DE · Poster

2016 · Cyan · DE · Poster

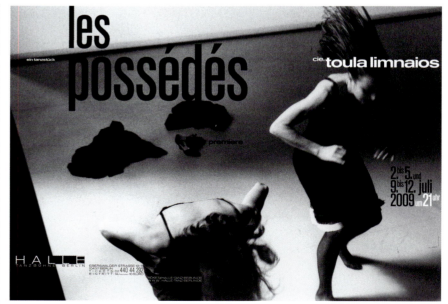

2009 · Cyan · DE · Poster

»A vision in graphic design has to respond to society, politics, economy, and culture. Impulses from outside are translated into visual language and in turn establish a possibility for communication and identification.«

Cyan, *Graphic Design for the 21st Century*, 2003

2004 · Cyan · DE · Poster

2016 · Cyan · DE · Poster

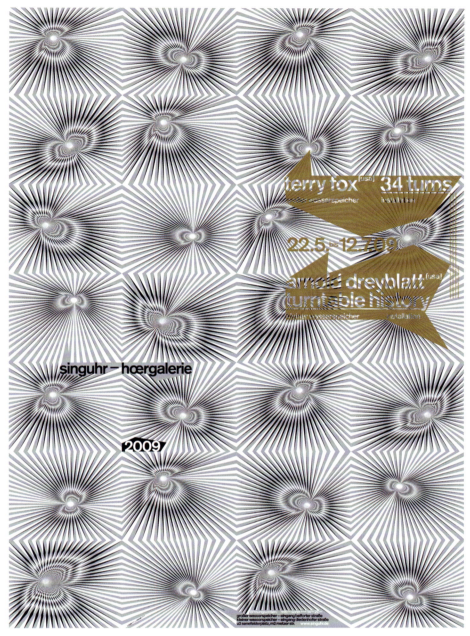

2009 · Cyan · DE · Poster

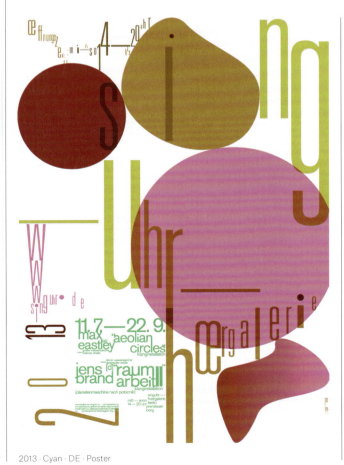

2013 · Cyan · DE · Poster

2003 · Cyan · DE · Poster

Cyan (1992) is a Berlin-based creative studio founded by Detlef Fiedler (1955, Schönebeck, Germany), an architect-turned-designer, and Daniela Haufe (1966, Berlin), a trained typesetter and typographer from East Germany. With a body of work ranging from visual identity to advertising campaigns, posters, books, magazines, and websites, the duo has consistently offered a contemporary approach. From 1996 to 2006 Fiedler and Haufe both taught as professors of graphic design at the Academy of Visual Arts, Leipzig; they were also co-editors of the critical design magazine *form+zweck*.

Cyan (1992) ist ein Kreativstudio mit Sitz in Berlin, das von Detlef Fiedler (1955, Schönebeck), einem ehemaligen Architekten, der auf Grafik umsattelte, und Daniela Haufe (1966, Berlin), einer ostdeutschen Drucksetzerin und Typografin, gegründet wurde. Das Duo kann auf ein vielfältiges Werk verweisen, von visuellen Identitäten bis hin zu Werbekampagnen, Plakaten, Büchern, Zeitschriften und Websites. Dabei haben die beiden Grafikdesigner immer einen Ansatz gewählt, der auf der Höhe der Zeit war. Von 1996 bis 2006 unterrichteten sowohl Fiedler als auch Haufe als Professoren für Grafik an der Hochschule für Grafik und Buchkunst in Leipzig; zudem waren sie Co-Herausgeber der kritischen Designzeitschrift *form+zweck*.

Cyan (1992) est un studio de création berlinois fondé par l'ex-architecte devenu designer Detlef Fiedler (1955, Schönebeck, Allemagne) et Daniela Haufe (1966, Berlin), compositrice et typographe de formation et originaire d'Allemagne de l'Est. Pour leurs projets qui englobent identités visuelles, campagnes publicitaires, affiches, livres, magazines et sites Internet, le duo a constamment proposé une approche contemporaine. De 1996 à 2006, Fiedler et Haufe ont enseigné le graphisme à l'École supérieure des arts graphiques et du livre de Leipzig. Ils ont par ailleurs été co-rédacteurs du magazine de design critique *form+zweck*.

2009 · BVD · SE/DE · Packaging

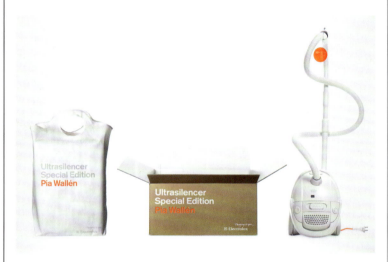

2007 · BVD · SE · Packaging

2009 · BVD · SE/DE · Packaging

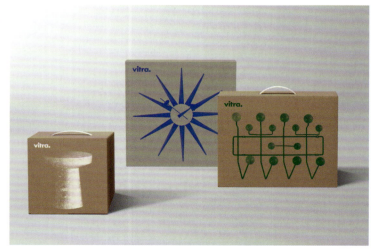

2013-15 · BVD · SE/DE · Packaging

BVD (1996) is an award-winning Swedish design agency with strong work in branding and visual communication. With an emphasis on simplifying brands and company identities, the studio has built an impressive client list, including Coca-Cola, Vitra, Skandia, H&M, and many others. Through its inquisitive approach, the Stockholm-based firm has evolved a working process and developed its own framework to achieve a high degree of clarity (Simplify to Clarify), attracting communication challenges from national as well as international companies. In over 20 years of work, BVD has created innovative package design, brand systems, editorial, and store concepts.

BVD (1996) ist eine preisgekrönte schwedische Designagentur, die insbesondere durch ihre Entwürfe in den Gebieten Branding und visuelle Kommunikation überzeugt. Bei der Arbeit geht es dem Studio insbesondere um die Schlichtheit von Brands und Firmensignets, und damit hat es eine eindrucksvolle Liste von Auftraggebern aufgebaut, unter anderem Coca-Cola, Vitra, Skandia und H&M. Die in Stockholm ansässige Firma hat mit ihrer Lust am Hinterfragen eine besondere Arbeitsweise und ein ganz eigenes Rahmenwerk entwickelt, dank deren sie ein hohes Maß an Klarheit erreicht: Simplify to Clarify. Schwedische ebenso wie internationale Unternehmen wandten sich wegen dieses Ansatzes mit ihren Kommunikationsbedürfnissen an die Agentur. In ihrer über 20-jährigen Arbeit hat sie innovatives Verpackungsdesign und Brandsysteme entworfen, aber auch Konzepte für Printmedien und Geschäfte.

BVD (1996) est une agence de design suédoise primée qui offre principalement des services de branding et de communication visuelle. Toujours en quête de simplifier des identités d'entreprises, le studio installé à Stockholm s'est constitué une impressionnante liste de clients comptant notamment Coca-Cola, Vitra, Skandia, H&M. À travers une approche très fouillée, l'équipe a défini un processus de travail et développé ses propres standards pour assurer un haut niveau de clarté – simplifier pour clarifier –, s'attirant ainsi des commandes du marché national et international. En plus de vingt ans de travail, BVD a innové dans le packaging, les systèmes de marques, le design éditorial et le concept de magasin.

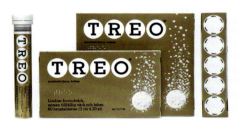

2007 · BVD · SE · Packaging

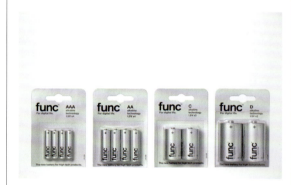

2003-10 · BVD · SE/NO · Packaging

2013 · BVD · SE · Packaging

APOTEK ♡

2009 · BVD · SE · Logo · Apotek

2009 · BVD · SE · Identity · Apotek

2009 · BVD · SE · Store design

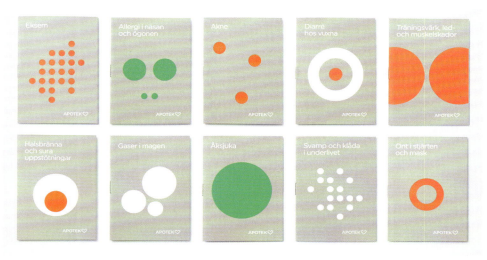

2009 · BVD · SE · Brochures

2009 · BVD · SE · Packaging

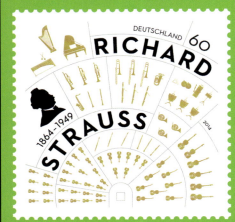

2014 · Jens Müller · DE · Stamp

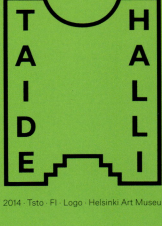

2014 · Tsto · FI · Logo · Helsinki Art Museum

2016 · Les Graphiquants · FR · Poster

2010

2017 · Craig & Karl, Christian Tönsmann (AD) · UK/US/DE · Magazine cover

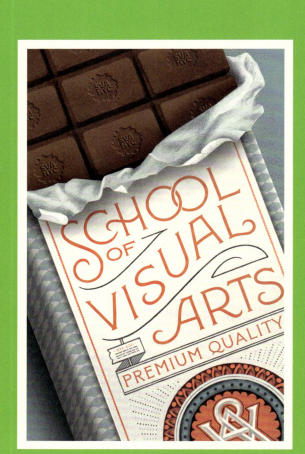

2016 · Louise Fili · US · Poster

2014 · Frost* Design · AU · Poster

2014 · Hvass & Hannibal · DK · Poster

2019

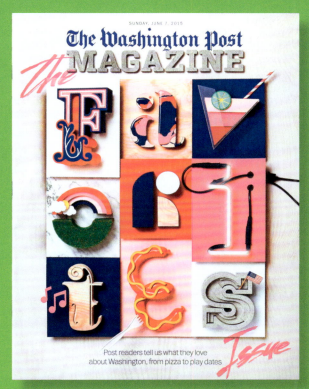

2015 · Snask · SE/US · Magazine cover

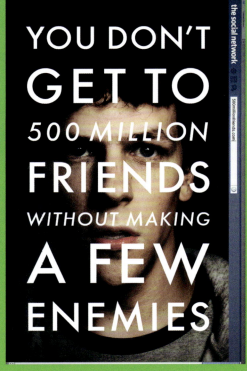

2010 · Neil Kellerhouse (AD), Frank Ockenfels (PH), Kellerhouse Inc. · US · Poster

The 2010s are already recognized as the age of social media, together with all the various aspects associated with it, both positive and negative. Never before has it been so easy to see such a diverse assortment of design works and to follow the creation of new styles in near-real time. Thus enabled, sophisticated designers work towards stronger positioning and an even clearer assertion of their own visual vocabulary. Sometimes, however, global networking can lead to big problems, for example, when the logo of a major sporting event in Japan looks too much like that of a provincial theater in Belgium, or the clientele of a fashion house protest vociferously when the company's trusted trademark is changed. Even so, the industry's persistent navel-gazing doesn't necessarily result in second-rate designs, and in fact in many cases it actually contributes to the stimulation of adventurous and innovative approaches. All of this makes it exciting to observe how new visual trends can, as always, develop at first at the local level, and likewise, how continuing technological advances are a firm guarantee that there will always be new designs.

Die 2010er-Jahre gelten schon heute als das Zeitalter der sozialen Medien – mit einer Reihe von positiven wie negativen Aspekten. Noch nie zuvor war es so einfach möglich, unterschiedlichste Arbeiten zu sehen und die Entstehung neuer Stilrichtungen nahezu in Echtzeit zu verfolgen. Anspruchsvolle Gestalterinnen und Gestalter zwingt dies zu einer noch stärkeren Positionierung und einem noch deutlicheren Bekenntnis zur eigenen visuellen Sprache. Manchmal führt die globale Vernetzung jedoch auch zu ganz handfesten Problemen, etwa wenn das Zeichen einer japanischen Großsportveranstaltung dem eines belgischen Provinztheaters zu ähnlich sieht oder wenn die Kunden eines Modekonzerns sich lautstark gegen die Überarbeitung des lange vertrauten Markenzeichens wehren. Die allgegenwärtige Nabelschau der Branche führt jedoch mitnichten zwingend zu zweitklassigen Entwürfen, sondern sie trägt in vielen Fällen zu gewagten und innovativen Ansätzen bei. Es ist dabei spannend zu beobachten, dass sich neuartige visuelle Tendenzen nach wie vor lokal entwickeln können. Ebenso bleibt die fortschreitende technische Entwicklung ein steter Garant für neue Gestaltung.

Les années 2010 sont déjà considérées aujourd'hui comme l'ère des médias sociaux, avec tous les aspects positifs et négatifs qui sont liés. Jamais auparavant il n'a été aussi simple de découvrir une variété de travaux et de suivre la genèse de nouvelles tendances quasiment en temps réel. Des graphistes de haut vol travaillent ainsi à un positionnement plus marqué et à une affirmation encore plus claire de leur langage visuel. Mais la mise en réseau globale soulève parfois aussi des problèmes de taille, par exemple quand le logo d'un grand événement sportif japonais ressemble trop à celui d'un théâtre de province belge, ou quand les clients d'une maison de couture s'opposent énergiquement au remaniement de leur marque de confiance. Cela dit, ce nombrilisme du secteur ne produit pas forcément que des projets de second rang et donne souvent lieu à des approches audacieuses et novatrices. Il est passionnant de voir qu'aujourd'hui comme toujours, les nouvelles tendances visuelles peuvent se développer d'abord en local, et que les progrès technologiques garantissent un éternel renouveau dans le graphisme.

left: A joint project created by the design studio Why Not Associates in collaboration with the artist Gordon Young, *Comedy Carpet* has been a show-piece at the English seaside resort of Blackpool since 2011.

above: The bus described as the Moscow Design Museum's "mobile exhibition hall" matching the visual identity created for the museum by the Dutch design studio Lava in 2012.

right: Advertising campaign developed by the Dutch studio Designpolitie for the 2014 *What Design Can Do* conference.

---

links: Ein vom Designbüro Why Not Associates gemeinsam mit dem Künstler Gordon Young entworfener *Comedy Carpet* ist seit 2011 eine Attraktion der englischen Küstenstadt Blackpool.

oben: Ein Werbebus des Moscow Design Museum, gestaltet gemäß der visuellen Identität, die das niederländische Designbüro Lava 2012 für das Museum entwickelte.

rechts: Kampagne des niederländischen Studios Designpolitie für eine 2014 veranstaltete Konferenz über die Wirkung von Design.

à gauche: le *Comedy Carpet*, conçu par le studio de graphisme Why Not Associates en collaboration avec l'artiste Gordon Young, est une attraction de la ville côtière anglaise de Blackpool depuis 2011.

en haut: bus publicitaire du Moscow Design Museum, conforme à l'identité visuelle de ce musée, telle qu'elle a été développée en 2012 par l'agence de graphisme néerlandaise Lava.

à droite: campagne du studio néerlandais Designpolitie pour la conférence *What Design Can Do* en 2014.

2010

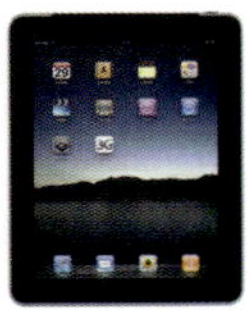

The release of Apple's first iPad marks the rise of tablet computers

In Chile, 33 miners are trapped in a copper and gold mine but all are rescued 69 days later

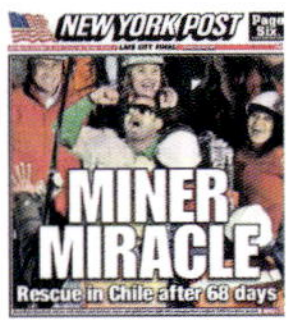

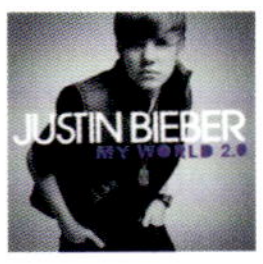

Justin Bieber releases his debut album *My World 2.0*

Piper Kerman's *Orange Is the New Black* is published, a memoir of her conviction and year spent in a women's prison

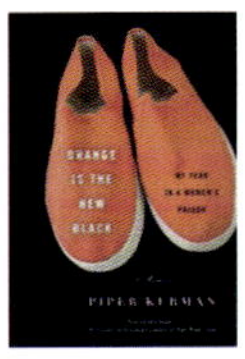

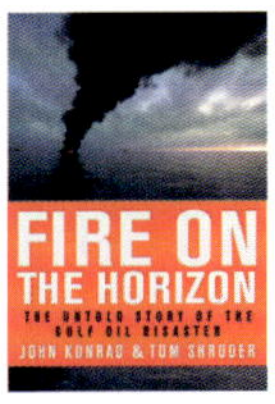

An explosion on the *Deepwater Horizon* drilling rig kills 11 crewmen and causes the largest oil spill in U.S. waters

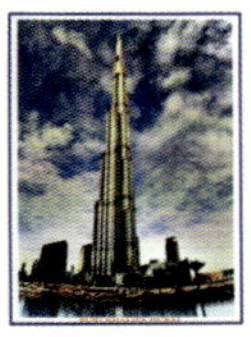

At 2,722 feet (830 m), the Burj Khalifa, the world's tallest building, opens in Dubai

The ash cloud from the eruption of the Icelandic volcano Eyjafjallajökull causes severe restrictions on traffic in European airspace

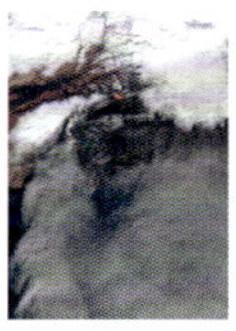

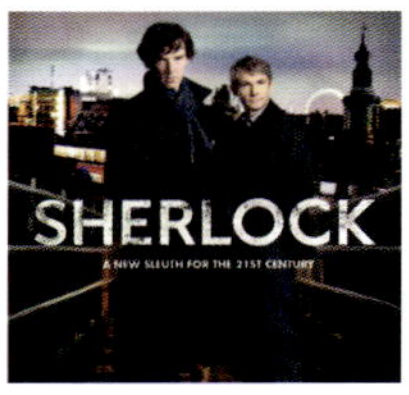

The first episode of British TV series *Sherlock* is aired

A crowd disaster at the Love Parade in Duisburg, Germany, results in the deaths of 21 people

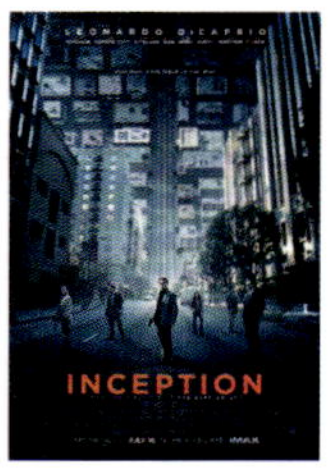

Christopher Nolan's sci-fi heist movie *Inception* premieres

2011

Prince William and Kate Middleton marry at Westminster Abbey in London

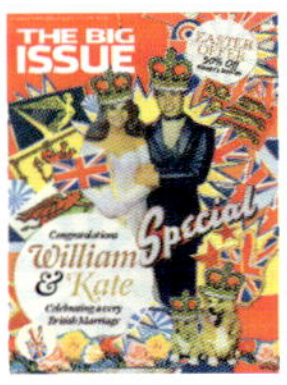

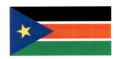

South Sudan gains independence

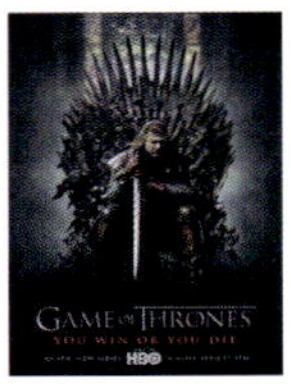

The first episode of TV series *Game of Thrones* is aired

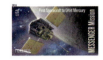

The NASA orbiter *Messenger* enters into orbit around Mercury after more than six years of traveling

Civil war breaks out in Syria

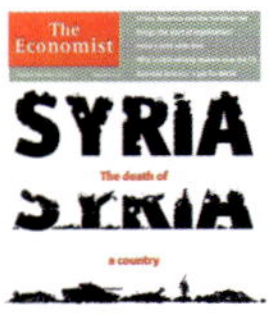

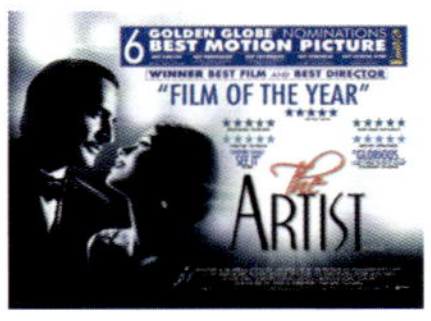

The French drama *The Artist* is released and goes on to win 92 film awards and nominations

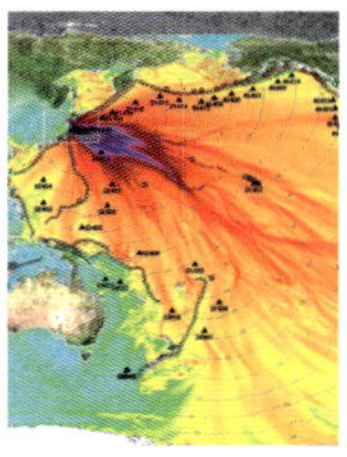

A tsunami brings about the Fukushima nuclear disaster in Japan

CHRISTIE'S

At Christie's in New York Andreas Gursky's *Rhein II* is auctioned for $4.3m and becomes the most expensive photograph ever sold

Al Qaeda leader Osama bin Laden is killed by U.S. special forces in Abbottabad

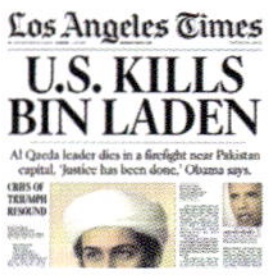

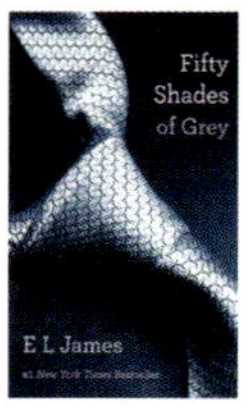

Popular BDSM page-turner *Fifty Shades of Grey* is published

2012

Sotheby's

A pastel version of Munch's *The Scream* sells for $120m at Sotheby's in New York and sets a new record for an auctioned work of art

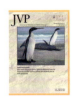

The remains of the giant prehistoric penguin *Kairuku grebneffi* are classified as a distinct species

Gillian Flynn's elusive thriller *Gone Girl* is published

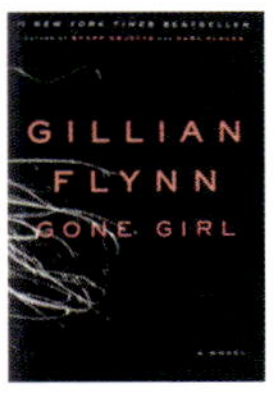

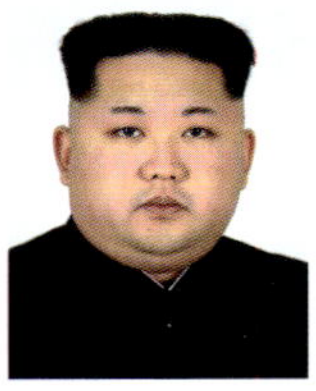

Kim Jong Un is officially appointed Supreme Leader of North Korea

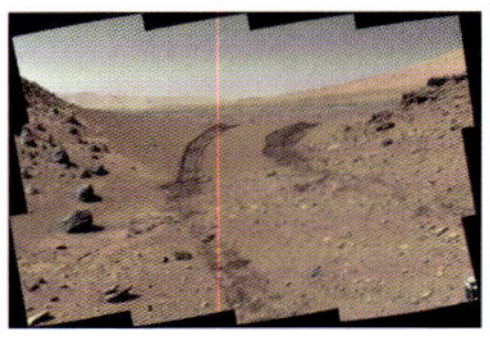

The NASA rover vehicle *Curiosity* lands on Mars

At 1,016 feet (310 m), the Shard opens in London as the tallest building in the European Union

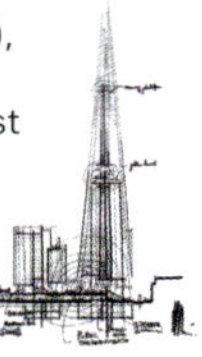

The European Union is awarded the Nobel Peace Prize

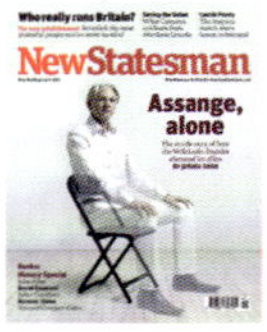

WikiLeaks founder Julian Assange seeks asylum in the Ecuadorian Embassy in London

Starring and directed by Ben Affleck, the movie *Argo* premieres

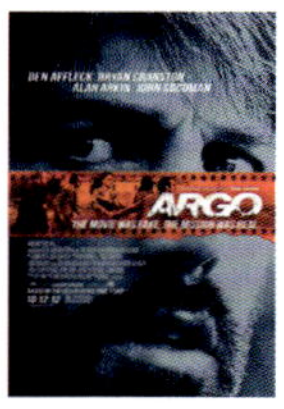

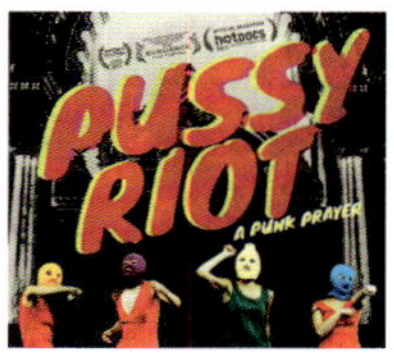

Three members of Russian punk feminist band Pussy Riot are jailed for their anti-Putin protest

2013

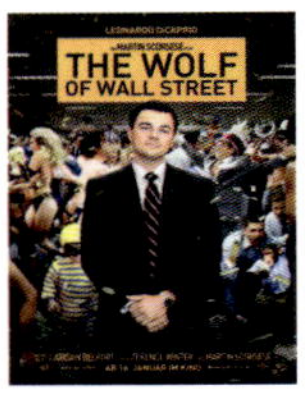

The Wolf of Wall Street premieres, starring Leonardo DiCaprio

Nelson Mandela dies at 95

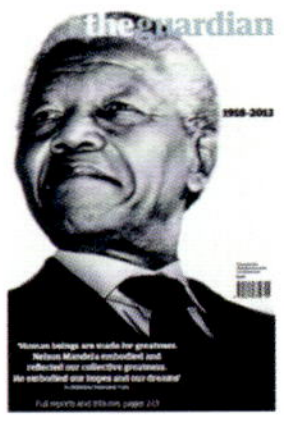

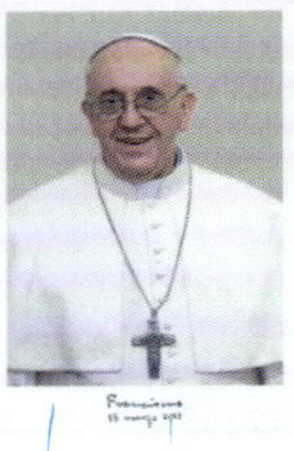

Cardinal Jorge Mario Bergoglio becomes pope and takes the name Francis

A meteor explodes above Chelyabinsk in Russia injuring 1,500 people

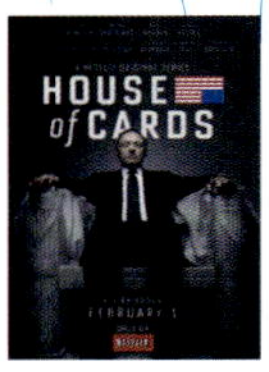

The political thriller *House of Cards* first airs on Netflix

The TrueSmart is the first smartwatch to claim it has the full capability of a smartphone

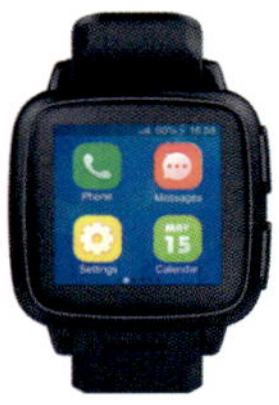

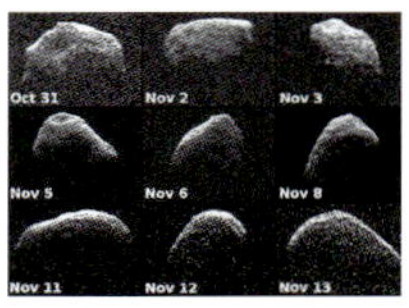

Micro-asteroid Duende passes within a very close 17,200 miles (27,700 km) of Earth

NO CRUEL COSMETICS

The European Union bans the sale of cosmetics that have been tested on animals

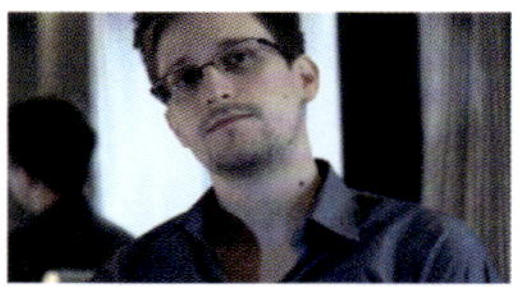

Edward Snowden reveals thousands of classified security documents to journalists

Lance Armstrong admits to doping in all of his Tour de France wins

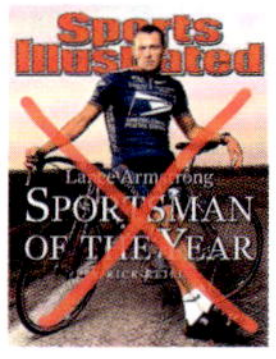

2014

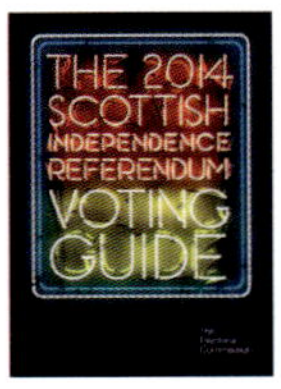

Scotland votes to remain part of the United Kingdom

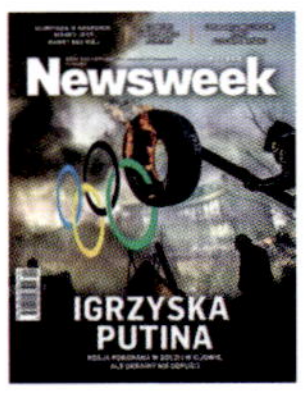

Civil war begins in Ukraine

At 17 the Pakistani activist Malala Yousafzai is the youngest person to receive the Nobel Peace Prize

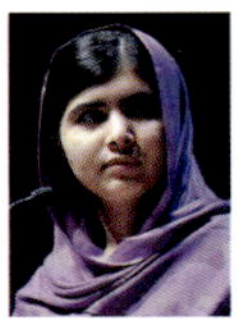

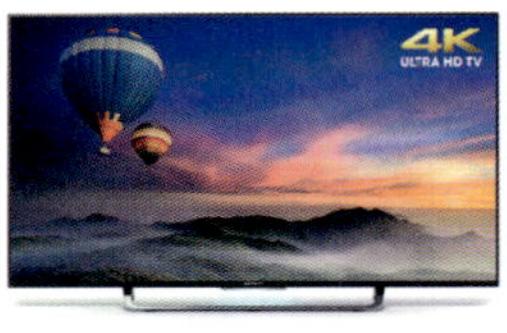

4K-resolution televisions become more common as prices fall dramatically

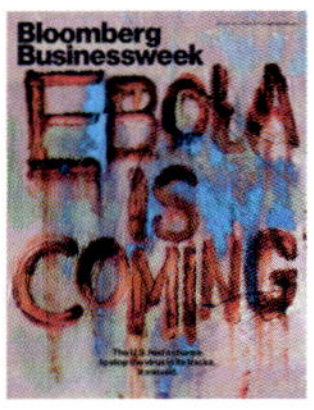

An epidemic of Ebola in West Africa becomes the most widespread outbreak yet for the viral disease

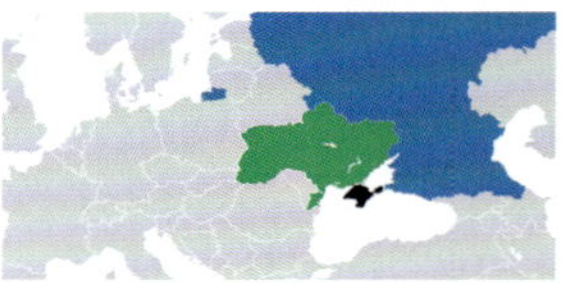

As a result of the revolution in Ukraine the Crimean peninsula is annexed by Russia

WORLD TRADE CENTER

The new One World Trade Center opens in New York City

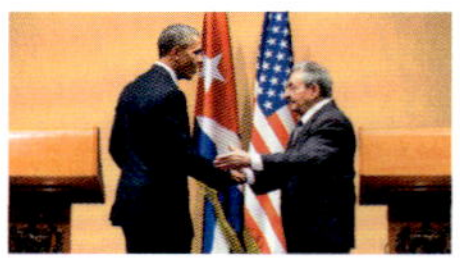

Cuba and the United States agree to restore diplomatic relations after 50 years

The terrorist organization Islamic State (IS) conquers large parts of Iraq and crosses into Syria

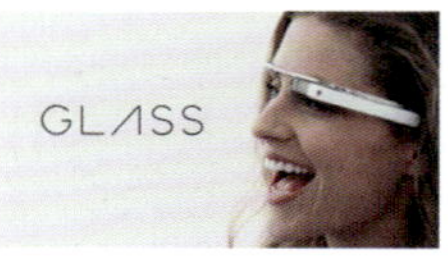

Google releases its smart glasses

2015

Ringo Starr's personal copy of the Beatles' *White Album*, numbered 0000001, sells for $790,000

A refugee crisis threatens to overwhelm Europe

A 1,111-carat gem discovered at the Karowe mine in Botswana is the largest diamond to be found in over a century

A terrorist attack in Paris on the offices of the satirical newspaper *Charlie Hebdo* leaves 12 dead

Paula Hawkins's novel *The Girl on the Train* is published and quickly becomes a bestseller

Volkswagen is alleged to have been involved in worldwide rigging of diesel emission tests

Six U.S. states allow self-driving cars to be tested on public roads

Terrorist attacks in Paris at several locations leave 130 dead and IS claims responsibility

The space probe *New Horizons* makes the first flyby of Pluto

Birdman, starring Michael Keaton, wins four Oscars including Best Picture and Best Director

2016

American singer-songwriter Bob Dylan is awarded the Nobel Prize for Literature

The United Kingdom votes to leave the European Union

Boxing legend Muhammad Ali dies

Pokémon Go, the real-world mobile game by Niantic, becomes a global phenomenon

The TV show *Westworld* premieres on HBO

Reality TV star Donald Trump is elected U.S. president

The WHO declares a public health emergency following the rapid spread of the Zika virus

Riots break out in North Carolina after a video is released showing police killing an unarmed Afro-American

Three coordinated suicide-bomb attacks in Brussels and its airport leave 32 dead

NASA's *Juno* spacecraft enters orbit around Jupiter

2017

Millions of people worldwide join the Women's March in Washington after Trump's inauguration as president

The Barry Jenkins film *Moonlight* wins the Oscar for Best Picture

Emmanuel Macron is elected president of France

North Korea provokes international condemnation for test-firing ICBMs

The movie *Blade Runner 2049* is released

The G20 banking forum held in Hamburg is marked by violent protests and vandalism

Allegations of sexual abuse against Hollywood producer Harvey Weinstein give rise to the Me Too movement

An overwhelming vote for Catalan independence is declared illegal by the Spanish government

Russia is banned from the 2018 Winter Olympics over state-sponsored doping

The Louvre Abu Dhabi art museum opens in the United Arab Emirates

2018

The Winter Olympics are held in Pyeong-chang, South Korea

Presidential elections are held in Russia and Putin remains in office

The Marvel Comics movie *Black Panther* is released

The Academy Awards turns 90

A fatal shooting at a school in Parkland, Florida, brings mass demonstrations in support of gun control

The test flight by SpaceX of its Falcon Heavy rocket is the second-most watched livestream ever on YouTube

The FIFA Soccer World Cup is held in Russia

President Moon Jae In welcomes Kim Jong Un to South Korea, the first leader from the north to cross the DMZ since it was created in 1953

Data from 87 million Facebook users is found to have been harvested by Cambridge Analytica

Prince Harry and Meghan Markle marry at Windsor Castle in London

General Data Protection Regulation (GDPR) comes into force in EU law

2019

2010

Hannes von Döhren creates the **Brandon** typeface

The independent graphic design publisher **Unit Editions** is founded by Tony Brook, Patricia Finegan, and Adrian Shaughnessy

The introduction of a new logo for the fashion brand **Gap** fails because of customers' negative reactions to it

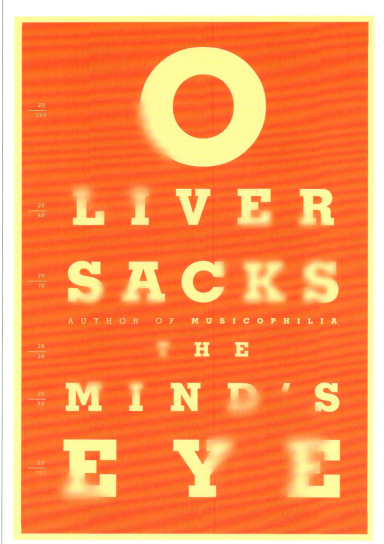

2010 · Chip Kidd · US · Book cover

2010 · Spin · UK · Logo · Unit Editions

MUSEO ITALIANO CULTURAL CENTRE

2010 · David Pidgeon · AU · Logo · Museo Italiano Cultural Centre

LIBRARY OF CONGRESS

2011 · Chermayeff & Geismar & Haviv · US · Logo · Library of Congress

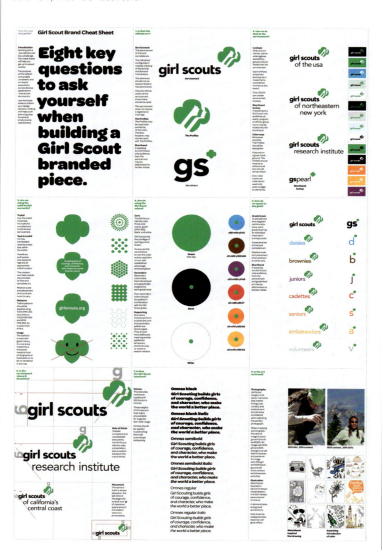

2010 · OCD · US · Identity · Girl Scouts of the United States

2010 · Ludovic Balland · CH · Poster

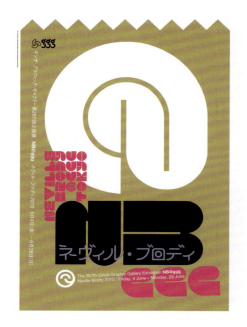

2010 · Neville Brody · UK/JP · Poster

2010 · Neville Brody · UK · Identity · Anti-Design Festival

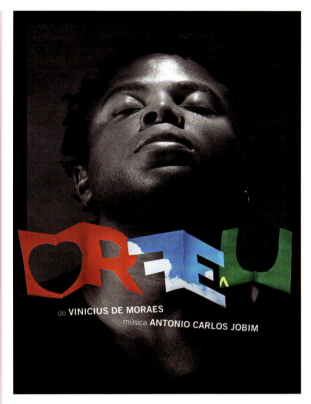

2010 · Felipe Taborda, Glaucio Ayala (PH) · BR · Poster

2010 · NB Studio · UK · Poster

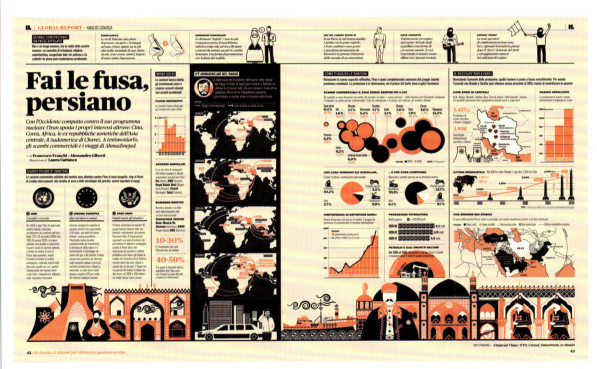

2010 · Francesco Franchi (AD) · IT · Magazine spread, Information graphic

2010 · 2xGoldstein · DE · Poster

2010 · Codefrisko · BE · Identity · Les Tartes de Françoise

2010 · Thonik · NL · Identity · VPRO

The rise in internet use at the turn of the 21st century had a drastic effect on print media circulation, so much so that a number of experts predicted its imminent demise. By the 2010s, however, fresh opportunities offered by digital media production, and the immediacy of online sales which functioned without the standard model for distribution, had resulted in the rise of new, non-mainstream magazines. Exciting publications, unhampered by the need to please a mass readership and hence able to make use of uncompromising design concepts, soon began to appear. The boom in such indie magazines led to the opening in several major cities of a new type of shop, a cross between a news kiosk and a bookshop, set up to sell the increasing numbers of intriguing magazines emerging around the world.

Mit dem Anstieg der Internetnutzung nach der Jahrhundertwende reduzierten sich die Auflagen von Printmedien drastisch, viele Experten prophezeiten gar deren Ende. Die neuen Möglichkeiten digitaler Medienproduktion und des Onlinevertriebs ohne klassische Vertriebsstrukturen führten spätestens ab den 2010er-Jahren jedoch auch zu einem Anstieg neuer Magazine jenseits des Mainstreams. Unabhängig von den Konventionen massentauglicher Publikationen entstanden faszinierende Hefte mit kompromisslosen Gestaltungskonzepten. Durch den Boom der Indiemagazine entstand in Großstädten sogar eine neue Gattung Shops zwischen Kiosk und Buchhandel, in denen sich immer wieder neue faszinierende Hefte aus aller Welt finden lassen.

Avec la montée en puissance d'Internet au tournant du millénaire, les tirages de la presse écrite ont radicalement chuté, à tel point que de nombreux experts prédisaient sa disparition. Dans les années 2010 néanmoins, les nouvelles possibilités offertes par la production de médias numériques et l'immédiateté de la vente en ligne en dehors des structures de distribution standard ont donné naissance à de nouveaux magazines en marge du courant dominant. D'intéressantes publications ont ainsi vu le jour à l'écart du grand public en recourant à des concepts graphiques sans concessions. Suite au boom de ces magazines indépendants, les grandes villes ont vu s'ouvrir un nouveau genre de boutiques entre le kiosque et la librairie, qui proposent un nombre croissant de revues singulières éditées dans le monde entier.

A Smart Magazine for Women
Issue 2

Riposte

N°2

In this issue:
Deborah Sussman,
Chimamanda
Ngozi Adichie,
Purple Milk,
and Lizzo.

UK 10, EU 11, US 16

www.ripostemagazine.com

2013 · Shaz Madani · UK · Magazine cover (front and back)

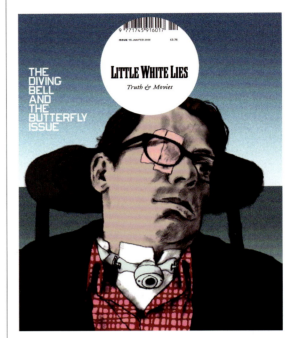

2008 · Paul Willoughby (AD, ILL), Rob Longworth (AD) · UK · Magazine cover

2010 · Paul Willoughby · UK · Magazine cover

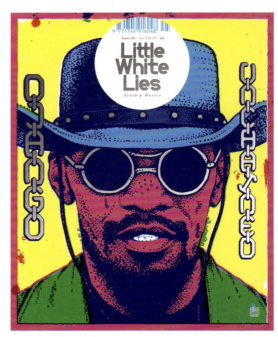

2013 · Paul Willoughby · UK · Magazine cover

2007 · Meiré und Meiré · DE · Magazine cover

2011 · Felix Burrichter, Dylan Fracareta · US · Magazine cover

2015 · David Lane, Harri Peccinotti (PH) · UK · Magazine cover

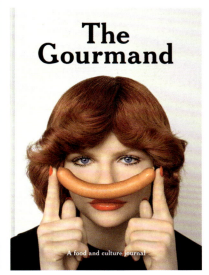

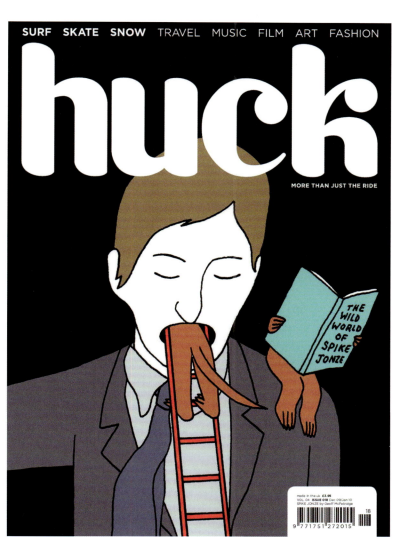

2009 · Rob Longworth, Geoff McFetridge (ILL) · UK · Magazine cover

2011 · Brian McMullen, Walter Green, Noriko Yamaguchi · US · Magazine cover

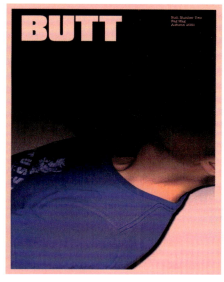

2001 · Jop van Bennekom · NL/UK · Magazine cover

2009 · Omar Sosa, Albert Folch · ES · Magazine cover

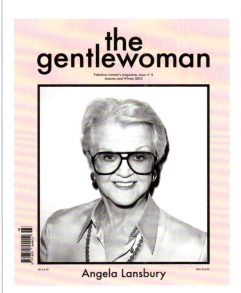

2011 · Jop van Bennekom · NL/UK · Magazine cover

2006 · Hort · DE/US · Poster

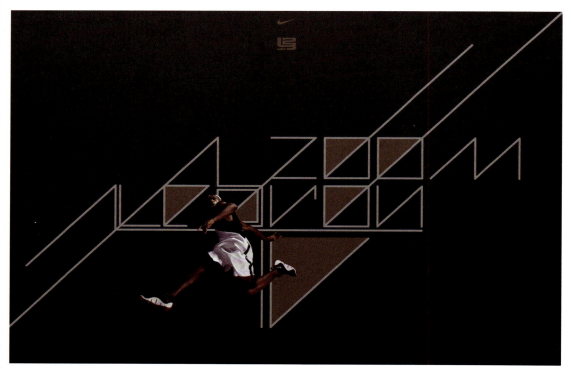

2007 · Hort · DE/US · Poster

2010 · Hort · DE · Identity · Bauhaus Dessau

Hort (1994) is the brainchild of designer Eike König (1968, Hanau, Germany), whose initial concept for his studio in Frankfurt (later moving to Berlin) was to create a collaborative design environment. Over the years König has managed to mix his own experimental work with commissions for clients such as Nike, *The New York Times*, and Walt Disney. After originally studying graphic design in Darmstadt, he worked as art director at Logic Records, before opening his own practice. König has taught regularly at the Bauhaus University in Weimar, at the University of Art and Design in Offenbach, and the University of Mainz.

Hort (1994) ist das Geisteskind des Grafikdesigners Eike König (1968, Hanau), dem es darum ging, in Frankfurt (und später Berlin) ein Designumfeld zu schaffen, das der Kooperation förderlich ist. Im Lauf der Jahre ist es König gelungen, seine Experimentalarbeit mit Aufträgen für Auftraggeber wie Nike, *The New York Times* und Walt Disney zu verbinden. Nach einem Grafikstudium in Darmstadt war er bei Logic Records als Artdirector tätig, ehe er sein eigenes Studio gründete. König unterrichtet regelmäßig an der Bauhaus-Universität Weimar, an der Hochschule für Gestaltung in Offenbach sowie an der Universität Mainz.

Hort (1994) est une création du graphiste Eike König (1968, Hanau, Allemagne). Le concept original du studio francfortois (installé plus tard à Berlin) était de créer un environnement de design collaboratif. Au fil des années, König a su intégrer son propre travail expérimental dans ses réalisations pour des clients comme Nike, *The New York Times* et Walt Disney. Après des études de graphisme à Darmstadt, il a été directeur artistique chez Logic Records, puis a ouvert son propre studio. König a enseigné régulièrement à la Bauhaus-Universität Weimar, à la Haute École d'art et de design d'Offenbach et à l'université de Mayence.

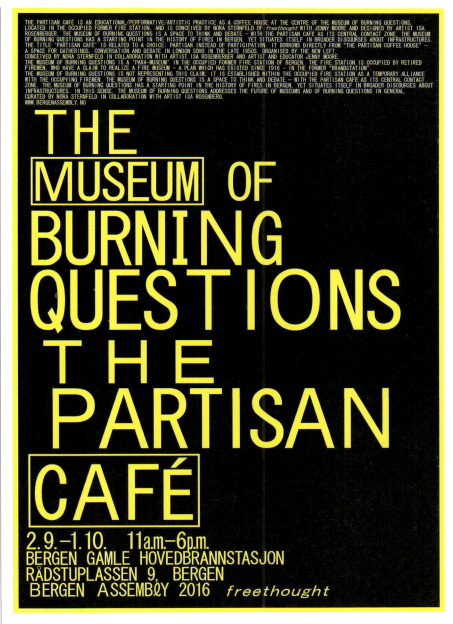

2016 · Hort · DE/NO · Poster

2016 · Hort · DE · Poster, Identity · Tanzplattform Deutschland

2010 · Hort · DE/DK · Poster

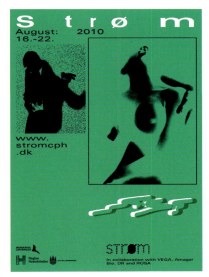

2010 · Hort · DE/DK · Poster

2010 · Hort · DE/DK · Poster

2011

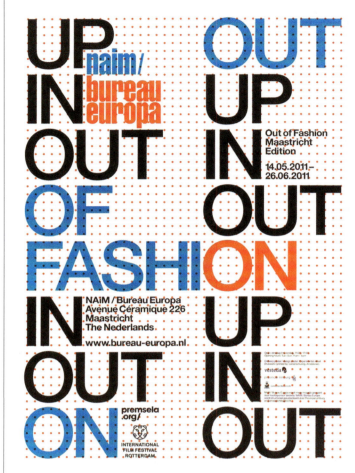

2011 · Experimental Jetset · NL · Poster

2011 · Thelab · US · Logo · Comedy Central

2011 · Kurppa Hosk · SE · Logo · Unit Portables

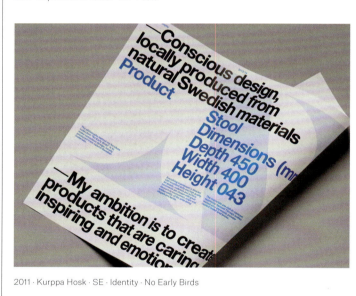

2011 · Kurppa Hosk · SE · Identity · No Early Birds

2011 · Lava · NL · Logo · THNK

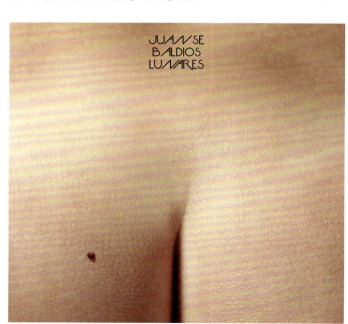

2011 · Alejandro Ros, Marcelo Setton (PH) · AR · Record cover

2011 · Kyle Cooper, Prologue Films · US · Opening titles

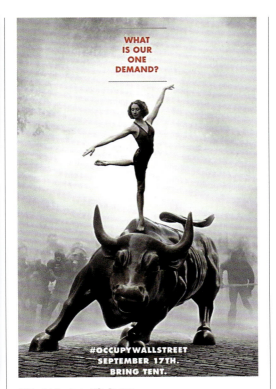

2011 · Ad Busters · US · Poster

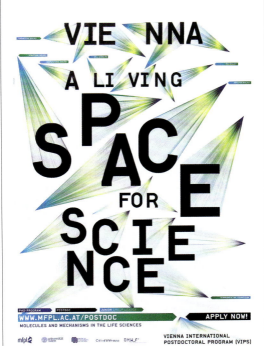

2011 · Buero Bauer · AT · Poster

2011 · Marian Bantjes · CA · Poster

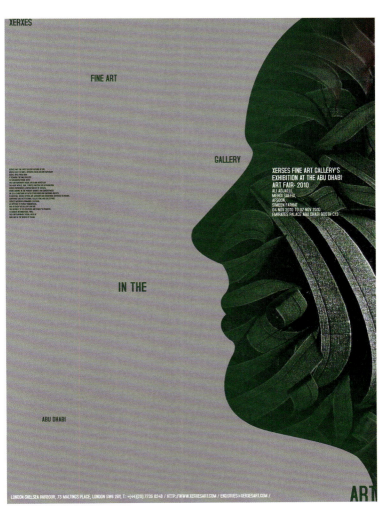

2011 · Mehdi Saeedi · IR · Poster

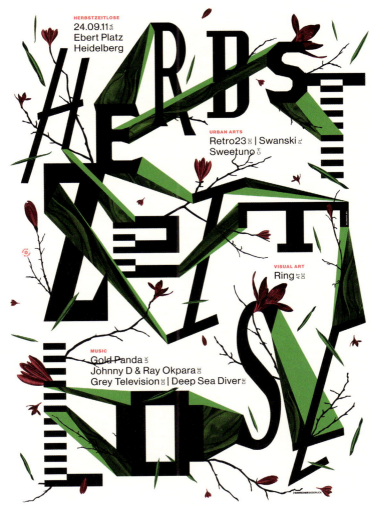

2011 · Götz Gramlich · DE · Poster

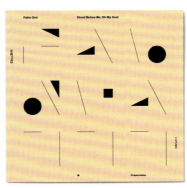
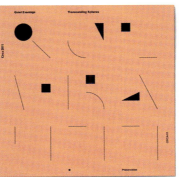
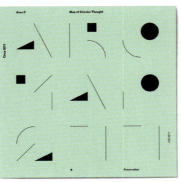
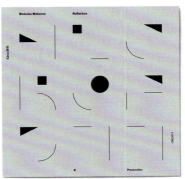
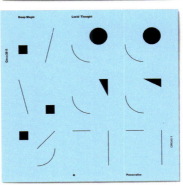
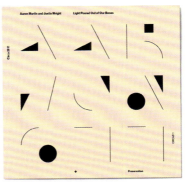

2011 · Mark Gowing · AU · Posters

The American business magazine *Business-week* was first published in 1929, and in 2009 the media company Bloomberg acquired and totally revamped the long-established publication. The young British art director Richard Turley introduced an entirely new design concept to the renamed *Bloomberg Business-week*, and it was above all his imaginative ideas for the front cover which gave the magazine a whole new look, earning it many "likes" on social networks.

Das erste Heft der amerikanischen Wirtschaftszeitschrift *Businessweek* erschien 1929. Der Medienkonzern Bloomberg kaufte das Traditionsblatt 2009 und überarbeitete es vollständig. Unter der Artdirection des jungen britischen Designers Richard Turley erhielt *Bloomberg Businessweek* ein neues Gestaltungskonzept. Vor allem die genialen Coverideen sorgten für eine völlig neue Wahrnehmung der Zeitschrift und für viele Likes in den sozialen Netzwerken.

La parution du premier numéro du magazine économique américain *Businessweek* remonte à 1929. Le groupe de médias Bloomberg acquit cette publication historique en 2009 et la transforma intégralement. Sous la direction artistique du jeune graphiste britannique Richard Turley, elle fut renommée *Bloomberg Businessweek* avec un concept graphique entièrement nouveau. Ce sont surtout les idées géniales des couvertures qui ont entièrement changé la perception du magazine et suscité quantité de *likes* sur les réseaux sociaux.

2011 · Richard Turley (AD) · UK/US · Magazine cover

2013 · Richard Turley (AD) · UK/US · Magazine cover

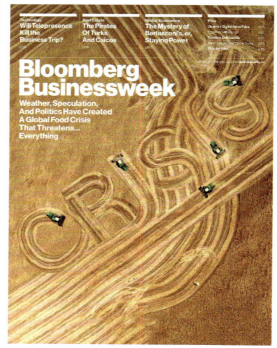

2011 · Richard Turley (AD) · UK/US · Magazine cover

2012 · Richard Turley (AD) · UK/US · Magazine cover

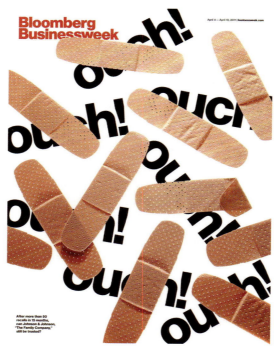

2011 · Richard Turley (AD) · UK/US · Magazine cover

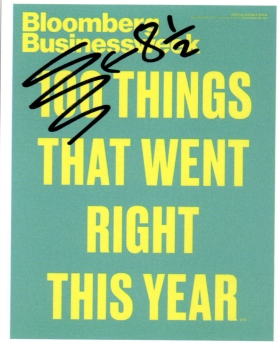

2013 · Richard Turley (AD) · UK/US · Magazine cover

2013 · Richard Turley (AD) · UK/US · Magazine cover

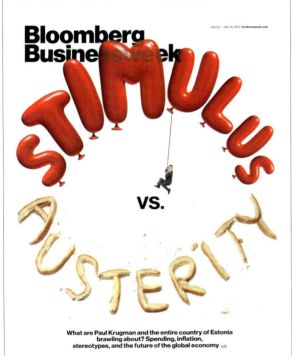

2012 · Richard Turley (AD) · UK/US · Magazine cover

2012 · Richard Turley (AD) · UK/US · Magazine cover

2010s · Richard Turley (AD) · UK/US · Magazine spreads

Richard Turley (1976, Bristol, England) is a creative director with a body of distinguished work in media. In 2010 he was responsible for the complete visual overhaul of *Bloomberg Businessweek*, and then went on to join MTV in 2014 as its first Senior Vice-President of Visual Storytelling. With a deep understanding of both design and editorial, Turley has expanded the remit of the creative director and its influence on the way information is communicated. Having studied at art school in Liverpool and worked at *The Guardian* in London, he has become a key force in transforming traditional media in the digital era.

Richard Turley (1976, Bristol, England) zeichnet sich als Kreativdirektor insbesondere durch seine Arbeit in den Medien aus. 2010 übernahm er die vollständige Neugestaltung der Zeitschrift *Bloomberg Businessweek*, 2014 ging er als erster Senior Vice-President of Visual Storytelling zu MTV. Durch sein Verständnis für die grafische ebenso wie die redaktionelle Seite des Mediums hat Turley den Aufgabenbereich des Kreativdirektors erweitert, aber auch seinen Einfluss auf die Art und Weise, Informationen zu kommunizieren. Nach dem Besuch der Kunstakademie in Liverpool und einer Anstellung bei der Tageszeitung *The Guardian* in London ist er zu einer maßgeblichen Gestalt beim Übergang der traditionellen Medien in die digitale Ära geworden.

Richard Turley (1976, Bristol, Angleterre) est un directeur créatif qui s'est distingué par un ensemble de projets dans les médias. En 2010, il a été chargé de la refonte visuelle de *Bloomberg Businessweek*, avant de rejoindre MTV en 2014 en qualité de premier vice-président pour la narration visuelle. Doté d'une profonde connaissance du graphisme et de l'édition, Turley a élargi son champ de compétences de directeur créatif et son influence sur la manière de communiquer l'information. Après des études artistiques à Liverpool et un passage par *The Guardian*, à Londres, il est devenu un acteur clé de la transformation des médias traditionnels à l'ère du numérique.

Flexible Branding

Already in the 1920s Lucian Bernhard had developed a design concept which was the first to allow companies to adopt a flexible trademark. For one particular wholesale business he designed more than 40 logos to present the firm's across-the-board activities. Some 90 years later, other designers came up with the same idea, for clients such as the internet service provider AOL and the city of Melbourne. The various design solutions included changing configurations or colors, shapes, or even typefaces, as in the case of the German art exhibition documenta. Stefan Sagmeister created an unusually innovative concept for Casa da Música, the concert hall in Porto. Software created especially for the project analyzed a number of possible motifs for use in the design of the logo, and then helped to combine different elements to construct a distinctive symbol.

Bereits in den 1920er-Jahren entwickelte Lucian Bernhard ein Gestaltungskonzept, das erstmals ein flexibles Markenzeichen für ein Unternehmen vorsah. Für einen Großhandelsvertrieb entwickelte er über vierzig variable Logos, um die inhaltliche Bandbreite der Firma zu visualisieren. Neunzig Jahre später kamen Gestalter auf die gleiche Idee, beispielsweise für den Internetkonzern AOL oder für die australische Stadt Melbourne. Die Varianz der Lösungen reichte von wechselnden Mustern, Farben, Formen und sogar Schriften, wie bei dem Erscheinungsbild der Kunstausstellung documenta. Ein besonders innovatives Konzept entwickelte Stefan Sagmeister für das Konzerthaus Casa da Música im portugiesischen Porto. Eine eigens für dieses Projekt entwickelte Software analysierte die im Kontext des Logos verwendeten Bildmotive und generierte ein darauf abgestimmtes individuelles Zeichen.

Dès les années 1920, Lucian Bernhard élaborait un concept graphique permettant pour la première fois aux entreprises de bénéficier d'une marque flexible. C'est ainsi qu'il développa pour un grossiste plus de quarante logos à l'image des activités globales de la société. Environ 90 ans plus tard, d'autres graphistes ont eu la même idée – notamment pour le fournisseur de services Internet AOL ou la ville de Melbourne. La palette de solutions incluait des variations sur les motifs, les couleurs, les formes et les caractères, comme pour l'exposition d'art documenta en Allemagne. De son côté, Stefan Sagmeister a développé un concept particulièrement novateur pour la salle de concerts Casa da Música à Porto. Un logiciel spécialement conçu pour ce projet a analysé divers motifs possibles pour le logo et généré un symbole spécifique à partir de différents éléments.

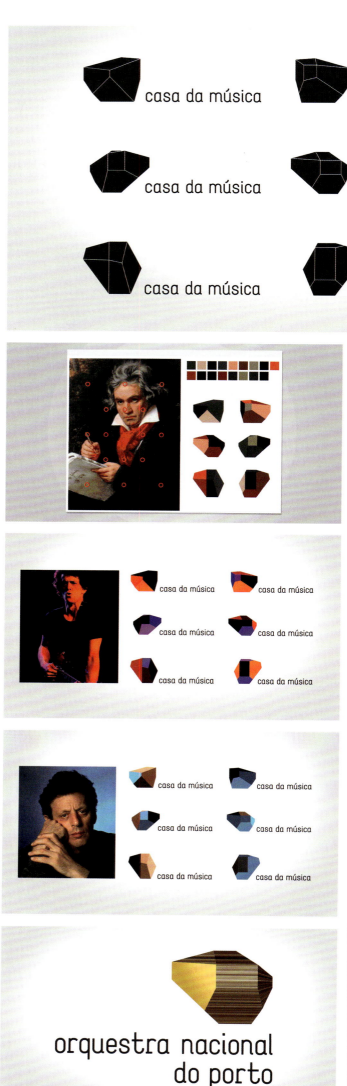

2007 · Stefan Sagmeister · US/PT · Identity · Casa da Música

2009 · Wolff Olins · UK/US · Identity · AOL

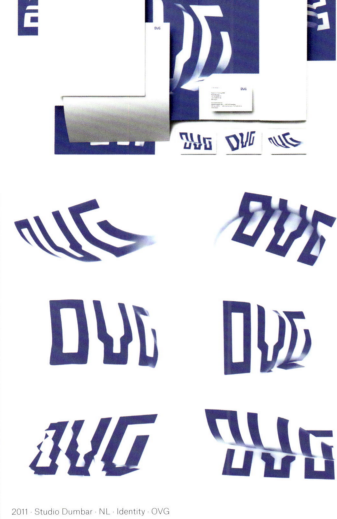

2011 · Studio Dumbar · NL · Identity · OVG

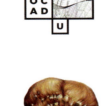

2011 · Bruce Mau Design · CA · Identity · OCAD University

2012 · Leftloft · IT/DE · Identity · documenta (13)

PROUD

2014 · Designpolitie · NL · Identity · Proud

2016 · Kurppa Hosk · SE · Identity · Stockholm concert hall

427

2012

Stefan Sagmeister's exhibition project **The Happy Show** opens at the Chicago Institute of Contemporary Art

The exhibition **The Printed Book: A Visual History** is shown in Amsterdam

The exhibition **Graphic Design: Now in Production** opens at the Walker Art Center

2012 · Chris Martin (ILL), Love Design · UK · Packaging

2012 · Michael Bierut, Pentagram · US · Packaging

2012 · Detail · IE · Logo · Merrion Square

2012 · Paula Scher, Pentagram · US · Logo · Windows 8

2012 · 2x4 · US · Logo · Pérez Art Museum, Miami

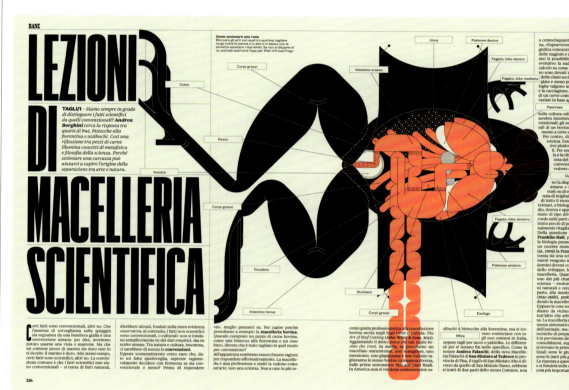

2012 · Francesco Franchi (AD) · IT · Magazine spreads

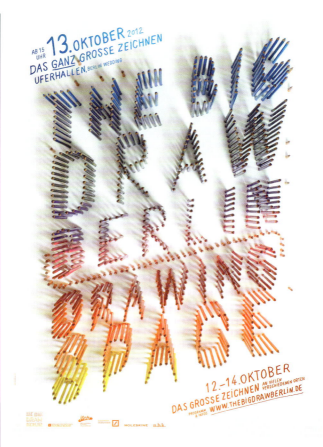

2012 · Ariane Spanier · DE · Poster

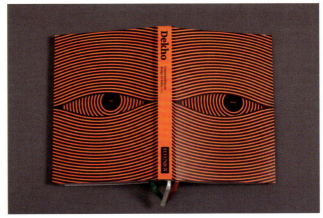

2012 · Oded Ezer · IL · Poster

2012 · Codesign · IN · Book cover

2012 · Anagrama · MX · Packaging

2017 · Craig & Karl, Thomas Alberty (AD) ·
UK/US · Magazine cover

2012 · Louise Fili · US · Stamp

2012 · Lamm & Kirch · DE · Poster

2012 · Sasha Vidakovic · BA/US · Poster

2012 · BVD · SE · Identity · Seven Eleven

2012 · Heine/Lenz/Zizka · DE · Packaging

2012 · Wolff Olins · UK/US · Identity · USA Today

2012 · Wolff Olins · UK/US · Newspaper design

2012 · Wolff Olins · UK/US · Newspaper design

WOLFF OLINS

Wolff Olins (1965, London) is an international brand consultancy whose many notable achievements include the identity for the London 2012 Summer Olympics. With offices in San Francisco and New York as well, the firm has established a global community of thinkers and makers with a unique design focus. Founded by graphic designer Michael Wolff (1933, London) and brand consultant Wallace Olins (1930–2014, London), the business was acquired in 2001 by the New York-based communications group Omnicom. Their works have been exhibited in London at the Design Museum and the V&A.

Wolff Olins (1965, London) ist eine internationale Brand Consultancy, zu deren renommierten Projekten unter anderem das Corporate Design für die Sommerolympiade 2012 in London gehört. Die Firma, die Büros auch in New York und San Francisco unterhält, bildet eine globale Gemeinschaft von Denkern und Machern, deren Augenmerk ganz auf dem Design liegt. Sie wurde von dem Grafikdesigner Michael Wolff (1933, London) und dem Brand Consultant Wallace Olins (1930–2014, London) gegründet und ging 2001 in den Besitz der Kommunikationsgruppe Omnicom mit Sitz in New York über. Ihre Arbeiten wurden in London im Design Museum sowie im V&A ausgestellt.

Wolff Olins (1965, Londres) est une agence internationale de conseil en identité de marque dont les nombreuses réalisations remarquées comptent notamment le visuel des jeux Olympiques d'été de Londres de 2012. Avec des bureaux à New York et San Francisco, la firme a constitué une communauté mondiale de concepteurs-réalisateurs portant une attention tout à fait unique au design. Fondée par le graphiste Michael Wolff (1933, Londres) et le consultant en marques Wallace Olins (1930–2014, Londres), elle a été rachetée en 2001 par Omnicom, le groupe de communication new-yorkais. Leurs travaux ont été exposés à Londres au Design Museum et au V&A.

1994 · Wolff Olins · UK · Logo · Orange

2003 · Wolff Olins · UK · Logo · British Telecom

2006 · Wolff Olins · UK/NO · Logo · Telenor

2012 · Wolff Olins · UK/US · Logo · Belkin

1997 · Wolff Olins · UK/PT · Logo · Portugal Telekom

2004 · Wolff Olins · UK · Logo · Unilever

2007 · Wolff Olins · UK/JP · Logo · Wacom

2012 · Wolff Olins · UK · Logo · London 2012

2000 · Wolff Olins · UK/DE · Logo · E.ON

2005 · Wolff Olins · UK · Logo · Manpower

2007 · Wolff Olins · UK/US · Logo · New York City

2012 · Wolff Olins · UK/ES · Logo · Repsol

2000 · Wolff Olins · UK · Logo · Tate Galleries

2005 · Wolff Olins · UK · Logo · Macmillan

2008 · Wolff Olins · UK/US · Logo · Booz & Co.

2016 · Wolff Olins · UK/US · Logo · The Met

2001 · Wolff Olins · UK/CH · Logo · Schaulager

2006 · Wolff Olins · UK · Logo · Djuice

2010 · Wolff Olins · UK/US · Logo · PWC

2016 · Wolff Olins · UK/IT · Logo · Enel

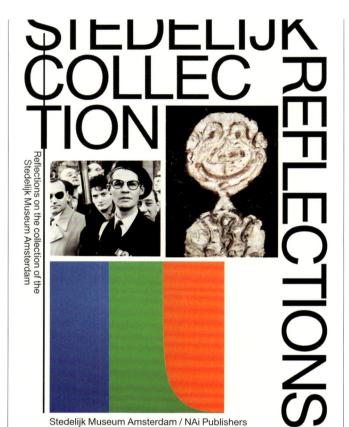

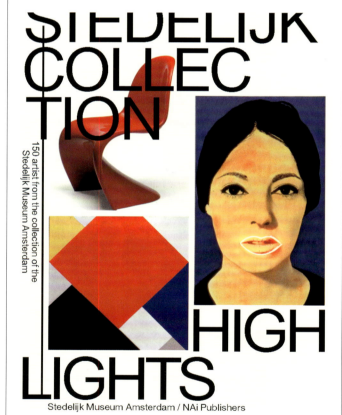

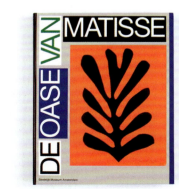

Mevis & Van Deursen (1986, Amsterdam) is the graphic design studio of Dutch partners Armand Mevis (1963, Oirsbeek) and Linda van Deursen (1961, Aardenburg). After graduating from the Gerrit Rietveld Academy in Amsterdam the pair have focused on publications and identities for artists, fashion designers, and architects, by exploring the interplay between imagery and typography. Commissions have included work for the Stedelijk Museum, the Museum of Contemporary Art in Chicago, and the New Institute in Rotterdam. Mevis is artist director of the Werkplaats Typography and van Deursen is senior critic at Yale School of Art.

Mevis & Van Deursen (1986, Amsterdam) ist das Grafikdesignstudio der niederländischen Partner Armand Mevis (1963, Oirsbeek) und Linda van Deursen (1961, Aardenburg). Nach dem Besuch der Gerrit Rietveld Academy in Amsterdam konzentrierte sich das Duo vorwiegend auf Publikationen und Identitäten für Künstler, Modedesigner und Architekten, und dabei galt ihr Augenmerk insbesondere dem Zusammenspiel von Bildsprache und Typografie. Damit bekamen sie Aufträge u. a. vom Stedelijk Museum, dem Museum of Contemporary Art in Chicago und dem New Institute in Rotterdam. Mevis ist zudem Design Critic am Werkplaats Typografie, und van Deursen ist Senior Critics an der Yale School of Art.

Mevis & Van Deursen (1986, Amsterdam) est le studio de graphisme des associés néerlandais Armand Mevis (1963, Oirsbeek) et Linda van Deursen (1961, Aardenburg). Après avoir obtenu leur diplôme à l'académie Gerrit Rietveld à Amsterdam, le duo s'est concentré sur des publications et des identités pour des artistes, des créateurs de mode et des architectes en explorant l'interaction entre images et typographie. Leurs commandes ont compté des réalisations pour le Stedelijk Museum Amsterdam, le musée d'art contemporain de Chicago et le Nouvel Institut de Rotterdam. Mevis est aussi le directeur artistique de Werkplaats Typografie et Linda est intervenante principale à la Yale School of Art.

2012 · Mevis & Van Deursen · NL · Identity · Stedelijk Museum

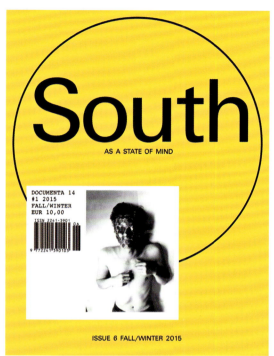

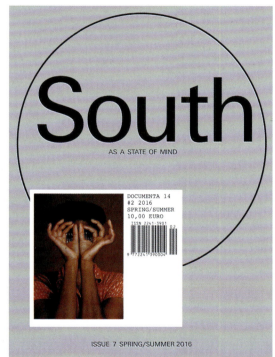

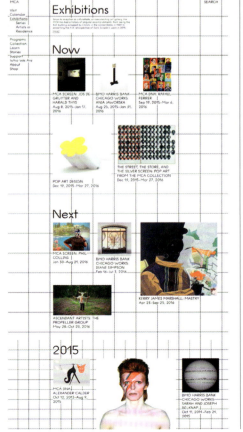

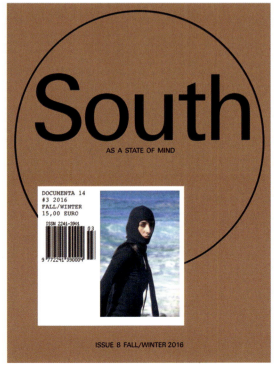

2015 · Mevis & Van Deursen, Dylan Fracareta, Tomas Celizna (WD) · NL/US · Identity · Chicago Museum of Contemporary Art

2016 · Mevis & Van Deursen · NL · Magazine covers

2013

2013 · Sascha Lobe, Simon Brenner · DE · Poster

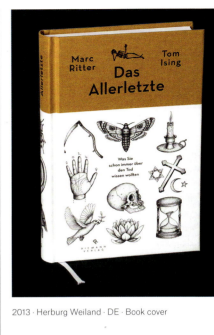

2013 · Herburg Weiland · DE · Book cover

2013 · Michael Bierut, Pentagram · US · Logo · Mohawk Fine Papers

ART**RIO**

2013 · Dupla Design · BR · Logo · Art Rio

TELEMARK

2013 · Snøhetta · NO · Logo · Telemark

2013 · Les Graphiquants · FR · Poster

2013 · Rodrigo Tovar, Sociedad Anónima · MX · Packaging

2013 · Alejandro Ros · AR · Record cover

2013 · Ludovic Balland · CH/PL · Poster

2013 · Gavillet & Cie · CH · Book series

2013 · Kurppa Hosk · SE · Identity · Spread the Sign

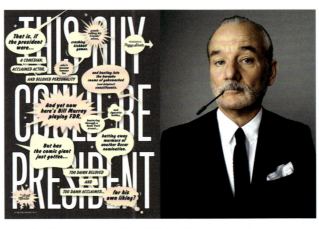

2013 · Fred Woodward, Peggy Sirota (PH) · US · Magazine spread

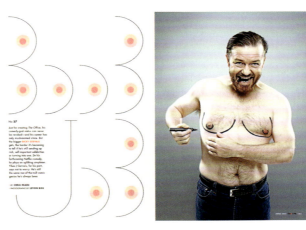

2013 · Fred Woodward, Levon Biss (PH) · US · Magazine spread

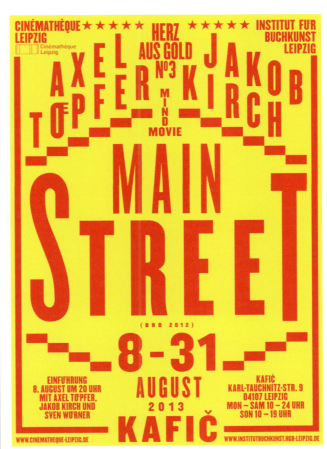

2013 · Lamm & Kirch · DE · Poster

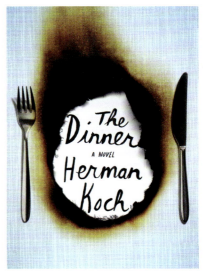

2013 · Chip Kidd · US · Book cover

2013 · MuirMcNeil · UK · Poster

2013 · Anna Berkenbusch · DE · Book cover

2013 · Antoine+Manuel · FR · Poster

Mirko Borsche · Germany

Mirko Borsche (1971, Tegernsee, Germany) is a German graphic designer whose work has a strong focus on editorial and branding design. After attending Kingston University in London, Borsche moved back to Germany to study communication design at Augsburg. Starting his career in advertising, he worked at the Springer & Jacoby advertising agency before going on to design the magazine for leading German newspaper *Süddeutsche Zeitung*. Since 2007 Borsche has been the art director of the highly influential weekly magazine for *Die Zeit*. His Munich-based studio is also responsible for innovative identity projects and work for clients such as the Bavarian State Opera, Nike, and the Munich design museum Die Neue Sammlung.

Mirko Borsche (1971, Tegernsee) ist ein deutscher Grafikdesigner, der sich in seiner Arbeit insbesondere dem Editorial und Branding Design widmet. Auf ein Studium an der Kingston University in London folgte ein Studium des Kommunikationsdesigns in Augsburg. Anschließend arbeitete Borsche zunächst in der Werbebranche bei Springer & Jacoby, später war er für das Gesicht des Magazins der *Süddeutschen Zeitung* verantwortlich. Seit 2007 ist Borsche Artdirector des Magazins der Wochenzeitung *Die Zeit*. Sein Studio mit Sitz in München übernahm auch die Gestaltung innovativer Identitäten für die Bayerische Staatsoper, Nike, das Münchner Designmuseum, Die Neue Sammlung und andere.

Mirko Borsche (1971, Tegernsee, Allemagne) est un graphiste allemand dont le travail porte principalement sur le design éditorial et l'image de marque. Après des études à l'université Kingston à Londres, Borsche rentre au pays pour suivre des études de design communicationnel à Augsbourg. Il débute ensuite dans la publicité pour l'agence Springer & Jacoby, avant de se charger du graphisme éditorial pour le magazine du grand quotidien allemand *Süddeutsche Zeitung*. Depuis 2007, Borsche est directeur artistique du très influent magazine de l'hebdomadaire *Die Zeit*. Son studio à Munich assure aussi des projets d'identité innovants et compte parmi ses clients le Bayerische Staatsoper, Nike ou le musée du design Neue Sammlung à Munich.

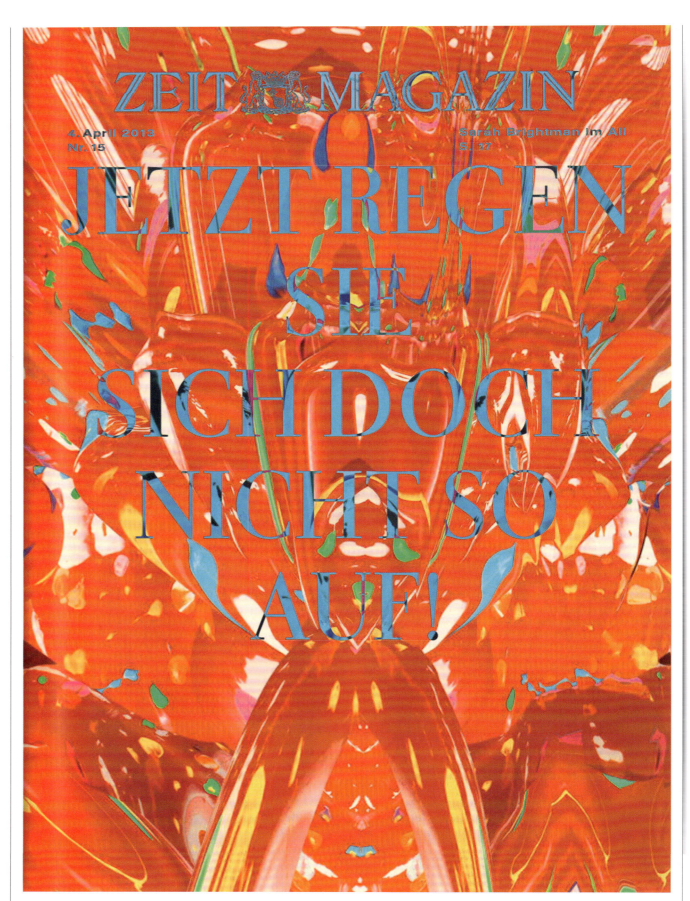

2013 · Mirko Borsche · DE · Magazine cover

In 2007 Mirko Borsche was appointed creative director of *Zeit Magazin*, the supplement to the German weekly newspaper *Die Zeit*. Since then, he has continued to surprise readers with his fresh ideas for designs which smoothly run alongside the magazine's discussion of a variety of social issues. One innovative example is the double cover, which presents contrasting visual ideas on two consecutive front pages.

Im Jahr 2007 wurde Mirko Borsche Kreativdirektor des *Zeit Magazins*, das der Wochenzeitung *Die Zeit* beiliegt. Seither überrascht er immer wieder mit neuen Gestaltungskonzepten unterschiedlicher Gesellschaftsthemen. Ein Beispiel sind die Doppelcover die visuelle Ideen im Spannungsfeld von zwei aufeinanderfolgenden Titelseiten präsentieren.

En 2007, Mirko Borsche fut nommé directeur créatif de *Zeit Magazin*, le supplément de l'hebdomadaire allemand *Die Zeit*. Depuis, il a régulièrement surpris les lecteurs avec de nouvelles approches graphiques en accord avec les articles sur une variété de sujets de société. Borsche est notamment l'auteur de la couverture double pour présenter des idées visuelles contrastées sur deux couvertures consécutives.

2006 · Mirko Borsche · DE · Magazine cover

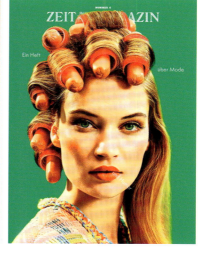

2017 · Mirko Borsche · DE · Magazine covers

2011 · Mirko Borsche · DE · Magazine covers

2011 · Mirko Borsche · DE · Magazine covers

2016 · Mirko Borsche · DE · Magazine spreads

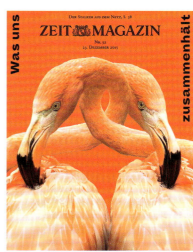

2015 · Mirko Borsche · DE · Magazine covers

2014

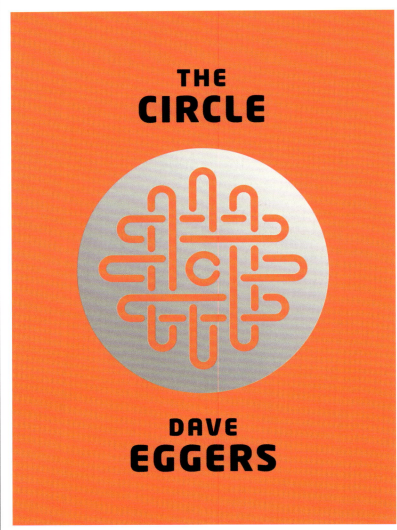

2014 · Jessica Hische · US · Book cover

2014 · Holger Jacobs, Mind Design · UK · Logo · Ecelctic

2014 · Michael Bierut, Pentagram · US · Logo · MIT Media Lab

2014 · DesignStudio · UK/US · Logo · Airbnb

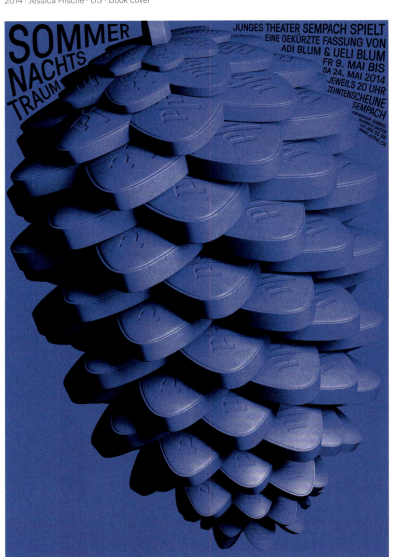

2014 · Erich Brechbühl · CH · Poster

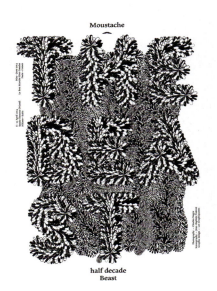

2014 · Les Graphiquants · FR · Poster

2014 · Ariane Spanier · DE · Magazine cover

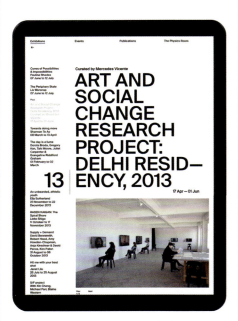

2014 · Timothy Kelleher, Matthew Arnold, Greg Brown, Sons & Co. · NZ · Website

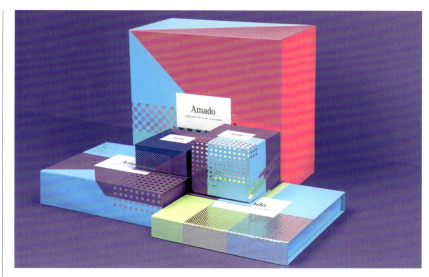

2014 · Anagrama · MX · Identity · Amado

2014 · Eduardo Aires, White Studio · PT · Identity · Porto

2014 · Snask · SE · Brochure cover

2014 · Frédéric Vanhorenbeke, Coast · BE · Poster

2014 · Majid Abbasi · IR · Poster

2014 · StudioStudio · BE · Poster

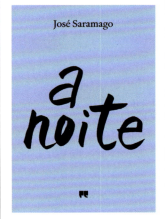
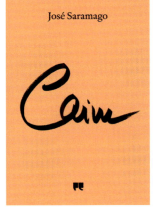

2014 · Jorge Silva · PT · Book covers

2011 · Elastic · US · Opening titles

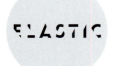

Elastic (2008, Santa Monica) is a creative firm based in California with acclaimed work in visual effects and animation. Elastic is a full-service studio whose work in motion graphics, live action, and CG has brought compelling visual identities to TV series such as Marvel's *Daredevil* (2015) and *Luke Cage* (2016), HBO's *Game of Thrones* (2011), the Academy Awards, and numerous feature films and advertising spots. Their clients have included prominent Hollywood studios and advertising agencies.

Elastic (2008, Santa Monica) ist ein Kreativbüro mit Sitz in Kalifornien, das mit Arbeiten im Bereich Visual Effects und Animation bekannt wurde. Als Full-Service-Studio hat Elastic mit Motion Graphics, Live Action und CG vielen Fernsehserien zu einer überzeugenden visuellen Identität verholfen, ob nun *Daredevil* (2015) und *Luke Cage* (2016) von Marvel, *Game of Thrones* (2011) von HBO, die Academy Awards oder zahlreiche Spielfilme und Werbespots. Zu den Auftraggebern von Elastic gehören namhafte Hollywood-studios und Werbeagenturen.

Elastic (2008, Santa Monica) est une firme créative basée en Californie, très remarquée pour son travail dans les domaines des effets spéciaux et de l'animation. Ce studio offre des services complets et son travail en graphisme animé, prise de vue réelle et images de synthèse a donné les identités visuelles fascinantes de séries télévisées comme *Daredevil* (2015) et *Luke Cage* (2016) de l'univers Marvel, *Game of Thrones* de HBO (2011), des Oscars et de nombreux longs métrages et spots publicitaires. Ses clients comptent de grands studios et agences publicitaires d'Hollywood.

2014 · Elastic · US · Opening titles

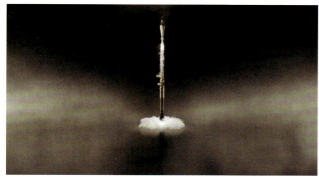

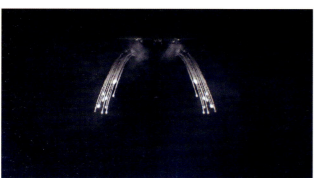

In the late 1990s, the American pay television service HBO revolutionized the whole concept of the TV series with its screening of shows such as *The Sopranos* and then *Game of Thrones* a few years later. Streaming platforms such as Netflix, founded in 1997, gave the genre a boost and a new lease of life, and TV series became ever more lavishly produced, often with production values to equal those seen in full-length movies. Such developments were also reflected in the ingenuity of the opening credits, some of the best known of which were designed by the American studio Elastic.

Ab den späten 1990er-Jahren revolutioniert der amerikanische Bezahlsender HBO mit Serien wie *The Sopranos* oder *Game of Thrones* das Genre der Fernsehserie. Durch Streamingdienste wie das 1997 gegründete Netflix wurde dieses Feld noch einmal belebt. Serien wurden zunehmend aufwendiger produziert und erreichten nicht selten Kinoniveau. Diese Entwicklung spiegelt sich auch in den kreativen Vorspannen wider, von denen einige der bekanntesten durch das US-Studio Elastic realisiert wurden.

À la fin des années 1990, la chaîne de télévision payante américaine HBO a révolutionné le concept de série télévisée, notamment avec *Les Soprano* et *Game of Thrones*. Ce domaine a aussi été fortement stimulé par les plateformes de diffusion comme Netflix, fondé en 1997. Les séries étaient produites avec des moyens considérables, et il n'était pas rare que leur valeur de production atteigne celle des longs métrages. La même évolution s'est constatée aussi dans la créativité des génériques dont certains des plus célèbres ont été réalisés par le studio américain Elastic.

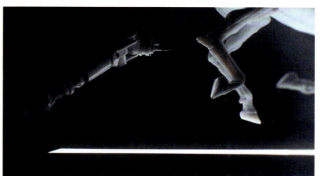

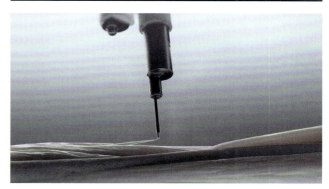

2016 · Elastic · US · Opening titles

2016 · Elastic · US · Opening titles

441

2015

Controversy erupts concerning the new logo for the **Tokyo 2020 Olympics**, claimed by some to be plagiarism

The Zurich **Museum für Gestaltung** moves to a new space at Toni-Areal, a former dairy factory

The first **Graphic Design Festival Scotland** is held in Glasgow

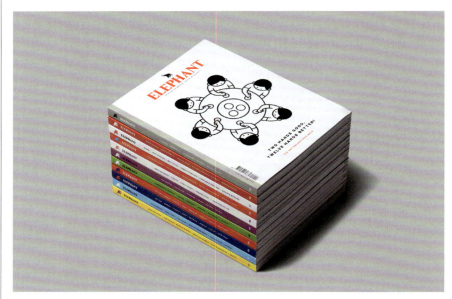

2015 · Atlas · ES · Magazine

2015 · Bruce Mau Design · CA · Identity · Sonos

FRANK DANDY

2015 · Kurppa Hosk · SE · Logo · Frank Dandy

2015 · Antoine+Manuel · FR · Logo · Villa Noailles-Hyères

2015 · Google design team · US · Logo · Google

2015 · Bureau Borsche · DE · Posters

A Kickstarter campaign to back the reissue
of the 1975 **NASA** graphics standards manual
raises almost a million dollars

French design magazine **Étapes**
celebrates its 20th anniversary

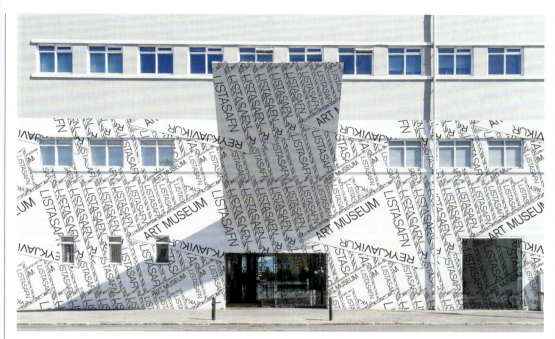

2015 · Karlssonwilker · US/IS · Identity · Reykjavik Art Museum

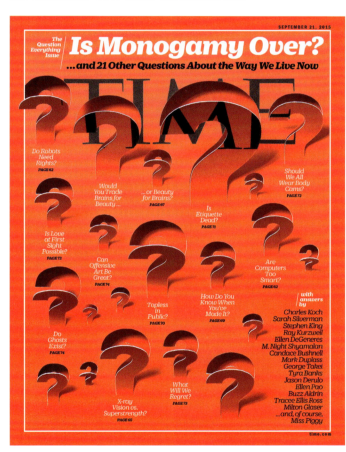

2015 · Ariane Spanier · DE/US · Magazine cover

2015 · Ermolaev Bureau · RU · Packaging

2015 · Jens Müller, Optik · DE · Magazine cover

2015 · Anna Berkenbusch · DE · Poster

2015 · Mainstudio · NL · Identity · De School

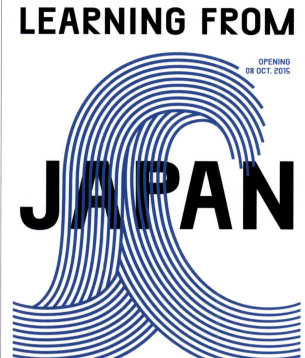

2015 · Studio Claus Due · DK · Poster

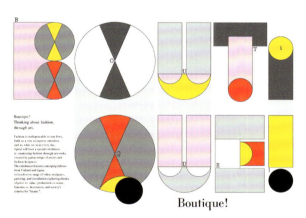

2015 · Ryosuke Uehara · JP · Poster

2015 · Fol · TR · Poster

Art Direction

While in recent years advertising agencies have gradually taken over tasks that were previously assigned to graphic designers, at the same time a reverse trend has also set in. Using the umbrella term "art direction", many design studios now undertake the entire visual design of individual campaigns. Their collaboration with photographers and stylists has enabled them to produce fascinating images in which even the minutest detail is not left to chance.

Während in den vergangenen Jahren Werbeagenturen zunehmend auch Aufgaben übernahmen, die traditionell im Grafikdesign verortet waren, ließ sich auch ein gegenläufiger Trend feststellen. Viele Designbüros übernahmen unter dem Überbegriff „Art Direction" die visuelle Gestaltung einzelner Kampagnen. In Zusammenarbeit mit Fotografen und Stylisten entstanden so faszinierende Bildmotive, bei denen kein Detail dem Zufall überlassen wurde.

Si les agences publicitaires ont dernièrement assumé des tâches relevant traditionnellement des graphistes, la tendance inverse a également été constatée. Sous le terme générique de direction artistique, nombre d'agences de graphisme se chargent à présent de la conception visuelle de campagnes. En collaboration avec des photographes et des stylistes, elles peuvent produire d'étonnantes images dans lesquelles aucun détail n'est laissé au hasard.

2013 · Sagmeister & Walsh · US · Ad

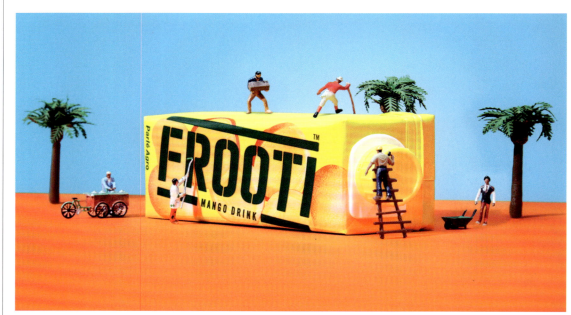

2015 · Sagmeister & Walsh · US · Ad

2015 · Sagmeister & Walsh, Jessica Walsh (AD), Sing-Sing (PH) · US · Ad

2015 · Snask · SE · Ad

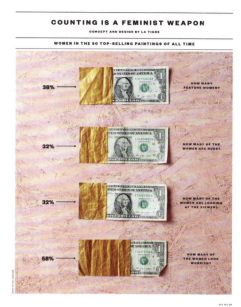

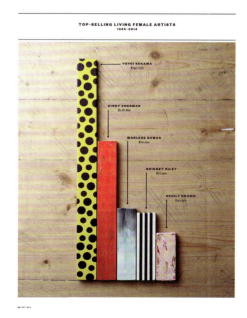

2016 · La Tigre, Atlas, Matteo Cremonini (PH) · IT/ES · Information graphics

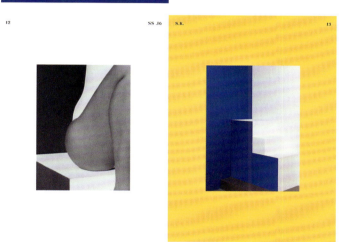

2015 · Les Graphiquants · FR · Brochure spreads

2015 · Lundgren+Lindqvist · SE · Poster

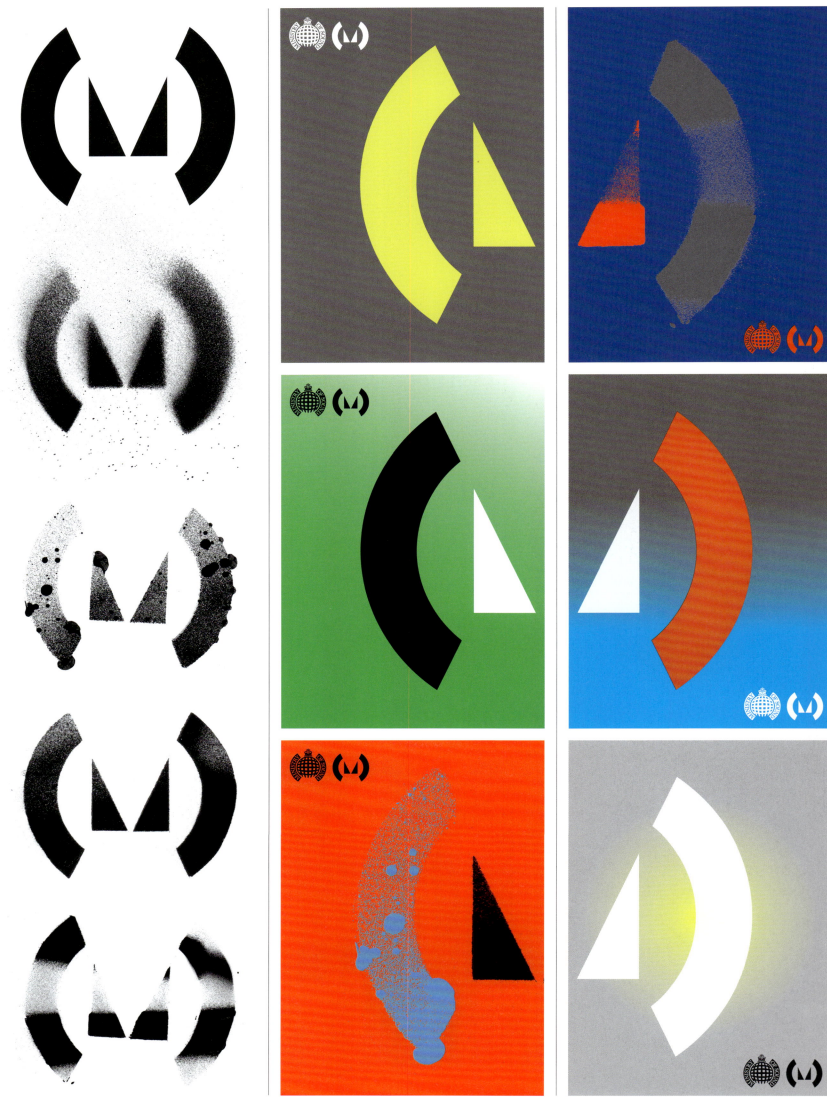

2016 · Tony Brook, Claudia Klat, Jonathan Nielsen, Spin · UK · Identity · Ministry of Sound

2016 · Tony Brook, Claudia Klat, Jonathan Nielsen, Spin · UK · Identity · Jigsaw

Spin (1992, London) is the creative firm of Tony Brook (1962, Halifax, England) and Patricia Finegan (1965, Manchester), widely acknowledged for its excellence in the design areas of identity, print, digital, posters, and typography. Spin's clients have included Deutsche Bank, Nike, Christie's, Channel Four, and many others. As active proponents of design and visual culture, in 2010 the duo co-founded Unit Editions—a small publishing venture—with designer and writer Adrian Shaughnessy (1953, Glasgow). Brook is a visiting professor at the School of Communication Design, UCA, in Epsom, and has also served as president of the UK chapter of the AGI.

Spin (1992, London) ist das Kreativbüro von Tony Brook (1962, Halifax, England) und Patricia Finegan (1965, Manchester), allgemein anerkannt wegen ihrer Meisterschaft in den Bereichen Identity, Print, Digital, Plakat und Typografie. Zu Spins Auftraggebern zählen u. a. die Deutsche Bank, Nike, Christie's und Channel Four. Als engagierte Fürsprecher einer Design- und visuellen Kultur rief das Duo 2010 zusammen mit dem Schriftsteller und Grafikdesigner Adrian Shaughnessy (1953, Glasgow) den kleinen Verlag Unit Editions ins Leben. Brook ist Gastprofessor an der School of Communication Design, UCA, in Epsom, England, und zudem Präsident des UK-Verbands der AGI.

Spin (1992, Londres) est le studio créatif de Tony Brook (1962, Halifax, Angleterre) et Patricia Finegan (1965, Manchester), largement reconnu pour ses réalisations majeures en matière d'identités, de matériel imprimé, de numérique, d'affiches et de typographie. Les clients de Spin incluent Deutsche Bank, Nike, Christie's, Channel Four et bien d'autres. Promoteur du design et de la culture visuelle, le duo a co-fondé en 2010 Unit Editions, une petite société d'édition avec le graphiste et écrivain Adrian Shaughnessy (1953, Glasgow). Brook est professeur invité à la School of Communication Design de l'UCA, à Epsom, et a aussi été président de la section anglaise de l'AGI.

2017 · Tony Brook, Claudia Klat, Spin · UK · Identity · Collect

Christoph Niemann · Germany/United States

2014 · Christoph Niemann · DE/US · Magazine cover

2011 · Christoph Niemann · DE/US · Magazine cover

2015 · Christoph Niemann · DE/US · Magazine cover

Christoph Niemann (1970, Waiblingen, Germany) is a designer, author, and visual artist with extensive work in editorial. His straightforward approach to vector illustration has brought Niemann plenty of commissions for magazine covers, including *The New Yorker*, *The New York Times Magazine*, and *The Atlantic*, amongst a host of others. A frequent lecturer on design and illustration, he has won several awards from the Art Directors Club, AIGA, and *American Illustration*. After living and working in New York for over a decade, Niemann moved to Berlin where his work is regularly exhibited in art galleries.

Christoph Niemann (1970, Waiblingen) ist ein Grafikdesigner, Autor und Illustrator, der insbesondere im Printbereich arbeitet. Seinen erfrischenden Umgang mit Vektorgrafik nutzten zahlreiche Magazine für ihre Coverillustrationen, unter vielen anderen *The New Yorker*, *The New York Times Magazine* und *The Atlantic*. Niemann ist ein vielfach gefragter Dozent zum Thema Design und Illustration, zudem wurde er mit Preisen vom Art Directors Club, des AIGA und vom *American Illustration* ausgezeichnet. Er lebte und arbeitete über zehn Jahre lang in New York, ehe er nach Berlin zog, wo seine Arbeiten regelmäßig in Galerien ausgestellt werden.

Christoph Niemann (1970, Waiblingen, Allemagne) est un graphiste, auteur et artiste visuel avec un vaste éventail de projets dans le domaine de l'édition. Son approche très directe de l'illustration vectorielle lui a valu une foule de commandes de couvertures de magazines, notamment pour *The New Yorker*, *The New York Times Magazine* et *The Atlantic*, parmi bien d'autres clients. Niemann donne souvent des conférences sur le design et l'illustration, et il a remporté plusieurs prix de l'Art Directors Club, de l'AIGA et d'*American Illustration*. Après avoir vécu et travaillé plus de dix ans à New York, Niemann s'est installé à Berlin, où son travail est régulièrement exposé dans des galeries d'art.

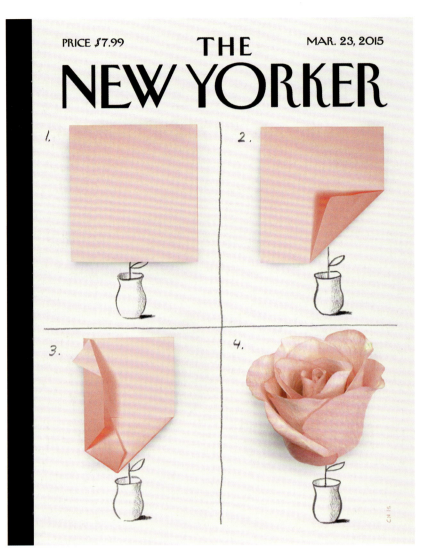

2015 · Christoph Niemann · DE/US · Magazine cover

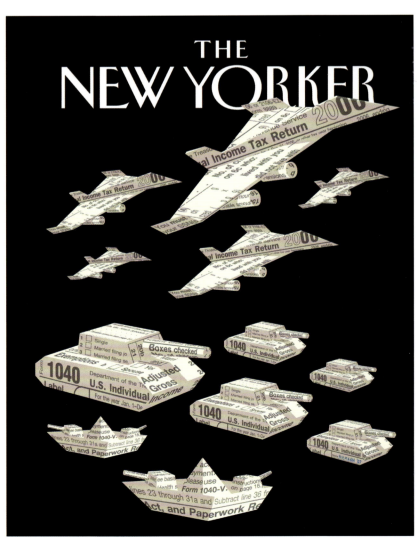

2007 · Christoph Niemann · DE/US · Magazine cover

For a number of years now, Christoph Niemann's cover designs for *The New Yorker* have demonstrated how the power of artwork can persist in an age when photography is omnipresent. Niemann not only experiments with different ideas for images but also with technology. In 2016, he produced a cover for the magazine which became an augmented reality when viewed using a Smartphone app, as well as a cover that could be accessed as a 360-degree video animation to be used in conjunction with various popular virtual reality interfaces (including iPads and Google Cardboard).

Mit seinen Coverentwürfen für das Magazin *The New Yorker* beweist Christoph Niemann seit einigen Jahren, wie kraftvoll Illustration gerade in Zeiten der omnipräsenten Fotografie ist. Dabei experimentiert er nicht nur mit unterschiedlichen Bildideen, sondern auch mit der Technik. 2016 entwickelte er ein Cover, das als Augmented Reality auf dem Smartphone weiterentwickelt wird, weiter ein Cover, das auch als begehbares 360-Grad-Video für die boomenden Virtual-Reality-Brillen entwickelt wurde.

Avec ses conceptions de couvertures pour le magazine *The New Yorker*, Christoph Niemann démontre depuis quelques années toute la puissance de l'illustration, particulièrement à une époque où l'image photographique est omniprésente. Il a pour cela recours non seulement à toutes sortes d'idées graphiques, mais aussi à la technologie. En 2016, il a conçu une couverture qui devenait une réalité augmentée si on la regardait avec une application pour smartphone. Il a également créé une couverture conçue comme une animation à 360 degrés pour diverses interfaces de réalité virtuelle, dont l'iPad et le Google Cardboard.

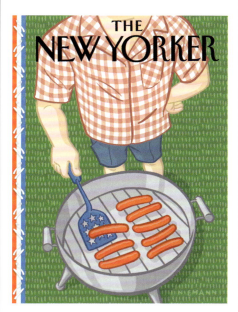

2003 · Christoph Niemann · DE/US · Magazine cover

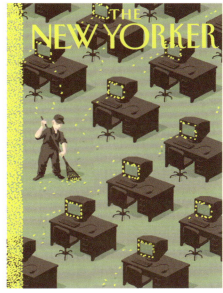

2004 · Christoph Niemann · DE/US · Magazine cover

2001 · Christoph Niemann · DE/US · Magazine cover

2016 · Christoph Niemann · DE/US · Magazine cover

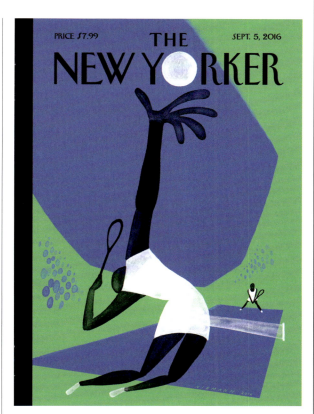

2016 · Christoph Niemann · DE/US · Magazine cover

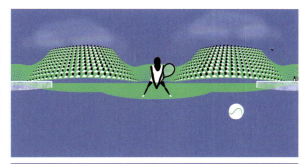

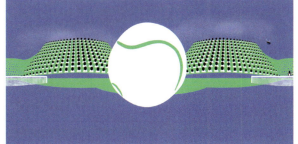

2016 · Christoph Niemann · DE/US · 360° animation

2016 · Christoph Niemann · DE/US · 3D animation

E se con la tua vecchia  ti comprassi un 📱? Basta 🚐. Il prossimo anno vacanze in ⛵. Cos'hanno in comune i nostri amici 👷 & 🕵? Hanno trovato lavoro grazie a subito!

2015 · Leftloft · IT · Identity · Subito

2015 · Leftloft · IT · Identity · Subito

Leftloft

Leftloft (1999, Milan) is an Italian design firm whose cohesive approach amalgamates work in identity, art direction, environmental, print, and digital design. The studio's varied portfolio has included work for Pirelli, documenta (13), Moleskine, and Mondadori, and they have been one of the few in Italy to embrace contemporary design on an international scale. Since 2009, Leftloft has had a branch in Brooklyn, which has further helped to extend their client base. In 2011, they embarked on an extensive rebranding for Inter Milan soccer club, which took three years to be completed.

Leftloft (1999, Mailand) ist eine italienische Designfirma, deren Arbeitsverständnis auf Kohäsion beruht und die sich mit CI-Projekten ebenso beschäftigt wie mit Artdirection, Umwelt-, Print- und digitalem Design. Zu ihren vielfältigen Arbeiten gehören Aufträge für Pirelli, die documenta 13, Moleskine und Mondadori. Als eines der wenigen italienischen Studios ist es ihnen gelungen, zeitgenössisches Grafikdesign international zu vertreten. Seit 2009 unterhält Leftloft auch ein Büro in Brooklyn, wodurch sich der Kundenkreis noch mehr erweitert hat. 2011 übernahm das Studio den Auftrag für das umfassende Neubranding des Fußballklubs Inter Milan, dessen vollständige Umsetzung drei Jahre in Anspruch nahm.

Leftloft (1999, Milan) est une firme de design italienne dont l'approche homogène combine des projets sur l'identité, la direction artistique, le design de l'environnement, le matériel imprimé et la conception numérique. Avec un portefeuille très diversifié de clients comme Pirelli, documenta (13), Moleskine et Mondadori, il s'agit de l'une des rares agences italiennes à traiter le design contemporain à un niveau international. En 2009, l'ouverture d'un bureau à Brooklyn lui a permis d'élargir sa clientèle. En 2011, le studio s'est attelé pendant trois ans à la refonte de l'identité du club de football Inter Milan.

»Our approach could be considered quite common. It's a mixture of rational practices and intuitive trial-and-error actions. It usually sparks off from a 'vision', which is then explored and tested by deep research and backed up by sketches, diagrams, or any other notes that might be helpful in order to share the initial intuition.« Andrea Braccaloni, *designboom.com*, 2014

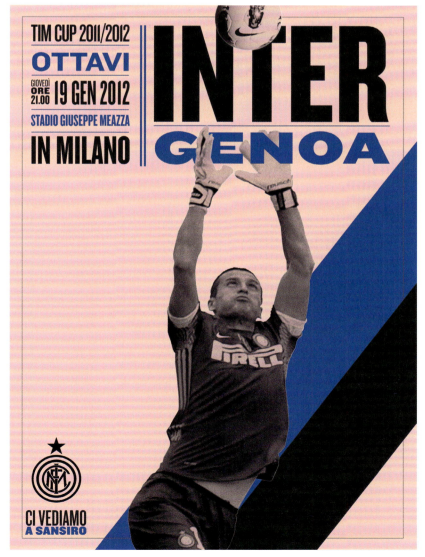

2014 · Leftloft · IT · Identity · Inter Milan

2010 · Leftloft · IT · Logo · Artadoo

SLOWEAR

2009 · Leftloft · IT · Logo · Slowear

2003 · Leftloft · IT · Logo · City Observer

NeTCO

2011 · Leftloft · IT · Logo · Netco

COVEN

2001 · Leftloft · IT · Logo · Coven

SINISTRA ITALIANA

2017 · Leftloft · IT · Logo · Sinistra Italiana

COLMAR

2015 · Leftloft · IT · Logo · Colmar

DIECI

2007 · Leftloft · IT · Logo · Dieci

ICON

2012 · Leftloft · IT · Logo · Icon

2008 · Leftloft · IT · Logo · Design Directory

2016

The **London Design Museum** moves into a new space in smart new premises in Kensington

The **International Poster Biennale of Warsaw** celebrates its 25th competition

Stefan Sagmeister's film documentary **The Happy Film** premieres at New York's Tribeca Film Festival

2016 · Herburg Weiland · DE · Book

2016 · StudioStudio · BE/IS · Brochure cover

2016 · Cyan · DE · Poster

2016 · Mainstudio · NL · Logo · Electriciteitsfabriek

2016 · Raffinerie · CH · Poster

2016 · Build · UK · Ad

2016 · Studio Koniak · IL · Logo · Leny

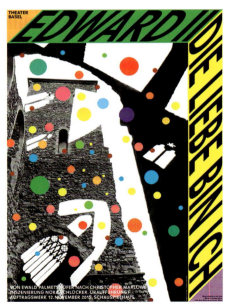

2016 · André Baldinger, Toan Vu-Huu, Baldinger Vu-Huu · FR · Logo · CCCOD

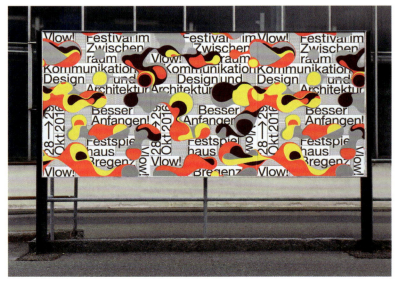

2016 · Felix Pfäffli, Studio Feixen · CH · Poster

2016 · Dupla Design · BR · Identity · Rio 2016 Olympic Games

2016 · Michael Bierut, Pentagram · US · Identity · Hillary for America

2016 · Snask · SE · Identity · Kaibosh

2016 · Kurppa Hosk · SE · Identity · Stockholm concert hall

2016 · Irma Boom · NL · Book

2016 · Erich Brechbühl · CH · Poster

2016 · Mousegraphics · GR/CN · Packaging

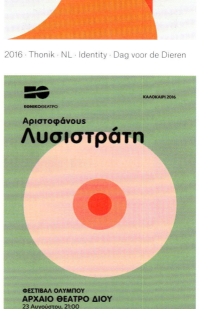

2016 · Thonik · NL · Identity · Dag voor de Dieren

2016 · G Design Studio · GR · Poster series

453

454

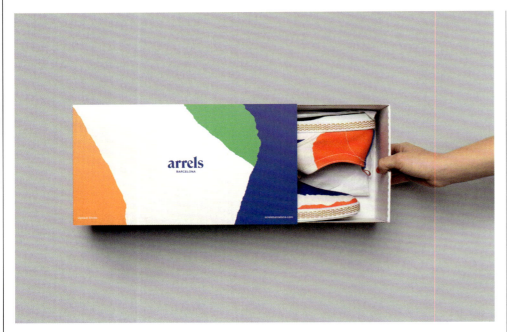

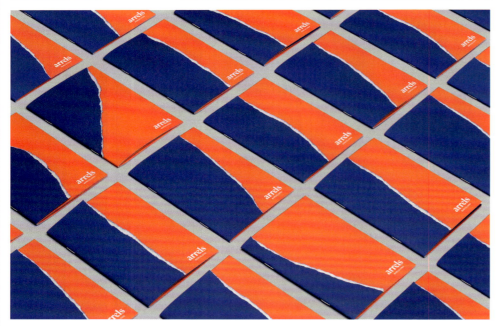

2015 · Hey · ES · Identity · Arrels

2014 · Hey · ES · Packaging/Identity

2014 · Hey · ES · Book cover

2010 · Hey · ES · Book series

2012 · Hey · ES/CL · Identity · Chile Film Commission

Hey

Hey (2007, Barcelona) is a design firm specializing in brand identity, editorial design, and illustration. The studio is a rare example in Spain of design work being undertaken for clients abroad, which includes Apple, Turkish Airlines, General Electric, *The Wall Street Journal*, CBS, and Penguin Random House. With a visual language based on geometry, color, and the application of direct typography, Hey have helped to bring a modern form of Spanish design to the world stage. Since 2014, they have also run their own online store.

Hey (2007, Barcelona) spezialisiert sich als Designfirma auf Brand Identity, Editorial Design und Illustration. Dem Studio ist es als einem der sehr wenigen in Spanien gelungen, einen internationalen Kreis an Auftraggebern aufzubauen, unter anderem Apple, Turkish Airlines, General Electric, *The Wall Street Journal*, CBS und Penguin Random House. Mit einer visuellen Sprache, die auf Geometrie, Farbe und direkter Typografie beruht, hat Hey dazu beigetragen, eine moderne Form des spanischen Designs international bekannt zu machen. Seit 2014 betreibt das Studio auch einen Onlineshop.

Hey (2007, Barcelone) est une firme de design spécialisée dans l'identité de marque, le design éditorial et l'illustration. C'est un des rares studios espagnols à s'être constitué une base de clients internationaux, parmi lesquels Apple, Turkish Airlines, General Electric, *The Wall Street Journal*, CBS et Penguin Random House. Basant son langage visuel sur la géométrie, la couleur et l'emploi d'une typographie directe, Hey a introduit une forme moderne du design espagnol sur la scène internationale. Depuis 2014, l'équipe gère sa propre boutique en ligne.

2016 · Hey · ES/FR · Poster

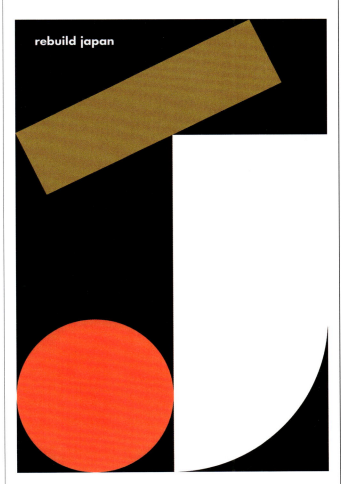

2015 · Hey · ES · Poster

2015 · Sawdust · UK/US · Magazine cover

2014 · Sawdust · UK/IT · Magazine cover

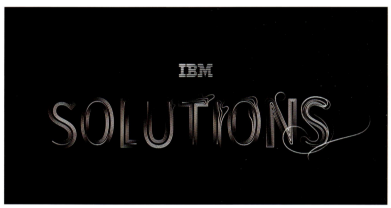

2014 · Sawdust · UK/US · Logos · IBM Solutions

2014 · Sawdust · UK · Record cover

2015 · Sawdust · UK · Magazine cover

2016 · Sawdust · UK/DE · Magazine cover

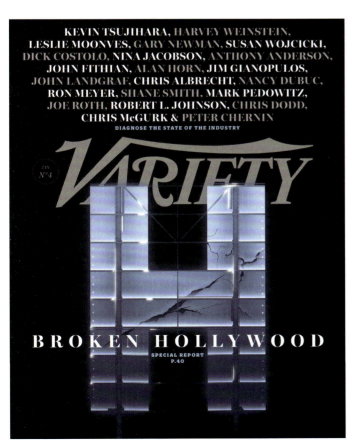

2015 · Sawdust · UK/US · Magazine cover

2016 · Sawdust · UK/US · Magazine cover

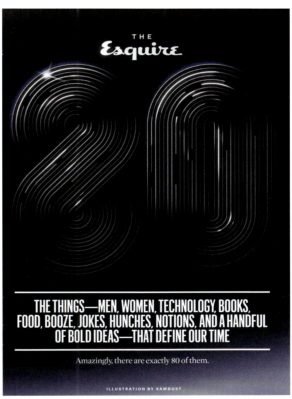

2013 · Sawdust · UK/US · Magazine illustration

Sawdust (2006, London) is the design partnership of Jonathan Quainton (1982, Oxford) and Rob Gonzalez (1980, Oxford). The pair met while they were both studying for national diplomas in graphic design prior to university, and they soon found themselves collaborating on a number of projects throughout the two-year course. Sawdust has built a reputation in bespoke and innovative typography work, applying it to editorial, branding, displays, visual identities, and image creation. Their client list includes Nike, *Wired*, *The New York Times*, Coca-Cola, AKQA, ESPN, among a number of others.

Sawdust (2006, London) ist die Designpartnerschaft von Jonathan Quainton (1982, Oxford) und Rob Gonzalez (1980, Oxford). Die beiden lernten sich noch vor dem Studium bei einem zweijährigen Ausbildungskurs in Grafikdesign kennen und arbeiteten bereits dort häufig an Projekten zusammen. Sawdust machte sich mit maßgeschneiderten und innovativen typografischen Arbeiten einen Namen, ob im Bereich Editorial oder Branding Design, Displays, visuelle Identität oder Imagebildung. Zu ihren Auftraggebern gehören u. a. Nike, *Wired*, *The New York Times*, Coca-Cola, AKQA und ESPN.

Sawdust (2006, Londres) est l'association des graphistes Jonathan Quainton (1982, Oxford) et Rob Gonzalez (1980, Oxford). Ils se sont connus lors d'une formation de deux ans, visant un diplôme national de graphisme avant l'université et pendant laquelle ils n'ont pas tardé à collaborer sur de nombreux projets. Sawdust a acquis une solide réputation grâce à des typographies innovantes et sur mesure dans les domaines de l'édition, du branding, de l'affichage, de l'identité visuelle et de la création d'image. Parmi leurs clients figurent Nike, *Wired*, *The New York Times*, Coca-Cola, AKQA, ESPN et bien d'autres.

2013 · Anette Lenz · DE/FR · Poster

2014 · Anette Lenz · DE/FR · Poster

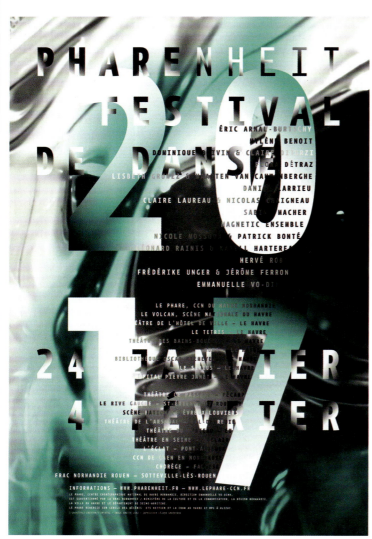

2017 · Anette Lenz · DE/FR · Poster

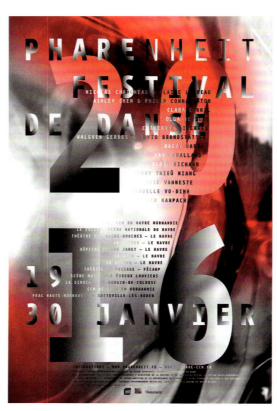

2016 · Anette Lenz · DE/FR · Poster

Anette Lenz (1964, Esslingen, Germany) is a German graphic designer who has lived in Paris since 1990, creating innovative posters and visual identities, mainly for cultural institutions. After completing her studies in Munich she joined French design group Grapus and later co-founded design collective Nous Travaillons Ensemble. In 1993 she opened her own studio and has since worked for clients including the Musée des Arts Décoratifs and Radio France. Her poster designs feature in major collections such as New York's MoMA and the Stedelijk Museum in Amsterdam. Lenz is also much in demand as a lecturer, teaching at institutions including the University of Art and Design (HEAD) in Geneva.

Anette Lenz (1964, Esslingen) ist eine deutsche Grafikdesignerin, die seit 1990 in Paris lebt und vor allem für kulturelle Institutionen innovative Plakate und Erscheinungsbilder geschaffen hat. Nach dem Studium in München wurde sie Mitglied des legendären französischen Designkollektivs Grapus und war Mitbegründerin des Nachfolgebüros Nous Travaillons Ensemble. 1993 gründete sie in Paris ihr eigenes Studio und ist seither für Auftraggeber wie das Musée des Arts Décoratifs oder Radio France tätig. Die von ihr realisierten Plakatentwürfe sind in wichtigen internationalen Sammlungen wie dem MoMA New York oder dem Stedelijk Amsterdam. Neben der gestalterischen Arbeit ist Lenz als Dozentin gefragt und unterrichtete unter anderem an der University of Art and Design (HEAD) in Genf.

Anette Lenz (1964, Esslingen, Allemagne) est une graphiste allemande établie à Paris depuis 1990, qui a surtout créé des affiches et des identités innovantes pour des institutions culturelles. Après ses études à Munich, elle devient membre de Grapus, le légendaire collectif de graphisme français, puis co-fonde Nous Travaillons Ensemble. En 1993, elle ouvre son propre studio à Paris et a travaillé depuis pour le musée des Arts décoratifs et Radio France. Ses créations d'affiches sont représentées au sein de prestigieuses collections internationales comme le MoMA de New York ou le Stedelijk Museum Amsterdam. Lenz est sollicitée pour des conférences et a enseigné notamment à la Haute École d'art et de design (HEAD) à Genève.

2016 · Anette Lenz · DE/FR · Poster

2018 · Anette Lenz · DE/FR · Poster

2013 · Anette Lenz · DE/FR · Poster

2015 · Anette Lenz · DE/FR · Poster

2016 · Anette Lenz · DE/FR · Posters

2016 · Anette Lenz · DE/FR · Brochure spreads

2016 · Anette Lenz · DE/FR · Poster

The first season of the Netflix documentary series **Abstract: The Art of Design** is aired, featuring Paula Scher, Christoph Niemann, and others

The final printed issues of American graphic design magazines **Print** and **How** are published

Briar Levit's film documentary **Graphic Means: A History of Graphic Design Production** is released

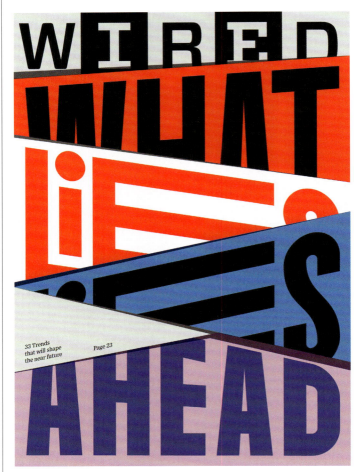

2017 · Felix Pfäffli, Studio Feixen · CH · Magazine cover

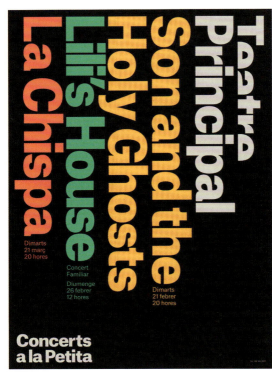

2017 · Atlas · ES · Poster

2017 · Interbrand Milan · IT · Logo · Juventus F.C.

2017 · Sociedad Anónima, Mauro Bonillo (AD) · MX · Signage

2017 · Ludovic Balland · CH · Poster

2017 · Johnson Banks · UK · Logo · Mozilla

2017 · Werklig · FI · Logo · City of Helsinki

2017 · Richard Turley (CD), Wieden+Kennedy · UK · Identity · Formula 1

2017 · Gavillet & Cie · CH · Book

Pentagram partner Marina Willer's first feature film **Red Trees** premieres at the Cannes Film Festival

IBM releases the **IBM Plex** type family, designed by Mike Abbink, to be shared and used by everyone for free

The world's first **Design Film Festival** is held in Singapore, curated by the local design studio Anonymous

2017 · Thonik · NL · Poster

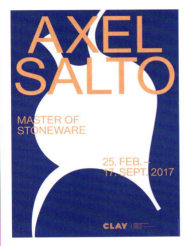

2017 · Studio Claus Due · DK · Poster

2017 · Götz Gramlich · DE · Packaging

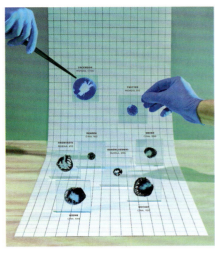

2017 · La Tigre · IT · Information graphics

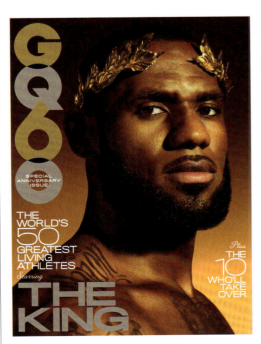

2017 · Fred Woodward, Pari Dukovic (PH) · US · Magazine cover

2017 · Raffinerie · CH · Poster

2017 · Milkxhake · HK · Poster

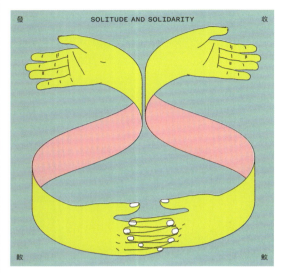

2016 · Jaemin Lee, Studio Fnt · KR · Record cover

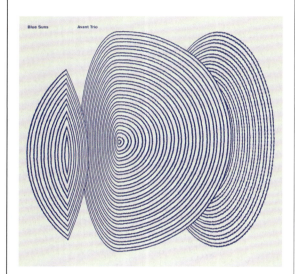

2016 · Jaemin Lee, Studio Fnt · KR · Record cover

2016 · Jaemin Lee, Studio Fnt · KR · Record cover

2016 · Jaemin Lee, Studio Fnt · KR · Identity · Seoul Record Fair

2016 · Jaemin Lee, Studio Fnt · KR · Poster

2016 · Jaemin Lee, Studio Fnt · KR · Poster

2016 · Jaemin Lee, Jisung Park, Studio Fnt · KR · Identity · Seoul Record Fair

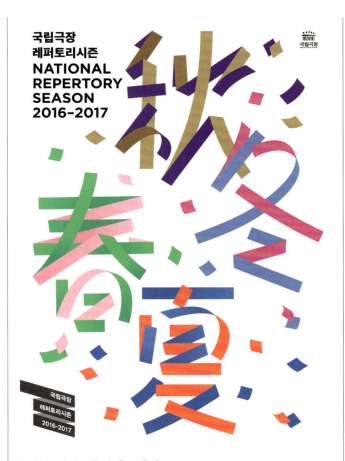

2016 · Jaemin Lee, Studio Fnt · KR · Poster

Jaemin Lee (1979, Seoul) is creative head of Studio Fnt (2006), a leading voice in contemporary graphic design in South Korea. With work in print, brand identity, and digital media, Lee has also been a frequent lecturer at two universities in Seoul. Since 2011 he has worked with the Junglim Foundation on architectural projects, and in the fields of culture, arts, and education, in particular exploring exchanges with the public on the social role of architecture and urban living. Lee's work has influenced the new generation of graphic design professionals both in his own country and across Asia.

Jaemin Lee (1979, Seoul), der Kreativleiter des Studio Fnt (2006), ist eine maßgebliche Stimme im zeitgenössischen Grafikdesign Südkoreas. Jaemin Lee arbeitet in den Bereichen Print, Brand Identity und digitale Medien, zudem lehrt er in Seoul häufig an zwei Universitäten. Seit 2011 arbeitet er mit der Junglim Foundation an Architekturprojekten, aber auch in den Bereichen Kultur, Kunst und Bildung. Dabei widmet er sich insbesondere dem Austausch mit der Öffentlichkeit über die gesellschaftliche Rolle der Architektur und des urbanen Lebens. Mit seiner Arbeit hat er die neue Generation professioneller Grafikdesigner nicht nur in seiner Heimat, sondern in ganz Asien beeinflusst.

Jaemin Lee (1979, Séoul) est le directeur créatif du Studio Fnt (2006), voix majeure du graphisme contemporain en Corée du Sud. Outre son travail en identités de marques et pour les médias imprimés et numériques, Lee a donné de nombreuses conférences dans deux universités à Séoul. Depuis 2011, il travaille sur des projets d'architecture avec la Fondation Junglim, ainsi que dans les domaines de la culture, des arts et de l'éducation, explorant en particulier les échanges avec le public sur le rôle social de l'architecture et de la vie urbaine. Lee a influencé la nouvelle génération de graphistes professionnels dans son pays comme dans le reste de l'Asie.

2011 · Jaemin Lee, Studio Fnt · KR · Poster

2016 · Jaemin Lee, Heesun Kim, Jeeook Choi (ILL), Studio Fnt · KR · Identity · 20th Bucheon International Fantastic Film Festival

2016 · Jaemin Lee, Heesun Kim, Jeeook Choi (ILL), Studio Fnt · KR · Poster

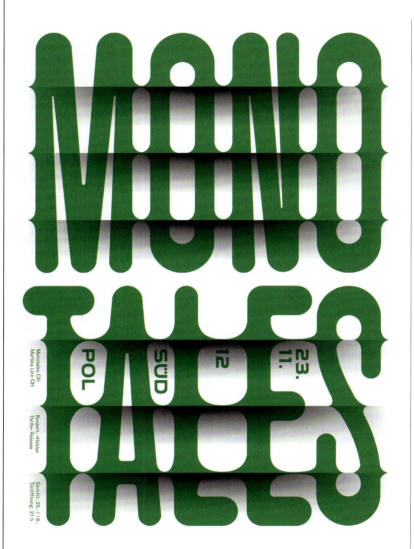

2012 · Felix Pfäffli, Studio Feixen · CH · Poster

2013 · Felix Pfäffli, Studio Feixen · CH · Poster

2013 · Felix Pfäffli, Studio Feixen · CH · Poster

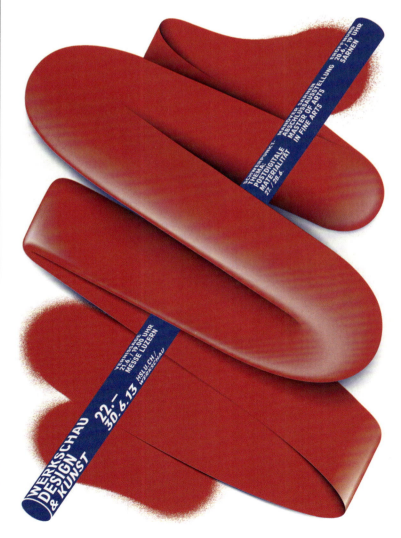

2013 · Felix Pfäffli, Studio Feixen · CH · Poster

2012 · Felix Pfäffli, Studio Feixen · CH · Poster

Felix Pfäffli (1986, Lucerne) is a Swiss designer and lecturer whose work in poster and motion design has been marked by a contemporary take on the use of typography. After studying design in Lucerne and founding in 2009 his own practice, Studio Feixen, Pfäffli has made his name by manipulating the shapes of letters, applying distortions and creating new perspectives. His clients have included Nike, Google, *The New York Times*, and the Nuits Sonores music festival in France. In 2011, Pfäffli started teaching typography, narrative design, and poster design at the Lucerne School of Graphic Design.

Felix Pfäffli (1986, Luzern) ist ein Schweizer Grafikdesigner und Dozent, dessen Werk im Bereich Plakat und Motion Design sich insbesondere durch einen zeitgenössischen Ansatz in der Typografie auszeichnet. Nach dem Grafikdesignstudium in Luzern gründete Pfäffli 2009 sein eigenes Büro, Studio Feixen. Einen Namen machte er sich mit dem Verformen von Buchstaben, wofür er mit Verzerrung arbeitet und dadurch neue Perspektiven schafft. Zu seinen Auftraggebern zählen Nike, Google, *The New York Times* und das französische Musikfestival Nuits Sonores. Seit 2011 unterrichtet Pfäffli Typografie, narratives Grafikdesign und Plakatgestaltung an der Fachklasse Grafik Luzern.

Felix Pfäffli (1986, Lucerne) est un designer et conférencier suisse dont le travail dans le domaine de l'affiche et du design d'animation obéit à une approche contemporaine de la typographie. Après des études de design à Lucerne, il a ouvert Studio Feixen en 2009 et s'est fait connaître en manipulant les caractères, en les déformant et en offrant de nouvelles perspectives à la typographie. Parmi ses clients figurent notamment Nike, Google, *The New York Times* et le festival de musique Nuits Sonores. Depuis 2011, Pfäffli enseigne la typographie, la création narrative et la conception d'affiche à la Haute École de Lucerne.

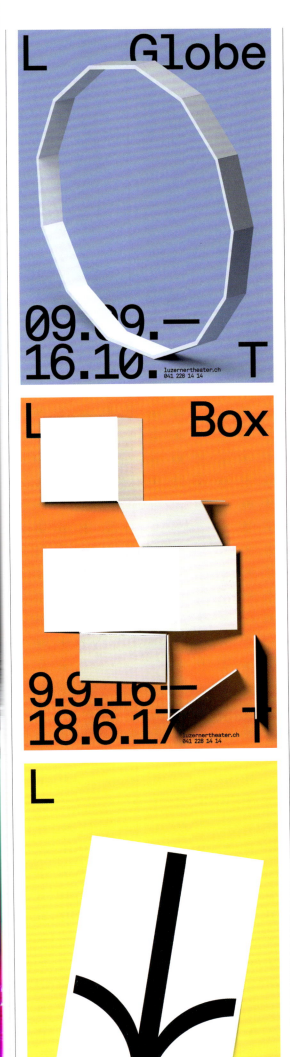

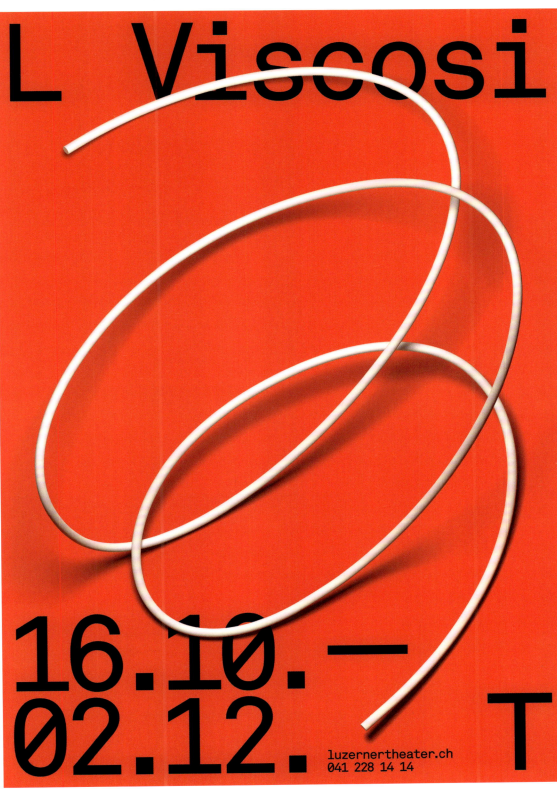

2016 · Felix Pfäffli, Studio Feixen · CH · Identity · Luzerner Theater

465

2018

The poster project **Footb-All Mix** is initiated by Felipe Taborda and Susana Machicao to celebrate the soccer World Cup in Russia

The exhibition **Design Studio** examines the creative design process at the Museum für Gestaltung in Zurich

Greg Durrell's film **Design Canada** is released

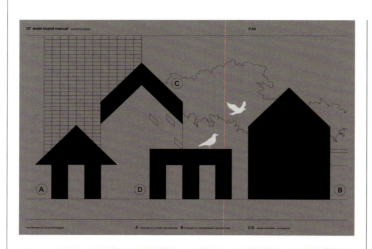

2018 · Lundgren+Lindqvist · SE · Identity · Enter Architecture

2018 · Craig & Karl, David Whitmore (AD) · US/UK · Magazine cover

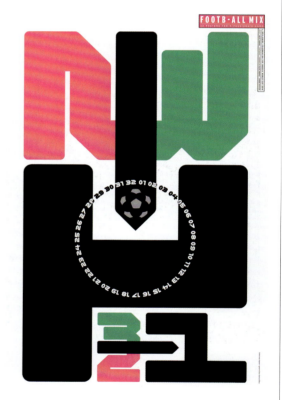

2018 · Neville Brody · UK · Poster

2018 · Chermayeff & Geismar & Haviv · US · Logo · US Open

2018 · Koto · UK · Logo · BlaBlaCar

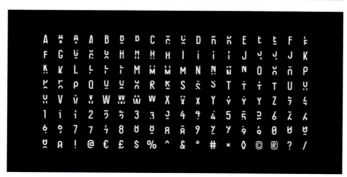

2018 · Wolff Olins, Agence Zélé (signage) · UK/FR · Identity · Lafayette Anticipations

2018 · Commission, Bureau Borsche · UK/DE · Identity · Rimowa

2018 · Vladimir Lifanov, Ilya Lazuchenkov, Egor Myznik, Denis Shlesberg, Erken Kagarov · RU · Logo · Tourism Russia

2018 · Sons & Co. · NZ · Website

2018 · Louis Byrne · UK · Record cover

2018 · Lufthansa Design, Martin et Karczinski · DE · Identity · Lufthansa

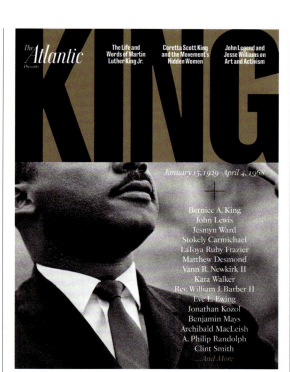

2018 · OCD · US · Magazine cover and spreads

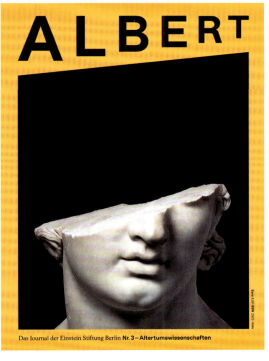

2018 · Fons Hickmann m23 · DE · Magazine cover

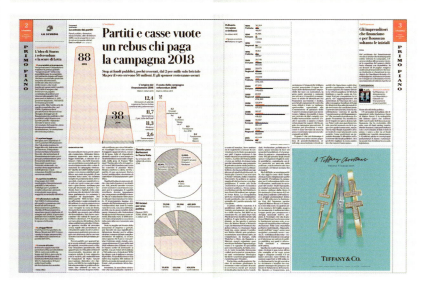

2018 · Francesco Franchi (AD) · IT · Newspaper

2018 · Francesco Franchi (AD) · IT · Newspaper

Francesco Franchi (1982, Rome) is a leading Italian information designer whose work has embraced new forms of visual storytelling by using graphics in an entertaining and informative manner. A graduate of the Politecnico di Milano, with a Master's in industrial design, Franchi has produced groundbreaking work at *Il Sole 24 Ore*, Italy's leading financial newspaper. He has received accolades at the European Design Awards, the D&AD, and SPD Awards, and his work has been exhibited at the V&A in London and New York's Cooper Hewitt, Smithsonian Design Museum.

Francesco Franchi (1982, Rom) ist ein bedeutender italienischer Informationsdesigner, der Grafik unterhaltsam und informativ einsetzt und damit neue Formen des visuellen Erzählens entstehen lässt. Nach dem Besuch des Politecnico di Milano machte Franchi einen Magister in Industriedesign. Für die namhafte italienische Wirtschaftstageszeitung *Il Sole 24 Ore* hat er bahnbrechende Arbeiten vorgelegt. Bei den European Design Awards, vom D&AD und bei den SPD Awards wurde er mit Preisen ausgezeichnet, sein Schaffen wurde im V&A in London und im Cooper Hewitt, Smithsonian Design Museum, in New York mit Ausstellungen gewürdigt.

Francesco Franchi (1982, Rome) est un chef de file italien en design de l'information qui se livre à de nouvelles formes de récit visuel en utilisant le graphisme d'une manière aussi ludique qu'informative. Diplômé de l'École polytechnique de Milan et titulaire d'un master en design industriel, Franchi a produit des travaux révolutionnaires pour le grand quotidien financier italien *Il Sole 24 Ore*. Il a été récompensé aux European Design Awards, aux D&AD Awards et aux SPD Awards, et son travail a été exposé au V&A à Londres, et au Cooper Hewitt, Smithsonian Design Museum à New York.

After more than eight years as art director of *Il Sole 24 Ore*, in 2016 Franchi was appointed managing editor of *La Repubblica*. As well as drawing up a highly innovative master plan for its graphic design, he also developed a content strategy, designed to infuse the daily newspaper with a new relevance to match the digital age. One part of the new concept is *Robinson*, the Sunday supplement which captivates readers with its constant visual reinventions and wonderfully lavish artistic touches.

Nach über acht Jahren als Artdirector der Zeitung *Il Sole 24 Ore* wurde Franchi 2016 zum Managing Editor von *La Repubblica*. Neben einem völlig neuen grafischen Gesamtkonzept entwickelte er auch eine neue inhaltliche Strategie, die der Tageszeitung im digitalen Zeitalter neue Relevanz verleiht. Teil des neuen Konzepts ist unter anderem die sonntägliche Magazinbeilage *Robinson*, die sich visuell immer wieder neu erfindet und durch eine geradezu verschwenderische Menge gestalterischer Details fasziniert.

En 2016, après plus de huit années à la direction artistique du journal *Il Sole 24 Ore*, Franchi est devenu rédacteur en chef de *La Repubblica*. Outre l'élaboration d'un plan graphique très novateur, il a aussi développé une nouvelle stratégie pour les contenus, conférant au quotidien une nouvelle pertinence à l'ère numérique. Le supplément dominical *Robinson* fait partie de cette nouvelle approche et se réinvente continuellement sur le plan visuel pour attirer les lecteurs avec de superbes touches artistiques.

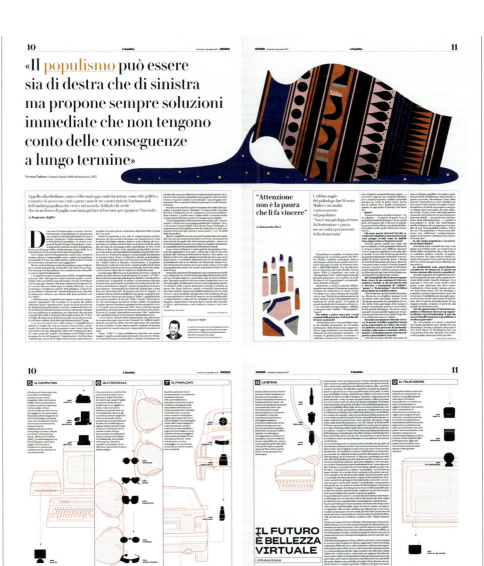

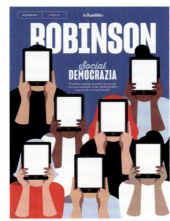

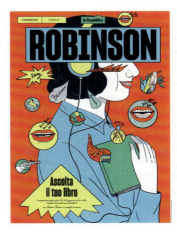

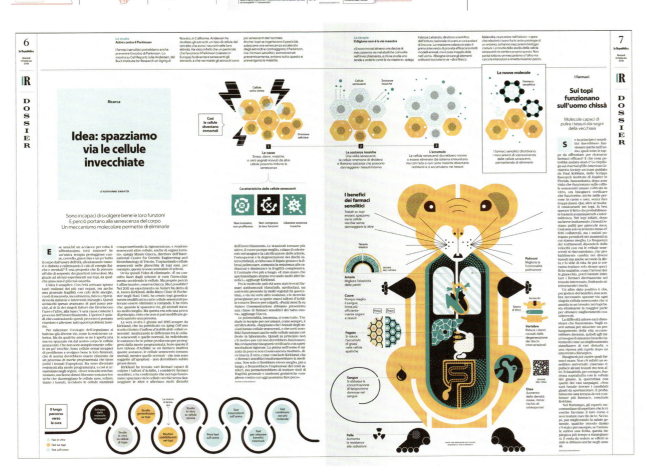

2017 · Francesco Franchi (AD) · IT · Newspaper

2016 · Edel Rodriguez · CU/US/DE · Magazine cover

2017 · Edel Rodriguez · CU/US · Magazine cover

2017 · Edel Rodriguez · CU/US/DE · Magazine cover

2017 · Edel Rodriguez · CU/US/DE · Magazine cover

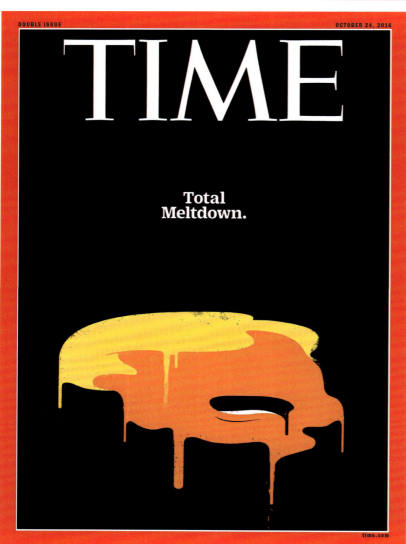

2016 · Edel Rodriguez, P.W. Pine (AD) · CU/US · Magazine covers

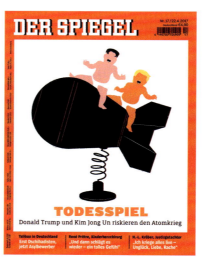

2017 · Edel Rodriguez · CU/US/DE · Magazine cover

2017 · Edel Rodriguez · CU/US/DE · Magazine cover

2017 · Edel Rodriguez · CU/US/DE · Magazine cover

2017 · Edel Rodriguez · CU/US · Magazine cover

2018 · Edel Rodriguez · CU/US/DE · Magazine cover

Edel Rodriguez (1971, Havana) is a Cuban-American artist and illustrator who rose to fame as a graphic designer with his political magazine covers. He studied painting at New York's Pratt Institute and received his Master's degree in 1998 from the city's Hunter College. As well as working as a freelance artist, Rodriguez has also worked as an illustrator for publishing houses and magazines, and during the 2016 U.S. election campaign he was commissioned by *Time* to design a cover depicting the presidential candidate Donald Trump. This much-admired "Meltdown" design attracted international attention and brought him many more assignments on the same subject.

2009 · Edel Rodriguez · CU/US · Magazine cover

2015 · Edel Rodriguez · CU/US · Magazine cover

2018 · Edel Rodriguez · CU/US · Magazine cover

Edel Rodriguez (1971, Havanna) ist ein kubanisch-amerikanischer Künstler und Illustrator, der im Bereich des Grafikdesigns mit politischen Illustrationen für Zeitschriftencover auf sich aufmerksam machte. Rodriguez studierte Malerei am Pratt Institute und erhielt seinen Master 1998 am Hunter College in New York. Neben seiner freien künstlerischen Arbeit war er parallel als Illustrator für Verlage und Zeitschriften aktiv. Im US-Wahlkampf 2016 beauftragte ihn das *Time* Magazine mit dem Entwurf eines Covers zum Präsidentschaftskandidaten Trump. Das viel beachtete „Meltdown"-Cover sorgte für internationale Aufmerksamkeit und brachte ihm zahlreiche weitere Aufträge zum Thema ein.

2011 · Edel Rodriguez · CU/US · Magazine cover

2015 · Edel Rodriguez · CU/US · Magazine cover

2018 · Edel Rodriguez · CU/US/UK · Magazine cover

Edel Rodriguez (1971, La Havane) est un artiste et illustrateur cubano-américain qui s'est fait remarquer dans le domaine du graphisme par ses couvertures politiques de magazines. Il a suivi ses études de peinture à l'Institut Pratt et obtenu un master en 1998 au Hunter College à New York. À côté de son travail d'artiste indépendant, il a exercé comme illustrateur pour des maisons d'édition et des magazines. Pendant la campagne présidentielle de 2016, le *Time* magazine l'a chargé d'un projet d'illustration du candidat à la présidence Trump. La très remarquée couverture «Meltdown» a attiré l'attention internationale sur Rodriguez et lui a valu de nombreuses autres commandes sur le même thème.

2011 · Edel Rodriguez · CU/US · Magazine cover

2016 · Edel Rodriguez · CU/US · Magazine cover

2018 · Edel Rodriguez · CU/US/IT · Magazine cover

2015 · Edel Rodriguez · CU/US · Magazine cover

2017 · Edel Rodriguez · CU/US/UK · Magazine cover

COUNTRY ABBREVIATIONS

AE	United Arab Emirates
AR	Argentina
AT	Austria
AU	Australia
BA	Bosnia and Herzegovina
BE	Belgium
BG	Bulgaria
BO	Bolivia
BR	Brazil
CA	Canada
CH	Switzerland
CL	Chile
CN	China
CU	Cuba
CZ	Czech Republic
DE	Germany
DK	Denmark
EC	Ecuador
ES	Spain
FI	Finland
FR	France
GDR	former German Democratic Rep.
GR	Greece
HK	Hong Kong
HR	Croatia
HU	Hungary
IE	Ireland
IL	Israel
IN	India
IR	Iran
IS	Iceland
IT	Italy
JP	Japan
KR	South Korea
LU	Luxembourg
LV	Latvia
MX	Mexico
MY	Malaysia
NL	Netherlands
NO	Norway
NZ	New Zealand
PL	Poland
PT	Portugal
PY	Paraguay
RU	Russia
SE	Sweden
SG	Singapore
SI	Slovenia
SK	Slovakia
TH	Thailand
TR	Turkey
UK	United Kingdom
US	United States
YU	former Republic of Yugoslavia
VE	Venezuela
ZA	South Africa

JOB ABBREVIATIONS

AD	Art Direction
CD	Creative Direction
ILL	Illustration
PH	Photography
TY	Typography
WD	Web Design

1993 · Mostafa Assadollahi · IR · Poster

1976 · Kurt Wirth · CH · Poster

NATIONAL LIBRARY WEEK APRIL 21-27, 1963

1963 · Arnold Blumberg, Grey · US · Ad

1962 · Wim Crouwel · NL · Poster

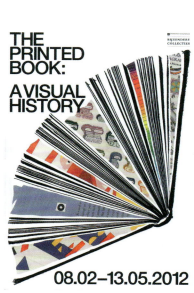

2012 · Experimental Jetset · NL · Poster

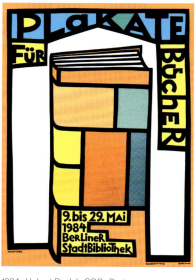

1984 · Hubert Riedel · GDR · Poster

BIBLIO— GRAPHY

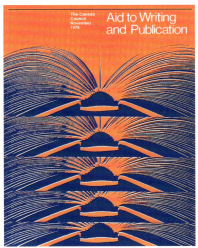

1976 · Burton Kramer · CA · Brochure cover

1901/76
75 ANIVERSARIO
BIBLIOTECA
NACIONAL
JOSE MARTI

1976 · Menede · ES · Poster

1963 · Leif Frimann Anisdahl · NO · Poster

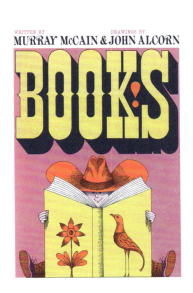

1962 · John Alcorn · US · Book cover

Abbasi, Majid (ed.): *Neshan. The Iranian Graphic Design Magazine* (several volumes); Tehran 2003–today

Ackermann, Marion (ed.): *Piktogramme. Die Einsamkeit der Zeichen*; Deutscher Kunstverlag, Munich 2006

Aicher, Otl: *Typographie*; Ernst & Sohn, Berlin 1988

Aicher, Otl: *The World as Design*; Ernst & Sohn, Berlin 1991

Alliance Graphique Internationale (ed.): *107 grafici dell'AGI*; Alliance Graphique Internationale, Milan 1974

Almeida, Victor; Baltazar, Victor João; Bártolo, José; Souto, Maria Helena (eds.): *Design Português* (8 vols.); Centro de Estudos Sociais da Universidade de Coimbra, Coimbra 2015

Almeida, Luis; Troconi, Giovanni: *Diseño gráfico en México. 100 años 1900–2000*; Universidad Autónoma Metropolitana, Mexico City 2010

Amstutz, Walter (ed.): *Who's Who in Graphic Art*; Amstutz & Herdeg Graphis Press, Zurich 1962

Amstutz, Walter (ed.): *Who's Who in Graphic Art*, vol. 2; Amstutz & Herdeg Graphis Press, Dübendorf 1982

Anceschi, Giovanni; Piazza, Mario: *Bob Noorda. Design*; Moleskine, Milan 2015

Anikst, Michail; Černevič, Elena Vsevolodovna: *Russian Graphic Design*; Abbeville, New York 1990

Annicchiarico, Silvana; Camuffo, Giorgio; Piazza, Mario; Vinti, Carlo (eds.): *TDM5. Grafica italiana*; Corraini, Milan 2012

Armstrong, Helen (ed.): *Graphic Design Theory. Readings from the Field*; Princeton Architectural Press, New York 2009

Aynsley, Jeremy: *Grafik-Design in Deutschland 1890–1945*; Verlag Hermann Schmidt, Mainz 2000

Bakker, Wibo; Kempers, Bram: *Droom van helderheid. Huisstijlen, ontwerpbureaus en modernisme in Nederland*; NAi, Rotterdam 2011

Bakos, Katalin: *100 + 1 Éves a Magyar Plakat*; Műcsarnok, Budapest 1986

Barré, François (ed.): *Design & Designer 21. Roman Cieslewicz*; Pyramyd, Paris 2004

Barthel, Tobias: *Photo Graphik international*; Callwey, Munich 1965

Bateman, Steven; Hyland, Angus: *Symbol*; Laurence King Publishing, London 2011

Beilenhoff, Wolfgang: *Das Filmplakat*; Scalo, Zurich 1995

Beyrow, Matthias: *Mut zum Profil. Corporate Identity und Corporate Design für Städte*; av-Edition, Stuttgart 1998

Bierut, Michael; Hall, Peter: *Tibor Kalman. Perverse Optimist*; Princeton Architectural Press, New York 2000

Bierut, Michael: *Forty Posters for the Yale School of Architecture*; Mohawk Fine Papers, Cohoes 2007

Bierut, Michael: *How to*; Harper, New York 2015

Bially, Jean-Christophe; Marhenke, Dorit: *Roman Cieslewicz. Plakate, Affiches, Posters, Collages*; Braus, Heidelberg 1984

Biesele, Igildo G.: *Graphic Design International*; ABC Verlag, Zurich 1977

Blauvelt, Andrew; Lupton, Ellen (eds.): *Graphic Design. Now in Production*; Walker Art Center, Minneapolis 2011

Booth-Clibborn, Edward; Baroni, Daniele: *The Language of Graphics*; Thames and Hudson, London 1980

Booth-Clibborn, Edward; Poynor, Rick; Why Not Associates: *Typography Now*; Booth-Clibborn, London 1991

Bos, Ben (ed.): *TD 63–73. Total Design and its Pioneering Role in Graphic Design*; Unit Editions, London 2011

Bos, Ben; Bos, Elly (eds.): *AGI. Graphic Design since 1950*; Thames & Hudson, London 2007

Brade, Helmut: *Helmut Brade. Plakate und andere Arbeiten*; Staatliche Galerie Moritzburg, Halle 1987

Brade, Helmut: *Helmut Brade. Plakate No. 2*; Stiftung Kulturfonds, Halle 1993

Brändle, Christian; Gimmi, Karin; Junod, Barbara; Reble, Christina; Richter, Bettina: *100 Jahre Schweizer Grafik*; Lars Müller, Zurich 2014

Braunstein, Cloé (ed.): *Ruedi Baur. Intégral and Partners*; Lars Müller, Baden 2001

Braus, Günter; Müller, Rolf (eds.): *HQ. High Quality* (several volumes); Heidelberger Druckmaschinen AG, Heidelberg 1985–1998

Breuer, Gerda; Meer, Julia (eds.): *Women in Graphic Design. 1890–2012*; Jovis, Berlin 2012

Brody, Neville; Wozencroft, Jon: *The Graphic Language of Neville Brody*; Bucher, Munich 1988

Brook, Tony; Shaughnessy, Adrian: *Lance Wyman. The Monograph*; Unit Editions, London 2015

Brook, Tony; Shaughnessy, Adrian: *Paula Scher. Works*; Unit Editions, London 2017

Burns, Diane; Igarashi, Takenobu: *Designers on Mac*; Graphic-sha, Tokyo 1992

Caban, Geoffrey: *A Fine Line. A History of Australian Commercial Art*; Hale & Iremonger, Sydney 1983

Caban, Geoffrey: *World Graphic Design. Grafikdesign aus Afrika, Fernost, Lateinamerika und dem nahen Osten*; Stiebner, Munich 2004

Calza, Gian Carlo (ed.): *Tanaka Ikko. Graphic Master*; Phaidon, London 1997

Carson, David: *The End of Print*; Bangert, Munich 1995

Carson, David; Blackwell, Lewis: *The End of Print*, vol. 2; Bangert, Munich 1997

Channaud, Michel (ed.): *étapes* (several volumes); Pyramyd, Paris 1996–today

Chase, Margo: *Really Good Logos Explained*; Rockport, Beverly 2008

Chermayeff, Ivan; Geismar, Tom; Geissbühler, Steff: *TM. Trademarks designed by Chermayeff & Geismar*; Lars Müller, Baden 2000

Chermayeff, Ivan; Geismar, Tom; Geissbühler, Steff: *Designing*; Graphis, New York 2003

Chermayeff, Ivan; Geismar, Tom; Kenedi, Aaron: *Identify. Basic Principles of Identity Design in the Iconic Trademarks of Chermayeff & Geismar*; Print Publishing, New York 2011

Chwast, Seymour: *The Push Pin Graphic. A Quarter Century of Innovative Design and Illustration*; Chronicle, San Francisco 2004

Chwast, Seymour; Heller, Steven: *Graphic Style*; Abrams, New York 1988

Chwast, Seymour; Heller, Steven: *Illustration. A Visual History*; Abrams, New York 2008

Chwast, Seymour; Scher, Paula: *Seymour. The Obsessive Images of Seymour Chwast*; Chronicle, San Francisco 2009

Codrington, Andrea: *Kyle Cooper*; Laurence King Publishing, London 2003

Constantine, Mildred; Fern, Alan Maxwell: *Word and Image*; MoMa, New York 1968

Coyne, Patrick (ed.): *Communication Arts* (several volumes); Coyne & Blanchard, Menlo Park 1959–today

Crosby/Fletcher/Forbes (ed.): *A Sign System Manual*; Praeger, New York 1970

Crouwel, Wim; Weidemann, Kurt: *Packaging. An International Survey*; Thames and Hudson, London 1968

Davenport, Peter; Thompson, Philip: *The Dictionary of Visual Language*; Bergstrom & Boyle, London 1980

de Bondt, Sara, (ed.): *Graphic Design. History in the Writing*; Occasional Papers, London 2012

de Burre, Gilles: *The Golden Age of Magazine Illustration. The 60s and 70s*; Vilo, Paris 2001

de Jong, Cees; Purvis, Alston W.: *The Poster. 1000 Posters from Toulouse-Lautrec to Sagmeister*; Abrams, New York 2010

Dheer, Sudarshan: *Symbols, Logos and Trademarks. 1500 Outstanding Designs from India*; Dover Publications, Mineola 1998

Diethelm, Walter J.; Diethelm, Marion: *Form + Communication. Wege zur Visualisierung*; ABC Verlag, Zurich 1974

Diethelm, Walter; Diethelm, Marion; Carmi, Eugenio (eds.): *Signet, Signal, Symbol. Handbuch internationaler Zeichen*; ABC Verlag, Zurich 1984

Dotz, Warren; Husain, Masud: *Meet Mr. Product*; Chronicle, San Francisco 2003

Drew, Ned; Sternberger, Paul Spencer: *By Its Cover. Modern American Book Cover Design*; Princeton Architectural Press, New York 2005

Durrell, Greg: *Burton Kramer. Identities. A Half Century of Graphic Design*; Lulu, 2011

Dydo, Krzysztof: *Polski Plakat Teatralny. Polish Theatre Posters. 1899–1999*; Galeria Plakatu, Krakow 2000

Erler, Johannes: *Hello I am Erik. Erik Spiekermann. Typographer Designer Entrepreneur*; Gestalten, Berlin 2014

Evamy, Michael: *Logo*; Laurence King Publishing, London 2007

Evamy, Michael: *Logotype*; Laurence King Publishing, London 2012

Evers, Bernd; Schneider, Katja: *Helmut Brade. Plakate No. 3*; Staatliche Galerie Moritzburg, Halle 2003

Experimental Jetset: *Statement and Counter-Statement. Notes on Experimental Jetset*; Roma, Rotterdam 2015

Farelly, Liz: *Cutting Edge. April Greiman*; Thames & Hudson, London 1998

Favier, Léo; Cowper, Simon: *What, You Don't Know Grapus?*; Spector Books, Leipzig 2014

Fiell, Charlotte; Fiell, Peter: *Graphic Design for the 21st Century*; TASCHEN, Cologne 2003

Fiell, Charlotte; Fiell, Peter: *Contemporary Graphic Design*; TASCHEN, Cologne 2007

Fili, Louise; Browe, Nicola Bednarek; Heller, Steven: *Elegantissima. The Design & Typography of Louise Fili*; Princeton Architectural Press, New York 2012

Fletcher, Alan: *The Art of Looking Sideways*; Phaidon, London 2001

Fondazione Pirelli (ed.): *Pirelli. Advertising with a Capital P*; Corraini Edizioni, Mantua 2017

Fontana, Rubén; Jalluf, Zalma: *Historia Gráfica del Di Tella*; Capital Intelectual, Buenos Aires 2017

Franchi, Francesco: *Designing News. Changing the World of Editorial Design and Information Graphics*; Gestalten, Berlin 2013

Franchi, Francesco: *The Intelligent Lifestyle Magazine. Smart Editorial Design, Storytelling and Journalism*; Gestalten, Berlin 2016

Fraser, James Howard: *The American Billboard. 100 Years*; Abrams, New York 1991

Fraser, James Howard; Dana, Gordon; Stehlíková, Blanka; Snider, Frederick: *The Czech Avant-Garde and Czech Book Design*; Fairleigh Dickinson University, Madison 1996

Friedl, Friedrich; Ott, Nicolaus; Stein, Bernard: *Typographie. Wann Wer Wie*; Könemann, Cologne 1998

Friedman, Mildred; Filler, Martin (eds.): *Design Quarterly* (several volumes); Walker Art Center, Minneapolis 1946–1993

Frutiger, Adrian: *Type, Sign, Symbol*; ABC Verlag, Zurich 1980

Frutiger, Adrian: *Adrian Frutiger. Schriften. Das Gesamtwerk*; Birkhäuser, Basel 2008

Fukuda, Shigeo: *Posters of Shigeo Fukuda*; Mitumura Tosho Shuppan, Tokyo 1982

Fukuda, Shigeo (ed.): *Idea Special Issue. Graphic Design in West Germany*; Seibundo Shinkosha, Tokyo 1976

Gallo, Max: *Geschichte der Plakate*; Pawlak, Herrsching 1975

Garfield, Simon: *Just My Type*; Profile Books, London 2010

Garland, Ken: *Graphics Handbook*; Studio Vista, London 1966

Gasser, Manuel (ed.): *Exempla graphica. 78 Graphiker der Alliance Graphique Internationale zeigen 78 Arbeiten*; Hug, Zurich 1967

Gassner, Christof: *Alltag, Ökologie, Design. Umweltzeitschriften gestalten*; Hermann Schmidt, Mainz 1994

Geiser, Roger; Verband Schweizerische Grafiker (eds.): *Schweizer Grafiker*; Käser, Zurich 1960

Gejko, Fjodor; Malsy, Victor; Teufel, Philipp: *Helmut Schmid. Gestaltung ist Haltung. Design is Attitude*; Birkhäuser, Basel 2006

Georges, Martina; Giudicelli, François (eds.): *Publimondial* (several volumes); Art et Publications, Paris 1942–1960

Gerstner, Karl: *Programme entwerfen*; Niggli, Teufen 1963

Gerstner, Karl: *Kompendium für Alphabeten*; Niggli, Teufen 1972

Gerstner, Karl: *Karl Gerstner. Review of 5 x 10 Years of Graphic Design*; Hatje Cantz, Ostfildern 2001

Gerstner, Karl; Kutter, Markus: *Die neue Grafik*; Niggli, Teufen 1959

Gil, Emilio: *Pioneers of Spanish Graphic Design*; Mark Batty Publishers, New York 2009

Ginza Graphic Gallery (ed.): *The Designers Republic (ggg Books 96)*; Ginza Graphic Gallery; Tokyo 2011

Giovannini, Joseph (ed.): *Graphic Design in America. A Visual Language History*; Walker Art Center, Minneapolis 1989

Giudici, Giovanni: *Design Process. Olivetti 1908–1983*; Ed. di Communità, Milan 1983

Glaser, Milton: *Milton Glaser. Graphic Design*; The Overlook Press, New York 1973

Glaser, Milton: *Drawing is Thinking*; The Overlook Press, New York 2008

Glaser, Milton: *Milton Glaser. Art is Work*; Duckworth, London 2008

Gluck, Felix; Mercer, Frank A.; Moody, Ella (eds.): *Modern Publicity*. Issue of *Art & Industry Annual of International Advertising Art* (several volumes); Studio Vista, London 1930–1986

Goldsholl, Morton; Sekiguchi, Yoshi: *Inside Design*, Graphic-sha, Tokyo 1987

Gorman, Paul: *The Story of the Face*; Thames & Hudson, London 2017

Grass, Tino (ed.): *Typorama. The Graphic Work of Philippe Apeloig*; Thames & Hudson, London 2013

Greiman, April: *It's Not What You Think It Is*; Artemis, Zurich 1994

Grignani, Manuela: *Franco Grignani. Alterazioni ottico mentali 1929–1999*; Umberto Allemandi, Turin 2014

Grohnert, René (ed.): *Plakatgestaltung Holger Matthies*; Folkwang/Steidl, Essen 2010

Grohnert, René (ed.): *Punktum. Plakatgestaltung von Uwe Loesch*; Folkwang/Steidl, Essen 2010

Grohnert, René (ed.): *Raumeroberungen. Plakatgestaltung von Gunter Rambow*; Folkwang/Steidl, Essen 2010

Grohnert, René (ed.): *Niklaus Troxler. Jazz 'n' More. Plakate*; Folkwang/Steidl, Essen 2017

Grohnert, René (ed.): *San Francisco 1967. Posters from the Summer of Love*; Folkwang/Steidl, Essen 2017

Hallam, Sophie; Rennie, Paul: *Modern British Posters*; Black Dog, London 2010

Hara, Kenya: *Designing Design*; Lars Müller, Baden 2007

Harper, Laurel: *Radical Graphics/Graphic Radicals*; Chronicle, San Francisco 1999

He, Jianping (ed.): *Design + Life. Christof Gassner*; Hesign, Berlin 2004

Hefting, Paul: *Tel Design. 1962–1992*; BIS Publishers, Amsterdam 1992

Heimann, Jim (ed.): *All-American Ads* (several volumes); TASCHEN, Cologne 2001–2004

Heller, Martin (ed.): *Who's Who in Graphic Design*; Benteli Werd, Zurich 1994

Heller, Steven: *Paul Rand*; Phaidon Press, London 1999

Heller, Steven: *Merz to Emigre and Beyond. Avant-Garde Magazine Design of the Twentieth Century*; Phaidon, London 2013

Heller, Steven: *100 Classic Graphic Design Journals*; Laurence King Publishing, London 2014

Heller, Steven; Ilić, Mirko: *Icons of Graphic Design*; Thames & Hudson, London 2001

Henrion, F.H.K.: *Design Coordination and Corporate Image*; Studio Vista, London 1967

Henrion, F.H.K.: *Top Graphic Design*; ABC Verlag, Zurich 1983

Herdeg, Walter (ed.): *Graphis* (several volumes); Graphis Press, Zurich 1944–1986

Herdeg, Walter (ed.): *Graphis Annual* (several volumes); Graphis Press, Zurich 1952–1986

Herdeg, Walter (ed.): *Graphis Diagrams*; Graphis Press, Zurich 1974

Hillebrand, Henri: *Graphic Designers in Europe* (3 vols.); Universe Books, New York 1971

Hillebrand, Henri: *Graphic Designers in the USA* (3 vols.); Universe Books, New York 1971

Hillman, David; Peccinotti, Harri: *Nova. 1965–75*; Pavilion, London 1994

Hillmann, Hans; Rambow, Gunter: *Ein Plakat ist eine Fläche die ins Auge springt. Plakate der Kasseler Schule*; Zweitausendeins, Frankfurt am Main 1979

Hochuli, Jost: *Detail in Typography*; Hyphen Press, London 2008

Hofmann, Armin: *Graphic Design Manual. Principles and Practice*; Reinhold, New York 1965

Hofmann, Dorothea: *Die Geburt eines Stils. Der Einfluss des Basler Ausbildungsmodells auf die Schweizer Grafik*; Triest, Zurich 2016

Hofstede, Dominic: *Les Mason. Epicurean Magazine 1966–1979*; The Narrows, Melbourne 2010

Hollis, Richard: *Graphic Design. A Concise History*; Thames & Hudson, London 1994

Hollis, Richard: *Swiss Graphic Design. The Origins and Growth of an International Style*; Yale University Press, New Haven 2006

Hölscher, Eberhard (ed.): *Gebrauchsgraphik. International Advertising Art* (several volumes); Bruckmann, Munich 1950–1971

Homem de Melo, Chico; Ramos, Elaine: *Linha do tempo do design gráfico no Brasil*; Cosac Naify, São Paulo 2011

Huygen, Frederike: *The Style of the Stedelijk*; nai010, Rotterdam 2013

Huygen, Frederike: *Wim Crouwel. Modernist*; Lecturis, Eindhoven 2015

Igarashi, Takenobu: *Igarashi Alphabets from Graphics to Sculptures*; ABC Verlag, Zurich 1987

Ishihara, Yoshihisa (ed.): *Idea Special Issue. Who's Who of European Designers. Belgium, Spain, Czechoslovakia, Poland*; Seibundo Shinkosha, Tokyo 1972

Ishihara, Yoshihisa (ed.): *Designers in Italy. Graphic, Photo, Illustration, Architecture, Product*; Seibundo Shinkosha, Tokyo 1981

Jaaks, Anke: *Wolfgang Schmidt. Worte und Bilder*; Schmidt, Mainz 1992

Johnson, J. Stewart: *The Modern American Poster*; Museum of Modern Art, New York 1983

Jones, Sydney R.: *Posters and Their Designers*; Studio Vista, London 1924

Kamekura, Yusaku: *Trademarks and Symbols of the World*; Reinhold, New York 1965

Kamekura, Yusaku (ed.): *Creation. International Graphic Design, Art & Illustration* (several volumes); Rikuyo-sha, Tokyo 1989–1994

Kern, Anita: *Grafikdesign in Österreich im 20. Jahrhundert*; Designaustria, Vienna 2008

Kern, Anita; Reinhold, Bernadette; Wekner, Patrick (ed.): *Grafikdesign von der Wiener Moderne bis heute – von Kolo Moser bis Stefan Sagmeister*; Springer, Vienna 2009

Kidd, Chip; Bloom, Amy; Melnick, Mark; Spear, Geoff: *Chip Kidd. Book One. 1986–2006*; Rizzoli, New York 2005

Kidd, Chip; Spear, Geoff: *Chip Kidd. Book Two. 2007–2017*; Rizzoli, New York 2017

Klanten, Robert; Losowsky, Andrew: *Turning Pages. Editorial Design for Print Media, Magazines, Books, Newspapers*; Gestalten, Berlin 2010

Koetzle, Hans-Michael; Wolff, Carsten (ed.): *twen. Revision einer Legende*; Klinkhardt & Biermann, Leipzig 1995

Koetzle, Hans-Michael; Wolff, Carsten (ed.): *Fleckhaus. Design, Revolte, Regenbogen*; Hartmann Books, Stuttgart 2017

Kristahn, Heinz-Jürgen; Schubert, Zdzisław: *Jan Lenica. Plakat- und Filmkunst*; Frölich & Kaufmann, Berlin 1981

Kršić, Dejan: *Mirko Ilić. Fist to Face*; Print, New York 2012

Kühnel, Anita (ed.): *Welt aus Schrift*; König, Cologne 2010

Kurlansky, Mervyn: *Masters of the 20th Century*; Graphis Press, New York 2001

Kuwayama, Yasaburo: *Trademarks & Symbols* (2 vols.); Van Nostrand Reinhold, New York 1973

Léger, Régis: *Cuba Gráfica. Histoire de l'affiche Cubaine*; L'Echappée, Paris 2013

Leslie, Jeremy: *Issues. New Magazine Design*; Laurence King Publishing, London 2000

Leufert, Gerd: *Gerd Leufert. Diseñador*; Museo de Bellas Artes, Caracas 1976

Leufert, Gerd; Sotillo, Alvaro: *La emblemática de Gerd Leufert*; Ediciones Galeria de Arte Nacional, Caracas 1984

Lewis, John: *Typography. Basic Principles*; Van Nostrand Reinhold, New York 1964

Loesch, Uwe: *Der Ort, die Zeit und der Punkt. Plakate von Uwe Loesch*; Museum für Kunsthandwerk; Frankfurt am Main 1991

Lohse, Richard Paul; Müller-Brockmann, Josef; Neuburg, Hans; Vivarelli, Carlo L. (eds.): *Neue Grafik* (several volumes); Otto Walter, Olten 1958–1965

Bibliography

Lupton, Ellen: *Thinking with Type*; Princeton Architectural Press, New York 2004

Lupton, Ellen: *How Posters Work*; Cooper Hewitt, New York 2015

Lupton, Ellen (ed.): *Design & Designer 70. Paula Scher*; Pyramyd, Paris 2008

Lüthy, Wolfgang (ed.): *Schweizer Plakatkunst. Die besten Plakate der Jahre 1941–1965 mit der Ehrenurkunde des Eidgenössischen Departements des Innern*; Visualis, Zurich 1968

Maiwald, Heinrich; Wannemacher, Alois (eds.): *Graphik. Konjunktur, Werbung & Formgebung* (several volumes); Maiwald Verlag, Stuttgart 1948–1956

Matsunaga, Shin: *Shin Matsunaga no dezain. The Design Works of Shin Matsunaga*; Kodansha, Tokyo 1992

Meggs, Philip B.; Purvis, Alston W.: *Meggs' History of Graphic Design* (5th edition); John Wiley & Sons, New York 2011

Mendell, Pierre: *At First Sight. Everyday Graphic Design*; Lars Müller, Baden 2001

Mendell, Pierre: *Pierre Mendell. Plakate für die Bayerische Staatsoper*; Lars Müller, Baden 2006

Menéndez, Pepe: *Cuba Gráfica. Una visión del diseño gráfico cubano*; Icograda, Havana 2007

Minick, Scott; Jiao, Ping: *Chinese Graphic Design in the Twentieth Century*; Thames and Hudson, London 1990

Mollerup, Per: *Marks of Excellence. The History and Taxonomy of Trademarks*; Phaidon, London 1999

Moser, Eva: *Otl Aicher. Gestalter*; Hatje Cantz, Ostfildern 2012

Moser, Horst: *Surprise Me*; Hermann Schmidt, Mainz 2002

Mott, Toby; Poynor, Rick: *Oh So Pretty. Punk in Print 1976–1980*; Phaidon, London 2016

Moya Peralta, Rómulo: *Diseño Gráfico Latinoamericano*; Ediciones Trama, Quito 2006

Mroszczak, Józef: *Polnische Plakatkunst*; Econ, Dusseldorf 1962

Mrowczyk, Jacek: *Very Graphic. Polish Designers of the 20th Century*; Adam Mickiewicz Institute, Warsaw 2015

Muir, Hamish; Holt, Mark (ed.): *8vo. On the Outside*; Lars Müller, Baden 2005

Müller, Jens: *A5/01. Hans Hillmann. The Visual Works*; Lars Müller, Baden 2009

Müller, Jens: *A5/08. Best German Posters*; Optik, Dusseldorf 2016

Müller, Jens; Weiland, Karen: *FilmKunstGrafik. Ein Buch zur neuen deutschen Filmgrafik der sechziger Jahre*; Deutsches Filmmuseum, Frankfurt am Main 2007

Müller, Jens; Weiland, Karen: *A5/05. Lufthansa. Visual History of an Airline*; Lars Müller, Baden 2010

Müller, Jens; Wiedemann, Julius (ed.): *Logo Modernism*; TASCHEN, Cologne 2015

Müller, Lars: *Helvetica. Homage to a Typeface*; Lars Müller, Baden 2002

Müller-Brockmann, Josef: *The Graphic Artist and his Design Problems*; Niggli, Teufen 1961

Müller-Brockmann, Josef: *Geschichte des Plakats*; ABC Verlag, Zurich 1971

Müller-Brockmann, Josef: *A History of Visual Communication*; Niggli, Teufen 1971

Müller-Brockmann, Josef: *Grid Systems in Graphic Design*; Niggli, Teufen 1981

Munari, Bruno: *Design as Art*; MIT Press, Cambridge (MA) 1987

Musée de l'Affiche et de la Publicité (ed.): *Grapus*; Veyrier, Paris 1982

Nagai, Kazumasa; Sato, Koichi; Toda, Seiju: *Graphics Japan. 46 Leading Graphic Designers*; Graphic-sha, Tokyo 1987

Olins, Wally: *Corporate Identity. Strategie und Gestaltung*; Campus, Frankfurt 1990

Oostens-Wittamer, Yolande: *L'Affiche belge*; Bibliothèque Royale Albert I, Brussels 1975

Owen, William: *Modern Magazine Design*; Rizzoli, New York 1991

Paos (ed.): *Paos Design. Corporate Aesthetics, Creative Identities and Management Culture*; Kodansha, Tokyo 1990

Passek, Jean-Loup: *Jan Lenica*; Centre Pompidou, Paris 1980

Paulo, Joaquim; Wiedemann, Julius (ed.): *Jazz Covers*; TASCHEN, Cologne 2008

Paulo, Joaquim; Wiedemann, Julius (ed.): *Funk & Soul Covers*; TASCHEN, Cologne 2010

Pedersen, B. Martin (ed.): *Graphis* (several volumes); Graphis, New York 1987–2005

Pedersen, B. Martin; Drasin, Ros; Hayden, Clare: *Graphis Magazine Design 1*; Graphis, New York 1997

Peignot, Charles (ed.): *Arts et Métiers Graphiques* (several volumes); Deberny & Peignot, Paris 1927–1939

Pelta, Raquel (ed): *D1. R2. Design de Comunicação*; Imprensa Nacional, Lisbon 2011

Phaidon Press (ed.): *Area. 100 Graphic Designers, 10 Curators, 10 Classics*; Phaidon, London 2005

Piazza, Mario (ed.): *La Grafica del Made in Italy. Comunicazione e aziende del design 1950–1980*; Aiap Edizioni, Milan 2012

Polano, Sergio; Vetta, Pierpaolo (eds.): *ABC of 20th-Century Graphics*; Electa, Milan 2002

Popitz, Klaus: *Plakate aus Israel*; Reimer, Berlin 1985

Poynor, Rick: *Typography Now Two. Implosion*; Internos, London 2000

Poynor, Rick: *No More Rules. Graphic Design and Postmodernism*; Laurence King Publishing, London 2013

Poynor, Rick: *Communicate. Independent British Graphic Design since the Sixties*; Laurence King Publishing, London 2014

Poynor, Rick; Walters, John L. (eds.): *Eye. The International Review of Graphic Design* (several volumes); Eye/Haymarket Media, London 1991–today

Purvis, Alston W.: *Dutch Graphic Design. A Century of Innovation*; Thames & Hudson, London 2006

Quinn, Anthony: *A History of British Magazine Design*; V&A Publishing, London 2016

Rademacher, Hellmut: *Gebrauchsgrafik in der DDR*; Verband Bildender Künstler der DDR, Berlin 1975

Rademacher, Hellmut: *P 40. Plakate aus der DDR*; Verband Bildender Künstler der DDR, Berlin 1988

Rand, Paul: *Paul Rand. A Designer's Art*; Yale University Press, New Haven 1985

Rathgeb, Markus: *Otl Aicher*; Phaidon, London 2006

Rattemeyer, Volker (ed.): *Rambow in Museum Wiesbaden. Plakate 1960–1980*; Museum Wiesbaden, Wiesbaden 1988

Reichert, Hans Dieter (ed.): *Baseline* (several volumes); Bradbourne Publishing, East Malling, Kent 1979–today

Rendgen, Sandra; Wiedemann, Julius (ed.): *Information Graphics*; TASCHEN, Cologne 2012

Ricci, Franco Maria; Ferrari, Corinna (eds.): *Top Symbols and Trademarks of the World* (11 volumes); Deco Press, Milan 1973–1983

Roberts, Caroline: *Graphic Design Visionaries*, Laurence King Publishing, London 2015

Robertson, Matthew: *Factory Records. The Complete Graphic Album*; Thames & Hudson, London 2006

Ruder, Emil: *Typography. A Manual of Design*; Niggli, Teufen 1967

Rudge, William Edwin; Kaye, Milton L.; Lyman, Nanci A. (eds.): *Print. America's Graphic Design Magazine* (several volumes); Rudge, New York 1940–today

Rüegg, Ruedi; Fröhlich, Godi: *Typografische Grundlagen*; ABC Verlag, Zurich 1972

Sagmeister, Stefan; Hall, Peter: *Sagmeister. Made You Look*; Abrams, New York 2009

Sandhaus, Louise: *Earthquakes, Mudslides, Fires and Riots. California & Graphic Design 1936–1986*; Thames & Hudson, London 2014

Sarowitz, Sam; Drate, Spencer; Kehr, Dave; Salavetz, Jütka: *Art of the Modern Movie Poster*; Chronicle, San Francisco 2008

Schindler, Herbert: *Monografie des Plakats*; Süddeutscher Verlag, Munich 1972

Schmid, Helmut: *Typography Today*; Seibundo Shinkosha, Tokyo 1980

Schmittel, Wolfgang: *Design, Concept, Realisation*; ABC Verlag, Zurich 1975

Schmittel, Wolfgang: *Process Visual. Development of a Corporate Identity*; ABC Verlag, Zurich 1978

Schmittel, Wolfgang: *Corporate Design International. Definition and Benefit of a Consistent Corporate Appearance*; ABC Verlag, Zurich 1984

Schnapp, Jeffrey T.: *Les Vagues révolutionnaires. L'art de l'affiche politique 1914–1989*; Skira, Stanford 2005

Schröder, Till (ed.): *I-d. Die Wirklichkeit des Unerwarteten. Holger Matthies im Museum der Arbeit*; Dölling und Galitz, Hamburg 2000

Schubert, Zdzisław; Kondziela, Henryk: *Waldemar Świerzy. Plakaty*; Muzeum Narodowe w Poznaniu, Poznań 1986

Seibundo Shinkosha (ed.): *IDEA* (several vols.); Seibundo Shinkosha, Tokyo 1953–today

Shaughnessy, Adrian; Brook, Tony (eds.): *Manuals. Design & Identity Guidelines* (2 vols.); Unit Editions, London 2014

Shaughnessy, Adrian: *Herb Lubalin. American Graphic Designer 1918–81*; Unit Editions, London 2012

Shaughnessy, Adrian: *FHK Henrion. The Complete Designer*; Unit Editions, London 2013

Sinclair, Mark: *TM. The Untold Stories Behind 29 Classic Logos*; Laurence King Publishing, London 2014

Society of Industrial Artists and Designers (ed.): *Designers in Britain* (several volumes); Wingate, London 1947–1971

Spencer, Herbert: *Pioneers of Modern Typography*; Lund Humphries, London 1969

Spencer, Herbert: *The Liberated Page. A Typographic Anthology*; Bedford Press, San Francisco 1987

Spiekermann, Erik; Ginger, E.M.: *Stop Stealing Sheep & Find Out How Type Works*; Adobe Press, Mountain View 1993

Stancheva, Magdalina: *Logo Book Stefan Kanchev*; Zhanet45, Plovdiv 2012

Stankowski, Anton: *Visuelle Kommunikation. Ein Design-Handbuch*: Reimer, Berlin 1989

Stermer, Dugald: *The Art of Revolution. 96 Posters from Cuba*; McGraw-Hill, New York 1970

Stiebner, Erhardt (ed.): *Novum Gebrauchsgraphik* (several volumes); Bruckmann, Munich 1972–today

Studinka, Felix; Massin, Robert: *Poster Collection 09. Ralph Schraivogel*; Lars Müller, Baden 2003

Studio Mendell & Oberer (ed.): *Mendell und Oberer. Graphic Design*; Hatje, Stuttgart 1976

Sutnar, Ladislav: *Visual Design in Action*; Hastings House, New York 1961

Sutnar, Ladislav; Lönberg-Holm, Knud: *Catalog Design*; Sweet's Catalog Service, New York 1944

Taborda, Felipe; Wiedemann, Julius (ed.): *Latin American Graphic Design*; TASCHEN, Cologne 2008

Tanaami, Keiichi: *The Work of Keiichi Tanaami*; Sano Garō, Ayauta 1990

Tanaka, Ikko: *Tanaka Ikko*; Electra, Tokyo 1997

Terragni, Emilia: *The Phaidon Archive of Graphic Design*; Phaidon, London 2012

Tschichold, Jan: *Die neue Typographie. Ein Handbuch für zeitgemäss Schaffende*; Verlag des Bildungsverbandes der Deutschen Buchdrucker, Berlin 1928

Troxler, Niklaus: *Jazz Blvd. Niklaus Troxler Posters*; Lars Müller, Baden 1999

Trulove, James Grayson: *New Design. Berlin*; Rockport, Gloucester 2000

Tufte, Edward R.: *The Visual Display of Quantitative Information*; Graphics Press, Cheshire (CT) 1983

van der Vlugt, Ron: *Logo Life. Life Histories of 100 Famous Logos*; BIS Publishers, Amsterdam 2012

van der Sman, Marie-Christine; Hefting, Paul: *Archief Studio Dumbar–PTT*; (Z)oo, Eindhoven 2010

van Nes, Irene (ed.): *Dynamic Identities. How to Create a Living Brand*; BIS Publishers, Amsterdam 2013

Verlag Die Wirtschaft (ed.): *Neue Werbung. Fachzeitschrift für Theorie und Praxis der sozialistischen Werbung* (several volumes); Verlag Die Wirtschaft, Berlin 1954–1991

Vignelli, Massimo: *The Vignelli Canon*; Lars Müller, Baden 2015

Vignelli, Massimo: *Vignelli. From A to Z*; RIT Press, Rochester (NY) 2017

Vit, Armin; Gomez-Palacio, Bryony: *Graphic Design Referenced*; Rockport, Palo Alto 2009

Walter Landor Associates (ed.): *Walter Landor Associates*; Seibundo Shinkosha, Tokyo 1980

Wasniewski, Jerzy (ed.): *Projekt. Visual Art and Design* (several volumes); RSW, Warsaw 1955–1989

Wasser, Jack; Wolf, Werner M. (eds.): *Siegfried Odermatt & Rosmarie Tissi. Graphic Design*; Wasser, Zurich 1993

Weidemann, Kurt: *Wo der Buchstabe das Wort führt. Ansichten über Schrift und Typographie*; Hatje Cantz, Ostfildern 1994

Weidemann, Kurt (ed.): *Der Druckspiegel. Ein Archiv für deutsches und internationales grafisches Schaffen* (several volumes); Blersch, Stuttgart 1950–1970

Weingart, Wolfgang: *Typography*; Lars Müller, Baden 2000

Widmer, Jean: *Jean Widmer*; Maison du livre de l'image et du son, Paris 1991

Wilhelm, Jürgen: *Plakate Morteza Momayez*; Wilhelm, Bergisch Gladbach 1989

Willinger, Brigitte: *Henry Steiner. Bridging East and West*; Designaustria, Vienna 2017

Wirth, Kurt: *Drawing. A Creative Process*; ABC Verlag, Zurich 1976

Wlassikoff, Michel: *The Story of Graphic Design in France*; Gingko Press, Corte Madera 2005

Yokoo, Tadanori: *The Complete Tadanori Yokoo*; Kodansha, Tokyo 1970

Zeegen, Lawrence; Roberts, Caroline: *Fifty Years of Illustration*; Laurence King Publishing, London 2014

Bibliography

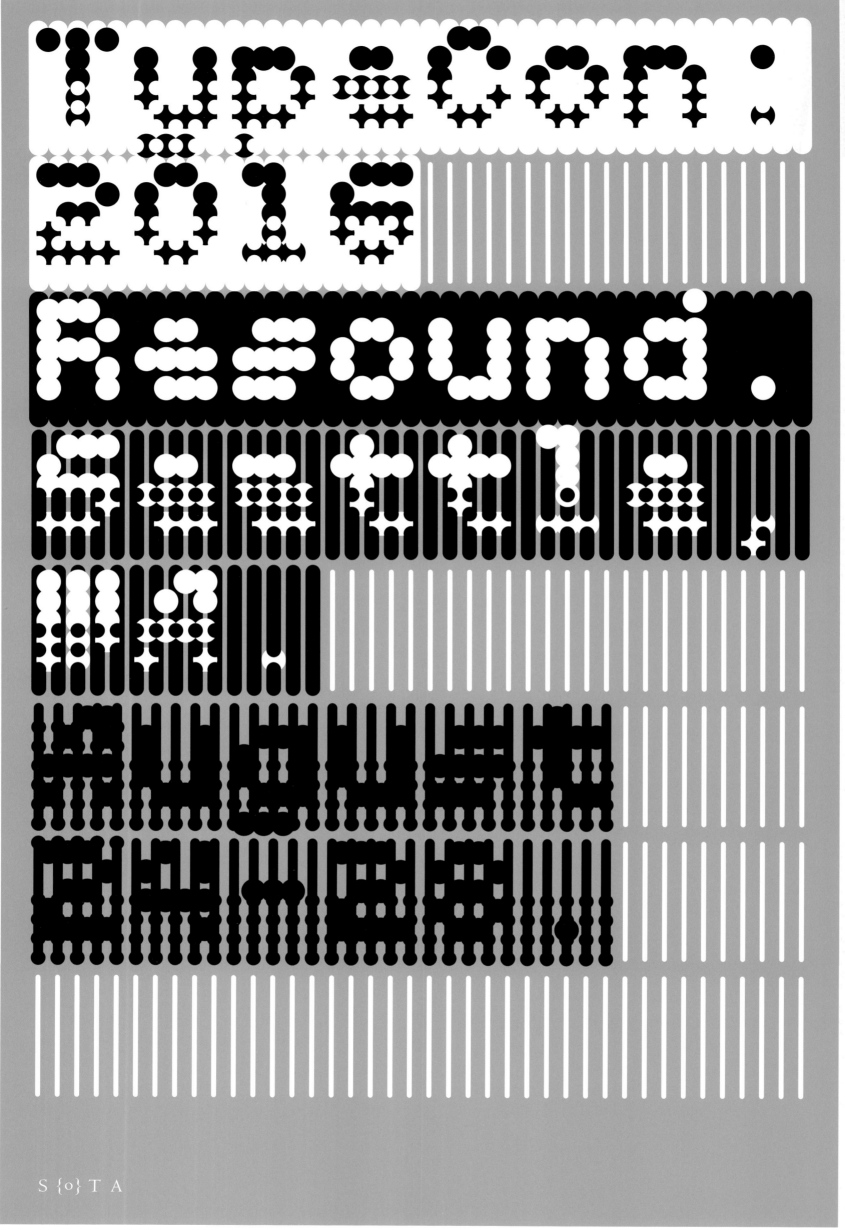

2016 · MuirMcNeil · UK · Poster

INDEX

1972 · René Ferracci · FR · Poster

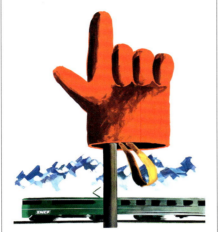

pour aller aux sports d'hiver
LE TRAIN

1973 · Anonymous · CH · Poster

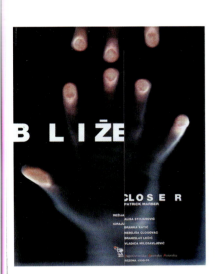

2000 · Slavimir Stojanovic · YU · Poster

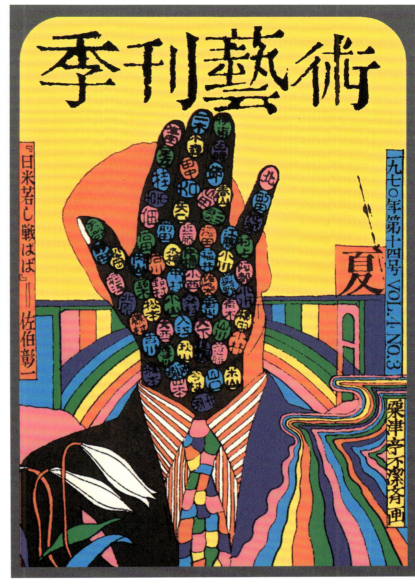

1970 · Kiyoshi Awazu · JP · Book cover

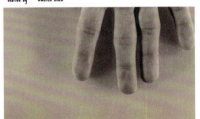

1990 · Chip Kidd · US · Book cover

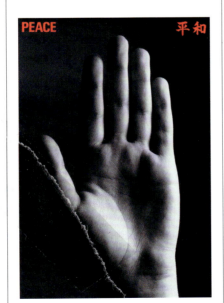

1985 · Tom Geismar, Chermayeff & Geismar · US · Poster

1976 · Morteza Momayez · IR · Poster

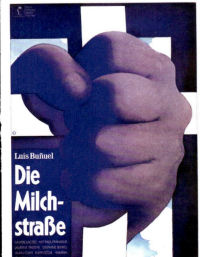

1969 · Hans Hillmann · DE · Poster

1960s · Benno Wissing · NL · Logo · Stichting Collectieve Propaganda van het Nederlandse Boek

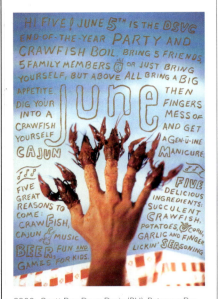

2000 · Scott Ray, Doug Davis (PH), Peterson Ray & Company · US · Poster

1983 · Anonymous · CZ · Poster

1982 · Radovan Jenko · SL · Poster

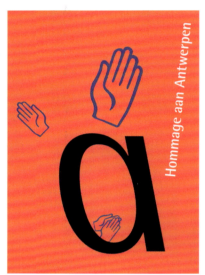

1993 · Uwe Loesch · DE · Poster

1977 · Mieczysław Wasilewski · PL · Poster

1980 · Anonymous · JP · Poster

2011 · Herburg Weiland · DE · Book cover

1975 · Horst Wendt · GDR · Poster

1978 · Terry Gilliam · US/UK · Logo · Hand Made Films

IMPRINT

EACH AND EVERY TASCHEN
BOOK PLANTS A SEED!

TASCHEN is a carbon neutral publisher.
Each year, we offset our annual carbon
emissions with carbon credits at the
Instituto Terra, a reforestation program
in Minas Gerais, Brazil, founded by Lélia
and Sebastião Salgado. To find out more
about this ecological partnership, please
check: www.taschen.com/zerocarbon

Inspiration: unlimited.
Carbon footprint: zero.

To stay informed about TASCHEN and
our upcoming titles, please subscribe
to our free magazine at www.taschen.com/
magazine, follow us on Twitter, Instagram,
and Facebook, or e-mail your questions
to contact@taschen.com.

© 2019 TASCHEN GmbH
Hohenzollernring 53
D-50672 Köln
www.taschen.com

Design
Jens Müller/optik
www.optik-studios.de

Editor
Julius Wiedemann

Editorial Coordination
Daniel Siciliano Brêtas

Collaboration
Nora Dohrmann

Production
Daniela Asmuth

English Translation
Isabel Varea-Riley

German Translation
Ursula Wulfekamp

French Translation
Wolf Fruhtrunk

English Revision
Chris Allen

German Revision
Eva Hembach
Maike Specht

French Revision
Valérie Lavoyer
for Delivering iBooks & Design

Printed in Italy
ISBN 978-3-8365-7037-4

Acknowledgements

The making of this book has truly turned
out to be a journey round the world and
through time as well. My first thanks go
to the many, many supporters of this project in all parts of the globe, who have so
generously shared their knowledge and
materials. When TASCHEN approached
me with the idea of producing a general
book on the international history of
graphic design it seemed like a virtually
impossible task. However, under the lead
of Julius Wiedemann and in close association with his experienced team of Nora
Dohrmann and Daniel Siciliano Brêtas,
the concept was developed and made
into a reality. My heartfelt thanks go out
to these three for their never-ending passion and enthusiasm throughout the production of this book. Big thanks must also
go to the translators, copy-editors, and
proofreaders who have been involved in
working on the text, and especially to the
production team at TASCHEN. I would
also like to thank my studio colleagues
Andreas Magino, Friederike Spielmann-
leitner, and Janine Uhlke, Esther Jakob,
and Valeria Sava for their long-standing
hard work and support. Last but not least
my very personal thanks go to my partner
Katharina Sussek for her invaluable judg-
ment and encouragement, and for continuing to bring joy and love to my life.

Jens Müller

dedicated to helmut schmid (1942–2018)
teacher, inspirer, and friend

Picture Credits